Lecture Notes in Artificial Intelligence 12960

Subseries of Lecture Notes in Computer Science

More information about this subseries at http://www.springer.com/series/1244

Mufti Mahmud · M Shamim Kaiser ·
Stefano Vassanelli · Qionghai Dai ·
Ning Zhong (Eds.)

Brain Informatics

14th International Conference, BI 2021
Virtual Event, September 17–19, 2021
Proceedings

Editors
Mufti Mahmud
Nottingham Trent University
Nottingham, UK

M Shamim Kaiser
Jahangirnagar University
Dhaka, Bangladesh

Stefano Vassanelli
University of Padua
Padua, Italy

Qionghai Dai
Tsinghua University
Beijing, China

Ning Zhong
Maebashi Institute of Technology
Maebashi, Japan

ISSN 0302-9743 ISSN 1611-3349 (electronic)
Lecture Notes in Artificial Intelligence
ISBN 978-3-030-86992-2 ISBN 978-3-030-86993-9 (eBook)
https://doi.org/10.1007/978-3-030-86993-9

LNCS Sublibrary: SL7 – Artificial Intelligence

This Springer imprint is published by the registered company Springer Nature Switzerland AG
The registered company address is: Gewerbestrasse 11, 6330 Cham, Switzerland

Preface

The Brain Informatics (BI) is an emerging interdisciplinary research field which aims to apply informatics when studying the brain. This combines efforts from diverse related disciplines such as computing and cognitive sciences, psychology, neuroscience, artificial intelligence, etc., to study the brain and its information processing capability. From the informatics perspective, the efforts concentrate on the development of new software tools, platforms, and systems to improve our understanding of the brain, its functionality, disorders, and their possible treatments. The BI conference is a unique avenue which attracts interdisciplinary researchers, practitioners, scientists, experts, and industry representatives who are using informatics to address questions pertaining to brain and cognitive sciences including psychology and neuroscience. Therefore, BI is more than just a research field, it is rather a global research community aiming to build improved, inspiring, intelligent, and transformative technologies through the use of machine learning, data science, artificial intelligence (AI), and information and communication technology (ICT) to facilitate fundamental research and innovative applications of these technologies on brain related research. The BI conference series started with the WICI International Workshop on Web Intelligence Meets Brain Informatics, held at Beijing, China, in 2006. It was one of the early conferences which aimed at focusing informatics application on brain sciences. The subsequent editions of the conference were held in Beijing, China (2009), Toronto, Canada (2010), Lanzhou, China (2011), and Macau, SAR China (2012). But in 2013, the conference title was changed to Brain Informatics and Health (BIH) with an emphasis on real-world applications of brain research in human health and well-being. BIH 2013, BIH 2014, BIH 2015, and BIH 2016 were held in Maebashi, Japan; Warsaw, Poland; London, UK; and Omaha, USA; respectively. In 2017, the conference went back to its original design and vision to investigate the brain from an informatics perspective and to promote a brain-inspired information technology revolution. Thus, the conference name was changed back to Brain Informatics in Beijing, China, in 2017. The editions in 2018 and 2019 were held in Arlington, Texas, USA and Haikou, China, respectively.

The novel COVID-19 pandemic has affected the organization of the last two editions of the conference. The 2020 edition was originally planned to be held at Padua, Italy, which was not possible due to the pandemic and was instead held virtually. It was reduced from the usual three-day conference to one day with the plan to hold the workshops, special sessions, panel discussions, and the networking events in 2021.

Fighting against the pandemic with massive support from everyone through development and administration of vaccines, restricted movement, maintenance of hygiene and social distancing, there seemed to be light at the end of the tunnel. However, due to the recent discovery of variants of the virus, travel remained restricted and therefore the 2021 edition of the conference – though planned to be held physically at Padua, Italy – was also held as a fully virtual event. To increase participation, we decided to go back to the usual three days with one day dedicated to workshops and special sessions, one day to the excellent keynote sessions, and one day to the technical sessions.

The BI 2021 online conference was supported by the Web Intelligence Consortium (WIC), the University of Padua, the Padua Neuroscience Centre, the Chinese Association for Artificial Intelligence, the CAAI Technical Committee on Brain Science and Artificial Intelligence (CAAI-TCBSAI), the Applied Intelligence and Informatics (AII) Lab, and the Nottingham Trent University.

The theme of BI 2021 was "Innovative Computational Approaches for Understanding Brain Functions and Treat its Disorders." The goal was to see how the world leading BI researchers are coping with this current pandemic situation and still continuing to contribute to the knowledge base and disseminate their amazing work on understanding brain functions and treating it's disorders. The BI 2021 addressed broad perspectives of BI research that bridges scales that span from atoms to thoughts and behaviour. These papers provide a good sample of state-of-the-art research advances on BI from methodologies, frameworks, techniques to applications and case studies. The selected papers cover five major tracks of BI, including: (1) Cognitive and Computational Foundations of Brain Science, (2) Human Information Processing Systems, (3) Brain Big Data Analytics, Curation, and Management, (4) Informatics Paradigms for Brain and Mental Health Research, (5) Brain–Machine Intelligence and Brain-Inspired Computing.

This edition of the BI 2021 conference attracted 90 submissions including 20 abstracts and 70 full papers from 24 countries belonging to all 5 BI 2021 tracks, relevant workshops, and special sessions. The submitted papers underwent a single blind review process, soliciting expert opinion from at least three experts: at least two independent reviewers and the respective track chair. After the rigorous review reports from the reviewers and the track chairs, finally 50 high-quality papers (including two short papers) from 22 countries were accepted for presentation at the conference. Additionally, 18 abstracts were also selected through the same peer-review process. Therefore, this volume of the BI 2021 conference proceedings contains these 50 full papers which were presented virtually during the conference days. Despite the COVID-19 pandemic situation, it was an amazing response from the BI community during this challenging time.

We would like to express our gratitude to all BI 2021 conference committee members for their instrumental and unwavering support. BI 2021 had a very exciting program which would not have been possible without the generous dedication of the Program Committee members in reviewing the conference papers and abstracts. BI 2021 could not have taken place without the great team effort and the generous support from our sponsors. We would especially like to express our sincere appreciation to our kind sponsors, including Springer Nature. Our gratitude goes to Springer for sponsoring student first-author registrations which were selected based on the quality of the submitted papers and their need for financial support. We are grateful to Aliaksandr Birukou, Ronan Nugent, Guido Zosimo-Landolfo, Anna Kramer, Celine Chang, Nick Zhu, Peter Strasser, Selma Somogy, Ramvijay Subramani and the LNCS/LNAI team from Springer Nature for their continuous support in coordinating the publication of this volume. Also, special thanks to Hongzhi Kuai, Vicky Yamamoto, and Yang Yang for their great assistance and support. Last but not least, we thank all our contributors and volunteers for their support during this challenging time to make BI 2021 a success.

September 2021

Mufti Mahmud
M Shamim Kaiser
Stefano Vassanelli
Qionghai Dai
Ning Zhong

Organization

Conference Chairs

Mufti Mahmud	Nottingham Trent University, UK
Stefano Vassanelli	University of Padua, Italy
M Shamim Kaiser	Jahangirnagar University, Bangladesh
Qionghai Dai	Tsinghua University, China
Ning Zhong	Maebashi Institute of Technology, Japan

Advisors

Amir Hussain	Edinburgh Napier University, UK
Guoming Luan	Capital Medical University and Sanbo Brain Hospital, China
Hanchuan Peng	SEU-Allen Institute for Brain and Intelligence, China
Heseng Liu	Harvard Medical School and Massachusetts General Hospital, USA
Maurizio Corbetta	Padua Neuroscience Centre, Italy
Shinsuke Shimojo	California Institute of Technology, USA

Organizing Committee

Alessandra Bertoldo	University of Padua, Italy
Michele Giugliano	SISSA, Italy
Michela Chiappalone	Italian Institute of Technology, Italy
Xiaohui Tao	University of Southern Queensland, Australia
Alberto Testolin	University of Padua, Italy
Marzia Hoque Tania	University of Oxford, UK
Yang Yang	Beijing Forestry University, China
Peipeng Liang	Capital Normal University, China
Gopikrishna Deshpande	Auburn University, USA
Cosimo Ieracitano	Mediterranean University of Reggio Calabria, Italy
Marco Dal Maschio	University of Padua, Italy
Marco Zorzi	University of Padua, Italy
Samir Suweis	University of Padua, Italy
Abzetdin Adamov	ADA University, Azerbaijan
Claudia Cecchetto	Okinawa Institute of Science and Technology, Japan
Francesco Morabito	Mediterranean University of Reggio Calabria, Italy
K. C. Santosh	University of South Dakota, USA
Saiful Azad	University of Malaysia, Pahang, Malaysia
Shouyi Wang	University of Texas at Arlington, USA
Vicky Yamamoto	USC Keck School of Medicine, USA

Zhiqi Mao	Chinese PLA General Hospital, China
Hongzhi Kuai	Maebashi Institute of Technology, Japan
Shuvashish Paul	Jahangirnagar University, Bangladesh

Technical Program Committee

Alessandra Pedrocchi	Politecnico di Milano, Italy
Alessandro Gozzi	IIT, Italy
Bernd Kuhn	OIST, Japan
Bo Song	University of Southern Queensland, Australia
Daniel Marcus	University of Washington, USA
Davide Zoccolan	SISSA, Italy
Dimeter Prodonov	Imac, Belgium
Egidio D'Angelo	University of Pavia, Italy
Eleni Vasilaki	University of Sheffield, UK
Francesco Papaleo	University of Padua and IIT, Italy
Gabriella Panuccio	IIT, Italy
Gaute Einevoll	Norwegian University of Life Sciences, Norway
Giacomo Indiveri	University of Zurich, Switzerland
Giancarlo Ferregno	Politecnico di Milano, Italy
Giorgio A. Ascoli	George Mason University, USA
Guenther Zeck	NMI, Germany
Gustavo Deco	Pompeu Fabra University, Spain
Jonathan Mappelli	University of Modena, Italy
Laura Ballerini	SISSA, Italy
Luca Benini	ETH, Switzerland
Luca Berdondini	IIT, Italy
Luciano Gamberini	University of Padua, Italy
M. Arifur Rahman	Jahangirnagar University, Bangladesh
M. Mostafizur Rahman	AIUB, Bangladesh
Manisha Chawla	IIT-Gandhinagar, India
Marco Mongillo	University of Padua, Italy
Martin McGinnity	Ulster University, UK
Mathew Diamond	SISSA, Italy
Mathias Prigge	Weizmann Institute of Science, Israel
Md. Atiqur Rahman Ahad	Osaka University, Japan
Michele Magno	ETH, Switzerland
Mohammad Shahadat Hossain	University of Chittagong, Bangladesh
Mohammad Shorif Uddin	Jahangirnagar University, Bangladesh
Muhammad Golam Kibria	University of Liberal Arts, Bangladesh
Muhammad Nazrul Islam	MIST, Bangladesh
Ofer Yizhar	Weizmann Institute of Science, Israel
Paolo Del Giudice	National Institute of Health, Italy
Paolo Massobrio	University of Genoa, Italy
Patrick Ruther	University of Freiburg, Germany

Ralf Zeitler	Venneos GmbH, Germany
Roland Thewes	Technical University of Berlin, Germany
Sergio Martinoia	University of Genoa, Italy
Shamim Al Mamun	Jahangirnagar University, Bangladesh
Silvestro Micera	Scuola Superiore Sant'Anna, Italy
Stefano Ferraina	Sapienza University of Rome, Italy
Themis Prodomakis	University of Southampton, UK
V. N. Manjunath Aradhya	JSS S&T University, India
Wolfgang Maas	Technische Universität Graz, Austria
Xiaofei Zhang	Jiangsu University of Science and Technology, China

Peer-Reviewed Abstracts

Innovative Interdisciplinary Brain Communication for IBSE High School Didactic

Marina Minoli

STEM DidaInnovaBiolab- Royal Society of Biology - National Biologists Order, Italy
marina.minoli@biologo.onb.it

Abstract. From the classroom to the public communication is the principal objective of this project about Brain science topic as interesting thematic to involve in inclusive way High School students in Learning by doing activities. All students that have participated at this project have also realized in previous years different activities in learning basics of neuroscience with innovative integrated ICT methodology. To promote awareness in brain science competences biology high school biologist-teacher has created innovative didactic active brain research with IBSE methodologies: students of different classes of Scientific High School Institute have created didactic and communication strategies in which participated as explores in interdisciplinary Neuroscience project about some modern aspects of brain science (also interconnections between Nanoscience and Neuroscience researches) with elements of bioinformatic working in neuroscience data banks, searching and elaborating information about proteins involved in neuroscience diseases as Alzheimer' disease. From History of brain science to modern evolution of Neuroscience also analyzing some important technique as Patch CLAMP and some neuroscientists' biographies of Nobel Prize. Very positive results are obtained also with strategies of debate: students have realized some brief talks with comparison of ideas interpreting different scientists and have compiled brain reports with significative brain images useful to represent the specific research and results analyzing some benefit for Society in the time. All students of different classes have divided in different little groups to realize research work with IBSE methodology and to present at the end of the project the results of different innovative activities in a Virtual Brain Science Conference and Brain social communication for local community as little neuroscientists with the guide of Biology Teachers as principal investigator simulating science research world. From Brain debate of classes to public Brain local debate into local community was very useful to involve all citizens in neuroscience historical and modern aspects of Neuroscience with High satisfaction of all actors of this project. In conclusion is possible to affirm that these activities of didactic research and neuroscience communication was one important opportunity to create Brain Science Communication with Society and for Society, one innovative proposal to realize also in future others innovative neuroscience communication with and for the public in scientific network of contacts.

Keywords: Brain science · Neuroinformatic · Neurodegenerative disease · Innovative virtual brain conference · IBSE methodology

Learning from Play: Mechanisms and Constraints

Jinyun Lyu, Yijin Fang, and Stella Christie

Tsinghua University, China
christie@tsinghua.edu.cn

Abstract. Learning—the process of acquiring new knowledge in order to apply it in future contexts—is a fundamental aspect of our cognition. What does early learning look like? We approach this question by examining young children's most ubiquitous activity: play. In three studies, we asked whether play results in learning and what mechanisms and constraints govern learning from play.

In Study 1, to investigate whether play results in learning, we compared Chinese three-year-olds' generalization learning in Free-Play (self-discovery) vs. Didactic (explicitly taught) conditions (N= 59; Mage = 3.25 years, SD = 0.49). Children saw a novel machine that made a sound when certain blocks were put atop it. A rule governed the sound activation (e.g., same-shape rule: the machine was activated if the block's shape matched the machine's). The question was whether children could learn and generalize this rule. Children in the Didactic condition were explicitly shown which blocks activated the machine (without being told the rule) while children in the Free-Play condition were simply given the machines and blocks to play with for 5 minutes. Following this, children in both conditions were given two tests: to select one of three blocks to activate a previously seen machine (First-order generalization) and a new machine (Second-order generalization). Children learned well in the Didactic condition: 77% correct in the First-order test (t-test against chance .5, t(29) = 3.40, p = .002), and 73% correct in the Second-order test (t(29) = 2.84, p =.008). However, children did not learn from Free-Play: accuracy of First-order test was 55% (t(28) = 0.55, p = .586), likewise for Second-order test (Accuracy = 48%, t(28) = −0.18, p =.856). These results differ from a previous study using an identical paradigm with US three-year-olds (Sim & Xu 2017), where generalization learning was equally high in both Didactic and Free-Play conditions. That is, we found that by three years of age, cultural difference had already influenced learning from play. To investigate the mechanisms and constraints of learning from play, in Study 2 we ran another Free-Play condition (N = 31), but this time with the promise of reward ("Play on your own; if you figure out how this machine works, you'll get a gift!"). Reward had no impact, as accuracy for First order (39%) and Second-order (45%) tests were again at chance. In Study 3 we tested whether children's own hypotheses (about which block activated the machine) impacted learning. To do this, we manipulated whether the child's first try during Free-Play led to activation (First-Positive-Evidence, N = 30) or not (First-Negative-Evidence, N = 30). Surprisingly, children could learn the rule from play if their first try was successful; accuracy across two tests were 77%, comparable to Study 1's Didactic condition. However, children did not learn the rule if their first try was negative (37% accuracy). Across three studies, we found evidence that play could result in learning and generalization, even as well as learning from explicit instruction. However, culture and the child's own hypotheses may constrain learning from play.

Keywords: Generalization learning · Free play · Reward · Hypotheses · Evidence

Comparison of Active Areas By Estimating Brain Activities Evoked By Verbal Stimuli Given from Speech and Text

Rikako Sumida[1], Hiroto Yamaguchi[2], Tomoya Nakai[2], Shinji Nishimoto[2], Ichiro Kobayashi[1]

[1] Ochanomizu University, Japan
sumida.rikako@is.ocha.ac.jp
[2] National Institute of Information and Communications Technology, Osaka University, Japan

Abstract. In this study, we aim to investigate the semantic representation in the brain evoked by verbal stimuli. The brain activity data was observed by means of fMRI while subjects were listening to speech in Japanese and reading transcription of the speech. We predict the state of the brain with a Ridge regression model. To build a model, an optimal regularization parameter of a Ridge regression model was assessed in each voxel with 5-fold cross-validation and evaluate predicted results with Pearson's correlation coefficient between predicted value and the observed value of the state of the brain. Significant differences were computed using a one-sided Student's t-test. The resulting p-values were corrected for multiple comparisons, using the false discovery rate (FDR) procedure. We conducted the following four experiments with the data. The first one is to estimate the state of the brain by regressing it from speech stimuli - the following five models were used to extract speech features from the spectrogram given by speech: (a) The model that directly estimates the brain activity data with audio spectrogram. This model is used as a baseline model for the following four models. (b) Bi-LSTM model. We regard speech as a series of spectrogram, and then it can be dealt with like a text by Bi-LSTM. (c) Bi-GRU model. (d) Bi-RNN model. (b) and (c) are used to compare the ability with (d). The second one is to estimate the state of the brain by regressing it from the intermediate feature of a speech-to-text deep learning model called ESPNet. The feature represents the one converting speech into texts. The third one is to estimate the semantic representation in the brain by using word embedding vectors. In this study, we used word2vec and BERT embedding vectors to represent the semantics of language and investigate the differences between those vectors. The last one is to investigate commonalities and differences between auditory and visual modalities in terms of representing semantic features in the brain. Firstly, using bidirectional sequential models, we have confirmed that the models showed better accuracy than the model (a). Secondly, although the input features of the ESPnet model (e) represent the intermediate state converting speech to text, which is different from those of the models (b)–(d), however, the visualization of the estimation result with ESPnet model is quite like that of (b)–(d). Additionally, the estimation of ESPnet model shows high reaction in language center of the brain. Thirdly, we found that BERT embedding is more suitable to estimate the semantic representation in the brain than word2vec embedding in both auditory and visual modality. Lastly, by investigating commonalities and differences of features between auditory and visual modality in the brain, a remarkable reaction was observed in Superior temporal gyrus and around the area, and Middle frontal gyrus. For both cases where textual information is provided as either speech stimuli or visual stimuli, we have confirmed that a remarkable reaction was observed in language center of the brain.

Keywords: Estimation of brain activity · BERT · Audio StimuliB243: Comparison of active areas by estimating brain activities evoked by verbal stimuli given from speech and text.

The Attentional Blink Effect of Emotional Face Recognition

Lu Hehe and Jiang Ke

School of Mental Health, Wenzhou Medical University, China
jiangke200@126.com

Abstract. Emotional face recognition plays an extremely important role in many areas of social interaction. However, it is still controversial that if there are two different perceptive processes of geometric features and emotional features of face images respectively in the field of face perception. And furthermore, there are also controversies of attentional bias within the domain of emotional face recognition: an angry superiority effect or a happiness superiority effect? The main purpose of this study is to explore the characteristics of emotional expression recognition. The experiments in this research were conducted on two dimensions. One was the control of time variables, the other was the interference between positive (PE), negative (NE) and neutral (N) expressions. Attentional blinking (AB) refers to the phenomenon that when an individual identifies two targets (T1 and T2) in a short time, the accurate identification of T2 will impair if T1 is properly processed. In this study, seven 2 (conditions: experimental/control) ×4 (SOAs: 0/235/706/1176 ms) in-subject design experiments were conducted in the reference of the SOA paradigm by Awh et al. (2004). Experiment a1 was a face recognition experiment (N-N, both T1 and T2 were neutral expressions), and experiments b1 ~ b6 were the emotional expression discrimination experiments with 6 combinations of T1 and T2 (PE-NE, NE-PE, PE-N, N-PE, NE-N, N-NE). In the experimental condition, participants had to report both targets, but in the control condition, only T2 was needed. SOAs (stimulus onset asynchronies) referred to the time interval between two points at which T1 and T2 began to appear. The results of experiment a1 showed that the main effects of condition variables and SOAs variables were significant, which indicated that the neutral expressions both as T1 and T2 could produce AB effect. The results of experiments b1 ~ b6 showed that, firstly, positive emotional face recognition had a higher accuracy. Secondly, the main effects of condition variable in experiments b1 ~ b2 (T1 and T2 were both emotional expressions) were significant, but in experiments b3 ~ b6 (one of T1 and T2 was an emotional expression, while the other was neutral), the results were not significant. Thirdly, when T1 and T2 were both emotional expressions, during the SOAs of 0 ms and 235 ms, the reduction of negative T1 on positive T2 recognition accuracy was greater than that of the opposite condition. Based on the above results, according to the research conclusion of Awh et al. (2004), which found AB effect can be generated if the processing channels of cognitive tasks are the same; on the contrary, if there are different processing channels of cognitive tasks, AB effect will not appear. Therefore, we conclude that in the emotional face recognition task, there is possible separability between geometric feature and emotional feature of face images.

Keywords: Attention blink · SOA paradigm · Face recognition · Emotion recognition · Evolutionary psychology

Gender Differences in Transitive Inference

Lingyun Cai[1], Gorka Navarrete[2], Cristian Modrono[3], Peipeng Liang[1], and Vinod Goel[4]

[1] School of Psychology and Beijing Key Laboratory of Learning and Cognition, Capital Normal University, China
[2] Laboratory of Cognitive and Social Neuroscience (LaNCyS), UDP-INECO Foundation Core on Neuroscience (UIFCoN), Universidad Diego Portales, Spain
[3] Department of Physiology, University of La Laguna, Spain
[4] Department of Psychology, York University, Canada
2193502037@cnu.edu.cn

Abstract. Problem Statement: Many previous studies consider transitive inference (TI) to be a process based on spatial ability (e.g., mental model theory). It is also the case that spatial demands can be modulated by problem difficulty and by presenting the material in linguistic or pictorial formats. Some data and evolutionary arguments suggest a male advantage in spatial ability. If this is the case, then it is possible that a male advantage may be found in TI. Objective: We set out to address this question by looking for relative sex-related differences in linguistically and spatially presented TI tasks of varying levels of difficulty. Methodology: Two studies utilizing the identical paradigm were conducted in two very different regions: Spain and China. Study 1 recruited 30 participants (15 females) in Tenerife and Study 2 recruited 40 participants (20 females) in Beijing. Participants completed spatially presented TI tasks (Pictorial TI task) and linguistically presented TI tasks (Linguistic TI task). Afterward, data were also collected on the Raven's Progressive Matrices, Digit Span, Similarities, and 3D Mental Rotation task. Results: The two studies showed that there was a significant male advantage in the linguistic TI task which recruits more spatial ability to explicitly determine and represent spatial relations, but no significant gender difference in the pictorial TI task where spatial relations were explicit and already represented in the problem statement. Furthermore, the male advantage increased with problem difficulty. No significant gender difference was found in the Raven's Progressive Matrices, Digit Span, and Similarities tasks. The males showed an advantage in the 3D Mental Rotation task. Correlation analysis found a significant positive correlation between males' 3D Mental Rotation score and their linguistic TI accuracy, in contrast, no such significant correlation was found in females. Conclusion: The results of the two studies provide converging evidence for gender difference in TI and suggest that different cognitive abilities may be engaged by males and females in doing TI. Spatial ability has a critical role to play in TI for males, but females may draw upon other (perhaps linguistic) resources. This suggests that future studies of TI, or even other reasoning problems, will need to control for sex differences before generalizing results across the population.

Keywords: Transitive inference · Gender difference spatial ability

Deep Learning-Based Difficulty Classification of Tracing Neuronal Signals in 3D Image Blocks

Bin Yang[1,2], Jiajin Huang[1,2], Gaowei Wu[3,4], and Jian Yang[1,2]

[1] Faculty of Information Technology, Beijing University of Technology, Beijing, China
jianyang@bjut.edu.cn
[2] Beijing International Collaboration Base on Brain Informatics and Wisdom Services, Beijing, China
[3] School of Artificial Intelligence, University of Chinese Academy of Sciences, Beijing, China
[4] Institute of Automation, Chinese Academy of Sciences, Beijing, China

Abstract. Quickly and accurately tracing neurons in a large-scale volumetric microscopy data is a very challenging task. Most latest automatic algorithms for tracing multi-neurons in a whole brain are designed under the Ultra Tracer framework, which begins the tracing of a neuron from its soma and tracing all signals via a block-by-block strategy. Some neuron image blocks are easy to trace, and their automatic reconstructions might be very accurate, and some others are difficult to trace and their reconstructions might be inaccurate or incomplete. The former are called Low Tracing Difficulty Blocks (Low-TDBs) and the latter are called High Tracing Difficulty Blocks (High-TDBs). We design a model called 3D-SSMto classify the tracing difficulty of 3D neuron image blocks, which is based on 3DResidual attention Network (3D-ResNet), Fully Connected Neural Networks (FCNNs) and Long Short-Term Memory (LSTM). 3D-SSM contains three parts: Structure Feature Extraction module (SFE), Sequence Information Extraction module (SIE) and Model Fusion module (MF). SFE utilizes 3D-ResNet and FCNN to extract two kinds of features in 3D neuron image blocks and reconstructions. SIE uses two LSTMs to extract sequence information hidden in features of sequential blocks produced by 3D-ResNet and FCNNs, respectively. MF adopts a concatenation operation and a full connection layer to combine outputs of two models in SIE. Neuron images of a whole mouse brain are segmented into many overlapped 3D image blocks along the gold standard reconstruction of each traced neuron. Corresponding to gold standard and APP2automatic reconstructions, 12732 training samples and 5342 test samples are constructed based on those 3D image blocks, respectively. The 3D-SSM model is trained by using training image blocks, neuron distances and L-measure features of reconstructions corresponding to these training samples. Its classification accuracy is 87.07% on training set and 83.88% on test set. Results of tracing difficulty classification produced by 3D-SSM model can be used as the stop condition of an automatic reconstruction algorithm in the Ultra Tracer framework. With that, neuronal signals are traced by the automatic algorithm in Low-TDBsand reconstructed by an annotator in High-TDBs. The introducing of interaction between automatic tracing and manual reconstruction is capable of promoting Ultra Tracer to generate more accurate neuronal reconstructions. The code and models are available at https://github.com/BingooYang/ Tracing-difficulty-classification-on-3D-neuron-image-block.

Keywords: Fully connected neural networks · Tracing difficulty classification · Tracing neurons · Long short-term memory · 3D residual neural network

Heath Older Adults Reduced Sensitivity to Premise Diversity Rather Than That to Premise Monotonicity During Category-Based Induction

Yuhang Ling and Changquan Long

Southwest Universuty, China
lcq@swu.edu.cn

Abstract. Problem Statement: Category-based induction (CBI) involves generalizing the properties from a known exemplar to novel cases by using the categorical relations. In category-based induction, both premise monotonicity effect and premise diversity effect are important during life-span development, but few previous studies have investigated the premise monotonicity and diversity effect during semantic category-based induction in health older adults. Moreover, inductive reasoning ability as an advanced cognitive ability, is vital in improving the life quality of older adults. In order to track the life-span development of premise monotonicity and diversity effect during category-based induction, we investigated premise monotonicity and diversity effect in health older adults and college students. Methodology & Results: In Experiment 1, health older adults and college students were randomly assigned into either premise diversity task group or premise monotonicity task group. Participants were instructed to compare the inductive strength of two sets of the premises (monotonic or non-monotonic; diverse or non-diverse), then make forced-choice decisions between two sets of premise pairs (monotonic or non-monotonic; diverse or non-diverse), indicating which set was more likely to lead them to believe a particular "claim" (or conclusion). Statistical results showed that, after controlling the years of education, there was no significant difference in the scores of the premise monotonicity task between health older adults and college students, while the scores of premise diversity task in health older adults were significantly lower than those in college students. In Experiment 2, health older adults and college students participated both premise monotonicity task and premise diversity task with the same experiment procedure as in Experiment 1. We found that, after controlling for the years of education, for health older adults, premise monotonicity task scores were significantly higher than premise diversity task scores; for college students, there was no significant difference between premise monotonicity task scores and premise diversity task scores; for premise monotonicity task, there was no significant difference between health older adults and college students; for premise diversity task, the scores of health older adults were significantly lower than the scores of college students. Those results verified the validity of results in Experiment 1. In Post-hoc Experiment, health older adults and college students should rate the similarity of the premises (diverse pairs and non-diverse pairs) from 1 to 7. Statistical results showed that, the main effect of pair (diverse, non-diverse) was significant after controlling the years of education, and the mean of similarity scores of the non-diverse pairs was significantly higher than that of the diverse pairs. Conclusion: Heath older adults reduced sensitivity to premise diversity rather than that to premise monotonicity, while college students retain sensitivity to both premise diversity and monotonicity semantic during category-based induction. Moreover, both health older adults and college students found the diverse premise are less diverse than the non-diverse premise, which means the decline of premise diversity effect during semantic category-based induction did not cause by the decline of sensitivity of similarity of premises during premise diversity task.

Keywords: Fully connected neural networks, Tracing difficulty classification, Tracing neurons, Long short-term memory, 3D residual neural network

Feature Representation Based on Kernel Canonical Correlation Analysis Enhancing Interpretability of Brain-Computer Interface Systems

Viviana Gómez Orozco, Iván De La Pava Panche, Miguel Ángel Espinosa Echeverry, David Augusto Cárdenas Peña, Paula Marcela Herrera Gómez, and Álvaro Ángel Orozco Guitiérrez

Universidad Tecnológica de Pereira, Colombia
vigomez@utp.edu.co

Abstract. Motivation: Brain-computer interface (BCI) systems allow users to control applications and devices from neuroimaging data. Among all kinds of neuroimages, electroencephalographic (EEG) signals non-invasively record brain electrical activity driven by stimuli or intentions. BCI applications for motor-disabled people include physical therapy, rehabilitation, and motion assistance. Problem statement: One of the most significant open issues in BCI relies on the extraction and selection of features relevant for performing an action and explaining the underlying brain dynamics. On the one hand, feature engineering approaches demand knowledge about brain physiology, which sometimes is either unknown or suffers from insufficient accuracy. On the contrary, the deep learning models outperform thanks to the hierarchically gained complexity. However, the reasons behind the outcomes become inscrutable, and the predictions result disbelieved in critical scenarios. Methods: This work proposes a feature representation methodology for BCI that decodes nonlinear relationships from EEG data through the Kernel Canonical Correlation Analysis (KCCA). KCCA identifies data nonlinearities through a linear combination on the kernel projections. The proposal highlights spatial and temporal patterns by analyzing EEG trials belonging to one of two classes. We consider a BCI processing pipeline as follows: Firstly, a filter bank decomposes EEG signals into nine non-overlapping 4 Hz wide subbands within the range of 4 to 40 Hz. Secondly, the common spatial patterns (CSP) technique band-wise extracts features from the first and last two spatial filters that best discriminates two tasks regarding their variance. Such a feature extraction yields 36 features holding spectro-spatial information. Then, a selection stage ranks resulting features according to the Mutual Information with the given task label. The proposed KCCA-based representation maps the characterized trials and task labels into a new joint space. We consider the radial basis function and the Dirac delta as the kernel mappings for the features and task labels. Lastly, the linear discriminant analysis (LDA), K-nearest-neighbor (KNN), and linear support vector machine (SVM) carry out the classification stage from the KCCA mapping of trial features. A nested 10-fold cross-validation scheme tunes the number of selected features and the KCCA regularization. Validation: We test the proposed methodology in the well-known BCI Competition IV dataset 2a containing EEG records from nine healthy subjects while performing four motor imagery (MI) tasks. We selected the left and right-hand MI tasks for a bi-class problem from the provided training and test subsets. Results evidenced that LDA, KNN, and SVM classifiers attained an average performance of 79.46%, 61.45%, and 81.25%, respectively. Further, features within 8-16 Hz from contralateral channels achieved 91.7% average accuracy on the four best performing subjects, which agrees with the MI physiological knowledge. Conclusion: The introduced feature representation using a classic linear SVM achieves accuracy rates competitive with the state-of-the-art BCI strategies. Besides, the processing pipeline allows identifying the spatial and spectral features driven by the underlying brain activity and best modeling the MI intentions.

Keywords: Kernel Canonical correlation analysis, Feature representation, Electroencephalogram, Brain-computer interface systems, Motor Imagery.

A Novel Phase-Based Transfer Entropy Estimator from a Kernel Approach

Iván De La Pava Panche[1], Viviana Gómez Orozco[1], Julián David Pastrana Cortés[1], Andrés Marino Álvarez Meza[2], Paula Marcela Herrera Gómez[1], and Álvaro Ángel Orozco Gutiérrez[1]

[1] Universidad Tecnológica de Pereira, Colombia
ide@utp.edu.co
[2] Universidad Nacional de Colombia - Sede Manizales, Colombia

Abstract. Problem Statement: Neural oscillations are observed in the mammalian brain at different temporal and spatial scales. These oscillations, and their interactions, have been linked to cognitive functions and information processing at large. Furthermore, their phases are fundamental for the coordination of anatomically distributed processing in the brain. The concept of phase transfer entropy (TE) refers to an information theory-based measure of directed connectivity among neural oscillations that allows studying such distributed processes. Methodology: In this work, we propose a novel methodology to estimate TE between phase time-series. Our approach combines a kernel-based TE estimator of Renyi's α entropy, which sidesteps the need for probability distribution computation, with phase time-series obtained by convolving the neural signals with a Morlet Wavelet. Our proposal is tested on simulated unidirectionally coupled data holding spectral properties that resemble those of electroencephalographic signals. The simulated data are generated using mathematical models of neural mechanisms that aim to capture the behavior of neural populations at the macroscopic level known as neural mass models. We evaluate our proposal's performance in the frequency range between 2 Hz and 60 Hz for different levels of coupling strength, noise, and signal cross-talk. For each case, we perform permutation tests based on randomized trial surrogates to determine which couplings or directed connections are statistically significant at a Bonferroni-corrected alpha level of 0.00033. Results and discussion: Obtained results show that our approach successfully captures the phased-based interactions present in the simulated data. It accounts for different coupling strengths, and it is robust to the presence of realistic noise levels and signal mixing. In that regard, the proposed methodology outperforms other explored approaches that involve conventional TE estimators, which depend on probability estimation as an intermediate step in TE computation. Finally, it is worth noting that unlike alternative methodologies for phase TE estimation that rely on trial collapsing, our method allows estimating the phase TE between individual pairs of signals. Therefore, the proposed approach can be readily used as a characterization strategy in brain-computer interface applications or other machine learning tasks involving directed interactions between neural signals.

Keywords: Effective connectivity, Transfer entropy, Phase interactions, Kernel methods

Measuring the Effect of Pre-sleep Activities in Sleep Quality from EEG Activity

Rafael Ramirez[1] and Rafael Raul Ramirez-Nethersole[2]

[1] Universitat Pompeu Fabra, Spain
[2] Institut Joaquima Pla i Farreras, Spain
rafael.ramirez@upf.edu

Abstract. Problem Statement: Neural oscillations are observed in the mammalian brain at different temporal and spatial scales. These oscillations, and their interactions, have been linked to cognitive functions and information processing at large. Furthermore, their phases are fundamental for the coordination of anatomically distributed processing in the brain. The concept of phase transfer entropy (TE) refers to an information theory-based measure of directed connectivity among neural oscillations that allows studying such distributed processes. Methodology: In this work, we propose a novel methodology to estimate TE between phase time-series. Our approach combines a kernel-based TE estimator of Renyi's α entropy, which sidesteps the need for probability distribution computation, with phase time-series obtained by convolving the neural signals with a Morlet Wavelet. Our proposal is tested on simulated unidirectionally coupled data holding spectral properties that resemble those of electroencephalographic signals. The simulated data are generated using mathematical models of neural mechanisms that aim to capture the behavior of neural populations at the macroscopic level known as neural mass models. We evaluate our proposal's performance in the frequency range between 2 Hz and 60 Hz for different levels of coupling strength, noise, and signal crosstalk. For each case, we perform permutation tests based on randomized trial surrogates to determine which couplings or directed connections are statistically significant at a Bonferroni-corrected alpha level of 0.00033. Results and discussion: Obtained results show that our approach successfully captures the phased-based interactions present in the simulated data. It accounts for different coupling strengths, and it is robust to the presence of realistic noise levels and signal mixing. In that regard, the proposed methodology outperforms other explored approaches that involve conventional TE estimators, which depend on probability estimation as an intermediate step in TE computation. Finally, it is worth noting that unlike alternative methodologies for phase TE estimation that rely on trial collapsing, our method allows estimating the phase TE between individual pairs of signals. Therefore, the proposed approach can be readily used as a characterization strategy in brain-computer interface applications or other machine learning tasks involving directed interactions between neural signals Background. Sleep commonly covers nearly one third of the lifespan of a person. While we sleep, body systems such as the circulatory, musculoskeletal, respiratory, and central nervous system are repaired. Sleep is also important for functions such as memory consolidation, learning, and emotion regulation, as well as for quality of life. Furthermore, due to sleep deprivation the immune system gets damaged and there is an increase in the risk of cardiovascular pathologies, hypertension, obesity, metabolic deregulation, and diabetes. Several studies have shown that patients with sleep disorders have high levels of beta EEG activity (13-32 Hz) at or around sleep onset and during NREM sleep. Objectives. The aim of this study is to investigate sleep quality, in particular sleep onset predisposition, by studying the impact of common daily actions on alpha, beta, delta, and theta EEG activity. We evaluate the extent to which 1) social media viewing in mobile devices, 2) reading in mobile devices, and 3) reading on paper, affect EEG frequency band activity. Methods. Participants took part in three individual sessions where they were asked to perform the three different activities (i.e. social media viewing in mobile devices, reading in mobile devices, and reading on paper) while their EEG activity was recorded. EEG recordings were obtained before starting the activity (2 minutes), during the activity (20 minutes) and after the activity (2 mins). EEG data were divided into frontal, parietal, temporal, and occipital lobe data according to the electrode positions. For each group, data were filtered to obtain delta (1–3 Hz), theta (4–7 Hz), alpha (8–12 Hz) and beta (13–32) waves. Time-based epoching was performed with a window size of 1 second and hop size of 0.1 seconds. Data was squared and arithmetic mean was computed. Finally, log(1 + x) was computed. For each lobe, frequency bands were obtained, as well as an average for all regions. The resulting data was compared to quantify the effect of each activity. Results. Results show that social media viewing on average caused a significant decrease in delta, theta, and alpha waves, while causing a significant increase in beta waves. In contrast, reading on paper caused a decrease in beta waves. Conclusions. Results seem to indicate that social media viewing increased the state of alertness (increase in beta waves) and decreased relaxation and drowsiness of the participants. In contrast, reading on paper caused a decrease in beta waves and a slight smaller decrease in alpha waves compared to social media viewing, which may be interpreted as favoring a state of relaxation and decreasing alertness, which in turn is beneficial for sleep onset quality.

Keywords: EEG · Sleep quality · Power spectral analyses

Can 13-/15-Month-Old Infants Make Transitive Inference of Social Dominance?

Jing Zhao, Xi Yao, Yumeng Wang, Xi Liang, Zhengyan Wang, and Peipeng Liang

School of Psychology, Capital Normal University, China
conanzj@126.com

Abstract. Transitive inference (TI) plays an important role in our daily life. Researchers have long been interested in the origin of TI. Given that infants are sensitive to the social hierarchies, some studies examined whether these young children are capable of TI in the context of social dominance. However, this issue remains largely unanswered and relevant findings are inconsistent. The conflicting findings might be ascribed to the differences in methodological factors, including end-of-trial criteria, the criteria of identifying valid participants, and subjective observation of infants' behavior. Experiment 1 in the present study replicated the study of Gaze et al. (2017) with similar settings of materials to examine whether the 13-month-old infants emerged TI by a violation-of-expectation (VoE) paradigm involving a dominance hierarchy (donkey>dog>frog; where '>' denotes greater dominance). In contrast to the previous study, more strict criteria were adopted in this study to identify valid participants, and eye-tracking technique was used to record the measurements of looking time more objectively. Infants viewed interactions between donkey and dog as well as interactions between dog and frog during the familiarization stage; While in the test stage, interactions between donkey and frog were presented, which included the congruent (donkey > frog) and incongruent (frog > donkey) conditions. Results of Experiment 1 showed that there was non-significant difference in looking time between congruent and incongruent conditions in the VoE task. Further, Experiment 2 added the experimental instruction to make infants pay more attention to the social relation between the agents. Similar patterns of results to Experiment 1 were observed in Experiment 2, revealing that infants of 13-month-old may not be able to make transitivity reasoning. Therefore, older infants with 15 months of age were invited to Experiment 3. With the same task and procedure as Experiment 2, a significantly congruent effect was detected. In particular, infants looked longer to incongruent than congruent display, indicating the emergence of TI in this cohort of participants. In order to examine the stability of the TI ability in 15-month-old infants, we changed to use a cartoon video including the interaction between chick, rabbit and pig in Experiment 4, in which the time of each motion in the video could be exactly arranged and manipulated. A marginally significant effect of congruence was then found for the looking time based on the VoE task. Moreover, in this experiment, the predictive looking paradigm was supplemented besides the VoE paradigm, which was set before the presence of results about the agents' interaction, so as to examine whether infants established the expectation about the social dominance in the test stage. Results on the predictive looking did not show any significant effects, suggesting a lack of stable expectation about the social relation. In sum, the current findings suggested that 15-month-old infants might emerge the TI ability, but not stable. The TI ability of 15-month-old infants might be affected by the test material, which closely associated with whether a reliable prediction of the social hierarchy was established or not. The present results supported the emergence of TI in young infants to some extent, and bring some enlightenments for early childhood education.

Keywords: Transitive inference · Violation of expectation · Looking time · Eye-tracking, infant

AI Block Design for Wired/Wireless Modularity Algorithms

Yoosoo Oh

Daegu University, Republic of Korea
yoosoo.oh@daegu.ac.kr

Abstract. In this paper, we propose an approach for creating a block-type module equipped with a machine learning algorithm. We design contact and contactless data communications. Contact data communication is a wired serial communication method for block modularization. Contactless data communication is a wireless block communication method for block modularization. We propose a novel technology that constructs multiple AI blocks that have machine learning algorithm modules. The multiple blocks are put together to create a high-level machine learning service. Each AI block can be an algorithm, processing, training data/test data, trained model, and database. Logically, a processing block connects with algorithms, training data, and models for a machine learning application. In the modeling phase, we can apply several machine learning algorithms as needed. The practical machine learning algorithm can be supervised/unsupervised/deep learnings such as kNN, SVM, random forest, Gaussian naive Bayesian, and neural network. We developed a wired serial communication method, which is a contact communication for modularity block. For wired communications, we designed a brick shape for each wired block. For the logical module, we physically put the raspberry PI in a brick-shaped block. The embedded raspberry PI can be the role of each module entity. Each brick-shaped block has four connectors, four pushbuttons, and one raspberry PI. The four connectors, serial ports for flexible connection, communicate machine learning data with the other blocks. The four pushbuttons can trigger the serial connection. We developed a wireless block communication method, which is a contactless communication for modularity block. For wireless communications, we designed a fruit shape for each wireless block. The wireless blocks consist of a fruit-shaped block and a plate-shaped block. The wireless blocks have a raspberry PI to construct a machine learning module entity and a trigger module for the connection of MQTT which determines a change status of MQTT grouping. The plate-shaped block is a processing block with a load cell that detects the connection of fruit-shaped blocks by measuring the weight of each fruit-shaped block. The weight of each fruit-shaped block is equivalent, and then the plate-shaped block notices whether a new block is connected or an existing block is released. Our suggested approach is different from the distributed machine learning research. Our approach is to build a machine learning block for wired/wireless modularity algorithms. Our suggested approach has features that enable free addition/deletion for linking AI block algorithms. Also, the proposed scheme enables easy and simple data communication settings. Moreover, the proposed scheme applies to various edge computing devices.

Keywords: AI · Machine learning · Modularity · Block technology

Parsing Grey Matter Heterogeneity of Autism Spectrum Disorder Using Normative Model

Xiaolong Shan, Jinming Xiao, Huafu Chen, and Xujun Duan

School of Life Science and Technology, MOE Key Lab for Neuro information, High-Field Magnetic Resonance Brain Imaging Key Laboratory of Sichuan Province, University of Electronic Science and Technology of China, Chengdu, 610054, People's Republic of China
duanxujun@uestc.edu.cn

Abstract. Background: Autism spectrum disorder (ASD) is a sever and complex neurodevelopmental disorder characterized by substantial clinical and biological heterogeneity, which is a major challenge in understanding and treating the ASD. However, the extent of individuals with ASD differ from neurotypical development (TD) in brain structure is still unclear. Participants and methods: Here, T1-weighted magnetic resonance imaging data from 560 TD and 496 subjects with ASD were selected from the ABIDE-I as an independent test cohort and 564 TD from the ABIDE-II were used to generate the model. Voxel-based morphometry (VBM) maps were obtained for each subject, and grey matter matrices with the dimension of the number of voxel × the number of subject were constructed for ABIDE_I_TD, ABDIE_I_ASD and ABIDE_II_TD. The non-negative matrix factorization (NMF) was employed to decompose the grey matter matrix of ABIDE_II_TD into six factors and the corresponding characteristic weights which represent the variability of individuals. Subsequently, the non-negative reconstruction algorithm was used to reconstruct ABIDE_I_ASD and ABIDE_I_TD grey matter matrix based on the six factors obtained from the former step. The strategy of reconstruction was iteratively updating weight matrix, while keeping the factor matrix obtained from ABIDE_II_TD grey matter matrix decomposition fixed. Next, weights of ABIDE _II_TD were used for normative modeling to map the deviation of factors in brain structure through the Gaussian process regression. Finally, a data-driven clustering analysis was utilized to identify biologically defined ASD subtypes based on their individual neuroanatomical deviation profiles. Results: Six latent factors including the medial cortex, cerebellum, perceptual region, parietal lobe, frontal lobe and limbic system, and corresponding weights were first obtained from the implementation of NMF on the gray matter matrix. Using case-control analysis, we found ASD showed increased weights and deviations of factors which were characterized by the medial cortex, perceptual region, parietal, frontal, and limbic system than TD. Three subtypes with distinct neuroanatomical deviation patterns were identified using the Gaussian mixture clustering. Specifically, subtype 1 and subtype 3 showed increased grey matter volume (GMV) in relation to neurotypical range across the whole brain. Conversely, subtype2 showed decreased GMV across the whole brain. Distinct clinical manifestations also were identified among these subtypes. Notably, case subjects in subtype 2 showed lower ADOS Communication scores and ADOS social scores. Conclusions: Our findings suggested that individuals with ASD have highly heterogeneous deviation patterns. The results highlight the need to test for subtypes, as different abnormal anatomical patterns were observed in three distinct subgroups. This study also presents a data-driven route for understanding the neuroanatomical heterogeneity.

Keywords: Autism spectrum disorder · Non-negative matrix factorization · Normative model · Deviation · Neuroanatomical heterogeneity

The Influence of Narrative Factors In Violent Online Games on the Aggression of Male Gamers

LiYan Li[1], Liang Zhao[2], Jiali Jiang[1], and Xiuya Lei[1]

[1] Beijing Forestry University, China
leixiuya@163.com
[2] Peking University, China

Abstract. The influence of violent online games on aggression has been widely concerned, but few studies have explored the specific factors affecting aggression in violent online games. With the continuous development of technology, more and more online games begin to try to add narrative factors into online games. Narrative factors in violent online games can affect game experience, cognitive process, and decision-making behavior of gamers. This research designs an experiment in order to explore the influence of narrative factors in violent online games on the aggression of male gamers. Sixty male college students were selected as subjects, using the hot sauce paradigm, the State of Hostility Scale, the Mental State Reading Test of Eye Zone, and the Implicit Association Test to explore the influence of narrative factors in violent online games on the explicit and implicit aggression of male gamers. In terms of explicit aggression, the score of the hot sauce paradigm in the narrative group was significantly higher than that of the non-narrative group ($F(1,54) = 19.89$, $P < 0.001$), and the score of hostility in the narrative group was significantly lower than that of the non-narrative group ($F(1,54) = 147.38$, $P < 0.001$). For implicit aggression, the reaction time of inconsistent tasks in the narrative group was significantly shorter than that in the non-narrative group ($t = -4.30$, $P < 0.001$). Compared with non-narrative violent games, male gamers have higher aggressive behaviors but lower aggressive emotions when playing narrative violent games. Narrative factors in the game will influence the implicit attack evaluation of male gamers. Related personnel can reduce the negative impact of violent online games by optimizing the narrative factors in violent online games.

Keywords: Violent online games · Narrative factors · Explicit aggression · Implicit aggression · Male gamers

The Influence of Cyberbullying on Adolescents' Non-suicidal Self-injury: Mediated Moderating Model

Jiali Jiang[1,2], LiYan Li[1,2], Yue Peng[1,2], and Xiuya Lei[1,2]

[1] Beijing Forestry University, China
[2] Peking University, China
leixiuya@163.com

Abstract. The influence of violent online games on aggression has been widely concerned, but few studies have explored the specific factors affecting aggression in violent online games. With the continuous development of technology, more and more online games begin to try to add narrative factors into online games. Narrative factors in violent online games can affect game experience, cognitive process and decision-making behavior of gamers. This research designs an experiment in order to explore the influence of narrative factors in violent online games on the aggression of male gamers. Sixty male college students were selected as subjects, using the hot sauce paradigm, the State of Hostility Scale, the Mental State Reading Test of Eye Zone, and the Implicit Association Test to explore the influence of narrative factors in violent online games on the explicit and implicit aggression of male gamers. Results: (1) In terms of explicit aggression, the score of the hot sauce paradigm in the narrative group was significantly higher than that of the non-narrative group ($F(1,54) = 19.89$, $P < 0.001$), and the score of hostility in the narrative group was significantly lower than that of the non-narrative group ($F(1,54) = 147.38$, $P < 0.001$). (2) For implicit aggression, the reaction time of inconsistent tasks in the narrative group was significantly shorter than that in the non-narrative group ($t = -4.30$, $P < 0.001$). Compared with non-narrative violent games, male gamers have higher aggressive behaviors but lower aggressive emotions when playing narrative violent games. Narrative factors in the game will influence the implicit attack evaluation of male gamers. Related personnel can reduce the negative impact of violent online games by optimizing the narrative factors in violent online games.

Keywords: Violent online games · Narrative factors · Explicit aggression · Implicit aggression · Male gamers

Irrational Expression in College Students' Online News Comments: Structure and Influencing Factors

Yue Peng, Yang Yang, Xiuya Lei, Leyi Zhu, Yinuo Lyv, Lu Qiao, Zhaoqi Jian, and Cancan Jin

Beijing Forestry University, China
jcctxdy@163.com

Abstract. With the continuous increase in the number of netizens, Internet irrational expression is a network phenomenon that has received more and more attention in recent years. This study aims to explore the structure of irrational expression in online news comments of college students, and the impact of self-control and life events on Internet irrational expression. The study selected 130 college students (sample 1) to complete the Internet Irrational Expression Questionnaire for item analysis and exploratory factor analysis, and 740 college students (sample 2) to complete the questionnaire for confirmatory factor analysis. In addition, 547 college students (sample 3) were selected to complete the Internet Irrational Expression Questionnaire, Self-Control Scale, as well as Adolescent Self-Rating Life Events Check List respectively. Results: (1) College students' Internet irrational expression could be divided into four dimensions: verbal violence, cynicism, self-centeredness, and influence of attachment; the confirmatory factor analysis suggested that the model fitted well, with $\chi 2/df = 4.22$, CFI = 0.95, TLI = 0.93, NFI = 0.94, RMSEA = 0.07, and the Cronbach's α of different dimensions ranging from 0.74 to 0.88; (2) Life events were positively correlated with Internet irrational expression, and self-control obviously played a mediating role between life events and Internet irrational expression; (3) Grades could significantly moderate the impact of self-control on Internet irrational expression, with the lower-grade group having a partial mediating effect, while the higher-grade group not having any. The Internet Irrational Expression Questionnaire can serve as a suitable tool for related studies; life events can cause college students to produce Internet irrational expression by reducing self-control, with the process moderated by grades.

Keywords: Internet irrational expression · Development of questionnaire · Life events · Self-control · Multi-group comparison

The Relationship Between Media Multitasking and Creativity: A Review

Ziying Li, Jiajing Li, Yue Peng, and Zelong Meng

Beijing Forestry University, China
declan_meng@163.com

Abstract. With the development of the Internet, the forms of media activities are gradually becoming diversifying. More and more people choose to use multiple media at the same time to meet the needs of current media activities, 60.3% of young people in China engage in media multitasking in their daily life. Media multitasking, as a new normal of media use, has attracted extensive attention because of its impact on individual cognitive abilities such as sustained attention, inhibitory control, working memory and long-term memory. Currently, many studies have concentrated on the relationship between media multitasking and creativity. However, there are still many controversies among these studies. The current study summarized a total of 75 relevant articles over the last 15 years concerning media multitasking and its relationship with creativity in order to sort out and reveal the systematic relationship. The results found a positive relationship between media multitasking and creativity. Specifically: (1) Media multitasking had different relationships with different aspects of individual creative thinking, that is, it was positively correlated with individual divergent thinking, but not aggregative thinking; (2) Media multitasking was positively related to creative personality; (3) Media multitasking was positively correlated with individual creative achievement; The correlation can be mainly explained from three perspectives: attention style, cognitive resources and emotional information. Future research can be carried out in three directions: longitudinal tracking design and more rigorous measurement methods to examine the causal relationship, more diverse samples to expand the external validity of the study and exploring the internal psychological mechanism.

Keywords: Media multitasking · Divergent thinking · Aggregative thinking · Creative personality · Creative achievement

Combining Machine Learning and Biophysical Modeling to Solve Computational Psychiatry Problems

Dimitris Pinotsis[1,2], Sean Fitzgerald[3], and Alik Widge[4]

[1] City, University of London, UK
[2] MIT, USA
pinotsis@mit.edu
[3] University of London, UK
[4] University of Minnesota, USA

Abstract. Computational Psychiatry is an exciting emerging field that focuses on mechanistic explanations of neurological diseases and disorders. The hope is that such explanations will allow us to gain a deeper understanding of the causes of such diseases and disorders, suggest effective treatments and prevent their onset. In this talk, I will review some recent work in this field. I will first consider differences in brain structure and function between schizophrenics, their relatives and controls and how these might relate to aberrant neuromodulation in frontal areas. I will show that schizophrenics have higher activity than normal and that this activity changes in the opposite direction for unexpected stimuli than what is observed in controls. Also, although stimuli are processed in lower (auditory) cortices these changes occur only in higher (frontal) cortices. These results are based on a biophysical large-scale network model of a Mismatch Negativity (MMN) paradigm together with Variational Inference algorithms from machine learning. They demonstrate our ability to identify inter-group differences using biophysical models. I will then discuss some recent results based on EEG data from MDD patients and healthy people performing a Multiple Source Interference Task (MSIT). I will show how a biophysical large-scale network model of the MSIT task allows us to better distinguish MDD patients and their subtypes compared to just using classical neuroimaging measures like ERP amplitudes and latencies. To assess the predictive power of different data features, I will use machine learning algorithms for supervised and unsupervised clustering and feature importance. Overall, the above results suggest a new way to dissect and explain neurological disorders: combine machine learning with biophysical modeling. This combination renders results of machine learning algorithms more interpretable: the corresponding data features these algorithms use describe brain pathophysiology.

Keywords: Computational psychiatry · Biophysical models · Machine learning

Contents

Investigations of Human Information Processing Systems

Brain Big Data Analytics, Curation and Management

Cognitive and Computational Foundations of Brain Science

Inferring Neural Circuit Interactions and Neuromodulation from Local Field Potential and Electroencephalogram Measures

Pablo Martínez-Cañada[1,2], Shahryar Noei[1,3], and Stefano Panzeri[1,4](✉)

[1] Neural Computation Laboratory, Center for Neuroscience and Cognitive Systems, Istituto Italiano di Tecnologia, Genova and Rovereto, Italy
{pablo.martinez,shahryar.noei}@iit.it,
stefano.panzeri@zmnh.uni-hamburg.de

[2] Optical Approaches to Brain Function Laboratory, Istituto Italiano di Tecnologia, Genova, Italy

[3] CIMeC, University of Trento, Rovereto, Italy

[4] Department of Neural Information Processing, Center for Molecular Neurobiology (ZMNH), University Medical Center Hamburg-Eppendorf (UKE), Hamburg, Germany

Abstract. Electrical recordings of neural mass activity, such as local field potentials (LFPs) and electroencephalograms (EEGs), have been instrumental in studying brain function. However, being aggregate signals that lack cellular resolution, these signals are not easy to interpret directly in terms of neural functions. Developing tools for a reliable estimation of key neural parameters from these signals, such as the interaction between excitation and inhibition or the level of neuromodulation, is important both for neuroscience and clinical applications. Over the years we have developed tools based on the combination of neural network modelling and computational analysis of empirical data to estimate neural parameters from aggregate neural signals. The purpose of this paper, which accompanies an Invited Plenary Lecture in this conference, is to review the main tools that we have developed to estimate neural parameters from mass signals, and to outline future challenges and directions for developing computational tools to invert aggregate neural signals in terms of neural circuit parameters.

Keywords: Local Field Potential (LFP) · Electroencephalogram (EEG) · Neural circuit · Neural network model · Leaky Integrate-and-Fire (LIF) neuron model · Neuromodulation

This work was supported by the European Union's Horizon 2020 research and innovation programme under the Marie Skłodowska-Curie (grant agreement No 893825 to P.M.C), the NIH Brain Initiative (grants U19NS107464 to S.P. and NS108410 to S.P.) and the Simons Foundation (SFARI Explorer 602849 to S.P.).

M. Mahmud et al. (Eds.): BI 2021, LNAI 12960, pp. 3–12, 2021.
https://doi.org/10.1007/978-3-030-86993-9_1

1 Introduction

Aggregate electrical brain signals such as Local Field Potentials (LFPs) or Electroencephalograms (EEGs) have major applications in both scientific research and clinical diagnosis because they are easy to record, capture activity at different organization levels from mesoscopic to macroscopic brain scales, and can reveal oscillatory activity over a wide range of frequencies [1,4,6,10,16,17]. However, these aggregate signals are more difficult to interpret than spiking activity of individual neurons, because they conflate and add together contributions from many complex neural processes [1,4,6,16,17]. Being able to separate the contributions of different neural phenomena to LFPs or EEGs, and to quantify how neural parameters change with manipulations of neural circuits or in brain disorders, will enhance our understanding of how best to use LFPs or EEGs to study brain function and dysfunction.

Over the years we have developed numerous computational tools to address this issue. Our approach includes advanced methods to identify regions of interest in the frequency domain in neural recordings, neural network models that predict key neural phenomena, and computationally-guided perturbation experiments to causally validate model predictions.

In this paper, which accompanies the Plenary Lecture, we review our approach and point to new directions and challenges for future research in this field.

2 Analytical Methods to Identify Regions of the Frequency Spectrum Capturing Different Neural Phenomena of Interest

The LFP and the EEG display prominent oscillatory activity. Thus, the LFP and EEG have been traditionally decomposed and interpreted in the frequency domain [4,16,17]. For example, Fourier analysis allows individual analysis of frequency bands such as the widely used delta, theta, alpha, beta and gamma bands. The validity of this approach is supported by the associations found between band-limited power signals and distinct behavioural states or sensory inputs [2,8,17,20,22]. However, the individuation, separation and definition of individual frequency bands are often largely arbitrary, based on heuristic criteria and vary substantially between studies [6]. Thus, a first major problem when trying to infer neural mechanisms from aggregate signals is to establish a correspondence between specific regions of the LFP or EEG frequency spectrum and specific neural mechanisms of interest.

One major difficulty in this endeavour is that the average of the power spectrum (either over time epochs or trials) of a typical recording (see Fig. 1A for an example of LFP recordings in visual cortex during naturalistic stimulation) is dominated by a power-law aperiodic component and often lacks easily identifiable oscillatory peaks. This could lead us to think that there is no distinctive structure in the power spectrum and, thus, there is no possibility for a clear and objective separation in frequency bands. However, the average spectrum may mask individual variations that correspond to different processing modalities or functions, especially for complex tasks or during stimulation with naturalistic sensory stimuli. To capture how individual Fourier coefficients vary their power over time in relation to stimulus variations, we developed an information theoretic algorithm that quantifies the stimulus information coding of each frequency. The theoretical foundations of information theory (see [19, 21]) demonstrate that mutual information is the most important measure to capture all possible ways in which a neural signal can carry information about any sensory variable of interest. The information spectrum computed for V1 data during naturalistic stimulation showed a clear structure that was invisible in the average spectrum: there are only two bands that carry stimulus information, a low-frequency (1–8 Hz) and a high-frequency gamma band (60–100 Hz), whereas middle frequencies carry little information (Fig. 1B).

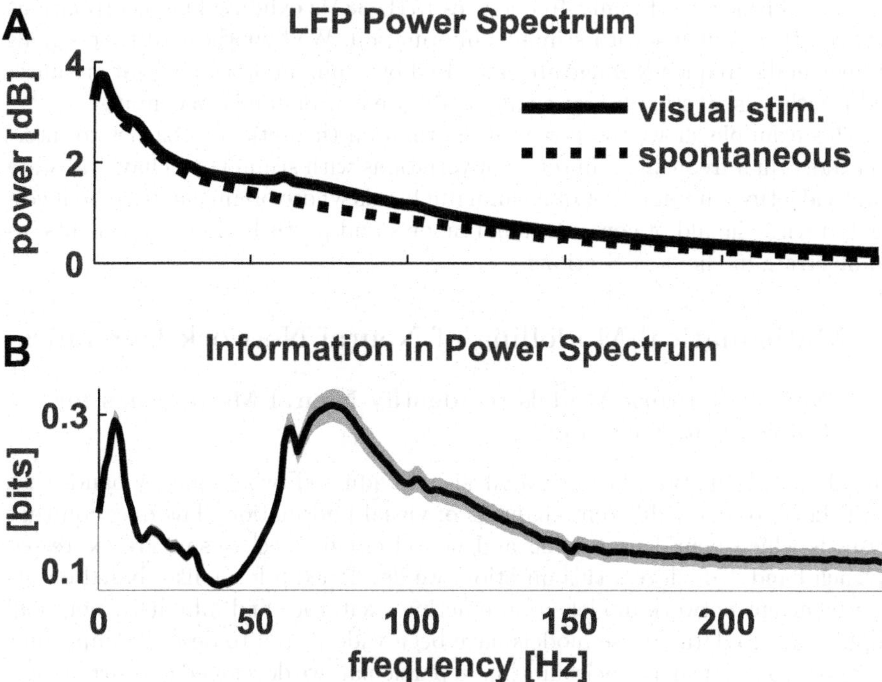

Fig. 1. Comparison of power and information spectra. Data are taken from primary visual cortex of anaesthetised macaques during stimulation with naturalistic movies. A) Power spectrum B) Information spectrum. Recomputed from data first published in [2,9].

Extending the information theory approach to the multivariate case of information carried by pairs of frequencies (see [18] for some of its theoretical foundations) allowed us to characterize specific regions of the information spectrum as belonging to only one or multiple bands. This partition into functionally meaningful bands can be achieved by quantifying patterns of redundancy or independence between the information carried by different frequencies. For example, if the information carried by one frequency is independent of amplitude variations in another frequency, then these two frequencies probably capture different neural contributions to the LFP. If the two frequencies carry redundant information instead, they likely originate from common neural phenomena. Application of this approach to visual cortical data has revealed three different functional bands in the information spectrum [2]. Frequencies in the gamma (60–100 Hz) range exhibited high visual information and also had large redundancy among them, indicating that neural responses at these frequencies have a common component that is stimulus-driven. The same applies to low frequencies (1–8 Hz), where there was high redundancy between frequencies. Importantly, low and high frequency frequencies carried totally independent information, indicating that they act as independent visual information channels and probably originate from separate neural processes. Finally, frequencies 15 Hz 38 Hz exhibited high correlations between them but not with stimulus information. We hypothesised that signals in this middle frequency range are generated by common processes that are unrelated to the visual stimuli - for example, diffuse neuromodulatory inputs.

This example shows the power of information theoretic approaches to interpret individual frequencies in terms of variations with stimuli or behavioral state and to identify a minimal set of meaningful bands whose origin can then be investigated with the aid of computational models and perturbation experiments, as we illustrate in the next Sections.

3 Mathematical Modelling of Neural Network Dynamics

3.1 Neural Network Models to Identify Neural Mechanisms for Information Encoding

The above information theoretic analysis individuated two frequency bands that were shown to carry different channels of visual information. The question that arises is which neural processing and neural circuit mechanisms are expressed by each band. To address this question, we developed a formalism based on fitting recurrent network models of interacting excitatory and inhibitory neuronal populations to data. These models have been widely used to describe important properties of cortical microcircuits [5]. In particular, we developed a recurrent network model [12,14,15] of leaky integrate-and-fire (LIF) neuronal populations that receive external inputs (both a sensory driven thalamic input and a noisy intracortical input) to predict some key aspects of neural activity in primary visual cortex during naturalistic visual stimulation and spontaneous activity. Specifically, in Mazzoni et al. [12,14], we found that the simulated network was able to capture the translation rules between stimulus dynamics and LFP frequency bands. Confirming theoretical results demonstrating that the gamma power in a recurrent network tends to increase with the strength of the input to the network [3], we found that the network encoded the overall strength of the input into the power of gamma-band oscillations generated by inhibitory-excitatory neural interactions.

In addition, we found that the network encoded slow dynamic features of the input into slow LFP fluctuations mediated (through entrainment to the inputs) by stimulus-neural interactions. Thus our recurrent network model could provide evidence for both the low frequency information channel (carrying temporal information of the dynamics of sensory-driven thalamic inputs) and the gamma band information channel (reflecting excitatory inhibitory interactions modulated by the strength of thalamic inputs). Interestingly, the model also reproduced other features of the dynamics of visual cortex, including the cross-frequency coupling between the EEG delta-band phase and gamma-band amplitude [15].

Importantly, our model [12,14,15] could not reproduce the excess in power and the strong within band correlations observed in real data for the mid-range (19–38 Hz) band in visual cortex [2]. Our model did not include changes in neural activity induced by neuromodulation, further corroborating the idea that stimulus-independent neuromodulatory factors are needed to model the dynamics of this mid-range band.

3.2 Realistic Computation of Field Potentials from Point-Neuron Network Models

The above studies compared qualitatively and quantitatively information patterns in neural network models and real data to make inferences about which neural pathway contribute to each frequency band. As demonstrated in Ref. [3] this question can be addressed even without having to compute a realistic LFP or EEG from the network models, because basic oscillation properties of the network can be observed both at the level of spiking activity of neurons and at the level of aggregate mass signals.

We have then begun to investigate the more difficult problem of trying to measure, or infer, the precise value of microscropic neural parameters, such as the activity of individual classes of neurons within a network, from mass activity measures such as EEG or LFP. To obtain a more precise estimation of network parameters, it is necessary to compute a realistic LFP or EEG from these model networks of point neurons. However, these models lack a neural spatial structure which prevents modellers from being able to compute the spatially separated transmembrane currents that generate LFPs and EEG in real biological networks.

In our initial studies [12,14,15] we estimated the LFP and EEG based on the sum of absolute values of synaptic currents from simulation of the network model. Other studies have proposed different approaches to compute extracellular potentials using other variables of the simulation, such as the average membrane potentials, the average firing rate or the sum of all synaptic currents. We then evaluated systematically [11,13] the limitations and caveats of using such ad-hoc simplifications to estimate the LFP or EEG from neuron models without spatial structure (i.e., point-neuron models). We compared how well different approximations of field potentials (termed proxies) proposed in the literature reconstructed a ground-truth signal obtained by means of the hybrid modelling approach [7]. This approach includes a network of unconnected multicompartment neuron models with realistic three-dimensional (3D) spatial morphologies. Each multicompartment neuron is randomly assigned to a unique neuron in the network of point neurons and receives the same input spikes of the equivalent point neuron. Since the multicompartment neurons are not connected to each other, they are not involved in the network dynamics and their only role is to transform the spiking activity of the point-neuron network into a realistic estimate of the LFP or EEG that is used as the ground-truth signal.

We found that a specific weighted sum of synaptic currents from the point-neuron network model, for a specific network state (i.e., asynchronous irregular), performed remarkably well in predicting the LFP [13]. We then extended our study to the EEG [11] by including a head model that approximated the different geometries and electrical conductivities of the head necessary for computing a realistic EEG signal recorded by scalp electrodes. We also validated our EEG proxies across the repertoire of network states displayed by recurrent network models, namely the asynchronous irregular (AI), synchronous irregular (SI), and synchronous regular (SR). We found that a new class of linear EEG proxies, based on an optimized weighted sum of synaptic currents, outperformed previous approaches and was able to predict local integration of the EEG signal in a spatially extended network model.

3.3 Changes in Excitation-Inhibition (E:I) Imbalance in Simulated Neural Mass Signals

Our realistic estimations of mass signals from simple point neuron networks allowed us to invert and use these models to estimate some neural parameters of circuit activity that are not directly accessible from the EEG and LFP. For example, we considered how we could use network models to estimate from such recordings the ratio between excitation and inhibition. The theory of neural network models [3] and the empirical electrophysiological data have reported that the E:I ratio has profound effects on the spectral shape of neural activity. Its imbalance has been implicated in neuropsychiatric conditions, including autism. In Trakoshis et al. [23], we investigated different biomarkers computed on the power spectrum of LFPs and blood oxygen level dependent (BOLD) signal that could be used to reliably estimate the E:I ratio: the exponent of the 1/f spectral power law, slopes for the low- and high-frequency regions of the spectrum and the Hurst exponent (H). We simulated the LFP and BOLD signal from our recurrent network model, and studied how these biomarkers changed when we manipulated the E:I ratio by independently varying the strengths of the inhibitory (g_I) and excitatory (g_E) synaptic conductances. Part of our results are shown in Fig. 2. A flattening of high-frequency slopes was found in the excitation-dominated region where the E:I ratio is shifted in favor of E than the reference value used previously [12,14,15] to capture cortical power spectra. We also observed that H decreased in the excitation-dominated region. However, shifting the E:I balance towards stronger inhibition had a weaker effect on slopes and H. We then validated our model against in-vivo chemogenetic manipulations in mice that either increased neurophysiological excitation or silenced the local activity in the network. When modelling effects of chemogenetic manipulations within the recurrent network model, we found that DREADD manipulations that enhanced excitability of pyramidal neurons reduced steepness of the high-frequency slopes and led also to a decrease in H. In Ref. [23], we used the predictions of our model of how the ratio g between inhibition and excitation affects spectral properties such as slopes and H (see Fig. 2 C,D and Ref. [23]) to interpret the spectra of resting state fMRI (rsfMRI) in the medial prefrontal cortex (MPFC) of autistic subjects. In this paper we found that H was reduced in the MPFC of autistic males but not females, and using our model we interpreted this change in spectral properties as an indicator of increased excitation in males [23].

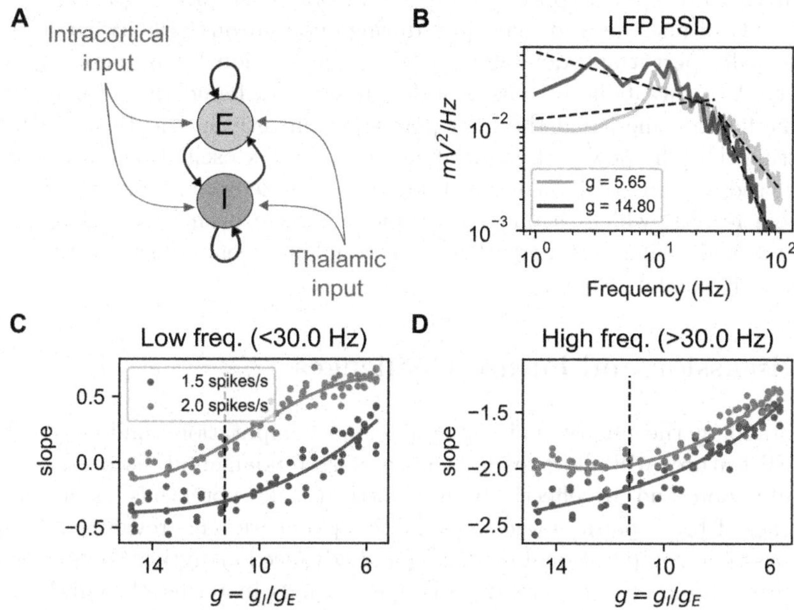

Fig. 2. A) Sketch of the point-neuron network that includes recurrent connections between two types of populations: excitatory cells (E) and inhibitory cells (I). Each population receives two types of external inputs: intracortical activity and thalamic stimulation. B) PSDs generated for two different ratios between inhibitory and excitatory conductances ($g = g_I/g_E$). The low- and high-frequency slopes of the piecewise regression lines that fit the log-log plot of the LFP PSDs are computed over two different frequency ranges (1–30 Hz for the low-frequency slope and 30–100 Hz for the high-frequency slope). The relationship between low-frequency slopes (panel C) and high-frequency slopes (panel D) are plotted as a function of g for two different firing rates of thalamic input (1.5 and 2 spikes/second). The reference value of g (which has shown in previous studies to reproduce cortical data well) is represented by a dashed black line. Recomputed and replotted from data first published in Ref. [23].

4 Perturbation Experiments Guided by Predictions of Computational Models

Biophysically realistic computational models and information theoretic methods can be used to generate predictions and test them with suitably designed perturbation experiments. Finding the best strategy to do it is an active topic of research. In what follows, we briefly review the attempts of us and others to address this challenge.

As reviewed above, based on our information theoretic analysis, we have proposed that the mid-frequency range (15–38 Hz approx.), which exhibited high correlations within frequency bands but contained little visual information, may reflect a single source of neuromodulatory inputs. We designed a perturbation experiment to test this hypothesis [24]. We recorded the LFP in primary visual cortex (V1) of anesthetized macaques during spontaneous activity while pharmacologically perturbing dopaminergic neuromodulation by systemic injection of L-DOPA (a metabolic precursor of dopamine). We found that dopaminergic neuromodulation increased the LFP power prominently in the 19–38 Hz band, suggesting that the power of endogenous visual cortex oscillations in this band can be used as a robust biomarker of dopaminergic neuromodulation [24].

These results, which in our view could not have been obtained by either computational analyses or perturbation experiments alone, illustrate the power of effectively combing them.

5 Discussion and Future Challenges

Understanding the microcircuit dynamics and computations underlying EEG and LFP features will allow researchers to make fundamental discoveries about brain function and to effectively use cortical field potentials as a reliable biomarker of brain pathophysiologies. In this paper we have reviewed our approach based on computational modelling and advanced analytical tools of neural network dynamics to interpret neural mass signals in terms of neural circuit parameters. Here we outline some limitations of our approach and the future challenges that we need to address them.

In Refs. [11,13] we have developed very accurate LFP and EEG proxies. These proxies open up the possibility of computing accurate EEG and LFP predictions from simple network models, which can be then compared to empirical EEGs and LFPs. However, to achieve this goal we need to accomplish several steps. First, we need to develop statistical tools that can infer neural parameters (such as the ratio between excitation and inhibition or properties of network connectivity) from EEG and LFP spectral features by fitting such models to empirically measured spectra. Second, we then need to carefully validate these statistical inference approaches on real brain data in which neural circuit parameters have been manipulated by the experimenter, for example by means of chemogenetic manipulations [23]. We could validate the inference algorithm by studying if it is able to predict which kind of controlled manipulation has been applied by the experimenter to the brain in each dataset (e.g. whether a manipulation increasing or decreasing excitation was applied). Third, although our models have some degree of realism, they do not capture the full complexity of the brain. It would therefore be particularly important to extend our models to include different classes of interneurons, to include interactions between different recurrent networks (which could generate wider oscillation ranges than the gamma oscillations mostly considered in our work), and to model the effects of different kinds of neuromodulators.

Given the above limitations, and although more work is needed to be able to interpret empirical EEGs and LFPs in terms of network model parameters and neuromodulation, we expect that future research can build on the encouraging results presented in this paper and lead to a credible, robust and biologically plausible estimation of neural parameters from neural mass signals.

References

1. Başar, E.: EEG-Brain Dynamics: Relation Between EEG and Brain Evoked Potentials. Elsevier-North-Holland Biomedical Press, Amsterdam (1980)
2. Belitski, A., et al.: Low-frequency Local Field Potentials and spikes in primary visual cortex convey independent visual information. J. Neurosci. **28**(22), 5696–5709 (2008)
3. Brunel, N., Wang, X.J.: What determines the frequency of fast network oscillations with irregular neural discharges? I. synaptic dynamics and excitation-inhibition balance. J. Neurophysiol. **90**(1), 415–430 (2003)
4. Buzsáki, G., Anastassiou, C.A., Koch, C.: The origin of extracellular fields and currents - EEG, ECoG LFP and spikes. Nature Rev. Neurosci. **13**(6), 407–420 (2012)
5. Einevoll, G.T.: The scientific case for brain simulations. Neuron **102**(4), 735–744 (2019)
6. Einevoll, G.T., Kayser, C., Logothetis, N.K., Panzeri, S.: Modelling and analysis of Local Field Potentials for studying the function of cortical circuits. Nat. Rev. Neurosci. **14**(11), 770–785 (2013)
7. Hagen, E., et al.: Hybrid scheme for modeling local field potentials from point-neuron networks. Cereb. Cortex **26**(12), 4461–4496 (2016)
8. Lakatos, P., Karmos, G., Mehta, A.D., Ulbert, I., Schroeder, C.E.: Entrainment of neuronal oscillations as a mechanism of attentional selection. Science **320**(5872), 110–113 (2008)
9. Magri, C., Schridde, U., Murayama, Y., Panzeri, S., Logothetis, N.K.: The amplitude and timing of the BOLD signal reflects the relationship between Local Field Potential power at different frequencies. J. Neurosci. **32**(4), 1395–1407 (2012)
10. Mahmud, M., Vassanelli, S.: Processing and analysis of multichannel extracellular neuronal signals: state-of-the-art and challenges. Front. Neurosci. **10**, 248 (2016)
11. Martínez-Cañada, P., Ness, T.V., Einevoll, G.T., Fellin, T., Panzeri, S.: Computation of the electroencephalogram (EEG) from network models of point neurons. PLoS Comput. Biol. **17**(4), e1008893 (2021)
12. Mazzoni, A., Brunel, N., Cavallari, S., Logothetis, N.K., Panzeri, S.: Cortical dynamics during naturalistic sensory stimulations: experiments and models. J. Physiol. Paris **105**(1), 2–15 (2011)

13. Mazzoni, A., Lindén, H., Cuntz, H., Lansner, A., Panzeri, S., Einevoll, G.T.: Computing the Local Field Potential (LFP) from integrate-and-fire network models. PLoS Comput. Biol. **11**(12), 1–38 (2015)
14. Mazzoni, A., Panzeri, S., Logothetis, N.K., Brunel, N.: Encoding of naturalistic stimuli by Local Field Potential spectra in networks of excitatory and inhibitory neurons. PLoS Comput. Biol. **4**(12), 1–20 (2008)
15. Mazzoni, A., Whittingstall, K., Brunel, N., Logothetis, N.K., Panzeri, S.: Understanding the relationships between spike rate and delta/gamma frequency bands of LFPs and EEGs using a local cortical network model. Neuroimage **52**(3), 956–972 (2010)
16. Mitra, P.P., Bokil, H.: Observed Brain Dynamics. Oxford University Press, Oxford (2008)
17. Nunez, P.L., Srinivasan, R., et al.: Electric Fields of the Brain: The Neurophysics of EEG. Oxford University Press, Oxford (2006)
18. Pola, G., Thiele, A., Hoffmann, K.P., Panzeri, S.: An exact method to quantify the information transmitted by different mechanisms of correlational coding. Network **14**, 35–60 (2003)
19. Quian Quiroga, R., Panzeri, S.: Extracting information from neuronal populations: information theory and decoding approaches. Nat. Rev. Neurosci. **10**, 173–185 (2009)
20. Ray, S., Maunsell, J.H.R.: Different origins of gamma rhythm and high-gamma activity in macaque visual cortex. PLoS Biol. **9**(4), e1000610 (2011)
21. Shannon, C.E.: A mathematical theory of communication. Bell Syst. Tech. J. **27**, 379–423 (1948)
22. Steriade, M., Hobson, J.: Neuronal activity during the sleep-waking cycle. Prog. Neurobiol. **6**, 157–376 (1976)
23. Trakoshis, S., et al.: Intrinsic excitation-inhibition imbalance affects medial prefrontal cortex differently in autistic men versus women. eLife **9**, e55684 (2020)
24. Zaldivar, D., Goense, J., Lowe, S.C., Logothetis, N.K., Panzeri, S.: Dopamine is signaled by mid-frequency oscillations and boosts output layers visual information in visual cortex. Curr. Biol. **28**(2), 224–235 (2018)

Intrinsic Motivation to Learn Action-State Representation with Hierarchical Temporal Memory

Evgenii Dzhivelikian[1], Artem Latyshev[1], Petr Kuderov[1,3](✉), and Aleksandr I. Panov[1,2,3]

[1] Moscow Institute of Physics and Technology, Dolgoprudny, Russia
kuderov.pv@phystech.edu
[2] Artificial Intelligence Research Institute, Moscow, Russia
[3] Federal Research Center "Computer Science and Control" of the Russian Academy of Sciences, Moscow, Russia

Abstract. In this paper, we propose a biologically plausible model for learning the decision-making sequence in an external environment with internal motivation. As a computational model, we propose a hierarchical architecture of an intelligent agent acquiring experience based on reinforcement learning. We use the basal ganglia model to aggregate a reward, and sparse distributed representation of states and actions in hierarchical temporal memory elements. The proposed architecture allows the agent to build a compact model of the environment and to form an effective strategy, which is experimentally demonstrated to search for resources in grid environments.

Keywords: Model-based reinforcement learning · Intrinsic motivation · Hierarchical temporal memory · Sparse distributed representations

1 Introduction

The ability to learn and accumulate knowledge on one's own is a distinguishing feature of intelligence. And how data is represented in memory, what learning mechanisms exist, and how learning can be autonomous are all central issues in Cognitive Sciences. Although computational Reinforcement Learning (RL) seeks to answer these questions as well, it has been criticized for being overly simplistic and lacking biological plausibility. However, the interaction between Cognitive Sciences and computational Reinforcement Learning has grown in popularity in recent years – RL now serves as a powerful testbed for neuroscientific models. In our work, we use a neurophysiologically inspired model in an RL setting to address the problems of data representation, learning, and autonomy.

Human behavior and the mental representations that accompany it are emphasized to have a hierarchical structure [13,20]. It allows us to learn and

M. Mahmud et al. (Eds.): BI 2021, LNAI 12960, pp. 13–24, 2021.
https://doi.org/10.1007/978-3-030-86993-9_2

apply spatial-temporal abstractions. While the classical Reinforcement Learning paradigm lacks the ability to work with abstractions, Hierarchical RL has several extensions, such as the Options Framework [18]. A model that could map Options Framework to prefrontal cortex neural structures was proposed [5], thereby bridging the gap between the RL model and Neurophysiology. Another study discovered that dopamine-driven TD-like learning mechanisms in the dorsal striatum play an important role in the development of a functional hierarchy in the prefrontal cortex [15].

In our work, we draw ideas from a cortical Hierarchical Temporal Memory model [10]. It enables unsupervised hierarchical learning of spatial-temporal data representation. This model, however, has limited utility because it only defines the memory's elementary building blocks. It does not define neither hierarchy, nor how to learn temporal abstractions, nor how the memory can be integrated into an intelligent agent model. Despite the fact that some works extend its usage in part [8,11,12], we address all of these issues in our original approach.

Many works are devoted to the problem of autonomy in relation to humans and artificial intelligence agents. Several models capable of performing actions even in the absence of an external sensory signal were proposed. One such model is based on the idea that constant brain activity and self-motivation are inherent in living organisms [6]. Another model introduces a causal network and describes the process of maintaining motivation based on a biological representation of the dopamine reward system which exists in the brain [19]. Santucci and colleagues investigated a variety of intrinsic motivation (IM) models in order to provide autonomy for a robotic agent exploring its surroundings, and the best results were compiled by their GRAIL model [16]. Works by [4,9] are linked with the similar concept of an agent's behavior being determined by intrinsic motivation and the interaction of numerous brain components (cortex, basal ganglia, thalamus, hippocampus, amygdala). We were inspired by this concept when designing our basal ganglia model.

In this paper, we present our approach to creating an autonomous agent called HIMA. We provide HIMA with a novel memory model with a hierarchical block structure. Although its Spatial Pooler and Temporal Memory blocks are heavily based on corresponding objects from the Hierarchical Temporal Memory model, we extend Temporal Memory with external modulation support via feedback connections and the higher-order sequences learning algorithm. The latter enables us to construct a hierarchy that can work with the state and action abstractions. We also propose the basal ganglia model as another memory building block, which is responsible for learning the action selection strategy while being driven by external and internal motivation. The sparse distributed representation of states and actions is another distinguishing feature of our model. As a result, our contribution is to investigate the representation of abstract context-dependent actions that denote behavioral programs, as well as the ability of the basal ganglia to learn the choosing strategy between partially overlapping actions. Finally, we validate HIMA's ability to aggregate experience in order to solve RL tasks.

The paper is organized as follows: in Sect. 3, we describe an agent's overall hierarchical model. We also outline the hypothesis that underpins the sparse distributed state-action value evaluation that we used for the Basal Ganglia model and, in addition, explain the choice of the baseline method for comparison in our experiments. The experimental setup is described in Sect. 4. Finally, in Sect. 5, we present the results of the experiments performed on a classic grid world environment, followed by a discussion of the proposed method's limitations.

2 Background

This section introduces the definitions and concepts that we will need in our work. We provide formalization in the first subsection that will be used to establish a link between our biologically inspired model and reinforcement learning. Other subsections explain biological concepts and computational models that we use as a foundation.

2.1 MDP, Options and TD

Consider an agent that must make sequential decisions while interacting with an environment. A common approach is to formalize such problem as Markov Decision Process (MDP) problem. Whereas experiment conditions force us to consider the partially observable MDP problem, we can consider s to be an estimate of a function of history of all previous observations. As a result, we use deterministic MDP formulation throughout the text to simplify derivations: $\langle S, A, P, R, \gamma \rangle$, where S – state space, A – action space, $P : S \times A \to S$ – transition function, $R : S \times A \to \mathbb{R}$ – reward function, $\gamma \in [0; 1]$ – discount factor.

For actions, we also employ temporal abstractions. The Options Framework is a popular way to generalize both elementary and high-level actions [3,18]. It defines an option as a tuple $\langle I, \pi, \beta \rangle$, where $I \subseteq S$ – initiation set, $\pi : S \times A \to [0, 1]$ – intra-option policy and $\beta : S \to [0, 1]$ – termination condition. Therefore a policy over options is a probability function $\mu : S \times O \to [0, 1]$, where O – set of options.

The agent's goal is to find such options and policy over options μ that maximize cumulative return $\mathbb{E}[\sum_{t=1}^{\infty} \gamma^{t-1} r_t \,|\, \mu, \pi, O]$.

We use the Temporal Difference Learning [17] to learn value function. This method has also proven to be biologically plausible [14]. State value defined as: $v_\pi(s) = \mathbb{E}_\pi[G_t | s_t = s] = \mathbb{E}_\pi[r_{t+1} + \gamma G_{t+1} | s_t = s] = \mathbb{E}_\pi[r_{t+1} + \gamma v_\pi(S_{t+1}) | s_t = s]$, where r_t, G_t – reward and return on t time step. In this approach the estimate of the value is updated according to the difference between current value $v(s_t)$ and its estimate bootstrapped from the value of the next observed state: $\hat{v}(s_t) = r_{t+1} + \gamma v_\pi(s_{t+1})$. This difference is called 1-step TD-error: $\delta_t = r_{t+1} + \gamma v(s_{t+1}) - -v(s_t)$. Thus the value update rule is: $v(s_t) \leftarrow v(s_t) + \alpha \delta_t$.

2.2 Basal Ganglia

The basal ganglia are the part of the brain that regulate movement and behavioral aspects of motivation. It is the most active part of the brain and the primary consumer of dopamine, and in terms of artificial intelligence, it realizes reinforcement learning. In this paper, we propose the basal ganglia model such as depicted in Fig. 1.

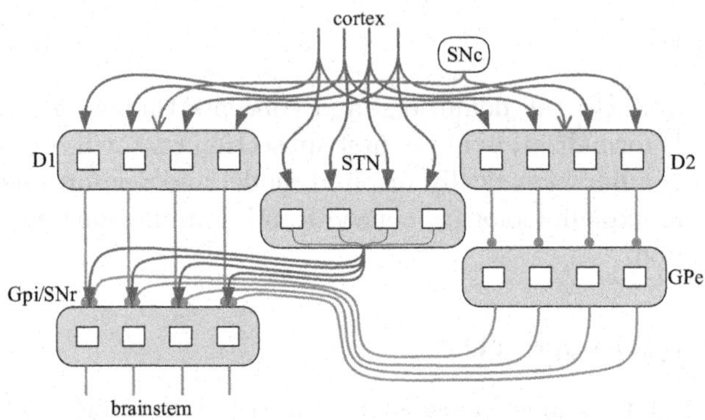

Fig. 1. The scheme of the basal ganglia model. Grey blocks represent corresponding biological objects: D1, D2 – dopamine receptors of striatal projection neurons; STN – subthalamic nucleus; GPi – globus pallidius internal segment; SNr – substantia nigra pars reticulata; GPe – globus pallidus external segment; SNc – substantia nigra pars compacta. Red arrows – excitatory connections; blue lines with circles – inhibitory connections; green arrows – dopamine connections. (Color figure online)

The input signal for the system $Cx \in \text{SDR}(d_{in})$ comes from the cortex to the D1 and D2 neurons of the striatum through fully-connected net: $D1_i \leftarrow \frac{1}{|Cx|}\sum_j W_{ij}^{D1} I[Cx_j = 1]$ and $D2_i$ is computed similarly. Where $\text{SDR}(d_{in})$ is an SDR [1] of size d_{in}; $W^{D1}, W^{D2} \in \mathbb{R}^{d_{out} \times d_{in}}$ are the weights of fully-connected net and d_{out} – the output signal size; $|Cx|$ – a number of nonzero components in Cx; $I[\text{condition}]$ – an indicator function of the condition. The D1 neurons are active selectors because they reduce the GPi's inhibition of the incoming signal. The D2 neurons, on the other hand, tend to suppress the corresponding signal by acting indirectly on the GPi via the GPe mediator. As a result, the incoming signal is subjected to dual control.

Also, the incoming signal Cx goes to subthalamic nucleus changing its activity: $STN_j \leftarrow \zeta I[Cx_j = 1] + (1 - \zeta)STN_j$, where $STN \in \mathbb{R}^{d_{in}}$. The general (average) excitation of the system is characterized by the subthalamic nucleus, which provides constant excitation of the GPi neurons. It is the system's only single source of excitation.

The output from the basal ganglia is formed in GPi ($GPi \in \mathbb{R}^{d_{out}}$) in several sequential steps. First, we calculate the difference between average activity and the expected value: $GPi_k \leftarrow \rho \sum_j STN_j - (D1_k - D2_k)$. Then GPi vector is normalized: $GPi_k \leftarrow \frac{GPi_k - \min GPi}{\max GPi - \min GPi}$. Finally, it is randomly binarized: $GPi_k \leftarrow I[RND_k < GPi_k]$, where RND is a random vector from uniform distribution. The resulting vector forms an output from the basal ganglia.

The dopamine release system (reward and punishment) is the system responsible for learning in the basal ganglia and, as a result, determines the effect of the BG on the input signal. It is based on signals coming from the SNc. Dopamine strengthens connections between the cortex and the striatum. In response to positive signals, it strengthens D1 receptors while weakening D2 receptors, and in response to negative signals, it has the opposite effect. The TD error, which is based on the reward from the environment as well as previous and current striatal activity, determines whether the signal is positive or negative.

2.3 Hierarchical Temporal Memory

To build a biologically consistent model of options we use cortical algorithms of Numenta, Hierarchical Temporal Memory [10], as building blocks and modify them to fit our hierarchy structure.

In our work we use Spatial Pooler [7] and Temporal Memory algorithms. Spatial Pooler (SP) is an algorithm that encodes binary input patterns into binary sparse distributed representation (SDR) [1]. It uses Hebbian learning rule to get robust pattern clusterization. Temporal Memory (TM) is a key algorithm that enables sequence learning. It is a sequence memory, so it can be used to predict the next sequence elements when a sequence has been learned. TM gets an SDR as input and returns the predicted next sequence element pattern.

3 Hierarchical Intrinsic Motivated Agent

Hierarchical Intrinsic Motivated Agent (HIMA) is an algorithm making decisions using a biologically plausible cortex model. The algorithm's general idea is to give an agent the ability to identify and memorize useful action sequences automatically to reuse them in similar tasks and environments.

For simplicity, consider a two-level version of the algorithm, which is schematically depicted in Fig. 2. Examine the functioning of the hierarchy from the level's perspective first, and then we will move to blocks.

The function of the first level is to learn sequences of sensory cell activation patterns. In order to form temporal abstractions on the second level, each first level sequence is associated with a single unique pattern, which we call as a name of a sequence. As a result, the second level memorizes sequences of names. The anomaly and confidence signals control the flow of information from the first to the second level (lines denoted with $\mathcal{A}$ and $\mathcal{C}$ in Fig. 2). These signals enable the detection of the beginning of the learned sequence. When the start is detected, the current active pattern is transferred from the first to the second level. This pattern is chosen as the sequence's name and remains active on the second level until the sequence's end or a transition to a new sequence is detected. In the

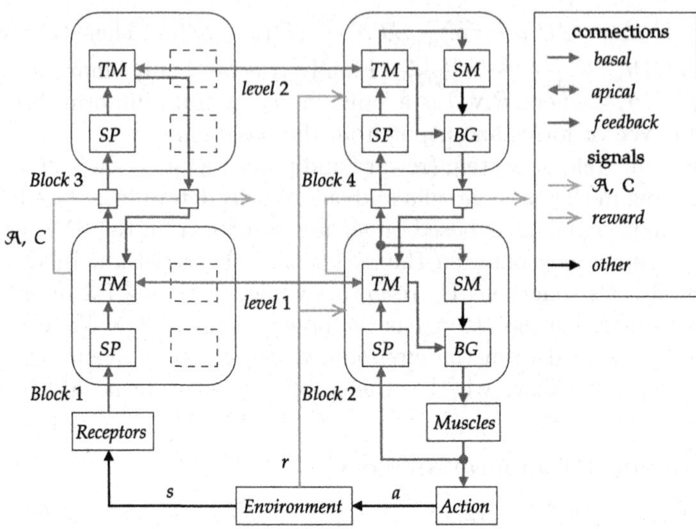

Fig. 2. HIMA with hierarchy of two levels and *Block 2* as an output block. (Color figure online)

most basic case, the name of a sequence is its first element (pattern). However, if two sequences share a prefix, only one of them will have their first element as a name, while the other will get a name from the first unique pattern (the first after shared prefix). This naming mechanism is accomplished through the use of feedback inhibitory connections (blue lines in Fig. 2). They suppress predictions that do not match the sequence with the name that is currently active on the second level.

In HIMA, sensory data is divided into two categories: environmental and muscular (Receptors and Muscles boxes in Fig. 2). We use two blocks on each level, resulting in two parallel vertical information flows along basal connections (red lines in Fig. 2). The activation of muscle cells corresponds to elementary actions $a \in A$ in the environment. *Block 2* handles these activations, while *Block 4* handles entire sequences of elementary actions that correspond to abstract actions. The other receptors represent the state of the environment $s \in S$. Similarly, *Block 3* handles sequences learned by *Block 1*. Furthermore, state and action sequence learning processes influence each other via apical connections. They represent casualty and help resolving ambiguity in input patterns.

So far, we've described HIMA as a passive structure that can learn and name sequences, forming temporal abstractions. The algorithm's main feature, however, is its ability to act in the environment using learned abstractions. The Basal Ganglia (BG) is in charge of action selection, whether elementary or abstract, as well as reward integration. On the first level, BG selects an action based on the current state's estimated value; actions with higher value are more likely to be selected. The second level, however, has the ability to shift the probability distribution towards actions that constitute the selected second level abstract action.

In the following sections, we describe the inner structure of blocks, the features of our BG model realization and reward encoding, and finally we establish a link between HIMA and the Options framework.

3.1 Block's Structure

Blocks consist of subblocks: Temporal Memory (TM), Spatial Pooler (SP), Spatial Memory (SM), and Basal Ganglia (BG). We used Spatial Pooler algorithm without making any changes for our model. Temporal Memory, on the other hand, has been modified by the addition of feedback and apical connections. Apical connections are used to resolve ambiguous basal input by incorporating information from other blocks. Feedback connections are critical in the formation of abstract actions and the hierarchical decision making process. Spatial Memory is the dynamic storage of block input patterns that is used in conjunction with the Basal Ganglia during decision making. The SM and BG subblocks are optional, as shown in Fig. 2.

In a block, two signals are generated that control vertical connections with other blocks. The first is anomaly $\mathcal{A}$, which is the Temporal Memory prediction error, and the second is confidence $\mathcal{C}$, which characterizes the quality of TM prediction. These signals are used to detect the beginnings and endings of sequences and to compute knowledge-based intrinsic reward. The intrinsic reward for the current step is calculated in *Block 1* as the difference between the mean and current anomaly levels if there was enough confidence in the previous step.

3.2 Basal Ganglia Model

The Basal Ganglia subblock gets as an input the list of predictions (patterns) with their weights $\{P_i, w_i\}$ and the condition (named as the signal from cortex Cx in Sect. 2.2). Each pattern is $P_i \in \text{SDR}(d_{in})$, where weights are real numbers and $Cx \in \text{SDR}(d_{in})$. The result of the computation process described in Sect. 2.2 is a signal from GPi. We use it to count the overlap with each pattern P_i and then, combined with the corresponding weights w_i, to form new pattern weights: $V_i = w_i \sum_j I[\neg(GPi_j = 1) \wedge P_{i,j} = 1]$. These pattern weights are normalized by the softmax function to be used as probabilities to choose between them. Resulting choice of a pattern is the output of the Basal Ganglia.

Learning in the striatum of the BG requires both current and previous patterns P^t and P^{t-1}, as well as current and previous input signals from cortex Cx^t and Cx^{t-1}. The value vector Q components are computed as following:

$$Q_i = \frac{1}{|Cx|} \sum_j (W_{ij}^{D1} - W_{ij}^{D2}) I[Cx_j = 1]$$

Only components i for which $P_i = 1$ are calculated, because the other components don't correspond to the pattern P, hence they should not affect its value. Then we compute an average value estimate using median: $q = \text{median}\ (Q)$. We chose median as a more stable estimate of an average than mean. The validity of an averaging for the sparse distributed value representation is covered in Sect. 3.3. Using the current reward and average value q^t, and the value vector Q^{t-1} for the previous time step we calculate TD-error, $\delta_i^{t-1} = \frac{r}{|P|} + \gamma q^t - Q_i^{t-1}$, and perform an update step for every weight that was active in the previous state:

$$W_{ij}^{D1} \leftarrow W_{ij}^{D1} + \alpha\delta_i^{t-1}; \qquad W_{ij}^{D2} \leftarrow W_{ij}^{D2} - \beta\delta_i^{t-1},$$

where i, j s.t. $P_i^{t-1} = 1$ and $Cx_j^{t-1} = 1$; α, β are learning rates.

3.3 Sparse Distributed Action Value Representation

The joint encoding of states and actions is critical for our model because it allows us to represent context-dependent actions. The basal ganglia learns the strategy for choosing among the currently available actions. In our work, it is accomplished by learning some form of the action value function (also known as the Q-value function in Reinforcement Learning). Because actions are represented by binary SDR patterns, the question is how to learn such a value function.

To answer this question, we considered the following approach: learn a distributed value function independently for each SDR component, and then use some form of aggregation to calculate the value for the corresponding action vectors. In this scheme, a binary vector space defines a sparse set of latent features that represent actions. The basal ganglia learns the Q-value function for each of these features individually and then aggregates them using averaging. Our hypothesis was that even linear averaging, such as mean, could provide a reasonable estimate of the action value. However, because encoded actions overlap, it is not obvious that the resulting Q-value after aggregation is a reasonable estimate of the real state-action value.

To put this theory to the test, we created sparse distributed adaptations of a classic RL Q-learning algorithm [17] and an exploratory method [2] that loosely mimics the intrinsically motivated optimistic exploratory behavior of living creatures in the face of uncertainty. Despite the fact that the latter method is not biologically plausible, it has been shown to be asymptotically optimal, so the resulting method was expected to represent a reasonable upper bound performance for HIMA. Following the confirmation of our hypothesis, we applied the concept to HIMA and continued to use this adaptation as a baseline measure of HIMA performance.

3.4 HIMA and Options

Now we can establish a connection between our model of cortex hierarchy and the options framework. First of all, we should notice, that resulting policy for an option depends not only on a state s but also on a previous action a, i.e.: $\pi = \pi(a'|s, a)$. However, we can include action as a part of a state. Thus consider states as $\tilde{S} = S \times A$, then a policy of an option is $\pi : \tilde{S} \times A \to [0, 1]$. BG of the *Block 4* defines a policy over options $\mu = \mu(o|s)$, where $s \in \tilde{S}$, $o \in O$. Here, o

corresponds to a feedback output pattern of the *Block 4*, and s corresponds to a concatenation of apical and basal inputs of a block. BG of the *Block 2* represents a policy of a chosen by *Block 4* option $\pi = \pi(a|s)$, where a corresponds to a pattern, that activates muscles that causes an action a in the environment and s has the same meaning as for *Block 4*. Every option can be chosen in any state of the environment, so $I = \tilde{S}$. The termination condition for an option is determined by $\mathcal{A}$ and $\mathcal{C}$ signals and corresponding thresholds in *Block 2*. For current time step t, this condition can be determined by an state $s \in \tilde{S}$, so the termination condition depends on time: $\beta = \beta_t(s)$. However, we can get rid of the time component if we stop TM's learning. *Block 2* and *Block 4* gather a reward with discount factor γ until their reinforce method will be called, so *Block 2* should be reinforced every action, but *Block 4* should be reinforced when an option is interrupted or ended. BG of *Block 4* gets as a reward $R_o = \sum_{t=1}^{m} \gamma^{t-1} r_t$, where m – duration of an option $o \in O$.

4 Experiments

In our experiments, we used classic grid world environments, which are represented as mazes on a square grid (see Fig. 3). Each state can be defined by an agent's position; thus, the state space S contains all possible agent positions. An agent begins in a fixed state s_0, with the goal of locating a single reward in a fixed position s_g. The environment's transition function is deterministic. The action space is made up of four actions that move the agent to each adjacent grid cell. However, when the agent attempts to move into a maze wall, the position of the agent remains unchanged. It is assumed that the maze is surrounded by obstacles, making it impossible for an agent to move outside. Every timestep, an agent receives an observation – a binary image of a small square window encircling it (we used 5×5 size with an agent being at its center). The observation has six channels: three color channels for the floor, walls, out-of-bounds obstacles, and the goal. We used maze floor coloring to add semantic clues to observations. When an agent achieves the goal state s_g, it receives a large positive value $+1.0$. Each step is also slightly punished with -0.002, causing an agent to seek the shortest path. We also set a time limit for episodes: 200 for an 8×8 environment and 350 for a 12×12 environment.

Every method was tested in twenty preselected randomly generated environments: ten in 8×8 environment and ten in 12×12. The testing environments were chosen to be not too easy, so that the optimal path from the starting point to the goal was between 8 and 20 steps. Three trials with different agent seeds were conducted in each environment, for a total of sixty testing trials. To avoid overfitting, we used a second validation set of randomly generated environments to select the agents' hyperparameters.

5 Results and Discussion

We compared our method's performance to the baselines: random strategy and sparsely distributed Q-learning adaptation (in our experiments, we call it UCB

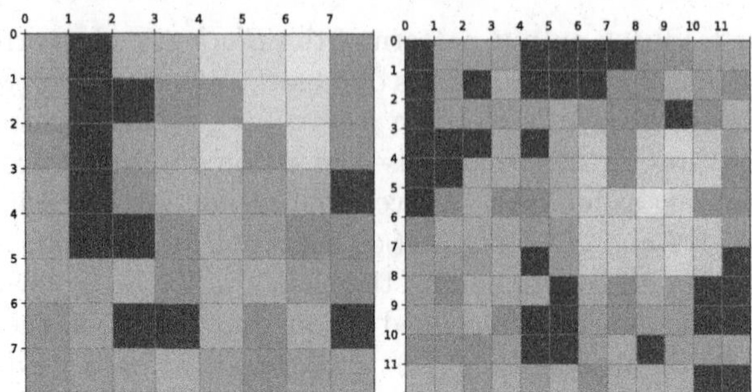

Fig. 3. Examples of the testing grid world environment with different sizes: 8 × 8 (left) and 12 × 12 (right). Yellow – the agent position; salad – a goal position; dark blue – walls; shades of light blue – different colors of the floor; lightened square area around the agent – its observation window. (Color figure online)

after the name of the exploration method). HIMA produced competitive results: fast conversion to optimal or near-optimal strategy. The HIMA agent has relatively high dispersion at early episodes compared to the baselines, as shown in Fig. 4. It's due to a more complex HIMA learning workflow and the exploration suboptimality, which is based solely on intrinsic motivation signals (anomaly and confidence), compared to UCB optimal exploration method. We also show that HIMA results outperform a random agent.

We demonstrated the ability of the HIMA model to exhibit adaptive behavior in simple goal-reaching tasks, however, we still lack experiments that justify the use of a two-level hierarchy. Also, our model lacks a visual system capable of semantic feature extraction which limits the use of the model in more challenging environments. In addition, we used only basic knowledge-based intrinsic motivation in this paper and did not test alternatives. Although our model is biologically plausible to some extent, some parts of the model are arbitrary and should be revised based on experimental data.

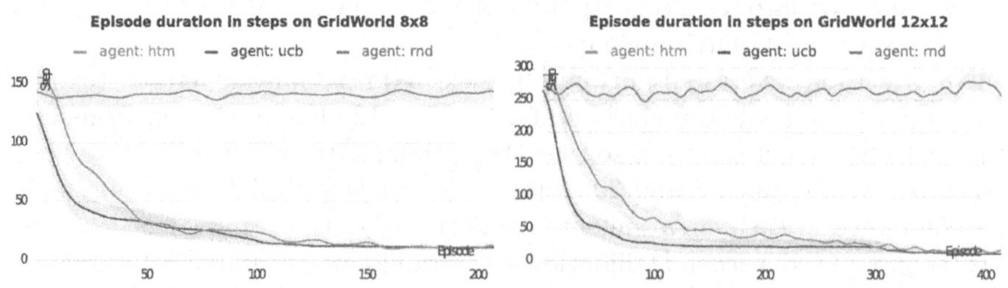

Fig. 4. Episode duration (in steps) on 8 × 8 (top) and 12 × 12 (bottom) grid world environment. Results are averaged over 10 different maps and 3 different initialization seeds, and also exponentially smoothed.

6 Conclusion

In our work, we proposed a biologically inspired model of an intelligent agent that autonomously acquires knowledge in an environment and then uses it to make better decisions. Our agent's hierarchical structure enables it to learn useful spatiotemporal abstractions while also building a compact model of the environment. We use the basal ganglia model to generate an intrinsic motivation signal, and sparse distributed representation of states and actions on different levels of the hierarchy. In our experiments on grid world environments, we demonstrate that the proposed architecture is capable of learning an effective resource-search strategy. It performed similarly to the classic RL method Q-learning combined with the asymptotically optimal exploration method UCB, which mimics intrinsically motivated optimistic exploration behavior.

In the future, we intend to investigate the benefit of reusing acquired options and utilizing hierarchical action space structure in multi-goal task settings. We also intend to experiment with different intrinsic motivation signals. Competence-based IM is particularly interesting because it can significantly aid in the learning of abstract actions. Another promising direction is to supplement HIMA with spatial hierarchy for better input semantics extraction. Finally, we're looking forward studying how the learned model can be applied, such as for dreaming or lookahead planning.

Acknowledgments. The reported study was supported by RFBR, research Project No. 18-29-22047.

References

1. Ahmad, S., Hawkins, J.: Properties of sparse distributed representations and their application to hierarchical temporal memory (2015)
2. Auer, P., Cesa-Bianchi, N., Fischer, P.: Finite-time analysis of the multiarmed bandit problem. Mach. Learn. **47**(2), 235–256 (2002). https://doi.org/10.1023/A:1013689704352
3. Bacon, P.L., Harb, J., Precup, D.: The option-critic architecture. In: Proceedings of the AAAI Conference on Artificial Intelligence, vol. 31 (2017)
4. Bolado-Gomez, R., Gurney, K.: A biologically plausible embodied model of action discovery. Front. Neurorobot. **7**(MAR), 1–24 (2013). https://doi.org/10.3389/fnbot.2013.00004
5. Botvinick, M.M., Niv, Y., Barto, A.G.: Hierarchically organized behavior and its neural foundations: a reinforcement learning perspective. Cognition **113**(3), 262–280 (2009). https://doi.org/10.1016/j.cognition.2008.08.011
6. Chang, O.: Self-programming robots boosted by neural agents. In: Wang, S., et al. (eds.) BI 2018. LNCS (LNAI), vol. 11309, pp. 448–457. Springer, Cham (2018). https://doi.org/10.1007/978-3-030-05587-5_42
7. Cui, Y., Ahmad, S., Hawkins, J.: The HTM spatial pooler-a neocortical algorithm for online sparse distributed coding. Front. Comput. Neurosci. **11**, 111 (2017). https://doi.org/10.3389/fncom.2017.00111

8. Daylidyonok, I., Frolenkova, A., Panov, A.I.: Extended hierarchical temporal memory for motion anomaly detection. In: Samsonovich, A.V. (ed.) BICA 2018. AISC, vol. 848, pp. 69–81. Springer, Cham (2019). https://doi.org/10.1007/978-3-319-99316-4_10
9. Fiore, V.G., et al.: Keep focussing: striatal dopamine multiple functions resolved in a single mechanism tested in a simulated humanoid robot. Front. Psychol. **5**(FEB), 1–17 (2014). https://doi.org/10.3389/fpsyg.2014.00124
10. Hawkins, J., Ahmad, S.: Why neurons have thousands of synapses, a theory of sequence memory in neocortex. Front. Neural Circuits **10**, 23 (2016). https://doi.org/10.3389/fncir.2016.00023
11. Hawkins, J., Ahmad, S., Cui, Y.: A theory of how columns in the neocortex enable learning the structure of the world. Front. Neural Circuits **11**, 81 (2017). https://doi.org/10.3389/fncir.2017.00081
12. Kuderov, P., Panov, A.: Planning with hierarchical temporal memory for deterministic Markov decision problem. In: Proceedings of the 13th International Conference on Agents and Artificial Intelligence - Volume 2: ICAART, pp. 1073–1081. INSTICC, SciTePress (2021). https://doi.org/10.5220/0010317710731081
13. Lashley, K.S.: The Problem of Serial Order in Behavior, vol. 21. Bobbs-Merrill, Oxford (1951)
14. O'Doherty, J., Dayan, P., Friston, K., Critchley, H., Dolan, R.: Temporal difference models and reward-related learning in the human brain. Neuron **38**(2), 329–337 (2003). https://doi.org/10.1016/S0896-6273(03)00169-7. Cited By 1014
15. Reynolds, J.R., O'Reilly, R.C.: Developing PFC representations using reinforcement learning. Cognition **113**(3), 281–292 (2009). https://doi.org/10.1016/j.cognition.2009.05.015
16. Santucci, V.G., Baldassarre, G., Mirolli, M.: GRAIL: a goal-discovering robotic architecture for intrinsically-motivated learning. IEEE Trans. Cogn. Dev. Syst. **8**(3), 214–231 (2016). https://doi.org/10.1109/TCDS.2016.2538961
17. Sutton, R.: Learning to predict by the methods of temporal differences. Mach. Learn. **3**(1), 9–44 (1988). https://doi.org/10.1023/A:1022633531479. Cited By 2498
18. Sutton, R., Precup, D., Singh, S.: Between MDPs and semi-MDPs: a framework for temporal abstraction in reinforcement learning. Artif. Intell. **112**(1), 181–211 (1999). https://doi.org/10.1016/S0004-3702(99)00052-1. Cited By 1269
19. Taj, F., Klein, M.C.A., van Halteren, A.: Computational model for reward-based generation and maintenance of motivation. In: Wang, S., et al. (eds.) BI 2018. LNCS (LNAI), vol. 11309, pp. 41–51. Springer, Cham (2018). https://doi.org/10.1007/978-3-030-05587-5_5
20. Zacks, J.M., Tversky, B.: Event structure in perception and conception. Psychol. Bull. **127**(1), 3–21 (2001). https://doi.org/10.1037/0033-2909.127.1.3

The Effect of Expected Revenue Proportion and Social Value Orientation Index on Players' Behavior in Divergent Interest Tacit Coordination Games

Dor Mizrahi(✉), Ilan Laufer, and Inon Zuckerman

Department of Industrial Engineering and Management, Ariel University, Ariel, Israel
Dor.mizrahi1@msmail.ariel.ac.il, {ilan1,inonzu}@ariel.ac.il

Abstract. Tacit coordination games are games in which players need to coordinate with one another, for example, on how to divide resources, while they are not allowed to communicate with each other. In divergent interest tacit coordination games, their interests are not always aligned. For instance, player may need to choose between a solution that maximizes their individual profit or a solution that is perceptually more salient to both players, i.e., a focal point, that will increase the chances for successful coordination. The goal of this study was to examine the effect of two key variables, the Expected Revenue Proportions (ERP) and the player's Social Value Orientation (SVO) on the probability of realizing a focal point solution in divergent interest tacit coordination games. Our results show that there is an interaction between the expected payoff and the SVO. For example, prosocial players tend to implement a social point solution although the expected payoff is less than that of their opponent. Thus, the implementation of a focal point depends on other contextual variables such as the SVO and the expected payoff. The main contribution of this work is showing that the probability to choose a focal point solution is affected by the interaction between SVO and the expected revenue of the player. This finding may contribute to the construction of cognitive models for decision making in diverge interest tacit coordination problems.

Keywords: Tacit coordination games · Decision making · Divergent interest · SVO; cognitive modeling

1 Introduction

A *tacit coordination game* is a game in which two or more individuals are rewarded for making the exact same choice from the same given and known set of alternatives, and any form of communication between the players is not possible [1]. These problems have been formally modeled in game theory as games with multiple Nash equilibria solutions with equal values [2]. Since Schelling's work [3] many experiments have shown that people somehow manage to converge to a solution more effectively than what was predicted by the game-theoretical analysis. The relative success is due to a set of solutions

M. Mahmud et al. (Eds.): BI 2021, LNAI 12960, pp. 25–34, 2021.
https://doi.org/10.1007/978-3-030-86993-9_3

called focal points (e.g. [4–7]). People often manage to see that these solutions somehow *stand out* from the rest of the solutions and can use them to successfully coordinate.

Previous research has demonstrated that there are many factors, such as cultural background [8], loss aversion [9] and gender [10], which can affect the players' behavior in coordination problems. The Social Value Orientation (SVO) theory describes the preferences or motivations of a decision maker. These motivations can vary on a wide scale, for example from motivation based solely on self-concern (individualist) to one that seeks to maximize the profit of all participants (prosocial). Previous studies have shown that the SVO variable has an effect on players in tacit coordination games (e.g. [11–13]), but in this research, we would like to examine it specifically in *divergent* interest tacit coordination games while examining the interaction with the expected revenue proportion in the coordination problem.

To that aim we have conducted an experiment to model the effect of social value orientation together with the expected revenue proportion on players' behavior in diverge interest tacit coordination games. Our results show that (1) as the SVO increases (towards cooperativeness) there is an increase tendency to implement a focal point solution. (2) When the boards present an unequal expected revenue proportion to the players, the tendency to implement a focal point decreases as well. (3) There is a statistically significant interaction between these two variables, SVO and ERP. That is, the probability of realizing a focal point solution as a function of one of the variables is affected by the value of the other variable.

2 Materials and Methods

2.1 Measuring Social Value Orientation

The social value orientation (SVO) theory describes the preferences or motivations of Decision Makers (DMs) when allocating joint resources between the self and another person [11, 14]. The model represents four main categories that describe those preferences: individualistic orientation – a DM who is only concerned with their own outcomes, Competitive orientation – a DM who aspires to maximize their own outcome, but in addition also minimizes the outcome of others, Cooperative orientation – a DM who tends to maximize the joint outcome, and Altruistic orientation – a DM who is motivated to help others at the expense of their own utility.

Over the years, a variety of methods have been developed for measuring and evaluating the value of SVO, with three methods being adopted as the most widely accepted. The first is called the Ring method [15], which consists of 24 social dilemma games in which the subject must choose between two alternatives that represent different combinations of outcomes for themselves as well as for another person. One of the main criticisms of the ring method was that it contains a large number of questions which causes the results to be skewed. Due to this the triple-dominance [16] method was introduced. The triple dominance method consists of nine items while in each of them the subject needs to select one out of three possible own-other outcomes.

The third and most recent measuring method is the Slider method [17], which is also considered to be the most accurate one because it provides a continuous measure of assessment (i.e., angle – see Eq. 1) and not a specific category. In the slider method, the participant must answer only 6 questions. These questions contain a continuous scale; each point on the scale produces a different allocation of resources between him or herself and an unknown other. The slider method is calculated as the arctangent of the ratio between the average payments of the unknown player and the average payments of the decision maker. Both average payments are centered on the ring by subtracting the fixed value of 50, as can be seen in the following Eq. (1):

$$SVO^{o} = \arctan\left(\frac{\overline{A_o} - 50}{\overline{A_s} - 50}\right) \tag{1}$$

Another strength of this measurement method is that it provides a way to discern the attitude of the subject towards two relatively selected categories (Each cross-section of different categories is applied in each one of the six different questions – as presented in Fig. 1). The six questions were designed to explore all the possible relationships between the four main categories mentioned in the Ring method. The SVO angle in the Slider.

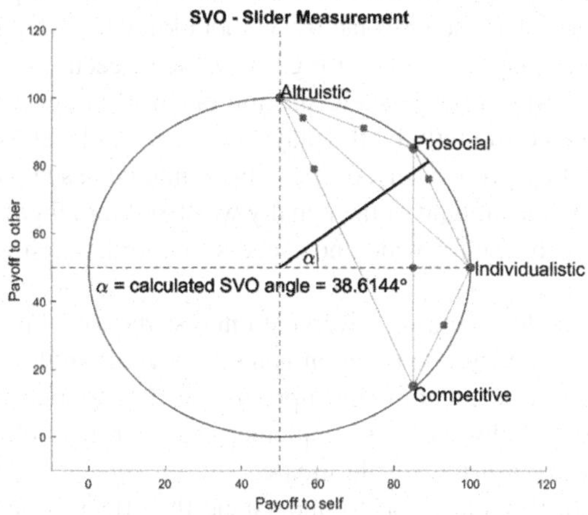

Fig. 1. SVO ring with slider method sub-graph between each two main categories

2.2 "Bargaining Table" Game

For our diverge interest tacit coordination game we have utilized the "Bargaining Table" Task [9, 18–20]. The "Bargaining Table" game is played on a 9 × 9 square board, with discs with varying numeric values scattered around the board. Alongside the discs, there are two squares of two different colors (see Fig. 2). The blue square denotes player 1 and is located at board position (2, 5); the orange square denotes player 2 and is located at board position (8, 5). The task of each player is to assign each of the discs to one of the squares (either blue or orange). The payoff for each player is the total sum of the numeric values of the discs that are assigned to their own square. For example, in Fig. 2 the blue player attained a payoff of [4 + 5] points, while the orange player attained a payoff of [1] point.

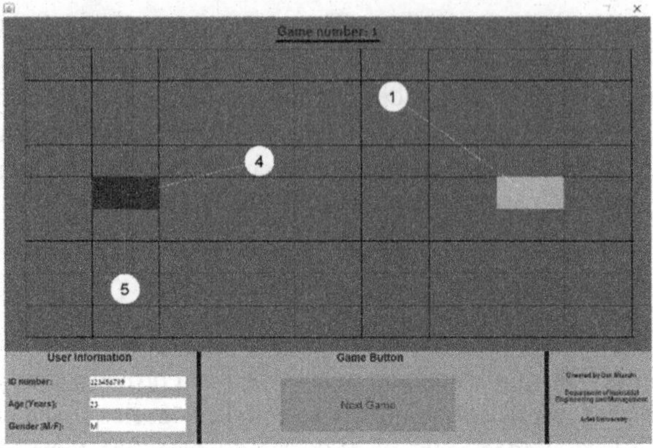

Fig. 2. "Bargaining Table" board game. (Color figure online)

The "Bargaining Table" poses a tacit coordination task since the players must assign each of the discs to one of the squares tacitly, without knowing what assignments were performed by the other player. In this setting, the value of each disc is given as payoff **only** if both players assign it to the same specific player (blue or orange square). If a given disc was assigned differently by the players (i.e., each player assigned the disc to a different square), both players received a penalty computed based on disc value. In the case of this experiment the amount of the penalty was fixed for all game boards and was 20% of the value of each disc for which no successful coordination was made between the two players.

The "Bargaining Table" game is a divergent interest version of the "Assign Circles" (e.g. [8, 12, 21–23]) pure tacit coordination games. Previous studies conducted on the latter [12, 21–23] have shown that the most prominent strategy players utilize to select a focal point is the rule of closeness. By implementing the rule of closeness, the player assigns each disc to the closest available square.

One of the aims of this study was to understand the effect of point distribution on the probability of realizing a Focal Point Solution (FPS). To do this we will define the concept of Expected Revenue Proportion (ERP). The ERP of each game board reflects the percentage of points that the player receives if both players implement a focal point solution according to the closeness rule. We have normalized this value to fit the [0, 1] range, where zero denotes that the player is not expected to receive any point, and one denotes the case in which the player is expected to get all the points in the game, if a focal point solution is implemented.

2.3 Experimental Design

Participants. The experiment involved 38 university students that were enrolled in one of the courses on campus (13 females; mean age = ~ 25, SD = 4.02). The study was approved by the IRB committee of the University. All participants provided written informed consent for the experiment.

Procedure. The study comprised the following stages. First, participants received an explanation regarding the overarching aim of the study and were given instructions regarding the experimental procedure and the interface of the application. Participants were offered a reward according to their level of coordination with their unknown counterpart that was chosen at random from the entire pool of participants. Following the instructions, each participant performed ten games that were included in the "Bargaining Table" application. All the game boards were randomly generated since we wanted to use a large variety of games for the construction of the behavioral model. To that end the following parameters were randomized by using a uniform distribution: the number of discs (~U [1, 8]); the numeric value of each disc (~U [1, 4]); and disc position (~U[1, 70]). Note that disc position excludes the two player's position and the vertical midline. In each game, the player type (blue/orange) was also randomly selected. Next, the SVO of each player was measured using the "slider" method [20]. Each player was presented with a "Slider" method application and answered six resource allocation tasks by using the slider. Finally, the output file with the experiment logs was uploaded also to a shared location for offline analysis.

3 Results and Discussion

3.1 The Effect of SVO Angle on FPS Realization Probability

In this section, we attempt to quantify the effect of the SVO index on the probability of focal point solution realization in diverge interest tacit coordination games. We have grouped the experimental results according to players' SVO variable at 5° resolution, and within each group calculated the mean focal point solution probability carried out from the experimental results and taking into account the standard error. Finally, the relationship was calculated between the mean focal point solution estimated probability and the SVO using linear regression, as can be seen in Fig. 3 and in Eqs. 2.1 and 2.2.

$$p_{FPS} = 0.3053 + 0.0023 * \text{SVO} \tag{2.1}$$

$$R^2 = 0.435; F - statistic = 7.6981; p - value = 0.0196 \tag{2.2}$$

It can be seen from the regression results that the relationship between the SVO and the mean predicted probability turned is *significant*. As the SVO angle increases, the greater the chance of realizing a focal point solution for a given game board. This result also in line with the SVO theory [15–17], as the angle increases players tend towards prosocial orientation. Despite the significant results, it can be seen in Fig. 3 that there is still another unexplained variance of different value for each SVO angle. That variance is explained by the other parameters, such as the ERP.

3.2 The Effect of ERP on FPS Realization Probability

The ERP reflects the percentage of points that the player receives if both players implement a focal point solution according to the closeness rule. In this section we will measure

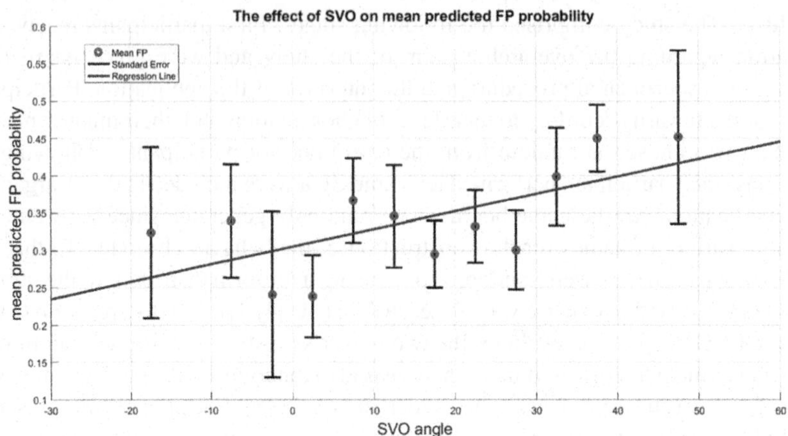

Fig. 3. The effect of SVO on mean focal point solution probability

the effect of the ERP variable on the probability of focal point solution realization. we will aggregate the experimental result according to the game board ERP value with a resolution of 0.1, and within each group calculate the mean focal point solution probability carried out from the experimental results and considering the standard error. The aggregate data is visualized in Fig. 4.

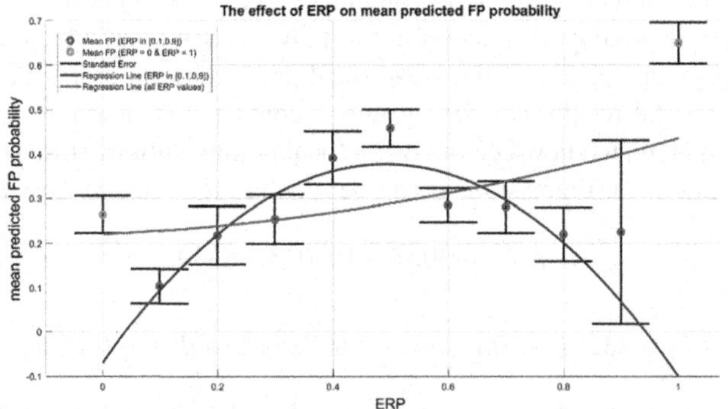

Fig. 4. The effect of ERP on mean FP probability

Modeling the data using a linear model did not produce statistically significant results ($p > 0.05$), therefore, we decided to raise the order of the model and tried to find the relationship by using a second-order polynomial. Ostensibly, this second-order model was also provided statistically insignificant results ($p > 0.05$), with high estimation errors. The model presented in the pink graph in Fig. 4.

An in-depth look at the data shows us that there are two exceptional points, ERP = 0 and ERP = 1. These points represent extreme situations in a game where one player receives all the points (ERP = 1) or none of the points (ERP = 0) when the FP solution is implemented. Understanding that these are extreme game situations is guiding us to model the data set in subgroups. When the ERP values in the range of $(0.1, 0.9)$ a general model is required. While in the other cases, where ERP = 0 or ERP = 1, a specific model will be tailored to these situations. The significant modeling results ($p < 0.05$) using a second-order polynomial for the cases where ERP is in the range $(0.1, 0.9)$ can be seen in Eqs. 3.1 and 3.2 together with the blue graph in Fig. 4.

$$p_{FPS} = -1.8475 * ERP^2 + 1.817 * \mathrm{ERP} - 0.07 \tag{3.1}$$

$$R^2 = 0.805; F - statistic = 10.32; p - value = 0.0168 \tag{3.2}$$

The results of the model clearly show that as you move away from the state in which the points on the board are evenly distributed (ERP = 0.5), the lower the probability of implementing the FP solution. Again, it should be emphasized that for each point there is a certain variance which is not explained by the ERP parameter alone and for exact revaluation we have to use additional various parameters, such the SVO. Another point to consider is the realization that there are extreme cases in the game that need to be modeled differently.

3.3 ERP and SVO Interaction Effect on FPS Realization Probability

To summarize the quantitative analysis of the data, since the two variables we chose to examine in this study, ERP and SVO, were accepted as having a significant effect on the probability of FPS realization, we examined whether there was an interaction between these two variables, and how it affects the probability of FPS realization. In order to perform the test, we will use a two-way ANOVA model to determine whether an interaction exists between them. For that end, we will discretize these variables to one of three possible levels so that the ANOVA array will be in size of 3×3.

The ERP value is divided into 3 possible levels. First level when ERP < 0.5, which means the player earns less than 50% of the points on the board. Second level is when ERP = 0.5, meaning that the points are evenly divided between the two players. Third level is ERP > 0.5, i.e., when the player earns more than 50% of the points on the board. The division can be seen mathematically in Eq. 4:

$$\text{quantized ERP} = \begin{cases} 0;\, if\ ERP < 0.5 \\ 1;\, if\ ERP = 0.5 \\ 2;\, if\ ERP > 0.5 \end{cases} \tag{4}$$

Most of the SVO values of the different participants in the experiment were clustered within the of 0 to 45 degrees boundary representing the range between cooperation and individualism. Therefore, the quantization of the SVO variable was performed uniformly in that range as described in Eq. 5:

$$\text{quantized SVO} = \begin{cases} 0;\, if\ SVO \leq 15 \\ 1;\, if\ 15 < SVO \leq 30 \\ 2;\, if\ SVO > 30 \end{cases} \tag{5}$$

The results of the ANOVA model showed that there was a significant main effect of the quantized ERP [$F(2,371) = 12.99$, $p < 0.001$], as well as of the quantized SVO [$F(2,371) = 5.87$, $p < 0.01$]. The interaction effect was also significant [$F(4, 371) = 3.77$, $p < 0.01$]. Figure 5 displays the interaction between the quantized ERP and SVO obtained within a 3 by 3 ANOVA array.

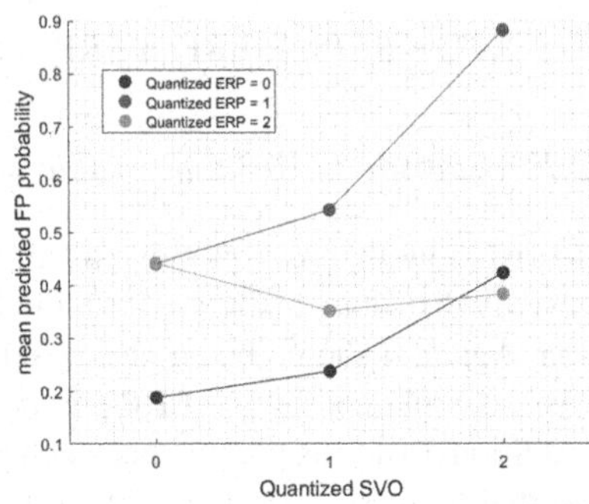

Fig. 5. The interaction between ERP and SVO

An interesting trend can be seen from the ANOVA model in the interaction between the parameters. For example, it can be seen that as the SVO value increases, the probability of realizing a focal point solution increases when ERP = 0.5 or ERP < 0.5 (the red and blue lines in Fig. 5), but when ERP > 0.5 the probability hardly changes (the green line in Fig. 5).

4 Conclusions and Future Work

The main purpose of this study was to show using mathematical tools that the SVO and ERP directly influence human behavior in divergent interest tacit coordination games. To that end we have an experiment which has collected individual data of players behavior and decision making actions in the "Bargaining Table" task [9, 18, 19]. Based on the players' SVO data together with behavioral data we have constructed models that link the probability of implementing a focal point solution with each of the variables, SVO and ERP, independently when it is statistically significant. When we examined the order of the relationship it could be seen that the relationship between SVO and the probability of realizing a focal point solution is linear (Eqs. 2.1 and 2.2), while for ERP the relationship is parabolic (Eqs. 3.1 and 3.2). Finally, we performed an analysis of the interaction between these two parameters using the ANOVA model, which is significant as well (Sect. 3.3).

There are some limitations in the current study that warrant consideration. First, in this study, we used a homogeneous sample of participants. Since it has been previously shown [8, 12] that the players' behavior in coordination games is sensitive to the effect of the cultural background, it is important to extend the study to include diverse populations. Second, [9] showed that loss-aversion is a significant factor in the individual behavior in divergent interest tacit coordination games. However, in our study the penalty for failed coordination was fixed and it is recommended to vary the amount of penalty in future studies.

Our findings open new avenues of research as follows. First, after conducting a group-level analysis in this study, it will be possible to try to break down the group level into individual models that represent different strategic profiles of players, as recently demonstrated for coordination games with a common interest [22, 24, 25]. Moreover, it might also be interesting to explore whether the behavioral differences which have reflected as a function of SVO and ERP parameters are accompanied by parallel changes in electrophysiological markers, such as the Theta-Beta ratio [26, 27] or other cognitive load measures [28], signifying potential differences in the functionality of the underlying brain networks. Finally, it will be interesting to see how these SVO and ERP relationships can be combined with an autonomous agent (e.g. [6, 20, 29–31]) who will optimize the divergent interest tacit coordination games profits against human players.

References

1. Bacharach, M.: Beyond Individual Choice: Teams and Frames in Game Theory. Wiley and Sons (2006)
2. Binmore, K.: Playing for Real: A Text on Game Theory. Oxford University Press, Oxford (2007)
3. Schelling, T.C.: The Strategy of Conflict. Cambridge (1960)
4. Poulsen, A., Sonntag, A.: Focality is intuitive - experimental evidence on the effects of time pressure in coordination games (2019)
5. Bardsley, N., Mehta, J., Starmer, C., Sugden, R.: Explaining focal points: cognitive hierarchy theory versus team reasoning. Econ. J. **120**, 40–79 (2009)
6. Zuckerman, I., Kraus, S., Rosenschein, J.S.: Using focal point learning to improve human-machine tacit coordination. Auton. Agent. Multi Agent Syst. **22**, 289–316 (2011)
7. Sugden, R.: A theory of focal points. Econ. J. **105**, 533–550 (1995)
8. Mizrahi, D., Laufer, I., Zuckerman, I.: Collectivism-individualism: strategic behavior in tacit coordination games. PLoS ONE **15**, e0226929 (2020)
9. Mizrahi, D., Laufer, I., Zuckerman, I.: The effect of loss-aversion on strategic behaviour of players in divergent interest tacit coordination games. In: Mahmud, M., Vassanelli, S., Kaiser, M.S., Zhong, N. (eds.) BI 2020. LNCS (LNAI), vol. 12241, pp. 41–49. Springer, Cham (2020). https://doi.org/10.1007/978-3-030-59277-6_4
10. Ortmann, A., Tichy, L.K.: Gender differences in the laboratory: evidence from prisoner's dilemma games. Econ. Behav. Organ. **39**, 327–339 (1999)
11. Bogaert, S., Boone, C., Declerck, C.: Social value orientation and cooperation in social dilemmas: a review and conceptual model. Br. J. Soc. Psychol. **47**, 453–480 (2008)
12. Mizrahi, D., Laufer, I., Zuckerman, I., Zhang, T.: The effect of culture and social orientation on player's performances in tacit coordination games. In: Wang, S., et al. (eds.) BI 2018. LNCS (LNAI), vol. 11309, pp. 437–447. Springer, Cham (2018). https://doi.org/10.1007/978-3-030-05587-5_41
13. Zuckerman, I., Cheng, K.L., Nau, D.S.: Modeling agent's preferences by its designer's social value orientation. J. Exp. Theor. Artif. Intell. **30**, 257–277 (2018). https://doi.org/10.1080/0952813X.2018.1430856
14. Balliet, D., Parks, C., Joireman, J.: Social value orientation and cooperation in social dilemmas: a meta-analysis. Gr. Process. Intergr. Relations **12**, 533–547 (2009)

15. Liebrand, W.B., Mcclntock, C.G.: The ring measure of social values: a computerized procedure for assessing individual differences in information processing and social value orientation. Eur. J. Pers. **2**, 217–230 (1988)
16. Van Lange, P.A.M., De Bruin, E.M.N., Otten, W., Joireman, J.A.: Development of prosocial, individualistic, and competitive orientations: theory and preliminary evidence. J. Pers. Soc. Psychol. **73**, 733 (1997)
17. Murphy, R.O., Ackermann, K.A., Handgraaf, M.J.J.: Measuring social value orientation. Judgm. Decis. Mak. **6**, 771–781 (2011)
18. Isoni, A., Poulsen, A., Sugden, R., Tsutsui, K.: Focal points and payoff information in tacit bargaining. Games Econ. Behav. **114**, 193–214 (2019)
19. Isoni, A., Poulsen, A., Sugden, R., Tsutsui, K.: Focal points in tacit bargaining problems: experimental evidence. Eur. Econ. Rev. **59**, 167–188 (2013)
20. Mizrahi, D., Zuckerman, I., Laufer, I.: Using a stochastic agent model to optimize performance in divergent interest tacit coordination games. Sensors **20**, 7026 (2020)
21. Mehta, J., Starmer, C., Sugden, R.: Focal points in pure coordination games: an experimental investigation. Theory Decis. **36**, 163–185 (1994)
22. Mizrahi, D., Laufer, I., Zuckerman, I.: Individual strategic profiles in tacit coordination games. J. Exp. Theor. Artif. Intell. 1–16 (2020)
23. Mehta, J., Starmer, C., Sugden, R.: The nature of salience: an experimental investigation of pure coordination games. Am. Econ. Rev. **84**, 658–673 (1994)
24. Mizrahi, D., Laufer, I., Zuckerman, I.: Modeling individual tacit coordination abilities. In: International Conference on Brain Informatics, Haikou, China, pp. 29–38. Springer, Cham (2019). https://doi.org/10.1007/978-3-030-37078-7_4
25. Zhao, W.: Cost of reasoning and strategic sophistication. Games **11**, 40 (2020)
26. Davis, F.D., Riedl, R., vom Brocke, J., Léger, P.-M., Randolph, A.B., Fischer, T. (eds.): NeuroIS 2020. LNISO, vol. 43. Springer, Cham (2020). https://doi.org/10.1007/978-3-030-60073-0
27. Mizrahi, D., Laufer, I., Zuckerman, I.: Topographic analysis of cognitive load in tacit coordination games based on electrophysiological measurements. In: NeuroIS Retreat 2021, Vienna, Austria (2021)
28. Fernandez Rojas, R., et al.: Electroencephalographic workload indicators during teleoperation of an unmanned aerial vehicle shepherding a swarm of unmanned ground vehicles in contested environments. Front. Neurosci. **14**, 1–15 (2020)
29. Kraus, S.: Predicting human decision-making: from prediction to action. In: Proceedings of the 6th International Conference on Human-Agent Interaction. p. 1 (2018)
30. Zuckerman, I., Kraus, S., Rosenschein, J.S.: The adversarial activity model for bounded rational agents. Auton. Agent. Multi Agent Syst. **24**, 374–409 (2012). https://doi.org/10.1007/s10458-010-9153-2
31. Bühler, M., Weisswange, T.: Theory of mind based communication for human agent cooperation. In: IEEE International Conference on Human-Machine Systems, Rome, Italy (2020)

On the Extraction of High-Level Visual Features from Lateral Geniculate Nucleus Activity: A Rat Study

Mai Gamal[1], Eslam Mounier[2,3], and Seif Eldawlatly[1,2(✉)]

[1] Computer Science and Engineering Department, Faculty of Media Engineering and Technology, German University in Cairo, Cairo, Egypt
mai.tharwat@guc.edu.eg, seldawlatly@eng.asu.edu.eg
[2] Computer and Systems Engineering Department, Faculty of Engineering, Ain Shams University, Cairo, Egypt
eslam.mounier@eng.asu.edu.eg
[3] Electrical and Computer Engineering Department, Faculty of Engineering and Applied Science, Queen's University, Kingston, ON, Canada

Abstract. The lateral geniculate nucleus (LGN) plays a vital role in visual information processing as an early stage in the visual system linking the retina with the visual cortex. Beyond its simple linear role, the LGN has been found to have a complex role in higher-order visual processing that is not fully understood. The aim of this study is to examine predicting high-level visual features from rat LGN firing activity. Extracellular neural activity of LGN neurons was recorded from 6 anesthetized rats in response to 4×8 checkerboard visual stimulation patterns using multi-electrode arrays. The first examined high-level feature is classifying the positions of the majority of white pixels in a visual pattern using the corresponding LGN activity. Three classes of patterns are identified in this task: majority in the top two rows, majority in the bottom two rows, or equal number of white pixels across the top and bottom halves of the pattern. The second examined high-level feature is estimating how far the white pixels are scattered in a visual stimulation pattern based on the corresponding LGN activity. Our results demonstrate that using LGN population activity achieves an F_1-score of 0.67 in the patterns classification and a root-mean-square error of 0.3 in the scatter estimation. Such performance outperforms that achieved using the visual stimulation patterns as inputs to the classification and scatter estimation methods. These results provide evidence that specific high-level visual features could be represented in the LGN; suggesting a critical role of the LGN in encoding visual information.

Keywords: LGN · Classification · Regression

1 Introduction

The lateral geniculate nucleus (LGN) is a subcortical structure in the thalamus that plays a crucial role in visual information processing [1, 2]. The axons from the retinal ganglion

M. Mahmud et al. (Eds.): BI 2021, LNAI 12960, pp. 35–45, 2021.
https://doi.org/10.1007/978-3-030-86993-9_4

cells form synaptic connections with LGN cells and axons from LGN cells project to the visual cortex [1]. Thus, the LGN has been known as a “relay nucleus” carrying visual information from the retina to the primary visual cortex. The LGN has been considered to be a simple linear early stage of visual processing. However, recent studies have shown that the LGN has a more complex role in visual information processing including various nonlinearities [2–5]. A main source of nonlinearity in the LGN is the feedback projections from the visual cortex that outnumber the feed forward retinal projections [2]. Accordingly, beyond its known role in low-level vision [6], the LGN is argued to have a role in higher-level cognitive processing [2].

The role of the LGN in higher-order visual processing has been studied in multiple studies. In a recent study, the categorization performance of human subjects was compared to a cortical object recognition model in the presence and absence of an LGN input-stage model [7]. The results showed that incorporating the role of LGN into the recognition model led to a performance closer to that of human subjects. In another study, it was found that the LGN has a role in processing orientation information which was traditionally thought to be attributed to the visual cortex [8]. Although these studies along with others show the role of LGN in object recognition and other higher-level processing, the complexity of the LGN role is not clearly understood. Moreover, high-level vision lacks a single agreed-upon definition, object recognition has been the focus of studying high-level vision. However, it is argued that there are important parameters of any object beyond its identity such as: how big it is? Or how close or far it is? [9]. Therefore, a better understanding of the LGN role would help in further understanding of the visual processing in the brain and would also help in developing more advanced high-level object recognition models [2].

In this paper, we aim to demonstrate two different visual features that can be extracted, in the form of classification and regression tasks, from LGN neural responses recorded from rats. In both tasks, we use machine learning techniques that are widely used in understanding biological data and neural data in particular [10, 11]. Moreover, we have used dimensionality reduction using Principal Component Analysis (PCA) to reduce the dimensions of the input data [12]. In the classification task, we classify the position of the majority of white pixels in a visual pattern into one of three classes: majority in the top half of the visual pattern, majority in the bottom half of the visual pattern, or equal number of white pixels across the two halves. In the regression task, we extract a nonlinear feature from the visual patterns, termed the Scatter Index (SI) hereafter, that quantifies the white pixels’ scatter. We recorded extracellular neural activity of LGN neurons in response to checkerboard visual stimulation patterns using multi-electrode arrays from 6 anesthetized rats. The neuronal firing rates per pattern were calculated and used in extracting visual features from the pattern. We compared the classification and regression accuracies achieved using the LGN neural activity with the accuracies achieved using the input visual patterns. We analyzed the performance achieved by the LGN activity at two levels: 1) single neurons, and 2) population of neurons. Our results show that the population of LGN neurons achieves the highest performance in both the classification and regression tasks compared to the input visual patterns and the single neurons. These results can help in demonstrating and understanding two high-level visual features that could be encoded in the LGN neural activity.

2 Methods

2.1 Data Collection

Six female Albino rats weighing ~120 g were used in this study. The procedures employed in this study were approved by the Research Ethics Committee at the Faculty of Medicine, Ain Shams University. Animals were fully anesthetized using Urethane (1 g/kg injected intraperitoneally; supplemented as needed) [13]. A craniotomy of size 4 mm × 4 mm (1–5 mm posterior and 1–5 mm lateral to Bregma) was drilled over the right LGN, and the underlying dura was resected [14]. In this study, we used 32-channel microelectrode silicon arrays (NeuroNexus Technologies, Ann Arbor, MI, USA) to record LGN neuronal activity. The array was lowered in 100 μm/min steps until the target location of the LGN is reached. Signals recorded were amplified and band pass filtered in the range 300–5000 Hz and sampled at 25 kHz (Tucker-Davis Technologies, Alachua, FL, USA). Once the LGN was reached, a 13-in. screen was used to present visual stimulation patterns to the rat's left eye. These patterns comprised dividing the screen into 4 × 8 pixels, in which 4 pixels are turned white at random, with the rest of the pixels kept black. A total of 32 different patterns were presented, 100 times each. For each pattern, the 4 flickered pixels were ON (White) for 200 ms and OFF (Black) for 300 ms. At the end of the recording sessions, rats were euthanized using an overdose of Thiopental Sodium injected intraperitoneally.

2.2 Data Preprocessing

In order to extract spike trains from the recorded extracellular activity, we used NeuroQuest as a MATLAB toolbox for neural data processing and analysis [15]. A spike detection threshold of 3 times the noise standard deviation was used. Detected spikes were aligned at their trough and PCA was applied to project the detected spikes into a 2-dimensional feature space. We used K-means clustering to sort the detected spikes into single units/neurons. A spike train was then formed with a resolution of 1 ms. For each trial, we then calculated the firing rate per neuron from the spike train by counting the number of spikes in 50 ms windows. Finally, to calculate the firing rate per pattern, we averaged the firing rate of each pattern for each neuron across 100 trials.

2.3 Classification Task

To examine the ability of the LGN activity to classify the visual patterns into 3 classes based on the location of the majority of white pixels, we used three different classifiers: Support Vector Machine (SVM), Naïve Bayes, and Linear Discriminant Analysis (LDA). The performance of these classifiers was compared across three different types of inputs: visual stimulation patterns, single neuron firing activity, and population firing activity. We applied dimensionality reduction to the input of the classifiers using PCA [16], and we used the number of principal components (PCs) resulting in the maximum accuracy. We also used the Leave-One-Out Cross-Validation (LOOCV) approach to compute the classification accuracy.

Support Vector Machine (SVM)
SVM classifies data by finding the hyperplane with the largest margin between the two classes to be separated. In linear SVM, which was used in this study, the hyperplane is found by maximizing the following objective function [17]

$$J = \sum_{i=1}^{N} \alpha_i - \frac{1}{2}\sum_{i=1}^{N}\sum_{j=1}^{N} \alpha_i \alpha_j y_i y_j \mathbf{x}_i^T \mathbf{x}_j \tag{1}$$

where $\mathbf{x}_i$ is an input vector, y_i is the class label of $\mathbf{x}_i$, α_i is a Lagrange multiplier, and N is the number of training data vectors.

Naïve Bayes
Naïve Bayes is a probabilistic classification algorithm that is based on Bayes' theorem with an assumption of independence between the data features. It assigns the most likely class (maximum a posteriori (MAP) class) to an input vector as [18]

$$C_{MAP}(\mathbf{x}_i) = \underset{k=1,\ldots,K}{\operatorname{argmax}} p(C_k) \prod_{j=1}^{M} p(x_{ij}|C_k) \tag{2}$$

where $C_{MAP}(\mathbf{x}_i)$ is the class assigned to $\mathbf{x}_i$, $p(C_k)$ is the prior probability of class C_k, $p(x_{ij}|C_k)$ is the probability of x_{ij} conditioned on C_k, K is the number of classes, and M is the number of features per input vector.

Linear Discriminant Analysis (LDA)
LDA is a method that was originally proposed by R. Fisher for separating classes by maximizing the between-class variance while minimizing the within-class variance. This criterion is achieved by maximizing the following objective function [19]

$$J(\mathbf{w}) = \frac{\mathbf{w}^T \mathrm{S_B} \mathbf{w}}{\mathbf{w}^T \mathrm{S_W} \mathbf{w}} \tag{3}$$

where $\mathbf{w}$ is the weight vector defining the hyperplane separating the classes, $\mathrm{S_B}$ is the between-class covariance matrix, and $\mathrm{S_W}$ is the within-class covariance matrix.

Classification Performance Evaluation
In this study, we have used the macro F_1-score to evaluate the classification accuracy which is calculated as [20]

$$Macro\ F_1 = \frac{1}{K}\sum_{k=1}^{K} F_{1k} \tag{4}$$

where F_{1k} is the F_1-score for class k, and K is the number of classes. F_1-score, which is also known as, F-measure, is calculated as follows [20]

$$F_{1k} = \frac{2P_k R_k}{P_k + R_k} \tag{5}$$

where P_k and R_k are the precision and recall values, respectively, for class k.

2.4 Regression Task

We have used linear regression in predicting the Scatter Index (SI); a metric that quantifies the scatter of the white pixels in the checkerboard patterns. The SI represents how far the white pixels are from their center in a pattern. The SI per pattern is calculated using the following equation:

$$SI = \frac{1}{P}\sum\nolimits_{i=1}^{P} d(\mathbf{z}_i, \overline{\mathbf{z}}) \tag{6}$$

where $\mathbf{z}_i$ is the position of the white pixel i in the pattern, $\overline{\mathbf{z}}$ is the mean position of all the white pixels in the pattern, $d(\mathbf{z}_i, \overline{\mathbf{z}})$ is the Euclidean distance between $\mathbf{z}_i$ and $\overline{\mathbf{z}}$, and P is the number of white pixels in the pattern.

As with the classification task, in the regression task, the performance achieved by the linear regression model is compared across three different types of inputs: visual patterns, single neuron firing activity, and population firing activity. We also applied PCA for better representation of the input data and we used the number of PCs with the best accuracy. LOOCV has also been used in the evaluation.

Linear Regression

Linear regression is a method that defines a linear relationship between a response variable and explanatory variables defined as [21]

$$\hat{y} = \beta_0 + \beta_1 x_1 + \cdots + \beta_L x_L \tag{7}$$

where $\hat{y}$ is the response variable (SI in this study), β_j is a model parameter/coefficient, x_j is an explanatory variable, and L is the total number of explanatory variables. The model parameters can be estimated using the least squares approach.

Regression Performance Evaluation

To evaluate the performance of the linear regression model, we used the root-mean-square error (RMSE) which is calculated as [22]

$$RMSE = \sqrt{\frac{1}{N}\sum\nolimits_{i=1}^{N} (\hat{y}_i - y_i)^2} \tag{8}$$

where $\hat{y}_i$ and y_i are the predicted and actual SI values, respectively, of sample i, and N is the number of samples.

3 Results

3.1 Classification Task

The objective of this task is to examine the utility of LGN firing in discriminating the position of the majority of white pixels in a pattern in comparison to the visual input patterns. The patterns are classified into one of three classes: Up, Down, or Equal. The "Up" class represents the patterns with the majority of white pixels in the upper half of the image (Fig. 1a), the "Down" class represents the patterns with the majority of white pixels in the lower half of the image (Fig. 1b), and the "Equal" class represents the patterns with an equal number of white pixels in the upper and lower halves (Fig. 1c). We first investigated the differences among the firing patterns of single neurons across the three classes. We computed the Post-stimulus Time Histogram (PSTH) per class by averaging the firing rate per each time bin (the bin is a 50 ms window) across all patterns belonging to that class where the firing rate per pattern is averaged across 100 trials. Figure 2a shows the PSTH plots of one sample neuron in one subject for the three classes of patterns. Despite the similarity in the PSTH across the three classes in terms of the bin at which the PSTH peaks, some differences can be observed such as the peak PSTH value for the case of the Down class compared to the other two classes. To visualize the population activity, we used PCA to project the firing rate activity of the population of neurons recorded from each subject into three-dimensional space as shown in Fig. 2b for a sample subject. In this case, the population activity per subject is the firing activity concatenated from individual neurons for all the 32 patterns. The figure illustrates separability between the points representing different classes, which indicates the possibility of discriminating between the three classes using machine learning classifiers.

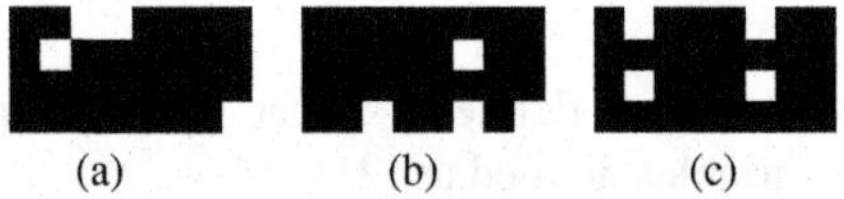

Fig. 1. Three classes of patterns. Each class is defined by the position of the majority of white pixels in the patterns (a) up, (b) down, and (c) equal.

We next examined the ability of machine learning classifiers to discriminate between the three classes when using as input the visual patterns, single neuron firing activity, or population firing activity. Figure 3 shows the classification accuracy, measured using the macro F_1-score, of the three classifiers (SVM, Naïve Bayes, and LDA). The accuracy reported for the single-neuron activity and population firing activity is averaged across the six subjects. The figure demonstrates that both the single-neuron activity and the population activity achieved above chance level accuracy. The single-neuron activity achieved macro F_1-score of 0.49 ± 0.12, 0.48 ± 0.11, and 0.49 ± 0.10, while the population activity achieved macro F_1-score of 0.67 ± 0.05, 0.64 ± 0.11, and 0.64 ± 0.08, using the SVM, Naïve Bayes, and LDA classifiers, respectively. On the other hand, the input patterns achieved macro F_1-score of 0.62, 0.57, and 0.64 using the SVM, Naïve Bayes, and LDA classifiers, respectively, which is lower than what is achieved using LGN population activity. These results demonstrate that the LGN population activity can be used to classify the position of the majority of the white pixels in an image, with an accuracy that is higher than what could be achieved using the corresponding visual stimulation patterns. This indicates that the visual information encoded in LGN neural activity could possess information beyond the simple representation of the single pixels in the image.

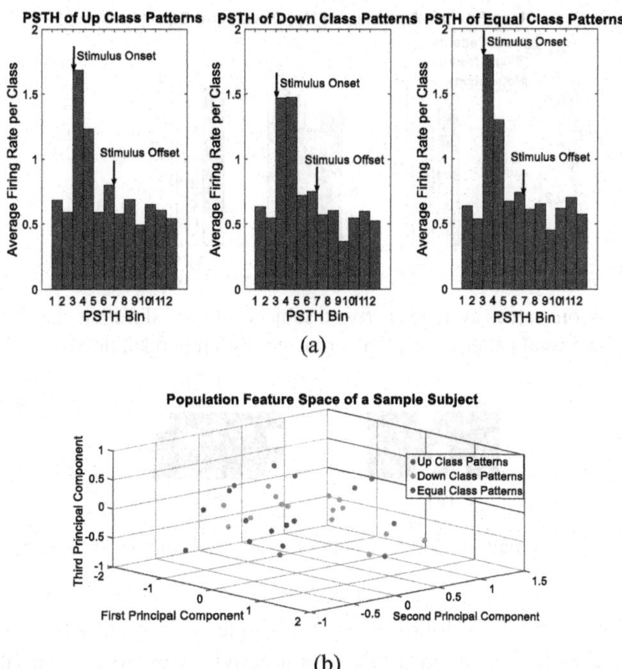

Fig. 2. Firing activity of one subject for the 32 patterns averaged across 100 trials. (a) PSTH of one sample neuron in one subject for the three classes of patterns (up, down, and equal). (b) feature space (first three PCs) of population activity of a sample subject after applying dimensionality reduction using PCA, where each dot represents one of the 32 patterns. Each pattern is colored based on its class: Up (red), Down (green), and Equal (blue) (Color figure online).

3.2 Regression Task

We next examine whether higher-level nonlinear features of the input pattern could be estimated from LGN firing. We predict a nonlinear feature; the SI, from the patterns using a linear regression model and three different types of inputs: visual patterns, single neuron firing activity, and population firing activity. Figure 4 shows two examples of images where one has a low scatter index of 1.3 (Fig. 4a), while the other has a high scatter index of 3.2 (Fig. 4b).

Figure 5a illustrates the actual SI values computed from the visual stimulation patterns versus the SI values estimated from the population activity of one subject. As shown in the figure, significant similarity can be observed between the actual and predicted SI values ($r^2 = 0.69$, $P < 5\text{e}^{-9}$). This indicates the ability of LGN neurons to encode the non-linear feature of scatter.

Figure 5b shows RMSE values of 0.39, 0.36 $\pm$ 0.05, and 0.30 $\pm$ 0.05 when using the input visual patterns, single-neuron activity, population activity for predicting the SI values using linear regression, respectively. As in the classification task, the accuracy reported for the single-neuron activity and population activity is averaged across 6 subjects. Figure 5b demonstrates that the LGN population activity achieves the highest

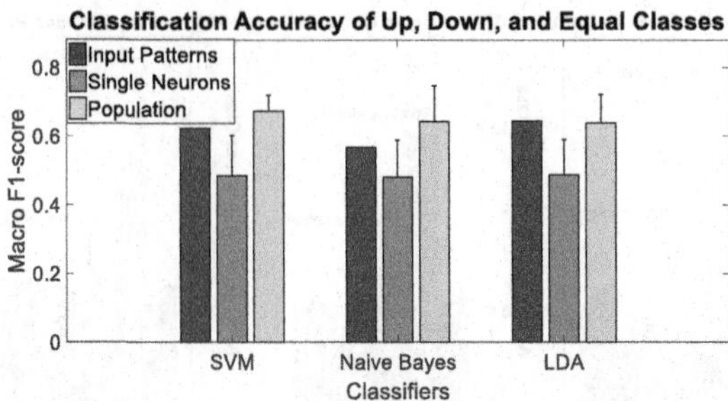

Fig. 3. Macro F_1-score values averaged across 6 subjects of three different classifiers comparing different inputs: raw visual patterns, single-neuron activity, and population firing activity.

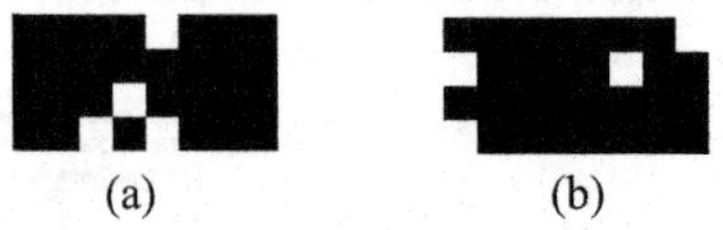

Fig. 4. Two examples of patterns. (a) Low scatter index (1.3) and (b) high scatter index (3.2).

performance (lowest RMSE), followed by the single-neuron activity and, finally, the visual patterns. This indicates that LGN neural activity can extract a nonlinear visual feature better than the corresponding visual stimulation patterns.

3.3 Performance Analysis

In order to analyze the performance achieved by the LGN firing activity in both the classification and the regression tasks, we examined the PC coefficients/loadings. The PC loadings at each time bin across all neurons can show which time bin contributes more to the performance achieved. Accordingly, we averaged the PC loadings, computed from applying PCA to the population firing activity of each rat, across all neurons at each time bin. We then normalized and averaged these values across all subjects. Figure 6 demonstrates, using the averaged normalized PCA loadings, that the first two-time bins, which are the first two frames after the stimulus onset, have the highest contribution to the performance achieved in the classification and regression tasks.

To further analyze the performance across the classification and regression tasks at the single-neuron level, we compared the performance achieved in both tasks (for the SVM classifier in the classification task) using the firing activity of each single neuron from the 6 subjects. Figure 7 demonstrates that there is no significant correlation between the classification and regression accuracies achieved by the single neurons. This result indicates that each neuron may have a different role in processing and discriminating the features in a given pattern. Moreover, we found that in 4 subjects out of 6, the classification accuracy of some single neurons did not surpass the accuracy of the population firing activity when using the SVM classifier. These results are consistent with other studies that demonstrated how the coordination between neurons constituting the population produces complex activity patterns that contribute to stimulus representation [23]. Information about stimulus encoding in different brain areas has been shown to be better

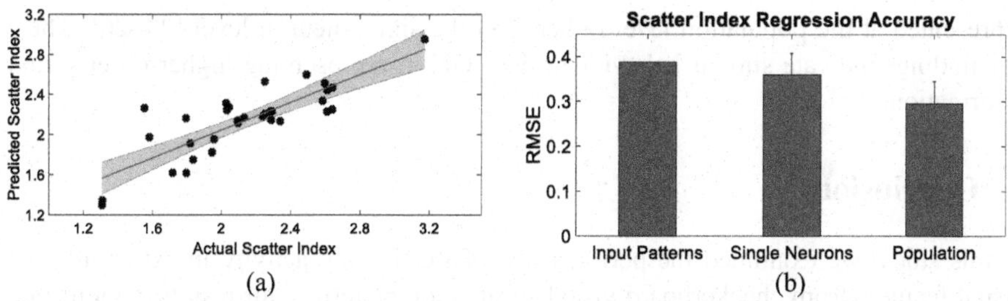

Fig. 5. Scatter Index (SI) prediction accuracy. (a) Actual SI values of the 32 examined patterns (each point represents a pattern) versus SI values predicted from the population firing activity of a sample subject fitted with a line ($r^2 = 0.69$). (b) RMSE values averaged across 6 subjects for predicting the SI values using linear regression model fitted either by raw visual patterns, single neuron firing activity, or population firing activity.

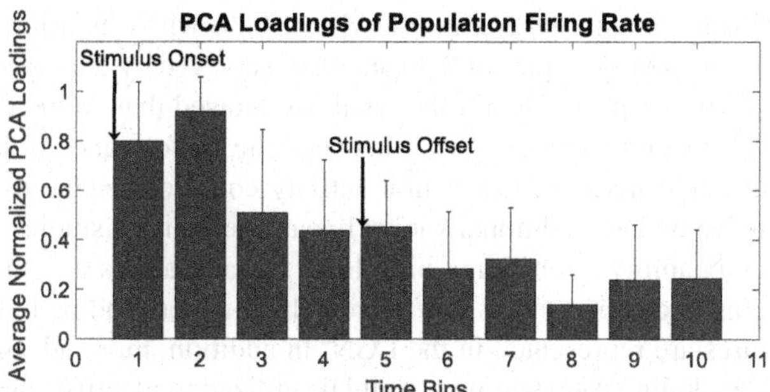

Fig. 6. Normalized PCA loadings of the population firing rate at each time bin (frame) averaged across 6 subjects and across all neurons per subject.

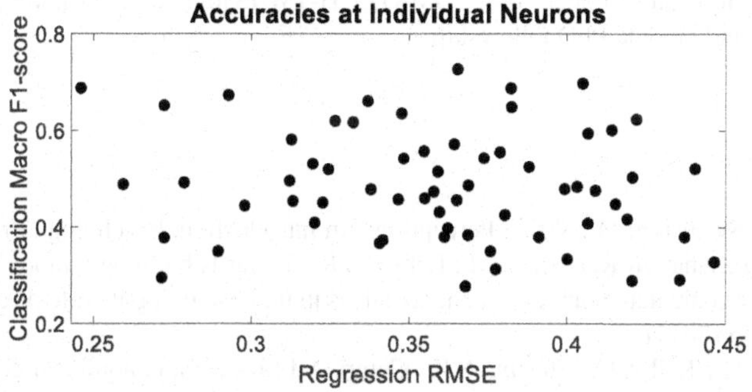

Fig. 7. Classification macro F_1-score (using SVM classifier) and regression RMSE achieved for each single neuron. Each point represents the accuracy achieved by one neuron and the plotted points represent all the neurons examined in the 6 subjects.

represented at the population level rather than the single-neuron level [24–26]. Thus, our findings indicate similar behavior in the LGN in representing higher-order visual information.

4 Conclusion

In this study, we examined the performance of LGN firing activity in extracting two visual features from checkerboard visual stimulation patterns. Our results demonstrate the success of the LGN population firing activity in extracting the two features with higher accuracy compared to the input visual patterns and single-neuron activity. In the classification task, using SVM classifier, the population firing activity achieved 0.67 average macro F_1-score across 6 subjects while the input patterns and single-neuron activity achieved scores of 0.62 and 0.49, respectively. Additionally, the population firing activity was able to predict, using linear regression, the SI values, a nonlinear feature, from the visual patterns with an average RMSE of 0.30 which is a lower prediction error compared to the RMSE values of 0.39 and 0.36 achieved by the input patterns and single-neuron activity, respectively. Further analysis showed that, at the level of single neurons, there is no significant correlation between the performance in both tasks. In sum, these results indicate that LGN neural activity could contribute to higher-order visual processing beyond its traditional known linear role. Further studies would enable examining the LGN ability in encoding high-level visual features of natural scenes in addition to building encoding models that could help in understanding how these high-level visual features are represented in the LGN. In addition, more advanced machine learning models, including deep learning, could be utilized to identify how the stimulus features are encoded and processed in the LGN.

Acknowledgments. This work was supported by the Science and Technology Development Fund (STDF) reintegration grant number 5168, COMSTECH-TWAS joint research grants program grant number 17-029, and Google PhD fellowship.

References

1. Wade, N.J., Swanston, M.: Visual Perception: An Introduction. Psychology Press (2013)
2. Ghodrati, M., Khaligh-Razavi, S.-M., Lehky, S.R.: Towards building a more complex view of the lateral geniculate nucleus: recent advances in understanding its role. Prog. Neurobiol. **156**, 214–255 (2017)
3. Solomon, S.G., Tailby, C., Cheong, S.K., Camp, A.J.: Linear and nonlinear contributions to the visual sensitivity of neurons in primate lateral geniculate nucleus. J. Neurophysiol. **104**(4), 1884–1898 (2010)
4. Alitto, H.J., Rathbun, D.L., Fisher, T.G., Alexander, P.C., Usrey, W.M.: Contrast gain control and retinogeniculate communication. Eur. J. Neurosci. **49**(8), 1061–1068 (2019)
5. Rathbun, D.L., Alitto, H.J., Warland, D.K., Usrey, W.M.: Stimulus contrast and retinogeniculate signal processing. Front. Neural Circuits **10**, 8 (2016)
6. Groen, I.I., Silson, E.H., Baker, C.I.: Contributions of low-and high-level properties to neural processing of visual scenes in the human brain. Philos. Trans. Royal Soc. B Biol. Sci. **372**(1714), 20160102 (2017)

7. Zabbah, S., Rajaei, K., Mirzaei, A., Ebrahimpour, R., Khaligh-Razavi, S.-M.: The impact of the lateral geniculate nucleus and corticogeniculate interactions on efficient coding and higher-order visual object processing. Vision Res. **101**, 82–93 (2014)
8. Ling, S., Pratte, M.S., Tong, F.: Attention alters orientation processing in the human lateral geniculate nucleus. Nat. Neurosci. **18**(4), 496–498 (2015)
9. Cox, D.D.: Do we understand high-level vision? Curr. Opin. Neurobiol. **25**, 187–193 (2014)
10. Majaj, N.J., Pelli, D.G.: Deep learning—using machine learning to study biological vision. J. Vis. **18**(13), 2 (2018)
11. Mahmud, M., Kaiser, M.S., McGinnity, T.M., Hussain, A.: Deep learning in mining biological data. Cogn. Comput. **13**(1), 1–33 (2021)
12. Cunningham, J.P., Byron, M.Y.: Dimensionality reduction for large-scale neural recordings. Nat. Neurosci. **17**(11), 1500–1509 (2014)
13. Mounier, E., Abdullah, B., Mahdi, H., Eldawlatly, S.: A deep convolutional visual encoding model of neuronal responses in the LGN. Brain Inform. **8**(1), 1–16 (2021). https://doi.org/10.1186/s40708-021-00132-6
14. Paxinos, G., Watson, C.: The Rat Brain in Stereotaxic Coordinates: Compact. Academic Press (2017)
15. Kwon, K.Y., Eldawlatly, S., Oweiss, K.: NeuroQuest: a comprehensive analysis tool for extracellular neural ensemble recordings. J. Neurosci. Methods **204**(1), 189–201 (2012)
16. Jolliffe, I.T., Cadima, J.: Principal component analysis: a review and recent developments. Philos. Trans. Roy. Soc. A: Math. Phys. Eng. Sci. **374**(2065), 20150202 (2016)
17. Cristianini, N., Shawe-Taylor, J.: An Introduction to Support Vector Machines and Other Kernel-Based Learning Methods. Cambridge University Press (2000)
18. Schütze, H., Manning, C.D., Raghavan, P.: Introduction to Information Retrieval. vol. 39. Cambridge University Press, Cambridge (2008)
19. Bishop, C.M.: Pattern Recognition and Machine Learning. Springer, New York (2006)
20. Opitz, J., Burst, S.: Macro f1 and macro f1. arXiv preprint arXiv:1911.03347 (2019)
21. Seber, G.A., Lee, A.J.: Linear Regression Analysis, vol. 329. John Wiley & Sons (2012)
22. Chai, T., Draxler, R.R.: Root mean square error (RMSE) or mean absolute error (MAE)?–arguments against avoiding RMSE in the literature. Geosci. Model Dev. **7**(3), 1247–1250 (2014)
23. Kohn, A., Coen-Cagli, R., Kanitscheider, I., Pouget, A.: Correlations and neuronal population information. Annu. Rev. Neurosci. **39**, 237–256 (2016)
24. Mendoza-Halliday, D., Martinez-Trujillo, J.C.: Neuronal population coding of perceived and memorized visual features in the lateral prefrontal cortex. Nat. Commun. **8**(1), 1–13 (2017)
25. Eldawlatly, S., Oweiss, K.G.: Millisecond-timescale local network coding in the rat primary somatosensory cortex. PLoS ONE **6**(6), e21649 (2011)
26. Fernandez, E., Ferrandez, J.-M., Ammermüller, J., Normann, R.A.: Population coding in spike trains of simultaneously recorded retinal ganglion cells. Brain Res. **887**(1), 222–229 (2000)

Disfluency as an Indicator of Cognitive-Communication Disorder Through Learning Methods

Marisol Roldán-Palacios and Aurelio López-López(✉)

Instituto Nacional de Astrofísica, Óptica y Electrónica, Luis Enrique Erro No. 1,
Sta. María Tonantzintla, 72840 Puebla, Mexico
{marppalacios,allopez}@inaoep.mx
https://ccc.inaoep.mx/

Abstract. The analysis of the different varieties of language alterations from several causes has become an indicator to support tentative diagnoses, not only physical but degenerative, functional or cognitive. In this study, we explore fluency-disfluency in language of participants after suffering a traumatic brain injury. From a linguistic-computational approach, covering one-year of periodic post-recovery stages samples, candidate subsets of features were evaluated with a pool of learning methods until obtaining comparable scores to a baseline taken as the maximums achieved with the same evaluation, but on the full feature set. Starting in three-months recovery stage, this was extended to six, nine, and twelve months. After setting a global overview during this period of the fluency response based on F1-score of the learning algorithms, the identified feature was the basis to work on a model in a longitudinal sense of the disfluency-response with dichotomous global linear mixed effects model.

Keywords: Cognitive-communication disorder · Traumatic brain injury · Disfluency · Machine learning · Global linear mixed effect models

1 Introduction

"Language is one of the most important products of human cerebral action, but also because the problems raised by the organization of language seem to me to be characteristic of almost all other cerebral activity." Lashley-1951 [9].

Cognitive-communication disorder is the term coined to describe anomalies in language as a consequence of a traumatic brain injury (TBI) [1,14]. Although *Western Aphasia Battery-Revised* is the most accepted instrument to examine a part of the affectations on language [2] caused by TBI, there are some sequelae not revealed by that test [17]. Besides, fluency has been identified as a possible factor guiding the exploration of the atypical language following a TBI [14].

Supported by CONACyT and partially by SNI.

M. Mahmud et al. (Eds.): BI 2021, LNAI 12960, pp. 46–56, 2021.
https://doi.org/10.1007/978-3-030-86993-9_5

Regarding fluency alteration, this work aims to find a feature subset of the indices measuring fluency, in addition to reveal changes across periodic stages of recovery, sampled after the injury. To achieve this, a principal component analysis along with the corresponding correlation analysis were performed to find the features contributing the best information for the discrimination task, and sensitive enough to reflect subtle modifications.

An evaluation step of the selected subset employing varied learning algorithms was added to determine the final selected subset. The results reported in this work consider three algorithms: Random Forest, SPAARC and Naïve Bayes. The approach followed to achieve a longitudinal response predictor was to elaborate a model based on the features evaluated with the learning methods considering multilevel modeling [7].

The contributions of our work are the following: a) The identification of a reduced group of *four features* of language fluency showing an F1 score above the whole feature set; b) we show that a learning method model based on trees operates accordingly to the worked context, language variations, in a wrapping step to evaluate this sort of variables; and c) A fused approach to define a part of the TBI-language reactions, first with learning methods to identify indicative features. Then, feeding them to a mixed model to know how language re-adapt during the recovery stage, a period barely studied.

The organization of the paper is as follows. After summarizing related work in Sect. 2, the initial whole feature group is described in Sect. 3. Then, experiments Sect. 4 includes the data description, its pre-processing, the methodology, selected feature set, results, discussions about features and learning methods, and ending with a revision of the longitudinal model applied. The work closes with conclusions and considerations of further analyses in Sect. 5.

2 Related Work

There is no consensus about the reliability of the inspection of features like repetitions, revisions and fillers (mazes) [17] in language impairment analysis. These and few other associated with disfluency were disregarded when assessing language discerning alterations in some cognitive skill after TBI [8], or revising discourse performance based on meaningful words [17].

While considering mazes, regression models were built to approximate an understanding of cognitive impairments related to sentence planning deficits observed in TBI-language [12]. Additionally, the number of fillers and abandoned words as speech fluency barometers, along other features, were examined with methods based on learning and language models, comparing their efficacy to determine language impairment [6].

After learning models were introduced [13], fed by language measures, to discern among different neuro-degenerative conditions, this angle has continued growing [3–5,15]. Such approach can complement those studies in which, declarative and working memory, attention, executive functions and social condition as *cognitive constructs* have been substantially investigated, and that started to shed some insights in their relationship with (non simulated) functional use of language [16] in TBI cases.

3 Feature Group

The package *flucalc* [10,19] extracts a pool of more than forty attributes. Among them, we find *#TD*, i.e. typical disfluencies (by definition the sum of phrase repetitions, word revision, phrase revision, pause counts, and filled pauses), *%TD* corresponding to the total typical disfluencies over the total words or total syllables, *#SLD* described as stutter-like disfluencies, including the sum of prolongations, broken words, words, part-word repetition (PWR), phonological fragments, and monosyllabic whole word repetition (WWR) along with *%SLD* proportion *#SLD* in reference to the total intended words. The *SLD Ratio* is calculated as $SLD/(SLD + TD)$, and the measure of *weighted SLD*, which is a relatively complex relation involving additions, subtractions, products and a ratio of PWR, mono-WWR, PWR-RU, mono-WWR-RU, prolongations and blocks, where *RU* stands for *repetition units.* All these features in addition to the measures in which they are based on, and some more, are addressed to assess fluency in the altered language. The complete list and description are in [11].

4 Experiments

The information collected for the experiments carried out for the analysis is reported with more detail in the next subsections, starting by the data set.

4.1 Data Collection

Regarding the studied group, a detailed description of the project of the data corpus [17] is given in [14]. Briefly, this consists of samples elicited to a selected cohort group of participants after being affected by a TBI, registered at three, six, nine, and twelve months, after the injury. The group consists of few more than fifty participants, however, a missing stage of recovery sample was allowed due to exceptional circumstances, that leaves an average of forty participants per period, mostly male.

From several tasks, the *recount of Cinderella story* was selected for this analysis. The negative set came from a different investigation [1], where the *generative story based on a picture* task was taken. Both data sets are in TBIBank [11,18]. So both task samples corresponding to study and negative cases respectively, were transcribed from recorded speech instances. Fluency attributes set, as described above, are obtained from those transcripts worked by experts.

4.2 Pre-processing

The indices extracted from *flucalc* package [11,19] condense densities, ratios, additions or other composed functions as *weighted SLD* (described in Sect. 3). These were pre-processed with a simple transformation to leave them all in a comparable interval, where the set of features varies.

4.3 Methodology

As shown in Fig. 1, the methodology starts with a *principal components analysis* (PCA) on the first recovery phase (i.e. the three months sample), the next step was to determine how many components derived from PCA were those contributing most, according to the problem at hand. Analyzing the evolution of language after the brain injury, during post-traumatic stages, we determined to keep as much information as possible. Based on customary *elbow graph* (Fig. 3) of a total of forty, the first twelve components were chosen after which the trajectory relatively stabilizes to a constant, covering so far 0.944 of the variance computed by PCA. Then, we established which features of each of the twelve linear combinations selected were strongest related to their corresponding PC and were taken as the initial subset. Noisy or neutral features were removed by correlation analysis. By the same criteria, the subset was extended, to then ablate while they are evaluated with learning methods to set the definitive selection.

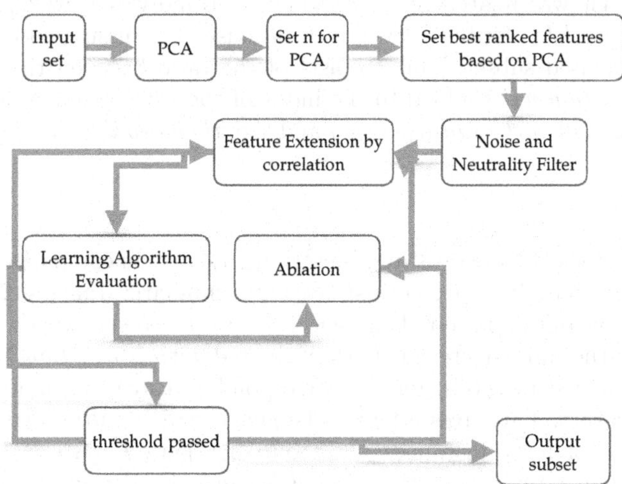

Fig. 1. Flucalc - feature selection - methodology

4.4 Selected Feature Set

Explicitly, the initial subset is $S_1 = \{mor\_Utts, mor\_Words, tot\_Prolongation, tot\_WWR, tot\_Phrase\_repetitions, prop\_Word\_revisions, prop\_Pauses, prop\_TD, Content\_words\_ratio\}$. The *prop_Broken_word* attribute, though associated to *PC6* was not included in that subset due to a poor correlation exhibited between them, along with the fact that it stays in the negative pole with respect to PC12. Promptly, *Content_words_ratio* and *tot_Prolongation* attributes were removed having a noisy or neutral influence with the rest. After shrinking and expanding successively the feature group, the definitive set is detailed in Table 1.

Table 1. Flucalc 4 features subset

FN	PC	FEATURE	DESCRIPTION
1	PC12	mor_Utts	Total utterances in the sample
24		Mean_RU	= (PWR-RU + WWR-RU)/(PWR + WWR)
27	PC4	tot_Phrase_repetitions	Total phrase repetitions
30	PC8, PC9	prop_Word_revisions	Proportion of word revisions

[a]RU, repetition units
[b]PWR, part-word repetition
[c]WWR, whole word repetition

Observe that *mor_Utts*, one of the most contributing feature, was selected after noting that was related to *PC12*. Having an individual weight of over 75 of efficacy, *Mean_RU* attribute was added because of a missing correlation with those in the revised subset. This consists of the ratio between the sum of the *part-word repetition units* added to the index of the *whole-word repetition units* and the addition of *part-word repetition* and the *whole-word repetition* (Table 1).

4.5 Results

The response of the 4-features subset describing fluency in comparison with full-set performance on the inspected instances are summarized in Fig. 2. This consists of the curve of evaluation of the selected features along side the base-curve calculated for the full feature set, both evaluated with *Näive Bayes, SPAARC*, and *Random Forest* methods, for the corresponding three, six, nine and twelve months of recovery. This gives a look of language changes after TBI.

An average of forty instances per group per period were evaluated with a *Leave-One-Out Cross Validation* (LOOCV) scheme. Periods of recovery are expressed in the X-axis and macro *F1-score* are plotted in Y-axis.

4.6 Feature Selection Discussion

We start by observing the principal components (PCs) related to three of the determined feature subset, showed in second column of Table 1. There, we can notice that they are distributed along the whole group of PCs considered, i.e. they do not lead the PC list. For instance, the total whole word repetitions *tot_WWR* associated with PC1 was removed due to having a negative role in the subset, when evaluated with the learning algorithms. Counter-intuitively, we did not find that some subset of measures defining typical disfluencies could lead the discriminating task. The first correlation showed certain negative effect of those features on some PCs then, learning algorithms evaluations evidence that densities and relations or functions associated with the concept of *typical disfluencies*

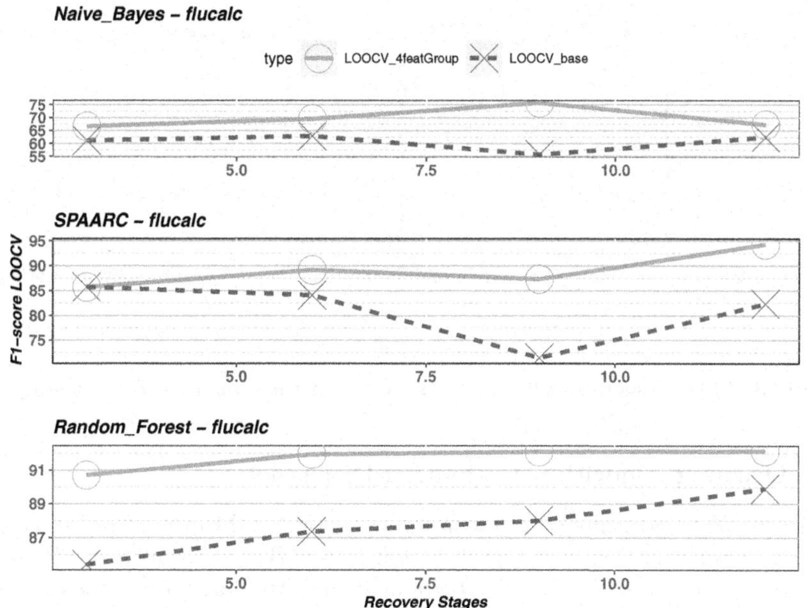

Fig. 2. (a) Naïve Bayes - (b) SPAARC - (c) Random Forest - fluency response - first year after traumatic brain injury

(TD) [11], in addition to those based on the concept of *stutter-like disfluencies* (SLD) do not work well together. In other words, they add noise if evaluated as a set along with other features, though individually some of them are relatively contributors for the task at hand. Further steps in the process led us to *Mean_RU* that was not revealed by any linear combination from the PCA analysis. Figure 2 shows that: $\forall p_i, F1_{score}$(4-features subset) $> F1_{score}$(full features), where $p_i \in \{recovery\_periods\}$, i.e. for each stage of recovery evaluated. This indicates that the $F1$-score curve corresponding to the 4-feature subset remains above the $F1$-score of the full-feature group, for each of the methods illustrated, suggesting that the 4-features subset encompasses the whole information of the full feature *flucalc* set. For instance, *Random Forest* is moving in the $[90.70, 92.13]$ interval regulating the discrimination task of negative versus study cases, and remains still sensitive to reflect the subtle changes in the *cognitive-communication disorder* analyzed with grounds on the fluency of the TBI-language samples inspected. Observing that none of the *TD* or the *stuttered-like disfluencies* [11], neither any composed function related to them, are part of this *4-features subset* (Table 1), together with the fact that none of them is correlated to PC1 or PC2 from PCA, provide evidence of the complexity in the characterization [14] of the *reorganized* language following a TBI.

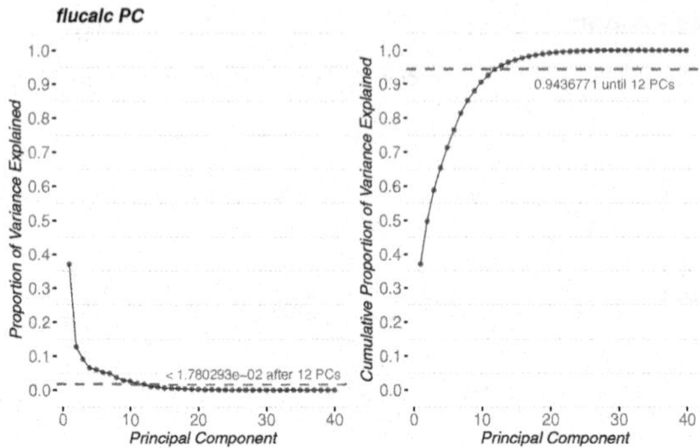

Fig. 3. 4-features subset - flucalc - correlation at three-months recovery stage.

4.7 Learning Algorithm Evaluation Discussion

Seven learning algorithms were taken into account for the evaluation step of the features: Sequential Minimal Optimization, Naïve Bayes, Bayes Net, SPAARC, Random Forest, Classification via Regression, and Adaboost. From these, results for the first, third and fourth are reported here. To judge how much information the *flucalc* feature set contains, the set was evaluated as a whole, and taken as baseline. A tenth (Table 1) of the original feature set [11] allows to achieve comparable efficacy measures in contrast with those obtained from the entire *flucalc* feature set. Though the comparison is illustrated with $F1$-score, calculated as $F1\text{-score} = \frac{2*TP}{2*TP+FP+FN}$, where TP, FP, FN respectively mean True-Positives, False-Positives and False-Negatives in the *confusion matrix*, to appropriately reflect the proportion of the elements in this latter. The *F1-score* values range in the $[0, 1]$ interval, but here they are expressed as percentages.

Contrasting response curves, *Random Forest* is indicating a more consistent behavior for both samples, negative versus study cases for the complete group of time points. The *base-set* curves move in a relatively similar scale for both tree based learning algorithms, but *SPAARC* reveals the existence of noisy features with a fall of around 15% in $F1$-score for the nine months stage of recovery. This is also evident in the trajectory that the response follows for the baseline set evaluated with *Naïve Bayes*, which in fact relatively mirrors the reaction illustrated for the flucalc base set evaluated with *SPAARC*, though the former moves to lower values than the latter. A common behaviour exhibited by the three learning methods is that *4-features subset* curve remains above the baseline trajectory for the four time points samples of the first year following TBI.

From what was described above, we can state that the discriminating task can be done with the chosen *4-features subset*. Moreover, though *Naïve Bayes* algorithm generally replicates the behavior between *4-features subset* and *baseline* curves, i.e. there is a gap between them, the former rests on the latter for the whole period considered, *baseline* moves in an interval around 60%, not giving much certainty about the registered efficacy. *SPAARC* and *Random Forest* keep consistency for both trajectories not only in the described aspects but both get acceptable measures, however, their response for each recovery stage oscillates dis-similarly, which does not allow to suggest anything regarding an amelioration or decline in the *cognitive-communication disorder* caused by a TBI.

4.8 Pattern Complexity

As a contribution to outline the intrinsic complexity of language in a *cognitive-communication disorder*, we include Fig. 4. Where every curve represents individual response by stage of recovery at 3, 6, 9, and 12 months. Each row represents one of the four features selected {*mor_Utts, Mean_RU, tot_Phrase_repetitions, prop_Word_revisions*}. The left side depicts TBI-language instances and right side draws negative responses. Same participants were evaluated in each side, though some graphs appears to have less, this is caused by the pattern of response. Presenting a more varied density, *mor_Utts* and *prop_Word_revisions* features allow to distinguish more than one response pattern. In the former, at least two clusters, one group of responses relatively stable remaining under 0.2 index and the other turning up and down from one time point to the next. The latter registers at least three patterns, one relatively steady resting below 0.25, one alternating valleys and peaks, and one more growing in the first three recovery stages and then drops. In *tot_Phrase_repetitions* attribute graph, in a minor or major grade. An *S* response group is differentiated from the cluster resting on zero. *Mean_RU* seems to exhibit two more conducts in addition to that leaving on zero, one for above 0.3 estimation and the other oscillating between zero and values equal or greater than this estimate. One last finding is that study group and negative cases seems to be comparable in density by feature.

4.9 Longitudinal Model

The next step was to work in determining the simplified expression to predict language disfluency-fluency over time. For that purpose, a longitudinal random intercept model with dichotomous response was tried, the elementary with only two nested structures, the repeated appraisals and the time. The features fed to the suggested model were the evaluated with the learning methods previously described, the four selected features *4-features set* = {*mor_Utts, Mean_RU, tot_Phrase_repetitions, prop_Word_revisions*}, in addition to the time points for the fixed effect part with random intercept in terms of a generalized linear mixed effects model. As proof of significance was applied, a *likelihood ratio test* which can be explained as the comparison of the likelihood of two models. Both inputs raise from the same structure but one *with* and the other *without* the factors of interest, the latter named *the null model.* The difference between these two models determines if a *fixed effect/variable* becomes significant, if the former is significant the latter will be. From one side, from the manageable tests, any confirmation of significance of the inspected characteristics was obtained, from another, examination brought to a singularity problem. The absence of some samples per period per participant in the current sample was one of the obstacles, given that the present study works in language impairment observing for

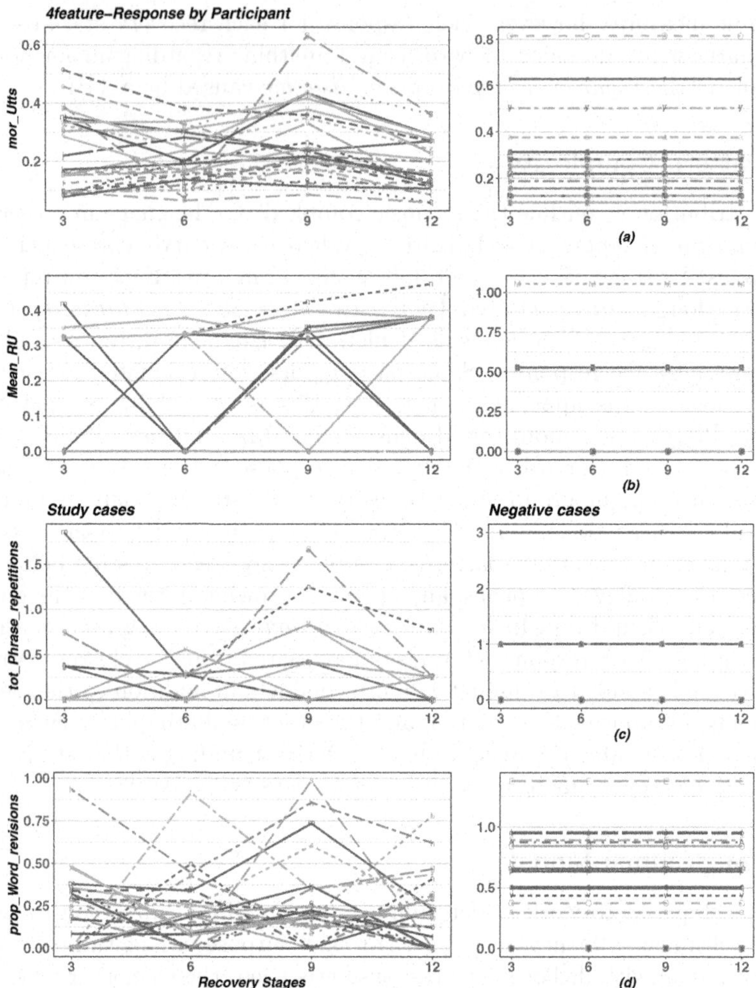

Fig. 4. (a) mor_Utts - (b) Mean_RU - (c) tot_Phrase_repetitions - (d) prop_Word_revisions - individual fluency response by feature - first year after TBI

any subtle adjustment in it, this could not be suitable to try any technique of data augmentation due to the inherently bias added and removing those incomplete records left different conditions for the learning algorithms in reference to multilevel modeling, situating us right beyond any determination of the complementarity of both techniques.

5 Conclusions and Further Work

The assessment in terms of $F1$-score supports the selection of the 4-features subset with indices moving in the interval [90.70, 92.13] for Random Forest and above 85 for SPAARC learning methods. Furthermore, the subset showed to include the information provided by the whole fluency feature.

However, setting a direct determination of a longitudinal model implementing a multilevel approach to predict the response across time was not completed, in part due to the combined techniques handle different conditions on the fed data. Results obtained removing noisy and neutral characteristics suggests that this is a proper approach to recognized contributors features, the extended analysis to predict TBI-language response over time have to be solved with a trade-off between a more scarcely data and the reliability of the results based on them.

A limitation of the followed approach is that, though results were summarized in F1–score, an additional detailed assessment of the learning methods can be carried out. Additionally, the sensitive factors of learning methods and mixed models have to be considered in advance to allow a less intricate *flow* of data from the learning algorithms to mixed effects model, to reach a good approximation of the response of the studied TBI-affected language.

References

1. Coelho, C.A., Grela, B., Corso, M., Gamble, A., Feinn, R.: Microlinguistic deficits in the narrative discourse of adults with traumatic brain injury. Brain Inj. **19**(13), 1139–1145 (2005)
2. Elbourn, E., et al.: Discourse recovery after severe traumatic brain injury: exploring the first year. Brain Inj. **33**(2), 143–159 (2019)
3. Fraser, K.C., et al.: Automated classification of primary progressive aphasia subtypes from narrative speech transcripts. Cortex **55**, 43–60 (2014)
4. Fraser, K.C., Hirst, G., Graham, N.L., Meltzer, J.A., Black, S.E., Rochon, E.: Comparison of different feature sets for identification of variants in progressive aphasia. In: Workshop on Computational Linguistics and Clinical Psychology: From Linguistic Signal to Clinical Reality, Baltimore, MD, USA, 27 June 2014, pp. 17–26 (2014)
5. Fraser, K.C., Hirst, G., Meltzer, J.A., Mack, J.E., Thompson, C.K.: Using statistical parsing to detect agrammatic aphasia. In: Proceedings on Biomedical Natural Language Processing (BioNLP), Baltimore, MD, USA, pp. 134–142 (2014)
6. Gabani, K., Sherman, M., Solorio, T., Liu, Y., Bedore, L.M., Peña, E.D.: A corpus-based approach for the prediction of language impairment in monolingual English and Spanish-English bilingual children. In: The 2009 Annual Conference of the North American Chapter of the ACL (NAACL), Boulder, CO, pp. 46–55 (2009)
7. Hair, J.F., Jr., Fávero, L.P.: Multilevel modeling for longitudinal data: concepts and applications. RAUSP Manag. J. **54**(4), 459–489 (2019)
8. Jorgensen, M., Togher, L.: Narrative after traumatic brain injury: a comparison of monologic and jointly-produced discourse. Brain Inj. **23**(9), 727–740 (2009)
9. Lashley, K.S.: The problem of serial order in behavior. In: Jeffress, L.A. (ed.) Cerebral Mechanism in Behavior, pp. 112–136. Wiley, New York (1951)
10. MacWhinney, B.: The Childes Project: Tools for Analyzing Talk, 3rd edn. Lawrence Erlbaum Associates, Mahwah (2000)
11. MacWhinney, B.: Tools for analyzing talk - electronic edition part 2: the CLAN programs. Carnegie Mellon University (2020)

12. Peach, R.K.: The cognitive basis for sentence planning difficulties in discourse after traumatic brain injury. Am. J. Speech Lang. Pathol. **22**, S285–S297 (2013)
13. Peintner, B., Jarrold, W., Vergyri, D., Richey, C., Gorno-Tempini, M.L., Ogar, J.: Learning diagnostic models using speech and language measures. In: 30th Annual International IEEE EMBS Conference, Vancouver, BC, Canada, pp. 20–24 (2008)
14. Power, E., et al.: Patterns of narrative discourse in early recovery following severe Traumatic Brain Injury. Brain Inj. **34**(1), 98–109 (2020)
15. Rentoumi, V., et al.: Automatic detection of linguistic indicators as a means of early detection of Alzheimer's disease and of related dementias: a computational linguistics analysis. In: 8th IEEE International Conference on Cognitive Infocommunications (CogInfoCom), pp. 11–14 (2017)
16. Rowley, D.A., Rogish, M., Alexander, T., Riggs, K.J.: Cognitive correlates of pragmatic language comprehension in adult traumatic brain injury: a systematic review and meta-analyses. Brain Inj. **31**(12), 1564–1574 (2017)
17. Stubbs, E., et al.: Procedural discourse performance in adults with severe traumatic brain injury at 3 and 6 months post injury. Brain Inj. **32**(2), 167–181 (2018)
18. TBI bank. https://tbi.talkbank.org/. Accessed 3 Mar 2021
19. Childes Project. https://talkbank.org/. Accessed 3 Mar 2021

Bidirected Information Flow in the High-Level Visual Cortex

Qiang Li(✉)

Image Processing Laboratory, Parc Cientific, University of Valencia, 46980 Valencia, Spain
qiang.li@uv.es

Abstract. Understanding the brain function requires investigating information transfer across brain regions. Shannon began the remarkable new field of information theory in 1948. It basically can be divided into two categories: directed and undirected information-theoretical approaches. As we all know, neural signals are typically nonlinear and directed flow between brain regions. We can use directed information to quantify feed-forward information flow, feedback information, and instantaneous influence in the high-level visual cortex. Moreover, neural signals have bidirectional information flow properties and are not captured by the transfer entropy approach. Therefore, we used directed information to quantify bidirectional information flow in this study. We found that there has information flow between the scene-selective areas, e.g., OPA, PPA, RSC, and object-selective areas, e.g., LOC. Specifically, strong information flow exists between RSC and LOC. It explained that functionally coupled between RSC and LOC plays a vital role in visual scenes/object categories or recognition in our daily lives. Meanwhile, we also found weak reverse-directed information flow in the visual scenes and objects neural networks.

Keywords: Bidirected information flow · Information theory · Nonlinear · Neural signal · Directed information

1 Introduction

Understanding how information flow in the brain conducts a specific cognitive task is a major scientific challenge. In the field of neuroscience, studying brain function entails learning about how the brain processes information. Researchers can figure out how information flows through different parts of the brain to gain such knowledge [8,9,12]. In most cases, information flow in the brain is random and directional. Granger causality [1,14], or Transfer Entropy [4,19], can be used to calculate directional information flow. However, the methods described above can only calculate one-way information flow from one area to another rather than bidirectional information and instantaneous information flow between functional brain regions. Directed information was designed to characterize channels with

M. Mahmud et al. (Eds.): BI 2021, LNAI 12960, pp. 57–66, 2021.
https://doi.org/10.1007/978-3-030-86993-9_6

feedback but the way that we applied it to neuroscience to solve the aforementioned problems [10]. It's mainly a tool for inference, some causality inference, and more along the lines of Granger causality in spirit [14]. Granger causality says that X causes Y because time series X causes a time series Y if you can predict Y if you also condition on the observations of X. Directed information encapsulates this by prediction reduction attribute so a decrease in randomness. Comparison of other information-theoretic methods applied in neuroscience, DI not only quantify measure feed-forward information but also feedback information. The brain is a complex system, and each region is densely connected to infer specific cognitive tasks. Therefore, directed information can help us understand how neural information flows among brain regions. This study uses a directed information method to measure information communication among visual scene category neural networks with fMRI dataset.

According to fMRI studies, some scene-selective regions in the human visual cortex have been discovered and linked to higher-order functions like scene perception or category, such as Primary Visual Cortex (V1), Fusiform Face Area (FFA) [7], Occipital Face Area (OFA), Occipital Place Area (OPA), Parahippocampal Place Area (PPA) [3], and retrosplenial cortex (RSC) [13]. Although all these regions respond well to scenes and objects, less research has been done on how these regions communicate with one another during the experience of natural scenes, specific bidirected information flow among these regions. That's also our primary motivation in this study.

2 Methods

2.1 Definition

Shannon Entropy. Assuming a random variable X, which can get a value like x as probability $\mathrm{P(X = x)}$, entropy of this variable can be expressed as:

$$\mathrm{H(X)} = -\sum_{\mathrm{x}} \mathrm{p(x)} \log_2 \mathrm{p(x)} = \langle -\log_2 \mathrm{p(x)} \rangle \tag{1}$$

Conditional Entropy. The conditional entropy of X given Y is the average uncertainty that remains about x when y is known:

$$H_{X|Y} = -\sum_{x,y} p(x,y) \log_2 p(x|y) = H_{X,Y} - H_Y p(x|y) = \frac{p(x,y)}{p(y)} \tag{2}$$

Mutual Information. Given two random variables X and Y, the mutual information can be calculate as the difference of sum of individual entropy and the entropy of the variables considered jointly as a single system. It can be mathematically formula expressed as:

$$\mathrm{H(X;Y) = H(X) + H(Y) - H(X,Y)} \tag{3}$$

Conditional Mutual Information. The conditional mutual information of X and Y given Z is the uncertainty that remains about x and y when z is known:

$$\begin{aligned} \mathrm{I(X;Y \mid Z)} &= \mathrm{H(X \mid Z) + H(Y \mid Z) - H(X,Y \mid Z)} \\ &= \left\langle \log_2 \frac{\mathrm{p(x \mid y,z)}}{\mathrm{p(x \mid z)}} \right\rangle \end{aligned} \tag{4}$$

Granger Causality. The Granger causality (GC) idea firstly proposed by Granger in 1969 [5]. The basic idea is, if two signal $\mathbf{X}$ and $\mathbf{Y}$ have caucal relationship, instead of history value of $\mathbf{Y}$, then $\mathbf{Y}$ also can be predicted given $\mathbf{X}$ information. Assuming $\mathbf{X}^n = [X_1, X_2, \ldots, X_n]$ and $\mathbf{Y}^n = [Y_1, Y_2, \ldots, Y_n]$ are two continue time series. The GC analysis can be expressed as a auto-regressive or line prediction model as follows:

$$Y_i = \sum_{j=1}^{P} a_j Y_{i-j} + e_i \tag{5}$$

$$Y_i = \sum_{j=1}^{P} [b_j Y_{i-j} + c_j X_{i-j}] + \tilde{e}_i \tag{6}$$

where e_i indicate error of prediction Y_i given only past valye of Y, $(Y_{i-1}, ..., Y_{i-P})$, and $\tilde{e}_i$ is the error of prediction Y_i given both history value of Y $(Y_{i-1}, ..., Y_{i-P})$ and previous value of X $(X_{i-1}, ..., X_{i-P})$. Based on GC properties above described, GC analysis gradually applied in the neuroscience disincline.

Transfer Entropy. Another widely applied causal measurement in neuroscience is Transfer Entropy (TE) [17]. How the prior knowledge affects the next state or predicts future state can use TE to address this question. TE can be defined as:

$$\begin{aligned} TE_{X\to Y} &= I\left(Y_{t+1} : X_{t-k:t} | Y_{t-l:t}\right) = H\left(Y_{t+1} | Y_{t-l:t}\right) - H\left(Y_{t+1} | Y_{t-l:t}, X_{t-k:t}\right) \\ &= \sum_{y_{t+1}} \sum_{x_{t-k:t}} \sum_{y_{t-l:t}} p\left(x_{t+1}, x_{t-k:t}, y_{t-l:t}\right) \log \frac{p\left(x_{t+1} | x_{t-k:t}, y_{t-l:t}\right)}{p\left(x_{t+1} | p\left(x_{t-k:t}\right)\right.} \end{aligned} \tag{7}$$

The TE can be used measured the directed information flow from $Y \to X$ or $X \to Y$. The basic theory of TE can be shown graphically in Fig. 1. In neuroscience studies, it is very used for defined the directed causality effects between neural signals. However, the real neural activity not just single directed information flow. Neurons can use resonance at the same time, that means $X \leftrightarrow Y$. The pitfall of TE is that it cannot measure the bi-directed information flow at the same time. A comprehensive review on TE estimate directed information flow could be found in [16].

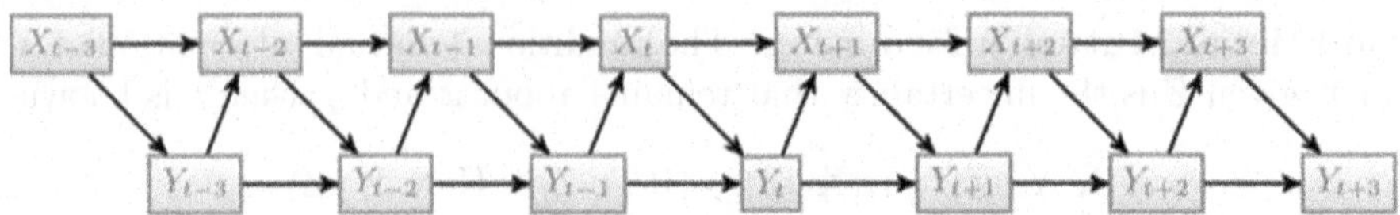

Fig. 1. The diagram of transfer entropy flow from $X \rightarrow Y$ (X causes Y) and vice versa. X_t and Y_t, with $t = 1, \cdots, n$ indicate two time series, respectively. The time series Y_t is caused not only by the previous history of X, X_t, X_{t-1}, X_{t-2}, and X_{t-3}, but also by the caused by self-previous history, Y_{t-1}, Y_{t-2}, and Y_{t-3}.

2.2 Directed Information

In this section, we are going to describe directed information from mathematics view. Assuming uppercase letters X and Y denoted random variables, and denote n-tuple $(X_1, X_2, \ldots, X_n)$ as X^n. The information flow from X^n to Y^n can be formula as,

$$I\left(X^n \rightarrow Y^n\right) \triangleq \sum_{i=1}^{n} I\left(X^i; Y_i \mid Y^{i-1}\right) = H\left(Y^n\right) - H\left(Y^n \| X^n\right) \tag{8}$$

Where $H\left(Y^n\right) - H\left(Y^n \| X^n\right)$ is *causally conditional entropy* [15], and it can be defined as,

$$H\left(Y^n \| X^n\right) \triangleq \sum_{i=1}^{n} H\left(Y_i \mid Y^{i-1}, X^i\right)$$

Comparison of mutual information,

$$I\left(X^n; Y^n\right) = H\left(Y^n\right) - H\left(Y^n \mid X^n\right)$$

The condition entropy instead of *causally conditional entropy* in the directed information. Meanwhile, directed information is not symmetric, e.g., $I\left(Y^n \rightarrow X^n\right) \neq I\left(X^n \rightarrow Y^n\right)$ in general. On the contrary, reverse information flow can be defined as,

$$I\left(Y^{n-1} \rightarrow X^n\right) = \sum_{i=1}^{n} I\left(Y^{i-1}; X_i \mid X^{i-1}\right) \tag{9}$$

It has a number of significant properties, some can be found in [1,15]. For the sake of brevity, we'll just reveal two enlightening conservation rules. Based on Massey and Massey [11] the conservation law,

$$I\left(X^n; Y^n\right) = I\left(X^n \rightarrow Y^n\right) + I\left(Y^{n-1} \rightarrow X^n\right) \tag{10}$$

Equation 10 is particularly enlightening in settings where X_i and Y_i appear alternately, as shown in Fig. 2.

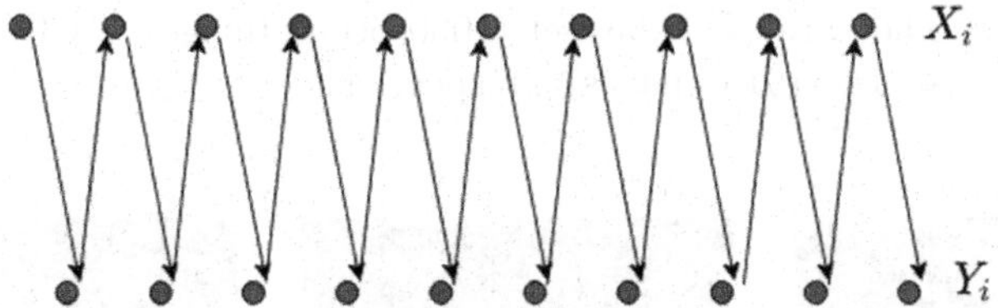

Fig. 2. The interaction between X^n and Y^n sequence.

In some cases, X^n, Y^n may happen simultaneously, such as neural network in the brain. The following is another conservation law stated in [1] which, in such situations, may be more insightful than that in Eq. 10. The *instantaneous influence* can be calculated through directed information and reverse directed information as shown in Fig. 3(c),

$$\sum_{i=1}^{n} I\left(X_i; Y_i \mid X^{i-1}, Y^{i-1}\right) = I\left(X^n \to Y^n\right) - I\left(X^{n-1} \to Y^n\right) \tag{11}$$

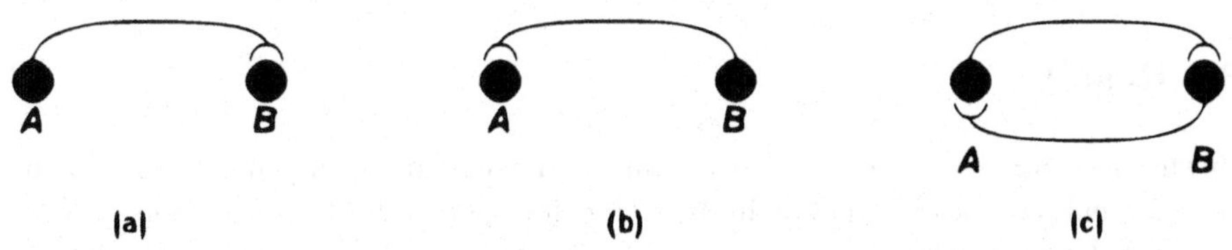

Fig. 3. The three possible way of neural information flow. (a) shown information flow from A to B, (b) shown information flow from B to A, (c) shown bidirectional information flow between A and B, respectively.

If $\sum_{i=1}^{n} I\left(X_i; Y_i \mid X^{i-1}, Y^{i-1}\right) = 0$. That is, they do not have an instantaneous effect on one another. In this study, the Context-Tree Weighting (CTW) algorithm proposed by Willims [18] was used to estimate DI [6] flow among visual scene neural networks and its powerful algorithms to compress data.

2.3 FMRI Dataset

The public BOLD5000 dataset[1] [2] used in this study when we estimated bidirected information flow among visual scene neural networks (see Fig. 4). The fMRI experiments used a dataset obtained from 4 subjects (aged 24 to 27 years) with normal or corrected-to-normal vision, who each viewed 5254 images over 15 scanning sessions. The stimuli images were selected from three classical computer

[1] https://bold5000.github.io/.

vision datasets. They are SUN dataset (1000 Scene Images)[2], COCO dataset[3], and ImageNet dataset (1916 images)[4], respectively.

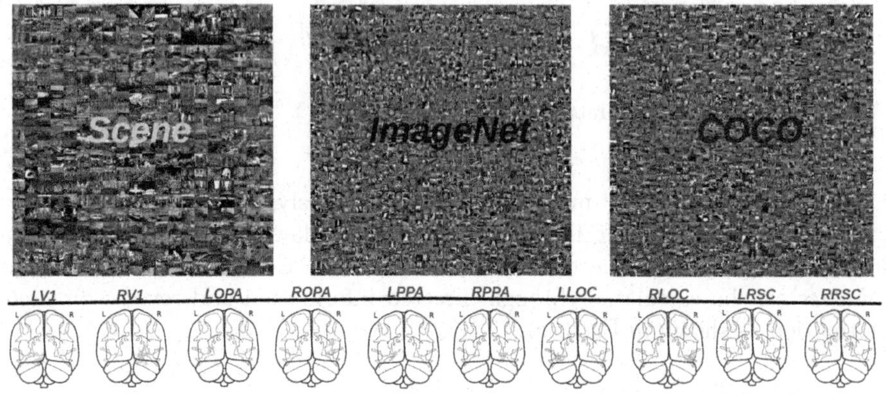

Fig. 4. Nature scenes and objects selective ROIs.

3 Result

In this section, we experimentally compared correlation, mutual information, transfer entropy, and directed information for quantifying information flow in the visual scenes neural networks. In Fig. 5, we have shown functional connectivity among visual scenes neural networks with correlation, mutual information, and transfer entropy approaches. We found that mutual information can capture more information than correlation, but both methods do not quantify information flow direction. In Fig. 6, the graphs depict the functional connectivity between visual scenes neural networks, and the strength of edges color represents connectivity weights in which consistence of functional connectivity matrix in Fig. 5. We found that information flow between the scene-selective areas, e.g., OPA, PPA, RSC, and object-selective areas, e.g., LOC, plays an important role in visual scene/object categories or recognitions. Nevertheless, we are interested in whether information feedback and resonance information flow in the high-level visual cortex. Therefore, in Fig. 7 and Fig. 8, we found consistent results with correlation and mutual information methods. However, we also found some unknown results that are resonance information exists in the high-level visual cortex.

[2] http://sun.cs.princeton.edu/.
[3] https://cocodataset.org/.
[4] http://www.image-net.org/.

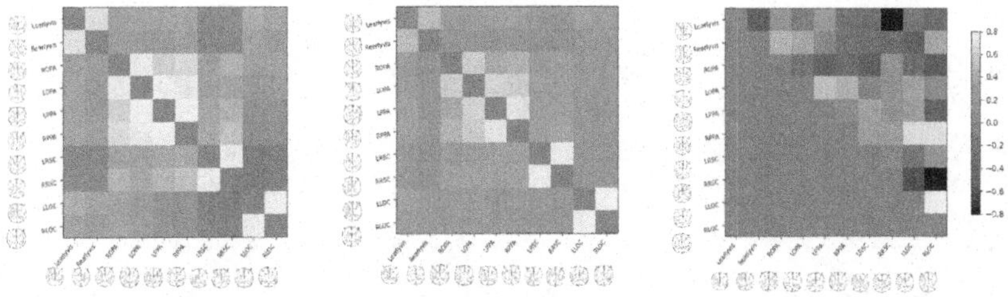

Fig. 5. The functional connectivity matrix between scene/object-selective ROIs was estimated with correlation, mutual information, and transfer entropy methods.

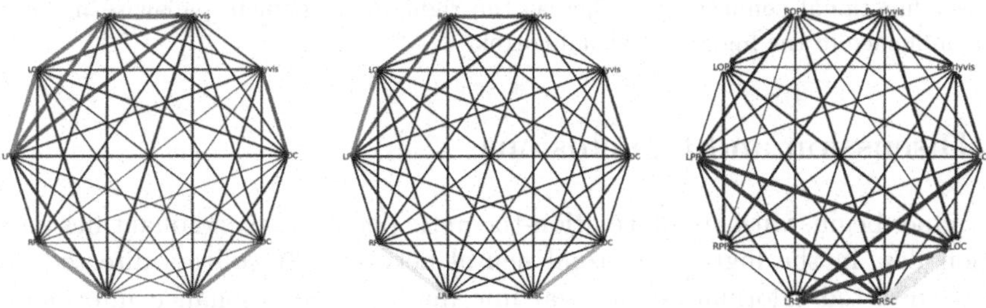

Fig. 6. The graphs depict functional connectivity in the high-level visual cortex with correlation with threshold 0.05, mutual information with threshold 0.1, and transfer entropy (arrow indicates the direction of information flow). Edge thickness is proportional to correlation coefficients, mutual information, and directed transfer entropy.

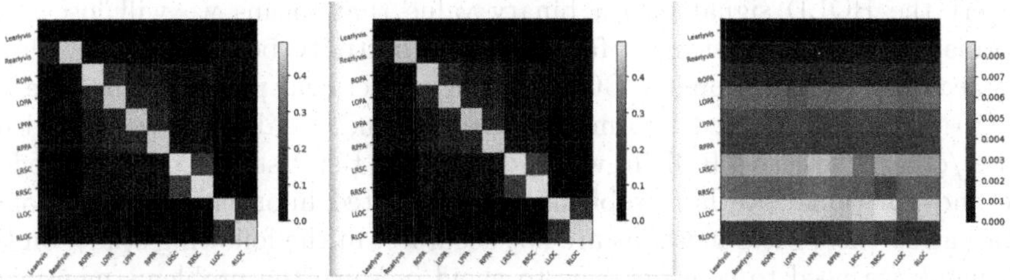

Fig. 7. The left matrix shows pair-wise directed functional connectivity. The middle image shows pair-wise instantaneous influence, and the right image indicates pair-wised reverse-directed functional connectivity in the high-level visual cortex. Therefore, there has a weak reverse-directed information flow in the visual scenes and objects neural networks.

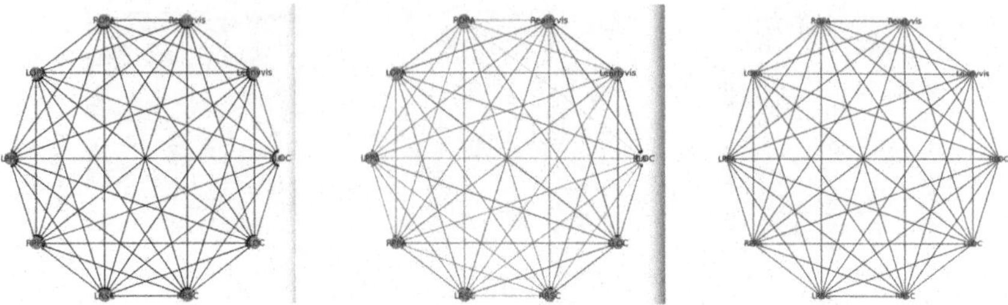

Fig. 8. The graph depicted functional connectivity of the representation from several scenes ROIs corresponding to Fig. 7, respectively. The graph on the left depicts pair-wise directed functional connectivity. The middle graph depicts pair-wise reverse directed functional connectivity, whereas the right figure depicts pair-wise instantaneous influence in the high-level visual cortex.

4 Discussion and Conclusions

This paper begins with an information-theoretic perspective and quantifies information flow in the high-level visual neural networks. It collects directed and reverse directed information, mutual information, and resonance information between the brain's left and right regions of interest. It opens up a new avenue for us to investigate what happens when pairwise neural signal entanglement occurs. It means a lot in understanding neural signal flow in the brain. However, there are some limitations in which we should point out in the following contents.

First, we got directed information through CTW estimator, and it needs to satisfy that input data should be binary value. In other words, we need to convert the BOLD signal into a binary value that means we will lose some information when we estimate functional connectivity between ROIs. Therefore accuracy estimate binary BOLD signal is a crucial problem when we are going to quantify directed information flow. Second, we directly used in visual scenes/objects selective-ROIs in which defined via t-statistics. Considered effect size and functional overlap problems, the estimated information flow through information-theoretical methods are not accurate. In the following study, on the one hand, we need to consider how to avoid or solve the problems mentioned above. On the other hand, we can reconstruct nature images from the BOLD signal to confirm the information flow in the high-level visual cortex.

Nevertheless, we still found some interesting results through estimated directed information. First, we found that there has information flow within the scene-selective areas, e.g., OPA, PPA, and RSC. Second, we also found that information flow between the scene-selective areas, e.g., RSC, and the object-selective areas, e.g., LOC. Third, we found that there has weak reverse-directed information flow in the high-level visual cortex.

5 Code Availability

The code used to reproduce result can be available under the request author.

References

1. Amblard, P., Michel, O.: Relating granger causality to directed information theory for networks of stochastic processes. IEEE Trans. Inform. Theory **53** (2009)
2. Chang, N., Pyles, J., Marcus, A., Mulam, H., Tarr, M., Aminoff, E.: BOLD5000, a public fMRI dataset while viewing 5000 visual images. Sci. Data **6** (2019). https://doi.org/10.1038/s41597-019-0052-3
3. Epstein, R., Kanwisher, N.: The parahippocampal place area: a cortical representation of the local visual environment. J. Cogn. Neurosci. **7** (1998). https://doi.org/10.1016/S1053-8119(18)31174-1
4. Gencaga, D.: Transfer entropy. Entropy **20**, 288 (2018). https://doi.org/10.3390/e20040288
5. Granger, C.: Investigating causal relations by econometric models and cross-spectral methods. Econometrica **37**, 424–38 (1969). https://doi.org/10.2307/1912791
6. Jiao, J., Permuter, H.H., Zhao, L., Kim, Y., Weissman, T.: Universal estimation of directed information. CoRR abs/1201.2334 (2012). http://arxiv.org/abs/1201.2334
7. Kanwisher, N., Mcdermott, J., Chun, M.: The fusiform face area: a module in human extrastriate cortex specialized for face perception. J. Neurosci. Official J. Soc. Neurosci. **17**, 4302–11 (1997). https://doi.org/10.3410/f.717989828.793472998
8. Mahmud, M., Kaiser, M.S., Hussain, A., Vassanelli, S.: Applications of deep learning and reinforcement learning to biological data. IEEE Trans. Neural Netw. Learn. Syst. PP (2017). https://doi.org/10.1109/TNNLS.2018.2790388
9. Mahmud, M., Kaiser, M.S., Mcginnity, T., Hussain, A.: Deep learning in mining biological data. Cogn. Comput. **13** (2021). https://doi.org/10.1007/s12559-020-09773-x
10. Massey, J.: Causality, feedback and directed information (1990)
11. Massey, J., Massey, P.: Conservation of mutual and directed information, pp. 157–158 (2005). https://doi.org/10.1109/ISIT.2005.1523313
12. Noor, M., Zenia, N.Z., Kaiser, M.S., Al Mamun, S., Mahmud, M.: Application of deep learning in detecting neurological disorders from magnetic resonance images: a survey on the detection of Alzheimer's disease, Parkinson's disease and schizophrenia. Brain Inform. **7**, 11 (2020). https://doi.org/10.1186/s40708-020-00112-2
13. Park, S., Chun, M.: Different roles of the parahippocampal place area (PPA) and retrosplenial cortex (RSC) in panoramic scene perception. NeuroImage **47**, 1747–56 (2009). https://doi.org/10.1016/j.neuroimage.2009.04.058
14. Tank, A., Covert, I., Foti, N., Shojaie, A., Fox, E.: Neural granger causality. IEEE Trans. Pattern Anal. Mach. Intell. PP, 1–1 (2021). https://doi.org/10.1109/TPAMI.2021.3065601
15. Tatikonda, S., Mitter, S.: The capacity of channels with feedback. IEEE Trans. Inf. Theory **55**, 323–349 (2009). https://doi.org/10.1109/TIT.2008.2008147
16. Vicente, R., Wibral, M., Lindner, M., Pipa, G.: Transfer entropy—a model-free measure of effective connectivity for the neurosciences. J. Comput. Neurosci. **30**, 45–67 (2011). https://doi.org/10.1007/s10827-010-0262-3

17. Wibral, M., Vicente, R., Lindner, M.: Transfer entropy in neuroscience. Underst. Complex Syst. 3–36 (2014). https://doi.org/10.1007/978-3-642-54474-3-1
18. Willems, F.M.J., Shtarkov, Y.M., Tjalkens, T.J.: The context-tree weighting method: basic properties. IEEE Trans. Inf. Theory **41**(3), 653–664 (1995). https://doi.org/10.1109/18.382012
19. Wollstadt, P., Martínez Zarzuela, M., Vicente, R., Díaz-Pernas, F., Wibral, M.: Efficient transfer entropy analysis of non-stationary neural time series. PLoS ONE **9** (2014). https://doi.org/10.1371/journal.pone.0102833

A Computational Network Model for Shared Mental Models in Hospital Operation Rooms

Laila van Ments[1], Jan Treur[2(✉)], Jan Klein[3], and Peter Roelofsma[3]

[1] AutoLeadStar, Jerusalem, Israel
laila@autoleadstar.com
[2] Social AI Group, Vrije Universiteit Amsterdam, Amsterdam, The Netherlands
j.treur@vu.nl
[3] Delft University of Technology Section Safety and Security Science, Delft, The Netherlands
{j.klein,p.h.m.p.roelofsma}@tudelft.nl

Abstract. This paper describes a network model for mental processes making use of shared mental models (SMM) of team performance. The paper illustrates the value of adequate SMM's for safe and efficient team performance. The addressed application context is that of a medical team performing a tracheal intubation executed by a nurse and a medical specialist. Simulations of successful and unsuccessful team performance have been performed, some of which are presented. The paper discusses potential further elaborations for future research as well as implications for other domains of team performance.

Keywords: Shared mental model · Network model · Hospital · Team performance · Healthcare safety

1 Introduction

A crucial aspect of the efficiency, effectiveness and safety of team performance concerns the adequacy of the shared mental model of the team members. The notion of shared mental model (SMM) - also called 'team mental model' – concerns a specific common knowledge structure held by members of a team or a group. More specifically, it refers to the alignment of the internal representations of the members concerning explanations on how reality works, or should work [6, 11, 12]. The aim of this paper is to present how a network-oriented modeling approach [18] can be used to model mental processes of team members using shared mental models. Besides representing the shared mental models themselves in a network-oriented manner, this also involves processing within the network model for the use of the mental model for internal (mental) simulations and using the outcomes of such internal simulations for decisions to undertake actions in the world via action ownership states mediating between the mental model and action execution. Thus, the paper contributes a first network model for the dynamics of the use of internal simulations of mental models and action ownership states to decide about actions to be undertaken.

M. Mahmud et al. (Eds.): BI 2021, LNAI 12960, pp. 67–78, 2021.
https://doi.org/10.1007/978-3-030-86993-9_7

First, in Sect. 2 some background for this is described. Section 2 also introduces the domain of the example scenario (use case) that is addressed, a team performance of a nurse and a medical specialist performing a tracheal intubation. In Sect. 3 the design of the network model using a shared mental model is presented. Section 4 presents some of the simulation examples. In this section a presentation of a successful team performance is given, and it is pointed out how a failure can be simulated. Section 5 summarizes the main conclusions and provides a discussion for further extensions of the obtained network model for shared mental models to support team performance.

2 Background

The network model introduced here is based on knowledge from a number of domains: mental models from psychology, team mental models from social sciences, hospital protocols from medical- and safety sciences and the domain of network-oriented modeling.

Mental Models. For the history of the mental models area, often Kenneth Craik is mentioned as a central person. Craik [3] describes a mental model as a *small-scale model* that is carried by an organism within its head as follows; see also [28]:

> 'If the organism carries a "small-scale model" of external reality and of its own possible actions within its head, it is able to try out various alternatives, conclude which is the best of them, react to future situations before they arise, utilize the knowledge of past events in dealing with the present and future, and in every way to react in a much fuller, safer, and more competent manner to the emergencies which face it.' ([3], p. 61)

Other authors also have formulated what mental models are. For example, with an emphasis on causal relations, Shih and Alessi ([16], p. 157) explain that.

> 'By a mental model we mean a person's understanding of the environment. It can represent different states of the problem and the causal relationships among states.'

De Kleer and Brown [4] describe a mental model as the envisioning of a system, including a topological representation of the system components, the possible states of each of the components, and the structural relations between these components, the running or execution of the causal model based on basic operational rules and on general scientific principles.

Shared Mental Models. A shared mental model consists of knowledge structures that overlap in contextual information and procedures. The lack of an adequate SMM in teams have been often been related to the occurrence of team errors [6, 11]. It is suggested that SSM play a major role in the effectiveness, efficiency of the group decision process and performance in a variety of domains, e.g., aviation decision making and medical team decision making and command and control [2, 8, 9, 12, 17, 29, 30]. Among others the adequacy of SSM have been related to patent safety in the operation room, e.g., open heart operation and tracheal intubation [10, 15].

Case Description. The setting of the addressed case is an emergency department where an emergency team is coming together for preparing to intubate a critically ill patient with deteriorating conscious state. The airway has been assessed as being normal and there is no expectation that there are going to be any difficulties with intubation. A doctor (D) is called to perform a tracheal intubation in collaboration with a nurse (N). In general, a tracheal intubation induces stress for D and A. The call of the doctor triggers the activation of the initial state of a shared mental model with separate roles and activities for the tracheal intubation for the D and N. The roles and activities are unique for D and N. The roles for the doctor are: team leader, prepare team, prepare for difficulties and the role of intubator. The roles for the nurse are: intubator's assistant, prepare patient, prepare equipment, prepare drugs, give drugs, monitoring patient, cricoid force, and the role of runner for help and/or additional equipment. In addition to the allocation of roles, the shared mental model contains the corresponding (temporal) sequence of activities for D and N. This consists of the following sequence. The nurse prepares the patient and performs the preparation of the equipment; then the nurse performs the preparation of the drugs. Doctor executes pre oxygenation and starts with the preparation of the team and the preparation for difficulties. The nurse listens and observes to the doctor's team preparation. The nurse give drugs to the patient and applies cricoid to the patient. Then the doctor initiates the executing of plan A Larynscopy and starts the first intubation attempt. The nurse assists the doctor in the intubation attempt. The nurse monitors the patient When the first attempt is finished the nurse seeks confirmation of its success by monitoring the capnograph. If this is OK, the attempt has succeeded.

Network-Oriented Modeling. The Network-Oriented Modelling approach based on temporal-causal networks from [18, 19] has been used to represent causal relations between mental and other states and to simulate the mental processes based on them, as needed for the use of mental models. Therefore, this approach was used to design a network model for using shared mental models in a team member's mental processing and acting. Network nodes X have state values indicated by real numbers $X(t)$ that vary over time t; nodes are also called states. The characteristics defining a network model are:

- **Connectivity characteristics**: *connections* from states X to Y, having *connection weights* $\omega_{X,Y}$ specifying their strengths
- **Aggregation characteristics**: each state Y has a *combination function* $\mathbf{c}_Y$ that specifies how impact from all incoming connections on Y is aggregated
- **Timing characteristics**: each state Y has a *speed factor* η_Y specifying how fast Y changes

The numerical representation created by the available dedicated software environment is based on the following equations based on the above network characteristics (where $X_1, \ldots, X_k$ are the states from which state Y gets incoming connections):

$$\mathbf{impact}_{X,Y}(t) = \omega_{X,Y} X(t) \tag{1}$$

$$\mathbf{aggimpact}_Y(t) = \mathbf{c}_Y(\mathbf{impact}_{X_1 Y}(t), \ldots, \mathbf{impact}_{X_k Y}(t)) = \mathbf{c}_Y(\omega_{X_1,Y} X_1(t), \ldots, \omega_{X_k,Y} X_k(t)) \tag{2}$$

$$
\begin{aligned}
Y(t+\Delta t) &= Y(t) + \eta_Y\big[\mathbf{aggimpact}_Y(t) - Y(t)\big]\Delta t \\
&= Y(t) + \eta_Y[\mathbf{c}_Y(\omega_{X_1,Y}X_1(t),\ \ldots,\ \omega_{X_k,Y}X_k(t)) - Y(t)]\Delta t
\end{aligned} \tag{3}
$$

Within this software environment based on the generic equations (3) the processing of all network states takes place, thereby using the network characteristics.

3 Design of the Network Model Using a Shared Mental Model

The introduced temporal-causal network model design for the scenario described in Sect. 2 has connectivity as depicted in Fig. 1. See Tables 1 and 2 for an explanation of the main states. The scenario describes a sequence of actions with actors performing them and their temporal order, according to the example scenario as described in Sect. 2.

The world states representing the steps in the world for this scenario are depicted in Fig. 1 by the blue nodes in the middle area with their connections. The green node on the left represents a contextual stress factor. The actor is indicated within a world state name by D for doctor or N for nurse. The mental models of the doctor and the nurse reflect this ordered structure (as discussed in the first part of Sect. 2); they are depicted by the red nodes and yellow nodes and their mutual connections, respectively (as indicated globally by the long red oval, and by the long yellow oval). The states within the mental models correspond to the world states and accordingly they also specify an actor, indicated by D for doctor or N for nurse. The two individual mental models are two instances of an overall team mental model addressing the course of actions and the roles of the different team members for these actions. As often not all team members will possess one and the same perfect team mental model, these individual instances of the team mental model can have differences. By each of the two team members, their own mental model is used to determine their actions in the world.

This goes through the members' action ownership states (indicated in light red for the doctor and in light yellow for the nurse). These ownership states are mental states but are not part of the mental models. Instead, they receive input from some of the mental model states and based on that initiate the execution of the indicated actions, which leads to affecting the related world states. By these causal pathways, the mental models affect the actions changing the world states. Connections from world states to corresponding mental model states are (at some points) used to generate information about the world as input for the mental models.

The combination functions from the combination function library available within the software environment used here are shown in Table 3.

4 Simulation for the Example Scenario

The network characteristics defining the network model introduced above have been specified in a standard table format (called role matrices) that can be used as input for the available dedicated software environment; see also the Appendix as Linked Data at URL https://www.researchgate.net/publication/350873959. When transferred to this software environment, they are automatically used by the incorporated differential equations (3)

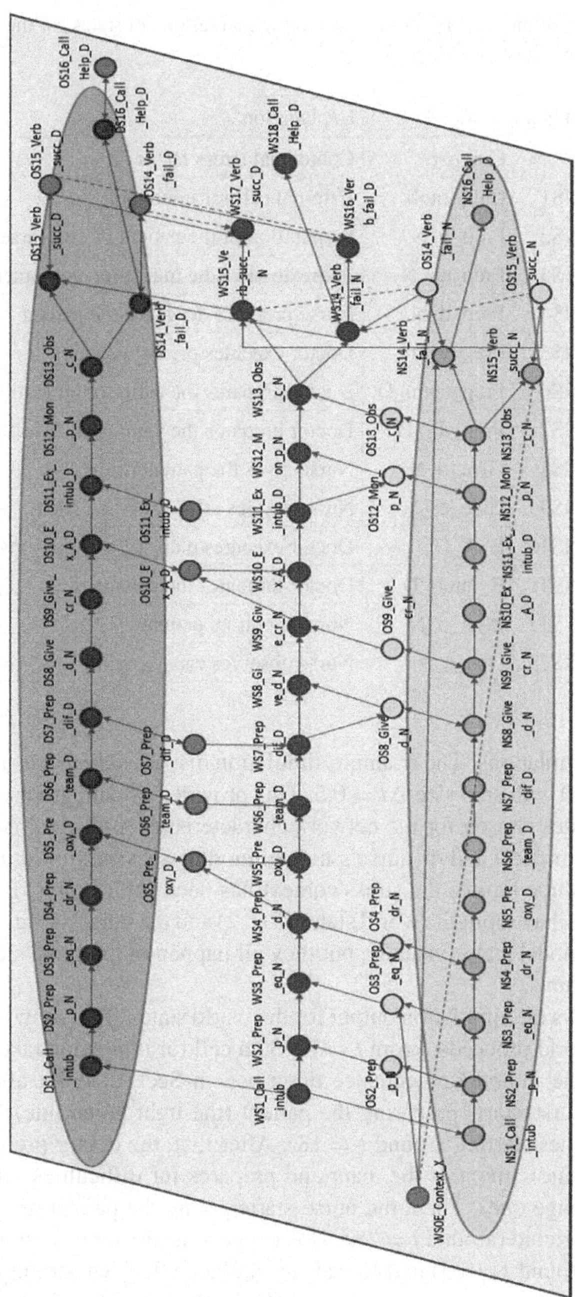

Fig. 1. Connectivity of the designed temporal-causal network model including the two mental models of the nurse (long yellow oval) and of the doctor (long red oval) (Color figure online)

Table 1. Overview of the world states (WS) and the mental model states for the doctor (DS) and nurse (NS) reflecting these world states

World, Doctor and Nurse				Explanation
WS0			Context	Contextual stress factor
WS1	DS1	NS1	Call_intub	External call for intubation
WS2	DS2	NS2	Prep_p_N	Preparation of the patient by the nurse
WS3	DS3	NS3	Prep_eq_N	Preparation of the intubation equipment by the nurse
WS4	DS4	NS4	Prep_d_N	Nurse prepares drugs for the patient
WS5	DS5	NS5	Pre_oy_D	Doctor executes pre oxygenation
WS6	DS6	NS6	Prep_team_D	Doctor prepares the team for intubation
WS7	DS7	NS7	Prep_dif_D	Doctor prepares the team for difficulties
WS8	DS8	NS8	Give_d_N	Nurse gives the patient drugs
WS9	DS9	NS9	Give_cr_N	Nurse applies cricoid to the patient
WS10	DS10	NS10	E_A_D	Doctor executes plan A Laryngoscopy
WS11	DS11	NS11	E_intub_D	Doctor intubates the patient
WS12	DS12	NS12	Mon_p_N	Nurse monitors patient
WS13	DS13	NS13	Obs_c_N	Nurse observes capnograph

when running simulations. The example simulation discussed here was run over a time interval of 0 to 80 with step size $\Delta t = 0.5$. This provides us with graphs of simulations based on the values chosen for the network characteristics. In Figs. 2 (world states), 3 (doctor's mental model) and 4 (nurse's mental model) a successful intubation process is shown. In all three figures the stress context has been set low (zero). For reasons of clarity, the figures have split the world states (Fig. 2) and the nurse's (Fig. 3) and doctor's (Fig. 4) mental model states visually, but they all happen in the same simulation at the indicated time points.

Figure 2 shows the simulation output for the world states. This shows how the actual process in the world proceeds. From $t = 10$–30 a call for intubation takes place, which sets in motion the intubation sequence described in Sect. 2. A bit after the call for intubation the Nurse starts preparing the patient (the light green line), the equipment and drugs (the lines starting around $t = 18$). After that, the doctor pre-oxygenates the patient (orange line), prepares the team and prepares for difficulties (blue and purple line after the orange one). Then, the nurse starts giving the patient drugs (around $t = 27$) and applies cricoid (around $t = 28$). This triggers the doctor to start the first attempt laryngoscopy (around $t = 33$) and to start to intubate after that (around $t = 37$). This triggers the nurse to monitor the patient, see the light blue line starting around $t = 37$, and to observe the capnograph. After this, the nurse will verbalize the success of the intubation (slowly starting at $t = 37$), and the doctor will then formally verbalize the success of the intubation (after $t = 47$).

Table 2. Overview of the ownership states for the doctor and nurse

Name		Explanation
DOS6	DOS for Pre_oxy_D	Ownership state for the action of preoxygenation
DOS7	DOS for Prep_team_D	Ownership state for the action of preparing the team
DOS8	DOS for Prep_dif_D	Ownership state for the action of preparing the team for difficulties
DOS11	DOS for E_A_D	Ownership state for the action of plan A Laryngoscopy by doctor
DOS12	DOS for E_intub_D	Ownership state for the action of intubating first attempt by doctor
DOS15	DOS for verb_fail_D	Ownership state for the action of verbalizing that attempt has failed by doctor
DOS16	DOS for Verb_succ_D	Ownership state for the action of verbalizing that attempt has succeeded by doctor
DOS17	DOS for Call_help_D	Ownership state for the action of call for help, by doctor
NOS3	NOS for Prep_N	Nurse Ownership State for Preparation patient
NOS4	NOS for Prep_eq_N	Nurse Ownership State for Preparation equipment
NOS5	NOS for Prep_dr_N	Nurse Ownership State for preparing drugs
NOS9	NOS for Give_d_N	Nurse Ownership State for Nurse gives drugs
NOS10	NOS for Give_cr_N	Nurse Ownership State for Nurse gives cricoid
NOS13	NOS for Mon_p_N	Nurse Ownership State for Nurse monitors patient
NOS14	NOS for Obs_c_N	Nurse Ownership State for observing capnograph
NOS15	NOS for Verb_fail_N	Nurse Ownership State for verbalizing that attempt has failed
NOS16	NOS for Verb_succ_N	Nurse Ownership State for verbalizing that attempt has succeeded

Table 3. Combination functions from the library used in the introduced network model

	Notation	Formula	Parameters
Steponce	**steponce**(V)	1 if $\alpha \leq t \leq \beta$, else 0	α start, β end time
Advanced logistic sum	**alogistic**$_{\sigma,\tau}(V_1, \ldots, V_k)$	$[\frac{1}{1+e^{-\sigma(V_1+\cdots+V_k-\tau)}} - \frac{1}{1+e^{\sigma\tau})}](1+e^{-\sigma\tau})$	Steepness $\sigma > 0$ Excitability threshold τ

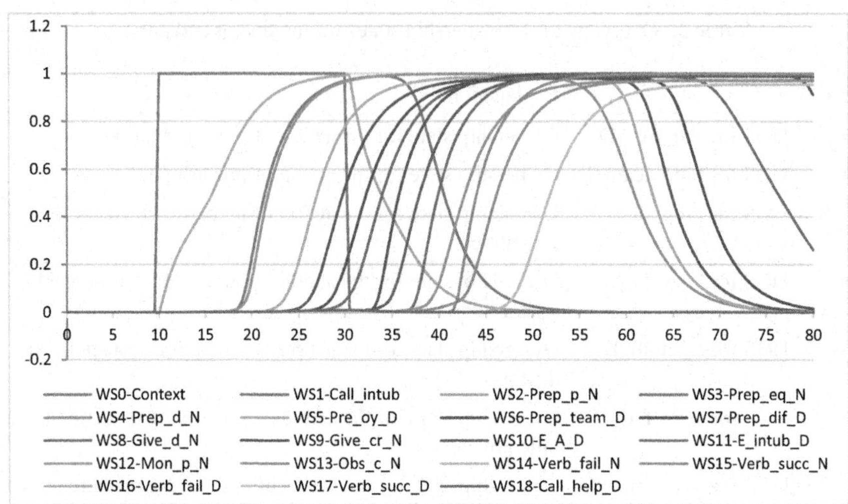

Fig. 2. World states of a successful intubation process (Color figure online)

Figures 3 and 4 show the successful intubation scenario described above, but for what precedes the world state activations described above: respectively the internal simulations by the doctor and nurse of their own mental model and activating accordingly their ownership states.

In Fig. 3, at $t = 10$ the world state for a call for intubation activates. This subsequently triggers the doctor's internal simulation of her mental model states for actions the nurse does, i.e., preparing the patient, equipment and drugs. When this sequence is finished, this internal simulation activates the doctor's mental model states for actions she has to do herself, which in turn activate her ownership states for these actions (dotted lines for pre oxygenating the patient, preparing the team and preparing for difficulties around $t = 18–22$). These actions trigger to subsequent mental model states that the nurse then makes her deciding for actions via the corresponding ownership states, giving the drugs and applying cricoid, which then activates the doctors mental model states and thus ownership states for his own next actions, starting to actually intubate (around $t = 28$). Around $t = 38$, the nurse's verbalization in the world states triggers the doctor's mental model state and ownership state of verbalization of a successful intubation.

Figure 4 shows a very similar pattern, just substituting the doctor's mental model states for the nurse's mental model states, and showing the nurse's ownership states instead of the doctor's ownership states.

The network model is also able to show a failed attempt, as illustrated in the Appendix by a scenario with a high contextual stress factor that was simulated. The high stress level leads to missing steps in the intubation scenario, leading to a failing intubation process.

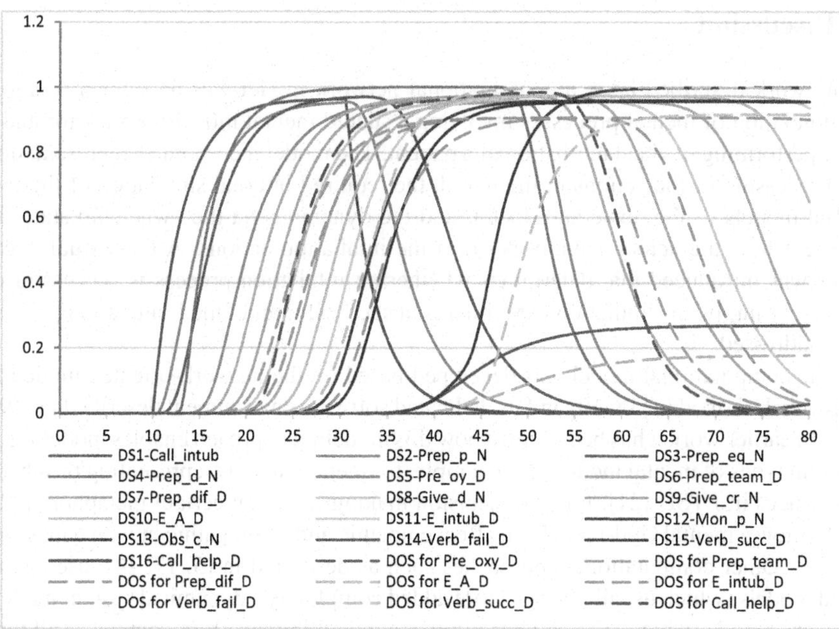

Fig. 3. The doctor's mental model and ownership states of a successful intubation process

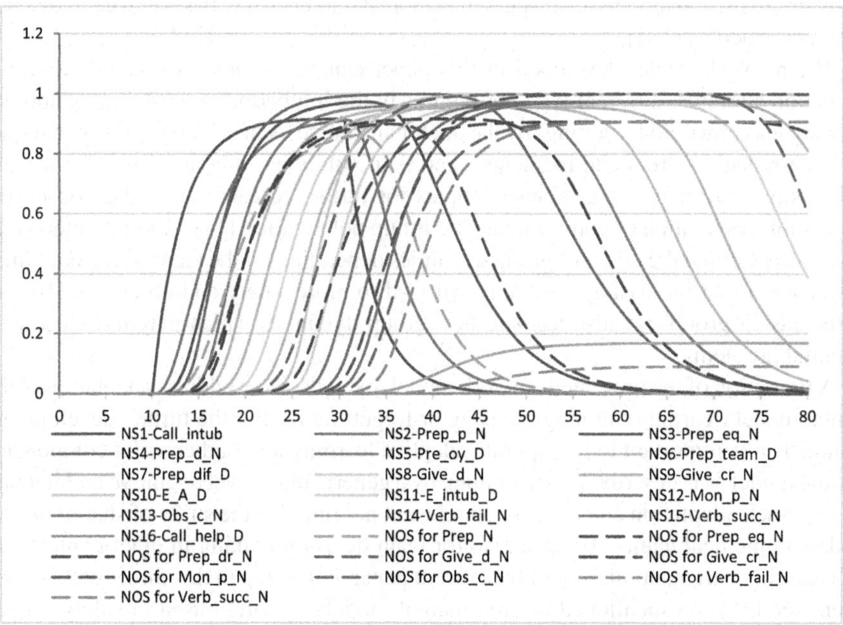

Fig. 4. The nurse's mental model and ownership states of a successful intubation process

5 Discussion

In the work described here, a computational network model was developed to allow for simulation of mental processes involving a shared mental model for a doctor and a nurse performing tracheal intubation of a patient. The model incorporates representation and processing of the actions in the world, the required internal simulation of the two mental models of the nurse and doctor, and the dynamics via the ownership states to represent how the actors actually perform the intubation actions. A contextual stress factor was introduced that determines whether an intubation process is successful or not. Accordingly, in simulation experiments, a successful and failed intubation process were addressed.

The computational model was developed based on the network-oriented modeling approach described in [18, 19] and its dedicated software environment described in [19], Ch 9. In earlier work it has been shown how this modeling approach enables modeling of different types of mental models, for example, for mental models representing flashback experiences in PTSD [21], for joint decision making based on certain metaphors [22], and for how a mental God-model can affect empathic and disempathic human behaviour [25–27]. Other computational approaches such as described in [5, 13, 14], use agent-based models (which usually brings more added complexity), dynamical system models or program code (which lacks a description at a modelling level). In contrast to all this, the current paper describes at a modelling level a first computational network model addressing hospital processes and shared mental models for teamwork for them. Neural correlates of mental models are discussed in more detail in [20] with several neuroscience references such as [1, 7].

The network model developed in this paper can be extended to include multiple intubation attempts, different types of failures in the intubation process, and adaptivity showing learning (and forgetting) by the doctor and nurse. A next step would be to model the occurrence of errors and incidents - and their solutions - that are specific for team and group performance. Examples of topics for further research are: false consensus, group think, escalation of commitment and group polarization [11]. Another interesting topic is to examine the effect of group dynamics depending on the team size. Sometimes it is claimed that increasing the team, will lead to more safety and efficiency [10] but an increasing group size also leads to new group dynamics which may introduce new potential problems.

A limitation of the presented network model that it does not address adaptation of the mental model (learning, refining, revising or forgetting it). For the further development of models it is important to incorporate adaptive learning and higher-order components into the model as is described, for example, by a generic multilevel cognitive architecture in [23]. Such adaptation and control are relevant not only for the study of shared mental models in medical teams [10], but also for team decision making in other contexts. In the meantime, after submission of the current paper a first step in this direction has been taken; see [24]. As mentioned, shared mental models are often used in safety-related situations such as aviation, firefighting teams, dealing rooms, shipping control, etc. An important line for future research is to analyse the validity of the introduced network model and further extensions of it for such domains.

References

1. Alfred, K.L., Connolly, A.C., Cetron, J.S., et al.: Mental models use common neural spatial structure for spatial and abstract content. Commun. Biol. **3**, 17 (2020)
2. Burtscher, M.J., Manser, T.: Team mental models and their potential to improve teamwork and safety: a review and implications for future research in healthcare. Saf. Sci. **50**(5), 1344–1354 (2012)
3. Craik, K.J.W.: The Nature of Explanation. University Press, Cambridge (1943)
4. De Kleer, J., Brown, J.: Assumptions and ambiguities in mechanistic mental models. In: Gentner, D., Stevens, A. (eds.) Mental models, pp. 155–190. Lawrence Erlbaum Associates, Hillsdale (1983)
5. Dionne, S.D., Sayama, H., Hao, C., Bush, B.J.: The role of leadership in shared mental model convergence and team performance improvement: an agent-based computational model. Leadersh. Q. **21**, 1035–1049 (2010)
6. Fischhof, B., Johnson, S.: Organisational Decision Making. Cambridge University Press, Cambridge (1997)
7. Garvert, M., Dolan, R., Behrens, T.: A map of abstract relational knowledge in the human hippocampal–entorhinal cortex. eLife. **6**, e17086 (2017)
8. Gehlert, S.: Developing a shared mental model of team functioning in the context of research. J. Psychiatry Psychiatr. Disord. **4**(3), 74–81 (2020)
9. Gisick, L.M., et al.: Measuring shared mental models in healthcare. J. Patient Saf. Risk Manag. **23**(5), 207–219 (2018)
10. Higgs, A., et al.: Guidelines for the management of tracheal intubation of critically ill adults. Br. J. Anaesth. **120**(2), 323–352 (2018)
11. Jones, P.E., Roelofsma, P.H.M.P.: The potential for social contextual and group biases in team decision making: biases, conditions and psychological mechanisms. Ergonomics **43**(8), 1129–1152 (2000)
12. Mathieu, J.E., Hefner, T.S., Goodwin, G.F., Salas, E., Cannon-Bowers, J.A.: The influence of shared mental models on team process and performance. J. Appl. Psychol. **85**(2), 273–283 (2000)
13. Outland, N.B.: A Computational Cognitive Architecture for Exploring Team Mental Models. College of Science and Health Theses and Dissertations. 289 (2019). https://via.library.depaul.edu/csh_etd/289
14. Scheutz, M.: Computational mechanisms for mental models in human-robot interaction. In: Shumaker, R. (ed.) Virtual Augmented and Mixed Reality. Designing and Developing Augmented and Virtual Environments. LNCS, vol. 8021, pp. 304–312. Springer, Heidelberg (2013). https://doi.org/10.1007/978-3-642-39405-8_34
15. Seo, S., Kennedy-Metz, L.R., Zenati, M.A., Shah, J.A., Dias, R.D., Unhelkar, V.V.: Towards an AI coach to infer team mental model alignment in healthcare. Department of Computer Science, Rice University Houston TX, USA (2021)
16. Shih, Y.F., Alessi, S.M.: Mental models and transfer of learning in computer programming. J. Res. Comput. Educ. **26**(2), 154–175 (1993)
17. Todd, J.: Audit of compliance with WHO surgical safety checklist and building a shared mental model in the operating theatre. BJM Leader **2**(1), 32–135 (2018)
18. Treur, J.: Network-Oriented Modeling: Addressing Complexity of Cognitive Affective and Social Interactions. Springer, Cham (2016). https://doi.org/10.1007/978-3-319-45213-5
19. Treur, J.: Network-Oriented Modeling for Adaptive Networks: Designing Higher-Order Adaptive Biological, Mental and Social Network Models. Springer, Cham (2020). https://doi.org/10.1007/978-3-030-31445-3

20. Treur, J.: Mental models in the brain: on context-dependent neural correlates of mental models. Cogn. Syst. Res. **79**, 83–90 (2021)
21. van Ments, L., Treur, J.: A higher-order adaptive network model to simulate development of and recovery from PTSD. In: Paszynski, M., Kranzlmüller, D., Krzhizhanovskaya, V.V., Dongarra, J.J., Sloot, P.M.A. (eds.) Computational Science – ICCS 2021. LNCS, vol. 12743, pp. 154–166. Springer, Cham (2021). https://doi.org/10.1007/978-3-030-77964-1_13
22. Van Ments, L., Treur, J.: Modeling adaptive cooperative and competitive metaphors as mental models for joint decision making. Cogn. Syst. Res. **69**, 67–82 (2021)
23. Van Ments, L., Treur, J.: Reflections on dynamics, adaptation and control: a cognitive architecture for mental models. Cogn. Syst. Res. **70**, 1–9 (2021)
24. Van Ments, L., Treur, J., Klein, J., Roelofsma, P.H.M.P.: A second-order adaptive network model for shared mental models in hospital teamwork. In: Nguyen, N.T., et al. (eds.) Proceedings of the 13th International Conference on Computational Collective Intelligence, ICCCI 2021, Lecture Notes in AI, Springer, Heidelberg (2021). To appear
25. Van Ments, L., Treur, J., Roelofsma, P.H.M.P.: A temporal-causal network model for the relation between religion and human empathy. In: Cherifi, H., Gaito, S., Quattrociocchi, W., Sala, A. (eds.) Proceedings of the 5th International Workshop on Complex Networks and Their Applications V. Lecture Notes in Computer Science, vol. 693, pp. 55–67. Springer, Heidelberg (2016)
26. Van Ments, L., Treur, J., Roelofsma, P.H.M.P.: Modeling the effect of religion on human empathy based on an adaptive temporal-causal network model. Comput. Soc. Netw. **5**(1), 1–23 (2018). https://doi.org/10.1186/s40649-017-0049-z
27. Van Ments, L., Treur, J., Roelofsma, P.H.M.P.: An adaptive network model for formation and use of a mental god-model and its effect on human empathy. In: Treur, J., van Ments, L. (eds.) Mental Models and their Dynamics, Adaptation, and Control: a Self-Modeling Network Modeling Approach. Springer, Heidelberg (2022)
28. Williams, D.: The Mind as a Predictive Modelling Engine: Generative Models, Structural Similarity, and Mental Representation. Ph. D. Thesis, University of Cambridge, UK (2018)
29. Wilson, A.: Creating and applying shared mental models in the operating room. J. Perioper. Nurs. **32**(3), 33–36 (2019)
30. Wise, S., Duffield, C., Fry, M., Roche, M.: A team mental model approach to understanding team effectiveness in an emergency department: a qualitative study. J. Health Serv. Res. Policy (2021). https://doi.org/10.1177/13558196211031285

System Level Knowledge Representation for Metacognition in Neuroscience

Paola Di Maio[1,2](✉)

[1] Center for Systems Knowledge Representation and Neuroscience, Edinburgh, UK
[2] Ronin Institute, Montclair, USA

Abstract. Neuroscience lies at the heart of a wide range of novel scientific and technological advances, from neurotechnology to computing and the cognitive sciences. Observing and studying the human brain allows glimpses into the most valuable resource resulting from evolution: the human mind. However abundant and widely available, neuroscience research data are knowledge and resource intensive to acquire and maintain, demanding a high level of skill and expertise to be produced, accessed and applied. As in all complex knowledge domains, reasoning with neuroscience relies on implicit metacognitive processes, and metacognition relies on high level cognitive models. This paper proposes a System Level Knowledge Representation schema as an abstraction for neuroscience data aimed at supporting explicit metacognition as well as knowledge organisation, understandability and to ease the cognitive load of processing systems neuroscience data.

Keywords: Knowledge · Representation · Neuroscience · System level · Metacognition

1 Introduction

Neuroscience research is producing vast amounts of data and insights, which need to be interpreted and understood so that these can be useful to inform scientific inquiry in diverse domains, from psychology to cognition, engineering, computer science, machine learning, AI and neuromorphic systems. To enable the interdisciplinary fruition of neuroscience data emerging from research, in addition to it being available, knowledge also needs to be cognitively intelligible and understandable for researchers and practitioners from disciplines others than neuroscience. This requires context and the availability of high level logical schemas. Although most publicly funded neuroscience research outputs have been historically shared openly in the public domain [1], in practice the usability of data sets remains limited because of the lack of syncretic knowledge schemas to explain their context. Neuroscience data models tend to be tightly coupled with software, ie, without the specific software that created the dataset, the dataset itself has limited usefulness and cannot be visualised in any other way. In some cases where the data models are software independent, representations are narrowly defined to suit the specific views and requirements of the researches and projects which motivated their

M. Mahmud et al. (Eds.): BI 2021, LNAI 12960, pp. 79–88, 2021.
https://doi.org/10.1007/978-3-030-86993-9_8

development. In addition, as the field of neuroscience expands and diversifies and novel advances produce new concepts and perspectives, even trained neuroscientists require ongoing learning and cognitive support as well as technical guidance to reference new constructs outside their original field of specialisation, which require new technology (such as AI based software) to be queried and used. As neuroscience becomes more diverse in terms of types, quality and quantity of data and data stores, the research landscape is becoming more demanding even for specialists. New methods, tools, techniques and devices are continually updated and the data model landscape is becoming increasingly vast and fragmented. This reflects a classical and common problem in data science, that the neuroscience research community has been trying to address for decades. This article proposes that approaches rooted in Knowledge Representation, such as for example Conceptual Graphs [2] and Formal Concept Analysis [3] can be leveraged to specify a knowledge object that supports the logical navigation of dataset and their mapping to a high level object modelled on a system level outline such as the Function Behaviour Structure framework [4]. In addition to supporting systems development by encoding logic, Knowledge Representation techniques and artefacts can also be used to facilitate the modelling of cognitive aspects of complex knowledge sharing [5], knowledge organisation, interpretability, and to enable the application of neuroethical principles [6]. A schematic named System Level Knowledge Representation Object is proposed to promote the automation of metacognition in neuroscience based systems. The rationale and motivation for a general System Level Knowledge Representation approach to handle complexity is described elsewhere [7].

2 Metacognition in Complexity

Neuroscience can be defined as the complex knowledge domain par excellence (together with astrophysics and a few others perhaps). Metacognition is considered necessary to handle cognitive complexity [8]. Metacognitive learning goals are essential in modern education and training, as learners are increasingly expected to acquire and exchange knowledge through constant interactions with different audiences, through a variety of tasks, purposes, and disciplines and be able to critically synthesize different resources and valuing sound evidence [9]. Defined as awareness of cognitive processes, metacognition is regarded inherently as implicit and occurring in the mind. Explicit metacognition is formalized and expressed with language leveraging deliberative (explicit) measures of attitudes [10] however, in particular metarepresentational metacognition leverage higher-order propositional or symbolic strategies [11] explicit metacognition is the basis for sharing explicit metarepresentation - defined as representation about representation. The study of human metacognition includes abstraction, metamemory, selfcontrol, uncertainty monitoring, heuristics, problem solving, strategy selection, implicit learning. Not only the research community is now coming to terms with handling exponential complexity in neuroscience, but it is also developing advanced information technology to support this complexity. Metacognition is not only necessary to handle the human cognitive processes in such tasks, but also, and increasingly relevantly so, the design, operation and maintenance of the automation of the technologies that support and mediate such cognitive processes. Corresponding machine learning techniques can be abstracted to automate at least to some extent this type of backend process supporting human intelligence [12, 13] Integrating AI technology and cognitive sciences requires the implementation of some level of artificial metacognition [14]. To facilitate the development of knowledge based systems capable of supporting metareasoning in neuroscience, metamodelling, namely a System Level model, is undertaken.

3 Accessing Data as Well as to the Context

Open Data can facilitate the reproducibility of research outcomes, accelerate discovery and diffusion of innovation, and can enable faster problem solving, better use and re-use of resources at a time where neuroscience is becoming very popular. However the knowledge required for reasoning and inference which is based on this data, must also be openly shared and as such, it also requires shared metacognitive artefacts. The explicit representation of the system level for example is required for the development of ethical AI systems [15]. This requires metarepresentation of abstract concepts such as ethical values, and which is also needed to meet neuroethics criteria which state that adhere to principles of ethics a system should ensure that the data is: (1) findable, with a rich assigned standardized metadata and persistent identifier; (2) accessible, via an identifier and an open, free, and universally implementable communications protocol; (3) interoperable, via broadly applicable language for knowledge representation (4), via domain-relevant community standards [16].

4 Knowledge Representation

KR consists of methods and techniques to capture, model and make explicit the necessary knowledge and reasoning, in short the "intelligence" required for the correct functioning of automated and autonomous systems. KR is a vast technical subject central to computer science since AI was first conceived [17–19] spanning logic, semantics, linguistics, formal systems supporting every aspect of computation. In computer science, it consists of well defined methods and techniques to model and encode inferential logic and knowledge, however in more general terms, it is applicable to a number of other disciplines, such as jurisprudence. The distinction can be made between KR as a technique/process - A set of activities in Knowledge Modeling and Knowledge Engineering applied to systems development and KR as the artifacts resulting from these activities - Knowledge encoded and implemented as a product of Knowledge modelling (for example a graph, an ontology or an algorithm). As with other complex knowledge domains, neuroscience meets with ongoing modelling challenges such as the identification of relevant dimensions in adequate scope and detail, such as the partial, temporal and computational scales, and the choice of adequate models and inferences to reach conclusions and gather insights. Knowledge Modelling and Representation On a large scale and with the necessary detail and complexity is non trivial, yet it impacts directly the outcome and meaning research and interpretation. One of the arguments against open sharing of brain data using higher level knowledge constructs that make data more accessible and interpretable is the risk of breach of privacy through the leakage of person data, but it is only through open models and agreed upon explicit representations that neuroscience can appropriately produce acceptable measures to protect person data, as well as to ensure validity and reproducibility of research outcomes. The lack of higher order explicit schema is more likely to disguise an inherent reluctance to share data in the first place than a concern for privacy of subjects. Sharing data without saying what it means is a form of data gatekeeping. It is only through explicit and shared knowledge representation that the validity and logical integrity of constructs and truth values can be ensured. In one recent case for example a user of BIDS[1] noted that after being processed using a particular tool, the source data itself had changed since it was first inputted. In public datasets, permutations that transform arbitrarily the data which is inputted, whether due to bugs or other system flaw or malfunction, can easily occur in records which are accessed and used by distributed teams of clinicians who may ot not have the necessary expertise and visibility to evaluate the correctness of the full data lifecycle at every step. Technically this results in high risk of error, with a very small pool of experts that have the ability to identify and address such data errors, that require considerable specialised resources to be resolved. Therefore in addition to the canonical roles for KR in AI described in textbooks [20], additional roles for KR are identified: such as supporting algorithmic fairness, to specify knowledge levels and dimensions in support of cognition/explainability, for identifying and resolving bias, to ensure stability consistency, integrity and truth values throughout permutations.

5 From Metacognition to Metarepresentation

The web with its open standards, shared schemas and ontologies is a major driver for the development of explicit knowledge representation. Declaring entities and attributes, classes, objects, properties and relations as well as specifying data models, schemas, metadata, vocabularies and their extensions, contribute to interoperability and ultimately to the usability and usefulness of knowledge. Good practices for open and shared knowledge are found on an ample spectrum of characteristics and desirable features [21]. Almost three decades of open access and knowledge sharing have driven web development research and practice. There is a vast body of literature and diverse communities agreeing on openness, accessibility, reusability and ultimately, open standards. Data sharing across the neuroscientific community has become an essential component of data-driven approaches to neuroscience as is evident from the number and scale of ongoing national and multinational projects, engaging scientists from diverse branches of knowledge [22]. At the time of writing, the standardization efforts for open and shared brain data is growing it remains increasingly fragmentary. Notable frameworks of reference are summarised in the Table 1, compiled via web searches and excerpted from literature [23].

6 Open Challenges, Current Trends

As the neuroscience body of knowledge expands, it is starting to seriously lack shape. While there is a lot of open and shared data available and accessible, the different open

[1] https://groups.google.com/g/bids-discussion/c/Geb28eMH2Qo/m/zxHymtFICAAJ?pli=1.

source datasets and projects tend to be 'islands', and will continue to be so, as standards, technology collection methods and frameworks are expected to evolve resulting from the diverse needs of an increasingly large research base. The proliferation of resources (tools, databases, materials) for neuroscientists available on the web is an incredible asset that new generations of researchers and scientists can leverage to advance the state of the art, at the same time it is becoming a challenge to cope with the volumes, and as such to channel resources appropriately and make novel contributions without extensive prior knowledge. Data modelling challenges for Neuroscience are not new: modelling and representing complexity at an appropriate scale, bridging fragmentation and adopting interoperable data models [24] remain open challenges. One of the problems encountered in many resources is referred to as overspecialization. In the case of BIDS, for example, data formats are developed with specific software architectures and corresponding classes and object models. This leads to situations where the key-value pairs of file names are tuned to a narrow class of software or concepts that cannot be used outside of that specific framework [25] This limitation in the data model contradicts the goal of data sharing and open software having a generic interface that is independent of a specific product, data format or narrow concept. When defining system extensions, it is good practice to generalize the data model rather than implementing a data structures that reflect the architecture of specific products. Data models should leverage generic patterns and common structures that underlie data. When modelled at the appropriate level of representation, data models are enormously simplified and the cognitive effort required to process them, both for humans and machines, is reduced accordingly. They also become transparent and are auditable in terms of fairness and ethics [6]. Although software systems may evolve and become deprecated, well designed data models are universal and withstand the test of time. To be able to evaluate research claims and results based on the datasets over time, explicit data models are necessary. This implies an explicit specification of concepts, architectures, implementations used for producing the results, together with function definitions, algorithms, parameters and variable settings. Table 1 includes the main examples of data models currently in use in neuroscience research. Not all of these use reference standard models (the explicit

Table 1. Examples of neuroscience data models in use

Resource	Description	Content	Interoperability
Neuroscience Information Network (Neuinfo.org)	Registry Vocabulary Web Index	Corpus	BFO
NeuroML Neural Open Markup Language (Neuroml.org) NeuroML (Goddard et al. 2001, Crook et al. 2007, Gleeson et al. 2010)	XML based language for describing detailed models of neural systems	MorphML, ChannelML and NetworkML	COMBINE (COmputational Modeling in BIology NEtwork)

(*continued*)

Table 1. (*continued*)

Resource	Description	Content	Interoperability
NineML http://incf.github.io/nineml-spec/	Description of computational neuroscience models of neuronal networks Restricted to Point Neuron Models	Network architecture, parameters and equations that govern the dynamics of a neuronal network, without taking into account model implementation details such as numerical integration methods	Computational! Neuroscience! Ontology! (CNO)
SBML, Systems Biology Markup Language, SBML, (Hucka et al. 2003)	Software independent schema to escribe biological processes incl metabolic pathways, cell signaling pathways	Specifying biological reaction networks	Miriam (http://www.ebi.ac.uk/miriam/)
CellML (Hedley et al. 2000, Lloyd et al. 2004) Model Repository (http://models.cellml.org)	Model/Component Description Language	Models Metadata	COMBINE Dublin Core
Simulation Experiment Description Markup Language (SED-ML) (Köhn and Le Novère 2008)	Language for encoding the details of simulation experiments	Description of which experimental data and models to use modifications to apply simulation procedures analysis results and how to presults them	MIASE (Minimal Information About a Simulation Experiment) guidelines (http://biomodels.net/miase)
The Neuroscience Simulation Data Format (NSDF; GitHub.com/nsdf/nsdf)	Designed for storing simulation data	File format for simulation data	HDF5 (Hierarchical Data Format 5)

(*continued*)

Table 1. *(continued)*

Resource	Description	Content	Interoperability
Neurodata without borders https://www.nwb.org/nwb-software/ Neuro Data Extensions (NDX)	Storage and organization of complex collections of neuroscience data Organize data hierarchically	Primitives e.g., Groups (similar to Folders), Datasets (n-D Arrays), Attributes (Metadata objects on Groups and Datasets), and Links (links to Groups and Datasets)	HDF5
Open Source Brain https://github.com/OpenSourceBrain/osb-model-validation	Tools for automated model validation in Open Source Brain projects, which can also be used for testing model behaviour on many simulation engines	Reference Model	NeuroML/Pynn
Brain Imaging Data Structure (BIDS) https://bids.neuroimaging.io/	Related to OpenNeuro Scheme for validation of imaging data formats	EEG iEEG MEG PET	https://openneuro.org/

knowledge schemas) such as BFO (Basic Formal Ontology) [26] and HDF (Hierarchical Data Format) [27]. The Lack of a unified data framework for neuroscience reflects the diversity of the research base but as the corpus expands rapidly it is a cause for concern in the scientific community [28, 29] Although efforts exist to provide unified frameworks/ontologies in the field of neuroscience, for various reasons a unified level of human and machine level interpretability for the data is still a long term vision [30] and may even be not entirely feasible.

7 System Level Knowledge Representation

System level web based applications that leverage integration are becoming available in neuroscience. The adoption of Task Oriented navigation, for example in Bioimage Suite [34], offers a GUI (Graphical User Interface) supporting generic users to load images and carry out intuitively basic research tasks without requiring specialized skills or expertise. It points to the emergence of new high level applications integrating generalization and abstraction, which are cognitive processes necessary to metacognition, as pointed out earlier [9]. A high level knowledge model which uses heuristic classification can support task based navigation [31]. Taking into account the evolutionary state of knowledge and data schemas for neuroscience, and the fact that fragmentation is inevitable and likely to continue, a System Level representation is proposed. From a systems science point of view system levels, states, processes, components [32] should be identified and made explicit. This can be achieved by merging Domain Analysis and Formal Concept Analysis techniques. On the whole, the resulting knowledge dimensions are less transient than at the level of individual resources and çomponents, therefore such a system view can provide a unifying conceptual model of reference to map the corresponding individual resources. This initial version of the schema outline (Fig. 1) consists of a representative set of categories to guide the conceptual representation of a structure, for component level representation (molecular, cellular, synaptic, regional, network and system) and with a provision to relate these vies to evolving theories. When devising a dataset, a tool, a method the proposed schema can be used to map artefacts to the corresponding level of reality thus, at a minimum simplifying the communication of the context to which it relates to. In essence the metamodel (also named KRO, Knowledge Representation Object) proposes that neuroscience data to be meaningful, should make explicit at a minimum the level of knowledge representation it references. A set of top level categories proposed here are intended as metacognitive metarepresentational dimension such as Concept Metacognition Metarepresentation Process Function and System, corresponding to a set of vertical dimensions such as Knowledge/Cognition (implicit) Language/expression (explicit formalism) Reasoning, inference (intelligent process) Decision, Action Behaviour. The model has been developed using a Formal Concept Analysis approach [33]. It is to be used as an example of metacognitive model and by no means limited to the categories currently serving as examples.

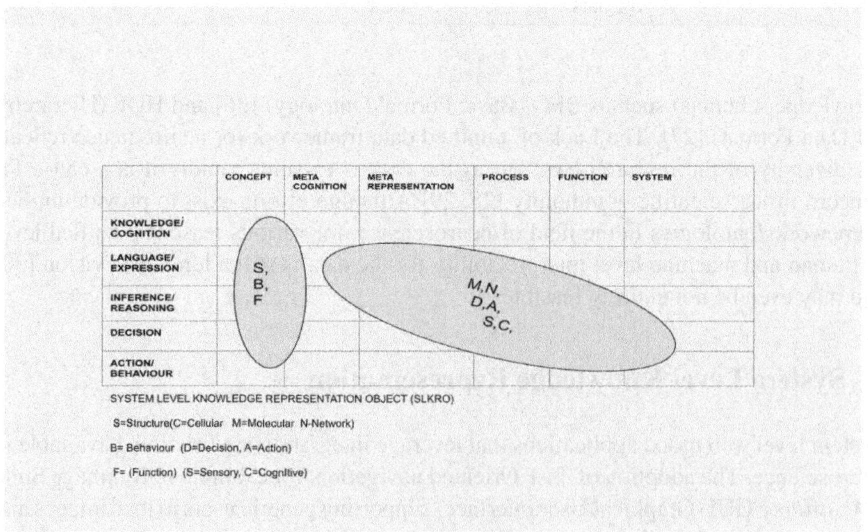

Fig. 1. Knowledge Representation Object (KRO)

8 Conclusion, Future Work

This paper discusses challenges related to complex knowledge domains, the role of metacognition and metarepresentation in relation to neuroscience research data. It makes the case for specifying high level representation corresponding to high level cognitive functions and proposes a knowledge representation object (KRO) for neuroscience to support data models that specify knowledge dimensions making explicit metacognition and metarepresentation. It can be used to guide the development of interfaces and system architectures and data models, as well for model verification and instruction purposes. Future work includes further developing evaluation and application of the object.

References

1. Gardner, W., Toga, A.W., Ascoli, G.A., et al.: Towards effective and rewarding data sharing. Neuroinformatics **1**(3), 289–295 (2003)
2. Sowa, J.F.: Conceptual graphs as a universal knowledge representation. Comput. Math. Appl. **23**, 75–93 (1992)
3. Kuznetsov, S.O., Poelmans, J.: Knowledge representation and processing with formal concept analysis. Wiley Interdisc. Rev. Data Min. Knowl. Disc. **3**, 200–215 (2013)
4. Gero, J.S., Kannengiesser, U.: Function-behaviour-structure: a model for social situated agents. In: Workshop on Cognitive Modeling of Agents and Multi-agent Interactions, International Joint Conference on Artificial Intelligence (2003)
5. Evermann, J.: Towards a cognitive foundation for knowledge representation. Inf. Syst. J. **15**(2), 147–178 (2005)
6. Di Maio, P.: Knowledge Representation for Neuroethics, Neuroethics Symposium (2020)
7. Di Maio, P.: System level knowledge representation for complexity. In: IEEE International Systems Conference (SysCon), pp. 1–6. IEEE (2021)
8. Rudolph, J., Niepel, C., Greiff, S., Goldhammer, F., Kröner, S.: Metacognitive confidence judgments and their link to complex problem solving. Intelligence **63**, 1–8 (2017)
9. Ozturk, N.: Assessing metacognition: theory and practices. Int. J. Assess. Tools Educ. **4**(2), 134–148 (2017)
10. Petty, R.E., Briñol, P.: A metacognitive approach to implicit and explicit evaluations: Comment on Gawronski and Bodenhausen (2006)
11. Fletcher, L., Carruthers, P.: Metacognition and reasoning. Philos. Trans. R. Soc. B: Biol. Sci. **367**(1594), 1366–1378 (2012)
12. Martinez, M.E.: What is metacognition? Phi Delta Kappan **87**(9), 696–699 (2006)
13. Shea, N.: Metacognition and abstract concepts. Philos. Trans. R. Soc. B: Biol. Sci. 373(1752) (2018)
14. Posner, I.: Robots Thinking Fast and Slow: On DualProcess Theory and Metacognition in Embodied AI (2020)
15. Peredo, A.M., Haugh, H.M., Hudon, M., Meyer, C.: Mapping concepts and issues in the ethics of the commons: introduction to the special issue. J. Bus. Ethics **166**(4), 659–672 (2020). https://doi.org/10.1007/s10551-020-04584-4
16. Wilkinson, A., Dumontier, M., Aalbersberg, I., et al.: The FAIR Guiding Principles for scientific data management and stewardship. Sci. Data **3**, 160018 (2016). https://doi.org/10.1038/sdata.2016.18
17. Minsky, M.: A Framework for Representing Knowledge. Technical Report. Massachusetts Institute of Technology, Cambridge, MA, USA (1974)

18. Goldstein, I., Papert, S.: Artificial intelligence, language, and the study of knowledge. Cogn. Sci. **1**(1), 84–123 (1977)
19. McCarthy, J.J., Minsky, M.L., Rochester, N.: Artificial intelligence. Research Laboratory ofElectronics (RLE) at the Massachusetts Institute of Technology (MIT) (1959)
20. Simmons, R., Davis, R.: The roles of knowledge and representation in problem solving. In: David, J.M., Krivine, J.P., Simmons, R. (eds.) Second Generation Expert Systems, pp. 27–45. Springer, Heidelberg (1993). https://doi.org/10.1007/978-3-642-77927-5_2
21. Di Maio, P.: Knowledge objects as shared system representation. Knowl. Manag. Res. Pract. **11**(1), 23–31 (2013)
22. Tsur, E.E.: Data Models in Neuroinformatics. Bioinformatics in the Era of Post Genomics and Big Data (2018)
23. McDougal, R.A., Bulanova, A.S., Lytton, W.W.: Reproducibility in computational neuroscience models and simulations. IEEE Trans. Biomed. Eng. **63**, 2021–2035 (2016)
24. Hucka, M., et al.: Promoting coordinated development of community-based information standards for modeling in biology: COMBINE initiative. Front. Bioeng. Biotechnol. **3**, 19 (2015)
25. BIDS Extension Proposal 032 (BEP032): BIDS Computational Model Specification version 0.9.0 (working copy) Available under the CC-BY 4.0 International license
26. BFO. https://basic-formal-ontology.org/
27. The HDF Group: Hierarchical Data Format, version 5 (1997–2015). http://www.hdfgroup.org/HDF5/
28. Rübel, O., Prabhat, M., Denes, P., Conant, D., Chang, E., Bouchard, K.: Brainformat: a data standardization framework for neuroscience data, vol. 2015, no. LBNL-188372. Lawrence Berkeley National Laboratory (LBNL), Berkeley (2015)
29. Bijari, K., Akram, M.A., Ascoli, G.A.: An open-source framework for neuroscience metadata management applied to digital reconstructions of neuronal morphology. Brain Inform. **7**(1), 1–12 (2020). https://doi.org/10.1186/s40708-020-00103-3
30. Flores Saiffe Farías, A., Mendizabal, A.P., Alejandro Morales, J.: An ontology systems approach on human brain expression and metaproteomics. Front. Microbiol. **9**, 406 (2018)
31. Clancey, W.: Heuristic classification. Artif. Intell. **27**, 289–350 (1985)
32. Kitano, H.: Systems biology: toward system-level understanding of biological systems. Found. Syst. Biol. 1–36 (2001)
33. Ganter, B., Wille, R.: Applied lattice theory: formal concept analysis. In: General Lattice Theory, G. Grätzer editor, Birkhäuser (1997)
34. Papademetris, X., et al.: Bioimage suite: an integrated medical image analysis suite: an update. Insight J. **2006**, 209 (2006)

Brain Connectivity Based Classification of Meditation Expertise

Pankaj Pandey[1], Pragati Gupta[2], and Krishna Prasad Miyapuram[1(✉)]

[1] Indian Institute of Technology Gandhinagar, Gandhinagar, India
{pankaj.p,kprasad}@iitgn.ac.in
[2] National Forensic Sciences University, Gandhinagar, India

Abstract. Recent developments in neurotechnology effectively utilize the decades of neuroscientific findings of multiple meditation techniques. Meditation is linked to higher-order cognitive processes, which may function as a scaffold for cognitive control. In line with these developments, we analyze oscillatory brain activities of expert and non-expert meditators from the Himalayan Yoga tradition. We exploit four dimensions (Temporal, Spectral, Spatial and Pattern) of EEG data and present an analysis pipeline employing machine learning techniques. We discuss the significance of different frequency bands in relation with distinct primary 5 scalp brain regions. Functional connectivity networks (PLV) are utilized to generate features for classification between expert and non-expert meditators. We find (a) higher frequency β and γ oscillations generate maximum discrimination over the parietal region whereas lower frequency θ and α oscillations dominant over the frontal region; (b) maximum accuracy of over 90% utilizing features from all regions; (c) Quadratic Discriminant Analysis surpasses other classifiers by learning distribution for classification. Overall, this paper contributes a pipeline to analyze EEG data utilizing various properties and suggests potential neural markers for an expert meditative state. We discuss the implications of our research for the advancement of personalized headset design that rely on feedback on depth of meditation by learning from expert meditators.

Keywords: Meditation · EEG · Machine learning · Phase Locking Value (PLV)

1 Introduction

EEG (Electroencephalography) is the most widely used noninvasive brain imaging technique to study the electrophysiological dynamics of the brain with direct implication in clinical, basic science, and several other fields [9]. EEG has been a significant methodology in the neuroscientific study of meditation and provides several avenues for exploration and insights into the human brain. EEG consumer headset technology develops brain training applications that aim to modulate features of the mental states and attributes related to particular meditation techniques.

M. Mahmud et al. (Eds.): BI 2021, LNAI 12960, pp. 89–98, 2021.
https://doi.org/10.1007/978-3-030-86993-9_9

EEG encodings consist of multidimensional information, characterizing brain states using temporal dynamics, frequency spectrum, spatial networks, and pattern recognition. EEG is traditionally considered to have excellent temporal resolution among the various brain imaging techniques. Several temporal trials can be concatenated to improve the signal strength and to observe the transient changes. Spectral analysis is a vital technique for several cognitive, systems, and clinical neuroscientists [14]. Exploiting the spatial representation of EEG data generates significant relationships between brain regions. Therefore, EEG has been effectively employed to construct functional brain networks to reveal important topological features, further classifying different conditions [27]. The existence of complex associations in EEG data limits its interpretation based on simple visualization. However, multiple machine learning algorithms [21] enable multivariate analysis and importance-based feature selection for a given task.

The most notable feature of EEG data is brain oscillations, which have been connected to perceptual, cognitive, motor, and affective functions in several studies. The generation of neural oscillations formed on the basis of different microcircuits with diverse cognitive contexts can have distinctive computational importance and cognitive ramifications [9]. Broadly, neural oscillations have been divided into five frequency bands delta (1–3 Hz), theta (3.5–7 Hz), alpha (8–13 Hz), beta (13–30), and gamma (30–100 Hz). Brain rhythms have been largely studied among meditators depicting their relation with various cognitive factors such as focussed attention, attentional engagements, internalized attention, etc. There are noticeable changes in electrographic activity, both regionally and globally, during intensive meditation. The predominant role of brain rhythms is observed through increased mid-frontal theta among various mediators such as among open monitoring, focused attention, transcendental, and loving-kindness meditators [3,8,24]. Other brain waves observed among meditators are low frequency alpha (somatosensory region) and high frequency gamma (parieto-occipital region) rhythms. Overall, Advanced Meditators are found to have consistent electrographic changes which can be classified as a trait with a more clear understanding of these neural oscillatory correlates.

With the advent of complex network theory in recent years [17], researchers have shown that EEG can be used to construct brain networks, and resulting networks preserve numerous crucial topological properties [27]. Long-term meditation practice generates trait effects in practitioners, which in turn is associated with changes in functional networks [13]. In our study, expert meditators may reflect the topological alterations in the networks that may lead to discrimination between the two groups. We employed Phase Locking Value (PLV) to estimate the functional connectivity networks. Synchronized Interaction between two signals is usually measured using Coherence and PLV. Coherence provides imprecise measures with increasing signal-to-noise ratios and poor performance for non-stationary signals [12]. While PLV is well suited for non-linear and non-stationary EEG signals. PLV is an effective technique to estimate the instantaneous phase relationship between two neural signals [15]. A more practical explanation for its use in neuroimaging studies is that it is robust to amplitude variations that may contribute less synchronized information than the relative phase does [2].

Feature extraction is the step to create an optimized feature set to enhance the classifier's performance. Recent studies on meditation examining neural signature between expert and non-expert have utilized spectral analysis [4], wavelet technique [21], and non-linear analysis [22,23]. A recent study classifying meditation traditions using Random Forest successfully generalizes meditation traditions based on the scalp distribution of gamma-band entropy [26]. In the current study, we utilize phase-locking connectivity matrices to generate features and then develop several ML models to obtain the most discriminatory region and associated brain wave between expert and non-expert meditators. To the best of our knowledge, PLV has not been utilized to generate features in the meditation literature. Our research, on the other hand, focuses on four dimensions of EEG data, presenting a complete pipeline from data collection to analysis. This study classifies the oscillatory signature between expert and non-expert meditators with an aim to identify a) the optimum number of trials to generate connectivity matrix b) discriminatory features of different frequency bands c) significance of different scalp regions during meditation d) best-performing machine learning classifier.

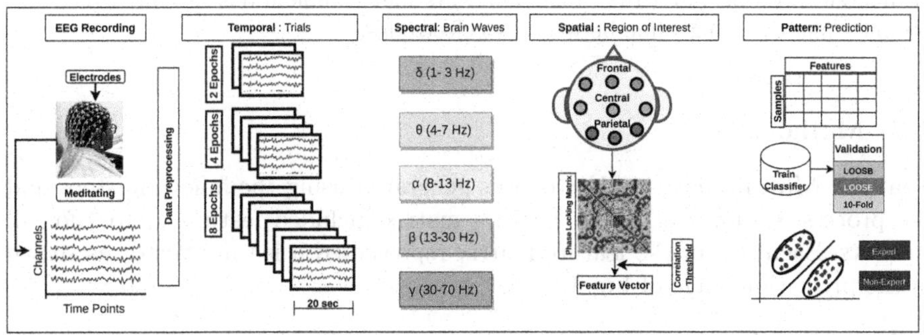

Fig. 1. Sequence of stages from EEG data acquisition to the prediction of brain state between expert and non-expert Himalayan Yoga meditators.

2 Materials and Methods

2.1 Data Description and Preprocessing

Data were obtained from an open access repository. The experimental paradigm with a detailed description is mentioned in the paper [4]. This study includes 24 meditators from the Himalayan Yoga tradition categorized as 12 experienced and 12 non-expert meditators. The expert group includes practitioners with a minimum of two hours of daily meditation for 1 year or longer, the non-expert group defines the practitioners who were acquainted with the meditation techniques but irregular in practice. Experience sampling probes were asked at random intervals ranging from 30 to 90 s, probe introduced to record the experience of the depth of the meditation, mind wandering and tiredness. Twenty second-epochs (trials) were extracted ranging from -20 s prior to the beginning of the question Q1. Standard EEG preprocessing steps were followed using EEGLAB software [11] and detailed steps are mentioned in this article [21].

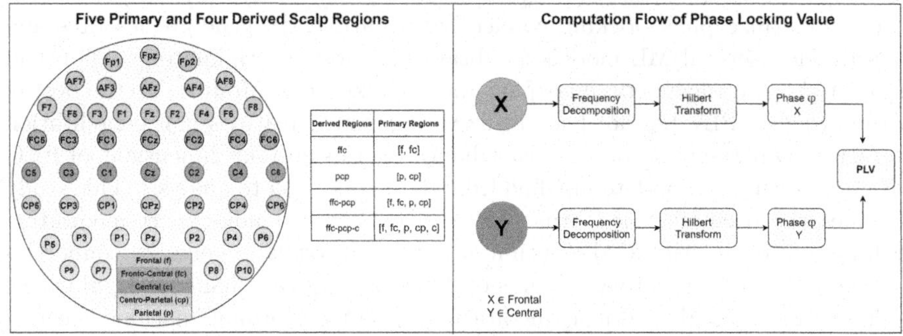

Fig. 2. [Left] Illustration of Five primary scalp regions based on the electrode placement in different positions, and the table defines its four combinations. [Right] Process to compute phase-locking value between two electrodes.

2.2 Methods

Feature Matrix. Feature Vector was generated using the following steps and the process is shown in Fig. 1. Feature matrix included feature vectors for all subjects. Each row of the feature matrix represented a feature vector as shown in the prediction stage of Fig. 1.

1. **Epoch Extraction:** Twenty second epochs (trials) were extracted and formed in two, four, and eight groups. It was because PLV computes the phase difference between two signals and average over several epochs.
2. **Decomposition and Regions of Interest:** Signals were filtered using the band-pass filter to obtain the frequency band of interest, for example, frequency range (1–3 Hz) and (4–7 Hz) denote delta and theta bands. Signals were classified based on the five scalp regions and their four combinations as described in Fig. 2.
3. **Hilbert Transform:** This was used to calculate the instantaneous phase value, which was further utilized to compute the phase-locking value. Analytic signal a(t) was computed for the provided EEG signal s(t) [25].

$$a(t) = s(t) + jH(t) = A(t)e^{\phi(t)} \tag{1}$$

where A(t) & $\phi(t)$ indicate the instantaneous amplitude and instantaneous phase of the signal s(t).

$$H(t) = \frac{1}{\Pi} P.V. \int_{-\infty}^{\infty} \frac{s(\tau))}{t - s(\tau)} d\tau \tag{2}$$

where H(t) is the Hilbert transform of s(t), P.V. indicates Cauchy principal value.

4. **Phase Locking Value:** Once the Hilbert Transform was computed, the phase-locking (pl) value was computed using the following equation [19]. Phase locking value varies from 0 (minimum) to 1 (maximum).

$$plv(t, a, b) = \left| \frac{1}{N} \sum_{j=1}^{n} e^{i(\phi_a(t) - \phi_b(t))} \right| \tag{3}$$

Here, $phi(t)$ is instantaenous phase at time point t, a & b are two channels, j represents the epoch (trial) and N indicates the total no. of trials.

5. **Averaging across time points:** Once the phase-locking value between the two signals was generated across timepoints, the phase-locking (PL) matrix was determined using the equation.

$$plv\_matrix(a, b) = \sum_{t=1}^{n} plv(t, a, b) \tag{4}$$

where t is the time points

6. **Correlation Threshold:** PL matrix was converted into a vector including correlated variables. Three thresholds 0.7, 0.75, and 0.8 were used to remove correlated variables and to create a feature vector. A model with fewer features is easier to interpret, less biased, and faster to train.

Machine Learning Classifiers. We trained five different models with hyperparameter tuning so that the variability of the data would be covered. Classifiers were SVM [Linear, C = 1], Adaboost (AB) [algorithm = SAMME.R, n_est = 50], Gaussian Process (GP) [optimizer = fmin_l_bfgs b,kernel = rbf], Random Forest (RF) [criterion = 'ginni', n_estimators = 30], and Quadratic Discriminant Analysis (QDA) [7].

Validation Techniques. Validation techniques made our study rigorous. We used three validation techniques to report the accuracy. The average accuracy of the testing sets is reported in this paper, keeping the accuracy from 0 to 1 as a minimum to maximum and rounded to 2 decimal places. It is a subject dependent analysis.

Leave One Out Subject (LOOSB): K-1 subjects were used for training and one subject for testing. Twenty four subjects were present in the dataset, each subject was considered for the testing and remaining subject used for training. Hence, there were 24 times of training and testing involved. It is a subject-independent analysis.

Leave One Out Session (LOOSE): The dataset had sessions for each participant varying from 1 to 3, depending on the willingness of a participant to sit comfortably for the experiment. In this technique, we iterated the session for testing and training. One session was left out for testing and remaining were included in the training. For example, the first subject has 3 sessions, so one session was considered for testing and the other two for training including other subjects also. This is a session-dependent analysis.

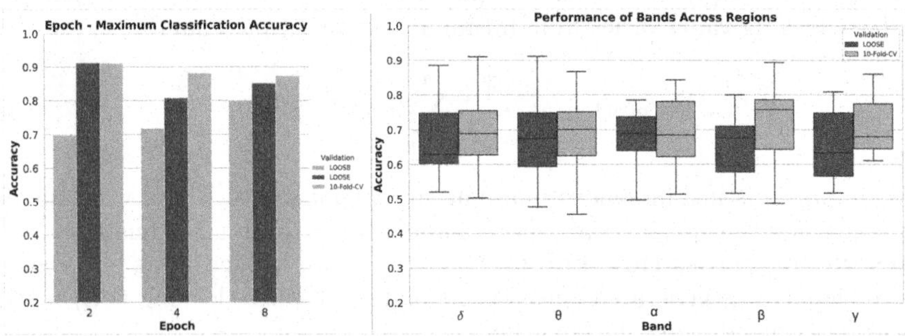

Fig. 3. [Left] Maximum classification accuracy obtained for each set of epochs, including all bands, regions, correlation thresholds, and classifiers. [Right] Performance of each frequency band during QDA classification, including all regions, two epochs, and correlation threshold of 80.

K-fold Validation: In this technique, the data matrix was divided into k-subsets and every subset was considered for training and testing set, K-1 subsets were used for training and the left out subset was used for validation. We used 10-fold validation. It is a subject dependent analysis.

3 Results

3.1 Identifying the Optimum Number of Epochs

In practice, varying the number of epochs has been suggested to obtain the best set for computing the connectivity matrix. We achieved a maximum classification accuracy of 91% in LOOSE and 10-Fold in 2 epochs and 80% in LOOSB in 8 epochs as shown in Fig. 3 [Left]. All three validation techniques performed above 80% accuracy in 8 epochs. We observed an increase in performance on LOOSB validation with an increase in epochs. Low performance of LOOSB validation possibly may occur due to inter-subject differences. Overall, our analysis suggests that 2 epochs are sufficient to measure the intra-subject performance, and more trials are required to increase subject-invariant learning.

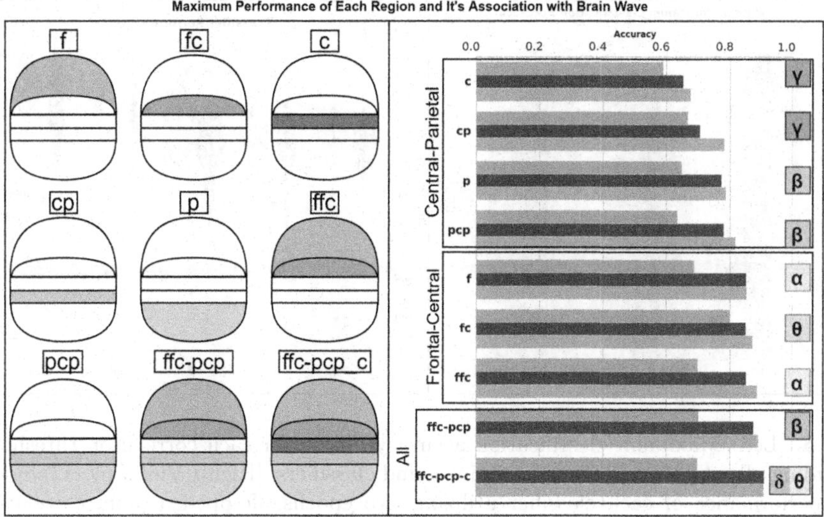

Fig. 4. [Left] Five primary regions (f to p) and their four derived regions (ffc to ffc-ppc-c). [Right] Maximum performance of each region, including all bands, correlation thresholds, and classifiers. Extreme right indicates the significance of the band with their respective region for maximum accuracy.

3.2 Significance of Brain Waves and Regions

We examined the role of frequency bands characterizing the difference between expert and non-expert meditators. Theta band showed maximum accuracy followed by the delta band as shown in Fig. 3 [Right]. Classification accuracy of 91% achieved in delta and theta whereas alpha, beta, and gamma obtained 84%, 89%, and 86%, respectively. We observed each band varied in their performance across regions, which led us to investigate each band's performance with respect to regions. In Fig. 4 [Right], the top box in the figure represents central, parietal, and their combinations. The middlebox indicates frontal and combinations of frontal and central, and the bottom box includes two frontal, central, and parietal combinations. The most dominant bands across central and parietal regions were beta and gamma. We found the most discriminatory characteristics from the frontal comprising of theta and alpha bands. Fronto-central region found to be a significant discriminator with an accuracy greater than 80% across three validation techniques. Region 'ffc_pcp_p' showed accuracy greater than 90% in 10-Fold and leave one out session. This performance may be due to each region's involvement, which increased more features for discrimination between two states of meditation.

3.3 Identifying the Best Feature Set and Classifier Performance

With few features, the model can learn efficiently and become more interpretable and less biased. We removed the correlated features and observed the highest

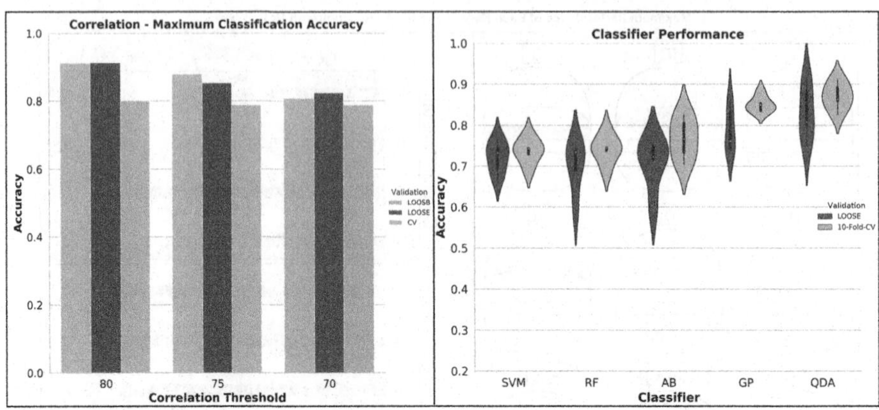

Fig. 5. [Left] Maximum classification accuracy obtain for each correlation threshold, including all sets of epoch, bands, regions, and classifiers. [Right] Violin plots indicate the performance of each classifier utilizing two epochs, ffc-ppc-c region, correlation threshold of 80, and all bands.

performance with correlation threshold of 80 as shown in Fig. 5 [Left]. QDA and Gaussian Process classifiers outperformed other mentioned classifiers. We obtained the highest accuracy in the 10-Fold and leave out one session. We observed a simple pattern of reducing accuracies with the elimination of sessions and subjects. Hence, this leads us to suggest that more data would boost the classifier's performance.

4 Discussion and Conclusion

In our current research, we explored features of expert Himlayana Yoga Meditators. We employed multidimensional features of EEG signals demonstrating a pipeline using functional brain networks (PLV) and machine learning techniques. Our findings revealed the enhancement of beta and gamma bands in the parietal electrodes and theta and alpha bands in the frontal electrodes. This finding, to some extent, is consistent with previous studies [4,8,16]. High-frequency bands such as beta and gamma indicate an attentive global state with a specific object in mind [10] and whereas theta and alpha rhythms are associated with attentional states of awareness [4]. Gamma and theta oscillations are identified as a trait effect based on hours of meditation practice. These findings were achieved using machine learning models. QDA outperformed all other classifiers and offered the opportunity for thorough inquiry to discover underlying structure or distribution from various meditative states. The poor performance in leave-one-out-subject (LOOSB) validation implies a shift in data distributions across subjects, indicating the well-known transfer learning problem. [20] and this may direct to utilize the state of the art deep learning techniques [18].

With three decades of contemplative research, meditation has been an effective tool to increase attentional engagement, well-being, and states of flow [6].

A key challenge for meditation training is absence of any feedback provided can be less rewarding and give rise to frustration for naive meditators. With recent advancements, Electroencephalography (EEG) headset technology [1] provides a mechanism for individuals to track their progress. However, processing those EEG signals and extracting features is crucial for classifying the different brain states, helping participants navigate their performance in a more customizable and flexible manner through neurofeedback [5]. Digital content and gadgets are now more widely available with significant advancements in digital technology and systems. As a result, there has been an increase in information overload possibly leading to overuse of the sensory, perceptual, and cognitive circuits involved in this process. In the long run, it can substantially impact our psychological and physical health. Meditation techniques, as a widely practiced mental training skill, are likely to exhibit increased cognitive control, attentional engagement, less mind-wandering, meta-cognitive awareness, compassion, etc. These skill sets can be mirrored into a Customized Meditation App to train individuals as per their needs. The respective computational models can be developed using state-of-the-art signal and machine learning techniques.

Acknowledgements. We thank SERB and PlayPower Labs for supporting PMRF Fellowship to Pankaj Pandey. We thank FICCI to facilitate this PMRF Fellowship.

References

1. Meditation made easy (2021). https://choosemuse.com/
2. Aydore, S., Pantazis, D., Leahy, R.M.: A note on the phase locking value and its properties. Neuroimage **74**, 231–244 (2013)
3. Baijal, S., Srinivasan, N.: Theta activity and meditative states: spectral changes during concentrative meditation. Cogn. Process. **11**(1), 31–38 (2010)
4. Brandmeyer, T., Delorme, A.: Reduced mind wandering in experienced meditators and associated EEG correlates. Exp. Brain Res. **236**(9), 2519–2528 (2018). https://doi.org/10.1007/s00221-016-4811-5
5. Brandmeyer, T., Delorme, A.: Closed-loop frontal midlineθ neurofeedback: a novel approach for training focused-attention meditation. Front. Hum. Neurosci. **14**, 246 (2020)
6. Brandmeyer, T., Delorme, A., Wahbeh, H.: The neuroscience of meditation: classification, phenomenology, correlates, and mechanisms. Prog. Brain Res. **244**, 1–29 (2019)
7. Buitinck, L., et al.: API design for machine learning software: experiences from the Scikit-learn project. In: ECML PKDD Workshop: Languages for Data Mining and Machine Learning, pp. 108–122 (2013)
8. Cahn, B.R., Delorme, A., Polich, J.: Occipital gamma activation during vipassana meditation. Cogn. Process. **11**(1), 39–56 (2010)
9. Cohen, M.X.: Where does EEG come from and what does it mean? Trends Neurosci. **40**(4), 208–218 (2017)
10. Colby, C.L., Goldberg, M.E.: Space and attention in parietal cortex. Annu. Rev. Neurosci. **22**(1), 319–349 (1999)

11. Delorme, A., Makeig, S.: EEGLAB: an open source toolbox for analysis of single-trial EEG dynamics including independent component analysis. J. Neurosci. Methods **134**(1), 9–21 (2004). https://doi.org/10.1016/j.jneumeth.2003.10.009
12. Deolindo, C.S., Ribeiro, M.W., Aratanha, M.A., Afonso, R.F., Irrmischer, M., Kozasa, E.H.: A critical analysis on characterizing the meditation experience through the electroencephalogram. Front. Syst. Neurosci. **14**, 53 (2020)
13. Hasenkamp, W., Barsalou, L.W.: Effects of meditation experience on functional connectivity of distributed brain networks. Front. Hum. Neurosci. **6**, 38 (2012)
14. Izhikevich, L., Gao, R., Peterson, E., Voytek, B.: Measuring the average power of neural oscillations. bioRxiv, 441626 (2018)
15. Lachaux, J.P., Rodriguez, E., Martinerie, J., Varela, F.J.: Measuring phase synchrony in brain signals. Hum. Brain Mapp. **8**(4), 194–208 (1999)
16. Lee, D.J., Kulubya, E., Goldin, P., Goodarzi, A., Girgis, F.: Review of the neural oscillations underlying meditation. Front. Neurosci. **12**, 178 (2018)
17. Li, X.J., Yang, G.H.: Graph theory-based pinning synchronization of stochastic complex dynamical networks. IEEE Trans. Neural Netw. Learn. Syst. **28**(2), 427–437 (2016)
18. Mahmud, M., Kaiser, M.S., McGinnity, T.M., Hussain, A.: Deep learning in mining biological data. Cogn. Comput. **13**(1), 1–33 (2021)
19. Namburi: Phase locking value. https://www.mathworks.com/matlabcentral/fileexchange/31600-phase-locking-value
20. Özdenizci, O., Wang, Y., Koike-Akino, T., Erdoğmuş, D.: Learning invariant representations from EEG via adversarial inference. IEEE Access **8**, 27074–27085 (2020)
21. Pandey, P., Miyapuram, K.P.: Classifying oscillatory signatures of expert vs non-expert meditators. In: 2020 International Joint Conference on Neural Networks (IJCNN), pp. 1–7. IEEE (2020)
22. Pandey, P., Miyapuram, K.P.: BRAIN2DEPTH: lightweight CNN model for classification of cognitive states from EEG recordings. arXiv preprint arXiv:2106.06688 (2021)
23. Pandey, P., Miyapuram, K.P.: Non-linear analysis of expert and non-expert meditators using machine learning (2021). https://doi.org/10.13140/RG.2.2.18323.60968. http://rgdoi.net/10.13140/RG.2.2.18323.60968
24. Pasquini, H.A., Tanaka, G.K., Basile, L.F.H., Velasques, B., Lozano, M.D., Ribeiro, P.: Electrophysiological correlates of long-term Soto Zen meditation. BioMed Res. Int. **2015** (2015)
25. Rosenblum, M.G., Pikovsky, A.S., Kurths, J.: Phase synchronization of chaotic oscillators. Phys. Rev. Lett. **76**(11), 1804 (1996). https://doi.org/10.1103/physrevlett.76.1804
26. Vivot, R.M., Pallavicini, C., Zamberlan, F., Vigo, D., Tagliazucchi, E.: Meditation increases the entropy of brain oscillatory activity. Neuroscience **431**, 40–51 (2020)
27. Zhang, B., Yan, G., Yang, Z., Su, Y., Wang, J., Lei, T.: Brain functional networks based on resting-state EEG data for major depressive disorder analysis and classification. IEEE Trans. Neural Syst. Rehabil. Eng. **29**, 215–229 (2020)

Exploring the Brain Information Processing Mechanisms from Functional Connectivity to Translational Applications

Hongzhi Kuai[1,2,6], Jianhui Chen[2,6], Xiaohui Tao[3], Kazuyuki Imamura[4], Peipeng Liang[5(✉)], and Ning Zhong[1,2,6(✉)]

[1] Department of Life Science and Informatics, Maebashi Institute of Technology, Maebashi, Gunma, Japan
zhong@maebashi-it.ac.jp
[2] International WIC Institute, Beijing University of Technology, Beijing, China
[3] School of Sciences, University of Southern Queensland, Toowoomba, Australia
[4] Maebashi Institute of Technology, Maebashi, Gunma, Japan
[5] School of Psychology and Beijing Key Laboratory of Learning and Cognition, Capital Normal University, Beijing, China
ppliang@cnu.edu.cn
[6] Beijing International Collaboration Base on Brain Informatics and Wisdom Services, Beijing, China

Abstract. Exploring information processing mechanisms in the human brain is of significant importance to the development of artificial intelligence and translational study. In particular, essential functions of the brain, ranging from perception to thinking, are studied, with the evolution of analytical strategies from a single aspect such as a single cognitive function or experiment to the increasing demands on the multi-aspect integration. Here we introduce a systematic approach to realize an integrated understanding of the brain mechanisms with respect to cognitive functions and brain activity patterns. Our approach is driven by a conceptual brain model, performs systematic experimental design and evidential type inference that are further integrated into the method of evidence combination and fusion computing, and realizes never-ending learning. It allows comparisons among various mechanisms on a specific brain-related disease by means of machine learning. We evaluate its ability from the brain functional connectivity perspective, which has become an analytical tool for exploring information processing of connected nodes between different functional interacting brain regions, and for revealing hidden relationships that link connectivity abnormalities to mental disorders. Results show that the potential relationships on clinical signs–cognitive functions–brain activity patterns have important implications for both cognitive assessment and personalized rehabilitation.

Keywords: Brain informatics · Cognitive neuroscience · Functional connectivity · Translational study

M. Mahmud et al. (Eds.): BI 2021, LNAI 12960, pp. 99–111, 2021.
https://doi.org/10.1007/978-3-030-86993-9_10

1 Introduction

Increasing evidence suggests that neuropsychiatries, such as depression, mild cognitive impairment and dementia, are associated with changes in the brain function and structure, which affect perception, attention, learning, memory, computation, reasoning, problem-solving and so forth. Many of these studies have integrated the quantitative assessments of clinical symptoms and pathophysiology into diagnostic and therapeutic procedures of neuropsychiatries. But recently, there are a growing number of studies to examine neuropsychiatries by exploring brain information processing mechanisms in cognition [1]. It is necessary to gain more insights into the information processing mechanisms of the brain and mental disorders with respect to various cognitive functions, which would be useful to develop contextually effective strategies and approaches from systems neuroscience to P4 (predictive, preventative, personalized, participatory) medicine.

In the last few years, advances in neuroimaging techniques such as functional magnetic resonance imaging (fMRI) have resulted in the explosion of studies related to the cognition and mental disorders. Especially, the graph theoretical approach for resting and task-related connectivity analyses has been employed to assess functional interactions in parameters of the regional node and global network. The study of mental disorders in brain cognition not only requires understanding the normal mechanisms of cognitive functions in the brain, but also needs a further understanding of abnormal mechanisms with potential linkages to various mental disorders. In the face of these challenges, the Brain Informatics methodology presents an opportunity for us to handle these issues, which investigates the brain information processing mechanisms with respect to the essential functions ranging from perception to thinking, and encompassing domains such as perception, attention, learning, memory, computation, reasoning and problem-solving [2]. Following this methodology, we propose a unique approach to uncover the brain information processing mechanisms related to thinking and perception through joint analyses of multiple experiments-related brain data continuously, hierarchically and incrementally. More specifically, our approach learns to capture the complex relationships between cognitive functions and brain activity patterns within a specific goal hypothesis. We show that it can evaluate the level of contribution of a certain brain activity pattern to a specific cognitive function through never-ending learning of experimental and computational brain data. Furthermore, these selected brain activity patterns at different levels would be transformed as features, and further be applied to clinical scenarios towards the translational study, to combine with the machine learning models.

In this paper, we evaluate the proposed approach by using task-related fMRI data from the connectivity perspective. The main contributions of this paper include the following: a conceptual Data-Brain model inspired by the Brain Informatics methodology is constructed; a systematic approach that realizes never-ending learning is proposed; and several case studies are presented from the functional connectivity to translational applications.

2 Method

2.1 Definition

The systematic approach is shown in Fig. 1, which is formalized as a loop towards never-ending learning of the brain information processing mechanisms and translational study.

Further details regarding the systematic approach are introduced as follows, including conceptual Data-Brain, systematic experimental design, evidential type inference, and evidence combination and fusion computing towards never-ending learning:

- *Conceptual Data-Brain.* The conceptual Data-Brain [3,4] provides a thinking space, which includes multiple knowledge graphs to represent the systematic brain investigation processes from four dimensions of function, experiment, data and analysis. It describes different scopes and their relations (including "include" and "related-to") at the conceptual level. If we solely consider the "include" relation in the subgraph of function, this graph will become a tree structure with "Function Dimension" being the root node.
- *Systematic Experimental Design.* Systematic experimental design indicates that the platform knows how to design the next experiment based on the heuristic from the previous experiments, depending on experimental types with similarity assessment through experiment dimension of the conceptual Data-Brain model. Experimental types have their own specificities and sequence characteristics, including the main experiment that corresponds directly to the goal hypothesis, as a starting point for systematic experimental design, and supplementary experiments that are inspired by the main experiment, as continuous supporting evidence for systematic fusion computing. To assess similarity ε between two experiments, it is necessary to describe the experimental profile such as paradigm- and stimuli-related factors, by which the design process is quantifiable. Here, we select three representative factors to realize this process, including experimental paradigm ($Edigm$), experimental protocol ($Eprot$) and explicit stimulus ($Estim$). Hence, the experimental similarity assessment can be realized on the basis of these experimental factors, $facs = \{Edigm, Eprot, Estim\}$, which is given by:

$$\varepsilon(T_M, T_S) = \frac{1}{the\ size\ of\ facs} \sum_{fac \in facs} BIN(T_M^{fac}, T_S^{fac}) \tag{1}$$

  where ε indicates the experimental similarity, T_M indicates the main experiment, T_S indicates a certain supplementary experiment; fac is the variable which indicates various factors in the $facs$; T_M^{fac} indicates the factor properties of the T_M at the fac, T_S^{fac} indicates the factor properties of the T_S at the fac; $BIN\left(T_M^{fac}, T_S^{fac}\right) = 1$ if the T_M^{fac} is consistent with T_S^{fac}.
- *Evidential Type Inference.* These evidences are classified into different types with evidence weight coefficient λ, namely Type-I and Type-II evidence,

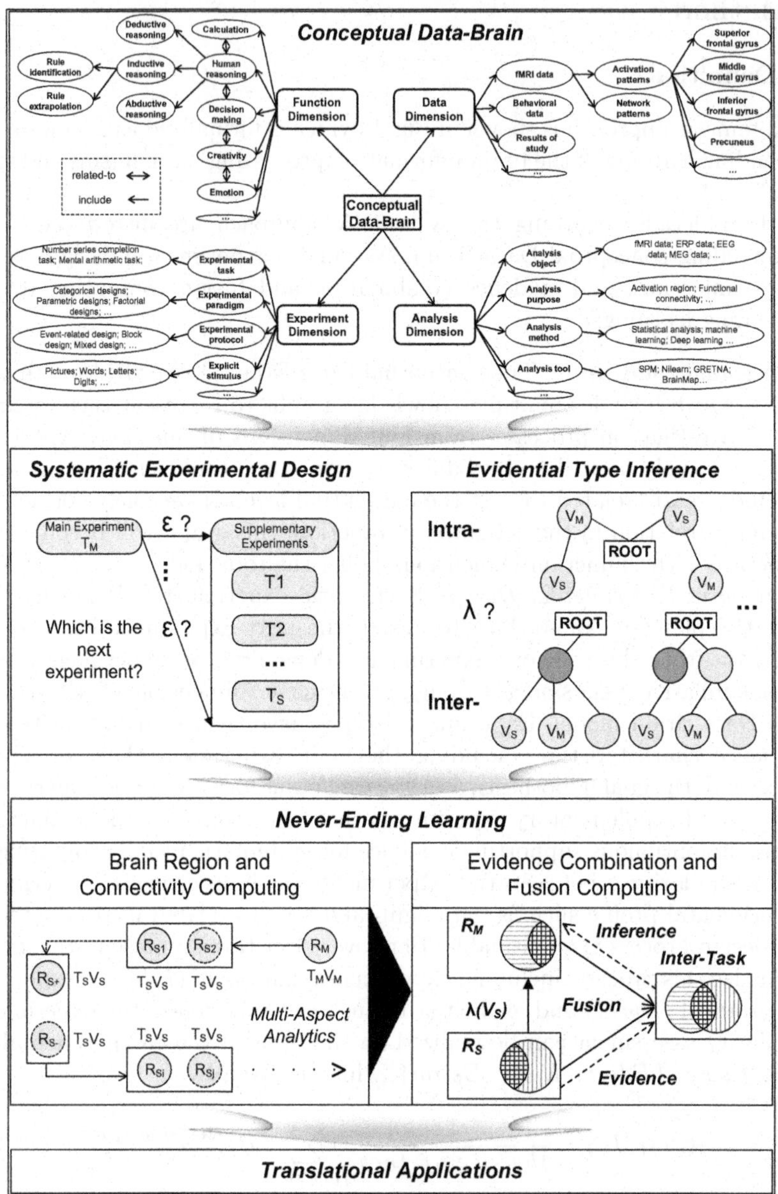

Fig. 1. The schematic diagram of the systematic approach. A conceptual Data-Brain model is constructed to guide systematic investigations of the complex brain science problems, systematic design of cognitive experiments, systematic brain data collection and management, as well as systematic brain data analysis and simulation stated in the Brain Informatics methodology. The hierarchical experimental design, evidential type inference, and evidence combination and fusion computing are performed to realize never-ending learning and translational applications.

which are identified by the inference capability in function dimension of the conceptual Data-Brain model. Here, the Type-I evidence is learned to help us strengthen credibility of the goal hypothesis, conversely, the Type-II evidence will increase the uncertainty of the goal hypothesis. In particular, if the evidence V_S corresponding to the supplementary experiment is identified as the Type-I evidence, it indicates that the functional domain of the V_S is the "ancestor" or "descendants" of the functional domain of the evidence V_M corresponding to the main experiment in function dimension of the conceptual Data-Brain model. Inversely, if the V_S is identified as the Type-II evidence, the functional domains of the V_M and V_S belong to other relationships that are different from the Type-I evidence, such as the "sibling" relationship. The λ coefficients are determined as follows: (1) if the functional domain of the V_S is the "descendants" of the functional domain of V_M, $\lambda = 1$; (2) if the functional domain of the V_S is the "ancestor" of the functional domain of V_M, $\lambda = \prod \frac{1}{degree\ of\ node}$, where the *node* is in the shortest path from the functional domain of the V_S to the parent of that of V_M in function dimension; (3) if the V_S belongs to the Type-II evidence, $\lambda = -1$.

- *Evidence Combination and Fusion Computing (ECFC).* Evidence combination indicates the selected evidence corresponding to multiple experiments is calculated on the basis of analysis dimension and aligned with a unified pattern type and size in such a loop. Furthermore, the computing results of these evidence are fused to measure the uncertainty distribution τ of brain functions on patterns (such as brain regions and/or network nodal information) underlying the goal hypothesis [5], which is given by:

$$\tau_{loop} = \sum_{i=1}^{N_{loop}} \lambda(V_i) \times Mask(GH_P) \times R(V_i) \tag{2}$$

where N_{loop} is the number of evidence that will be fused by the intersection of computing results in a loop, $\lambda(V_i)$ indicates the weight coefficient of the ith evidence, $Mask(GH_P)$ indicates the mask of patterns of interest from the goal hypothesis, $R(V_i)$ indicates the computing results of the ith evidence.

- *Never-ending Learning (NEL).* The never-ending learning indicates the new experiments, together with new evidence, are designed and combined by ECFC to test the goal hypothesis continuously. More specifically, along with iteration and evolution of the loop, the τ distribution is calculated and updated to interpret the multi-layer specificities of the brain functions on various patterns, which is given by:

$$\tau_{NEL} = \sum_{loop=1}^{\infty} \tau_{loop} \tag{3}$$

where τ_{NEL} indicates the τ distribution obtained by the cumulation of τ_{loop} from various loops. Theoretically, as the brain data is continuously acquired, the learning process can be performed forever. In addition to this mechanism, an end condition is also designed to ensure expected results that can

be observed. For more details, the τ distribution obtained by the Type-II evidence in a certain loop is used to exclude those parts where there is overlapping with the cumulative τ_{NEL}, until the τ_{NEL} is empty.
- *Translational Applications.* The learned multi-aspect patterns will be verified to build potential translational relationships with various clinical outcomes. In this part, the computational models are constructed.

2.2 Implementation

The general definition of the systematic approach is given in the previous section. We now implement this approach for systematic brain computing from the functional connectivity perspective. We quantify the properties of each network node to test the goal hypothesis – which brain patterns significantly support a specific cognitive function. Therefore, a goal hypothesis GH can be formalized as $GH = \{GH_F, GH_P\}$, where GH_F indicates the functional domain from function dimension and GH_P is a set of network nodes from the brain atlas. During never-ending learning process, each evidence is analyzed by graph theory, and then the effect of each node is evaluated to gain computing results R. The computing results of multiple evidence are fused to give the τ distribution for GH_P. Meanwhile, the ψ values of network nodes are recorded to determine whether the end condition is reached, where the initial value of ψ is zero. In particular, the ψ value of a network node is set to 1, if the effect of the network node is significant through evaluation of the Type-I evidence. Conversely, the ψ value of a network node is set to 0 and remains until the end of the program, if the effect of the network node is significant through evaluation of the Type-II evidence. In a certain loop, if the ψ values of all nodes in GH_P are 0, the end condition is reached.

3 Experiments

3.1 Sample Library

The fMRI data obtained by various experiments are summarized in Table 1, which is a fragment of the sample library. More specifically, each sample in this library is regarded as a chain of evidence that contains the functional neuroimaging data, purposes and results of studies, and their contexts such as experimental designs and processing methods.

3.2 Processing Pipeline

Data Preprocessing. The raw fMRI data were processed by the Statistical Parametric Mapping software (SPM, http://www.fil.ion.ucl.ac.uk/spm/software/) with the standard procedures, including slice-time correction, realignment to the median image, co-registration to the individual T1-weighted structural images, normalization to the Montreal Neurological Institute (MNI) template with a resampled voxel size of $3 \times 3 \times 3$ mm^3, spatial smooth with an 8 mm full-width at half-maximum (FWHM) Gaussian kernel, and temporal filtering with 0.008 Hz high-pass.

Table 1. A fragment of the sample library from multiple sources. In this library, each sample is regarded as a traceable "Function–Experiment–Brain Data–Analysis–Features" chain with the objective evidence, which is an instantiation of conceptual Data-Brain, including functional domain, experimental paradigm, experimental protocol, explicit stimulus, and so forth.

ID	*Fdomn*	*Edigm*	*Eprot*	*Estim*	Subjects (#)	
D1 [6]	Reasoning	Factorial	Event-related	Digits, Symbols	Healthy (11)	
D2 [6]	Social	Factorial	Event-related	Faces, Shapes	Healthy (30)	
D3 [7]	Reasoning, Calculation	Categorical	Block	Digits, Symbols	Healthy (15)	
D4 [8]	Reasoning	Factorial	Block	Digits,Letters	Healthy (23)	⋮
D5 [9]	Calculation	Categorical	Block	Digits, Symbols	Healthy (22)	
D6 [10]	Emotion, Calculation	Factorial	Block	Pictures	Healthy (13), MDD (13)	
D7 [11]	Reasoning	Factorial	Event-related	Digits	Healthy (15)	
			...			

MDD: Major Depressive Disorder; #: The number of subjects; Fdomn: functional domain.

Network Construction. Following previously published work [6], we used a structure-based automated anatomical atlas (AAL) with 90 nodes to construct connectome-wide networks [12]. The time series from the processed data for each node were extracted to build a 90×90 pairwise correlation matrix for each scan during each experiment using partial correlations. The derived correlation coefficients were normalized to Fisher's z score and the positive values were considered. Afterwards, these matrices were transformed to binary networks based on the various densities, where edges with value "1" were defined to the connections with coefficients higher than the given threshold.

Connectivity Measure. We quantified nodal contribution within the whole-brain functional network by two centrality measures, including: degree centrality and eigenvector centrality. For more details, these graph theoretical measures were described in [13]. All measures were calculated by using the NetworkX package (https://networkx.org).

3.3 Model Architecture

The GH_F of the goal hypothesis contained the functional domain of human reasoning. The GH_P was defined to 90 nodes using the AAL atlas. The significance of each node was determined by the ANOVA approach-based statistical comparisons of different conditions during each experiment for derived networks at 50 densities ranging from 0.01 to 0.5 with an increment interval of 0.01. After determination, the summation of the significant nodes was counted across all densities for each experiment and normalized to gain R as evidence. All evidences were further calculated to generate the multi-level τ distributions by the systematic approach mentioned above. Furthermore, the predication model was built on the basis of the support vector machine (SVM) algorithm to recognize patients with major depressive disorder (MDD) and the healthy control group, where the data were from D6 summarized in Table 1.

4 Results and Discussion

4.1 Estimating Functional Connectivity Property

Figure 2 shows the analytical processes of brain functional connectivity towards understanding the brain information processing mechanisms of human reasoning through Data-Brain driven never-ending learning. Four task-state fMRI data were matched and calculated, including: one human reasoning dataset generated by numeric and symbolic reasoning experiments from D1 summarized in Table 1, the emotional face dataset generated by happy and fear face matching experiments from D2, the mental arithmetic dataset generated by the addition and subtraction operation experiments from D5, and another human reasoning dataset generated by complex and simple numerical reasoning experiments from D7. Figure 2(a) shows the first case of analyzing functional connectivity through measuring nodal degree centrality in each loop, where the number of significant nodes changes accompanying with the combination of new evidence. Meanwhile, the τ distribution for some nodes also changes accompanying with fusion computing of evidential results. Figure 2(b) shows the second case based on the measures of eigenvector centrality, which reflects a similar situation with that of the degree centrality but shares some different nodal patterns. For instance, at the endpoints of two cases, some nodes (such as Precentral_L, Frontal_Inf_Orb_L and Postcentral_L) obtained by the measures of eigenvector centrality own higher τ values than that of degree centrality.

4.2 Prediction Experiments for Translational Study

The D6 dataset summarized in Table 1 includes the resting-state and emotional pictures-elicited fMRI data from patients suffering from MDD and the healthy controls, which is matched to verify the results of never-ending learning towards translational applications. The classification accuracies of both groups under different task states of resting and emotion are shown in Fig. 3, which are generated by using the SVM model with 10-fold cross-validation. These features are extracted on the basis of the face matching-related patterns provided in the previous section, where the D2 dataset is assigned as the main experiment followed by never-ending learning. The first 12 significant nodes with higher τ values are extracted as candidates, every three nodes of which are given as a feature pattern corresponding to a level. Hence, we got 10 levels from L1 with the highest τ distribution to L10 with the lowest τ distribution. Figure 3(a) shows the classification accuracies at various levels by using the feature patterns learned from the measures of degree centrality. Figure 3(b) shows the classification accuracies corresponding to the feature patterns learned from the measures of eigenvector centrality.

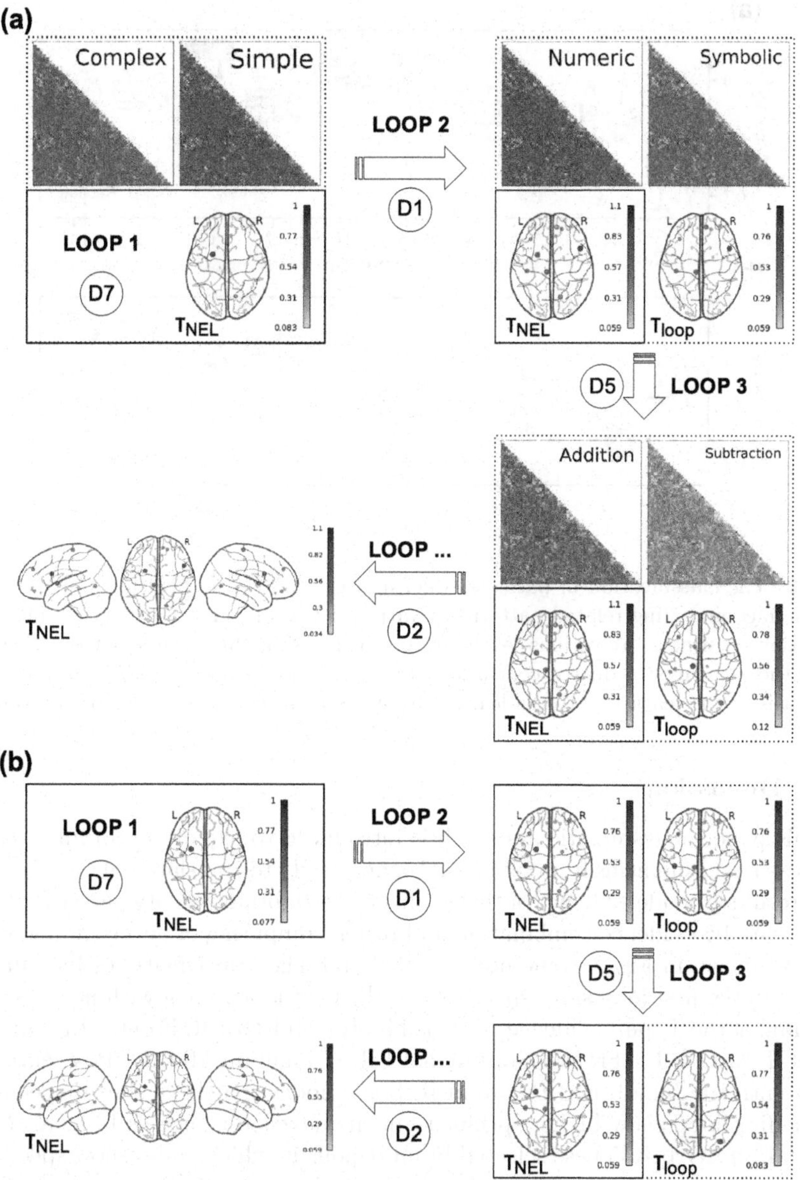

Fig. 2. The selected results of the functional connectivity analysis on human reasoning through Data-Brain driven never-ending learning. (a) The degree centrality is measured and their contrasts of both conditions for each experiment are performed to realize evidence combination and fusion computing in each loop. (b) The eigenvector centrality is also measured to realize never-ending learning. These fMRI datasets (including D1 obtained by the human reasoning task, D2 obtained by the face matching task, D5 obtained by the mental arithmetic task and D7 obtained by the human reasoning task) are matched, as summarized in Table 1.

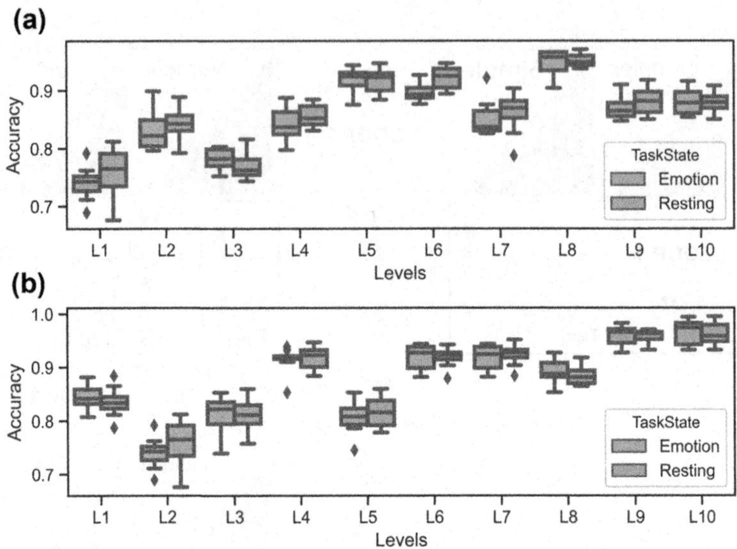

Fig. 3. The classification of patients suffering from MDD and healthy controls based on the face matching related patterns at various levels of τ distribution. (a) The classification accuracies at various levels are given by using the feature patterns learned from the measures of degree centrality; (b) the classification accuracies are given on the basis of the feature patterns learned from the measures of eigenvector centrality.

4.3 Discussion

In this paper, a systematic approach is introduced to explore brain information processing mechanisms from functional connectivity to translational applications. The results provide evidence of that ability to learn brain activity patterns at various levels by evidence combination and fusion computing of never-ending learning. As shown in Fig. 2, some nodes that do not show specificity for human reasoning in the first loop show specificity in the next loop, along with never-ending learning of the Type-I evidence, such as Frontal_Mid_Orb_R, Frontal_Inf_Oper_R, Frontal_Inf_Orb_L, Frontal_Sup_Medial_LR, Cingulum_Mid_R, Postcentral_L, Paracentral_Lobule_L and Pallidum_R. Some nodes that have shown specificity in the first loop show higher specificity in the next loop, such as Lingual_R and Frontal_Sup_Orb_R. These selected brain regions in which nodes show specificity for human reasoning were also taken into account in previous work, such as the prefrontal cortex [14]. Meanwhile, we can find that some of those node-related brain regions are also related to other functional domains, which are explored by combinations of the Type-II evidence, such as executive control, language, emotion and episodic memory [15,16]. For instance, as shown in Fig. 2, some nodes that have shown high specificity for human reasoning show lower specificity in the next loop, including Frontal_Mid_Orb_R, Postcentral_L, Pallidum_R and so forth. In this paper, the nodes are given various τ values that reflect the level of participation of brain regions and their contributions for a specific functional domain through never-ending learning of functional connectivity. On that basis, the nodes can be further divided into different feature patterns to achieve an extensive validation of the systematic approach for translational applications. Especially, the abnormal brain functions are evaluated to help perform objective diagnoses and personalized rehabilitation. From Fig. 3, we can find that such layered feature patterns obtained by the τ distribution play a meaningful role in this process, through the comprehensive comparison of classification accuracies at various levels. On the one hand, the classification accuracies with better and more stable trends have been observed from L1 to L10. It would be concluded that the MDD group in this experiment performs the abnormal function that is not closely related to the face matching-related cognition, but others. On the other hand, there are no significant differences between classification results of task states on resting and emotion, which can be interpreted by the independence, differentiation and specificity of the selected face matching-related feature patterns.

Most of the studies that focus on modeling multi-task brain data primarily adopt the flattening strategies, but overlook the differential contributions of each task in various contexts [17,18]. In such a systematic approach, the brain data generated by various cognitive experiments can be computed by selecting various machine learning and data analytic methods that are defined in the conceptual Data-Brain model. Furthermore, the computed results of which are taken as different types of evidence for evidential inference and learning from the never-ending perspective [19]. Our approach is a learning engine that narrows the gap among brain mechanisms, functional domains and mental health through the multi-level interpretations of the τ distribution. In the future, it will be important to develop more techniques that allow the systematic approach to handle brain science problems with multi-modal and multi-scale brain computing. Meanwhile, the learned data, information and knowledge for cognition, emotion and diseases will be refined and linked to the conceptual Data-Brain model continuously, which extend the scope of the sample library to make it suitable for more scenarios.

5 Concluding Remarks

Although the great improvements have been made in the field of brain science, it is difficult to give a clear mapping from various brain activity patterns to cognition, emotion and diseases, the crucial issue of which reflects uncertainty. Recent progress in Brain Informatics has opened up an avenue for investigating the complex brain science problems systematically by means of the experimental and computational neuroscience in the big data era. In this paper, we introduce the Data-Brain model inspired by the Brain Informatics methodology to support a systematic representation of the complex brain and cognition big data. We also propose a new "learning" paradigm, namely Data-Brain driven never-ending learning, to process brain data continuously, hierarchically and incrementally, as well as give multi-aspect interpretations for such uncertainty. This systematic approach could leverage the advantages of variety and volume of brain data, hence speed up the process of translational applications under various scenarios.

Acknowledgements. This work is partially supported by grants from the JSPS Grants-in-Aid for Scientific Research of Japan (19K12123), the National Natural Science Foundation of China (61420106005), the National Basic Research Program of China (2014CB744600), the National Key Research and Development Project of China (2020YFC2007302) and the Key Research Project of Academy for Multi-disciplinary Studies of Capital Normal University (JCKXYJY2019019).

References

1. Cuijpers, P.: Targets and outcomes of psychotherapies for mental disorders: an overview. World Psychiatry **18**(3), 276–285 (2019). https://doi.org/10.1002/wps.20661
2. Zhong, N., Bradshaw, J.M., Liu, J., Taylor, J.G.: Brain informatics. IEEE Intell. Syst. **26**(5), 16–21 (2011). https://doi.org/10.1109/MIS.2011.83
3. Zhong, N., Chen, J.: Constructing a new-style conceptual model of brain data for systematic brain informatics. IEEE Trans. Knowl. Data Eng. **24**(12), 2127–2142 (2011). https://doi.org/10.1109/TKDE.2011.139
4. Kuai, H., Zhong, N.: The extensible data-brain model: architecture, applications and directions. J. Comput. Sci. 101103 (2020). https://doi.org/10.1016/j.jocs.2020.101103
5. Kuai, H., et al.: Multi-source brain computing with systematic fusion for smart health. Inf. Fusion **75**, 150–167 (2021). https://doi.org/10.1016/j.inffus.2021.03.009
6. Kuai, H., Zhang, X., Yang, Y., Chen, J., Shi, B., Zhong, N.: Thinking-loop: the semantic vector driven closed-loop model for brain computing. IEEE Access **8**, 4273–4288 (2020). https://doi.org/10.1109/ACCESS.2019.2963070
7. Liang, P., Jia, X., Taatgen, N.A., Borst, J.P., Li, K.: Activity in the fronto-parietal network indicates numerical inductive reasoning beyond calculation: An fMRI study combined with a cognitive model. Sci. Rep. **6**(1), 1–10 (2016). https://doi.org/10.1038/srep25976
8. Liang, P., Jia, X., Taatgen, N.A., Zhong, N., Li, K.: Different strategies in solving series completion inductive reasoning problems: an fMRI and computational study. Int. J. Psychophysiol. **93**(2), 253–260 (2014). https://doi.org/10.1016/j.ijpsycho.2014.05.006
9. Yang, Y., et al.: The functional architectures of addition and subtraction: network discovery using fMRI and DCM. Hum. Brain Mapp. **38**(6), 3210–3225 (2017). https://doi.org/10.1002/hbm.23585
10. Yang, Y., et al.: Task and resting-state fMRI reveal altered salience responses to positive stimuli in patients with major depressive disorder. PLoS ONE **11**(5), e0155092 (2016). https://doi.org/10.1371/journal.pone.0155092
11. Zhong, N., Liang, P.P., Qin, Y.L., Lu, S.F., Yang, Y.H., Li, K.C.: Neural substrates of data-driven scientific discovery: an fMRI study during performance of number series completion task. Sci. China Life Sci. **54**(5), 466–473 (2011). https://doi.org/10.1007/s11427-011-4166-x
12. Tzourio-Mazoyer, N., et al.: Automated anatomical labeling of activations in SPM using a macroscopic anatomical parcellation of the MNI MRI single-subject brain. Neuroimage **15**(1), 273–289 (2002). https://doi.org/10.1006/nimg.2001.0978
13. Zuo, X.N., et al.: Network centrality in the human functional connectome. Cereb. Cortex **22**(8), 1862–1875 (2011). https://doi.org/10.1093/cercor/bhr269

14. Crescentini, C., Seyed-Allaei, S., De Pisapia, N., Jovicich, J., Amati, D., Shallice, T.: Mechanisms of rule acquisition and rule following in inductive reasoning. J. Neurosci. **31**(21), 7763–7774 (2011). https://doi.org/10.1523/JNEUROSCI.4579-10.2011
15. Bubb, E.J., Metzler-Baddeley, C., Aggleton, J.P.: The cingulum bundle: anatomy, function, and dysfunction. Neurosci. Biobehav. Rev. **92**, 104–127 (2018). https://doi.org/10.1016/j.neubiorev.2018.05.008
16. Balsters, J.H., Laird, A.R., Fox, P.T., Eickhoff, S.B.: Bridging the gap between functional and anatomical features of cortico-cerebellar circuits using meta-analytic connectivity modeling. Hum. Brain Mapp. **35**(7), 3152–3169 (2014). https://doi.org/10.1002/hbm.22392
17. Cole, M.W., Reynolds, J.R., Power, J.D., Repovs, G., Anticevic, A., Braver, T.S.: Multi-task connectivity reveals flexible hubs for adaptive task control. Nat. Neurosci. **16**(9), 1348–1355 (2013). https://doi.org/10.1038/nn.3470
18. Cao, H., et al.: Cross-paradigm connectivity: reliability, stability, and utility. Brain Imaging Behav. **15**(2), 614–629 (2020). https://doi.org/10.1007/s11682-020-00272-z
19. Mitchell, T., et al.: Never-ending learning. Commun. ACM **61**(5), 103–115 (2018). https://doi.org/10.1145/3191513

Investigations of Human Information Processing Systems

Spectral Properties of Local Field Potentials and Electroencephalograms as Indices for Changes in Neural Circuit Parameters

Pablo Martínez-Cañada[1,2(✉)] and Stefano Panzeri[1,3]

[1] Neural Computation Laboratory, Center for Neuroscience and Cognitive Systems, Istituto Italiano di Tecnologia, Genova and Rovereto, Italy
pablo.martinez@iit.it

[2] Optical Approaches to Brain Function Laboratory, Istituto Italiano di Tecnologia, Genova, Italy

[3] Department of Neural Information Processing, Center for Molecular Neurobiology (ZMNH), University Medical Center Hamburg-Eppendorf (UKE), Hamburg, Germany
stefano.panzeri@zmnh.uni-hamburg.de

Abstract. Electrical measurements of aggregate neural activity, such as local field potentials (LFPs) or electroencephalograms (EEGs), can capture oscillations of neural activity over a wide range of frequencies and are widely used to study brain function and dysfunction. However, relatively little is known about how to relate features of such aggregate neural recordings to the functional and anatomical configurations of the underlying neural circuits that produce them. An important neural circuit parameter which has profound effects on neural network dynamics and neural function is the ratio between excitation and inhibition (E:I), which has been found to be atypical in many neuropsychiatric conditions. Here we used simulations of recurrent networks of point-like leaky integrate-and-fire (LIF) neurons to study how to infer parameters such as the E:I ratio or the magnitude of the external input of the network from aggregate electrical measures. We used approximations (or proxies), validated in previous work, to generate realistic LFPs and EEGs from simulations of such networks. We computed different spectral features from simulated neural mass signals, such as the 1/f spectral power law or the Hurst exponent (H), and studied how these features changed when we changed the E:I ratio or the strength of the external input of the network model. We discuss how different spectral features of aggregate signals relate to the E:I ratio or the strength of the external input and outline our efforts to fit our model, in future work, to multiple measures extracted from empirical recordings of aggregate neural activity.

This work was supported by the European Union's Horizon 2020 research and innovation programme under the Marie Skłodowska-Curie (grant agreement No. 893825 to P.M.C), the NIH Brain Initiative (grants U19NS107464 to S.P. and NS108410 to S.P.) and the Simons Foundation (SFARI Explorer 602849 to S.P.).

M. Mahmud et al. (Eds.): BI 2021, LNAI 12960, pp. 115–123, 2021.
https://doi.org/10.1007/978-3-030-86993-9_11

Keywords: Biomarker · Excitation · Inhibition · Local field potential (LFP) · Electroencephalogram (EEG) · Neural network model

1 Introduction

Electrical recordings of aggregate neural activity, such as local field potentials (LFPs) or electroencephalograms (EEGs), have been a mainstream technique for studying large-scale brain dynamics, with important applications for both scientific research [5,10,13,19] and clinical diagnosis [2,3,21,24]. These recordings have been shown to capture how oscillatory aspects of neural activity change, over a wide range of frequencies, with cognitive or sensory tasks or in brain dysfunction [6,8,10,12]. Aggregate neural signals conflate different neural processes within and among different classes of cells and different spatial locations. This makes them difficult to interpret in terms of contributions of the different underlying neural phenomena. Determining the individual neural mechanisms that give rise to the different features of LFPs and EEGs, and quantifying how these features change with manipulations of neural circuits or in brain disorders, would significantly enhance our ability to understand the brain. Yet, how to accomplish this remains a major and largely unaddressed challenge.

An important parameter that describes local neural circuit dynamics is the excitation and inhibition (E:I) ratio. This ratio has been theorized to be a potential biomarker of many medical conditions, including autism [20,22]. Neural network models [4,11] have demonstrated that changes in the E:I ratio of the network have a direct effect on the spectral shape of neural activity, which suggests that features of power spectra of neural time-series data could be used to predict the E:I ratio. In previous work [23], we investigated different measures computed on the power spectrum of LFPs and blood oxygen level dependent (BOLD) signal that could be used to reliably estimate the E:I ratio: the exponent of the 1/f spectral power law, slopes for the low- and high-frequency regions of the spectrum and the Hurst exponent (H). We simulated the LFP and BOLD signal from our recurrent network model [7,15,17,18] of leaky integrate-and-fire (LIF) neuronal populations, and studied how these spectral measures changed when we manipulated the E:I ratio by independently varying the strengths of the inhibitory (g_I) and excitatory (g_E) synaptic conductances.

In this paper we take steps forward from our prior work [23] and present new results in the following directions. First, we used more realistic models to generate neural mass signals. In previous work [23], we computed the network's LFP as the sum of absolute values of synaptic currents. This is a simple and reasonable approximation (or proxy), which has been shown to work fairly well in describing both real cortical data [1,15,17] and field potentials and EEGs generated by simulations with networks of realistically-shaped 3D neurons [14, 16]. However, our recent work has demonstrated that it is possible to obtain better approximations of the LFP/EEG from networks of point neurons [14,16]. Second, in addition to previous spectral measures based on frequency slopes or H, here we analyze other metrics of power spectra to perform a systematic study of how different spectral features may contribute to the underlying changes in neural network parameters. We thus investigated how frequency slopes, H and other spectral properties (e.g., gamma peak frequency and gamma band power) of the different proxies change as a function of the ratio between inhibitory and excitatory conductances ($g = g_I/g_E$). Consistent with previous results [4, 17], we increased the firing rate of the external input of the network model to produce stronger and faster gamma oscillations in the proxy power spectra and we evaluated how these spectral measures are affected by this oscillatory activity. This led us to identify complementary ways in which different spectral features of aggregate neural signals encode changes in the network parameters.

Based on these encouraging results, in the Discussion, we pursue the idea that a suitable combination of spectral properties of LFPs/EEGs could be used to isolate such biomarkers of E:I ratio in power spectrum curves that have both 1/f aperiodic and periodic components.

2 Results

2.1 Simulation of Power Spectra of Neural Mass Signals from a Recurrent Network Model

As described in previous work [7,14,15,17,23], we used a network model of excitatory and inhibitory LIF neurons recurrently connected to simulate realistic cortical dynamics. The network was composed of 5000 neurons: 4000 were excitatory and 1000 inhibitory. The neurons were randomly connected with a connection probability between each pair of neurons of 0.2. This means that, on average, the number of incoming excitatory and inhibitory connections onto each neuron was 800 and 200, respectively. The network receives external synaptic input that carries sensory information and stimulus-unrelated inputs representing slow ongoing fluctuations of cortical activity.

From simulation of the point-like neuron network model, we computed different approximations (termed proxies) of aggregate electrical signal based on a weighted sum of synaptic currents. The first proxy is the average sum of absolute values of all synaptic currents ($\sum |I|$). The second proxy is a parametrized linear combination of AMPA and GABA currents that was found to perform well in approximating the LFP [16]: the LFP reference weighted sum (LRWS). We also evaluated a new class of current-based proxies whose parameters were optimized to fit the EEG across different network states of the point-neuron network [14]: the EEG reference weighted sum 1 (ERWS1) and the EEG reference weighted sum 2 (ERWS2). The difference between ERWS1 and ERSW2 is that parameters of ERWS2 adapt theirs values as a function of the strength of the external input ν_0, whereas the parameters of ERWS1 are not dependent on ν_0.

We then generated a large set of numerical simulations by systematically varying two parameters of the network model that are of interest to our study: the ratio between inhibitory and excitatory conductances ($g = g_I/g_E$), which is hypothesized to be related to the E:I ratio in the brain, and the firing rate ν_0 of the external input, which can elicit entrainment of gamma oscillations in the model.

For each simulation, we computed the power spectral density (PSD) functions of all the proxies and their spectral features were parametrized in the (1–150) Hz frequency range by two fitting algorithms. The first one is the FOOOF algorithm [9], which automatically splits neural PSDs into 1/f aperiodic and periodic (oscillatory) components. Parameters of the FOOOF algorithm were selected as follows. Maximum number of peaks: 2 ($\nu_0 = 1.5$ spikes/s), 3 ($\nu_0 = 2$ spikes/s) and 4 ($\nu_0 =$ 3 spikes/s). Peak width limits: (5–100) Hz. Peak threshold: 2 standard deviations. We also computed the piecewise linear regression functions that fit the proxy PSDs over two different frequency ranges (with a cutoff frequency that was 30 Hz for ν_0 = 1.5 or 2 spikes/s and 40 Hz for $\nu_0 = 3$ spikes/s).

Some example PSDs and their spectral fittings are shown in Fig. 1 for 3 levels of strength of external input ν_0 (1.5, 2 and 3 spikes/s) and 3 values of g (5.6, 11.3 and 14.8). The PSDs generated by our model exhibited both periodic and 1/f aperiodic components whose properties were modified by the choice of values of g and ν_0. For the reference value $g = 11.3$ [15,17], when the external rate was low ($\nu_0 = 1.5$ spikes/s), the power spectrum was dominated by the aperiodic component that has a 1/f-like distribution, with exponentially decreasing power across increasing frequencies. An increase of ν_0 ($\nu_0 = 2$ and 3 spikes/s) added periodic oscillatory peaks to the 1/f curve, which were more prominent in the gamma range (30–100 Hz). The dependence of the gamma oscillation on the input rate shows that, consistent with previous results [7,17], the gamma oscillation becomes stronger and faster as the input is increased.

2.2 Changes in the Ratio Between Inhibitory and Excitatory Conductances and External Input Strength Modulate Spectral Features

Changing g from the reference value shifted the network dynamics to different neural regimes, an excitation-dominated regime ($g < 11.3$) or an inhibition-dominated regime ($g > 11.3$), and modified properties of gamma oscillations. We computed from our model three measures to quantify spectral features in the gamma band: peak frequency, power modulation and peak bandwidth. We plotted them in Fig. 2 as a function of the inhibition-excitation ratio (g). Overall, a decrease of g from the reference value (that is, g is shifted in favor of excitation) produced more prominent changes in parameter values of the gamma oscillation than an increase of g. When g was decreased, we observed a decrease of the peak frequency, a weaker power modulation and a reduction of the peak bandwidth. While the peak frequency and the peak power modulation were the two metrics that produced the most similar values across proxies, the peak bandwidth values showed more variability across proxies and also over the values of g. It is important to note that the relationship between g and spectral parameters in the inhibition-dominated regime flattens out for low values of strength of external input ($\nu_0 = 2$ spikes/s). However, an increase of the strength of external input ($\nu_0 = 3$ spikes/s) produced variations of parameters of gamma oscillations in the inhibition-dominated regime that were sizeable.

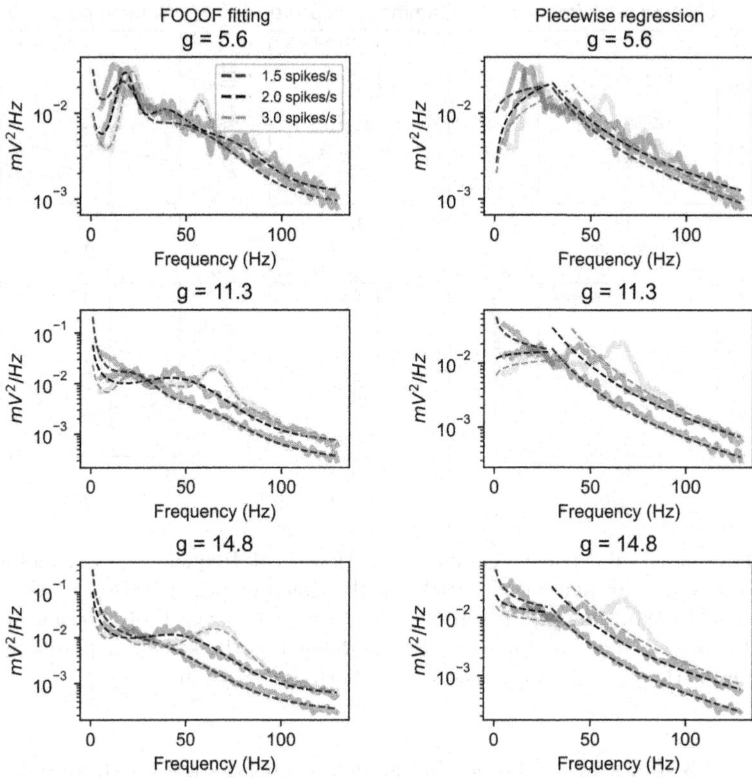

Fig. 1. Examples of proxy PSDs (solid lines) and spectral fittings (dashed lines) using the FOOOF algorithm [9] or a piecewise linear regression, plotted for 3 levels of strength of external input ν_0 (1.5, 2 and 3 spikes/s) and 3 values of g (5.6, 11.3 and 14.8). The PSDs were computed using the ERWS2 proxy.

Based on our previous work [23], we calculated slopes for the low- and high-frequency regions, slope of the 1/f aperiodic component generated by the FOOOF algorithm and the Hurst exponent (H) as a function of g, but here (Fig. 3) we extended our previous work by computing and comparing these spectral metrics for different proxy PSDs and for a stronger gamma oscillation ($\nu_0 = 3$ spikes/s). The different proxies produced similar values of low-frequency slopes for all rates of external input ($\nu_0 = 1.5$, 2 and 3 spikes/second). The high-frequency slope, aperiodic slope and H of the different proxies showed similar shapes as a function of g but with different offsets that depended on the external input rate. As the external input rate increased, the proxies produced values of slopes and H that were clustered in two groups: one formed by $\sum|I|$ and LRWS and the other by ERWS1 and ERWS2.

In agreement with our previous results [23], an increase in g beyond the reference value (shifting g towards stronger inhibition) had a weaker effect on slopes and H for $\nu_0 = 1.5$ or 2 spikes/s. However, when we increased the external

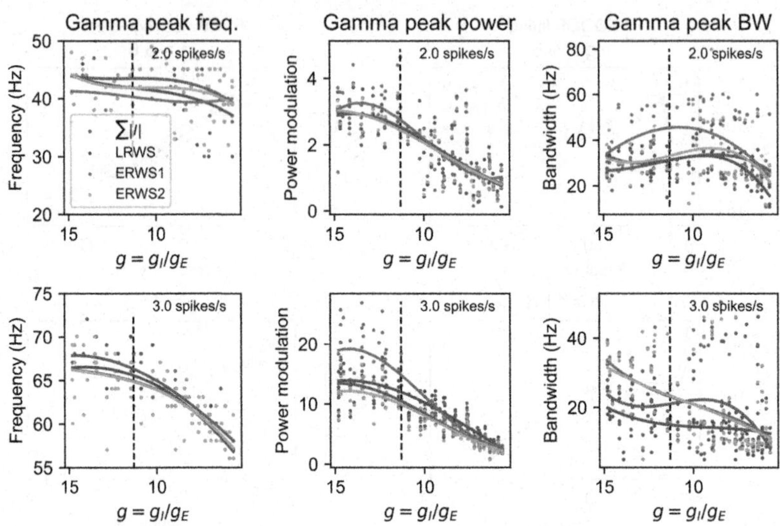

Fig. 2. Parameter values of the gamma oscillation (peak frequency, power modulation of the peak and peak bandwidth - BW) of the different proxy PSDs ($\sum|I|$, LRWS, ERWS1 and ERWS2), as a function of g for 2 levels of strength of external input ν_0 (2 and 3 spikes/s). The gamma oscillation is defined as the strongest power peak for frequencies 30 Hz ($\nu_0 = 1.5$ or 2 spikes/s) or 40 Hz ($\nu_0 = 3$ spikes/s).

input ($\nu_0 = 3$ spikes/s), we found that slopes (especially the low-frequency slope and aperiodic slope) in the inhibition-dominated regime showed changes comparable to changes in the excitation-dominated regime. Slopes in the excitation-dominated regime ($g < 11.3$) increase, that is, slopes flatten with decreasing g, although the relative amount of increase of the slopes is different depending on the value of ν_0. Analogously, H decreases with decreasing g below the baseline reference value for $\nu_0 = 1.5$ or 2 spikes/s. Changes in H as a function of g are less clear for $\nu_0 = 3$ spikes/s.

2.3 Major Limitations of the LFP and EEG Proxies

In the definition and computation of LFP and EEG proxies, we made some simplifying assumptions [14,16]. We considered a single cortical layer in the generation of LFPs/EEGs (L2/3) instead of the multi-layer structure of cortex. Although we have shown that our proxies generalize well for different L2/3 pyramidal-cell morphologies [14,16], it will be important to extend our work to quantify contributions from other cortical laminae and cell morphologies to the LFPs/EEGs. Another limitation is that our simple recurrent network model cannot produce internally generated oscillations in the canonical lower-frequency bands (delta, theta, alpha, and beta) commonly observed in EEG and MEG. The connectivity of the recurrent network model was distance-independent, which approximates the local connectivity of a cortical column. Since the EEG signal

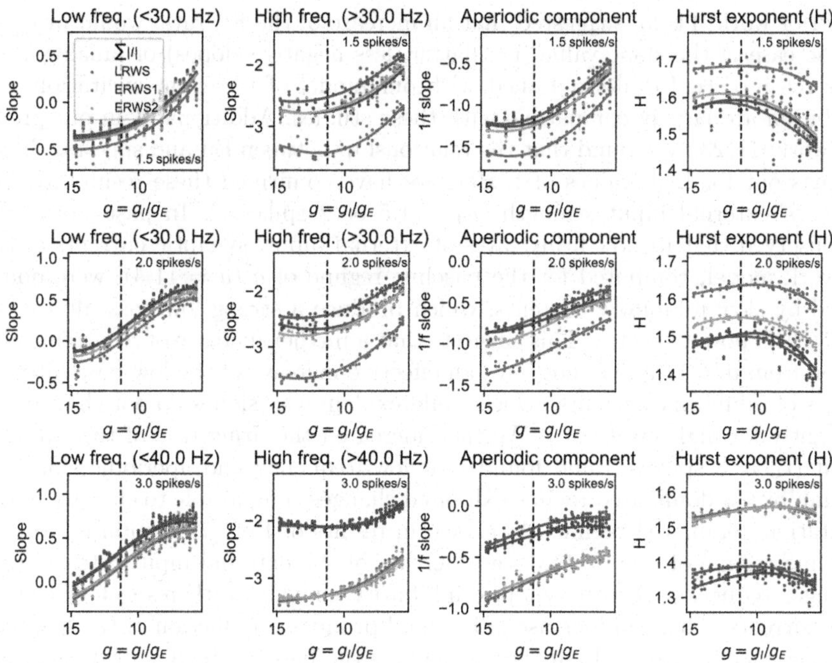

Fig. 3. Low- and high-frequency slopes, 1/f aperiodic component and H values, computed for the different proxy PSDs ($\sum|I|$, LRWS, ERWS1 and ERWS2), plotted as a function of g for three different firing rates of external input ν_0 (1.5, 2 and 3 spikes/second).

may integrate neural activity from distances typically larger than a cortical column, it will be essential to include realistic distance-dependent connectivity in future versions of the EEG proxies.

3 Discussion

In this work we explored the idea that spectral properties of neural mass signals (e.g., LFPs or EEGs) could be used to isolate key descriptors of the underlying neural circuit, such as the E:I ratio. We used a recurrent network model [7, 15,17,18] to simulate power spectra of aggregate neural signals and studied how spectral properties changed when manipulating the ratio between inhibitory and excitatory conductances ($g = g_I/g_E$). The metrics that we used are based on spectral properties commonly used in the literature to analyze the spectral shape of neural activity [9,11], such as the 1/f slope or the Hurst exponent (H). Here we have extended our previous work [23] by studying the effects of gamma oscillatory activity on these spectral metrics and by utilizing, and comparing, different proxies proposed in the literature to generate the LFP or EEG from networks of point neurons.

Prior work [11,23] suggested that an increase of the E:I ratio would produce an increase of the slope value (i.e. flatter, less negative slopes) or, analogously, a decrease of H. Results obtained with our model of recurrent excitation and inhibition are largely compatible with these studies. Additionally, in our previous work [11,23], we found that the relationship between E:I and spectral slopes flattens out for high values of I. Here we have confirmed these results for low levels of external input strength ($\nu_0 = 1.5$ or 2 spikes/s). In past work [14], we observed that for low firing rates of external input, synaptic currents of the network model, computed for the baseline regime of g ($g = 11.3$), were dominated by slow inhibitory currents, which produce a strong low-pass filtering of LFP/EEG power spectra. This suggests that a further increase of recurrent inhibition from $g = 11.3$ may not have an effective increase of the low-pass filtering effects of inhibitory currents, which could explain why slopes do not change significantly for high values of I. We then increased the firing rate of the external input ($\nu_0 = 3$ spikes/s) and found that low-frequency and aperiodic slopes in the inhibition-dominated regime exhibited changes comparable to changes in the excitation-dominated regime. As shown in results of Ref. [7], computed for the baseline regime of g ($g = 11.3$), an increase of the external input rate led to a stronger reduction of post-synaptic inhibitory currents with respect to excitatory currents. Thus, an increase of ν_0 could produce a reduction of the low-pass filtering effect of slow inhibitory currents for the baseline regime of g, resulting in flatter aperiodic slopes for $g = 11.3$ (as shown in Fig. 3, third column), and may leave room for a further reduction of the aperiodic slope for high values of I.

Taken together, our results suggest that the different metrics of neural power spectra evaluated in this work could be combined to reliably predict changes in the E:I ratio for power spectra that have different features of 1/f aperiodic and periodic components. By fitting our network model, in future work, to multiple measures extracted from empirical recordings of neural mass signals, estimates of the E:I ratio (or other key properties of the neural circuit such as the strength of the external input) could be obtained from EEG and LFP spectra or evoked potentials. This will give us the possibility to use the recurrent network model as a tool to interpret measurements of aggregate neural activity in terms of neural circuit parameters.

References

1. Barbieri, F., Mazzoni, A., Logothetis, N.K., Panzeri, S., Brunel, N.: Stimulus dependence of local field potential spectra: experiment versus theory. J. Neurosci. **34**, 14589–14605 (2014)
2. Bosl, W., Tierney, A., Tager-Flusberg, H., Nelson, C.: EEG complexity as a biomarker for autism spectrum disorder risk. BMC Med. **9**(1), 1–16 (2011)
3. Bosl, W.J., Loddenkemper, T., Nelson, C.A.: Nonlinear EEG biomarker profiles for autism and absence epilepsy. Neuropsychiatric Electrophysiol. **3**(1), 1–22 (2017)
4. Brunel, N., Wang, X.J.: What determines the frequency of fast network oscillations with irregular neural discharges? i. synaptic dynamics and excitation-inhibition balance. J. Neurophysiol. **90**(1), 415–430 (2003)

5. Buzsáki, G., Anastassiou, C.A., Koch, C.: The origin of extracellular fields and currents - EEG, ECoG. LFP and spikes. Nat. Rev. Neurosci. **13**(6), 407–420 (2012)
6. Buzsáki, G., Wang, X.J.: Mechanisms of gamma oscillations. Ann. Rev. Neurosci. **35**, 203–225 (2012)
7. Cavallari, S., Panzeri, S., Mazzoni, A.: Comparison of the dynamics of neural interactions between current-based and conductance-based integrate-and-fire recurrent networks. Front. Neural Circuits **8**, 12 (2014)
8. Colgin, L.L., et al.: Frequency of gamma oscillations routes flow of information in the hippocampus. Nature **462**(7271), 353–357 (2009)
9. Donoghue, T., et al.: Parameterizing neural power spectra into periodic and aperiodic components. Nat. Neurosci. **23**(12), 1655–1665 (2020)
10. Einevoll, G.T., Kayser, C., Logothetis, N.K., Panzeri, S.: Modelling and analysis of local field potentials for studying the function of cortical circuits. Nat. Rev. Neurosci. **14**(11), 770–785 (2013)
11. Gao, R., Peterson, E.J., Voytek, B.: Inferring synaptic excitation/inhibition balance from field potentials. Neuroimage **158**, 70–78 (2017)
12. Herrmann, C., Demiralp, T.: Human EEG gamma oscillations in neuropsychiatric disorders. Clin. Neurophysiol. **116**(12), 2719–2733 (2005)
13. Mahmud, M., Vassanelli, S.: Processing and analysis of multichannel extracellular neuronal signals: state-of-the-art and challenges. Front. Neurosci. **10**, 248 (2016)
14. Martínez-Cañada, P., Ness, T.V., Einevoll, G.T., Fellin, T., Panzeri, S.: Computation of the electroencephalogram (EEG) from network models of point neurons. PLoS Comput. Biol. **17**(4), e1008893 (2021)
15. Mazzoni, A., Brunel, N., Cavallari, S., Logothetis, N.K., Panzeri, S.: Cortical dynamics during naturalistic sensory stimulations: experiments and models. J. Physiol. Paris **105**(1), 2–15 (2011)
16. Mazzoni, A., Lindén, H., Cuntz, H., Lansner, A., Panzeri, S., Einevoll, G.T.: Computing the Local Field Potential (LFP) from integrate-and-fire network models. PLoS Comput. Biol. **11**(12), e1004584 (2015)
17. Mazzoni, A., Panzeri, S., Logothetis, N.K., Brunel, N.: Encoding of naturalistic stimuli by local field potential spectra in networks of excitatory and inhibitory neurons. PLoS Comput. Biol. **4**(12), e1000239 (2008)
18. Mazzoni, A., Whittingstall, K., Brunel, N., Logothetis, N.K., Panzeri, S.: Understanding the relationships between spike rate and delta/gamma frequency bands of LFPs and EEGs using a local cortical network model. NeuroImage **52**(3), 956–972 (2010)
19. Pesaran, B., et al.: Investigating large-scale brain dynamics using field potential recordings: analysis and interpretation. Nat. Neurosci. **21**(7), 903–919 (2018)
20. Rubenstein, J., Merzenich, M.M.: Model of autism: increased ratio of excitation/inhibition in key neural systems. Genes Brain Behav. **2**(5), 255–267 (2003)
21. da Silva, F.L.: EEG and MEG: relevance to neuroscience. Neuron **80**(5), 1112–1128 (2013)
22. Sohal, V.S., Rubenstein, J.L.: Excitation-inhibition balance as a framework for investigating mechanisms in neuropsychiatric disorders. Mol. Psychiatry **24**(9), 1248–1257 (2019)
23. Trakoshis, S., et al.: Intrinsic excitation-inhibition imbalance affects medial prefrontal cortex differently in autistic men versus women. eLife **9**, e55684 (2020)
24. Wang, J., Barstein, J., Ethridge, L.E., Mosconi, M.W., Takarae, Y., Sweeney, J.A.: Resting state EEG abnormalities in autism spectrum disorders. J. Neurodevelopmental Disord. **5**(1), 1–14 (2013)

Identifying Individuals Using EEG-Based Brain Connectivity Patterns

Hadri Hussain[1(✉)], Chee-Ming Ting[2], M. A. Jalil[3], Kanad Ray[4], S. Z. H. Rizvi[5], J. Kavikumar[6], Fuad M. Noman[2], A. L. Ahmad Zubaidi[7], Yin Fen Low[8], Sh-Hussain[1], Mufti Mahmud[9], M. Shamim Kaiser[10], and J. Ali[11]

[1] HealUltra PLT, No 20 Jalan Pulai 18, Taman Pulai Utama, 81300 Skudai, Johore, Malaysia
sh.hussain@tutanota.com

[2] School of Information Technology, Monash University Malaysia, 47500 Bandar Sunway, Selangor, Malaysia
{ting.cheeming,fuad.noman}@monash.edu

[3] Department of Physics, Faculty of Science, Unversiti Teknologi Malaysia, 81310 Skudai, Johor, Malaysia
arifjalil@utm.my

[4] Amity School of Applied Sciences, Amity University, Rajasthan 303001, India

[5] Department of Physics and Chemistry, Faculty of Applied Sciences and Technology, Universiti Tun Hussein Onn Malaysia, Edu Hub Pagoh, 84600 Muar, Malaysia
syedzuhaib@uthm.edu.my

[6] Department of Mathematics and Statistics, Faculty of Applied Sciences and Technology, Universiti Tun Hussein Onn Malaysia, Edu Hub Pagoh, 84600 Muar, Malaysia
kavi@uthm.edu.my

[7] Faculty of Medicine, Universiti Sultan Zainal Abidin, Medical Campus, 20400 Kuala Terengganu, Terengganu, Malaysia

[8] Faculty of Electronics and Computer Engineering, Universiti Teknikal Malaysia Melaka, Melaka, Malaysia
yinfen@utem.edu.my

[9] Nottingham Trent University, Clifton Lane, Nottingham NG11 8NS, UK

[10] Institute of Information Technology, Jahangirnagar University, Savar, Dhaka 1342, Bangladesh
mskaiser@juniv.edu

[11] Asia Metropolitan University 6, Jalan Lembah, Bandar Baru Seri Alam, 81750 Masai, Johor, Malaysia
jalilali@amu.edu.my

Abstract. Considering the recent rapid advancements in digital technology, electroencephalogram (EEG) signal is a potential candidate for a robust human biometric authentication system. In this paper the focus of investigation is the use of brain activity as a new modality for identification. Univariate model biometrics such as speech, heart sound and electrocardiogram (ECG) require high-resolution computer system with special devices. The heart sound is obtained by placing the digital stethoscope on the chest, the ECG signals at the hands or chest of the client and

M. Mahmud et al. (Eds.): BI 2021, LNAI 12960, pp. 124–135, 2021.
https://doi.org/10.1007/978-3-030-86993-9_12

speaks into a microphone for speaker recognition. It is challenging task when adapting these technologies to human beings. This paper proposed a series of tasks in a single paradigm rather than having users perform several tasks one by one. The advantage of using brain electrical activity as suggested in this work is its uniqueness; the recorded brain response cannot be duplicated, and a person's identity is therefore unlikely to be forged or stolen. The disadvantage of applying univariate is that the process only includes correlation in time precedence of a signal, while the correlation between regions is ignored. The inter-regional could not be assessed directly from univariate models. The alternative to this problem is the generalization of univariate model to multivariate modeling, hypothesized that the inter-regional correlations could give additional information to discriminate between brain conditions where the models or methods can measure the synchronization between coupling regions and the coherency among them on brain biometrics. The key issue is to handle the single task paradigm proposed in this paper with multivariate signal EEG classification using Multivariate Autoregressive (MVAR) rather than univariate model. The brain biometric systems obtained a significant result of 95.33% for dynamic Vector autoregressive (VAR) time series and 94.59% for Partial Directed Coherence (PDC) and Coherence (COH) frequency domain features.

Keywords: Electroencephalogram · Multivariate autoregressive · Vector autoregressive · Partial directed coherence · Coherence · Electrocardiogram

1 Introduction

Electroencephalogram (EEG) is an appropriate signal for brain biometric identification and its effective connectivity features are resistance to spoof attacks and impossible to use under pressure and coercion states.Biometrics is based on the client identification and verification system can be divided into physiological, behavioural and biosignals features associated with the clients. Data analysis procedure for biometric system usually involve pre-processing, feature extraction, and classification techniques [2,4,8,19,22,24,30,32,34], which address the complexity of the input space and the possibility of using reduced amount of training data before the classifier model can learn to generalize. In contrast, the data-driven models for speaker verification task uses a large amount of labeled data which is not only time consuming, but also requires a huge amount of training data for better generalization. Thus, proper selection of feature extraction and classification techniques is important for the design and performance of the biometric system. Other types of biometrics, such as palm, finger print, signature, and keystroke [6,11–13,27,29], are based on univariate model types of biometric systems. These traditional biometric systems rely on a single biometric with some form of limitations.

Researchers have shown that biometric traits extracted from a person (i.e., speech) tend to vary with time and vary from one person to another. Noisy biometric data such as inconvenient ambient conditions like heart sounds with loud background noise are example of noisy input that affects the performances of the system. Non universality can arise in speech technology. Similar to a fingerprint failure to enrol, some voice print might also be impossible to acquire its trait because of the poor quality of the voice, which in turn cause its failure to enrol the system. Most of the limitations of biometric systems are mainly because of their implementation by using unimodal biometric strategy. This unimodal biometric is totally relied on a single biometric trait. In order to address such issues, researcher works in this area overcome it by multi-biometric systems and using efficient fusion type to combine these systems. The information then is presented in a multiple biometric trait.

This paper propose a methodology based on specific features and classification techniques involving EEG data analysis for identification for healthy subjects. Thus, biometrics with multiple tasks or modalities can improve the system performance reliability of person recognition and also increase the difficulty of forging biometric data. This paper address the gap of impeding the implementation using EEG effective connectivity multivariate signal modal for biometric system.

2 Methods

2.1 Multi-channel EEG Biometric System

The application of multivariate EEG biometric utilizes the multi-channel time series modeling to infer the dynamic of physiological system. The Hidden Markov Model (HMM), is a well know classification method and has been proven tremendous performance, however with big data availability, and high computing power in processing, Deep Learning approach would be more reliable as it able to sustain good performance as parameter increased. In the last two decades, Deep Learning (DL) [1,31,36], a form of classifier is a family of Machine Learning (ML) or a traditional approach methods has gained considerable attention in the scientific community. In the exploration of DL it have succeeded in breaking the benchmark, in areas such as mining in biological data [17], reinforcement learning to biological data [16], classifying ECG signals [26,28] and many more.

For this paper, HMM is used. The method of using HMM, has shown to provide a reliable performance in estimating single-channel EEG, heart sound, ECG, speech signal and etc., however, the limitation of using univariate data is the process includes only correlation in time precedence of a signal, while the correlation between the other input signals is ignored. The alternative to this problem is the generalization of univariate model to multivariate modeling.

Using multivariate model, the inter-channel correlation could give additional information to discriminate between the different input signals where the models or methods can measure the synchronization between these signals and the coherency among them. One distinct disadvantage of a multivariate signals with different inputs stand in its difficulty to implement multiple sensors input and it can be costly. An alternative solution is the use of multivariate signal such as EEG where it is one of the promising and potent biosignals for brain biometrics [3,5,18,20,23,25,35,37]. The use of functional magnetic resonance imaging (fMRI) time series multivariate analysis with Independent Component Analysis (ICA) is also frequently used by researchers to analyse this type of signal [14,33]. However, the main drawback of this multivariate method is that it only assesses the spatial correlation, while the temporal correlations were ignored which can lead to results misinterpretation. Thus, not only it requires specialized equipment, it may not be suitable for task-related or highly non-stationary time series signals.

The multivariate EEG biometric system experimental set up, where the raw data time series is modeled using MVAR or Time-Varying Vector Autoregressive (TV-VAR) as time-domain feature extraction method. Later, this MVAR will be converted to PDC or COH as the frequency domain features. The analysis of the model performance is based on different biometric EEG signals, the complexity of the HMM classifier hyperparameters (i.e. states and Gaussian mixtures). The dataset consists of EEG biosignals of multi-subjects, multi-channels, with multi-trails as password-stimulated data. The first evaluation of the biometric system is the client identification experiments. Clint identification requires a close community only, which mean the data are train and test within the client's group.

EEG Database. We use a locally recorded EEG data obtained from the Computational Intelligence and Technologies (CIT) Research Group from Universiti Teknikal Malaysia Melaka (UTeM), to carry out experiments and validate the proposed methodology in this study. A summary of the data base is discussed here, and the full detail of the work can be found in [15]. During the data acquisition, eight Visual Evoked Potential (VEP) electrodes are used to record the EEG signals of control subjects. These occipital electrodes (i.e., PO7, PO3, POZ, PO4, PO8, O1, OZ and O2) were placed on subject's scalps which the EEG signals are digitized 256 Hz for intervals of one-second. A total of 37 subjects with each subject involved in 120 trials where 60 trials were shown different stimuli and 60 trials for password stimuli.

The 37 subject trials were randomly partitioned into 50% for training and 50% for testing. The HMM is trained using the training set to construct the subject-specific client's individual models. The system utilized continuous density HMM which further evaluated on different experiment setups, where different number of Markov states and Gaussian mixtures are used to construct the HMM models with different complexities. The number of trials conducted wss 1 s password-stimulli and 1.5 s of inter stimulus intervals.

The data were collected with the subject seated on a back-rested chair in front of a computer display which located 1 m away from the subject's eye level. The random or password pictures were displayed in sequence at the screen center with a fixation point. The collected data are divided into two conditions, a quiet environment and a noisy environment where an external audio clip of recorded office noise effects played through the audio speaker.

Subjects were asked to recognized the pre-selected password picture among the sequentially visualized pictures on the screen. The inter-stimulus interval for each trial was set to 1.5 s and the picture remained on the computer screen for 1 s followed by 1.5 s of white-blank screen. A short break of 5 min was interspersed in between the recording sessions to provide rest time to the subject to ensure good attention from the subject during the experiments [15].

Feature Extraction for Multi-channel EEG. VAR is a stochastic process model which can be used to capture the linear inter-dependencies among multiple time series of the EEG signals. VAR models generalize the univariate Autoregressive (AR) model by allowing for more than one evolving variable. VAR captures the spatial underlying dynamics of these variable using their own lagged values. These dynamics are represented by coefficient matrices and an error term. The only prior knowledge required is the past observations of all variables which can be hypothesized to affect each other inter-temporally. The EEG signals can be presented as a stationary piece-wise TV-VAR process $\mathbf{\Phi}_{\ell}$. TV-VAR is a natural extension of the VAR model to dynamic multivariate time series.

The rapid changes of the EEG signals can be efficiently modeled using TV-VAR model $\mathbf{\Phi}_{\ell t}$. The VAR model can be utilised to estimate time–domain directed EEG connectivity between various scalp regions. If the signal $\mathbf{y}_t = [y_{1t}, \ldots, y_{Nt}]'$,
$t = 1, \ldots, T$ represent the EEG signal then:

$$\mathbf{y}_t = \sum_{\ell=1}^{L} \boldsymbol{\Phi}(\ell t)\mathbf{y}_{t-\ell} + \boldsymbol{\epsilon}_t, \quad \boldsymbol{\epsilon}_t \sim N(\mathbf{0}, \boldsymbol{\Sigma}) \tag{1}$$

where $[\boldsymbol{\Phi}_{\ell t}]_{\ell=1}^{L}$ are $N \times N$ matrices of time-varying AR coefficients at time t and $\boldsymbol{\epsilon}_t$ is a $N \times 1$ i.i.d. Gaussian observational noise with mean zero and covariance matrix $\boldsymbol{\Sigma}$, $\boldsymbol{\epsilon}_t \sim N(\mathbf{0}, \boldsymbol{\Sigma}) \sim W(\mathbf{0}, \boldsymbol{\Sigma})$.

TV-VAR is an extension of the stationary AR model that can describe instantaneous correlation in time series, by allowing the coefficient matrix to change with time. Hence, a sequential implementation of Ordinary Least Square (OLS) algorithm is used to estimate the TV-VAR coefficients. To estimate the state noise covariance Q and the autoregressive coefficients, Φ, for each state dynamics, the OLS method was used.

$$\hat{\Phi} = (y'_{t-1}y_{t-1})^{-1}(y'_{t-1}y) \tag{2}$$

where y_{t-1} is 1 × P and contains the P = 1 lag observations of Y as an example. The OLS procedure is to estimate VAR coefficient using raw EEG data that is needed as the input features to the HMM. The classification potential of the static frequency-domain EEG connectivity to our knowledge is rarely explore in this area. For this purpose, the frequency domain of Generalized Partial Directed Coherence (GPDC), PDC, Directed Coherence (DC), and COH was extracted from the VAR parameters.

2.2 Classification (Hidden Markov Model)

The HMM model is a probabilistic model relies on Markov chains theory, wherein each Markov state does not directly correspond to observation data, instead it connects to a set of probability distributions of a state. The HMM is a common effective model which has shown to be successful in speech processing, biometrics, and medical applications [7,9,10,21].

The input to HMM is the vectorized matrices of wither Mel Frequency Cepstral Coefficents (MFCC), VAR, or TV-VAR connectivity coefficients. The HMM uses dynamic programming (Vertibi algorithm) to maximize the objective function of log likelihood. The model states are initialized using K-means clustering to distribute the VAR frames for the Gaussian mixture.

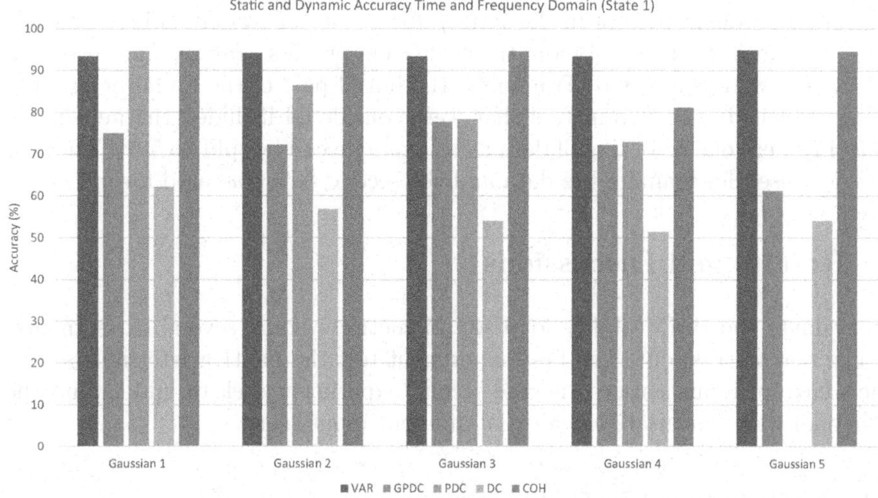

Fig. 1. Show the flow of the block diagram of training the HMM. Vector Quantization (VQ) was used to obtain the mean and the variance to train the model with specific parameters (A,B,π).

As shown in Fig. 1 the input features of the univariate or the multivariate signal, either as a static or dynamic (windowed) features are fed to the HMM classifier. The continuous HMM was used to model such univariate or multivariate features for the 37 classes representing the enrolled 37 clients. The HMM is a probabilistic method that can be used to statistically model the dynamical changes of the different types of input signals by making inferences about the likelihood of being in certain discrete states. In this study, a continuous HMM with Gaussian mixtures consisting of five states (left-to-right) and different Gaussian mixtures Probability Density Functions (PDF) for each state was used. In specific cases where the whole trial of the signals is assumed to be stationary, the Gaussian model is the preferred choice rather than HMM. An HMM can be defined as $\lambda = (A,\ B,\ \pi)$, where, π is the initial state probability vector, $A = [a_{ij}]$, $1 \leq i, j \leq N$ is the state transition matrix, and $B = [b_j(X)], 1 \leq j \leq N$, is the observation probability function for each state j.

The observation probability B can be modeled by the continuous PDF of predefine Gaussians mixtures, such that, $b_j(X)$ can be calculated as in Eq. (3).

$$b_j(x) = \sum_{m=1}^{M} C_{jm} \mathcal{N}(x, \mu_{jm}, \Sigma_{jm}), \quad 1 \leq j \leq N \tag{3}$$

where x represents the vector that is modelled, C_{jm} refers to the mixture coefficient of mth mixture component present in the state j, $\mathcal{N}(x, \mu_{jm}, \Sigma_{jm})$ is a multivariate Gaussian probability distribution function with mean vector $\mu_{jm} = [\mu_{jmd}]$ and the covariance matrix of $\Sigma_{jm} = [\Sigma_{jmd}]$ in the case of the mth mixture component present in the state j, for $1 \leq d \leq D$, where D is the dimension of the feature vectors. Before the evaluation process, training and testing of the system were conducted. Training is the initial part of the signal before it is being modelled. The parameters that were considered included the percentage split, in where one recording of data as an example can be split to 50%. The first 50% was used for training the data and the second 50% was used for testing.

3 Results and Discussions

To evaluate the HMM ability for EEG biometric system, several experimental setups were carried out. The first experiment test the multivariate signals with one source of input sensors and the second experiment seek to understand the unimodal with univariate signal from different input sensors.

3.1 Multi Channel EEG Biometric

The proposed model of biometric system used EEG data of healthy subjects which were processed with VAR to extract more meaningful effective brain network features. This section compares the performance of the stationary and non-stationary of the visual cortex area by modeling the signals using TV-VAR and TV-frequency domain, respectively.

With window size set at 25 ms and 10 ms overlaps, the TV-VAR performed sightly better with an accuracy of 95.33% using three Markov states and 6 Gaussian mixture as shown in Table 1. The initial findings suggest that the biometric system can use the static VAR (assume the brain signal is stationary across the entire scanning time) or the TV-VAR model, however, further experiments should be carried out to confirm the reliability of the two system.

Table 1. Shows the performance of different time-series TV-VAR features of multivariate EEG biometric system using Markov state. The performance is based on accuracy averaged over 37 subjects.

No of Gaussians	State 1	State 2	State 3	State 4	State 5
Gaussian 1	93.37	89.93	89.43	86.73	89.93
Gaussian 2	94.10	93.37	89.68	91.64	91.15
Gaussian 3	93.37	93.61	92.87	93.37	94.84
Gaussian 4	93.37	94.10	94.59	93.61	94.59
Gaussian 5	94.84	92.87	92.38	92.38	92.87
Gaussian 6	93.61	94.84	**95.33**	94.35	93.85
Gaussian 7	93.61	95.09	94.84	94.35	92.87
Gaussian 8	94.59	94.59	94.10	94.84	Inf

The time series approach TV-VAR shows almost similar between the state performance results while the frequency domain also perform but significantly depends on frequency features used. The results show the presence of the effective connectivity of the VAR changes over time. These changing connectivity structures can be said to reflect the behaviour of underlying brain states from the 37 subjects. To detect the state related change of brain activities based on effective connectivity, the next experiment will explore on the frequency domain of the EEG brain signal.

Table 2. Shows the performance of different frequency-domain features of multivariate EEG biometric system using single Markov state. The performance is based on accuracy averaged over 37 subjects.

No of Gaussians	GPDC	PDC	DC	COH
Gaussian 1	75.00	**94.59**	**62.16**	**94.59**
Gaussian 2	72.22	86.47	56.76	94.59
Gaussian 3	**77.77**	78.38	54.05	94.59
Gaussian 4	72.22	72.97	51.35	81.08

Table 2, shows the static EEG brain signal in the frequency domain performance using one state and different Gaussian parameters. The best performance form different type of feature of HMM in the frequency domain from GPDC gives an accuracy of 77.77%, PDC, 94.59%, DC, 62.16%, and COH 94.59%.

Figure 2, shows the performance of TV-VAR (1 state) and the frequency domain features. The best performance is obtained from TV-VAR (1 state) time domain with an accuracy of 94.84% with Gaussian 5 State 1 complexity. As for the frequency domain features for PDC and COH was able to achieve almost the same performances with the Gaussian 1 State 1 complexity when compared with

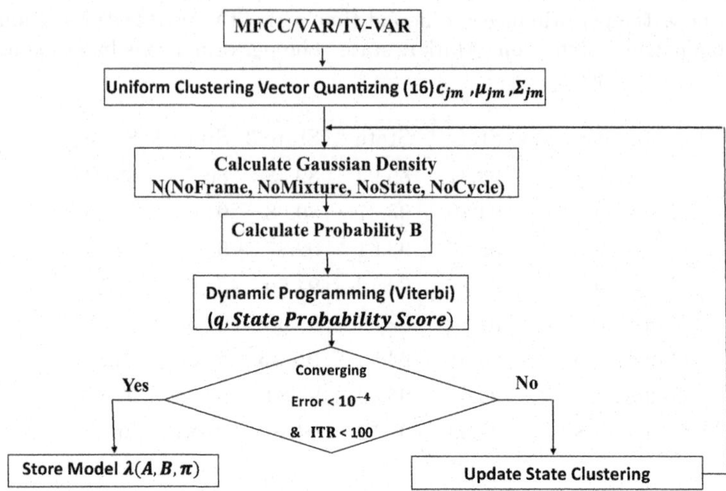

Fig. 2. Model performance accuracies based on different frequencies and time domain features.

the VAR model. However, extensive experiments conducted by the TV-VAR at different state have shown a slight improvement of 95.33% for a Gaussian 6 State 3 complexity.

3.2 Conclusion

The use of unimodel biometric system such as speech, does suffer from specific condition such as the speech can be contaminated with noise or a cold can seriously affect its performance. On the other hand, heart sound biometric can be exposed to non-universality where a faint heart sound from a overweight client or heart sound which can be contaminated with the sound of lungs and artefact can seriously damage the information of heart sound. This may result in the possibility of a client being unable to enrol into the biometric system. Furthermore, the univariate model is also likely to be exposed to spoof attack. The disadvantage of the univariate modal biometric is its reliance on a single biometrics trait. In order to address the said issues, an extension to the univariate model, we applied the multi model biometric system. The biometrics with multiple modalities have shown to improve the accuracy of client recognition and also increase the difficulty of forging biometric data. Acquiring data from a variety of input sensors such as discussed above can be time-consuming because the tasks must be performed sequentially. We proposed a new design scenario for multiple tasks in a biometric system, where, it only involve a series of tasks in a single paradigm rather than having users perform several tasks one by one. The key issue is to handle the single task paradigm proposed in this paper with multivariate signal EEG classification using MVAR rather than univariate model. The study on univariate model is limited with unrealistic assumptions such as stationary and linearity which are far from real in relationship to the behavioural signal (speech) as well as the biosignal (heart sound, ECG and EEG) for the biometric task.

3.3 Future Work

The discussions are part of the proposed framework to estimate the underlying dynamic effective connectivity in brain imagery EEG time series and the frequency domain. This paper applied the time series VAR as well as two derived frequency domain measures, example, PDC, to investigate dynamic causal interactions between parietal-occipital (PO) and occipital (O) areas in discriminating visual imagery. These findings result in some unanswered questions which will be address in future work. As an example, is it reliable to assume the brain signal to be stationary across the entire scanning time or it is dynamically changing and thus how to handle the effective connectivity of the brain? In addition, the time domain as well as the frequency domain seems to provide significant performance. Which type of features would be appropriate to estimate the dynamic changes in effective connectivity as well as how to design a proper multi model biometric that will increase the performance of this system?

References

1. Artzi, Y., Eisenstein, J.: Proceedings of the 56th Annual Meeting of the Association for Computational Linguistics: Tutorial Abstracts (2018)
2. Bennani, Y., Gallinari, P.: On the use of TDNN-extracted features information in talker identification. In: [Proceedings] ICASSP 91: 1991 International Conference on Acoustics, Speech, and Signal Processing, pp. 385–388. IEEE (1991)
3. Campisi, P., La Rocca, D.: Brain waves for automatic biometric-based user recognition. IEEE Trans. Inf. Forensics Secur. **9**(5), 782–800 (2014)
4. Chen, X., Wang, Y., Wang, L., et al.: Arrhythmia recognition and classification using ECG morphology and segment feature analysis. IEEE/ACM Trans. Comput. Biol. Bioinform. **16**(1), 131–138 (2018)
5. Chen, Y., et al.: A high-security EEG-based login system with RSVP stimuli and dry electrodes. IEEE Trans. Inf. Forensics Secur. **11**(12), 2635–2647 (2016)
6. Fei, L., Lu, G., Jia, W., Teng, S., Zhang, D.: Feature extraction methods for palmprint recognition: a survey and evaluation. IEEE Trans. Syst. Man Cybern. Syst. **49**(2), 346–363 (2018)
7. Feng, K., Liu, G.: Obstructive sleep apnea detection based on unsupervised feature learning and hidden Markov model. In: BIBE 2019; The Third International Conference on Biological Information and Biomedical Engineering, pp. 1–4. VDE (2019)
8. Homayon, S., Salarian, M.: IRIS recognition for personal identification using Lamstar neural network. arXiv preprint arXiv:1907.12145 (2019)
9. Hussain, H., Salleh, S., Ting, C., Ariff, A., Kamarulafizam, I., Surya, R.: Speaker verification using Gaussian mixture model (GMM). In: Osman, N.A.A., Abas, W.A.B.W., Ting, H.N. (eds.) IFMBE Proceedings, vol. 35, pp. 560–564. Springer, Heidelberg (2011). https://doi.org/10.1007/978-3-642-21729-6_140

10. Hussain, H., et al.: Analysis of ECG biosignal recognition for client identifiction. In: 2017 IEEE International Conference on Signal and Image Processing Applications (ICSIPA), pp. 15–20. IEEE (2017)
11. Kaur, G., Singh, D., Kaur, S.: Electrocardiogram (ECG) as a biometric characteristic: a review. Int. J. Emerg. Res. Manage. Technol. **4**(5), 202–206 (2015)
12. Kaur, R., Choudhary, P.: Handwritten signature verification based on surf features using hmm. Int. J. Comput. Sci. Trends Technol. (IJCST) **3**(1), 187–195 (2015)
13. Kumar, A., Prathyusha, K.V.: Personal authentication using hand vein triangulation and knuckle shape. IEEE Trans. Image Process. **18**(9), 2127–2136 (2009)
14. Liao, W., et al.: Evaluating the effective connectivity of resting state networks using conditional granger causality. Biol. Cybern. **102**(1), 57–69 (2010)
15. Liew, S.H., Choo, Y.H., Low, Y.F., Yusoh, Z.I.M.: EEG-based biometric authentication modelling using incremental fuzzy-rough nearest neighbour technique. IET Biometrics **7**(2), 145–152 (2017)
16. Mahmud, M., Kaiser, M.S., McGinnity, T.M., Hussain, A.: Deep learning in mining biological data. Cogn. Comput. **13**(1), 1–33 (2021)
17. Mahmud, M., Kaiser, M.S., Hussain, A., Vassanelli, S.: Applications of deep learning and reinforcement learning to biological data. IEEE Trans. Neural Networks Learn. Syst. **29**(6), 2063–2079 (2018)
18. Marcel, S., Millán, J.D.R.: Person authentication using brainwaves (EEG) and maximum a posteriori model adaptation. IEEE Trans. Pattern Anal. Mach. Intell. **29**(4), 743–752 (2007)
19. Maren, A.J., Harston, C.T., Pap, R.M.: Handbook of Neural Computing Applications. Academic Press, Cambridge (2014)
20. Min, B.K., Suk, H.I., Ahn, M.H., Lee, M.H., Lee, S.W.: Individual identification using cognitive electroencephalographic neurodynamics. IEEE Trans. Inf. Forensics Secur. **12**(9), 2159–2167 (2017)
21. Noman, F., Salleh, S.H., Ting, C.M., Samdin, S.B., Ombao, H., Hussain, H.: A Markov-switching model approach to heart sound segmentation and classification. IEEE J. Biomed. Health Inform. **24**(3), 705–716 (2019)
22. Oglesby, J., Mason, J.: Optimisation of neural models for speaker identification. In: International Conference on Acoustics, Speech, and Signal Processing, pp. 261–264. IEEE (1990)
23. Paranjape, R., Mahovsky, J., Benedicenti, L., Koles, Z.: The electroencephalogram as a biometric. In: Canadian Conference on Electrical and Computer Engineering 2001. Conference Proceedings (Cat. No. 01TH8555), vol. 2, pp. 1363–1366. IEEE (2001)
24. Pirale, D., Nirgude, M.: Biometric techniques using neural networks. Int. J. Adv. Res. Comput. Commun. Eng. **5**(4), 256 (2016)
25. Poulos, M., Rangoussi, M., Chrissikopoulos, V., Evangelou, A.: Person identification based on parametric processing of the EEG. In: ICECS 1999. Proceedings of ICECS 1999. 6th IEEE International Conference on Electronics, Circuits and Systems (Cat. No. 99EX357), vol. 1, pp. 283–286. IEEE (1999)
26. Rahman, S., Sharma, T., Mahmud, M.: Improving alcoholism diagnosis: comparing instance-based classifiers against neural networks for classifying EEG signal. In: Mahmud, M., Vassanelli, S., Kaiser, M.S., Zhong, N. (eds.) BI 2020. LNCS (LNAI), vol. 12241, pp. 239–250. Springer, Cham (2020). https://doi.org/10.1007/978-3-030-59277-6_22
27. Rowe, R.K., Nixon, K.A., Corcoran, S.P.: Multispectral fingerprint biometrics. In: Proceedings from the Sixth Annual IEEE SMC Information Assurance Workshop, pp. 14–20. IEEE (2005)

28. Satu, M.S., Rahman, S., Khan, M.I., Abedin, M.Z., Kaiser, M.S., Mahmud, M.: Towards improved detection of cognitive performance using bidirectional multilayer long-short term memory neural network. In: Mahmud, M., Vassanelli, S., Kaiser, M.S., Zhong, N. (eds.) BI 2020. LNCS (LNAI), vol. 12241, pp. 297–306. Springer, Cham (2020). https://doi.org/10.1007/978-3-030-59277-6_27
29. Shirke, S.D., Rajabhushnam, C.: Biometric personal IRIS recognition from an image at long distance. In: 2019 3rd International Conference on Trends in Electronics and Informatics (ICOEI), pp. 560–565. IEEE (2019)
30. Wang, M., El-Fiqi, H., Hu, J., Abbass, H.A.: Convolutional neural networks using dynamic functional connectivity for EEG-based person identification in diverse human states. IEEE Trans. Inf. Forensics Secur. **14**(12), 3259–3272 (2019)
31. Wilaiprasitporn, T., Ditthapron, A., Matchaparn, K., Tongbuasirilai, T., Banluesombatkul, N., Chuangsuwanich, E.: Affective EEG-based person identification using the deep learning approach. IEEE Trans. Cogn. Dev. Syst. **12**(3), 486–496 (2019)
32. Will, C., et al.: Radar-based heart sound detection. Sci. Rep. **8**(1), 1–14 (2018)
33. Winkler, I., Brandl, S., Horn, F., Waldburger, E., Allefeld, C., Tangermann, M.: Robust artifactual independent component classification for BCI practitioners. J. Neural Eng. **11**(3), 035013 (2014)
34. Xie, Q., Tu, S., Wang, G., Lian, Y., Xu, L.: Feature enrichment based convolutional neural network for heartbeat classification from electrocardiogram. IEEE Access **7**, 153751–153760 (2019)
35. Yeom, S.K., Suk, H.I., Lee, S.W.: Person authentication from neural activity of face-specific visual self-representation. Pattern Recogn. **46**(4), 1159–1169 (2013)
36. Zemouri, R., Zerhouni, N., Racoceanu, D.: Deep learning in the biomedical applications: recent and future status. Appl. Sci. **9**(8), 1526 (2019)
37. Zhao, Q., et al.: Improving individual identification in security check with an EEG based biometric solution. In: Yao, Y., Sun, R., Poggio, T., Liu, J., Zhong, N., Huang, J. (eds.) BI 2010. LNCS (LNAI), vol. 6334, pp. 145–155. Springer, Heidelberg (2010). https://doi.org/10.1007/978-3-642-15314-3_14

A Novel Hybrid Model for Brain Functional Connectivity Based on EEG

Yan Li[1], Haolan Zhang[2(✉)], Yifan Lu[3], and Huiming Tang[1]

[1] Zhejiang University, Hangzhou, China
{ly21121,tanghm}@zju.edu.cn
[2] SCDM Center, NIT, Ningbo Research Institute, Zhejiang University, Hangzhou, China
haolan.zhang@nit.zju.edu.cn
[3] Ningbo Tech University, Ningbo, China
yifan.lu@nbt.edu.cn

Abstract. In this paper, we introduce a novel model for establishing brain functional connectivity based on noninvasive Electroencephalogram (EEG) data sources. We reviewed the main methods used in EEG brain functional connectivity, and the current research progress of analyzing EEG datasets. In this paper, we proposed a new model for bridging the missing link between human brain functions and real time brain wave activities. The proposed model combines graph theory/complex network methods with fuzzy logic method to deliver an explicit connection in a real time environment. We conducted the EEG data preprocessing experiments for our new model.

Keywords: EEG data · Brain network · Fuzzy logic

1 Introduction

Brain functional connectivity is one of the key aspects of studying human brain activities. The commonly used noninvasive methods for brain analysis include functional Magnetic Resonance Imaging (fMRI), EEG, and Magnetoencephalography (MEG). Compared with the other methods, EEG has better real-time performance, which allows EEG based methods to capture brain activities and determine the relative strengths and positions of electrical activities in different brain regions through electrodes in real time. Therefore, EEG has a high temporal resolution. Moreover, the EEG is a much more economical solution than MRI and MEG. However, the spatial resolution of EEG is limited by the volume conduction problem as well as brain signal reverse traceability.

Advantage of EEG systems are noninvasiveness and the relative ease of use. Information conveyed in EEG signals can be highly informative about the underlying functional brain networks if those signals are appropriately processed to extract the relevant information. Since that EEG has excellent temporal resolution, which offers the irreplaceable opportunity to not only track large-scale brain networks over very short durations like in many cognitive tasks but to also analyze fast and dynamic changes that can occur during the resting state or in brain disorders [1]. However, most of the studies on EEG functional

M. Mahmud et al. (Eds.): BI 2021, LNAI 12960, pp. 136–145, 2021.
https://doi.org/10.1007/978-3-030-86993-9_13

connectivity analyses were performed at the sensor level, which is not straightforward for the interpretation of corresponding networks, as the signal are strongly corrupted by the volume conduction effect due to the electrical conduction properties of the head and the fact that multiple scalp electrodes collect the activity arising from the same brain sources [2].

Brain functional connectivity can be modeled and quantified with different techniques, and measurements of real-time and off-line electrodynamics of the human brain have evolved over the years. In recent years, much work has been done about brain function, and EEG biofeedback to control robotic limbs coupled with PET and fMRI cross-validation of the location of the sources of the EEG shows that the future of quantitative EEG or QEEG is very bright and positive because of the current trend of the neurophysics of the brain and high-speed computers [3]. EEG source connectivity approaches involve several steps, each related to important topics in signal processing, such as the preprocessing of raw EEG data, EEG inverse solutions, estimation of statistical couplings between signals and graph theory-based analysis. However, a complete overview of EEG source connectivity in terms of methodological choices and limitations at each stage and the available tools are still missing [4]. In this paper, we focus on the research of brain connectivity related methods based on EEG, and we propose a method to eliminate the volume conduction effect of EEG and use fMRI for result verification.

2 Methods of Brain Connectivity

In this section, we introduce several common methods of brain connectivity, and evaluate the advantages and disadvantages of these methods.

2.1 Graph Theory

Graph theory, especially the theory of directed graphs, is of special interest as it applies to structural, functional and effective brain connectivity at all levels [7]. Graphs of brain networks can be quantitatively examined for vertex degrees strengths, degree correlations (assortativity), subgraphs (motifs), clustering coefficients, path lengths (distances), and vertex, edge centrality, among many other graph theory measures. In graph theory, a specific network can be abstracted into a graph composed of a set of nodes ($N \equiv \{n_1, n_2, \ldots, n_N\}$) and a set of edges ($L \equiv \{l_1, l_2, \ldots, l_K\}$). An edge ($l_{i,j}$) indicates that there is a certain relationship between the two connected nodes (n_i, n_j).

A brain network can be represented as graphs that consists of nodes and their connections referred as edges. From these representations, a variety of graph measures can be calculated that are informative about the network topology. Several standard measures are used to describe the network's topology [8]: the average degree (k), which denotes the average number of edges per node; the degree distribution, which indicates the distribution of the network's nodal degree values; the characteristic path length (L), which is the average number of edges in the shortest paths between every pair of nodes in the network; and the average clustering coefficient (C) that represents the probability which neighbors of a node are also connected. C indicates the occurrence of clusters or cliques in the network.

Moreover, the characteristic path length and betweenness centrality can also be used to measure the overall characteristics of the network. The characteristic path length of the network is defined as the average value of the distance between any two nodes in the network to describe the global connection characteristics of the network, taking the following form:

$$D = \sum\nolimits_{n_i, n_j \varepsilon N i \neq j} d_{i,j} / (N(N-1)) \tag{1}$$

The importance of each node in the network can be expressed by the betweenness, and the number of the shortest path through a node is called the betweenness of the node, nodes or edges with high betweenness are usually important to maintain the effectiveness of the entire network communication.

Table 1. Analytical expressions for graph measures of theoretical networks [8, 9].

Network type	Path length (L)	Clustering coefficient (C)
Ring lattice	$\frac{N}{2k}$	$\frac{3(k-2)}{4(k-1)}$
Random network	$\frac{\ln(N)}{\ln(k)}$	$\frac{k}{N}$
Small-world network with rewiring probability p	$\frac{N}{k} f(pkN) with$ $f(u) = \begin{cases} const & if\ u \ll 1 \\ \frac{\ln(u)}{u} & if\ u \gg 1 \end{cases}$	$\frac{3(k-2)}{4(k-1)}(1-p)^3$
Scale-free network	$\frac{\ln(N)}{\ln\ln(N)}$	$N^{-0.75}$

In order to illustrate the size-dependency and degree-dependency of graph measures, C and L were listed for several canonical topologies [8]. Expressions depend either on k or N, or both and are specific for a particular network type [9]. See Table 1 for more details. The brain's structural and functional networks are intimately related and share common topological features, and topological network of the brain is shown in Fig. 1 [12].

2.2 Complex Brain Networks

Complex networks refer to a network with a complex topology between random networks that has small characteristic paths and small clustering coefficients and a regular network that has large characteristic path lengths and large clustering coefficients. Two of the most famous complex networks are small-world networks and scale-free networks. At present, brain networks have been proven to have small-world characteristics, which means this network has the shortest path length similar to the random network and larger clustering coefficient than the random network.

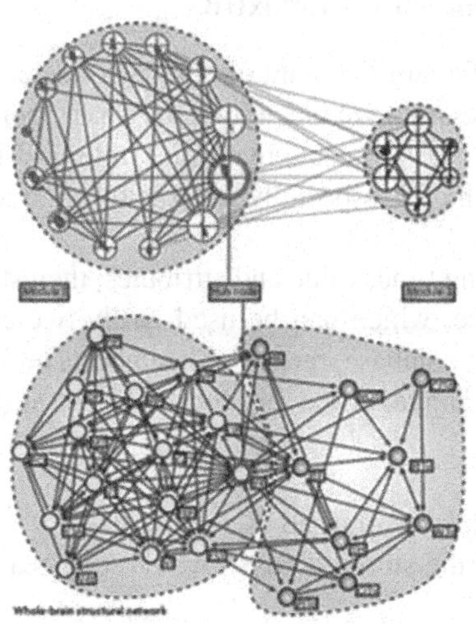

Fig. 1. The whole-brain networks demonstrate consistent topological features [12]. The brain's structural and functional net-works are intimately related and share common topological features.

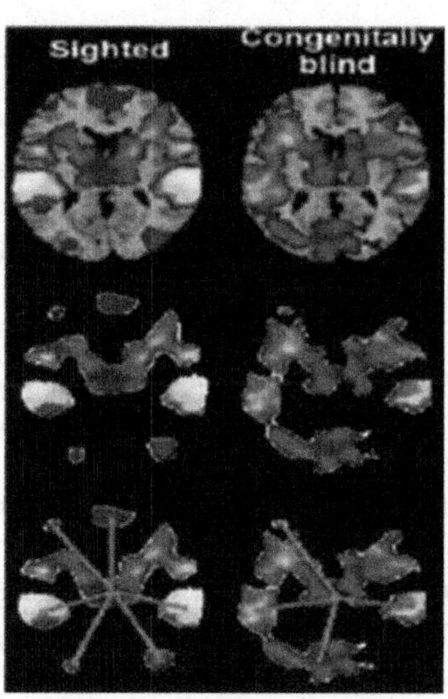

Fig. 2. Global graphs based on fMRI data [16]. The global graph is developed by connecting the centroids of the brain areas that show high level of activities for the frequencies under investigation.

Use C_p^{real}, C_p^{rand} to represent the clustering coefficients of the brain network and the random network separately, L_p^{real}, L_p^{read} to represent the shortest path length of the brain network and the random network, then the small-world network has:

$$\gamma = C_p^{real}/C_p^{rand} > 1 \tag{2}$$

$$\lambda = L_p^{real}/L_p^{read} \approx 1 \tag{3}$$

The small-world properties of the network can be summarized as $\sigma = \gamma/\lambda > 1$. The small-world attribute of the human brain network has important functional significance, which characterizes that the brain network is an efficient system with separation and integration of functions.

The process of using EEG to build a complex brain network includes filtering and artefact reduction, followed by feature extraction, which involves computing the FC measures and quantifying the measures using a number of reduced dimensionality neurobiological features by applying the Brain Connectivity Toolbox (BCT) [10].

A long-term goal of neuroscience is to develop models that integrate brain structures and functions to predict the human perception, cognition and behavior [11]. However, these models often lack characterization at the level of individual subjects. Nowadays, the development of innovative technologies enables the study of the computational architecture of brain connection individually [5].

2.3 EEG Analytics Based on Time Serial Database – InfluxDB

Since EEG data is recorded in time series, and a large amount of data is collected in a very short time, in order to facilitate data processing, we use influxDB, a very popular time series processing database to store and process the data real time. InfluxDB is an open-source distributed time series database, which is especially suitable for time series related data.

The data we sampled is recorded its sampling time, value and attributes, then stored in influxDB. InfluxDB built-in HTTP interface, which can be used easily, we could directly call the interface to read and write to the database, moreover it supports multiple query language, we can use flux or influxQL language to query the data. The steps to use influxDB to process data are as follows:

- First, the sampled EEG data is directly input into influxDB.
- InfluxDB supports python language to read the stored data, so we directly read the data.
- Process the data according to the above processing algorithm to obtain the frequency and amplitude of each individual waveform directly.

3 Combining Graph Theory with Fuzzy Logic for EEG Brain Functional Connectivity Analysis

In this section, we propose a novel method that combine the MRI image and EEG data to verify the brain connectivity. We use a graph method to create brain dynamic networks that contain information about the activity of the regions such as intensities and magnitudes [16]. Then according to the brain network based on the MRI image, we use T2 FL classifier to assign the EEG signal examined to classes of the specific subjects.

3.1 Brain Connectivity Graphs

In order to create the brain networks, the original RGB images need to be converted to CIELAB and then the activated brain regions are segmented [17]. After detecting the ROIs, the global graph is generated to represent the functional brain patterns. The local graph representation for the ROIs can be represented as the following:

$$L = N_1 a_{12}^l N_2 a_{23}^l \ldots N_{\text{k}} a_{\text{kl}}^l N_l \otimes N_i a_{ij}^s N_j \otimes \ldots \otimes N_n a_{nm}^{rd} N_m \tag{4}$$

In which, $\otimes$ represents the graph relationship operator, and each N_i represents the *i-th* graph nodes and contains both structural and functional attributes of the corresponding active brain regions. After defining the local graphs, the global graph connects the region's centroid to graphically illustrate which brain regions are active during a certain state and additionally presents the functional patterns generated among these regions. The expression of the Global Graphs can be shown as below:

$$GG = (L_1 R_{12} L_2)\Phi_{23}(L_1 R_{13} L_3)\ldots(L_1 R_{1n-1} L_{n-1})\Phi_{n-1n}((L_1 R_{1n} L_n) \tag{5}$$

where L_i is a global graph node or a local graph that represents a distinct active region and holds all crucial information about the local attributes that describes the brain activities such as magnitude, color scale and intensity. *Rij* represents the relative distance between two active regions Li and Li + 1, and lastly, *Φij* represents the relative angle between the distances of consecutive brain regions. The global graph based on MRI images is shown in Fig. 3 [16].

3.2 T2 FL Classification Based on EEG Data

(1) Type 2 Fuzzy Logic System

Fuzzy logic (FL) is a class of artificial intelligence [13], FL has many applications in many fields. FL is rule based, which is basically based on multivalued logic. Fuzzy logic (FL) has proven its potential for estimating and minimizing the effect of uncertainties that are present in the modeling environment [14]. Here we describe some basic information about T2 FL. The structure of a rule-based type-2 FLS is shown in Fig. 2 [15], including four components which are the most popular kind of T2 FL.

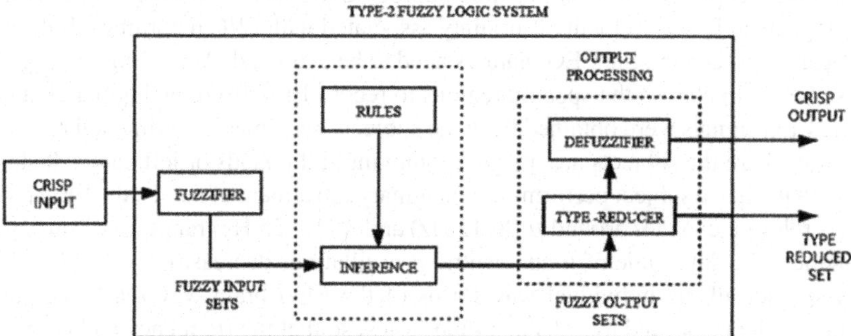

Fig. 3. The structure of a type-2 FLS [15], including Fuzzifier, Inference, Type-reducer and Defuzzifier.

T2 FL gives the degree of fuzziness of the membership value in the set, enhancing the ability of traditional fuzzy systems to describe and deal with uncertainties. The illustrated fuzzy rule contains fuzzy variables, which are defined, respectively, by a number of fuzzy sets. Each fuzzy set is defined by a linguistic variable, which is again defined by a multivalued membership function (MF). For each $x \in X$ (the membership grade), the T2 fuzzy set has fuzzy grades (fuzzy sets in J_X) can be represented as:

$$\mu_{\tilde{A}}(x) = \frac{f_x(u_1)}{u_1} + \frac{f_x(u_2)}{u_2} + \ldots + \frac{f_x(u_m)}{u_m} = \sum_i \frac{f_x(u_i)}{u_i}, \quad u_i \in J_x \tag{6}$$

The f_X represents the membership function of the membership grade x [15]. After measurements are fuzzified, the resulting input fuzzy sets are mapped into fuzzy output sets by the inference block. In the inference block, considering having *p* inputs ($x_1 \in X_1, x_2 \in X_2, \ldots, x_P \in X_P$) and one output ($y \in Y$), the *lth* rules have the form:

$$if\ x_1\ is\ \widetilde{F}_1^l\ and\ x_2\ is\ \widetilde{F}_2^l\ and\ \ldots\ and\ x_p\ is\ \widetilde{F}_p^l\ then\ y\ is\ \widetilde{G}^l$$

The membership function can be written as (7), $\widetilde{B}^l$ denotes $\widetilde{X}' \circ \widetilde{F}_1^l \times \widetilde{F}_2^l \times \ldots \times \widetilde{F}_p^l$, $\widetilde{X}'$ represents the fuzzy set, to which x' belongs [15].

$$\mu_{\widetilde{B}^l}(y) = \mu_{\widetilde{F1}^l}(x_1) \sqcap \mu_{\widetilde{F2}^l}(x_2) \sqcap \ldots \sqcap \mu_{\widetilde{G}^l}(y) \tag{7}$$

As for the type reduction of T2 FLS, the type-reducer combines all these output sets in some way and then performs a centroid calculation on this type-2 set. Except Centroid Type Reduction, there are other methods of Type Reduction, here we won't go into details.

In practice, the brain dynamics as a time-varying data-generating mechanism is accounted for by the concept of an extended T2 fuzzy set (FS) that can embrace the range of its possible behaviors. Interpretability and transparency of models obtained with FL-based approach are also worth emphasizing. Since multi-model anatomical approaches and functional connectivity studies brought renewed attention to the topic, better understanding of the theoretical and methodological implications of fuzzy boundaries in brain science can be conceptually useful.

(2) Classification of EEG Data

The emphasis is placed on T2 fuzzy methodology due to its capabilities to account for physiological and measurement uncertainty associated with EEG recordings. Before the classification procedure, the EEG features need to be extracted. According to the global graphs, we could choose the specific regions to record EEG from the bipolar channels. And the EEG signals were obtained from the subjects in a timed experimental recording procedure where the subjects are imagining moving right hands or left hands. It should be clear that when a subject performs the imaginary movement of hands, the EEG record displays relevant changes around μ (8–12 Hz) and β (18–25 Hz) ranges (i.e., during the imagination, the amplitude of μ and central β oscillations decrease).

We extract all the individual waveforms of the EEG brain waves and record the positions of the peaks and troughs in a time series, so that the frequency and amplitude of the brain waves can be calculated. Then we count the frequency within a time window (window length is set as *win*) and calculate the square norm of these frequency values, which could be represented as y_i^n, where n is an index of a recording channel and i is the index of the time windows. The feature vector could be written as (8):

$$R = \left(y_1^1, y_2^1 \ldots y_{win}^1, y_1^2, \ldots y_{win}^2, \ldots, y_{win}^n\right) \tag{8}$$

The fuzzy rule can be expressed as following:

$$IF\ R_1\ is\ A^1\ AND\ R_2\ is\ A^2\ AND \ldots AND\ R_n\ is$$
$$THEN\ class\ is\ C = \left[c_{lefts}, c_{rights}\right]$$

where $A^1, A^2, \ldots, A^n$ denote the uncertain means of the T2 FLs and C is the centroid of the consequent representing the class that input features are assigned to. The initial rule base that reflects the distribution of the EEG features and their corresponding class assignments in the input-output space could be created by clustering the training data with a mapping-constrained agglomerative algorithm or the single-pass algorithm [18]. Theoretically the consequent that obtained by the T2 FL classifier should be consistent with the results obtained by MRI.

3.3 Experiment

In this section, we design the experiment of extracting the individual waveform of EEG signal and calculating the frequency and introduce a new method for real time EEG data processing the influx dB combined dataset and propose the further work that could be done.

Data Collecting

The EEG signals were obtained from several subjects, including the imagining moving the hands, image moving the feet and meditation in a timed recording procedure. We select a specific subject that have the most stable performance. Thirty-two bipolar EEG channels were measured, and the EEGs were sampled at the frequency of 1000 Hz, and the EEG recording equipment is a Brain Amp DC amplifier.

The EEG signal recording time lasts for 120 s, all data are recorded into csv files in chronological order. In order to avoid the influence of clutter as much as possible, we only intercept the signal for a period of time when the attention is more concentrated for the experiment.

EEG Data Preprocessing

In the preprocessing step, we need to extract the individual waveform in continuous time and calculate the amplitude and frequency of the single waveform. The distribution of EEG data sampled in chronological order of one of the thirty-two bipolar channels is shown in Fig. 4.

The algorithm for intercepting the turning points of the waveform can be described as:

```
Procedure waveform_capture(N: integer);
  var i ,t ,j : integer ;
  begin
  i = 0;
    for t := 1 to N do:
    begin
      if sampled[t] > sampled[t + 1]&& sampled[t] > sampled[t − 1] then
        points[i] = sampled[t] ;
        i = i + 1;
      if sampled[t] < sampled[t + 1]&& sampled[t] < sampled[t − 1] then
        points[i] = sampled[t] ;
        i = i + 1;
     if sampled[t] == sampled[t + 1] then
        points[i] = sampled[t] ;
       i = i + 1;
   end
 end
```

N represents the number of sampled points. After extracting all the turning points of the EEG wave, we could get the start and end time of the single waveform and the height of a waveform from its lowest point to its peak.

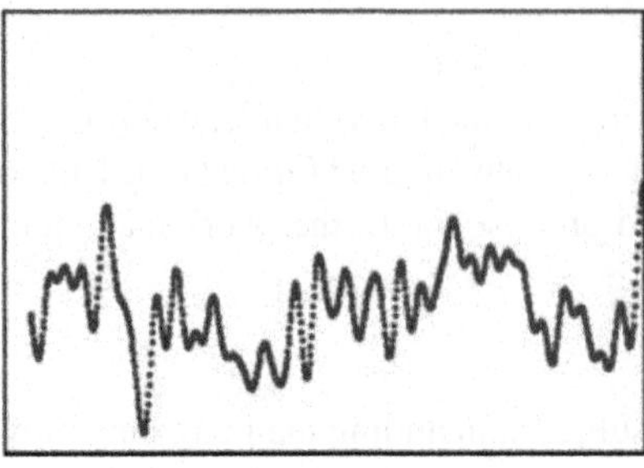
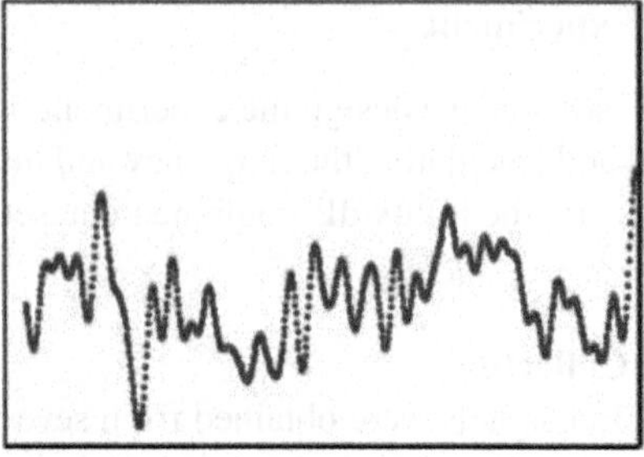

Fig. 4. The sampled wave and the individual waveform interception.

4 Conclusion

In this paper, we proposed a new method to verify the connectivity of the brain that combines the MRI and EEG data, according to the MRI image to construct the brain network and find the relationships of the different brain regions, then we introduce the type-2 fuzzy logic system which is used to get the relationship of different channels. Then according to the distribution of the bipolar channels, we could get the relationships of different regions, if the relationships of different channels are consistent with the results that we get from MRI image, we could verify the spatiality of EEG data.

We use influxDB database to store and process the data, which could support real-time data processing. We extract all the turning points of the sampled data, and according to the turning points, calculate the amplitude and the frequency of the EEG data, which are used in the T2 FLS as the input data. The construction of the brain network based on MRI and the identification of the structure of the T2 FL classifier will be the further work on the basis of our existing work.

Acknowledgment. This work is partially supported by Zhejiang Natural Science Fund (LY19F030010), Zhejiang Philosophy and Social Sciences Fund (20NDJC216YB), Ningbo Innovation Team (No. 2016C11024), Ningbo Natural Science Fund (No. 2019A610083), Zhejiang Provincial Education and Science Scheme 2021 (GH2021642).

References

1. Hassan, M., Benquet, P., Biraben, A., Berrou, C., Dufor, O., Wendling, F.: Dynamic reorganization of functional brain networks during picture naming. Cortex **73**, 276–288 (2015)
2. Brunner, C., Billinger, M., Seeber, M., Mullen, T., Makeig, S.: Volume conduction influences scalp-based connectivity estimates. Front. Comput. Neurosci. **10**, 121 (2016)
3. Thatcher, R.W., Biver, C.J., et al.: EEG and Brain Connectivity: A Tutorial (2004)
4. Hassan, M., Wendling, F.: Electroencephalography source connectivity: aiming for high resolution of brain networks in time and space. IEEE Sig. Process. Mag. **35**(3), 81–96 (2018)
5. Bullmore, E., Sporns, O.: Complex brain networks: graph theoretical analysis of structural and functional systems. Nat. Rev. Neurosci. **10**, 186–198 (2009)
6. Tomoyasu, Y., Wheeler, S.R., Denell, R.E.: Ultrabithorax is required for membranous wing identity in the beetle Tribolium castaneum. Nature **433**, 643–647 (2005)

7. Sporns, O.: Brain connectivity. Scholarpedia **2**(10), 4695 (2007)
8. Rubinov, M., Sporns, O.: Complex network measures of brain connectivity: uses and interpretations. Neuroimage **52**, 1059–1069 (2010)
9. van Wijk, B.C.M., Stam, C.J., Daffertshofer, A.: Comparing brain networks of different size and connectivity density using graph theory. PLoS ONE **5**(10), e13701 (2010). https://doi.org/10.1371/journal.pone.0013701
10. Rubinov, M.: Complex network measures of brain connectivity: uses and interpretations. J. NeuroImage **52**, 1059–1069 (2013)
11. Pal, C., Biswas, D., Maharatna, K., Chakrabarti, A.: Architecture for complex network measures of brain connectivity. IEEE International Symposium on Circuits and Systems (ISCAS), Baltimore, MD **2017**, 1–4 (2017). https://doi.org/10.1109/ISCAS.2017.8050239
12. Bullmore, E., Sporns, O.: Complex brain networks: graph theoretical analysis of structural and functional systems. Nat. Rev. Neurosci. **10,** 186–98 (2009). https://doi.org/10.1038/nrn2575
13. Bose, B.K.: Expert system, fuzzy logic, and neural network applications in power electronics and motion control. Proc. IEEE **82**, 1303–1323 (1994)
14. Mendel, J.M.: Uncertain Rule-Based Fuzzy Logic Systems: Introduction and New Directions. Prentice-Hall, Upper Saddle River (2001)
15. Karnik, N.N., Mendel, J.M., Liang, Q.: Type-2 fuzzy logic systems. IEEE Trans. Fuzzy Syst. (2000). https://doi.org/10.1109/91.811231
16. Manganas, S., Bourbakis, N., Michalopoulos, K.: Brain structural and functional representation based on the local global graph methodology. In: 2018 IEEE 18th International Conference on Bioinformatics and Bioengineering (BIBE), Taichung, Taiwan, pp. 139–142 (2018). https://doi.org/10.1109/BIBE.2018.00033
17. Bourbakis, N., Makrogiannis, S., Kapogiannis, D.: A synergistic model for monitoring brain's changes: a case study. In: 2011 23rd IEEE International Conference on Tools with Artificial Intelligence (ICTAI), pp. 1093–1098, November 2011
18. Wang, J.-S., Lee, C.S.G.: Self-adaptive neuro-fuzzy inference systems for classification wapplications. IEEE Trans. Fuzzy Syst. **10**(6), 790–802 (2002)

Emojis Pictogram Classification for Semantic Recognition of Emotional Context

Muhammad Atif[1], Valentina Franzoni[2](✉), and Alfredo Milani[2]

[1] University of Florence, Florence, Italy
muhammad.atif@unifi.it
[2] University of Perugia, Perugia, Italy
{valentina.franzoni,milani}@dmi.unipg.it

Abstract. In online interactions, users frequently add emojis (e.g., smileys, hearts, angry faces) to text for expressing the emotions behind the communication context, aiming at a better interpretation to text especially of polysemous short expressions. Emotion recognition refers to the automated process of identifying and classifying human emotions. If text-based emoticons (i.e., emojis created by textual symbols and characters) can be directly understood by semantic-based context recognition tools used in the Web and Artificial Intelligence and robotics, image-based emojis need instead image recognition for a complete semantic context interpretation. This study aims to explore and compare systematically different classification models of emoticon pictograms collected from the Internet, with different labels according to the Ekman model of six basic emotions. A first comparison involves supervised machine learning classifiers trained on features extracted through neural networks. In the second phase, the comparison is extended to different deep learning models. Results indicate that deep learning models performed excellent, and traditional supervised algorithms also achieve very promising outcomes.

Keywords: Machine learning · Deep learning · Emotion recognition · Transfer learning · Emoticons

1 Introduction

The need to express emotional context to text message or to give emotional feedback, lead to the spread of *emojis* (i.e., image-based emoticons) and *memes* in web-based social interactions. While emoticons were initially codified by standard sequences of characters, the large variety of pictograms available on different platforms and devices, allow denoting a wide range of emotional nuances. Emotion recognition of image-based emoticons for context interpretation became,

This work is partially supported by the Italian Ministry of Research under PRIN Project "PHRAME" Grant n. 20178 XXKFY.

M. Mahmud et al. (Eds.): BI 2021, LNAI 12960, pp. 146–156, 2021.
https://doi.org/10.1007/978-3-030-86993-9_14

thus, a novel task for web-based semantics. For instance, in social networks, social media websites and applications, as well as in video-calling tools (e.g., Zoom, Webex, Teams, Meet) image-based emotional pictograms (e.g., emojis, GIFS, memes) are integrated to be used to communicate messages in an emotional context or to send emotional feedback, usually called *reaction*. If humans convey their messages by using different facial expressions, in textual communication over different social media platforms, people like to add emotional clues through emojis to convey the emotional meaning when the face visual is not available or limited, and to add reactions as feedback to live video communication (e.g., live streaming, video calls). Images are among the most immediate clues to arouse emotional communication and empathy through media.

Most studies conducted regarding emotion recognition, based on real facial expressions, and speech, use a limited set of emotions. The most used and simple for a universal emotion recognition without cultural or geographical biases is the Ekman model of emotions with its six basic emotions categories (i.e., fear, anger, joy, sadness, disgust, and surprise) [8]. Classification of real facial images [9] has been done with high precision into the six basic emotion of the Ekman categorization, based on micro-expressions [10–12]. Also, the semantic analysis of textual messages in social networks is well studied, using term semantics or textual emoticons. To the best of our knowledge, there is no automatic system focused on the recognition of emotions from emojis pictograms, which hype of use is still recent.

We study and compare the application to pictogram emojis of emotional classification by traditional supervised machine learning techniques and deep learning approaches. From traditional machine learning techniques, we leverage k-nearest neighbors (K-NN) [1], Support Vector Machine (SVM) [2], Decision Tree [3] and Linear Discriminant Analysis (LDA) [4] classifiers. In deep learning approaches, to solve the problem of the extremely high number of samples required for training we have used transfer learning techniques based on pre-trained classification models for AlexNet [5,18], GoogleNet [14] and InceptionV3 [6]. Experimental results indicate that deep-learning classifiers with transfer learning perform better compared to traditional machine learning classifiers on a limited number of samples and balanced classes. The rest of the paper is organized as follows. Section 2 reports the research methodology and data set used for conducting this study. Section 3 describes deep learning models, traditional supervised classifiers, and feature descriptors used in this study. Section 4 presents the experimental results followed by the discussion. Finally, Sect. 5 concludes this study and outlines some future directions.

2 Classification Methodology

In this study, two approaches have been compared for classifying emojis pictograms into the six basic emotional categories of the Ekman model. Pre-trained deep models, i.e., *AlexNet*, *InceptionV3*, and *GoogleNet*, have been used, then applying a fine-tuning (i.e., a re-training) phase using transfer learning, which specializes the training on the six categories of emotions. In addition, traditional machine learning classifiers, i.e., *k-Nearest Neighbors (k-NN)*, *Support Vector Machines (SVM)*, *Decision Tree*, and *Linear Discriminant Analysis (LDA)* are also trained on the deep features extracted through the AlexNet and Resnet18 [13,18] neural networks (NN) [7].

2.1 Feature Extraction for Supervised Machine Learning

Supervised machine learning requires features and labels for classification. In our experiments using traditional supervised algorithms, the label is provided by the image emotion class, while the classification features are extracted from the image training set using deep neural networks. In particular, we used the AlexNet and ResNet18 Convolutional Neural Networks (CNNs) for feature extraction [7]. CNNs are a specialized type of Deep Neural Network, able to reduce the information explosion: in the convolutional layers, the image information is filtered, generating a feature map. The number of final feature maps will be equal to the amount of filters used in the convolutional layers. In the fully connected layers following the pooling layer which samples the size of each feature map to reduce the computation, the filtered information is converted to a feature vector which can be given as output after a weighting phase. Such a final weighted vector is extracted and fed to machine learning algorithms. In particular, AlexNet features are extracted from the *fc7* fully-connected layer and Resnet18 features from the *pool5* global pooling layer.

2.2 Knowledge Transfer for Deep Learning

Deep learning models can be trained from scratch, requiring high computational power and a large number of training samples. On the other hand, using Knowledge Transfer (i.e., Transfer Learning) a neural network pre-trained on large data sets of general images is used because already capable of recognizing the low-level features of images, e.g. color distribution, shapes, edges, and corners [17]. The neural network is then fine-tuned with additional fully connected layers according to our data set of emojis, to recognize the emotional categories. This method is proved efficient on image and emotion classification, using the knowledge acquired by the NN on images, i.e., the abilities to recognize low-level features, as the foundation to create a new model for a new problem.

2.3 Emojis Pictogram Classification Framework

Figure 1 shows the structure of our emojis pictogram recognition framework. The figure shows two blocks representing the flow of the training (left) and testing (right) phases. The top part shows the training and testing process of traditional machine learning classifiers; the bottom part shows how deep learning models are trained and tested. After feature extraction, the images go through the preprocessing phase (i.e., cleaning from text and frames), then data augmentation techniques are used to have more samples and to recognize emojis that are not perfectly even. Machine learning or deep learning using knowledge transfer are used for classification.

3 Experimental Setup

3.1 Data Set Collection and Balancing

The data set used in this work has been built by authors collecting emojis pictograms from different social media and devices. Emotion terms related to the Ekman model were used to search the Web for the images, with a focus on selecting visualizations from different software and devices, which may show with different facets the images related to the same emoticon. Image-based emoticons have been added to images related to different visualizations of text-based emoticons. The labels have been assigned to images based on the Ekman model, using the same emotional words used in the web-based search phase. Data augmentation techniques i.e., rotation, translation, shear, and reflection, allowed to diversify the samples and balance classes. The balanced number of samples for each class in the data set is 624 training images and 156 test images for each class, for a total of 4680 images, split for training and testing at an 80%–20% rate.

3.2 Preprocessing of Input Images and Experimental Setup

Initially, images are preprocessed to filter out textual or noise elements. Then, data augmentation techniques are applied to balance categories increasing the number of samples in the data set for the required categories, as explained in Sect. 2.1. Then images are resized according to the input of the models i.e., [227 227 3], [224 224 3], and [299 299 3] pixels for AlexNet, GoogleNet, and InceptionV3 deep neural networks respectively. The data set is divided into training and testing sets, i.e., 80% samples in training, while 20% images in the test set used for validation. Features are extracted through AlexNet and ResNet-18 pre-trained deep models, that are fed as input to traditional machine learning classifiers for the training and testing phase. Each traditional classifier is trained independently on both deep features using their own parameters setup. Using

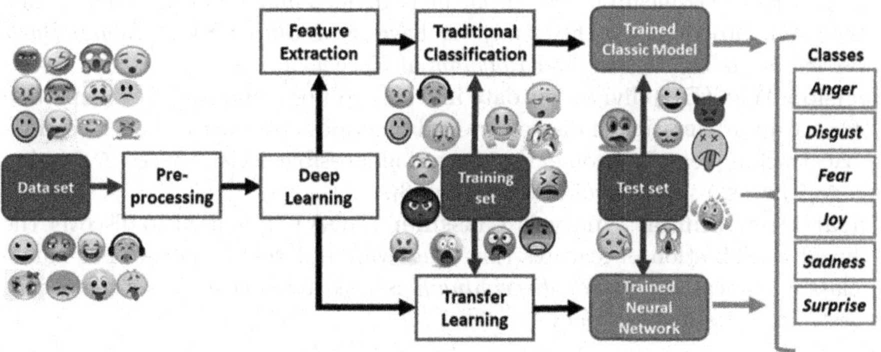

Fig. 1. Framework of the image-based emojis classification

transfer learning, the last fully connected layers of pre-trained deep models are fine-tuned on the emotion categories.

3.3 Feature Descriptors

To train and test traditional machine learning classifiers, fixed-size feature descriptors have been extracted [7] using the two pre-trained deep models of AlexNet [5] and Resnet18 [13]. The length of the feature descriptors, i.e. vectors, extracted through AlexNet and ResNet18 deep models is 1×4096 and 1×512 respectively for each emoji pictogram. Higher-level layers give low-level features and the feature descriptors length will be long, while deeper layers give us higher-level features with reduced size feature descriptors that can be easily processed. These features are extracted to train and test traditional machine learning classifiers.

3.4 Supervised Machine Learning Classifiers

The following supervised machine learning classifiers trained on the feature extracted through AlexNet and ResNet18 deep models.

K Nearest Neighbors (K-NN) [1] finds the k data points that are nearest to a given sample data point. The number of k neighbors is tuned by the user. For each sample of the testing data, the algorithm output associates membership to each emotion class, which depends on the value of k i.e., how many nearest neighbors are voting to a specific class. Experiments for K-NN have been performed with different k values i.e., odd values between 1 and 15. The value of K i.e., the number of neighbors which will contribute to the final decision, is tuned by the user and odd values are recommended to have fewer chances of a tie.

Support Vector Machine (SVM) [2], is designed for binary classification. To classify the data points (i.e., our emoji samples), the objective is to find the partition of the input space through hyper-planes as decision boundaries. For multi-class classification, the problem is divided into multiple binary classification problems. In this study we have used *Linear SVM*, *Radial Basis Function (RBF) Kernel*, and *Polynomial Kernel*.

Decision Tree (DS) divides the data into sub-groups recursively. It is a method for the approximation of discrete-valued functions. DS learns a heuristic, non-backtracking search, through the space of all possible decision trees. A pruning algorithm is given to avoid over-fitting [3].

Linear Discriminant Analysis Classifier (LDA) [4] is used to discover the linear combination of features that effectively isolates categories. For multi-class classification, *Fisher discriminant* is used to discover a subspace that restrains class inconsistency.

3.5 Deep Learning Classifiers

Three deep learning classifiers, i.e., AlexNet, GoogleNet, and InceptionV3 are pre-trained on the ImageNet database including 14,197,122 images of over 1000 different general object categories. Then, transfer learning is applied.

AlexNet [5] contains 8 layers, i.e., the first 5 layers are convolutional layers and the last 3 are fully connected layers. The input image is fed to the pre-trained network with a size of $[227 \times 227 \times 3]$ pixels. The softmax function receives the output of the last fully connected layer, which produces a distribution over the given categories.

InceptionV3 [6] is a deep convolutional neural network with 48 layers. The InceptionV3 pre-trained neural network has 3 main blocks: the basic convolutional block, Inception module, and classification block. The training process of InceptionV3 is accelerated by using a 1×1 convolutional kernel by decreasing the number of feature channels.

GoogleNet [14] is a 22 layers deep convolutional neural network. The input of the GoogleNet RGB images is of size $[224 \times 224 \times 3]$ pixels.

For fine-tuning deep neural networks, 3 different independent training functions/optimizers are used, i.e., Adaptive Moment Estimation (adam) [15], stochastic gradient descent with momentum (sgdm) [16], and Root Mean Square Propagation (rmsprop). *Adam* is an extension of stochastic gradient descent that has a small memory requirement and requires only first-order gradients, while *sgdm* uses stochastic gradient descent with momentum, i.e. a moving average of gradients, used to update the weights. *rmsprop* uses an adaptive learning rate instead of setting it as a hyper-parameter.

4 Experimental Results

This section describes and compares the experimental results achieved through traditional and deep learning classifiers. Accuracy is used as a performance metric to grade different classification algorithms, chosen as the most commonly used metric both for supervised and deep learning.

4.1 Traditional Machine Learning Classifiers Performance

This section expands on the experimental results achieved using traditional machine learning classifiers described in Sect. 3.2. Figure 3(a) highlights an accuracy achieved through k-NN classifiers using different odd values of k ranging from 1 to 15. We used features that are extracted through AlexNet and ResNet18. Experimental results indicate that for k = 1, we achieved the highest accuracy 94.66% and 94.97% using features extracted through AlexNet and Resnet18deep models, respectively. With a higher k, the classification performance keeps on degrading. K-NN Achieves higher performance on features extracted through Resnet18 model. SVM classifier trained using Linear, Radial Basis Function

(RBF), and Polynomial Kernels. Results Fig. 3(b) indicates that Linear SVM gives better performance compared to RBF and polynomial kernels i.e., 94.97% accuracy is achieved using features extracted through AlexNet, while SVM with RBF kernel gives less than 25% accuracy, which is very low. Unlike K-NN, SVM performs better on AlexNet extracted features. When data is linearly separable, Linear SVM performs better. K-NN achieved the highest accuracy 94.97% with k = 1 on Resnet18 feature descriptor, while linear SVM achieve the same highest accuracy of 94.97% through AlexNet feature descriptor. Results show that K-NN and SVM achieve the same highest accuracy (94.97%), while LDA and Decision tree performance is low compared to SVM and K-NN. Decision Tree achieves less than (66%) accuracy, which is very low compared to the other three traditional supervised classifiers.

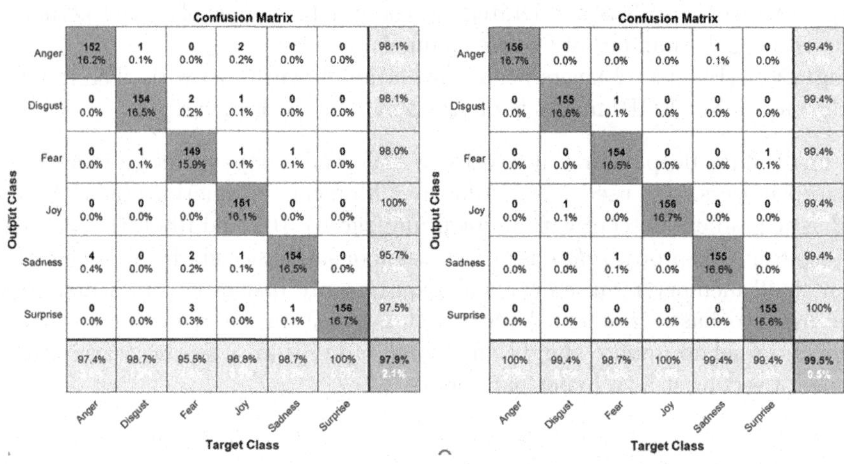

Fig. 2. **(a)** and **(b)**: on left confusion matrix of AlexNet and right confusion matrix of the best performing InceptionV3 NN (accuracy achieved: 99.47%)

4.2 Deep Classifiers Performance

This paragraph shows the results of the experimented deep neural networks.

GoogleNet and InceptionV3 perform better compared to AlexNet. We achieved the highest accuracy of 97.86%, 98.40%, and 99.47% through AlexNet, GoogleNet, and InceptionV3 model respectively. For training of these neural networks, we have used three different training functions (optimizer) i.e. *adam*, *sgdm*, and *rmsprop*. Table 1 shows the details of the experiments performed using different training functions and Learning Rates. The loss for InceptionV3 is lower compared to GoogleNet. The highest accuracy (97.47%) is achieved using InceptionV3 model with a learning rate 0.0001 and training function *adam*, while GoogleNet achieve highest performance 98.40% using training function *rmsprop* and learning rate 0.0001. The possible reason for the highest accuracy achieved

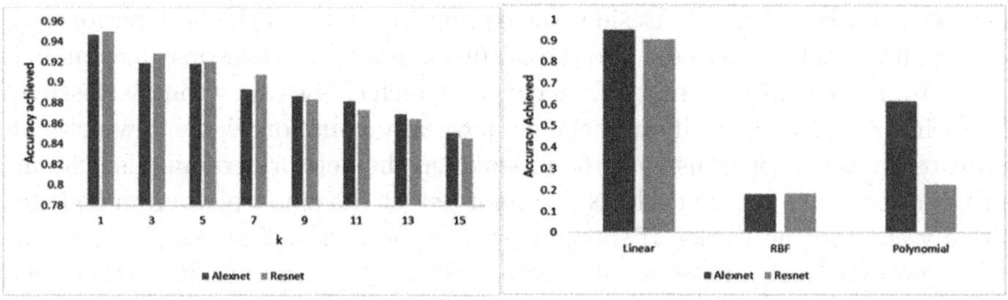

Fig. 3. (a) and (b): on the left, performance of K-NN for different k values; on the right, performance of SVM with different kernels on deep features

through InceptionV3 model may be the number of layers of the model, InceptionV3 has more layers compared to GoogleNet and AlexNet. AlexNet achieves highest accuracy 97.86% using training function *adam* and learning rate 0.00001. Another important observation is that for both AlexNet and InceptionV3, the highest accuracy is achieved through *adam*, while GoogleNet achieves the highest accuracy through *rmsprop*.

4.3 Discussion

Figure 4 shows the comparison of the deep learning (DL) and traditional supervised classifiers trained on the features extracted through AlexNet and Resnet18. InceptionV3 achieves the highest performance, while deep learning outperforms traditional machine learning. Among traditional classifiers, K-NN and SVM have the same best performance around 95%, similar to the LDA in the second place around 92%. Decision Tree has the worst performance, i.e. around 65%.

Further analysis of the performance of InceptionV3 (IV3) and AlexNet (AN), i.e., the best and the worst DL classifiers, can be achieved with the help of confusion matrices shown in Fig. 2(a) and (b), to show the overall and class-wise performance. IV3 achieved an overall accuracy of 99.47%, while AN achieved 97.86%. IV3 perfectly classified all the images of class Joy and Anger, while AN

Table 1. Validation accuracy (%) achieved using different learning rates (LR) and training functions.

Classifier	AlexNet			GoogleNet			InceptionV3		
Optimizer	*adam*	*sgdm*	*rmsprop*	*adam*	sgdm	rmsprop	*adam*	*sgdm*	*rmsprop*
Learning rate	Accuracy achieved								
0.01	16.67	16.67	16.67	16.67	16.67	16.67	82.37	98.4	79.81
0.001	16.67	16.67	16.67	84.72	97.86	16.67	95.51	98.61	96.37
0.0001	94.55	96.69	92.95	98.29	97.33	**98.40**	**99.47**	93.91	98.18
0.00001	**97.86**	95.51	97.65	96.69	82.26	97.54	93.91	75.53	94.76

misclassified several images. Besides the confusion matrix of the best-performing network, it is interesting to see also the confusion matrix of the worse deep model. In fact, from the confusion matrix, we can see which classes are wrongly classified in which classes, and see if such classes have any common element which can motivate the errors or if instead, the mistake on the network training is evident. In this case, we can see that AlexNet cannot detect the emoji pictogram features as easily as other networks. If some errors can depend on the samples, such as the Angry emotions mistaken into Sad or Disgust, where we have the same downward direction of lips, in other cases such as joy mistaken as Sad, Fear, and Angry, something went wrong in the network training. The final result is a high accuracy, but the single mistakes are heavier than the ones made by InceptionV3. In the latter, Joy, which is the emotional class that also in face detection is easier to recognize, does not present any mistake. The errors are apparent in the Fear class mistaken as Sad or Disgust, sharing similar features, Sad is one time mistaken as Angry, Surprise as Fear one time, having the big open mouth as a shared element. Only in the case of disgust mistaken as Joy, the training issue is more evident. Results achieved through InceptionV3 model are better compared to the other tested classifiers of this study.

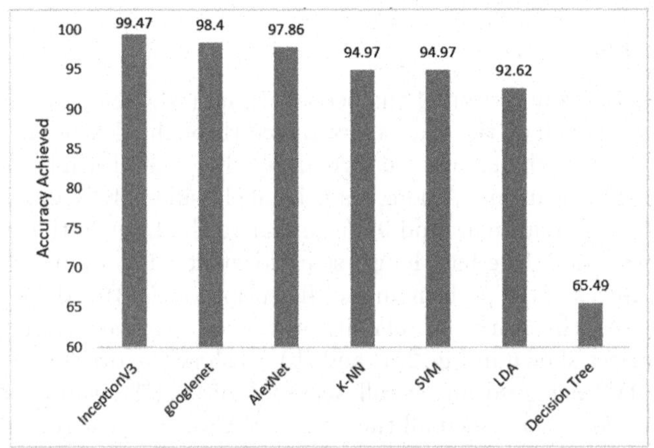

Fig. 4. Highest performance achieved by deep learning models & traditional classifiers

5 Conclusion

In this study, systematic experiments are performed to classify emojis pictograms into six basic classes of Ekman emotions. We run the experiments on traditional supervised classifiers trained on deep features extracted through AlexNet and Resnet18 pre-trained networks, and three deep learning pre-trained NNs, trained using transfer learning. Traditional classifiers K-NN and SVM achieved 94.97% accuracy using Resnet and AlexNet features respectively, while Decision Tree achieved the lowest accuracy i.e., 65.49% and 58.01% using AlexNet and ResNet features respectively. The highest 99.47% accuracy is achieved by InceptionV3 model, while AlexNet and GoogleNet performances are better compared to traditional supervised classifiers.

A fruitful extension of this work is to use multi-modal approaches e.g., merging our work with Natural Language Processing techniques for a deeper context analysis.

References

1. Guo, G., Wang, H., Bell, D., Bi, Y., Greer, K.: KNN model-based approach in classification. In: Meersman, R., Tari, Z., Schmidt, D.C. (eds.) OTM 2003. LNCS, vol. 2888, pp. 986–996. Springer, Heidelberg (2003). https://doi.org/10.1007/978-3-540-39964-3_62
2. Chih-Wei, H., Chih-Jen, L.: A comparison of methods for multiclass support vector machines. IEEE Trans. Neural Netw. **13**(2), 415–425 (2002)
3. Mitchell, T.M.: Machine learning (1997)
4. Şener, B., Çokluk-Bökeoğlu, Ö.: Discriminant function analysis: concept and application. Eurasian J. Educ. Res. (EJER) **33**, 73–92 (2008)
5. Li, W., Li, D., Zeng, S.: Traffic Sign Recognition with a small convolutional neural network. In: IOP, vol. 688, no. 4 (2019)
6. Krizhevsky, A., Sutskever, I., Hinton, G.E.: ImageNet classification with deep convolutional neural networks. In: Advances in Neural Information Processing Systems, vol. 25, pp. 1097–1105 (2012)
7. Sahoo, J., Prakash, S.A., Patra, S.K.: Hand gesture recognition using PCA based deep CNN reduced features and SVM classifier. In: IEEE International Symposium on Smart Electronic Systems (iSES), pp. 221–224 (2019)
8. Ekman, P.: An argument for basic emotions. Cogn. Emot. **6**(3–4), 169–200 (1992)
9. Jain, D.K., Shamsolmoali, P., Sehdev, P.: Extended deep neural network for facial emotion recognition. Pattern Recogn. Lett. **120**, 69–74 (2019)
10. Yan, J., Wenming, Z., et al.: Sparse kernel reduced-rank regression for bimodal emotion recognition from facial expression and speech. IEEE Trans. Multimed. **18**(7), 1319–1329 (2016)
11. Martin, W., Metallinou, A., et al.: Context-sensitive multimodal emotion recognition from speech and facial expression using bidirectional LSTM modeling. In: Proceedings of INTERSPEECH, pp. 2362–2365 (2010)
12. Liu, X., Fan, F., et al.: Image2Audio: facilitating semi-supervised audio emotion recognition with facial expression image. In: Proceedings of the IEEE/CVF, pp. 912–913 (2020)
13. He, K., Zhang, X., et al.: Deep residual learning for image recognition. In: Proceedings of the IEEE Conference on Computer Vision and Pattern Recognition, pp. 770–778 (2016)
14. Szegedy, C., Liu, W., et al.: Going deeper with convolutions. In: Proceedings of the IEEE Conference on Computer Vision and Pattern Recognition, pp. 1–9 (2015)
15. Ba, J.L., et al.: Adam: a method for stochastic gradient descent. In: ICLR, pp. 1–15 (2015)

16. Liu, Y., Gao, Y., Yin, W.: An improved analysis of stochastic gradient descent with momentum. arXiv preprint arXiv:2007.07989 (2020)
17. Franzoni, V., Biondi, G., Perri, D., Gervasi, O.: Enhancing mouth-based emotion recognition using transfer learning. Sensors **20**(18), 5222 (2020)
18. Gervasi, O., Franzoni, V., Riganelli, M., Tasso, S.: Automating facial emotion recognition. Web Intell. **17**(1), 17–27 (2019)

An Artificial Intelligence Based Approach Towards Inclusive Healthcare Provisioning in Society 5.0: A Perspective on Brain Disorder

Shamim Al Mamun[1,2(✉)], M. Shamim Kaiser[1,2], and Mufti Mahmud[3,4,5]

[1] Institute of Information Technology, Jahangirngar University, Savar, Dhaka 1342, Bangladesh

[2] Applied Intelligence and Informatics Lab (AII-Lab), Jahangirngar University, Savar, Dhaka 1342, Bangladesh
{shamim,mskaiser}@juniv.edu

[3] Department of Computer Science, Nottingham Trent University, Clifton Lane, Nottingham NG118NS, UK

[4] Medical Technologies Innovation Facility, Nottingham Trent University, Clifton Lane, Nottingham NG118NS, UK

[5] Computing and Informatics Research Centre, Nottingham Trent University, Clifton Lane, Nottingham NG118NS, UK
mufti.mahmud@ntu.ac.uk

Abstract. Face detection and sparse facial feature analysis is popular as a non-invasive approach to diagnosis special disease. In futuristic intelligent healthcare system, the confined way of preliminary computer aided diagnosis of diseases becoming more inclusive and faster than usual time. Therefore, face spacial feature analysis can be an elegant way of measuring attempt in tele-medicine industry. In this research paper, we investigate thorough review on disease diagnosis techniques, healthcare management and, data security features being used currently. Moreover, this work propose a i-health care monitoring and examining system of neuronal/brain disorder in layer base approach. Overall, this paper reviews about diseases which have already been detected by spacial feature of face using deep learning algorithm or feature based learning with a proposal of a monitoring system with its research area and challenges in smart intelligent healthcare system in society 5.0.

Keywords: Features · Face detection · Deep learning · Cloud system

1 Introduction

Face detection, a rapid growth of technology in the recent days, can predict the age, sex, race, and even social status and personality. Face detection techniques is also used in different application: liveliness detection in security system, criminal identification, bio-metric attendance system etc. Besides, a skilled observation

M. Mahmud et al. (Eds.): BI 2021, LNAI 12960, pp. 157–169, 2021.
https://doi.org/10.1007/978-3-030-86993-9_15

of the face is also relevant in the diagnosis and assessment of mental, physical, neurological disorder, non-communicable (NCD) diseases. The face appearance of a patient may indeed provide diagnostic clues to the illness, the severity of the disease and some vital patient's values.

Due to the large number of possible syndromes and their rarity, achieving the correct diagnosis involves a lengthy and expensive process. However, early diagnosis of disease syndromes improves outcomes and increase the efficiency of prevention of a disease. That's why, the confined way of preliminary computer aided diagnosis of diseases becoming more popular and safer than usual time. Therefore, face spacial feature analysis is an elegant way of measuring attempt of disease diagnosis techniques [21].

Face detection and sparse facial feature analysis can be a vital role to determine different kind of diseases: Autism Spectrum Disorder, Alzheimer, Acromegaly, Dementia, Cornelia de Lange syndrome (CdLS), Parkinson, Heartbeat Measurement, Strabismus, Traumatic Brain Injury, Oculomotor abnormalities, Schizophrenia and also can be used in different healthcare goal: ASD Assessment, Ophthalmology, Attention Monitoring, Brain Injury Assessment, Pain Monitoring, Depression Monitoring, Home Therapy Control, Vital Parameters Monitoring etc. [26].

Distinguish Healthcare research taxonomy introduced the facial feature of face. Some facial features which can be vital features to predict and detect the diseases: eyes, mouth, muscles, skin, and shape. Face detection and recognition system analyze each facial feature and the related healthcare goals that are pursued in detailed in our proposed approach.

Over the last decade machine learning (ML), Deep Learning (DL) [29] and, explainable AI has been successfully applied to biological data mining [28], image analysis and, disease detection & prediction. Recently, Many advance technology is applied to detect and predict the diseases based on facial features analysis using DL and ML approaches with outstanding performance and accuracy. Particularly, DL is now prominent approaches to detect the diseases from sparse facial features analysis.

Our contribution in this paper is as follows-

(i) to review about neural diseases which have already been detected by spacial feature of face using deep learning algorithm or feature based learning.
(ii) to conclude with a proposal of a monitoring system with its research area and challenges in smart intelligent healthcare system
(iii) layered proposal of healthcare facilities in Society 5.0.

The rest of the paper is organized as following. In Sect. 2, we discussed some literature review of existing researches. Disease identification methods in Sect. 3. In Sect. 4, i-Health Monitoring System in Society 5.0 is discussed. In Sect. 5, reports studies concentrate on opportunities and challenges. Finally, conclusion discussed in Sect. 6.

2 Disease Identification Methods

Face analysis has become a significant area of research for identifying faces that may be masked or unmasked, recognition of expression, emotion analysis, detection of diseases i.e. Parkinson's, Autism, Schizophrenia, Alzheimer's, pain detection and so on. For face detection, an early study [22] has utilized a system made up of two parts where the first part is for face detection and the following is for skin color detection (TSCD). The skin color detection neural network of this study [22] has been utilized for reducing the face search area to skin regions. An improved deep neural network, Mask R-CNN has been proposed in [2] for both detection and segmentation of human face by utilizing 101 layers deep Convolutional Neural Network (CNN) 'ResNet-101' for highlights separation, a Region Proposal Network for Region of Interests (ROIs) creation, and RoIAlign for the preservation of the exact spatial locations to generate the binary mask.

Individual picture of the faces has been detected with the closest neighbor classifier [35] and moreover, facial expressions testing and processing has been done by neural substrate pattern and Convolutional Neural Networks [10,25].

In futuristic society, researchers have done a lot of works on diseases detection based on facial features to identifying the face with emotion [8,14]. Almost all kind of neurological disorder diseases have been investigated with average accuracy of 95% [11,15,15,16,32]. Neuro-diseases like depression, anxiety, stress, schizophrenia, Parkinson and Alzheimer's diseases have been detected from the above research and the accuracy is appreciated. In addition, Pain detection and genetic diseases are also testifying with facial features [30,32]. Cardiocascular [34] and heartbeat measurement also taken into account for finding diagnosis of diseases. Moreover, Eye diseases and diabetes with average accuracy 96% have been tested in [1,3]. Tables 1 and 2, illustrated the summery of the diseases that have been state-of-art research for disease detection using deep learning with facial features. Explainable AI getting much assistive to give more explanation for the proper diagnosis of the doctors and hospital settings. In society 5.0, people will be more concern about their daily lifestyle to get fit without hassling to go clinical diagnosis rather they wanted to get medical service as much as at home suggests as a method for health care, AI was not created directly. And while AI is poised to answer "pain points" in indurate medical practice, it is neither astute nor intuitive. Humans would however remain key to the informed use of AI in medical practice.

3 Society 5.0

Society 5.0 is an idea of a human-focused future society in Japan that profoundly coordinates virtual space and real space, offsetting the economic headway with the resolution of social problems. This idea was proposed to lessen the constraints of the current society, in particular the trouble of investigating enormous data by a human for tracking down the essential one, the inconvenience of sharing information sufficiently for all in responding enough because of the limitations

Table 1. Detected diseases analysing human face

Ref	Detected disease	Performance
[14]	Depression, anxiety, stress	Accuracy: 93% for healthy vs depressed or stressed
[8]	Schizophrenia	Pearson's Correlation Coefficient (PCC): .42 (For Positive and Negative Syndrome Scale)
[32]	Genetic Diseases	Accuracy: 97.66%
[34]	Neurological disorders	Accuracy: 94.44%
[30]	Pain detection	Accuracy: 98%
[6]	Parkinsons	Accuracy: 95.6
[11]	Autism	Area Under Curve (AUC): .792
[17]	Beta-thalassemia, Hyperthyroidism, Down Syndrome, and Leprosy	Accuracy: 90%
[15]	Hypomimia	Sensitivity/Specificity: 0.58/0.54
[1]	Diabetic retinopathy	Accuracy: 92%
[16]	Alzheimer's Disease	Accuracy high [16], 95.04%
[23]	Acromegaly	sensitivity of 96% and a specificity of 96%
[13],	Diabetes	Accuracy: 97%
[3]	Retinal and Eye Diseases	Accuracy: 95%

Table 2. Datasets and features of diseases

Ref	Used Datasets	Detected diseases
[14]	Own collected dataset: total 128 subjects (46 effected and 82 normal)	Depression, anxiety, stress
[8]	EmotioNet [7], ExpW [36], CelebA [27], CEW [33]	Schizophrenia
[32]	eLife database consists of 12 classes of genetic syndromes of 1567 images [12]	Rare genetic diseases
[34]	Radboud Face Database (RaFD) [24]	Neurological disorders
[6]	Own collected dataset: 1812 videos of 604 individuals. (61 with PD and 543 without PD)	Parkinsons
[11]	Own collected dataset: 104 children with and without autism	Autism

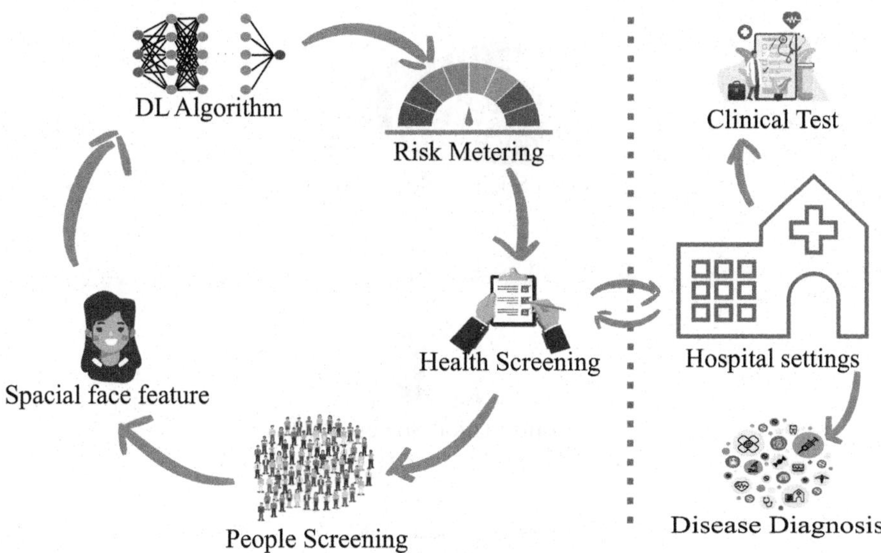

Fig. 1. Smart Healthcare in Society 5.0. From the people, smart healthcare facilities will identified facial feature to identifying the risk of being ill, the smart decision have been made for further clinical test through appropriate diagnosis in the hospital or at home.

on issues like a diminishing birthrate and maturing populace and nearby elimination. In Society 5.0, people, things, and systems are entirely related to the internet, and ideal results got by AI outperforming the individuals' capacities are dealt with back to physical space. Along these lines, society 5.0 targets making a new society fusing with cutting-edge innovations. Every individual can lead a functioning, top calibre, and pleasant life, having shared respect for one another eliminating provincial, age, sexual orientation and language gaps.

Healthcare, the most necessary domains for ensuring the characteristics of society 5.0, is one space that seems advantageous most through the utilization of cutting-edge innovations [5,31]. In society, the healthcare framework in organization 5.0 ought to incorporate things like a coherent healthcare framework, create next-generation pharmaceuticals, build a biological healthcare system, or collect, connect, and utilize life-course information. In society 5.0, the data can be managed by broadening the utilization of genomic tests, extending wellbeing exam checklists, utilization of wearable gadgets, digitization, and standardization of therapeutic and care information. Connecting the collected information can be done by creating individual data-linked IDs, Personal Data Store (PDS), and restorative blockchains, or creating Electronic Health Record (EHR), Personal Health Record (PHR). The collected and connected information can form a Healthcare information platform with open entry to National Data Base (NDB) with expanded utilization by the private division. The PDS will observe using a biometric confirmation in future healthcare framework. Moreover, different

Fig. 2. Definition of Society 5.0: The birth of human beings before 13000 BC when human coexisted with animal. After that humans are socialize with agricultural activities in middle age. Around 18th century industrial revulsion occurs and now industrial revulsion 4.0 is running which is called society 4.0. The supper smart society in the days to come where human will surrounded by robot, IoT devices, Big Data analysis for logic and AI support daily life style.

information in PDS with individual assent, dietary database, and dietary plans custom that fitted to the person is beneficial to detect PDS. Making next-generation pharmaceuticals, drugs can be personalized by progression in genomic determination and treatment supporting dignified revelation with AI. Regenerative medications can be fabricated, the symptomatic bolster can be given for doctor analysis, demonstrative imaging, liquid biopsies, progressed helpful instrumented can be created, digital therapy can be promoted, nursing care back can be encouraged by IT upgrades, inquire about on robotized respect, and medications for dementia, bio-security can be ensured. In futuristic smart helathcare, a collaboration between the medical and diagnosis field can be advanced with open development. In addition, serviceable separation at the community level can be energized and faster.

4 Methodology of Society 5.0 Healthcare

Mass people will be screened using a CCTV camera. An individual patient can check their health checkup using a mobile camera associated with various IoT sensors like temperature, smartwatch for heartbeat measurement, facial images from a web camera and other sensor input. Facial features are gathered using a camera and diagnosis with a pre-trained DL algorithm to find risk factor of his/her health. If the health condition is serious, then the online personnel doctor will suggest hospital settings for further diagnosis and clinical tests. Furthermore, virtual doctors are also employed in the web services to check the current health status from facial recognition and fuse that features with the sensors data to suggest patients for early treatment. Figure 2, illustrated the methodological cycle of the disease identification in the early stage of the patient's condition. In Society 5.0, daily life will be so fast and convenient that patients will not bother to go clinical test to identify his/her condition to move on.

5 Layer Architecture of Intelligent Health Service

In some cases where an urgent medical assistant is needed, we usually go to the hospital, such as having an accident or a heart attack, or a brain stroke. In this case, the online health assistant can play a very valuable role in the super society. Accordingly, the online assistant can review the form and give quick advice and contact the nearest hospital. But suppose all the daily ailments like glucose level measurement, eye pain, depression, body aches, heartbeat irregularity etc. are reported to the online assistant from home. In that case, the online assistant machine learning approach to the patient is a timely advice. In this case, we are proposing the following service level Architecture for Society 5.0 illustrated in Fig. 3.

5.1 Logic Layer

Many organizations will work on this logic layer. The government, hospitals, insurance companies, and pharmaceuticals play a vital role in this layer. The Logic layer have been build in such a way that all the business rule imposed by the government is implemented with easily accessible network. Web services, mobile accessibility, data query rules for the entire system are attributed here. In addition, it will perform administrative and research functions. The logic layer permits the government ministry for health directives to the doctors and third parties to handle Electronic Medical Record (EMR) data [28]. Hospital settings and insurance companies are directly associated to the transaction logic and pharmaceuticals will take initiatives for customization of drag management.

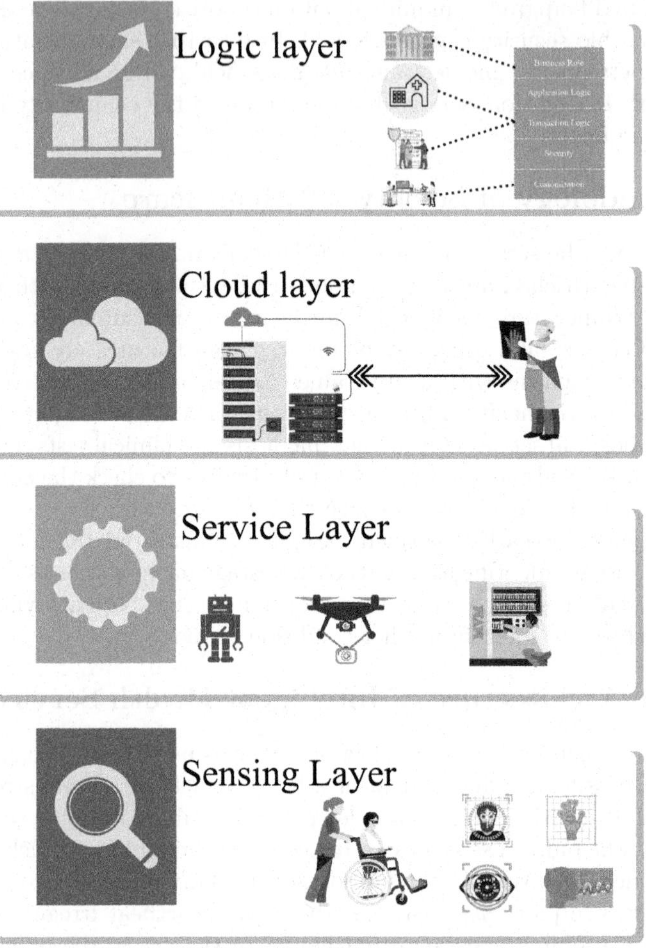

Fig. 3. Layer architecture of services in society 5.0. The Logic layer manages the residential inpatient neurological treatment Center with business logic. In contrast, the Cloud layer provides network connectivity of this center. The service layer ensures all possible healthcare assistive devices and machines for the patient to contact for the services. The sensing layer is the client access layer where facial recognition with computer vision-aided diagnosis will provide to the service—in a nutshell, the sensing layer act as a data acquisition provider.

5.2 Cloud Layer

The cloud layer's computing [9] burden is because all sorts of computing for disease diagnosis using facial features have tremendous data pressure on handheld devices. The cloud off-loading techniques will manage the mobile device power for long-term access. Moreover, The communication between other layers will establish using REST. Web services APIs will access cloud resources and operate them. Most importantly, the EMR data will be stored on the permanent storage servers or analyzed for decision-making by the medical personnel at this layer.

5.3 Service Layer

Disease diagnosis services will be completed by the end player like service robot [4,18,19], drone, and vending machine will be used to deliver medicine and clinical record. In addition, if a patient needs a further clinical test, the patient will use the above service machine that governs by the hospital settings. We will use different services in this society created by artificial intelligence, big data, IoT, and machine learning. Diagnosis from facial images will be sent to the primary health service via cloud service via mobile. From there, this service layer will use advanced 6G mobile connectivity [20], high-speed internet, and Optical device to fill up the necessary medical care.

5.4 Sensing Layer

In this layer, the patient's facial images scan by CCTV or handheld device. Moreover, IoT sensors will be available in society 5.0, where people can measure their heartbeat, blood pressure, blood sugar level even though heart attack/brain stroke symptoms. All the sensors for monitoring the health vitals of patients and older adults. Mobiles, Arduino, Raspberry Pi, will transmit data in real-time to the nearby cloud node.

6 Opportunity and Challenges

The quality of services is the main challenge of society 5.0 healthcare. However, many efforts have been directed in this area by researchers. The accurate disease prediction and automated prescription with delivery services in the next generation are the primary goals. Moreover, Service Level Agreement (SLA) violations will be looked after by the healthcare providers. Many researchers propose a high level of node connectivity in cloud and IoT, but latency is still problematic and Far-fetched. Though wireless Body Sensor Nodes (WBSN) have been working well, they exploit emerging technologies to reduce energy consumption and enhance performance

A facial feature collection is another challenge through the image. Though DL networks work well, researchers are not getting a proper explanation of the features, and accuracy is questionable. Here, XAI is introduced, and researchers are delivering state-of-art works on it. Shortly, quantum computing, cloud edge services, and high-speed network will cover all those challenges.

Our future goal is to detect non-communicable diseases using facial features and find the associated disease like the kidney problem, heart-attack prediction, diabetes type-2 detection.

7 Conclusion

An information-based society is highly dependent on cross-sectional knowledge but it is very difficult to manage and incorporate. Because there is a curtailment of human beings and the flowing information in such a society. So, social reformation is needed in a futuristic society to gather all the services under one umbrella. Our objective in this paper was how we can give society beautiful and tidy healthcare where impatient management of this neurological disordered patients. Moreover, cognitive therapeutic method needs more care and sometimes it needed residential inpatient neurological treatment Center. This paper shown that the best health brain/neuro-care systems can be developed using a variety of services for the brain or neurological health patients with facial recognition technologies and artificial intelligence. The layered architecture ensures the services in different labels and moreover, this paper concludes with the future research gap and challenges in the healthcare management sector.

References

1. Abràmoff, M.D., Lavin, P.T., Birch, M., Shah, N., Folk, J.C.: Pivotal trial of an autonomous AI-based diagnostic system for detection of diabetic retinopathy in primary care offices. NPJ Digit. Med. **1**(1), 1–8 (2018). https://doi.org/10.1038/s41746-018-0040-6, https://www.nature.com/articles/s41746-018-0040-6, number: 1 Publisher: Nature Publishing Group
2. Lin, K., et al.: Face detection and segmentation based on improved mask R-CNN. In: MDPI (2020). https://doi.org/10.1155/2020/9242917
3. Limkar, S., et al.: Detection of Retinal and Eye Diseases by using Convolutional Neural Network, December 2020. https://jusst.org/detection-of-retinal-eye-diseases-by-using-convolutional-neural-network/
4. Al Mamun, S., Chowdhury, Z.I., Kaiser, M.S., Islam, M.S.: Techno-financial analysis and design of on-board intelligent-assisting system for a hybrid solar-DEG-powered boat. Int. J. Energy Environ. Eng. **7**(4), 361–376 (2016)
5. Mamun, S.A., Lam, A., Kobayashi, Y., Kuno, Y.: Single laser bidirectional sensing for robotic wheelchair step detection and measurement. In: Huang, D.-S., Hussain, A., Han, K., Gromiha, M.M. (eds.) ICIC 2017. LNCS (LNAI), vol. 10363, pp. 37–47. Springer, Cham (2017). https://doi.org/10.1007/978-3-319-63315-2_4
6. Ali, M.R., Myers, T., Wagner, E., Ratnu, H., Dorsey, E.R., Hoque, E.: Facial expressions can detect parkinson's disease: preliminary evidence from videos collected online. arXiv:2012.05373 (2020). http://arxiv.org/abs/2012.05373
7. Benitez-Quiroz, C.F., Srinivasan, R., Martinez, A.M.: EmotioNet: an accurate, real-time algorithm for the automatic annotation of a million facial expressions in the wild. In: 2016 IEEE Conference on Computer Vision and Pattern Recognition (CVPR), pp. 5562–5570. IEEE (2016). https://doi.org/10.1109/CVPR.2016.600, http://ieeexplore.ieee.org/document/7780969/
8. Bishay, M., Palasek, P., Priebe, S., Patras, I.: SchiNet: automatic estimation of symptoms of schizophrenia from facial behaviour analysis. In: IEEE Transactions on Affective Computing, p. 1 (2019). https://doi.org/10.1109/TAFFC.2019.2907628, conference Name: IEEE Transactions on Affective Computing

9. Biswas, S., Anisuzzaman, Akhter, T., Kaiser, M.S., Mamun, S.A.: Cloud based healthcare application architecture and electronic medical record mining: an integrated approach to improve healthcare system. In: 2014 17th International Conference on Computer and Information Technology (ICCIT), pp. 286–291 (2014). https://doi.org/10.1109/ICCITechn.2014.7073139
10. Blair, R.J.R., Morris, J.S., Frith, C.D., Perrett, D.I., Dolan, R.J.: Dissociable neural responses to facial expressions of sadness and anger. Brain J. Neurol. **122**(5), 883–893 (1999). https://doi.org/10.1093/brain/122.5.883
11. Carpenter, K.L.H., et al.: Digital behavioral phenotyping detects atypical pattern of facial expression in toddlers with autism. In: Autism Research n/a (2021). https://doi.org/10.1002/aur.2391, https://onlinelibrary.wiley.com/doi/abs/10.1002/aur.2391
12. Ferry, Q., et al.: Diagnostically relevant facial gestalt information from ordinary photos. eLIFE **3**, e01883 (2014). https://doi.org/10.7554/eLife.02020
13. Gadekallu, T.R., et al.: Early detection of diabetic retinopathy using PCA-firefly based deep learning model. Electronics **9**(2), 274 (2020) https://doi.org/10.3390/electronics9020274, https://www.mdpi.com/2079-9292/9/2/274, number: 2 Publisher: Multidisciplinary Digital Publishing Institute
14. Gavrilescu, M., Vizireanu, N.: Predicting depression, anxiety, and stress levels from videos using the facial action coding system. Sensors **19**(17), 3693 (2019) https://doi.org/10.3390/s19173693, https://www.mdpi.com/1424-8220/19/17/3693, number: 17 Publisher: Multidisciplinary Digital Publishing Institute
15. Grammatikopoulou, A., Grammalidis, N., Bostantjopoulou, S., Katsarou, Z.: Detecting hypomimia symptoms by selfie photo analysis: for early parkinson disease detection. In: Proceedings of the 12th ACM International Conference on PErvasive Technologies Related to Assistive Environments, pp. 517–522. PETRA 2019, Association for Computing Machinery (2019). https://doi.org/10.1145/3316782.3322756
16. He, T., Zhang, X., Zhu, L.: Early diagnosis of Alzheimer's disease based on face recognition using M-Health technology. Int. J. Eng. Intell. Syst. 28(2), 235 (2020). https://website-eis.crlpublishing.com/index.php/eis/article/view/1467, number: 2
17. Jin, B., Cruz, L., Gonçalves, N.: Deep facial diagnosis: deep transfer learning from face recognition to facial diagnosis. IEEE Access **8**, 123649–123661 (2020). https://doi.org/10.1109/ACCESS.2020.3005687
18. Kaiser, M.S., Al Mamun, S., Mahmud, M., Tania, M.H.: Healthcare robots to combat COVID-19. In: Santosh, K.C., Joshi, A. (eds.) COVID-19: Prediction, Decision-Making, and its Impacts. LNDECT, vol. 60, pp. 83–97. Springer, Singapore (2021). https://doi.org/10.1007/978-981-15-9682-7_10
19. Kaiser, M.S., et al.: iWorksafe: Towards healthy workplaces during Covid-19 with an intelligent Phealth app for industrial settings. IEEE Access **9**, 13814–13828 (2021). https://doi.org/10.1109/ACCESS.2021.3050193
20. Kaiser, M.S., et al.: 6G access network for intelligent internet of healthcare things: opportunity, challenges, and research directions. In: Kaiser, M.S., Bandyopadhyay, A., Mahmud, M., Ray, K. (eds.) Proceedings of International Conference on Trends in Computational and Cognitive Engineering. AISC, vol. 1309, pp. 317–328. Springer, Singapore (2021). https://doi.org/10.1007/978-981-33-4673-4_25
21. Kaiser, M.S., et al.: Advances in crowd analysis for urban applications through urban event detection. Trans. Intell. Transport. Syst. **19**(10), 3092–3112 (2018) https://doi.org/10.1109/TITS.2017.2771746

22. Karungaru, S., Fukumi, M., Akamatsu, N.: Detection of human faces in visual scenes. In: The Seventh Australian and New Zealand Intelligent Information Systems Conference, pp. 165–170. IEEE (2001). https://doi.org/10.1109/ANZIIS.2001.974070, http://ieeexplore.ieee.org/document/974070/
23. Kong, X., Gong, S., Su, L., Howard, N., Kong, Y.: Automatic detection of acromegaly from facial photographs using machine learning methods. EBioMedicine **27**, 94–102 (2018) https://doi.org/10.1016/j.ebiom.2017.12.015, http://www.sciencedirect.com/science/article/pii/S2352396417304966
24. Langner, O., Dotsch, R., Bijlstra, G., Wigboldus, D.H.J., Hawk, S.T., Knippenberg, A.V.: Presentation and validation of the radboud faces database. Cogn. Emotion 24(8), 1377–1388 (2010). https://doi.org/10.1080/02699930903485076, publisher: Routledge _eprint
25. Leo, M., et al.: Computational assessment of facial expression production in ASD children. Sensors **18**(11), 67 (2018). https://doi.org/10.3390/s18113993
26. Leo, M., Carcagnì, P., Mazzeo, P.L., Spagnolo, P., Cazzato, D., Distante, C.: Analysis of facial information for healthcare applications: a survey on computer vision-based approaches. MDPI **11**(3), 128 (2020). https://doi.org/10.3390/info11030128, https://www.mdpi.com/2078-2489/11/3/128
27. Liu, Z., Luo, P., Wang, X., Tang, X.: Deep learning face attributes in the wild. In: Proceedings of International Conference on Computer Vision (ICCV), December 2015
28. Mahmud, M., et al.: A brain-inspired trust management model to assure security in a cloud based IoT framework for neuroscience applications. Cogn. Comput. **10**(5), 864–873 (2018)
29. Mamun, S.A., Daud, M.E., Mahmud, M., Kaiser, M.S., Rossi, A.L.D.: ALO: AI for least observed people. In: Mahmud, M., Kaiser, M.S., Kasabov, N., Iftekharuddin, K., Zhong, N. (eds.) AII 2021. CCIS, vol. 1435, pp. 306–317. Springer, Cham (2021). https://doi.org/10.1007/978-3-030-82269-9_24
30. Menchetti, G., Chen, Z., Wilkie, D.J., Ansari, R., Yardimci, Y., Çetin, A.E.: Pain detection from facial videos using two-stage deep learning. In: 2019 IEEE Global Conference on Signal and Information Processing (GlobalSIP), pp. 1–5 (2019). https://doi.org/10.1109/GlobalSIP45357.2019.8969274
31. Rahman, M.M., Mamun, S.A., Kaiser, M.S., Islam, M.S., Rahman, M.A.: Cascade classification of face liveliness detection using heart beat measurement. In: Kaiser, M.S., Bandyopadhyay, A., Mahmud, M., Ray, K. (eds.) Proceedings of International Conference on Trends in Computational and Cognitive Engineering. AISC, vol. 1309, pp. 581–590. Springer, Singapore (2021). https://doi.org/10.1007/978-981-33-4673-4_47
32. Singh, A., Kisku, D.R.: Detection of rare genetic diseases using facial 2D images with transfer learning. In: 2018 8th International Symposium on Embedded Computing and System Design (ISED), pp. 26–30 (2018). https://doi.org/10.1109/ISED.2018.8703997
33. Song, F., Tan, X., Liu, X., Chen, S.: Eyes closeness detection from still images with multi-scale histograms of principal oriented gradients. Pattern Recogn. **47**(9), 2825–2838 (2014). https://doi.org/10.1016/j.patcog.2014.03.024, https://linkinghub.elsevier.com/retrieve/pii/S0031320314001228
34. Yolcu, G., et al.: Facial expression recognition for monitoring neurological disorders based on convolutional neural network. Multimedia Tools Appl. **78**(22), 31581–31603 (2019). https://doi.org/10.1007/s11042-019-07959-6, http://link.springer.com/10.1007/s11042-019-07959-6

35. Zaaraoui, H., Abderrahim, S., Rachid, E.A., Mustapha, A.: A new local descriptor based on strings for face recognition. J. Electr. Comput. Engi. **2020**, (2020)
36. Zhang, Z., Luo, P., Loy, C.C., Tang, X.: From facial expression recognition to interpersonal relation prediction. arXiv:1609.06426 (2017). http://arxiv.org/abs/1609.06426

Sentiment Analysis Model Based on the Word Structural Representation

Gulmira Bekmanova[1,2], Banu Yergesh[1(✉)], and Altynbek Sharipbay[1,2]

[1] L.N. Gumilyov Eurasian National University, Nur-Sultan, Kazakhstan
[2] Nuclear University MEPhI, Moscow, Russian Federation

Abstract. Over the past year, distance learning has become an integral part of our lives and a rapidly developing field. Compared to traditional classroom learning, online learning has advantages such as no place restrictions and a wide range of interactions. At the same time, distance learning lacks interaction between teachers and learners, and teachers cannot observe learners face to face. Identifying students' emotions during distance learning can have a positive impact on learning, improve learning outcomes and improve the effectiveness, quality of learning. This paper describes a theoretical model for determining sentiment/emotion from audio data based on speech recognition. The recognition model based on generalized transcription was proposed. This method can be used to determine the student's emotions during the distance learning and online exam.

Keywords: Natural language processing · Speech recognition · Emotion recognition · Sentiment analysis · Kazakh language · Distance learning

1 Introduction

Emotion recognition is the process of identifying human emotions. People differ from each other in their emotions. Human emotion recognition technology is a new area of research.

The latest advances in the artificial intelligence, deep learning methods, human-friendly Robotics, Cognitive Sciences are used to develop the field of affective computing and approach to creating emotional machines [1–3].

Currently, there are works on the automation of facial emotion recognition from video [4–8], by the rhythm of the voice from audio information [9–12], by the style of writing from texts [13–15].Based on various studies, emotions play a vital role in e-learning [5, 16, 17]. Likewise, improving the emotion recognition learning environment has been focused by researchers in the past few decades in the field of computer-based collaborative learning [18]. Teachers can change their teaching style according to the needs of the students.

Emotions act an important role in the analysis of a student's interest and learning outcomes in the course. Understanding emotions by facial expression is the fastest way to detect emotions [19, 20]. Results on sentiment analysis, emotion recognition in the Kazakh language published in [21–25].

M. Mahmud et al. (Eds.): BI 2021, LNAI 12960, pp. 170–178, 2021.
https://doi.org/10.1007/978-3-030-86993-9_16

Recently, distance learning has become a major formal in education. Distance learning has become a safe and viable option for lifelong learning due to COVID-19 pandemic.

In the new epidemic realities, the role of distance learning in education have greatly increased all over the world, a huge number of people have switched to remote work, schoolchildren and students study remotely. More than 91% of the world's students have been affected by school closures due to the COVID-19 pandemic, according to UNESCO. Even before the pandemic, the global e-education market was already seeing massive annual global growth. The mass transition of education to the distance format has become a serious challenge, both for the University, teachers, and for the students themselves.

Accordingly, the education system provisioning all students with same access to quality education during this crisis.

This gave a powerful impetus to the development of distance learning. According to the UNESCO study, most of the 61 countries surveyed have implemented some form of distance learning. The digital format of education is likely to become more popular in the post-pandemic period. Because this education format is effective and affordable [26, 27].

Our university switched to a distance learning format as well. During distance learning, the Microsoft Teams corporate platform is used, where online classes are recorded on video. And during the session, a proctoring system is used to pass computer testing. We have a database of video recordings of computer testing process. The video is recorded from the webcam and the audio from the microphone. During the examination, many students pronounce questions, talks to themselves, their speech have recorded, and their emotionality was kept by the proctors, so we decided to use the resulting audio material to analyze emotions. This paper describes a theoretical method for determining sentiment/emotion based on speech recognition. This method can be used to measure student emotions during distance learning and online examinations without geographic or cultural limitations.

2 Speech Recognition

Since this experimental work was carried out only to determine sentiment based on special words using generalized transcription recognition method. The recognition method based on generalized transcription, described in [28] used for general Kazakh word recognition before [29], for the first time it is proposed to apply this model for emotion recognition.

2.1 Structural Classification of Kazakh Words and Use of Generalized Transcriptions

This section represents some established statistical about Kazakh words structure. They are, as it seems to us, interesting by them and besides could serve a basis for using the generalized transcriptions. Let's divide all the symbols of the Kazakh alphabet into several natural classes:

W - аұыоеәүіөу
C - бвгғджзйлмнңр
F - сш
P - кқптфх

"W" – vowels plus the consonant "У", which, when pronounced, remains the vocal tract opened; "C" – voiced consonants; "F" – voiceless hush consonants; "P" – voiceless consonants, which when pronounced represent a pause in a word. Let us assume there is a significantly large dictionary of Kazakh words. Now it shall be a dictionary of initial forms containing 41791 words. Let's mark it out, replacing each symbol by the number of its class.

The words with the same marks shall be deemed to have a similar structure. Thus, the structure – is some model of gradation of vowels, consonants, hush sounds, etc. It appears that the number of Kazakh words with a similar structure is relatively small. For example, all the words with a structure WCCWFPWC are as follows:

алжасқан WCCWFPWC
алмастыр WCCWFPWC
ойластыр WCCWFPWC
үндескен WCCWFPWC
алдаспан WCCWFPWC

Here are the words with a structure WCWCWCPW:
ағарыңқы WCWCWCPW
амазонка WCWCWCPW
ұғыныңқы WCWCWCPW

Maximum number of words with the same structure CWCWC equal to 201, that is, And so on. Maximal number of words with a similar structure CWCWC is equal to 201, that amounts to about 0.5%. Moreover it is practically an exclusive case. All other structures contains much lesser words. We have proved it by the program which automatically marks out and selects words with the similar structure. Besides the selection of classes could be changed [30, 31].

The generalized transcription described is developed in the following way. First the voiceless consonants are distinguished from the recorded and processed sound signal as it was above described. The basis for it serves processing of a signal by a band pass filter with the range of transmission interval from 100 to 200 Hz as describes in the work, the coefficients of this filter are estimated according to the following equation:

$$a_k = a_{k,2} - a_{k,1} \tag{1}$$

where $a_{k,2}$ - is the coefficients of audio frequency band-pass filter which band-pass range is equal to 200 Hz, and $a_{k,1}$ - is the coefficients of audio frequency band-pass filter which band-pass range is equal to 100 Hz.

Audio frequency band-pass filters are estimated according to the following equation:

$$a_k = a_{-k} = \frac{2f_0}{f}\frac{\sin\left(k2\pi\frac{f_0}{f}\right)}{k2\pi\frac{f_0}{f}} \tag{2}$$

where k filter order, f_0 - is a transmission frequency of filter, f is a sampling frequency of signal.

The sounds noted differ from all the other ones by the fact that after such filtration their fragments become similar to a pause and contain a large number of constancy points. Thus, at these fragments the difference between the number of inconstancy points and the number of constancy points would be negative, that allows distinguishing them in the massive of such differences developed for the sequence of windows containing 256 counts.

Further the hush and pauselike sounds are selected in the resulted fragments. The analogue of total variation with variable upper limit is estimated:

$$V(0) = 0, V(n) = \sum\nolimits_{i=0}^{n-1} |x_{i+1} - x_i| \tag{3}$$

Let N_1 - maximal number so that $V(N_1) \leq 255$.

N_2 - maximal number so that $W(N_1) \leq 255$ and so on. As a result the following massive of numbers appears

$$N_1, N_2 - N_1, N_3 - N_2 \ldots \tag{4}$$

At the hush segment the value (3) increases rapidly, i.e. the numbers (4) are relatively small. At the pause segment the value (3) increases slowly and consequently the numbers (4) are relatively large. To distinguish between the hush and the pause, introduce a threshold in the system, it is taken as 120.

When the hushes and the pauses are distinguished, the vowels and the voiced consonants are selected. The remaining fragments are divided into windows containing 256 counts and for them the value of total variation is calculated by Eq. (3), then the average of these values is estimated which is considered as the limit. All the values that are above the average are marked "B", below the average – "H". Then the interval, which the described procedure is conducted at, is moved one window to the right and the procedure is repeated. It continues up to the moment when the end of the interval falls outside the boundaries of the fragment (Fig. 1).

The marks of segmentations are entered at the points where the symbols "H" are changed into "B", or "B" into "H". B-fragment is deemed corresponding to the vowel (the symbol W is put near the left mark). H-fragment is deemed corresponding to the voiced consonant (the symbol C is put near the left mark) [30–32].

This algorithm could help to develop even more generalized transcription, namely to divide all the sounds into 2 natural classes: vowels and consonants. Such division gives good results in little dictionaries as well.

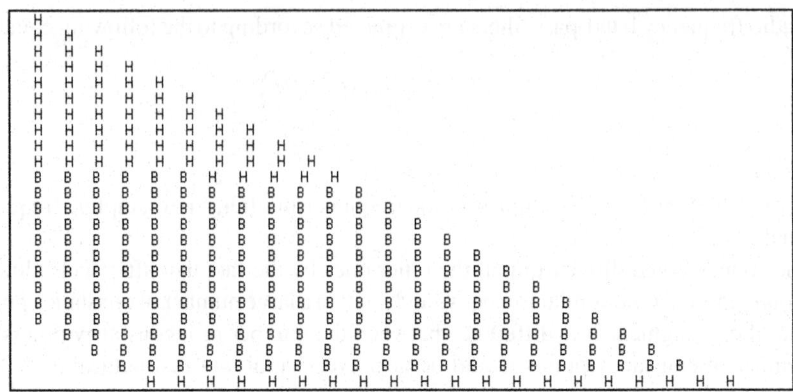

Fig. 1. Signal segmentation

2.2 Construction of Generalized Transcriptions of Sentiment Dictionary

The dictionary of generalized transcriptions of the sentiment dictionary obtained in [34] allows us to construct its generalized transcriptions and apply them to search for emotionally colored words.

Example of emotional words in the Kazakh language with generalized transcription:

Table 1. Example of sentimental words with generalized transcription

Sentiment words	Generalized transcriptions
onai (easy)	WCWC
quanyshtymyn (I'm glad)	PWWCWFPWCWC
senimdimin (I'm sure)	FWCWCCWCWC
daiyndaldym (prepared)	CWCWCCWCCWC
bilemin (I know)	CWCWCWC
aqymaq (stupid)	WPWCWP
qobalzhimyn (I'm worried)	PWCWCCWCCWC
bilmeimin (I don't know)	CWCCWCCWC
qorqamyn (I'm afraid)	PWCPWCWC
qiyn (difficult)	PWCWC

3 Sentiment Analysis

3.1 Dataset

Table 1 below shows the number of videos with audio recordings of the exam process (Table 2).

Table 2. Number of videos with audio recordings

Academic period	Number of videos with audio recordings
1 Semester	14606
2 Semester	4732
Total	19338

3.2 Sentiment Detection Process

The recorded speech is recognized, and then the text is analyzed to determine the sentiment. The process described in Fig. 2. Models and methods for determining the sentiment of texts in the Kazakh language are described in the works [22, 24, 33, 35].

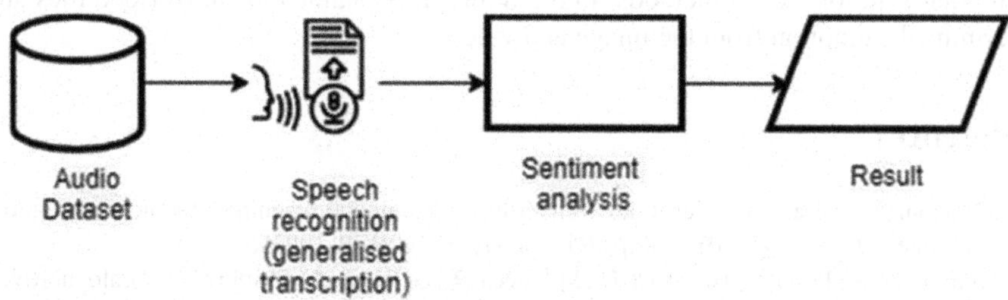

Fig. 2. Sentiment detection process

After speech recognition, words that express emotions are highlighted and tagged into 3 classes Positive, Neutral and Negative (Table 3). This tagged dataset will be used as test set.

Table 3. Sentiment classes

Polarity	Emotion	Number of audio recordings
Positive	Happy	1502
Neutral	Calm, neutral	1000
Negative	Sad, angry, fearful	500

Example:

Recognized words	Sentiment class
senimdimin (I'm sure)	Positive
daiyndaldym (prepared)	Positive
bilemin (I know)	Positive
aqymaq (stupid)	Negative
qobalzhimyn (I'm worried)	Negative

4 Conclusion

This work is devoted to the study and solution of the problem of sentiment analysis of students' speech. As a result of the study of models and methods of speech sentiment analysis of Kazakh language, a semantic base of emotional words with generalized transcription was obtained. Emotion detection models of audio sounds recorded during the distance exam were proposed and implemented. Experimental works in progress now. The implementation and application of this model can improve the interaction between the teacher and the student, improve the quality of distance learning, and help to personalize education. We are planning to complete experimental work and compare with other state-of-the-art methods. In the future, it is planned to study video files and determine the emotion from the image and video.

References

1. Franzoni, V., Milani, A., Nardi, D., Vallverdú, J.: Emotional machines: the next revolution. Web Intell. **17**(1), 1–7 (2019). https://doi.org/10.3233/WEB-190395
2. Majumder, N., Poria, S., Hazarika, D., Mihalcea, R., Gelbukh, A., Cambria, E.: DialogueRNN: an attentive RNN for emotion detection in conversations. In: Proceedings of the AAAI Conference on Artificial Intelligence, Honolulu, pp. 6818–6825 (2019). https://doi.org/10.1609/aaai.v33i01.33016818
3. Biondi, G., Franzoni, V., Poggioni, V.: A deep learning semantic approach to emotion recognition using the IBM Watson Bluemix Alchemy language. In: Gervasi, O., et al. (eds.) ICCSA 2017. LNCS, vol. 10406, pp. 718–729. Springer, Cham (2017). https://doi.org/10.1007/978-3-319-62398-6_51
4. Stappen, L., Baird, A., Cambria, E., Schuller, B.W., Cambria, E.: Sentiment analysis and topic recognition in video transcriptions. IEEE Intell. Syst. **36**(2), 88–95 (2021). Article no. 9434455
5. Yang, D., Alsadoon, A., Prasad, P.W.C., Singh, A.K., Elchouemi, A.: An emotion recognition model based on facial recognition in virtual learning environment. Procedia Comput. Sci. **125**, 2–10 (2018)
6. Gupta, O., Raviv, D., Raskar, R.: Deep video gesture recognition using illumination invariants. ArXiv abs/1603.06531 (2016)

7. Kahou, S.E., et al.: Combining modality specific deep neural networks for emotion recognition in video. In: Proceedings of the 15th ACM on International Conference on Multimodal Interaction, pp. 543–550. ACM (2013)
8. Ozdemir, M., Elagoz, B., Alaybeyoglu, A., Akan, A.: Deep learning based facial emotion recognition system. In: 2020 Medical Technologies Congress (TIPTEKNO), pp. 1–4 (2020). https://doi.org/10.1109/TIPTEKNO50054.2020.9299256
9. Franzoni, V., Biondi, G., Milani, A.: Emotional sounds of crowds: spectrogram-based analysis using deep learning. Multimedia Tools Appl. **79**(47–48), 36063–36075 (2020). https://doi.org/10.1007/s11042-020-09428-x
10. Salekin, A., et al.: Distant emotion recognition. Proc. ACM Interact. Mob. Wear. Ubiquit. Technol. **1**(3), 1–25 (2017). https://doi.org/10.1145/3130961
11. Fayek, H.M, Lech, M, Cavedon, L.: Towards real-time speech emotion recognition using deep neural networks. In: Proceedings of the 9th International Conference on Signal Processing and Communication Systems, ICSPCS 2015, pp. 1–5 (2015). https://doi.org/10.1109/ICSPCS.2015.7391796
12. Mirsamadi, S., Barsoum, E., Zhang, C.: Automatic speech emotion recognition using recurrent neural networks with local attention. In: ICASSP, IEEE International Conference on Acoustics, Speech and Signal Processing (2017). https://doi.org/10.1109/ICASSP.2017.7952552
13. Franzoni, V., Biondi, G., Milani, A.: A web-based system for emotion vector extraction. In: Gervasi, O., et al. (eds.) ICCSA 2017. LNCS, vol. 10406, pp. 653–668. Springer, Cham (2017). https://doi.org/10.1007/978-3-319-62398-6_46
14. Franzoni, V., Li, Y., Mengoni, P.: A path-based model for emotion abstraction on Facebook using sentiment analysis and taxonomy knowledge. In: Proceedings of International Conference on Web Intelligence, WI 2017, Leipzig, pp. 947–952 (2017)
15. Canales, L, Martinez-Barco, P.: Emotion detection from text: a survey. In: Processing of the 5th Information Systems Research Working Days (JISIC 2014), pp. 37–43 (2014)
16. Immordino-Yang, M.H., Damasio, A.: We feel, therefore we learn: the relevance of affective and social neuroscience to education. Mind Brain Educ. **1**(1), 3 (2007). https://doi.org/10.1111/j.1751-228X.2007.00004.x
17. Durães, D., Toala, R., Novais, P.: Emotion analysis in distance learning. In: Auer, M.E., Rüütmann, T. (eds.) ICL 2020. AISC, vol. 1328, pp. 629–639. Springer, Cham (2021). https://doi.org/10.1007/978-3-030-68198-2_58
18. Baker, M., Andriessen, J., Järvelä, S.: Affective Learning Together. Social and Emotional dimension of collaborative learning. Routledge, Abingdon (2013)
19. Krithika, Lb., Lakshmi, G.G.: Student emotion recognition system (SERS) for e-learning Improvement based on learner concentration metric. Procedia Comput. Sci. **85**, 767–776 (2016). https://doi.org/10.1016/j.procs.2016.05.264
20. Franzoni, V., Biondi, G., Perri, D., Gervasi, O.: Enhancing mouth-based emotion recognition using transfer learning. Sensors 5222 (2020). https://doi.org/10.3390/s20185222
21. Yergesh, B., Bekmanova, G., Sharipbay, A., Yergesh, M.: Ontology-based sentiment analysis of Kazakh sentences. In: Gervasi, O., et al. (eds.) ICCSA 2017. LNCS, vol. 10406, pp. 669–677. Springer, Cham (2017). https://doi.org/10.1007/978-3-319-62398-6_47
22. Yergesh, B., Bekmanova, G., Sharipbay, A.: Sentiment analysis of Kazakh text and their polarity. Web Intell. **17**(1), 9–15 (2019). IOS Press. https://doi.org/10.3233/WEB-190396
23. Zhetkenbay, L., Bekmanova, G., Yergesh, B., Sharipbay, A.: Method of sentiment preservation in the Kazakh-Turkish machine translation. In: Gervasi, O., et al. (eds.) ICCSA 2020. LNCS, vol. 12250, pp. 538–549. Springer, Cham (2020). https://doi.org/10.1007/978-3-030-58802-1_38

24. Yergesh, B., Bekmanova, G., Sharipbay, A.:Sentiment analysis on the hotel reviews in the Kazakh language. In: Proceedings of 2nd International Conference on Computer Science and Engineering (UBMK), Antalya, pp. 790–794 (2017)
25. Bekmanova, G., Yelibayeva, G., Aubakirova, S., Dyussupova, N., Sharipbay, A., Nyazova, R.: Methods for analyzing polarity of the Kazakh texts related to the terrorist threats. In: Misra, S., et al. (eds.) ICCSA 2019. LNCS, vol. 11619, pp. 717–730. Springer, Cham (2019). https://doi.org/10.1007/978-3-030-24289-3_53
26. Facts and Stats that Reveal the Power of eLearning. https://www.shiftelearning.com/blog/bid/301248/15-facts-and-stats-that-reveal-the-power-of-elearning. Accessed 01 May 2021
27. Online Education Statistics: 2020 Data on Higher Learning & Corporate Training. http://www.guide2research.com/research/online-education-statistics. Accessed 01 May 2021
28. Shelepov, V.Yu., Nitsenko, A.V.: On the recognition of Russian words using generalized transcription. Probl. Artif. Intell. **1**(8), 50–56 (2018). (in Russian)
29. Sharipbayev, A.A., Bekmanova, G.T., Shelepov, V.Yu.: Formalization of phonologic rules of the Kazakh language for system automatic speech recognition. https://kze.docdat.com/docs/411/index-1914530.html. Accessed 01 June 2021
30. Nitsenko, A.V., Shelepov, V.: Algorithms for phonemic recognition of words for a given dictionary. Artif. Intell. [Iskusstvennyy intellekt] **4**, 633–639 (2004). (in Russian)
31. Shelepov, V.Yu.: The concept of phonemic recognition of separately pronounced Russian words. Recognition of syntactically related phrases. In: Materials of International Scientific-Technical Conference "Artificial Intelligence", Donetsk-Taganrog-Minsk, pp. 162–170 (2007). (in Russian)
32. Shelepov, V., Nitsenko, A.V.: To the problem of phonemic recognition. Artif. Intell. [Iskusstvennyy intellekt] **4**, 662–668 (2005). (in Russian)
33. Yergesh, B., Sharipbay, A., Bekmanova, G., Lipnitskii, S.: Sentiment analysis of Kazakh phrases based on morphological rules. J. Kyrgyz State Tech. Univ. named after I. Razzakov **2**(38), 39–42 (2016). Bishkek
34. Yergesh, B.Zh.: Sentiment determination of the Kazakh language texts based on the dictionary of emotional vocabulary. In: Proceedings of 5th International Conference on Computer Processing of Turkic Languages "TurkLang 2017", vol. 1, pp. 62–67. Publishing House of the Academy of Sciences of the Republic of Tatarstan, Kazan (2017). (in Russian)
35. Yergesh, B., Sharipbay, A., Bekmanova, G.: Models and methods of sentiment analysis of texts in the Kazakh language. In: Computational Processing of the Kazakh Language: Collection Of Scientific Papers, Chapter 5. Kazakh University, Almaty (2020). (in Russian)

Towards Learning a Joint Representation from Transformer in Multimodal Emotion Recognition

James J. Deng[1(✉)] and Clement H. C. Leung[2(✉)]

[1] MindSense Technologies, Pok Fu Lam, Hong Kong, PRC
james@mindsense.ai

[2] The Chinese University of Hong Kong, Shenzhen, People's Republic of China
clementleung@cuhk.edu.cn

Abstract. Emotion recognition has been extensively studied in a single modality in the last decade. However, humans express their emotions usually through multiple modalities like voice, facial expressions, or text. This paper proposes a new method to learn a joint emotion representation for multimodal emotion recognition. Emotion-based feature for speech audio is learned by an unsupervised triplet-loss objective, and a text-to-text transformer network is used to extract text embedding for latent emotional meaning. Transfer learning provides a powerful and reusable technique to help fine-tune emotion recognition models trained on mega audio and text datasets respectively. The extracted emotional information from speech audio and text embedding are processed by dedicated transformer networks. The alternating co-attention mechanism is used to construct a deep transformer network. Multimodal fusion is implemented by a deep co-attention transformer network. Experimental results show the proposed method for learning a joint emotion representation achieves good performance in multimodal emotion recognition.

Keywords: Multimodal emotion recognition · Multimodal fusion · Transformer network

1 Introduction

Deep learning like convolution neural network (CNN), recurrent neural network (RNN), and other deep models have proven extremely useful in many domains, including computer vision, speech and audio processing, and natural language processing. Many applications like face recognition, speech recognition, and machine translation have achieved great success. Research on emotion recognition also yields significant importance. However, as emotion is complex and determined by a joint function of pharmacological, cognitive, and environmental variables, emotion recognized by different people may be ambiguous or even opposite. The single modality for emotion recognition is insufficient and incomplete. For example, in a conversation, people's voices, text of speech content,

M. Mahmud et al. (Eds.): BI 2021, LNAI 12960, pp. 179–188, 2021.
https://doi.org/10.1007/978-3-030-86993-9_17

facial expressions, body language, or gestures all convey emotional meaning. Thus, it is inappropriate to recognize people's emotions only through a single modality. Multimodal modeling is a natural and reasonable process for emotion recognition. Although multimodal analysis has been extensively studied and some have achieved remarkable results in specific constraints, it cannot simply apply these methods in different environments. Therefore, learning a joint representation for emotional information from multiple modalities is necessary and useful in downstream tasks like multimodal emotion recognition. In this paper, we propose a learning method to find a joint emotion representation using both speech audio and text information from a transformer netowrk with co-attention.

Training models using mega dataset consumes huge resource and have become more and more difficult and less affordable for most of researchers, institutes or companies. For example, training GPT-3 would cost at least $4.6 million, because training deep learning models is not a clean, one-shot process. There are a lot of trial and error and hyperparameter tuning that would probably increase the cost sharply. Transfer learning provides a powerful and reusable technique to help us solve resource shortages and save model training costs. This paper adopts this strategy and employs the excellent fruits of pre-trained models by mega datasets of audio and text as the basis of our work. A model named VGGish is an audio feature embedding produced by training a modified VGGNet model to predict video-level tags from this dataset, which is widely used for audio classification. In addition, another model TRIpLet Loss network (TRILL) is trained from AudioSet again and achieves good results for several audio tasks like speaker identification, and emotion recognition. We use the fine-tuned TRILL model to extract the speech audio features as the representation for the modality of speech audio. As for text representation, we adopt fine-tuned Text-To-Text Transfer Transformer (T5) [18] model trained by a common crawl (C4) dataset to extract text embeddings. Operations of transfer learning have greatly accelerated model training and that being applied in specific domains. To reuse the fruits of transfer learning especially for learning embeddings from speech audio and text, we adopts the strategy of transfer learning to obtain speech features and text embedding.

We expect the fused feature of speech and text are more informative and synthetic. To retain more hidden emotional information for multimodal fusion, we use the transformer network architecture to process modalities, with each modality passed to a dedicated transformer. Considering that speech audio and speech content obviously have some extent of correlation, and both exert an effect on emotion recognition, the co-attention mechanism is adopted here. This operation can well reflect internal influence of each modality. A quantitative evaluation shows that learned fused features can outperform the existing methods in emotion recognition. The main contribution of this paper is summarized as follows: (1) we propose an effective method to learn a joint emotion representation; (2) we evaluate the performance of the proposed method and validate the co-attention mechanism. Section 2 describes the literature review; Sect. 3 discusses the proposed methodologies and overall architecture; Sect. 4 explains the experimental setup and results, and Sect. 5 summarizes our work.

2 Literature Review

Many research works of emotion recognition have been done in a single modality setting in past decades. A survey [4] of methods is summarized to address three important aspects of the design of a speech emotion recognition system. The first one is the choice of suitable features for speech representation. The second issue is the design of an appropriate classification scheme and the third issue is the proper preparation of an emotional speech database for evaluating system performance. Domain expert knowledge makes significant for manually constructing high-quality features [16]. Recent research has mostly focused on deep representation learning methods, either supervised, semi-supervised, or unsupervised. Successful representations improve the sample efficiency of ML algorithms by extracting most information out of the raw signal from the new data before any task-specific learning takes place. This strategy has been used successfully in many application domains. Many deep learning methods like CNN [9], Deep Belief Network (DBN) [8], Long Short-Term Memory (LSTM), Autoencoder [2,11] have been used to construct various deep neural networks, achieving good performance in speech emotion recognition. Sentiment analysis [14] is the task of automatically determining from the text the attitude, classified by positive, negative, and neutral attitude. Knowledge-based and statistical methods are usually used to extract text features like word embedding (e.g., Word2Vec), pair-wise correlation of words, and parts-of-speech (POS) tag of the sentence. Recently, transformer architecture [20] is rather popular in dealing with natural language processing like General Language Understanding Evaluation (GLUE). The model of Bidirectional Encoder Representations from Transformers (BERT) [3] is constructed by 12 Encoders with bidirectional self-attention mechanism. A unified text-to-text format, in contrast to BERT-style models that can only output either a class label or a span of the input, can flexibly be used on the same model, loss function, and hyperparameters on any NLP tasks. This provides valuable insight for performing semantic classification like recognizing emotion from the text. This paper inherits this text-to-text transformer architecture.

Transfer learning and domain adaptation have been extensively practiced in machine learning. In specific domains, there is often only a few dataset available, and it is difficult to train an accurate model by using these small datasets. However, many modalities (e.g., speech, text) have the same essence and low-level elements. Thus, transfer learning can well overcome the small dataset limitation. A sharing learned latent representation [5] or deep models like VGGish or BERT is transferred to be used on another learning task, usually achieving an exciting performance. [12] uses DBN of transfer learning to build sparse autoencoder for speech emotion recognition. [10] introduces a sent2affect framework, a tailored form of transfer learning to recognize emotions from the text. Another Universal Language Model Fine-tuning (ULMFiT) [7] is carried out to evaluate several text classification and outperforms state-of-the-art models. Therefore, to make full use of pre-trained models by mega dataset, we adopt transfer learning of multiple modalities. Though there exists some work on multimodal emotion recognition, for example, canonical correlational analysis [15], joint feature representation

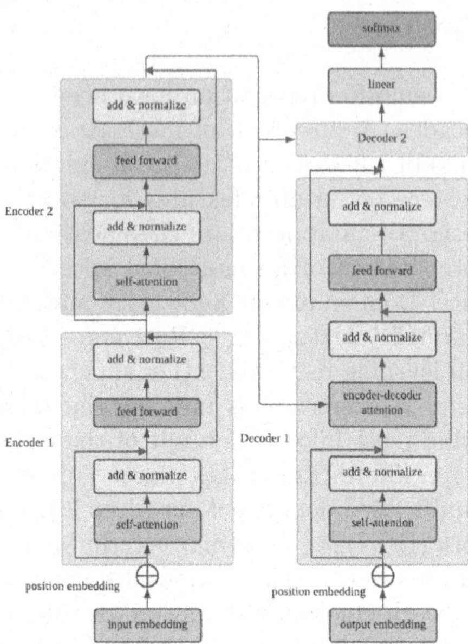

Fig. 1. An encoder-decoder transformer architecture with residual skip connections.

[17,19], or generative adversarial network (GAN) for multimodal modeling, there is less work on the aspect of transfer learning on multimodal. The co-attention mechanism [13] has showed good performance on visual question answering. This inspires us to use transfer learning, transformer network, and multimodal fusion to learn a joint emotional representation of modalities.

3 Methodology

This paper concentrates on dual modalities: speech and text. The aim is to learn a joint representation of emotional information from these dual modalities. This section will first introduce the emotional features extracted from speech audio, and text, respectively. Then the proposed method for joint emotion representation from transformer will be interpreted.

3.1 Feature Extraction from Modalities

Speech recognition has been extensively researched and achieved great success in the last decade, and many speech emotion recognition tasks adopt acoustic features like Mel-frequency Cepstral Coefficient (MFCC), deep auto-encoders in Deep Neural Network (DNN), or end-to-end with attention-based strategy that usually are used in speech recognition. However, the same content of speech usually expresses the different emotions corresponding to different voice attributes like pitch, rhythm, timbre, or context. Emotional aspects of the speech signal generally change more slowly than the phonetic and lexical aspects used to explicitly convey meaning. Therefore, we need to find a suitable representation for emotion-related tasks to be considerably more stable in time than what is usually adopted in speech recognition. To consider the temporal characteristic of speech audio, we represent a large and unlabeled speech collection as a sequence of spectrogram context windows $X = x_1, x_2, \ldots, x_N$, where each $x_i \in^{F \times T}$, F and T denotes for the dimensionality of spectrogram. We aim to learn a embedding $g :^{F \times T} \rightarrow^{d}$ from spectrogram context windows to a $d-$dimensional embedding space such that $\|g(x_i) - g(x_j)\| \leq \|g(x_i) - g(x_k)\|$ when $i - j \leq i - k$. We can express this embedding formulated by learning a triplet loss function. Suppose a large collection of example triplets is represented by $z = (x_i, x_j, x_k)$, where $|i - j| \leq \tau$ and $|i - k| > \tau$ for some suitably chosen time scale τ. The τ represent the specific duration of each given audio clip. The whole loss function $\Theta(z)$ is expressed as follows:

$$\Theta(z) = \sum_{i=1}^{N} [\|g(x_i) - g(x_j)\|_2^2 + \|g(x_i) - g(x_k)\|_2^2 + \delta] \tag{1}$$

where $\|\bullet\|$ is the L_2 norm, $[\bullet]$ represents standard hinge loss and δ is non-negative margin hyperparameter.

Considering that the transformer architecture has achieved high performance in a number of NLP tasks like The General Language Understanding Evaluation (GLUE) benchmark, Sentiment analysis (SST-2), SQuAD question answering, we adopt the transformer architecture as well. Given a sequence of text obtained from speech, we first map the tokens of the initial input sequence to an embedding space, and then input the embedded sequence to the encoder layer. The encoder layer is composed of a stack of blocks, and each block consists of a self-attention layer followed by a small feed-forward network. Layer normalization in the self-attention layer and feed-forward network is considered, where the activations are only re-scaled and no additive bias is applied. In addition, a residual skip is connected from input to output of the self-attention layer and feed-forward network, respectively. After that, the dropout is calculated within the feed-forward network, on the skip connection, on the attention weights, and at the input and output of the entire stack. As for the decoder layer, except for the similar block in the encoding layer, it contains a standard attention operation after each self-attention layer. The self-attention mechanism in the decoder also uses a form of auto-regressive or causal self-attention, which only allows the model to attend to past outputs. The output of the final decoder block is fed into a dense layer with a softmax output, whose weights are shared with the input embedding matrix. All attention mechanisms in the transformer are split up into independent "heads" whose outputs are concatenated before being further processed. The whole text-to-text transformer architecture is illustrated in Fig. 1. In a transformer, instead of using a fixed embedding for each position, relative position embeddings produce a different learned embedding according to the offset between the "key" and "query" being compared in the self-attention mechanism. We use a simplified form of position embeddings where each "embedding" is simply a scalar that is added to the corresponding logit used for computing the attention weights.

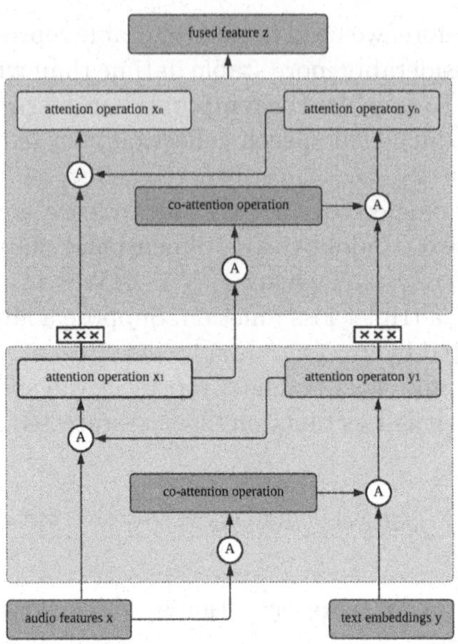

Fig. 2. Multimodal fusion by learning a joint emotion representation through a deep network with alternating co-attention operations.

3.2 Joint Emotion Representation from Transformer Network

After we obtain emotional representation of speech and text, it is natural to concatenate speech audio features and text embeddings, and feed them to a network. Here, we make some changes. Each modality is processed by a dedicated transformer. That's to say, speech audio features are passed to a transformer, and text embeddings are sent to another. Given a piece of speech, people recognize emotion both from speech audio and speech content. Speech audio and speech content obviously have some extent of correlation, and both exert an effect on emotion recognition. Thus, the co-attention mechanism is adopted. Taking the aforementioned Speech audio features X and text embedding Y as input, we pass the input features to a transformer network with a deep co-attention model. The network architecture of this deep co-attention is illustrated in Fig. 2. We sequentially alternate between speech and text attention. We first attend to the speech based on the text embedding vector. Then we attend to the text based on the attended speech feature. The co-attention operations are represented by

$$\begin{aligned} \hat{x} &= \Lambda(X; g_x) \\ \hat{y} &= \Lambda(Y; g_y) \end{aligned} \tag{2}$$

where attention guidance g_x derived from speech, and attention guidance g_y derived from text. The detailed computation is given as follows:

$$\begin{aligned} H &= tanh(W_x X + (W_{g_x} g_x)V^T) \\ \hat{a} &= softmax(w_{hx}^T H) \\ \hat{x} &= \sum a_i^x x_i \end{aligned} \tag{3}$$

where V is a vector with all elements equalling one. W_x and W_{g_x} denotes for $k \times d$ matrix parameter, and w_{hx} refers to k dimensional vector parameter. a^x is the attention weight of speech feature X. The computations of $\hat{y}$ follows the same process in Eq. 3. At the first step of alternating co-attention, g_x is 0. At the second step, g_y is intermediate attended text embedding from the first step. At last, we use the speech feature $\hat{x}$ as the guidance to attend the text again. We use a linear function to fuse attended features $\hat{x}$ and $\hat{y}$. The fused feature z is represented by

$$z = LayerNorm(W_x^T \hat{x} + W_y^T \hat{y}) \tag{4}$$

Finally, the binary cross-entropy is used as loss function to train a classifier.

4 Experiments and Results

We briefly introduce the necessary background topics required to understand the experiments and results before presenting the results from our empirical study. Youtube-8M dataset is a benchmark dataset that expands ontology of 632 audio event classes and a collection of 2,084,320 human-labeled 10-s sound clips drawn from YouTube videos. This dataset have been used in a number of audio tasks like speaker identification, emotion recognition. Several famous models like VGGish, Yamnet, and TRILL are trained by this benchmark dataset. VGGish is audio embedding generated by training a modified VGGNet model, and Yamnet employs Mobilenet_v1 depthwise-separable convolution architecture to predicts 521 audio event classes. TRILL is trained to find a good non-semantic representation of speech and exceeds state-of-the-art performance on a number of transfer learning tasks. Another new open-source pre-training dataset, called the Colossal Clean Crawled Corpus (C4) is used in many NLP tasks. The text-to-text transfer transformer, named T5 model, also achieves state-of-the-art results on many NLP benchmarks. Therefore, in our experiments, we reuse these pre-trained models in single modality, respectively. To evaluate the results of multimodal fusion through transfer learning, we choose two emotion datasets. Emotional Dyadic Motion Capture (IEMOCAP) [1] is a multimodal and multi-speaker database, containing approximately 12 h of audiovisual data, including video, speech, motion capture of face, text transcriptions. Another dataset is SAVEE [6] database recorded from four native English male speakers, supporting 7 emotion categories: anger, disgust, fear, happiness, neutral, sadness, and surprise. In the experiment of transfer learning, we select both the final output and intermediate representations of the given pre-trained models. As for speech

Table 1. Comparison of multimodal fusion by learning a joint emotion representation performance with single modality through the different embeddings on different emotion datasets.

Models	IEMOCAP	SAVEE	Mean
VGGis FC1	65.3%	57.7%	61.5%
VGGish finetuned	61.4%	59.3%	60.4%
YAMNet layer 10	63.2%	62.3%	62.8%
YAMNet finetuned	67.6%	62.7%	65.2%
TRILL distilled	70.5%	67.8%	69.2%
TRILL finetuned	73.8%	68.6%	71.2%
Text-to-Text transformer (T5)	75.7%	72.3%	75.5%
TRILL-T5 multimodal fusion	81.7%	75.9%	78.8%

audio, in the TRILL model, we use the final 512-dimensional embedding layer and the pre-ReLU output of the first 19-depth convolutional layer. For Vggish, we use the final layer and the first fully connected layer. For YAMNet, we use the final pre-logit layer and the 5 depth-separable convolutional layer outputs. We use the emotion dataset of IEMOCAP and SAVEE for fine-tune training. As for text processing, we use the Text-to-Text transformer model with a maximum sequence length of 512 and a batch size of 128 sequences. During fine-tuning, we continue using batches with 128 length-512 sequences, and a constant learning rate of 0.001. The number of embedding dimensionality is set to 512. We set 4-layer deep co-attention network for learning a joint emotion representation.

We used different pre-trained models like VGGish, YAMNet, TRILL, and T5 to fine-tune for emotion recognition in a single modality. The obtained emotion representation of speech audio and text embedding are concatenated to pass through a transformer network. Multimodal fusion of emotional information through a transformer network generates a unified representation for emotion recognition. Table 1 shows the comparison of several single modalities and multimodal fusion results for emotion recognition. We can see that fine-tuning the final embedding of pre-trained models gives a clear boost to emotion recognition. In addition, TRILL shows better performance than VGGish and YAMNet. Text-to-Text Transformer (T5) model shows better performance in emotion recognition from the text. The average of Text-to-Text Transformer accuracy achieves up to 75.5% in the emotion dataset. Multimodal fusion by learning a joint emotion representation shows better results than single modality for emotion recognition. This explains that multiple modalities like speech and text convey more emotional information than a single modality. The multimodal fusion can well employ complementary information. As the length of each speech in dataset of SAVEE is short, corresponding text numbers are rather small. Thus, the performance is lower than that of IEMOCAP dataset.

As speech audio samples of IEMOCAP datasets in some emotion categories are rather small, we only used four emotion categories (e.g., happy, sad, anger,

Table 2. Average performance of the different emotion representations on four selected emotion categories.

Models + Dataset	Happy	Anger	Sad	Natural	Mean
TRILL (IEMOCAP_Audio)	77.2%	81.9%	72.3%	66.8%	74.6%
TRILL (SAVEE_Audio)	73.3%	84.3%	73.3%	66.7%	74.4%
T5 (IEMOCAP_Text)	79.6%	82.7%	72.2%	64.9%	74.9%
T5 (SAVEE_Text)	75.0%	81.7%	71.7%	66.7%	73.8%
Multimodal fusion (IEMOCAP)	83.1%	84.6%	76.3%	71.1%	78.9%
Multimodal fusion (SAVEE)	84.7%	85.2%	74.5%	70.3%	78.7%

and natural) for analysis of differences in both two emotion datasets. Table 2 shows the comparison of single and multiple modalities on different emotion categories. We can see that the emotion category happy and anger achieves the best recognition results than that of sad and neutral. Through studies of false-positive results, we find that in the above-mentioned emotion datasets, it is not obvious and easy for a human to recognize samples that convey neutral or sad emotional meaning. Table 2 also shows the same conclusion that the performance of multimodal fusion through a transformer network exceeds single modality.

5 Conclusion

This paper proposed a new method for learning a joint emotion representation for multimodal emotion recognition. Considering that deep neural network models trained by huge datasets exhaust a lot of unaffordable resources, large excellent pre-trained models like TRILL and Text-to-Text Transformer from a single modality are used and fine-tuned on the used emotion datasets. The extracted emotional information from speech audio and text embedding are processed by dedicated transformer networks. The alternating co-attention mechanism is constructed in a deep transformer network. The fused features of each modality for emotional information are used in a classifier. The experiments compared the performance of single modality and multiple modalities (speech and text) for emotion recognition which showed noticeable advantages of the latter over the former. We showed that our proposed method for learning a joint emotion representation achieves good results and can be used in other zero-shot or one-shot emotion learning tasks.

References

1. Busso, C., et al.: IEMOCAP: interactive emotional dyadic motion capture database. Lang. Resour. Eval. **42**(4), 335–359 (2008)
2. Cibau, N.E., Albornoz, E.M., Rufiner, H.L.: Speech emotion recognition using a deep autoencoder. Anales de la XV Reunion de Procesamiento de la Informacion y Control **16**, 934–939 (2013)

3. Devlin, J., Chang, M.-W., Lee, K., Toutanova, K.: BERT: pre-training of deep bidirectional transformers for language understanding. arXiv preprint arXiv:1810.04805 (2018)
4. El Ayadi, M., Kamel, M.S., Karray, F.: Survey on speech emotion recognition: features, classification schemes, and databases. Pattern Recogn. **44**(3), 572–587 (2011)
5. Hamel, P., Davies, M.E., Yoshii, K., Goto, M.: Transfer learning in MIR: sharing learned latent representations for music audio classification and similarity (2013)
6. Haq, S., Jackson, P.J., Edge, J.: Speaker-dependent audio-visual emotion recognition. In: AVSP, pp. 53–58 (2009)
7. Howard, J., Ruder, S.: Universal language model fine-tuning for text classification. arXiv preprint arXiv:1801.06146 (2018)
8. Huang, C., Gong, W., Fu, W., Feng, D.: A research of speech emotion recognition based on deep belief network and SVM. Math. Probl. Eng. **2014** (2014)
9. Huang, Z., Dong, M., Mao, Q., Zhan, Y.: Speech emotion recognition using CNN. In: Proceedings of the 22nd ACM International Conference on Multimedia, pp. 801–804 (2014)
10. Kratzwald, B., Ilić, S., Kraus, M., Feuerriegel, S., Prendinger, H.: Deep learning for affective computing: text-based emotion recognition in decision support. Decis. Support Syst. **115**, 24–35 (2018)
11. Latif, S., Rana, R., Khalifa, S., Jurdak, R., Epps, J., Schuller, B.W.: Multi-task semi-supervised adversarial autoencoding for speech emotion recognition. IEEE Trans. Affect. Comput. (2020)
12. Latif, S., Rana, R., Younis, S., Qadir, J., Epps, J.: Transfer learning for improving speech emotion classification accuracy. arXiv preprint arXiv:1801.06353 (2018)
13. Lu, J., Yang, J., Batra, D., Parikh, D.: Hierarchical question-image co-attention for visual question answering. Adv. Neural Inf. Process. Syst. **29**, 289–297 (2016)
14. Medhat, W., Hassan, A., Korashy, H.: Sentiment analysis algorithms and applications: a survey. Ain Shams Eng. J. **5**(4), 1093–1113 (2014)
15. Mittal, T., Bhattacharya, U., Chandra, R., Bera, A., Manocha, D.: M3ER: multiplicative multimodal emotion recognition using facial, textual, and speech cues. In: Proceedings of the AAAI Conference on Artificial Intelligence, vol. 34, pp. 1359–1367 (2020)
16. Nwe, T.L., Foo, S.W., De Silva, L.C.: Speech emotion recognition using hidden Markov models. Speech Commun. **41**(4), 603–623 (2003)
17. Poria, S., Chaturvedi, I., Cambria, E., Hussain, A.: Convolutional MKL based multimodal emotion recognition and sentiment analysis. In: 2016 IEEE 16th International Conference on Data Mining (ICDM), pp. 439–448. IEEE (2016)
18. Roberts, A., Raffel, C.: Exploring transfer learning with T5: the text-to-text transfer transformer. Accessed 23 July 2020
19. Tzirakis, P., Trigeorgis, G., Nicolaou, M.A., Schuller, B.W., Zafeiriou, S.: End-to-end multimodal emotion recognition using deep neural networks. IEEE J. Sel. Top. Signal Process. **11**(8), 1301–1309 (2017)
20. Vaswani, A., et al.: Attention is all you need. arXiv preprint arXiv:1706.03762 (2017)

Virtual Reality for Enhancement of Emotional Mindset in the First Lockdown of United Kingdom for the Covid-19 Pandemics

Valentina Franzoni[1(✉)], Niccolò Di Marco[2], Giulio Biondi[2], and Alfredo Milani[1]

[1] Department of Mathematics and Computer Science, University of Perugia, Perugia, Italy
valentina.franzoni@dmi.unipg.it

[2] Department of Mathematics and Computer Science, University of Florence, Florence, Italy
{niccolo.dimarco,giulio.biondi}@unifi.it

Abstract. From 20 March to 10 May 2020, the "stay at home" countermeasures for the Covid-19 emergency lockdown were defined in the United Kingdom (UK) as leaving home for only the following reasons: "Key worker travelling to work", "Shopping for basic necessities", "Any medical need" or "Exercise once a day". Data collected from the UK Office for National Statistics through online and telephone questionnaires are an exceptional baseline data set on people behaviour during the Covid-19 pandemics. In this paper, data from demographic surveys from the UK are compared to statistical and feedback data from the Virtual Reality app called TRIPP for meditation in the experiences called Focus and Calm. Our data analysis shows that during lockdown the psychological and emotional mindset, severely challenged, has been successfully enhanced with the use of Virtual Reality.

Keywords: Artificial intelligence · Emotion recognition · Coronavirus · Affective computing · Lockdown

1 Introduction

In late 2019, the Covid-19 epidemic began to spread and referred to as The Pandemic. The first continent to host the new coronavirus after Asia was Europe, with Italy leading collective defence strategies. Soon the United Kingdom (UK) had to follow and pioneer the vaccination campaign. Italy and United Kingdom were among the first to decide and apply in March 2020 collective protection

Idea VF, data acquisition VF GB, data analysis VF NDM, experiments setting VF NDM, R statistics NDM, outcome evaluation VF NDM, supervision VF AM, data formatting GB VF, paper writing VF, paper revision GB.

M. Mahmud et al. (Eds.): BI 2021, LNAI 12960, pp. 189–198, 2021.
https://doi.org/10.1007/978-3-030-86993-9_18

measures, included long before in national plans for pandemics but mostly never tested before on real cases, considering that Ebola arrived in few vectors, contained without spreading in the UK. Such policies included social distancing, self-isolation in case of symptoms, and the state of emergency. From 20 March to 10 May 2020 the United Kingdom government introduced three new measures, with the same "stay at home" slogan followed by Italy:

- Requiring people to stay at home, except for very limited purposes.
- Homeschooling (i.e., carry out school activities remotely), and closing certain businesses and venues.
- Stopping all gatherings of more than two people or one family unit in public.

The prolongation of social distancing led to the emergence and exacerbation of psychological distress and pathologies such as anxiety and depression. During the first lockdown, people applied personal resources that become popular, including the rediscovery of cooking, exercise at home, and gaming. Among game consoles, Facebook put on the market the *Oculus Quest 2*, a standalone device for Virtual Reality (VR), just with the beginning of the worldwide state of emergency. The most comprehensive app at that time for relaxation and meditation in virtual reality was *TRIPP* [13], which recorded a significant boost in users. TRIPP [13] is a science-based platform for well-being experiences, which implements a broad range of AI and VR techniques for mental and emotional health [6], e.g., VR techniques to elicit awe [2,3], psychological reduction of conflict between self and reality such as mindfulness for clinical change and self-compassion [1,4], use of VR technology in treating anxiety [10], the impact of binaural beats [12], the impact of music and games in emotional well-being [9,14], the study of colors for mental clarity [7,8].

At the same time, to figure out how the pandemic was impacting lives in the United Kingdom, the *Office for National Statistics* (ONS) undertook to collect weekly information on people's experiences and opinions regarding the pandemic [11]. By comparing TRIPP users' feedback and session data with UK government baseline data, after the spike for VR had reached the hype settlement stage with the post-Christmas season, in this preliminary work we explore how the first lockdown influenced the emotional mindset of the population, and how Virtual Reality could change the emotional well-being in the United Kingdom.

2 Lockdown Data from the United Kingdom Office for National Statistics and the TRIPP VR App

The United Kingdom Office for National Statistics (OPN) from March 20 to March 30 reports outcomes from the very first week of the block. Statistical data from April 3 to May 10 combine five rounds of collection through surveys. Survey answers were collected using an online self-completion questionnaire, with the option to participate by phone.

TRIPP users feedback is given through in-app surveys on initial and final wellness state on a scale from 1 to 10 (1 is low and 10 is high wellness), initial and final moods (with 10 moods available and the selection order), and a final rating of the experience on a Likert scale of five stars.

2.1 Collected Data

ONS data include surveys covering the period between 20 March 2020 and 31 January 2021. Lockdown data are from 20 March 2020 to 10 May 2020. Data are averaged in variable days ranges. Indicators from the ONS Opinions and Lifestyle Survey include the impacts of the coronavirus pandemic on people, households and communities mindsets [11].

TRIPP data are used under non-disclosure agreement, and the results of this study are published with permission. Data are anonymized and include anagraphical data (e.g., age, gender, country), session data (e.g., device, duration, type of experience), and feedback. Anagraphical data analysis is reported in forms that do not disclose personal data (e.g., the age distribution is given as a histogram voluntarily limited in the readability of specific numbers but still very informative).

We selected the same ranges in the TRIPP data set for comparison and correlation finding.

2.2 Data Preprocessing

The data set was filtered, removing noise. From the whole data set, we selected sessions from the UK in the considered time range. We deleted aborted sessions. Accesses with missing feedback and age were not considered for related statistics.

The main extension regards calculated values and moods. We assigned weights to moods on a bipolar negative/positive weighted scale to calculate mood changes after the Focus or Calm experiences (see Table 1).

Table 1. Weights assigned to TRIPP moods

Mood	Upset	Tense	Distracted	Worried	Bored	Content	Relaxed	Calm	Focused	Inspired
Weight	−2	−2	−1	−1	−1	1	1	2	2	1

2.3 Strength and Limitations

TRIPP data are a relevant baseline for statistics on well-being, even given the possible selection bias for the app users, who might be willing to change their mindset. Studying correlations between TRIPP and ONS well-being data allows to reinforce the meaning of the data, and to analyze the effect of Virtual Reality experiences for well-being, on a tested range of anagraphical variety of users. The limits of this study are on data but are compensated with the comparison of the two data sources: if in the case of ONS data the anagraphical data have not been disclosed at all, from TRIPP data we could better analyze the population as suggested for scientific analysis, still without disclosing any data critical for personal privacy. On the other hand, if TRIPP users are not supervised, thus free to introduce noise to the data, required outliers identification and deletion,

Table 2. Users and feedback data breakdown for TRIPP

Users	Sessions	Males	Females	Prefer not say Gender	Teenagers	Young Adults	Seniors	Elders
2890	31274	17375	11993	1906	119	5624	23921	1610

Focus or Calm Users	Users with feedback	Feedbacks on scale	Feedbacks on mood
2762	2581	2497	2384

ONS conducts surveys with strict rules. For ONS data, an important strength is the adjustments of voluntary feedbacks for demographic characteristics, while TRIPP data relate to the VR sessions without adjustments different from what explained in Subsect. 2.2

3 Data Analysis

From ONS data, weighted responses to survey questions ensure that the estimates are representative of the target population, where weights indicate the number of people represented in the population.

More accurate weighting is based on the latest population estimates available for that period. When new population estimates become available, the data may be re-weighted to ensure better representation and thus greater accuracy of the estimates. March 2019 data have been re-weighted data to produce our quarterly estimates of personal well-being and remained fixed until 2021.

Regarding TRIPP data, the data set includes users sessions. We analyzed general data with a statistical data breakdown and then produced calculated data to measure the mindset and wellness state from user feedback given through the app. The data set also includes feedback about moods, which could be analyzed also with semantic emotion recognition tools [5].

3.1 Data Breakdown

ONS Data. We report here the information given on the surveys from the official website [11]. Data include weekly surveys from 6,430 people aged 16 years and over, self-reporting mental health voluntarily. ONS adjusted data for age, sex, ethnic group, and socio-economic classification. About ethnic groups, during the lockdown, over a quarter (27%) of those from Black, African, Caribbean or Black British ethnic groups reported finding it very or quite difficult to get by financially, significantly more than those from White Irish (6%), Other White (7%), Indian (8%) and Pakistani or Bangladeshi (13%) ethnic groups.

TRIPP Data. Relate to the Focus and Calm in-app experiences and include data about users, sessions, and feedback on the emotional mindset before and after the experience. Users data are detailed in Table 2. All the data are related only to the studied period. Statistics on sessions are grouped by user and time

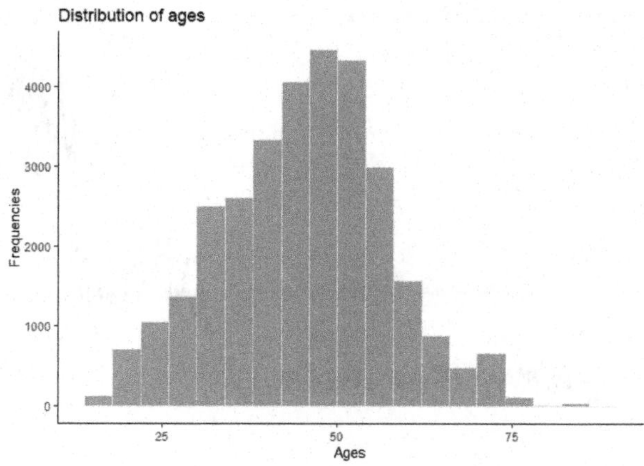

Fig. 1. Age distribution for TRIPP users of the whole period

range and shown in Table 3. TRIPP users in the UK in the defined period are mostly adults. We notice that most of TRIPP access come from the *Oculus Quest 2* VR device, which rules require a Facebook account, possible only over the age of 12 years (i.e., teenagers and over). The age distribution for sessions is shown in Fig. 1. The number of interactions per day is shown in Fig. 2. It is important to notice that a high peak is visible in the Christmas period. Both users (related to Christmas presents of VR devices) and accesses (related to testing the VR devices received) is present in the global TRIPP data set both in 2020 and 2021, higher for richer countries. After January the peak goes down in both cases, so it cannot be considered relevant for the Covid-19 emotional well-being comparison. The interaction variation is relevant for a correct interpretation of the feedback time series in Fig. 3–4.

Table 3. TRIPP statistics summary by user and by same period subdivisions as ONS

Statistics	Min	Median	Mean	Standard deviation	Max
Per-user access count	1	6	10.8	19.9	376
Access per time-range	165	371	727.3	740.7	3932

4 Experiments on the Impact of Covid-19 on Well-Being

Experiments compare by time series the data from ONS and TRIPP. We implement two main analyses: a first phase compares the emotional feedback from the ONS data set to the users' feedbacks on TRIPP moods, both in the whole analyzed period (including emotional changes before and after the end of the lockdown) and during the lockdown.

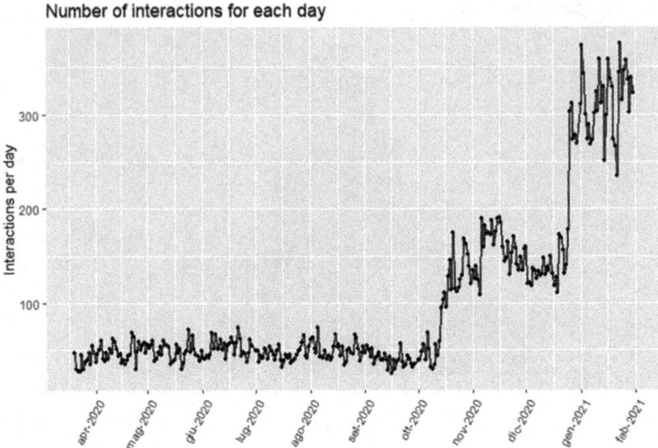

Fig. 2. Number of accesses to TRIPP by day

A second phase implements an in-depth analysis of TRIPP feedback before and after the Focus and Calm experiences, to test the efficacy of VR meditation exercises for the enhancement of the emotional mindset in the analyzed period.

4.1 Time Series

Figure 3 shows time series for positive moods of TRIPP and positive well-being perception on ONS data. As for the negative counterparts, on the left side of the vertical dotted line is the trend during the lockdown: the zoomed section is shown on the right. The scales of ONS and TRIPP data are very different: we transformed them in logarithmic scale, but a direct comparison on the y axis is not feasible. Also the amount of data is critically different: ONS surveys are around once a week, showing evident peaks, while TRIPP data relate to each day thus having a curved variation. Nonetheless, we can observe some similarities and correlations.

The trend of positive feelings can be correlated: TRIPP *Content* mood has a similar trend of *Happiness* in ONS data, rising initially during the lockdown probably because of an initial relaxation (as we all experienced), then going down, and up again just before and after the lockdown ended, showing hope for freedom. The trend stays up during summertime, then goes down again for ONS data, while has clear peaks for Christmas and holidays in TRIPP data. *Life Satisfaction* also goes up and down initially and then slowly falls down, while *Worthiness* of life goes slowly down over time, starting from the lockdown.

In TRIPP data, it is interesting to see that, except for an initial variation in the lockdown, *Calm* shows a similar trend on lower frequency to *Focused*. The two classes are close to *Inspired* and *Relaxed* respectively: this reinforces the observation that the Calm and Focus TRIPP experiences are helpful, but is

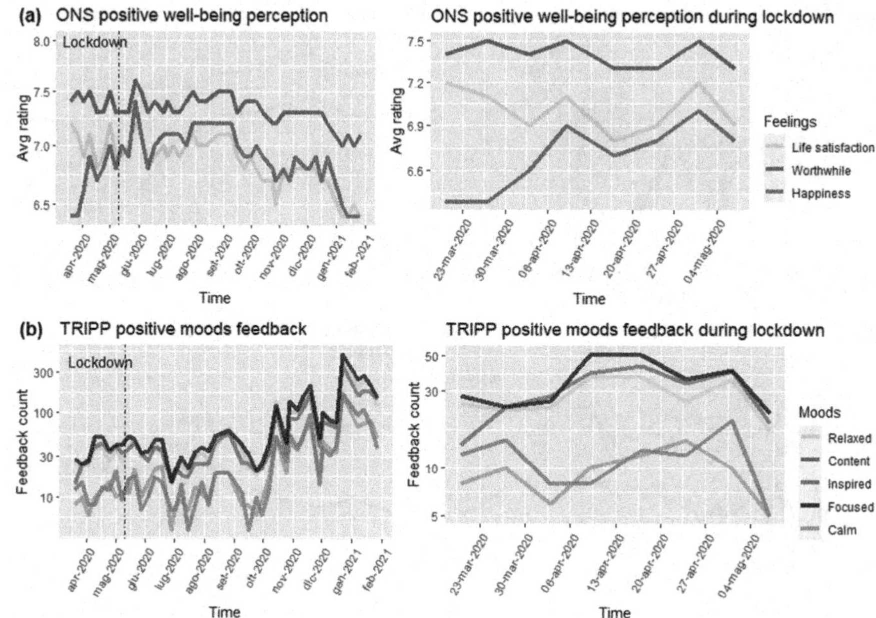

Fig. 3. Emotional feedback over time on positive classes, with a zoom about the lockdown on the right: (a) ONS feelings, (b) TRIPP moods as initial state

also slightly correlated to the general sense of happiness that we can find in the ONS data.

Figure 4 shows time series for negative moods of TRIPP and negative well-being perception on ONS data. As for the positive counterparts, some moods and feelings trends can be correlated. Almost all TRIPP negative moods show a similar waving trend with different frequencies: *Bored* is close to *Distracted*; *Upset* and *Tense* follow similar waves with less *Upset* than *Tense*, meeting in a falling trend at the end of the lockdown and at the beginning of 2021, where users declare a high peak of *Tense* and a *Upset*, which stays almost always close to *Worried*.

Being collected less frequently, the trend is less evident in ONS data. We can see that *Anxiety* is the most prevalent feeling, over loneliness and the feeling that Covid-19 affected well-being. *Anxiety*'s trend is slightly similar to TRIPP's *Tense*. A relevant observation is that, despite the data source, *Focused* seems to have an opposite trend to *Anxiety*, which is in line with science on mindfulness.

4.2 Enhancement of Emotional Mindset

Table 4 shows an enhancement of emotional mindset after TRIPP sessions for each type of user feedback.

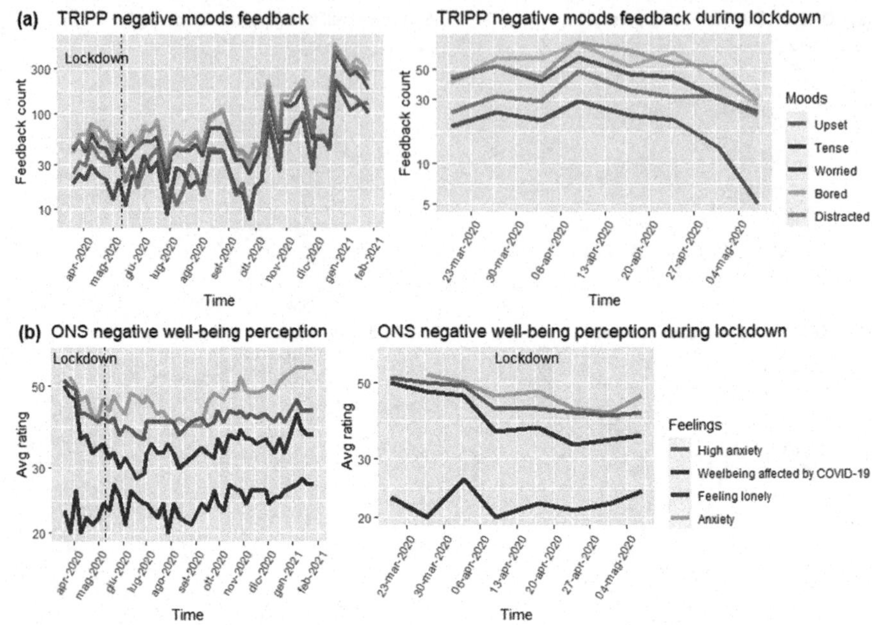

Fig. 4. Emotional feedback over time on negative classes, with a zoom about the lockdown on the right: (a) ONS feelings, (b) TRIPP moods as initial state

Table 4. Number of sessions of Focus and Calm with positive or negative user feedback

Feedback	Positive experience	Non-positive experience
Scale rating	1221	326
Mood weighted rating	9369	7739
First mood ranking	393072	5459

In Fig. 5 users feedback is shown where moods before (left side) and after (right side) the experience are shown in a colour scale from red (i.e., very negative) to green (i.e., very positive). It is noticeable a clear correlation between positive or negative moods and mindset scale. It is visible that also in this case negative moods are largely prevalent before the experience, and positive ones fill almost all the histogram after the experience. From this graph, we can see which moods were prevalent, and link them to the time series seen in Fig. 3–4.

In Fig. 6 feedback during the lockdown is shown, before and after the experience, on the 1 (negative) to 10 (positive) rating scale for the emotional mindset state. It is apparent that the emotional state before the VR experience was negative (i.e. reddish parts) for almost half the sessions, and not very positive (reddish plus very light green) for most people. It is also evident that the emotional mindset was largely enhanced by the VR experience: the pie on the right showing the ratings after the session is largely green.

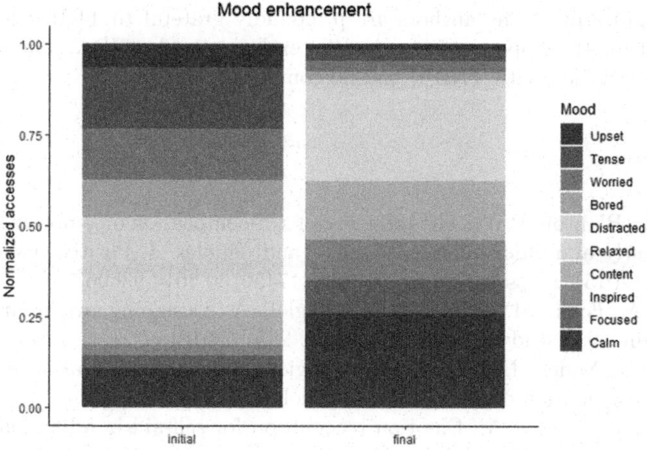

Fig. 5. Mood enhancement after TRIPP sessions during lockdown (Color figure online)

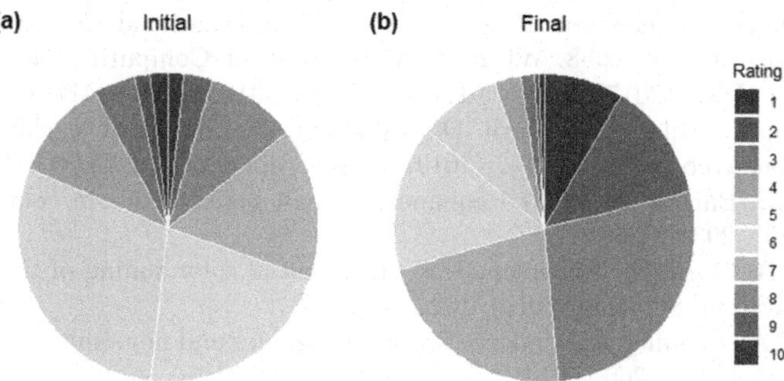

Fig. 6. Mindset enhancement after TRIPP sessions during lockdown (Color figure online)

5 Conclusions

We can conclude that data from the United Kingdom Office for National Statistics (ONS) and the TRIPP app for Virtual Reality (VR) show a prevalence of negative feelings during the studied period of the Covid-19 pandemics but also an evident enhancement of the emotional mindset for every VR session of *Calm* and *Focus*. An in-depth data analysis shows correlations and other interesting trend similarities between the two data sets, between, e.g., the TRIPP *Content* and the ONS *Happiness* classes, TRIPP *Tense* and ONG *Anxiety*, while *Anxiety* inversely correlates to TRIPP *Focused*, reinforcing the assumption that mindfulness exercises can enhance emotional mindset. Future works will include a broader analysis of the worldwide TRIPP data set to study if cultural biases happen on emotional mindset enhancement through VR experiences.

Acknowledgements. The authors are profoundly grateful to TRIPP for providing the data and for their openness to scientific exchange under NDA. The authors also declare no association with TRIPP and no conflict of interest.

References

1. Bluth, K., Blanton, P.W.: The influence of self-compassion on emotional well-being among early and older adolescent males and females. J. Positive Psychol. **10**(3), 219–230 (2015). https://doi.org/10.1080/17439760.2014.936967
2. Chirico, A., Ferrise, F., Cordella, L., Gaggioli, A.: Designing awe in virtual reality: an experimental study. Front. Psychol. **8**, 2351 (2018)
3. Chirico, A., Yaden, D.B., Riva, G., Gaggioli, A.: The potential of virtual reality for the investigation of awe. Front. Psychol. **7**, 1766 (2016)
4. Franzoni, V., Milani, A.: Emotion recognition for self-aid in addiction treatment, psychotherapy, and nonviolent communication. In: Misra, S., et al. (eds.) ICCSA 2019. LNCS, vol. 11620, pp. 391–404. Springer, Cham (2019). https://doi.org/10.1007/978-3-030-24296-1_32
5. Franzoni, V., Milani, A., Biondi, G.: Semo: A semantic model for emotion recognition in web objects. In: Proceedings of the International Conference on Web Intelligence, pp. 953–958. WI 2017. Association for Computing Machinery, New York, NY, USA (2017). https://doi.org/10.1145/3106426.3109417
6. Franzoni, V., Milani, A., Nardi, D., Vallverdú, J.: Emotional machines: the next revolution. Web Intell. **17**, 1–7 (2019). https://doi.org/10.3233/WEB-190395
7. Hill, R.A., Barton, R.A.: Red enhances human performance in contests. Nature **435**(7040), 293 (2005)
8. Hu, K., De Rosa, E., Anderson, A.K.: Differential color tuning of the mesolimbic reward system. Sci. Rep. **10**(1), 10223 (2020)
9. Jones, E.A.: Gaming well: links between videogames and flourishing mental health. Front. Psychol. **5**, 260 (2014)
10. Maples-Keller, J.L., Bunnell, B.E., Kim, S.J., Rothbaum, B.O.: The use of virtual reality technology in the treatment of anxiety and other psychiatric disorders. Harvard Rev. Psychiatry **25**(3), 103–113 (2017)
11. UK ONS survey data on Covid-19, July 2021. https://www.ons.gov.uk/peoplepopulationandcommunity/healthandsocialcare/healthandwellbeing
12. Reedijk, S., Bolders, A., Hommel, B.: The impact of binaural beats on creativity. Front. Hum. Neurosci. **7**, 786 (2013)
13. About tripp, July 2021. https://www.tripp.com/about/
14. Villani, E.A.: Videogames for emotion regulation: a systematic review. Games Health J. **7**(2), 85–99 (2018). https://doi.org/10.1089/g4h.2017.0108

Study on the Influencing Factors of Short Video Users' Subjective Well-Being

Jiajing Li, Jie Bai, Ziying Li, Yang Yang(✉), and Xiuya Lei

Department of Psychology, School of Humanities and Social Science, Beijing Forestry University, Beijing, China

Abstract. As one of the types of mobile social media, short video has a huge number of users in China, which is over 873 million, accounting for 88.3% of the total number of Internet users by December 2020. The purpose of this study is to understand the emotional and psychological state of users in process of using short video and improve the subjective well-being level of the users. Methods: The Study conducted in-depth interviews with 12 short video users to explore the factors that affect the subjective well-being of short video users. Results: (1) The influential factors affecting the subjective well-being of short video users in the process of using social media usage were information overload and social pressure in environmental factors; physical condition, emotional state, aesthetic fatigue, social comparison, fear of missing out, self-expectation and self-control in personal factors; passive use and diving factors in behavioral factors; (2) It was further generalized that boredom proneness and time management proneness are the two most important factors that affect users' subjective well-being. Conclusion: The most important factors influencing the subjective well-being of short video users are boredom proneness and time management proneness.

Keywords: Short video users · Use of mobile social-media · Boredom proneness · Time management proneness · Subjective well-being/SWB

1 Introduction

The 47th Statistical Report on the Development of the Internet in China shows that by December 2020, there were 989 million Internet users in China, an increase of 85.4 million compared to March last year, and the Internet usage rate reached 70.4%, an increase of 5.9% points compared to March 2020. Among them, the number of Internet users using mobile phones in China totaled 986 million, an increase of 88.85 million compared with March, and the proportion of Internet users using mobile phones to access the Internet reached 99.7%, an increase of 0.4% points compared with March [1].

Mobile social media has grown rapidly in recent years, using mobile devices such as mobile phones and ipads as carriers. Mobile social media is one of the ways for people to interact online and is a typical medium that can provide social networking services. The more famous mobile social media abroad include Facebook and Twitter, while the more popular mobile social media in China mainly include WeChat, Weibo, Zhihu and other social software, which penetrate all aspects of people's study, work and

M. Mahmud et al. (Eds.): BI 2021, LNAI 12960, pp. 199–210, 2021.
https://doi.org/10.1007/978-3-030-86993-9_19

life through pictures, videos and texts, with short video social networking sites rapidly gaining a large number of users in recent years. The number of online video users in China has reached 927 million, accounting for 93.7% of the overall number of Internet users; among them, the number of short video users has reached 873 million, accounting for 88.3% of the overall number of Internet users (data as of December 2020).

Previous research has shown that social relationships can influence individuals' perceptions of well-being [2], and online communication through the internet has brought about a new way of socializing, and individuals' well-being has become more dependent on mobile social media [3]. With the widespread use of mobile social media and the large proportion of short-form video users, this study aims to explore the factors that influence the subjective well-being of short-form video users, with a view to helping them to improve their well-being through the use of mobile social media.

Studies have shown that mobile social media use has been increasing in recent years [4, 5], and short video users have become a major component of internet users. The use of mobile social media can help people maintain better social relationships, which can provide social support and reduce depression [6]. However, excessive or inappropriate use of mobile social media can cause users to experience more negative emotions, such as increased anxiety and experience more loneliness [7]. These negative emotions can affect users' psychological well-being, which in turn affects their level of subjective well-being. Individuals with stronger time management tendencies have a greater sense of control over their time during the use of mobile social media, and are also able to use mobile social media more appropriately, reducing the occurrence of negative experiences and thus increasing their level of subjective well-being.

First, previous studies have focused more on the pathological feature of addiction, such as internet addiction [8] and mobile phone addiction [9, 10], but addiction is more extreme for most people. People use social media frequently due to work, school or other reasons, and this process may lead to an over-reliance on mobile social media, and this overuse may affect all aspects of the user, such as perceptions of emotions (experiencing more negative emotions) [11], physical health status [12], life satisfaction [13], etc. With the satisfaction of material life, people begin to seek satisfaction in the spiritual world, mainly in the form of the pursuit of happiness, and in such a general environment as the Internet, it is important to explore the relationship between mobile social media and individuals' subjective well-being.

Secondly, boredom is a negative emotion, but it is easier to ignore because it does not manifest itself too strongly, but boredom can also have negative consequences. Therefore, it should also receive attention. It is common for people to use mobile social media when they are bored, have nothing to do, or even feel a bit irritable, but it is not known whether the presence of mobile social media will alleviate this state or worsen it. At the same time, individuals with a high propensity for boredom are more likely to experience negative emotions such as boredom, which in turn has a negative impact on subjective well-being. This suggests a strong relationship between mobile social media use, boredom and subjective well-being.

Third, time management tendency is an individual's ability to perceive and control time. Those with high boredom tendency overestimate time and are more inattentive, while those with low boredom tendency underestimate time, suggesting that an individual's ability to perceive time has an impact on boredom perception, and that propensity to problematic mobile social media use is also related to time management, suggesting a possible association between the three.

Fourthly, previous studies have explored the factors that influence the subjective well-being of short video users more in terms of behavioral approaches as an entry point, without delving into the impact of the emotional and psychological states that arise from users' use of mobile social media on their levels of subjective well-being.

The purpose of this paper is to explore the Influencing Factors of Short Video Users' Subjective Well-Being.

2 Method

This study is based on the theory of rooting, the collection of relevant information in a state of nature and the use of oneself as a tool to analyze the phenomenon and the information collected, leading to a theory. "Coding" is the basic work of rooted theory and is divided into open coding, axial coding and selective coding. This method is therefore used in this study to analyze the data collected.

2.1 Study Subjects

Interviews with short video users were conducted both online and offline, and the basic information of the 12 interviewees is shown in Table 1.

Table 1. Basic situation of interviewees

No.	Gender	Age	Occupation	Length of interview (min)
Yu (A01)	Female	23	Student instructor	≈49
Lin (A02)	Female	20	Junior student	≈46
Kun (A03)	Female	48	Primary school teacher	≈51
Jia (A04)	Female	23	Student instructor	≈56
Sha (A05)	Female	22	Senior year	≈45
Yuan (A06)	Male	21	Senior year	≈48
Yue (A07)	Male	25	Postgraduate student	≈47
Ping (A08)	Female	25	Marketing planner	≈70
Zi (A09)	Male	19	Sophomore	≈46
Sheng (A10)	Male	50	Self-employed	≈60
Xia (A11)	Female	51	Freelancer	≈41
Hui (A12)	Male	58	Logistician	≈58

2.2 Qualitative Research Tools

In this study, the interviews were recorded using a voice recorder and transcribed into word text after the interviews were completed. The text was collated and analysed using

Nvivo 12.0 qualitative analysis software to form nodes and codes, and finally the codes were sorted.

2.3 Qualitative Research Procedures

Pre-interview Procedures

An interview outline was prepared and pre-interviews were conducted by reading relevant literature. The pre-interviews were conducted with two graduate students in psychology. The interviewees were asked: whether the interview questions were clear and easy to understand; whether the interview time was appropriate; and whether the interview content was suitable. The suggestions made by the pre-interviewees were summarized to form the final outline of the formal interview.

Formal Interview Procedures

One-to-one structured interviews were conducted with 12 short video users. During the interviews, the researcher does not give judgmental discourse on the interviewees' responses and only conducts the interviews based on objective facts, maintaining a neutral attitude.

Transcription and Coding of Interview Results

Transcriptions of the interviews were transcribed verbatim and, to ensure accuracy, the transcriptions also retained the verbal words of the interviewees in addition to the basic content; any content that would reveal information about the interviewees was removed to protect the privacy of the interviewees. After transcription, the results were compounded and reviewed.

Coding of Interview Results

The coding of the transcribed text was done independently by the researcher. A bottom-up, three-level coding of the transcribed text was done. Firstly, the interview texts were coded word by word and word frequencies were recorded to form primary codes; secondly, secondary codes were used to collate the primary coded words to form genera; thirdly, tertiary codes were used to analyze again against the texts and genera to form relationships between the genera.

Research Methodology

Determining the Outline of the Interview

Based on the literature review and experts' opinions, an outline of the interview was prepared, and the interview was conducted based on the following basic outline: 1) Please talk about your understanding of happiness. 2) Do you think you are happy in your life? What is the specific performance? 3) In what kind of scenes do you feel the above-mentioned in the process of watching short videos? 4) How do you think short videos and mobile social media affect your happiness and how do they manifest?

Data Collection Method

The methodological framework was based on the rooting theory in qualitative research, and a semi-structured, face-to-face interview was conducted by the researcher himself with 12 mobile social media users of different age groups according to the interview outline. One interview was conducted for approximately 30–60 min, excluding environmental noise and maintaining privacy. The researcher explained the significance and methodology of this study in detail to the interviewees, and the interviewees agreed to record and transcribe the interviews on site, and the transcribed information was given to the interviewees for verification and commitment to confidentiality. When handling interview materials, names were anonymized and replaced by a single word number. Within 4 h after each interview, two researchers manually transcribed the audio materials word by word and sentence by sentence into Word text materials based on the recordings and audio recordings made during the interviews, using the interviewees' text code numbers as file names and comparing them to form the final version.

Data Organization and Analysis
Based on the content analysis method of rooting theory, the audio recordings were imported into Nvivo12.0 software in the form of Word text, and the text was coded at three levels: open coding, associative coding, and selective coding. As the Word text data was entered, the researcher continuously coded the interview data into new or existing nodes.

3 Results

Through coding analysis, it was concluded that the factors affecting the happiness of short video users are environmental factors, personal factors negative behavioral factors. The coding results are shown in Tables 2, 3, 4 and 5.

Table 2. Coding table of factors affecting short video users' subjective well-being

Three-level coding	Secondary codes	Level 1 code	Reference points
Environmental factors	Invalid information	Too much information	6
		Too much information	5
		Distortion of information	3
	Invalid social	Too many friends in the address book	4
		Repeated communication	4
		Focus on pressure	1
Personal factors	Health status	Affects sleep	2
		Headaches	1
		Bad for the eyes	3

(*continued*)

Table 2. (*continued*)

Three-level coding	Secondary codes	Level 1 code	Reference points
	Positive emotions	Happy	19
		Satisfaction	2
		Warmth	3
		Happiness	15
	Negative emotions	Unhappy	1
		Irritable	1
		Resentment	1
		Sense of emptiness	4
		Anger	6
		Boredom	1
		A sense of self-recrimination	2
	Conflict emotions	Pleasure and sin go hand in hand	4
	Aesthetic fatigue	Get tired of it	4
		Adaptation	6
		Decline in quality	2
	Social comparison	Upstream comparison	7
		Downside comparison	3
	Fear of missing out	Worried about missing messages	9
	Self-expectation	Looking forward to following	2
		Feeling neglected	4
		Seeking recognition	1
		Finding presence	3
		Being noticed	13
		Gaining recognition	7
	Self-control	Difficult to control	7
		Forgetting time	2
		Control yourself	3
Negative behaviors	Passive use	Passive processing of messages	2
		Message mute	1
	Diving	Avoiding the spotlight	6
		Avoidance of comments	1
		Not emotionally invested	4

Table 3. Three level coding of influencing factors of time management

Three-level coding	Secondary codes	Level 1 code	Reference points
Environmental factors	Information overload	Too much information	6
	Invalid social	Too many friends in the address book	4
		Repeated communication	4
Personal factors	Cognition	Self-control	12
		Fear of missing out	9
	Emotions	Positive emotions	39
		Negative emotions	16
		Conflict Emotions	4
	Behavior	Passive use	3

Table 4. Three level coding of influencing factors of boredom proneness

Three-level coding	Secondary codes	Level 1 code	Reference points
Environmental factors	Invalid information	Too much information	5
		Distortion of information	3
	Invalid social	Poor communication	3
		Too many friends in the address book	4
Personal factors	Cognition	Aesthetic fatigue	12
		Self-expectation	9
	Emotions	Positive emotions	39
		Negative emotions	16
		Conflict Emotions	4
	Behavior	Passive use	3

Table 5. Three level coding of other influencing factors

Three-level coding	Secondary codes	Level 1 code	Reference points
Social factor	Social pressure	Focus on pressure	1
	Social comparison	Upstream comparison	7
		Downside comparison	3

(*continued*)

Table 5. (*continued*)

Three-level coding	Secondary codes	Level 1 code	Reference points
Personal factors	Sense of neglect	Feelings of neglect	4
	Recused	Recusal behavior	7
		Emotional avoidance	4
	Physiological factors	Health status	6

4 Analysis and Discussion

Based on the content of the interviews and the analysis of the text, the results are that the main factors affecting the happiness of short video users are the time management factor and the boredom factor, on which the factors affecting the role of both environmental and personal factors (Fig. 1).

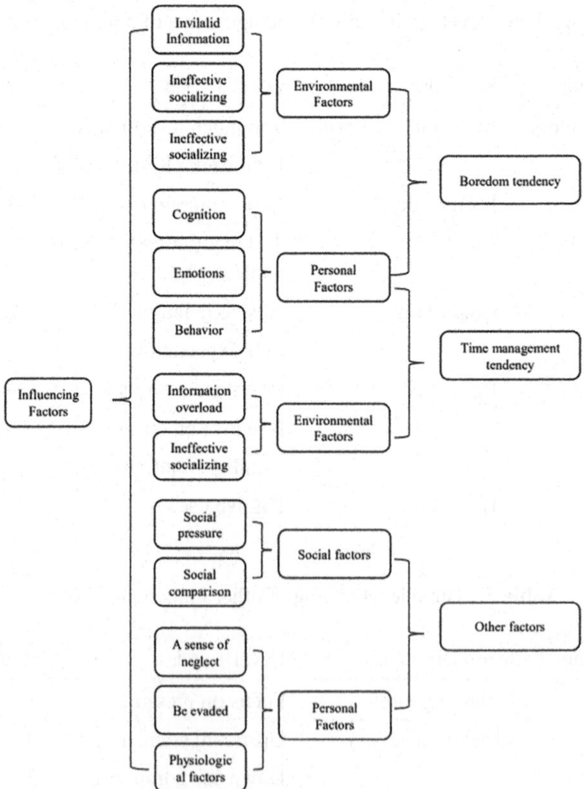

Fig. 1. Result flow chart

4.1 The Influence of Environmental and Personal Factors on Subjective Well-Being Under Time Management Proneness

Information Overload

The development of the Internet has led to the development of various mobile social media software, which has also gained a large number of users. On the one hand, mobile social media provides people with a large number of channels to obtain information; through mobile social media, they can contact with people all over the world, but on the other hand, although users can obtain a large amount of information from social media anytime and anywhere, it consumes a lot of energy and time for users to filter and filter from a large amount of information, and individuals with poor time management skills are more likely to be trapped in the complicated information. Individuals with poor time management skills are more likely to be trapped in the clutter of information. At the same time, due to the current fast-paced life, users are prone to cognitive depletion when dealing with the information overload, which leads to a sense of emptiness and fatigue.

Ineffective Socialization

One of the features of social media is that it is easier to connect with people, but it also brings many people in your address book who are not your friends in the traditional sense, you may have only met them on one occasion, or you may not even know who they are. A01 said, some people in my circle of friends may only know each other, but they don't have much interaction with each other either.

Cognitive Factors

If you can control more of the time you spend in swiping short videos when watching short videos, it will less affect your life, your body, your mental state and it will not affect your work tasks. When there is less time to generate such guilt, users will feel more in control of their lives, and they can have fun from it, which will increase their happiness. If users have less self-control and always interfered with their task plans for swiping short videos, they will be more likely to feel self-condemned, being in such state for a long time will affect their sense of well-being.

Emotional Factors

As mobile social media is primarily hedonistic, users expect more pleasure and relief from fatigue when using it. When users are more likely to watch funny short videos or get interesting news, they will experience more positive emotions in the moment. When individuals experience more positive emotions, it has a facilitating effect on happiness. Users also get information from mobile social media about social events, national news, etc. The variety of categories, combined with the differences in users' experiences, result in different emotions towards different events. The interviews revealed that such conflicting emotions occur more often when users indicate that they are watching short videos. Short videos are short in length and interesting, which makes each short video stimulate the user's brain and instantly grab their attention; the feedback period is short and easy to obtain a sense of satisfaction. But it is also due to such characteristics that users are often controlled by performance without realizing it, and a brush is often several hours. After reacting, they often carry a sense of guilt.

Behavioral Factors

When users feel negative emotional states such as stress, fatigue or a sense of being watched during mobile social media use, they may have the intention to withdraw from mobile social media use, but may not be able to do so completely due to circumstances, for example, and may then be forced to use or avoid negative behavior on mobile social media interactions. For example: (A11) I don't usually comment, people say online that you don't like, but it's good to take a comma, but I sometimes don't comment blindly. One time I commented on someone scolding me, because like I did once, it wasn't me, it was like saying what about Henan people, I forget what I commented on, but they scolded me, I was angry and a bit unjust.

4.2 The Influence of Environmental and Personal Factors on Subjective Well-Being Under the Tendency of Boredom

Invalid Information

Users can be confronted with a multitude of information, and it takes a lot of energy for users to filter and filter out the information they need from a multitude of information; at the same time, due to the current fast-paced lifestyle, people do not have the time and will not have the patience to read long-form content, which also makes the current mobile social media information fragmented and disorganized. Instead, users need to consume more cognition to piece together the information. Due to the competitive market pressure, media companies, in order to get a lot of traffic, will put out a lot of headlines with eye-catching content, but without any substantial content to push, which appears to be characterized by low quality information. When faced with more and more of this, users will easily experience cognitive exhaustion when processing this overload of information, and will then experience a sense of emptiness and fatigue.

Ineffective Socialization

One of the features of social media is that it is easier to connect with others, and because it is so easy to add friends to each other, there are many people in the address book who are not friends in the traditional sense, and they may only know each other on one side or even have no communication with each other. A01: Among these people, some may only know each other on one side or not very well. Some people may only know each other, but there is not much communication.

Cognitive Factors

Aesthetic fatigue mainly occurs in short video viewing. Short video will push similar types of video content according to users' viewing preferences and habits, and when users watch too much similar content, they will feel "bored". When the user lives with this kind of stimulation, the feeling of fatigue will arise and the feeling of happiness will gradually decline. I don't feel that I feel very bright or anything less and less, so the feeling of happiness may not be as strong as when I first used it (A04). The aesthetic fatigue of users also makes it easier to feel empty after the short video, plus the guilt users are more likely to self-blame, such negative emotions and behaviors will hinder the user's perception of happiness.

Through the interviews, it was found that users, on the one hand, express themselves positively and, on the other hand, want to show their presence and gain the attention of others by posting updates. In other words, when users use mobile social media, if the actual situation differs too much from their self-expectation, they are more likely to have negative emotions and their perception of happiness will be weakened: on the contrary, it will be enhanced.

Emotional Factors

Users also get information about social events, national news, etc. from mobile social media. The variety of categories, coupled with the differences in users' experiences, result in different emotions for different events. When users see irritating social news events, they are more likely to have an emotional state of anger. When a user sees a social media post that contradicts their own views, they will feel very disgusted. Some people will post something they find interesting, but I think it might go against my own social values, and then it will cause my own resentment (A02).

Through the interviews, it was found that when interviewers were asked to give some descriptions of what was funny, they tended to be more general in saying that it was funny happy things, but when asked what kind of things they would feel more unhappy about, they tended to be more specific in their descriptions. Some interviewees indicated that he would laugh at the funny content.

The interviews revealed that such conflicting emotions would occur more often when users said they would watch short videos. Some interviewees said that this kind of guilt will exist from the beginning of the brush, but because the short video is nice, meaningful and fun, they will still brush on even though they feel guilty. When there is no task for the user, this guilt will be slightly reduced, more from the fact that if you do not brush the short video then you can have more time to do meaningful things, such as: reading, fitness.

Behavioral Factors

When users feel negative emotional states such as stress, fatigue, or a sense of being watched during mobile social media use, they may have the intention to quit mobile social media use, but may not be able to completely quit due to environmental reasons, etc., and then they may be forced to use or avoid negative behavior of interacting on mobile social media.

4.3 Relevant Factors that Jointly Influence Both

The common influences on both are invalid information and social interaction in the environment, and emotional and behavioral factors in the individual. When individuals receive more invalid information, it will deplete their cognitive resources, which will lead to fatigue and boredom, and too much invalid information will not only prevent them from getting useful content, but also take up a lot of their time and spend time looking for useful information. If individuals can manage their time well during the use of mobile social media and reduce the boredom caused by ineffective information and prolonged use, this will improve their subjective well-being.

When users experience more positive emotions during their use of mobile social media, it will reduce the impact of negative emotions such as boredom, which in turn will increase the level of subjective well-being of the individual. When individuals have better control over their emotions, their time management skills will also increase and their subjective well-being will improve.

5 Conclusion

Boredom proneness and time management proneness are the two most important factors that affect short video users' subjective well-being.

References

1. CNNIC (2021). http://cnnic.cn/gywm/xwzx/rdxw/20172017_7084/202102/t20210203_71364.htm
2. Diener, E., Suh, E.M., Lucas, R.E., Smith, H.L.: Subjective well-being: three decades of progress. Psychol. Bull. **125**(2), 276–302 (1999)
3. Qiu, L., Lin, H., Leung, A.K., Tov, W.: Putting their best foot forward: emotional disclosure on Facebook. Cyberpsychol. Behav. Soc. Netw. **15**(10), 569–572 (2012)
4. Li, S., Wang, Y., Xue, J., Zhao, N., Zhu, T.: The Impact of COVID-19 epidemic declaration on psychological consequences: a study on active Weibo users. Int. J. Environ. Res. Publ. Health **17**(6), 2032 (2020)
5. Gao, J., et al.: Mental health problems and social media exposure during COVID-19 outbreak. PLOS ONE **15**(4), e0231924 (2020)
6. Frison, E., Subrahmanyam, K., Eggermont, S.: The short-term longitudinal and reciprocal relations between peer victimization on Facebook and Adolescents' well-being. J. Youth Adolescence **45**(9), 1755–1771 (2016). https://doi.org/10.1007/s10964-016-0436-z
7. Chou, C., Hsiao, M.-C.: Internet addiction, usage, gratification, and pleasure experience: the Taiwan college students' case. Comput. Educ. **35**(1), 65–80 (2000)
8. Wang, X., Yu, H., Lei, A., et al.: Generation of gene-modified goats targeting MSTN and FGF5 via zygote injection of CRISPR/Cas9 system. Sci. Rep. **5**, 13878 (2015)
9. Feng, J., Cao, G.: A review of studies on the relationship between mobile phone addiction and impulsiveness (2017)
10. Gang, D., Ying, X., Xin, Z., et al.: Relationship among college students' mobile phone addiction tendency, life events and social support. China J. Health Psychol. (2014)
11. Steers, M.-L.N., Wickham, R.E., Acitelli, L.K.: Seeing everyone else's highlight reels: how Facebook usage is linked to depressive symptoms. J. Soc. Clin. Psychol. **33**(8), 701–731 (2014)
12. Hawi, N.S., Samaha, M.: The relations among social media addiction, self-esteem, and life satisfaction in university students. Soc. Sci. Comput. Rev. **35**(5), 576–586 (2016)
13. Yang, Y., Liu, K., Li, S., Shu, M.: Social media activities, emotion regulation strategies, and their interactions on people's mental health in covid-19 pandemic. Int. J. Environ. Res. Publ. Health **17**(23), 8931 (2020)

Assessment of Machine Learning Pipelines for Prediction of Behavioral Deficits from Brain Disconnectomes

Marco Zorzi[1,3](✉), Michele De Filippo De Grazia[3], Elvio Blini[1], and Alberto Testolin[1,2]

[1] Department of General Psychology, University of Padova, 35141 Padova, Italy
{marco.zorzi,alberto.testolin}@unipd.it
[2] Department of Information Engineering, University of Padova, 35141 Padova, Italy
[3] IRCCS San Camillo Hospital, Venice-Lido 30126, Italy

Abstract. Recent studies have shown that brain lesions following stroke can be probabilistically mapped onto disconnections of white matter tracts, and that the resulting "disconnectome" is predictive of the patient's behavioral deficits. Disconnectome maps are sparse, high-dimensional 3D matrices that require unsupervised dimensionality reduction followed by supervised learning for prediction of the associated behavioral data. However, the optimal machine learning pipeline for disconnectome data still needs to be identified. We examined four dimensionality reduction methods at varying levels of compression and used the extracted features as input for cross-validated regularized regression to predict the associated language and motor deficits. Features extracted by Principal Component Analysis and Non-Negative Matrix Factorization were found to be the best predictors, followed by Independent Component Analysis and Dictionary Learning. Optimizing the number of extracted features improved predictive accuracy and greatly reduced model complexity. Moreover, the choice of dimensionality reduction technique was found to optimally combine with a specific type of regularized regression (ridge *vs.* LASSO). Overall, our findings represent an important step towards an optimal pipeline that yields high prediction accuracy with a small number of features, which can also improve model interpretability.

Keywords: Stroke · Structural connectome · Disconnections · Machine learning · Feature extraction · Dimensionality reduction · Predictive modeling

1 Introduction

Stroke is a major cause of serious disability for adults and it can affect multiple behavioral domains, from motor control to language and cognition [1]. A classic approach in cognitive neuroscience is to establish which brain lesion is associated to a specific behavioral deficit [2]. The reverse inference is more challenging because lesion information is used to predict the behavioural performance of new (i.e., held out) patients despite the considerable individual variability of lesion-behavior relationships [3]. Moreover,

M. Mahmud et al. (Eds.): BI 2021, LNAI 12960, pp. 211–222, 2021.
https://doi.org/10.1007/978-3-030-86993-9_20

white-matter lesions cause structural disconnections that produce widespread dysfunction of brain networks [4] and can be better predictors of behavioral deficits than lesion site [1, 5, 6].

Assessing damage to the structural connectome requires complex neuroimaging methods (i.e., diffusion tensor imaging) that are difficult to implement in clinical practice. However, Foulon et al. [7] recently proposed an indirect method for estimating structural disconnection from clinical structural Magnetic Resonance Imaging (MRI) scans. Using the connectome of healthy individuals as reference atlas, the method estimates the probability that a lesion at any given location (voxel) causes disconnection of white matter tracts. Therefore, a disconnectome map indicates, for each voxel in a standard brain template, the probability of structural disconnection. Salvalaggio et al. [6] showed that disconnectome maps can be used to predict behavioral deficits. Their machine learning pipeline was adapted from previous work on structural lesions [1, 8] and was not optimized for disconnectome data. In short, Principal Component Analysis (PCA) was used for dimensionality reduction and the components cumulatively explaining 95% of the variance were retained as features for prediction. The latter was based on cross-validated ridge regression using a behavioral score as outcome variable.

Unsupervised dimensionality reduction is a necessary step for neuroimaging data, which typically have a much greater number of features than observations [9]. A variety of techniques can be used to extract a limited number of features that can compactly describe the data distribution. Prediction from a compact set of brain-related features can then be carried out using regularized regression methods such as ridge regression [4] or Least Absolute Shrinkage and Selection Operator (LASSO) [10]. Regularized regression includes a penalty term that pushes the estimated coefficients of irrelevant features toward zero, limiting the risk of multicollinearity and overfitting [11, 12]. Moreover, regularized methods often also improve model interpretability [13, 14], making them particularly suitable for the analysis of neuroimaging data [15].

In the present study, we systematically investigated the effect of both feature extraction techniques and regularized regression on predictive accuracy, in order to identify the most effective machine learning pipeline for disconnectome data. Indeed, different methods can show considerable variability in performance depending on the type of neuroimaging data and task considered [9, 15, 16]. We recently investigated this issue in the context of resting-state functional connectivity data [10]. Here we extended our approach to disconnectome maps of stroke patients, which were used to predict behavioral scores in the language and motor domains. Disconnectome maps were first processed using different dimensionality reduction methods: Principal Component Analysis, Independent Component Analysis, Non-Negative Matrix Factorization and Dictionary Learning. The extracted features were then used as predictors for cross-validated regularized regression. We assessed the predictive performance while systematically varying the number of extracted features for each dimensionality reduction method as well as a function of the type of regularization method used for supervised learning. Finally, we examined the quality of the brain maps that display disconnectome voxels that are most predictive of behavioral performance in each domain.

In summary, structural disconnectomes [7] represent a relatively new type of neuroimaging data that has not been systematically approached with machine learning techniques. With respect to the state-of-the-art [6], the main contributions of the present work include: i) the consideration of a broad range of dimensionalty reduction techniques; ii) the evaluation of different types of regularized regression; iii) the inclusion of feature selection to reduce the number of predictors; iv) the assessment of predictive accuracy across multiple measures that also consider model complexity.

2 Materials and Methods

2.1 Participants and Data Acquisition

Behavioral and MRI data were obtained from a previously published study [1], in which 132 symptomatic stroke patients underwent MRI scanning and behavioral testing 1–2 weeks after the stroke occurred. The data for each patient consisted of a 3D image of the lesion, reconstructed from the original MRI image (see [1] for details) and registered to a common coordinate space provided by the Montreal Neurological Institute (MNI space, 2 mm isovoxel resolution) using affine and diffeomorphic deformations. Structural disconnections for 131 patients were computed in [6] from the lesion image with the BCB-toolkit [7], using 176 healthy controls from the "Human Connectome Project" 7T diffusion-weighted imaging dataset as a reference to track fibers passing through each lesioned voxel. In the resulting disconnectome map, the value in each voxel indicates the probability of disconnection from 0 to 1 (see Fig. 1). Note that each map is a sparse high-dimensional 3D matrix, with size $91 \times 109 \times 91$.

Behavioral assessment spanned several cognitive domains [1]. In the present work we focus on language and motor scores, which are available for $n = 116$ and $n = 108$ patients, respectively. For each domain we used an overall "factor score" [1, 6], which

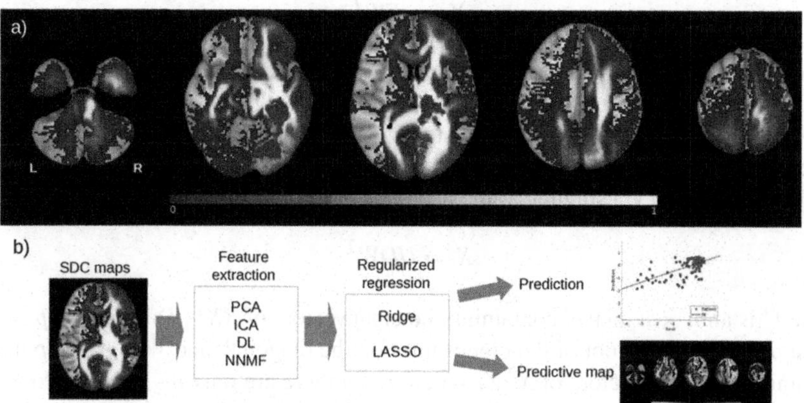

Fig. 1. a) The 3D disconnectome map of a sample stroke patient is displayed here using 5 axial slices. A localized right hemisphere lesion involving the thalamus and the lateral occipital cortex (overlayed on the map in blue color) produces more widespread white matter disconnections (with probability indexed by the red-yellow scale) that include posterior thalamic radiation, superior corona radiata, and extend to the left hemisphere through the splenial part of the corpus callosum. b) Machine learning pipelines assessed in our study. At each processing stage, the performance of different methods was systematically compared to establish the optimal combination of feature extraction and regularized regression techniques. (Color figure online)

captures the shared variance of several sub-tests. For example, the language factor score is the first principal component accounting for 77.3% of the variance across a variety of language tasks. The motor factor score expresses contralesional motor performance (e.g., right limb for left hemisphere damage and vice versa). Each factor score was normalized to represent impaired performance with negative values.

2.2 Unsupervised Feature Extraction

Unsupervised feature extraction was performed using the entire dataset ($n = 131$ and $p = 902{,}629$), to take advantage of all patients' data regardless of the availability of specific neuropsychological scores. All feature extraction methods used in the present work are linear, which means that they aim to find a weight matrix W that can transform the original $n \times p$ data matrix X into a new set of k features, with $k < p$ and usually $k < n$, such that:

$$F = XW \tag{1}$$

where F is the feature space. Since choosing the value of k is nontrivial, we systematically varied k from 5 to $n-1$, with step size = 5, where n is the number of patients entered in the regularized regression. A cross-validation procedure was then used to select the optimal value of k (see Sect. 2.4 below). To compare the compression ability of the different feature extraction methods, the reconstruction error was calculated as the mean squared error (MSE) between the original disconnection maps X and the reconstructed maps X_R, for each value of k. The original maps can be reconstructed by simply backprojecting the feature set into the original input space using the transposed weight matrix:

$$X_R = FW^T \tag{2}$$

Principal Component Analysis (PCA). PCA linearly transforms the input data into a smaller set of uncorrelated features called principal components, sorted by the explained data variance [17]. The input data is first centered, so that it has zero-mean. The eigenvalues and eigenvectors of the $p \times p$ covariance matrix X^TX are then computed using matrix factorization via singular value decomposition:

$$X = UDW^T \tag{3}$$

where U is an $n \times n$ matrix containing the eigenvectors of XX^T, D is an $n \times p$ matrix containing the square root of the eigenvalues on the diagonal, and W is a $p \times p$ matrix containing the eigenvectors of X^TX. When $p > n$ there are only $n - 1$ non-zero eigenvalues, so only the first $n - 1$ columns of D and W are kept. Eigenvectors are sorted in descending order of explained variance. Hence, W contains $n-1$ principal components, expressed as a set of p weights that can map the original variables in a new (compressed) feature space. Since PCA is a deterministic method, it was performed only once, and the first k features were then iteratively selected. The other feature extraction methods are probabilistic in nature, so the procedure was repeated for each value of k.

Independent Component Analysis (ICA). ICA assumes that a *p*-dimensional signal vector $X_{i,*}^T$ is generated by a linear combination of *k* features (with $k < = p$) that are assumed to be independent and non-gaussian [18], leading to:

$$X_{i,*}^T = AF_{i,*}^T \tag{4}$$

where A is a $p \times k$ unmixing matrix, which maps the signal in the sources, and F is the feature vector. Hence, the features can be obtained by:

$$F_{i,*}^T = WX_{i,*}^T \tag{5}$$

where W is the inverse of the unmixing matrix A. The input data is first centered, and then further pre-processed through whitening so that a new vector with uncorrelated components and unit variance is obtained. The *FastICA* function of the scikit-learn library was used, and PCA was used for data whitening [18].

Non-negative Matrix Factorization (NNMF). NNMF is a form of matrix factorization into non-negative factors W and H [19], such that the linear combination of each column of W weighted by the columns of H can approximate the original data X:

$$X \approx WH \tag{6}$$

NNMF aims to minimize the following loss function:

$$\begin{gathered} \|A - WH\|_F^2 \\ \textit{subject to } W, H \geq 0 \end{gathered} \tag{7}$$

The *nnmf* MATLAB function with the "multiplicative update algorithm" was used.

Dictionary Learning (DL). The DL algorithm, sometimes known as *sparse coding*, jointly solves for a $p \times k$ dictionary W and the new set of features F that best represent the data. To obtain only few non-zero entrances an additional L_1 penalty term is included in the cost function:

$$\begin{gathered} (W, F) = \min_{(W,F)} \frac{1}{2} \left\| X - FW^T \right\|_2^2 + \lambda \|F_1\| \\ \textit{subject to } \left\| W_j \right\|_2 \leq 1, \forall j = 1, \ldots, k \end{gathered} \tag{8}$$

where λ is the L_1 penalty coefficient, controlling for the sparsity of the compressed representation [20]. The *DictionaryLearning* function of the scikit-learn library was used.

2.3 Regularized Regression

The features extracted by each unsupervised learning method were then used as regressors for the prediction of the language and motor scores. Note that only the subjects with available target scores were kept in this phase. The regressors were normalized and then entered in either a ridge regression or a LASSO regression [10, 21]. In both cases the loss function can be defined as:

$$\min_{\beta}\left(\frac{1}{2n}\sum\nolimits_{i=1}^{n}\left(y_i - x_i^T\beta\right)^2 + \lambda R\right) \tag{9}$$

where n is the number of observations, y_i is the prediction target, x_i is the data observation, β represents the p regression coefficients, and R is the regularization term, weighted by the non-negative coefficient λ. In the case of ridge regression, the regularizer is defined as:

$$R(\beta) = \sum\nolimits_{j=1}^{p} \beta_j^2 \tag{10}$$

while in the case of LASSO regression the regularizer is defined as:

$$R(\beta) = \sum\nolimits_{j=1}^{p} |\beta_j| \tag{11}$$

The main difference is that LASSO forces the estimates of non-predictive coefficients to have exactly-zero values, whereas the ridge regularization shrinks those coefficients towards near-zero values [21]. The optimal λ was chosen among 100 values in the range $[10^{-5}, 10^5]$ with logarithmic step.

2.4 Cross-Validation Setup and Model Comparison

To find the optimal values for the hyper-parameters λ and k while controlling for overfitting, we employed a search procedure over a range of possible values using cross-validation (CV). The complete dataset was thus split into a *training* set and a *test* set: the training set was used for tuning the hyper-parameters, and the resulting model was then evaluated on the left-out test set. We adopted a Leave-One-Out (LOO) cross validation setup, where just one sample was circularly included in the test set. As a control analysis, we also explored hyper-parameter tuning using nested CV [22]. However, since this method led to negligible differences compared to the standard CV, for computational convenience we did not include it in the final analyses.

To compare the models generated by the different feature extraction methods, both the R^2 and the Bayesian Information Criterion (BIC) [23] were calculated (note that only the non-zero coefficients were used for BIC calculation). Finally, for each method, the optimal regression coefficients were backprojected in the original space, by means of a linear transformation through the features' weights, and restored in the 3D volume of the template brain [6]. This provides a brain map that displays the predictive voxels for a given behavioral domain. The machine learning pipeline is depicted in Fig. 1b.

3 Results

The feature extraction methods were first assessed based on their reconstruction error. For all methods, the reconstruction error decreased when increasing the number of features (Fig. 2a), and NNMF showed generally higher reconstruction error. Systematic variation of the number of features (k) used as input for regression revealed a pattern of predictive accuracy (in terms of R^2) that was strongly influenced by the feature extraction method (Fig. 2b). PCA- and NNMF-based models were largely insensitive to k, whereas performance of the ICA- and DL-based models deteriorated for large k values. For ICA the performance loss was almost linear and markedly steep when the number of independent components exceeded the optimal k (here 10), suggesting that over-decomposition introduces noise and makes the components less informative. In contrast, the strict order of components' extraction in PCA implies that increasing k has no effect on previously extracted features. Nonetheless, at the optimal value of k, all models showed very good predictive performance with R^2 around 0.40.

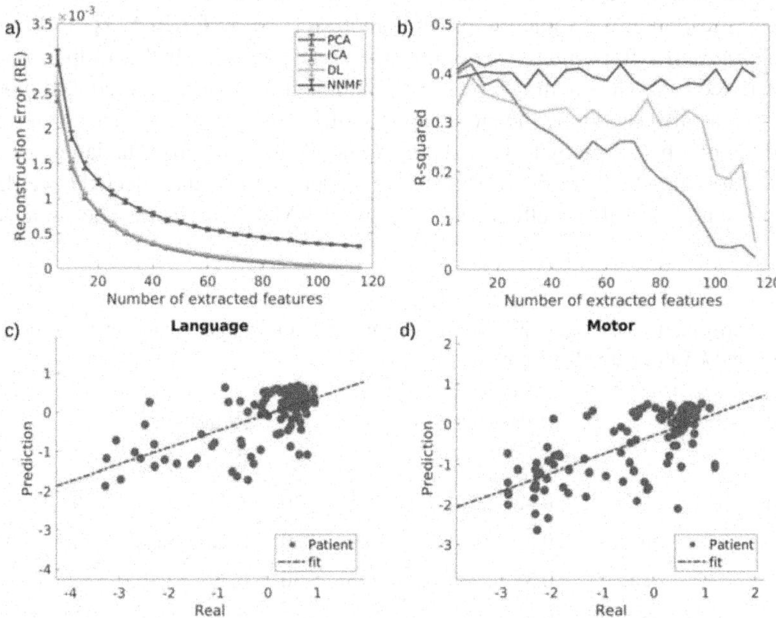

Fig. 2. a) Reconstruction error as a function of the number of extracted features, separately reported for each feature extraction method. b) R^2 values of the models in predicting language scores as a function of the number of extracted features. c) PCA + ridge model predictions with LOO CV for the language domain and d) NNMF + LASSO model predictions for the motor domain.

Performance of the selected model (i.e., optimized for k) for each feature extraction method and behavioral score (language vs. motor) is reported in Table 1 (ridge) and Table 2 (LASSO). The tables also report the optimal hyper-parameters values, as well as the number of non-zero weights in the LASSO regression model after training. Interestingly, different feature extraction methods led to slightly different optimal hyper-parameters. The ICA- and DL-based models were chosen with fewer features than the PCA- and NNMF-based models. A marked difference can be observed between NNMF and the other methods, with k up to six times larger. Regarding the regularization coefficient, the variability was more substantial for ridge regression than for LASSO.

PCA and NNMF yielded the best predictive accuracy across types of regularization and behavioral domains in terms of R^2. NNMF combined with LASSO regression reached the best performance in the prediction of both motor and language scores, although by a tight margin with respect to PCA + ridge (see model predictions in Fig. 2c and d). When considering the BIC, on the other hand, the PCA + ridge pipeline was favored by the lower model complexity (smaller number of weights). We also report as baseline the performance of models with non-optimized (i.e., fixed) number of features (Tables 1 and 2). For PCA, we used the principal components cumulatively accounting for 95% of the variance ($k = 30$), as used in previous studies [6]. The level of reconstruction error yielded with these components was matched across feature extraction methods to select corresponding k values as baseline models ($k = 30$ for ICA, $k = 30$ for DL, $k = 65$ for NNMF). Importantly, the optimized models were in all cases superior to the baseline (fixed k) models both in terms of prediction performance and reduced models' complexity, as also shown by the large gap in terms of BIC. LASSO regression further reduced the number of predictors by setting some weights to zero. The latter seems to be particularly important for the NNMF-based models because the selected k was larger in comparison to the other methods (accordingly, NNMF + ridge was poor in terms of BIC).

Table 1. Performance of ridge regression in the prediction of language and motor scores. The selected λ and k values are also reported.

Method		Ridge (fixed k)				Ridge			
		R^2	BIC	λ	k	R^2	BIC	λ	K
Lang (n = 116)	PCA	0.42	413.4	475.1	30	0.43	316.8	298.4	10
	ICA	0.31	433.3	46.4	30	0.42	318.7	14.5	10
	DL	0.33	430.6	756.5	30	0.39	323.5	117.7	10
	NNMF	0.42	580.2	1519.9	65	0.42	580.2	1519.9	65
Motor (n = 108)	PCA	0.43	428.9	298.4	30	0.44	333.4	187.4	10
	ICA	0.32	446.9	29.2	30	0.43	334.8	9.1	10
	DL	0.22	461.7	475.1	30	0.42	312.1	11.5	5
	NNMF	0.36	603.7	954.6	65	0.42	571.2	475.1	60

The back-projected weights for the best two models in each domain are depicted in Fig. 3. The language score was predicted by a broad white matter network encompassing tracts traditionally associated with linguistic processing, including the superior longitudinal/arcuate fasciculus, predominantly in the left hemisphere. For the motor domain, the predictive map shows a more circumscribed, subcortical, and bilateral set of white matter tracts surrounding the basal ganglia (e.g., internal and external capsule) as well as, more dorsally, parts of the corona radiata.

Table 2. Performance of LASSO regression in the prediction of language and motor scores. The selected λ, and k values and the number of non-zero features (NZ) is also reported.

		LASSO (fixed k)				LASSO			
		R^2	BIC	λ	k(NZ)	R^2	BIC	λ	k(NZ)
Lang (n = 116)	PCA	0.41	358.2	0.055	30(18)	0.42	336.9	0.055	20(14)
	ICA	0.30	435.8	0.043	30(30)	0.42	319.3	0.022	10(10)
	DL	0.24	354	0.11	30(11)	0.35	316.7	0.055	10(7)
	NNMF	0.41	358	0.087	65(18)	0.43	317	0.069	25(10)
Motor (n = 108)	PCA	0.38	405	0.055	30(23)	0.43	335	0.022	10(10)
	ICA	0.24	459.6	0.003	30(30)	0.43	335.1	0.022	10(10)
	DL	0.14	397.3	0.11	30(14)	0.42	313.6	0.001	5(5)
	NNMF	0.23	502.5	0.043	65(39)	0.45	451.6	0.055	60(36)

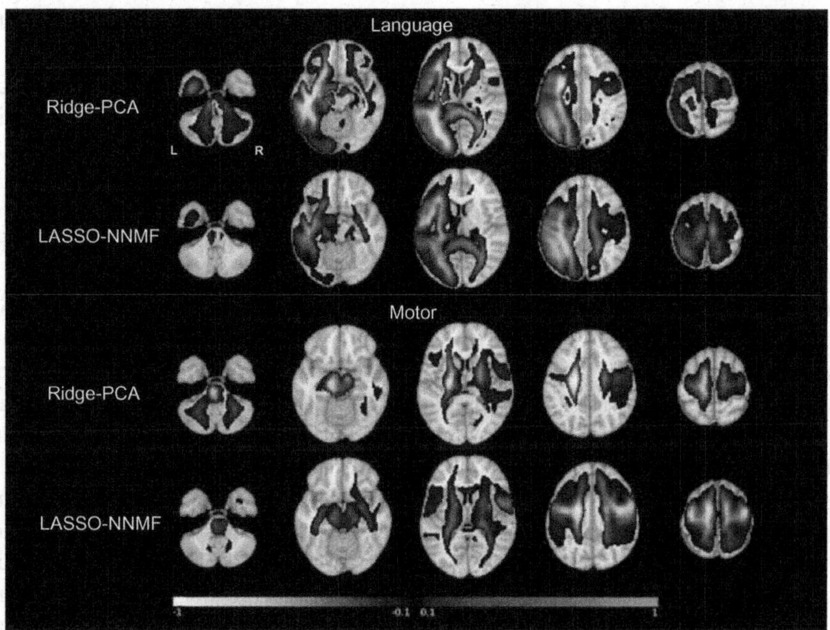

Fig. 3. Back-projected weights for the best two models for prediction of each behavioral score, highlighting the most predictive white matter tracts.

4 Discussion

In this work we systematically compared four unsupervised dimensionality reduction methods in their ability to extract relevant features from probabilistic structural disconnection maps of stroke patients at different levels of compression. We then assessed how these methods influence a regularized regression model trained on the features to predict patients' behavioral performance.

Overall, PCA and NNMF turned out to be the best methods for extracting robust predictors, followed by ICA and DL. Optimizing the number of extracted features (k) to be entered as predictors for regression was crucial for the predictive accuracy of ICA- and DL-based models, but not for PCA and NNMF. Nevertheless, when compared to non-optimized models (fixed k), we observed that the optimization of k improved the accuracy for all methods and greatly reduced model complexity, thereby leading to large gains in terms of BIC. This suggests that good predictive accuracy can be obtained with a limited number of features. A compact representation is desirable as it improves model interpretability and it might favor out-of-sample generalization. Interestingly, while LASSO regression can further reduce model complexity by setting some weights to 0, we found that it was not superior to ridge regression when the optimization of k was in place.

Finally, the type of regularizer interacted with the feature extraction method: PCA optimally combined with ridge regression, whereas NNMF optimally combined with LASSO regression. These two pipelines achieved the best performance, but PCA + ridge regression was more consistently the best approach when also considering the BIC score. However, the differences between these two pipelines (given the optimal hyperparameters) were small. Indeed, the back-projection of the most relevant features for the two best models in each domain were similar and neuroanatomically sound.

Overall, our findings represent an important step towards the definition of the optimal pipeline for disconnectome data. Compared to the previous state-of-the-art [6], the gain in terms of r-squared is marginal (e.g., 2% of variance for language scores) but this is achieved with a much more parismonius model with just one third of the number of predictors (10 vs. 29 in [6]). A potential limitation of the study is due to the relatively small sample size of the patient group, but this simply reflects the lack of large-scale stroke datasets including both neuroimaging and behavioral data. Further efforts should be spent in assembling larger-scale datasets, which would allow to deploy even more powerful predictive models, such as those based on deep learning [24]. Future work should also extend these results to the prediction of a broader range of behavioral scores, to better assess whether some feature extraction methods could be more general than others and to further compare them in terms of interpretability and neuroscientific accuracy of the predictive maps.

Acknowledgments. This work was supported by grants from the Italian Ministry of Health (RF-2013–02359306 to MZ, Ricerca Corrente to IRCCS Ospedale San Camillo) and by MIUR (Dipartimenti di Eccellenza DM 11/05/2017 n. 262 to the Department of General Psychology). We are grateful to Prof. Maurizio Corbetta for providing the stroke dataset, which was collected in a study funded by grants R01 HD061117–05 and R01 NS095741.

References

1. Corbetta, M., et al.: Common behavioral clusters and subcortical anatomy in stroke. Neuron **85**, 927–941 (2015)
2. Rorden, C., Karnath, H.O.: Using human brain lesions to infer function: a relic from a past era in the fMRI age. Nat. Rev. Neurosci. **5**, 813–819 (2004)
3. Price, C.J., Hope, T.M., Seghier, M.L.: Ten problems and solutions when predicting individual outcome from lesion site after stroke. Neuroimage **145**, 200–208 (2017)
4. Siegel, J.S., et al.: Disruptions of network connectivity predict impairment in multiple behavioral domains after stroke. Proc. Natl. Acad. Sci. USA **113**, E4367–E4376 (2016)
5. Thiebaut de Schotten, M., Foulon, C., Nachev, P.: Brain disconnections link structural connectivity with function and behaviour. Nat. Commun. **11**, 5094 (2020)
6. Salvalaggio, A., de Filippo De Grazia, M., Zorzi, M., de Schotten, M.T., Corbetta, M.: Post-stroke deficit prediction from lesion and indirect structural and functional disconnection. Brain **143**, 2173–2188 (2020)
7. Foulon, C., et al.: Advanced lesion symptom mapping analyses and implementation as BCBtoolkit. Gigascience **7**, 1–17 (2018)
8. Chauhan, S., et al.: A comparison of shallow and deep learning methods for predicting cognitive performance of stroke patients from MRI lesion images. Front. Neuroinf. **13**, 53 (2019)
9. Mwangi, B., Tian, T.S., Soares, J.C.: A review of feature reduction techniques in Neuroimaging. Neuroinformatics **12**, 229–244 (2014)
10. Calesella, F., Testolin, A., De Filippo De Grazia, M., Zorzi M.: A comparison of feature extraction methods for prediction of neuropsychological scores from functional connectivi-ty data of stroke patients. Brain Inf. **8**, 8 (2021)
11. Guyon, I., Elisseeff, A.: An introduction to variable and feature selection. J. Mach. Learn. Res. **3**, 1157–1182 (2003)
12. Hua, J., Tembe, W.D., Dougherty, E.R.: Performance of feature-selection methods in the classification of high-dimension data. Pattern Recogn. **42**, 409–424 (2009)
13. Carroll, M.K., Cecchi, G.A., Rish, I., Garg, R., Rao, A.R.: Prediction and interpretation of distributed neural activity with sparse models. Neuroimage **44**, 112–122 (2009)
14. Teipel, S.J., Kurth, J., Krause, B., Grothe, M.J.: The relative importance of imaging markers for the prediction of Alzheimer's disease dementia in mild cognitive impairment - beyond classical regression. NeuroImage Clin. **8**, 583–593 (2015)
15. Cui, Z., Gong, G.: The effect of machine learning regression algorithms and sample size on individualized behavioral prediction with functional connectivity features. Neuroimage **178**, 622–637 (2018)
16. Jollans, L., et al.: Quantifying performance of machine learning methods for neuroimaging data. Neuroimage **199**, 351–365 (2019)
17. Jolliffe, I.T.: Principal component analysis. In: Encyclopedia of Statistics in Behavioral Science (2002)
18. Hyvärinen, A., Oja, E.: Independent component analysis: algorithms and applications. Neural Netw. **13**, 411–430 (2000)
19. Lee, D.D., Seung, H.S.: Algorithms for non-negative matrix factorization. In: Advances in Neural Information Processing Systems, pp. 556–562 (2001)
20. Mairal, J., Bach, F., Ponce, J., Sapiro, G.: Online dictionary learning for sparse coding. In: ACM International Conference Proceeding Series, pp. 689–696 (2009)
21. Tibshirani, R.: Regression shrinkage and selection via the lasso. J. Roy. Stat. Soc. Ser. B (Methodol.) **58**, 267–288 (1996)

22. Hastie, T., Tibshirani, R., Friedman, J.: The Elements of Statistical Learning. Springer Series in Statistics. Springer, New York (2009). https://doi.org/10.1007/978-0-387-84858-7
23. Schwarz, G.: Estimating the dimension of a model. Ann. Stat. **6**, 461–464 (1978)
24. Vieira, S., Pinaya, W.H., Mechelli, A.: Using deep learning to investigate the neuroimaging correlates of psychiatric and neurological disorders: methods and applications. Neurosci. Biobehav. Rev. **74**, 58–75 (2017)

Brain Big Data Analytics, Curation and Management

System Level Knowledge Analysis and Keyword Extraction in Neuroscience

Paola Di Maio(✉)

Ronin Institute, Montclair, USA

Abstract. Vast amounts of knowledge resources are emerging from Neuroscience research, thanks to increasingly widely available imaging and analysis technologies and open data sets. Learning, processing and keeping up to date with developments however imply steep learning curves. Advances in Neuroscience research provide insights into the human brain and the mind for brain specialists, but also inform other scientific disciplines such as to complexity science, cognitive computing, medicine in general and general technology and policy sectors. With a few exceptions however, the majority of Neuroscience research outcomes can still be accessed and leveraged mostly only by highly trained neuroscientists and brain informatics researchers in their respective specialisations, as the knowledge and skill sets required to query and manipulate such data is only meaningful for individuals with specific training. This paper identifies and addresses the need to lower the cognitive barriers to accessing Neuroscience research, as it is becoming very relevant to other fields, and to widen its accessibility to a broader range of scholars of other disciplines - such as Computer Science and Information Technology for example, reducing the efforts required in tracking innovation and facilitate knowledge acquisition. Keeping up with the state of the art is a challenge in any field, yet increasing number of researchers, students and practitioners from diverse professions and with a wide range of interests and goals, and multi disciplinary and linguistic backgrounds. The approach proposed here leverages a combination of elementary core methods from semantic technology, including simple corpus and linguistic analysis techniques, and devises a low tech instrument that can be adopted irrespective of the availability of software and level of English language proficiency to acquire the necessary familiarity to handle Neuroscience topics The same method can also be leveraged in other complex knowledge domains. A set of experiments to evaluate the effectiveness of the method is described with preliminary results.

Keywords: Neuroscience · Concept analysis · Terminology · Vocabulary extraction · Cognitive load

1 Introduction

The size of the Neuroscience body of knowledge is vast and incalculable, and growing. It has reached the level that it is almost humanly impossible to master without significantly narrowing qualitatively and quantitatively the scope and focus of the knowledge

M. Mahmud et al. (Eds.): BI 2021, LNAI 12960, pp. 225–234, 2021.
https://doi.org/10.1007/978-3-030-86993-9_21

being measured [1]. This impacts the ability of tracking advances and the state of the art, which is particularly relevant to education and research. On the other hand, meta cognitive Neuroscience is emerging based on a system view of the field, requiring comprehensive models of the knowledge domain being studied [2]. Information science and research in semantic web technologies over the years have produced a rich portfolio of computational resources to address the cognitive demands of increasingly complex knowledge and data intensive fields. There is no shortage of lexical analysis and corpus analysis methods with many online tools offering free functionalities [3]. Increasingly specialized resources, software and services supporting the querying and retrieval of Neuroscience data are available, including very large open data sets that in principle should facilitate knowledge extraction, tagging and organization [4]. However, the goal post keeps shifting: while the data sets are becoming bigger, the applications offering more and more functionality are becoming increasingly specialized and complex to use. In addition, the literature and research data in Neuroscience tends to be fragmented and epistemically unorganized [5]. This paper offers a practical method based on a meta cognitive approach and the adoption of vocabulary extraction techniques, taxonomy development and concept mapping, to cut through the dense fragmentation and facilitate learning and reasoning especially for practitioners with limited background knowledge or from a multidisciplinary background, as well as students and early stage research scholar entering the field. They contributions in this paper are:

- an analysis of the challenges for learners and practitioners in Neuroscience to keep up to date and comprehend the scope and range of the vast amount of knowledge in the field
- a summary of state of the art domain and knowledge analysis techniques
- a method of analysis and extraction that facilitates and simplifies the acquisition of knowledge that emphasizes system and network level requirements capable of supporting at least in part the multidimensionality and cognitive complexity of the corpus.

2 Goals, Method and Scope

The main purpose of this paper is to provide a simple takeaway method with examples to support pragmatic knowledge acquisition in the field of Neuroscience for non specialists, based on a combination of semantic technologies, such as vocabulary extraction and a synthesis of domain knowledge acquisition instruments such as concept and lexical analysis, Specific goals include:

1. To reduce the cognitive load and facilitate learning, with emphasis on discovering correlations among structures functions and behaviors of brain regions.
2. To minimize the need to rely on sophisticated and expensive technology resources and maximize knowledge acquisition.
3. To facilitate the evaluation of claims of novelty in scholarly proceedings.

The research adopts a mixed method approach with meta analysis. The specific goals outlined in the preceding paragraph are identified via the participation in student forums and communities of practice, and graduate programs, data is gathered via mixed methods (qualitative and quantitative) including questionnaires and quizzes, and then combined and analyzed. The methods offered such as vocabulary extraction are not novel, but they are used in a novel context in relation to the scenarios and problem spaces discussed. In addition this research paves the way for the development of an integrated method to ease the cognitive load for Neuroscience learners and practitioners The scope of the paper is limited to identifying and documenting areas of concern, to introduce the overview of the techniques leveraged in the method. Exploratory experiments and preliminary results are described to understand how can the proposed method increase the efficiency of learning. Pointers to future work are provided.

3 Scenarios and Problem Statement

Neuroscience is one of the most dynamic cognitively demanding fields in research, It studies the most sophisticated and complex biological system: the human brain. It leverages the convergence of science, engineering and computation, with results, new concepts, terminology and claims being introduced on an ongoing basis. No single human expert, nor team of experts, can reasonably maintain state of the art scholarship in the field of Neuroscience as a whole for very long. Professionals and researchers tend to focus on one or more specializations, and follow innovations and scientific advances by subscribing to specialized journals, and conferences that best reflect their sphere of competence, but tracking the state of the art is an ongoing challenge. Observable scenarios include:

1. The specialized knowledge from one field of Neuroscience research is becoming relevant to other fields of medicine and health practice
2. The specialized knowledge from one field of Neuroscience needs to be accessed by non specialists, or by specialists of other fields.
3. Researchers, developers, funding councils and investors working with Neuroscience need to keep up with the latest advances in more than one field of specialization (such as machine learning, research ethics, clinical research as well as the broader field of bio informatics) yet have limited resources to devote to this effort

Considering the growing importance of brain science to other fields, developing tools to facilitate knowledge acquisition, processing and management of Neuroscience knowledge is now a priority. Based on a survey of requirements of international communities of practice, there following requirements can be defined:

1. To ease the Cognitive Load.
2. To facilitate knowledge acquisition, storage, query and visualization.
3. To identify and evaluate novelty and track the state of the art.

4 Overview

Advanced ontologies and data schemas exist and are widely in use that represent various aspects of the Neuroscience corpus [10] however they address different requirements and satisfy the criteria of diverse specializations. Concept analysis, Vocabulary extraction and taxonomy development, briefly described in Sect. 5 of this paper, are not generally adopted in teaching despite offering benefits in knowledge acquisition and management. In addition, scholarly resources such as conference proceedings rarely include a terminology index to facilitate their consultation. Indexing is necessary basic and fundamental analytical tool for any large text and body of knowledge from which valuable qualitative insights can easily be gathered. Without an index it is impossible to evaluate for example what novel concepts and terms are added to existing concepts and research in the proceedings published in previous years, for example. Answering the question *what's new this year* can be done with relative ease by comparing key terms and concepts. This paper demonstrates that concept analysis and vocabulary extraction, which can be performed even with limited resources, using freely available tools or even manually, are valuable artifacts that enable faster understanding and reduce the cognitive load for learners and practitioners who want to be up to date, and can be used as qualitative and quantitative metric to evaluate and manage knowledge acquisition efforts.

4.1 The Growing Neuroscience Body of Knowledge

The Neuroscience body of knowledge is vast. Research produces thousands (more than 30,000) scholarly papers per year, with 40% in the 2006–2015 period [11, 12]. Large publicly funded projects to track the state of the art, The Human Brain Project in the EU (stalled) and the BRAIN Initiative in the US despite maximum availability of human power and resources, face unprecedented hurdles due to the sheer heterogeneity of the landscape. Advanced analytical combinatorial approaches can deliver new understanding of human brain and its workings [13]. These advances point clearly to a view of the brain and associated functions (sensory, motor and cognitive) as increasingly integrated and to some extent interdependent, Yet the body of knowledge in research does not reflect the conceptual integration needed to study the brain as a whole [14]. Innumerable Knowledge Extraction and Representation techniques are available, with varying degrees of complexity (from ontologies to taxonomies) that can be used to formulate an ontology for brain science, and although efforts in this direction have been ongoing for over a decade [15] available ontologies are encoded in languages that require specialist skills and tools such as ontology editors, constraining the accessibility of domain knowledge. There is a need to expose the knowledge which partly exists in Neuroscience ontologies using natural language and easily accessible visualization and indexing tools, such as vocabularies written in plain English and concept maps using simple visual diagrams, for example. Researchers, scholars and students need to maximize their ability to identify and understand and evaluate novel constructs emerging from research at increasing speed while minimizing the amount of resources invested in achieving this without having to study ontology engineering and learn how to use ontology editors and languages. The same applies for containerization[1], the trend towards storing data in digital containers in Neuroscience has resulted in entire labs devoting far too much time to figure out how to configure containers.

Semantic web technologies on a large scale are bench marked to optimize computational performance, in terms of resources, for example load and speed of query executing and processor capacity. However they are not designed to take into account the need to reduce the cognitive load for learners and scholars, in fact, they increase it. The sections below summarize key analytical techniques that have been applied experimentally using low tech, and which have been valuated for usefulness in terms of reducing the cognitive load.

4.2 Cognitive Load Theory

One of the benefits of structured knowledge acquisition using automated vocabulary extraction over a vast corpus is to reduce the cognitive load to identify novel concepts and terminology arising from research. The same technique can be applied to automate the creation of book and proceedings indexes as quick lists of references. According to cognitive load theory, tasks requiring some level of cognitive engagement can be evaluated according to neurophysiological parameters, overall mental performance is a multidimensional construct, and that measurement of cognitive load typically adopts either direct or indirect metrics [6]. According to cognitive load theory [7] learning helps to promote schema development and acquisition. The method proposed provides an instrument to directly measure a learner's working memory resources and takes steps toward exploring further how cognitive load relates to specific forms of knowledge representation addressing not only the broader need to increase learners efficiency, but also open questions in cognitive load theory research [8, 9].

4.3 Knowledge Analysis

Established approaches exist for knowledge acquisitions in new domains, from classical literature reviews, to more formal complex and linguistic analysis of a corpus. Furthermore an AI based future for automated literature reviews is looming. Although research still requires human level skills to be carried out, increasingly sophisticated semantic technology tools exist capable of knowledge extraction and categorization, facilitating literature reviews and knowledge analysis, however they constitute a research domain of their own and are not the focus of this paper. Research in Knowledge Acquisition methods and technologies has grown exponentially and have become scholarly disciplines in their own right.

A handful of pointers is provided below to techniques relevant to the experiments. Although the development of advanced corpus and linguistic technologies is not the main focus of this paper, the adoption of simple tools such as knowledge visualization and extraction is also leveraged in the experiments.

Domain Analysis (DA) is concerned with identifying what kind of knowledge is needed by specialists working in a specific subject field and what approaches are used to produce

[1] https://www.globenewswire.com/news-release/2021/02/18/2178094/0/en/Global-Application-Container-Market-2021-to-2026-Growth-Trends-COVID-19-Impact-and-Forecasts.html.

domain-specific knowledge. It includes methods such as classifications and thesauri, research on indexing and retrieving specialities, empirical user studies, bibliometrical, historical, epistemological and critical studies, terminological studies, LSP (languages for special purposes), discourse studies; studies of structures and institutions in scientific communication and in professional cognition and artificial intelligence [16, 17] DA is also an established research technique in software engineering, carried out via multiple approaches and can include ontology engineering techniques [18]. Ontologies can automate domain analysis by ingesting knowledge resources which represent the corpora to be acquired, however software can be expensive to develop and maintain.

Vocabulary Extraction lies at the heart of ontology engineering [19] and domain analysis - is relatively much more feasible and less resource intensive,

Literature Reviews are still the most common way of searching for scholarly background however as scholarly knowledge grows exponentially, it is necessary to approach literature review following a strategy [20] which can include the systematic data processing approach comprised of three steps, namely: (a) literature search and screening; (b) data extraction and analysis; and (c) writing the literature review.

Corpus Linguistics consists of advanced and specialized language analysis techniques including qualitative methods [21] for scholarly body of knowledge [22] A number of different Concept Analysis methodologies exist, traced in a healthcare context [23] such as nursing.

Formal Concept Analysis (FCA) [24] is an applied branch of Lattice Theory, a mathematical discipline which enables formalisation of concepts as basic units of human thinking and analyzing data in the object-attribute form. Originated in early 80s, it became a popular human-centred tool for knowledge representation and data analysis with numerous applications. FCA topics include Information Retrieval with a focus on visualization aspects, Machine Learning, Data Mining and Knowledge Discovery, Text Mining and several others.

Lexical Analysis: Technical and Scientific language tells about the world by means of hypotheses, create new concepts, make new discoveries, create novel explanations and methods. Technical vocabularies can be considered either words associated with professional communication and learned words. Terminology may refer to the study of terms, to the practical aspect of doing terminographical work, and to a set of specialized terms. The lexical components of specialized languages emerge from theoretical and technological innovation: new scientific insights and novel tools enrich the conceptual and practical environment of the specialists, and in the process expand their vocabularies. Vocabularies are the product of dynamic cognition, of the transition from a concept (mental category) to a verbalized concept associated with some theory to conceptualize a particular field of knowledge or activity [25].Terminology is what connects the structures of language and tacit knowledge. Lexicalization of -ing and -ed verb forms and their transition into adjectives and nouns; [26, 27]. Knowledge Analysis and Linguistic expression using specialized vocabularies is central to knowledge acquisition and communication and can be used as a tool to measure and manage cognitive load in

Neuroscience learning and research The methods briefly outlined are used in different combinations and measure in the experiment described.

5 Method

The proposed method leverages a combination of Knowledge and Language analysis techniques described in the previous sections. It is summarized in the following steps (Fig. 1).

1. Identify the target topics and sources of knowledge - depending on the tasks at hand, these could be as broad as an entire discipline say, Cognitive Neuroscience as a whole - or as narrow as a single unit of knowledge, say a physiological component or an observation, a behavior or a specific research method or bio-marker.
2. Extract key concepts via the identification of keywords - this can be done manually or using term extraction software.
3. Map the keywords to concept spaces or pre defined knowledge schemas (for example structure, function behavior),
4. Pair the keyword to related keywords by making explicit their relation.
5. Identify, discover and evaluate semantic relations between keywords.

A simplified example of data resulting from this method of conceptual analysis is a list of terms/keywords (roughly corresponding to an index), a list of sources (where the keywords are taken from) a concept map, a set of relations between terms/concepts, a memorization device in the form of a checklist or cheat sheet (things to know).

	Source	Concept Map	Things to Know	Dependencies	Relational Index
Topic					
Term					
Context					
Description					
Related Terms					
Index					

Fig. 1. Summary of method

6 Experiment Design

The overall aim of the method is to develop a compendium of teaching resources for Neuroscience with emphasis on concept analysis that captures the relations and dependency between the components to facilitate the discovery of integrated functions and behaviors. The goal of the experiments is to evaluate whether the method meets this aim. Reported is an outline of the experimental protocol and preliminary results. The preparation phase consists of corpus and participant selection, protocol definition:

1. **Corpus Selection** A sample corpus is selected, consisting of four main resources

   Fundamental Neuroscience, Squire Textbook [28].
   Neuroscience Online resource from MGovern Medical School[29].
   Brain Informatics 2020, Proceedings [30].
   Journal issues [31].

2. **Protocol** A set of core terminology and concept maps is extracted manually for each of the resources
3. **Participants Selection** Participants from diverse disciplinary background are included in a focus group [32] They are recruited via career department and job board with specific demographic profile (undergraduate considering neuroinformatics careers or electives, and graduates seeking to pursue further studies in neuroinformatics)
4. **The Tasks:** concept and term identification, and assessment of novelty claims are assessed qualitatively via self evaluation (questionnaire) More specific tasks are quantitatively evaluated using tests/quizzes using standard evaluation parameters such as number of right answers/time to answer with and without the artifacts (the vocabularies and concept maps) These include: a)Identify and define novel concepts and terms between two sets of scholarly resources for the purpose of evaluating novelty. The resource used in this experiment is data set from a related study [1] b) Identify and enumerate concepts and terminology in conference proceedings (Brain Informatics 2020 Book, Springer) c) Relate a set of concepts and terms from a given resource (Fundamental Neuroscience Textbook) to a meta level analysis of the domain from Systems Neuroscience.

7 Results and Evaluation

Initial tests were carried out during online sessions where the participants (12) were given access to a subset (i.e., only a part of) of the learning resources and given a time frame to answer some questions, and the results scored. In a second session the same group of participants were given the complete set of resources (the full resource) together with a set of keywords and concept map, and were asked to answer the same questions over a more extensive body of knowledge and the results scored. In addition, to scoring the results for an objective evaluation, participants were asked to carry out self assessment in terms of qualitative evaluation to describe if the artifacts made a difference to their ability to answer the questions. In terms of the following criteria time saving and Cognitive load reduction (self reported) The qualitative evaluation shows that overall, based on self reporting, the resources contributed to ease the cognitive load and save the learner time. Learners using the resources were able to achieve higher scores given the same amount of time to answer the question, compared to those who did not use the resources.

7.1 Resulting Artifacts and Unplanned Outcomes

Resources generated during the method development include list of terms, concept maps, concept lattices and indices, including an index for the Brain Informatics 2020 book of proceedings. The impact and usefulness of these artifacts is sill under evaluation with planned iterative refinement before they are released for general use.

8 Conclusion and Future Work

The Neuroscience body of knowledge is of inestimable value for humankind, expected to trigger advances. however its complexity and sheer size contribute to inhibit its impact outside limited academic circles. Simple text extraction and concept analysis routines can be of considerable value to learners and anyone wishing to gain insights in this important field. Future work includes comprehensive experimental data and results and the publication of the artifacts (the vocabularies and concept maps) and an educational compendium.

References

1. Kenkel, W.: Corpus colossal: a bibliometric analysis of neuroscience abstracts and impact factor front. Integr. Neurosci **13**, 18 (2019)
2. Fleming, S.M., Frith, C.D.: Meta cognitive neuroscience: an introduction. In: Fleming, S., Frith, C. (eds.) The Cognitive Neuroscience of Metacognition. Springer, Berlin, Heidelberg (2014). https://doi.org/10.1007/978-3-642-45190-4_1
3. Bonacchi, N., Gaelle, C., et al.: Data architecture for a large-scale Neuroscience collaboration. BioRxiv, pp. 827–873 (2020)
4. Bassett, D.S., et al.: Reflections on the past two decades of Neuroscience. Nat. Rev. Neurosci. **21**(10) (2020)
5. Abraham, F.D.: Chapter six epistemology of the neurodynamics of mind a fractal epistemology for a scientific psychology: bridging the personal with the transpersonal (2020)
6. Martin, S.: Measuring cognitive load and cognition: metrics for technology-enhanced learning. In: Educational Research and Evaluation (2014)
7. Sweller, J.: Cognitive load theory and educational technology. Education Tech. Research Dev. **68**(1), 1–16 (2019). https://doi.org/10.1007/s11423-019-09701-3
8. Brünken, R., Plass, J.L., Moreno, R.: (eds.) Current issues and open questions in cognitive load research. In: Plass, J.L., Moreno, R., Brünken, R. (eds.) Cognitive Load Theory, pp. 253–272. Cambridge University Press, New York (2010)
9. Paas, F., Alexander, R., Sweller, J.: Cognitive load theory: instructional implications of the interaction between information structures and cognitive architecture. Instr. Sci. **32** (2004)
10. Gupta, A., Ludascher, B., Martone, M.E.: Knowledge-based integration of Neuroscience data sources. In: Proceedings. 12th International Conference on Scientific and Statistica Database Management, pp. 39–52. IEEE (2000)
11. Yeung, A.W.K., Tazuko, K.G., Keung, W.: The changing landscape of Neuroscience research, 2006–2015: a bibliometric study. Front. Neurosci. **11** (2017)
12. Keshava, R.: Growth analysis of neuroscience research in Asian Countries, 1989–2018: a scientometric study (2020)
13. Kocoń, J.M.: M Mapping WordNet onto human brain connectome in emotion processing and semantic similarity recognition. In: Information Processing & Management (2021)

14. Bassett, D.S., Sporns, O.: Network neuroscience. Nat. Neurosci. **20**(3) (2017)
15. Larson, S., Martone, M.: Ontologies for neuroscience: what are they and what are they good for? Front. Neurosci. **3** (2009)
16. Hjørland, B.: Domain analysis in information science. J. Doc. (2002)
17. Dines, B.: Domain analysis and description principles, techniques, and modelling languages. ACM Trans. Softw. Eng. Methodol. (2019)
18. Prieto-Díaz, R.: Domain analysis: an introduction. SIGSOFT Softw. Eng. Notes **15** (1990)
19. Heilman, M., Eskenazi, M.: Application of automatic thesaurus extraction for computer generation of vocabulary questions. In: Workshop on Speech and Language Technology in Education (2007)
20. Paré, G., Spyros, K.: Methods for literature reviews In: Handbook of eHealth Evaluation: An Evidence-Based Approach Internet. University of Victoria (2017)
21. Onwuegbuzie, A.J., Leech, N.L., Collins, K.M.T.: Qualitative analysis techniques for the review of the literature. Qual. Rep. **17**, 56 (2012)
22. Adorján, M.: Introducing corpus linguistic tools to EFL undergraduates and trainee teachers. Education 4.0 revolution: transformative approaches to language teaching and learning, assessment and campus design (2020)
23. Dennis, C.L.: Peer support within a health care context: a concept analysis. Int. J. Nurs. Stud. **40**(3), 321–332 (2003)
24. Ganter, B.W.: Applied lattice theory: formal concept analysis. In: Grätzer, G., (ed.) General Lattice Theory, Birkhäuser (1997)
25. Rusko, T.: Lexical features of scientific discourse. Santalka Filologija Edukologija **22**(1), 82–88 (2014)
26. Kockaert, H., Steurs, F.: Handbook of Terminology, vol. 1. John Benjamins Publishing Co., Amsterdam (2015)
27. Kandrashkina, O.O., Revina. E.V.: Lexical analysis of technical terms in the field of materials science. IOP Conference Series: Materials Science and Engineering. IOP Publishing (2020)
28. Squire, L., Berg, D., Bloom, F.E., Du Lac, S., Ghoshand, A., Spitzer, N.C. (eds.) Fundamental Neuroscience. Academic Press (2012)
29. Neuroscience Online McGovern Medical School at UTHealth Department of Neurobiology and Anatomy
30. Mahmud, M., Vassanelli, S.K., Zhong, N., (eds.) Brain Informatics: 13th International Conference, BI 2020, Padua, Italy Springer Nature (2020)
31. Same as 1 (datasets from Article Corpus Colossus article)
32. Wilkinson, S.: Focus group methodology: a review. Int. J. Soc. Res. Methodol. **1**, 181–203 (1998)

ConnExt-BioBERT: Leveraging Transfer Learning for Brain-Connectivity Extraction from Neuroscience Articles

Ashika Sharma[1,2(✉)], Jaikishan Jayakumar[3], Namrata Sankaran[5], Partha P. Mitra[3,4], Sutanu Chakraborti[2], and P. Sreenivasa Kumar[2]

[1] Center for Artificial Intelligence and Robotics, DRDO, Bangalore 560093, India
[2] Department of Computer Science and Engineering, Indian Institute of Technology Madras, Chennai 600036, India
[3] Center for Computational Brain Research, IIT Madras, Chennai 600036, India
[4] Cold Spring Harbour Laboratory, Cold Spring Harbour, New York 11724, USA
[5] Vellore Institute of Technology, Chennai 600127, India

Abstract. Study about brain connectivity provides important biomarkers for predicting brain related disorders and also for analyzing normal human functions. Findings of this study are reported in the form of neuroscience research articles. We propose a tool, *ConnExt-BioBERT*, to mine relevant scientific literature for curating a large resource of reported connections between regions of the brain. We have utilized the popular transfer learning technique that has been trained on large datasets, the Bidirectional Encoder Representations for Transformers (BERT) to apply it to a narrowband subject area of extracting brain regions and potential connection mentions from a set of 53,000 full-text neuroscience articles (*53kNeuroFullText*) indexed on PubMed. Evaluation of ConnExt-BioBERT has been performed on a benchmark dataset of abstracts and on a dataset of seven full-text articles annotated by a domain expert. Additionally, connections retrieved by the tool on *53kNeuroFullText* have been evaluated using a manually curated resource, Brain Architecture Management System (BAMS). A web-application has been developed for search over extracted brain region connections on *53kNeuroFullText*. This application is currently being used by neuroscience researchers to quickly retrieve brain connectivity information reported by various authors. Large scale text mining of brain-connectivity information reported in neuroscience literature, aids in progressing research in the area of neurological disorders and further helps diagnosis and treatment of the same.

Keywords: Brain region connectivity extraction · Text mining · Machine learning · Natural language processing

1 Introduction

Brain connectivity is the study of associations between various regions of the brain of an organism. This study is crucial for understanding and detecting

M. Mahmud et al. (Eds.): BI 2021, LNAI 12960, pp. 235–244, 2021.
https://doi.org/10.1007/978-3-030-86993-9_22

various neurological disorders and treating them. Research conducted in this direction is reported and published in several scientific forums as free-form text. Manual curation of a centralized resource for brain-conectivity from scientific literature is a laborious task. Moreover, such a resource needs to be continuously updated to keep up with new findings. As of May 2021, PubMed [5] contains over 32 million indexed articles, with a significant number of them from neuroscience domain. Over 3000 new articles get published every day in peer-reviewed journals from biomedical domain [14] and over a million get published every year. Scale of the published scientific literature poses a challenge for human curation. Efforts in the past have used biomedical Natural Language Processing (NLP) techniques, to compile brain region connectivity information by mining relevant scientific literature.

Let us consider an example sentence from a neuroscience article.

"*The organization of the efferent projections from the* ***pontine parabrachial area*** *to the* ***amygdaloid complex***" [1].

The terms *pontine parabrachial area* and *amygdaloid complex* represent brain region mentions. This sentence denotes existence of a connection between the two brain regions.

Earlier methods have used lexical-based NER [11,17] using a dictionary of brain regions and conditional random fields (CRFs) [7,9] to identify brain region mentions. Methods for brain-connectivity extraction range from shallow linguistic kernel [8,9], pre-defined regular expressions for relation patterns [17], pre-defined patterns on dependency parse trees [11], to using deep linguistic features from link parse structure of sentence [18,19]. These methods use supervised Machine Learning (ML) techniques for brain-connectivity extraction.

Machine Learning models are trained for a specific task by using relevant labeled data. Conventionally, this training knowledge gained by a machine learning model on one task cannot be applied for a different task. Human beings on the other hand, use knowledge derived from learning previous tasks to improve the way a new task is learned. Building machine learning models to understand the complexities of human language not only requires large sets of labeled data, but also powerful computers and trained human experts, both of which are costly resources, and data that is abundantly available, is mostly unlabeled.

Transfer learning [15] is a machine learning paradigm that reuses knowledge gained from a particular task/corpus to build models that learn from the widely available unlabeled data, thereby not requiring many expensive machines, trained experts or large sets of labeled data.

In this paper, we have used transfer learning for extracting brain regions and connections among them from research articles. The Bidirectional Encoder Representations from Transformers (BERT) [6] architecture and its variants in biomedical domain have been used for brain-connectivity extraction. In the past, BERT has been used for extracting protein-protein interactions [10] from text.

Efforts towards brain-connectivity extraction [8,9,11,17–19], have used a benchmark dataset compiled from sentences of PubMed abstracts. ConnExt-BioBERT handles entire full-text articles irrespective of the number of brain region mentions in each sentence. Further, connections retrieved by ConnExt-BioBERT are compared with the manually compiled resource, Brain Architecture Management System (BAMS) [3]. Several techniques have been applied to normalize and map the brain regions mentions and connections between ConnExt-BioBERT and BAMS. Evaluation of ConnExt-BioBERT on a dataset of seven full-text articles is also presented. A web application has been developed for quick brain region based search for connections extracted from a large dataset of 53,000 neuroscience articles. The application aids researchers in the field to quickly sift through large amounts of scientific literature to find required brain region and connectivity information.

2 Methods

2.1 BERT and Its Variants in Biomedical Domain

BERT is a deep neural network based on transformer architecture [22], which is more efficient than convolution neural networks and recurrent neural networks, due to its enhanced ability to handle long-range dependencies and perform GPU-based parallel computation. BERT uses transfer learning to pre-train bi-directional language representations from large unlabeled datasets comprising entire Wikipedia of around 2.5B words and the Books corpus [24] of around 0.8B words. BERT serves as a general-domain language model for performing various downstream tasks like text classification, sequence modeling, question-answering *etc.* During the adaptation phase, BERT model is fine-tuned with limited labeled data corresponding to the downstream task. Lee *et al.*, [14] proposed BioBERT, the first domain specific model based on BERT for biomedical domain. Domain-specific text has many proper nouns and terms due to which, performance of a general-domain model suffers. With this hypothesis, BERT model was further pre-trained on PubMed abstracts (4.5B words) and PMC full-text articles (13.5B words). BioBERT language model inherits vocabulary from general domain to leverage knowledge from both general domain as well as biomedical corpora, thus making it an effective model for biomedical text-mining tasks. PubMed-BERT [12] proposed a new paradigm for biomedical language model pre-training by moving from mixed-domain pre-training as used in BioBERT, to exclusively in-domain pre-training from scratch using abstracts from PubMed and full-text articles from PubMedCentral. The idea of PubMedBERT is, biomedical domain has enough domain-specific text for entire pre-training and does not need the model to be trained on any general domain corpus.

2.2 ConnExt-BioBERT Architecture

ConnExt-BioBERT is an end-to-end tool for large scale curation of brain-connectivity information from full-text articles in the neuroscience domain. Architecture of the tool is depicted in Fig. 1.

A set of 53,000 full-text articles (*53kNeuroFullText*) from the neuroscience domain has been used to compile a resource for brain region connectivity.

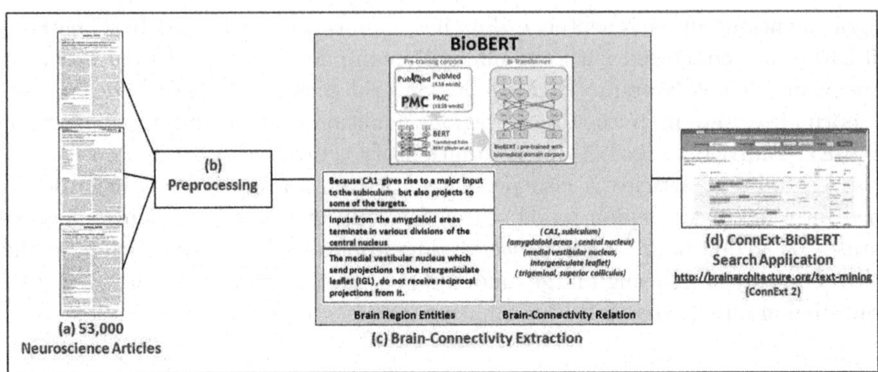

Fig. 1. Architecture of ConnExt BioBERT. (a) Full-text articles from neuroscience domain. (b) Preprocessing performed on articles to eliminate metadata, tables, figures and consider only textual content from paragraphs. (c) Brain region identification and connectivity prediction per sentence in the corpus using BioBERT (d) Web based search application on connections extracted from 53,000 neuroscience articles.

The set of articles are initially pre-processed to remove noise using RegEx pattern matching. Following are considered as noise in the research articles: *Journal names, Institute names and addresses, List of author names and contact details, References, Tables and figures, Copyright lines, Acknowledgments Author affiliations and Journal issue dates.*

In this study, *Brain-connectivity* is treated as a binary relation and hence connectivity is extracted only between two brain regions at a time. *53kNeuroFullText* articles have sentences with number of brain region mentions ranging from none to sentences having more than ten region mentions. All sentences having more than two brain regions are pre-processed and replicated multiple times such that, only two regions are considered at a time for predicting connectivity.

Brain-connectivity extraction is performed in two steps, first is to identify the brain region mentions and next is to extract connections between the regions. BERT and its biomedical variants described in Sect. 2.1 have been explored to find the most suitable neural architecture for brain-connectivity extraction. Based on experiments described further in this Section, BioBERT [14] was chosen to perform the following downstream tasks:

1. Named Entity Recognition (NER) for identifying *'Brain region'* entity
2. Relation Extraction (RE) for identifying *'Brain-connectivity'* relation

To perform these tasks using BioBERT, an additional linear layer is appended to the pre-trained model above the transformer output. The augmented model is trained on the corresponding downstream task, using limited task-specific labeled data. During this fine-tuning process, the model parameters are refined by gradient descent using standard backpropagation. NER is posed as a sequence tagging task, where the output layer predicts token-level probabilities to classify a token into one of the pre-defined entity classes. On the other hand, RE is considered as a text classification task. The aggregate sequence representation of the entire sentence is fed into the output layer for classification of the sentence.

Finally, connections extracted by ConnExt-BioBERT on *53kNeuroFullText* are made available as a web-based search application. The web application is further detailed in Sect. 2.4.

Experiments. Benchmark dataset, *WhiteText* [8,9] has been used in this study for performance evaluation of different models described in Sect. 2.1. To the best of our knowledge, *WhiteText* is the only benchmark dataset for brain region connectivity extraction. Fine-tuning was done for NER and RE using both versions of *WhiteText* dataset [8,9]. For vanilla BERT, the pre-trained model *"BERT-Base-Cased"* [6], for BioBERT, the pre-trained model, *"BioBERT-Base v1.0 (+PubMed 200k + PMC 270K)"* [14] and for PubMedBERT, the pre-trained model, *"PubMedBERT-base-uncased-abstract-fulltext"* [12] was used to initialize the neural network. All three BERT models used in the experiment were set to a sequence length of 512, with 12 encoder blocks and 12 attention heads. Hidden size was set to 768 and GELU was used as the activation function. Table 1 shows results of NER and Table 2 shows results of RE, both in 10-fold cross-validation setting for the three BERT variants.

Table 1. Precision (P), Recall (R) and F_1 score computed on *WhiteText* [8,9] dataset for NER task, fine tuned to extract *'Brain Region'* entity. Numbers highlighted in bold indicate best performance with respect to dataset and the considered evaluation measure.

Dataset	Approach	P	R	F_1
WhiteText (*French et al.*, 2012) [8] I dataset	BERT	83.30	85.59	0.84
	BioBERT	**84.05**	**86.30**	**0.85**
	PubMedBERT	82.94	85.36	0.84
WhiteText (*French et al.*, 2015) [9] II dataset	BERT	82.25	86.28	0.84
	BioBERT	**83.53**	**87.00**	**0.85**
	PubMedBERT	82.11	85.41	0.84

In case of NER (Table 1), all three BERT models have comparable performance in recognizing the brain region entities. However BioBERT has performed marginally better than the other two models on both datasets of *WhiteText* with F_1 score of 0.85.

The Relation Extraction task (Table 2) also follows a similar trend. BioBERT again demonstrated superior performance on both datasets of *WhiteText* with a maximum precision of around 74% and F_1 score of 0.75. This proves that mixed domain pre-training involving both general-domain as well as domain-specific data has paid off well for BioBERT compared to vanilla BERT and PubMedBERT for both NER and RE tasks. As seen in Tables 1 and 2, among all variants of BERT, BioBERT gave the best performance in terms of F_1 score

Table 2. Precision (P), Recall (R) and F_1 score computed on *WhiteText* [8,9] dataset for RE task, fine tuned to extract *'Brain Region Connectivity'* relation. Numbers highlighted in bold indicate best performance with respect to dataset and the considered evaluation measure.

Dataset	Approach	P	R	F_1
WhiteText (*French et al.*, 2012) [8] I dataset	BERT	71.77	72.78	0.72
	BioBERT	**73.65**	**75.89**	**0.75**
	PubMedBERT	67.90	68.75	0.68
WhiteText (*French et al.*, 2015) [9] II dataset	BERT	63.68	63.75	0.63
	BioBERT	**69.35**	**68.11**	**0.68**
	PubMedBERT	58.85	61.53	0.60

and hence BioBERT was used for brain region and connection extraction from the *53kNeuroFullText* articles.

Experiments on the large corpus of 53,000 full-text neuroscience articles could not be entirely validated due to lack of ground truth labels for this real-world corpus. We resorted to manual evaluation of results on a small subset of seven full-text articles (*7NeuroFullText*) from the 53,000 article set. Sentences in *7NeuroFullText* were annotated by a domain expert for brain-connectivity. The brain region mentions in *7NeuroFullText* were identified using BioBERT NER, trained on *WhiteText* [8]. *7NeuroFullText* contains 3181 sentences after pre-processing the articles for noise removal and sentence expansion to consider two brain regions per input sentence. Number of positive instances/connections in *7NeuroFullText* is limited to 263. Experiments were performed by running BioBERT in inference mode on *7NeuroFullText*.

To analyze the effect of quantity and nature of labeled data on the fine-tuning process, we trained the BioBERT model with different labeled datasets as shown in Table 3.

Table 3. Precision (P), Recall (R) and F_1 score computed on *7NeuroFullText* dataset for extracting *'Brain Region Connectivity'* using different training datasets.

Training dataset	Precision	Recall	F_1 score
WhiteText (*French et al.*, 2012) [8] I dataset	69.76	65.75	0.68
WhiteText (*French et al.*, 2015) [9] II dataset	63.05	59.70	0.61
WhiteText I dataset [8] + *WhiteText* II dataset [9] II dataset	67.92	68.44	0.68
10NeuroPubMed [18]	84.62	4.18	0.08

Experiment depicted in Table 3 analyzes performance of ConnExt-BioBERT on *full-text articles*. Precision and recall values have reduced compared to the models tested only on abstracts as shown in Table 1 and Table 2. This can be explained by the observation, sentences in abstracts generally tend to be short and to-the-point without many long range dependencies and brain region coreferences across sentences. But full-text articles have lengthy sentences with many brain regions and long-range dependencies. We validated this observation by computing sentence level statistics on *53kNeuroFullText.* Full-text articles on *53kNeuroFullText* contained around 300 sentences on an average with 241 characters being the average length and 48 being the average number of words in a sentence. On the other hand, abstracts in the corpus, on an average contained around 10 sentences with average sentence length being 159 characters and average number of words being 26.

Let us now analyze the performance when model is trained on full-text articles, instead of abstracts. We have used *10NeuroPubMed* [18], a set of 10 full-text articles from neuroscience. Brain Connection mentions in *10NeuroPubMed* have been manually annotated by a domain expert. The model has high precision, but poor recall. This can majorly be attributed to the very small size of *10NeuroPubMed*, which contains only 2435 sentences with 275 positive instances/connections. On the other hand, *WhiteText* I dataset [8] contains 22547 sentences with 3096 connections and *WhiteText* II dataset [9] contains 11825 sentences with 2111 connections.

2.3 Comparison with BAMS

ConnExt-BioBERT is evaluated on a small dataset of seven neuroscience articles based on connection ground truth annotated by a domain expert as described in Sect. 2.2. However, to get a better estimate of performance, results of ConnExt-BioBERT are compared to a standard database of connectivity, the Brain Architecture Management system (BAMS) [2]. BAMS is a comprehensive and manually curated reference database of brain connectivity information and is used extensively by the neuroscience community. BAMS stores the hierarchical taxonomy of brain along with axonal connections between brain regions. This information has been manually collated from literature and recorded by researchers.

Comparing the results of ConnExt-BioBERT with the brain connections in BAMS or any other standard database of connectivity, needs mapping of brain regions and connections between the two lists. ConnExt-BioBERT processed 53,000 neuroscience articles (*53kNeuroFullText*) and found over 0.5 million connections and 56,000 unique brain regions. BAMS database has 615 distinct brain regions and 7,606 distinct connections between the regions. To analyze the percentage of connections retrieved by ConnExt-BioBERT that can be validated with BAMS, we applied multiple techniques for normalizing the brain region names and connections present in the two lists. The steps given below were followed for the mapping.

1. Lookup brain regions retrieved by ConnExt-BioBERT in BAMS list using exact string match
2. Apply inexact match to handle variations in spelling and out-of-order words. The inexact matching method uses Levenshtein Distance [23] to match the sequence of words.
3. Normalize brain region names across different nomenclatures used by different authors. BAMS was originally curated using Swanson-98 [20] and Swanson-

04 [21] nomenclatures (*53kNeuroFullText*). Whereas, connections in literature are authored using Swanson (1998, 2004) [20,21], Paxinos, Franklin (2014) [16], Hof *et al.,* [13] and several other nomenclatures. Neuronames [4] has been referred to map and resolve variations in nomenclature and abbreviations of brain region names.

4. Once both brain regions in a connection retrieved by ConnExt-BioBERT are mapped to regions in BAMS, we check if the connection is reported in BAMS. Connections in the BAMS ontology [3] are up-propagated in the anatomical hierarchy to find a mapping. The idea is, if brain regions, *BR1* and *BR2* are connected, then all their ancestors/enclosing regions are also connected [8].

Mapping brain regions of ConnExt-BioBERT with that of BAMS revealed 371 common brain regions between the two lists. Comparison of connectivity matrices corresponding to ConnExt-BioBERT and BAMS for these 371 brain regions is shown in Table 4. Initially, on applying inexact match and nomenclature match, 575 distinct connections in the matrix were found by both ConnExt-BioBERT and BAMS. Further, on up-propagating connections in the hierarchy, additional 104 connections could be validated with BAMS. Among all connections possible between the 371 brain regions in BAMS, ConnExt-BioBERT was able to predict around 33% of the connections. The reason ConnExt-BioBERT failed to report 1356 connections in **(ii)** could be because the articles from which these connections were compiled in BAMS, were not part of *53kNeuroFullText*. Connections in **(iii)**, identified by ConnExt-BioBERT could be considered as potential augmentation to BAMS.

Table 4. Statistics on comparison of connections reported by ConnExt-BioBERT and BAMS among a set of 371 brain regions

	Reported by BAMS	Reported by ConnExt-BioBERT	No. of connections
(i)	✓	✓	575 +104
(ii)	✓	X	1356
(iii)	X	✓	6835
(iv)	X	X	59869

2.4 Web Application ConnExt-BioBERT

ConnExt-BioBERT is hosted as a search engine over the 53,000 full-text neuroscience articles. It is currently being used by neuroscience researchers to query for connections between brain region mentions. The tool provides login based facility for multiple users to search using the tool (with additional confidence scores) and also annotates correctness of each query result. This helps the domain expert using the tool to validate the output, as well as create ground truth for sentences in the repository, which can be further used to re-train the learning model for improving its performance. The tool has the ability to compare across different available NLP models. The application is powered by Elastic search with a Django front-end and MySQL back-end. The tool can also be used to search for connections validated by BAMS, a manually curated database of brain connections, and can be accessed as Connext-2 at http://www.braincircuits.org/text-mining/.

3 Conclusion

The paper presents ConnExt-BioBERT, a large-scale biomedical text mining approach to curate brain-connectivity information from neuroscience text articles. A web application is developed for quick brain region based search for connections extracted from a dataset of 53,000 neuroscience articles. The application aids researchers in the field to quickly sift through large amount of scientific literature to find required brain region and connectivity information. There are few limitations of the method, namely the data specific, species specific nomenclature, where there is no consensus within the neuroscience community, and the public accessibility of full text articles and subsequent processing through our application. Further, connectivity extraction can be made species specific to augment the corresponding centralized connectivity resource. Brain connectivity information coupled with automated extraction of brain disorders will make a useful resource for analyzing the effect of connectivity structure of the brain in the diagnosis and treatment of brain disorders.

References

1. Bernard, J.F., Alden, M., Besson, J.M.: The organization of the efferent projections from the pontine parabrachial area to the amygdaloid complex: a phaseolus vulgaris leucoagglutinin (PHA-L) study in the rat. J. Comp. Neurol. **329**(2), 201–229 (1993)
2. Bota, M., Dong, H.W., Swanson, L.W.: Brain architecture management system. Neuroinformatics **3**, 15–47 (2005). https://doi.org/10.1385/NI:3:1:015
3. Bota, M., Swanson, L.W.: BAMS neuroanatomical ontology: design and implementation. Front. Neuroinform. **2**, 2 (2008)
4. Bowden, D.M., Dubach, M., Park, J.: Creating neuroscience ontologies. In: Crasto, C.J., Koslow, S.H. (eds.) Neuroinformatics. MIMB, vol. 401, pp. 67–87. Springer, Heidelberg (2007). https://doi.org/10.1007/978-1-59745-520-6_5
5. Canese, K., Weis, S.: PubMed: the bibliographic database. In: The NCBI Handbook, 2nd edn. National Center for Biotechnology Information (US) (2013)
6. Devlin, J., Chang, M.W., Lee, K., Toutanova, K.: BERT: pre-training of deep bidirectional transformers for language understanding. arXiv:1810.04805 (2018)
7. French, L., Lane, S., Xu, L., Pavlidis, P.: Automated recognition of brain region mentions in neuroscience literature. Front. Neuroinform. **3**, 29 (2009)
8. French, L., et al.: Application and evaluation of automated methods to extract neuroanatomical connectivity statements from free text. Bioinformatics **28**(22), 2963–2970 (2012)
9. French, L., et al.: Text mining for neuroanatomy using WhiteText with an updated corpus and a new web application. Front. Neuroinform. **9**, 13 (2015)

10. Giles, O., et al.: Optimising biomedical relationship extraction with BioBERT. bioRxiv (2020). https://doi.org/10.1101/2020.09.01.277277
11. Gökdeniz, E., Özgür, A., Canbeyli, R.: Automated neuroanatomical relation extraction: a linguistically motivated approach with a PVT connectivity graph case study. Front. Neuroinform. **10**, 39 (2016)
12. Gu, Y., et al.: Domain-specific language model pretraining for biomedical natural language processing. ArXiv (2020)
13. Hof, P.R.: Comparative Cytoarchitectonic Atlas of the C57BL/6 and 129/Sv Mouse Brains. Elsevier, Amsterdam (2000)
14. Lee, J., et al.: BioBERT: pre-trained biomedical language representation model for biomedical text mining. arXiv preprint arXiv:1901.08746 (2019)
15. Pan, S.J., Yang, Q.: A survey on transfer learning. IEEE Trans. Knowl. Data Eng. **22**(10), 1345–1359 (2010). https://doi.org/10.1109/TKDE.2009.191
16. Paxinos, G., Franklin, K.: Stereotaxic Coordinates. Second (2001)
17. Richardet, R., Chappelier, J.C., Telefont, M., Hill, S.: Large-scale extraction of brain connectivity from the neuroscientific literature. Bioinformatics **31**(10), 1640–1647 (2015)
18. Sharma, A., Jayakumar, J., Mitra, P.P., Chakraborti, S., Kumar, P.S.: Application of supervised machine learning to extract brain connectivity information from neuroscience research articles. Interdiscip. Sci. Comput. Life Sci. 1–20 (2021). https://doi.org/10.1007/s12539-021-00443-6
19. Sharma, A., Sharma, A., Deodhare, D., Chakraborti, S., Kumar, P.S., Mitra, P.P.: Case representation and retrieval techniques for neuroanatomical connectivity extraction from PubMed. In: Goel, A., Díaz-Agudo, M.B., Roth-Berghofer, T. (eds.) ICCBR 2016. LNCS (LNAI), vol. 9969, pp. 370–386. Springer, Cham (2016). https://doi.org/10.1007/978-3-319-47096-2_25
20. Swanson, L.: Structure of the rat brain: a laboratory guide with printed and electronic templates for data, models an schematics. In: Brain Maps: Structure of the Rat Brain, 2nd edn. Elsevier Science, Amsterdam (1998)
21. Swanson, L.: Brain maps: structure of the rat brain: a laboratory guide with printed and electronic templates for data, models and schematics. In: Brain Maps: Structure of the Rat Brain, 3rd edn. Elsevier, Amsterdam (2004)
22. Vaswani, A., et al.: Attention is all you need. In: Advances in Neural Information Processing Systems (2017)
23. Wagner, R.A., Fischer, M.J.: The string-to-string correction problem. J. ACM (JACM) **21**(1), 168–173 (1974)
24. Zhu, Y., et al.: Aligning books and movies: towards story-like visual explanations by watching movies and reading books. In: Proceedings of the IEEE International Conference on Computer Vision (2015)

An Attention-Based Mood Controlling Framework for Social Media Users

Tapotosh Ghosh[1(✉)], Md. Hasan Al Banna[1], Tazkia Mim Angona[1], Md. Jaber Al Nahian[1], Mohammed Nasir Uddin[1], M. Shamim Kaiser[2], and Mufti Mahmud[3]

[1] Bangladesh University of Professionals, Dhaka, Bangladesh
nasiruddin@bup.edu.bd

[2] Jahangirnagar University, Savar, Dhaka, Bangladesh
mskaiser@juniv.edu

[3] Nottingham Trent University, Clifton Campus, Nottingham NG11 8NS, UK
mufti.mahmud@ntu.ac.uk

Abstract. In this digital age, social media is an essential part of life. People share their moments and emotions through it. Consequently, detecting emotions in their behavior can be an effective way to determine their emotional disposition, which can then be used to control their negative thinking by making them see the positive aspects of the world. This study proposes an emotion detection-based mood control framework that reorganizes social media posts to match the user's mental state. An emotion detection model based on Attention mechanism, Bidirectional Long Short Term Memory (LSTM), and Convolutional Neural Network (CNN) has been proposed which can detect six emotions from Bangla text with 66.98% accuracy. It also demonstrates how emotion detection frameworks can be implemented in other languages as well.

Keywords: Mood · Emotion · Attention · LSTM · Detection

1 Introduction

People typically express emotion through their communication and it can take various forms, like verbal, texts, non-verbal interactions such as gestures and facial expressions. Despite the fact that texting is more popular, social media has elevated it to a whole new dimension. Social media provides an easy means of expressing emotions. Platforms such as Twitter, Reddit, and Facebook are heavily used by people across the planet to express themselves. Due to the extensive use of these platforms, textual data became humongous, creating a new research question in the domain of natural language processing. A number of these questions have a substantial impact on diverse fields, including the detection of the emotional content sent through a text.

The rapid growth of social media has been a huge boon for the communication of emotions. Social media can create a quite impact on one's current mood.

M. Mahmud et al. (Eds.): BI 2021, LNAI 12960, pp. 245–256, 2021.
https://doi.org/10.1007/978-3-030-86993-9_23

A series of negative posts on a user's social media may affect their thoughts and increase risk for depression, loneliness, anxiety, self-harm and even suicidal thoughts. For improving mental health, posts of user's newsfeed can be filtered based on their current mood. An Attention-based Bidirectional LSTM-CNN model has been proposed in this paper to detect an user's emotion through their shared posts and filter out negative posts from their feed. To control negative emotions or change their mood, inspirational or positive energy posts can be visualized to the user.

To identify emotions conveyed in social media, textual information is very useful for assessing human perception in contexts such as product analysis, movie review, acceptance of a recently amended state policy, and so on, which has stimulated a need to identify it. As social media expands, people strive for convenience and naturally gravitate to informal ways of representation, making classification a difficult task for a machine. It is very easy for the human brain to detect this type of emotions attached with a text, whereas it is extremely challenging for a machine to do so. Emotion detection is very difficult in Bengali language due to the scarcity of data and use of emoji-mixed patterns in social media. A huge number of words in the Bangla dictionary and diversity in spelling make the classification process more difficult. Because of the absence of annotated corpus in the Bangla language domain and lack of an appropriate standard model, this research domain is still undergoing exploratory work.

Some researches have been conducted in order to detect emotion and sentiment of the Bangla text. Alam et al. [10] adopted transformers for emotion detection (5 classes) from Bangla YouTube comments. A computational approach based on Naïve Bayes classifier was proposed by Ruposh et al. [26] to classify 6 emotion classes from Bangla text. Das et al. [16] annotated emotions of blog posts using a syntactic model which was created by taking argument structure of the sentences with respect to the verbs. Tripto et al. [28] used LSTM with embedding to determine the emotion of YouTube comments. Azamin et al. [11] used Naïve Bayes classifier to classify 3 emotions from Bangla text. He performed n-gram, pos-tagging and TF-IDF in the feature extraction phase. Das et al. [16] tracked the emotions of Bangla block using Bangla wordnet. Rahman et al. [25] used classical machine learning algorithms to detect 6 different emotions from Bangla text where SVM with unigram and tf-idf feature was found as the best performing combination. Sarkar et al. [27] suggested the Naïve Bayes classifier to detect polarity of Bangla text. Nabi et al. [23] analyzed different features and machine learning classifiers to detect 3 sentiments from Bangla text.

As social media has become the media of the mass people, a social media based framework has been proposed in the framework which will be helpful in controlling negative mood of the user. The main contribution of the paper is given below:

- A framework has been proposed for controlling user moods.
- An Attention-based Bi-Directional LSTM-CNN model has been proposed to detect emotion from Bangla text. To the best knowledge of the authors, Attention based architectures have not been used in Bangla emotion detection.

- A comparison of the performance of the proposed model with the machine learning and deep learning models was presented.

Rest of paper is organized in the following manner: Sect. 2 describes the proposed mood control framework. Methodology for emotion detection has been discussed in Sect. 3. Section 4 sheds light on the obtained emotion detection result and provides comparison with similar architectures. This article comes to an end with a conclusion which is in Sect. 5.

2 Framework for Controlling Negative Mood Using Social Media Data

This work outlines a framework which can aid people in maintaining emotional balance. People become emotionally affected by their own personal matters, the environment at work, or what they witness around him. Most people are likely to feel negatively if they view contents that are downbeat or posts that are about death or other negative sentiments. A person's current mood and his mental state need to be analyzed before recommending social media content to control negative mood.

Here, a deep learning-based approach for detecting emotions from text data is proposed. Social media is used more often by people to share life events and express emotions. They write and share everything on social media as if it were a diary. Therefore, it can be helpful to observe the emotional state of their social media activity to gain insight of their mental state. In this framework, a post ranking methodology has been proposed to control negative emotion using social media.

Initially, the posts, comments, and reactions that have been posted in social media in the past would be analyzed by means of an Attention-based Bidirectional LSTM-CNN model. In the preprocessing stage, punctuation and stop words will be removed as well as tokenization and stemming would be performed. Following that, the input tensor was formed and the words got replaced by the pretrained Embedding layer. Finally, the proposed model classified these texts into six emotions: Joy, Surprise, Anger, Fear, Sad, and Disgust. In this work, a proposed model of this kind was built on the Bangla language. Bangla was selected due to its lack of development of natural language processing and usage by a large population worldwide. However, this emotion detection method can be applicable for any language.

As part of the framework, the posts of the potential users, advertisements, and posts of friends will also be subjected to a sentiment detection model. These texts will be categorized as positively and negatively to provide input for the ranking phase of the framework. Since there has been a lot of research related to sentiment analysis of textual data [1,12,21], we did not propose any model for this task.

Post ranking would consider two factors: the user's current emotion and the sentiment of the posts that will be viewed by that user. If the current emotion is positive, such as Joy or Surprise, no ranking will be applied to the potential posts, so all posts will be shown in regular order. However, in case there are many posts of negative emotions (Sad, Anger, Disgust, Fear) posted or reacted by the user, a ranking would be carried out (Fig. 1).

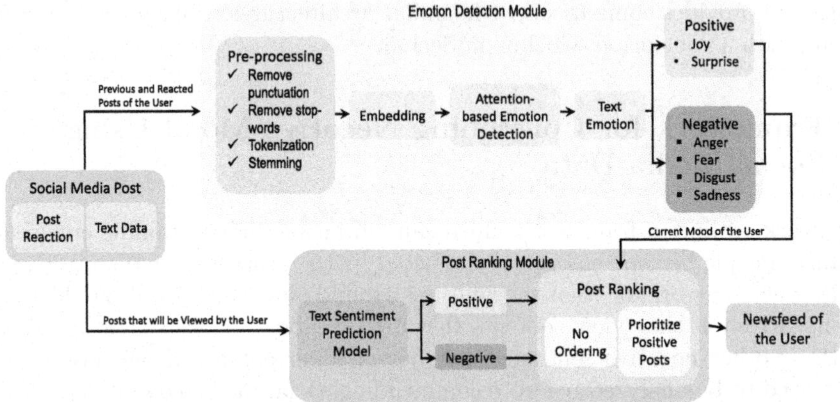

Fig. 1. Proposed framework for controlling negative emotion. An Attention-based Bidirectional LSTM-CNN framework would be used for detecting emotions of the previous posts, where potential posts that would be viewed by the user would be classified into positive and negative sentiment. If the user viewed or posted content of negative emotions, a ranking would be performed based on the sentiment of the posts where the user would be able to view the posts of positive sentiment first.

The user will be able to see posts with positive sentiment first, as they would have been promoted to the top position by the ranking phase, whereas negative sentiment posts would be found later. This will enable social media users to regulate their negative mood that may be triggered by social media or their daily life events. Figure 2 illustrates the proposed framework. This framework can be adopted in any language by training the Attention-based emotion detection model for that specific language.

3 Methodology for Detecting Emotions of Bangla Text

Machine learning and deep learning algorithms have been widely used in several classification and detection tasks [2–9,19]. A study on emotion detection using Attention-based Bidirectional LSTM-CNN hybrid architecture has been carried out in this paper. Bangla is a language with a very enriched diversity. It has 50 basic characters and more than 400 compound characters [20]. There are several characters which produce same kind of pronunciations [17,18], and due to this reason, people are more likely to do spelling mistakes during writing statuses. Many English words such as status,depression,challenge, and so on have been already used largely in between Bangla words in non formal Bangla writings. These things make it tough to classify emotion from Bangla text. In this work, we have collected a dataset of labelled Bangla emotion dataset, preprocessed the text, and extracted several features such as word2vec, fastText, and Glove embeddings. After that, several neural networks and machine learning based models were used to detect six different emotions from these features.

3.1 Dataset

BEmoD [14,15] dataset has been used in this paper for Bangla emotion detection purpose. This dataset contains 6243 Bangla text samples which are labelled into 6 emotions: anger, disgust, fear, joy, sadness, and surprise. After preprocessing the samples, 19169 words were found out in total. Out of 6243 samples, 4950 samples were used for training purpose and 1293 samples were kept aside for testing and evaluating the performance of the proposed architecture. Properties of the dataset has been provided in Table 1.

Table 1. Dataset properties

Total samples	6243	
Training sample	4950	
Testing samples	1293	
Total No. of words	19169	
Classes	**Training samples**	**Testing samples**
Anger	634	141
Disgust	1249	334
Fear	711	177
Joy	935	240
Sadness	964	258
Surprise	607	143

3.2 Text Preprocessing

In the text preprocessing phase, punctuation and bad symbols were removed at first. Then, stop words were removed from the text. These samples were tokenized. In the next step, a stemming was performed on each and every word. Then, the preprocessed texts were converted to numeric values by creating a word dictionary. All the samples were converted to a numerical vector having a length of 140 where blank spaces were filled with 0.

3.3 Feature Extraction

For extracting features from text, word embeddings have been utilized. In the word embedding, words were replaced by a distinct dimension vector which is created from a huge amount of text. In word embedding, similar words are represented by similar vectors. In this work, Word2Vec [22], fastText [13] and Gensim [24] word embedding techniques have been used. In Word2Vec, the embedding model is trained to find out similar numerical representation for similar words. In this work, a 300 dimensional pretrained Word2Vec was used which was trained on Bangla Wikipedia Dataset. Glove is quite similar as Word2Vec but it creates co-occurrence matrix where it values the frequency of a word to create the vector. A pretrained glove with 300 dimensional vector was used in this case which was trained on news articles and wikipedia. fastText represents each characters for training where words are considered in Word2Vec and Glove. fastText is quite efficient in generating word embedding in rarely used words which was found useful in this research.

3.4 Proposed Model

An Attention-based Bidirectional LSTM-CNN hybrid model has been proposed to classify six emotion from Bangla text. The model contains an embedding layers which converts the tensor into vector based on pretrained embeddings in the feature extraction phase. Then, the vector goes through an Bidirectional LSTM layer of 100 neurons and a LSTM layer of 100 neurons. Output of the 2nd LSTM layer is fed to a 1D convolutional layer with 50 neurons to find out higher level features. An attention layer was introduced in the following layer to memorize long sequence by creating shortcuts between the source and the context vector. This layer takes the output of convolutional layer as input. The output of the attention layer was given input to a max pooling layer to downsample the representation. Then, 3 Dense layers with 250, 50 and 6 neurons were used to find out the class from the extracted features of the previous layers. Dropouts were used to reduce overfitting problem. All the layer used ReLU activation function apart from the last Dense layer that used Softmax.

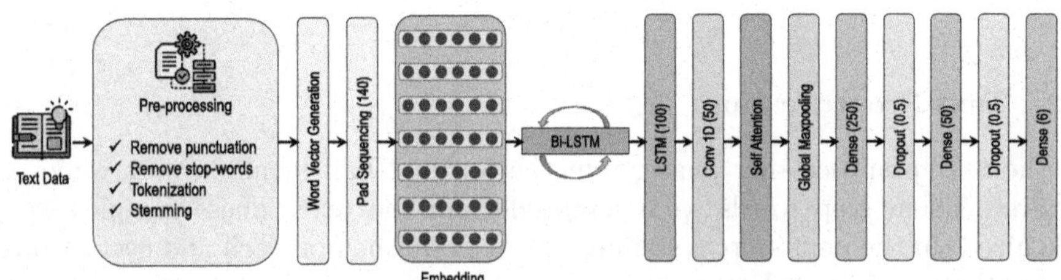

Fig. 2. Proposed Attention-based bidirectional LSTM-CNN architecture. The texts were first preprocessed. Then, it was converted to input tensor. After that, pretrained word embeddings were used to extract features. The proposed model consisting 1 BiLSTM layer, 1 LSTM layer, 1 Convolutional layer, 2 dropout layers and 3 dense layers classified the input tensor into six different emotions.

3.5 Training and Testing

During training, learning rate was set to 0.001 and the optimizer was Adam. It was trained for 30 epochs. These hyperparameters were chosen after trying out several combinations. The model was then tested with a completely different set of 1293 samples. Experiments were run on Kaggle Kernel which provided 4 CPU Cores, NVIDIA Tesla P100 GPU, and 16 GB of RAM.

4 Result and Discussion

The proposed Attention-based BiLSTM-CNN architecture achieved 66.97% accuracy in classifying six emotions when it used fastText Embedding. It achieved 67.31% precision and 64.84% precision in this case. It correctly classified 866 out of 1293 samples. The proposed model was most successful in classifying samples labelled as "Disgust" (77.54%) where it performed poorly in classifying "Surprise" (56.64%) and "Anger" (58.15%) texts due to the inadequate samples for training of these classes. This architecture classified Fear, Joy and Sadness with 63.84%, 65.42%, and 67.44% accuracy respectively. Confusion matrix is provided in Fig. 3(a). In case of using Word2Vec and Gensim Embedding, the proposed model achieved 66.43% and 65.66% accuracy respectively. Precision and recall during using Word2Vec Embedding was 67.06% and 64.92% respectively. Proposed model with Gensim Embedding achieved a precision of 66.43% where recall was 65.66%. Proposed model with fastText embedding performed better compared to other two embeddings which can be illustrated from Fig. 3(b). Classwise performance of all 3 embeddings is provided in Table 2.

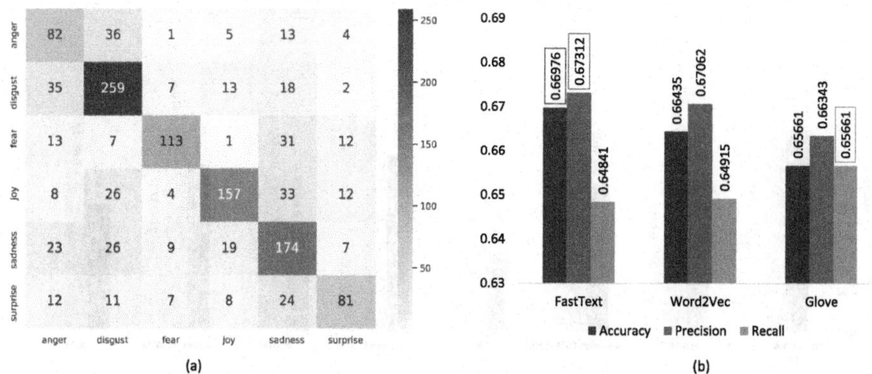

Fig. 3. (a) Confusion matrix of the proposed model. It performed quite good in classifying disgust, joy, and sadness. (b) Performance of the proposed model while using 3 different types of embedding. The proposed architecture performed better when it used the fastText embedding.

Table 2. Classwise accuracy of the proposed model

Embedding	Anger	Disgust	Fear	Joy	Sadness	Surprise
fastText	0.5816	0.7754	0.6384	0.6542	0.6744	0.5664
Word2Vec	0.5319	0.6856	0.7288	0.7333	0.6628	0.5524
Glove	0.4894	0.7395	0.5989	0.7000	0.6899	0.5664

Table 3. Different architecture to detect emotion

Model	Layer
BiLSTM-CNN	Embedding - Bidirectional LSTM (100) - LSTM (100) - Conv1D (50) - MaxPool - Dense (250) - Dropout (0.5) - Dense (50) - Dropout (0.5) - Dense (6)
Attention-LSTM-CNN	Embedding - LSTM (100) - Conv1D (50) - Attention - MaxPool - Dense (250) - Dropout (0.5) - Dense (50) - Dropout (0.5) - Dense (6)
LSTM-CNN	Embedding - LSTM (100) - Conv1D (50) - MaxPool - Dense (250) - Dropout (0.5) - Dense (50) - Dropout (0.5) - Dense (6)
Attention-BiLSTM	Embedding - Bidirectional LSTM (100) - LSTM (100) - Attention - Flatten - Dense (250) - Dropout (0.5) - Dense (50) - Dropout (0.5) - Dense (6)
BiLSTM	Embedding - Bidirectional LSTM (100) - LSTM (100) - Flatten - Dense (250) - Dropout (0.5) - Dense (50) - Dropout (0.5) - Dense (6)
Attention-LSTM	Embedding - LSTM (100) - LSTM (100) - Attention - Flatten - Dense (250) - Dropout (0.5) - Dense (50) - Dropout (0.5) - Dense (6)
LSTM	Embedding - LSTM (100) - LSTM (100) - Flatten - Dense (250) - Dropout (0.5) - Dense (50) - Dropout (0.5) - Dense (6)

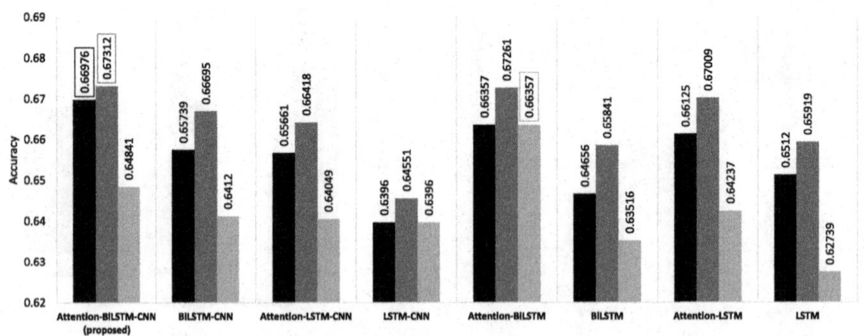

Fig. 4. Performance comparison with other LSTM, CNN and Attention based models. Proposed model performed better than other models in terms of precision, recall and accuracy. Attention based model showed greater performance in classifying six emotions.

We have also tried out 5 different LSTM, CNN and Attention based architectures. The detail of these architectures are provided in Table 3. Performance comparison of these architecture with proposed architecture has been illustrated in Fig. 4. The proposed architecture outperformed all the architectures in terms of accuracy. Attention-BiLSTM and Attention-LSTM achieved more than 66% accuracy which was close to the achieved performance of the proposed model. It is also noticeable that Attention-based models performed better than the rest of the models. fastText Embedding was used in all the above cases.

Ensemble approaches are capable of achieving a very high performance. A voting approach consisting of Attention-BiLSTM-CNN, Attention-BiLSTM, Attention-LSTM was tried out which yielded an accuracy of 66.05%. The precision and recall was 66.232% and 66.048%. Therefore, performance degraded when an ensemble approach was taken. Ensemble approaches are time consuming and also need larger in parameters and size. Considering all this issues, the proposed model was better choice than the voting ensemble approach.

Machine learning models are capable of classifying with a significant level of efficiency in case of texts. To evaluate classical machine learning algorithms, we have used TF-IDF vectorizer to extract features. These features were fed to Logistic Regression, Decision Tree, Naive Bayes, Random Forest and SVM models. Among these models, Logistic Regression performed the best with 59.8% accuracy where Decision Tree achieved the lowest accuracy (52.36%). SVM performed quite well by achieving an accuracy of 58.78%. No machine learning classifier performed better than the proposed architecture which achieved an accuracy of 66.98%. Table 4 provides a performance comparison between the machine learning classifiers and the proposed model.

Table 4. Performance comparison with machine learning classifiers

Model	Accuracy	Precision	Recall
Logistic Regression	0.598608	0.627712	0.598608
Decision Tree	0.523589	0.515763	0.523589
Random Forest	0.559165	0.586259	0.559165
Naive Bayes	0.527456	0.625344	0.527456
SVM	0.587780	0.654867	0.587780
Proposed Model	**0.66976**	**0.67312**	**0.64841**

5 Conclusion

Negativity, cynicism, and emotional despair are some of the most important causes of depression. In today's world, social media makes a huge impact on the user's mental state. Reports of violence, toxicity, and hatred can make the users mentally unstable. People with unstable mental health can observe severity viewing these contents. In this paper, to solve this problem, an emotion detection model was proposed for Bangla text data. For the detection of six distinct emotions, the proposed model achieved an accuracy of 66.98%. The performance of the model was compared with the shallow machine learning and deep learning models. The proposed model showed superior performance than these models. Based on this model, a mood control framework is proposed where the social media posts are rearranged based on the emotional state of the user. This may not be a permanent solution, but it can definitely decrease the depression invoked suicides. In the future research, the improvement of the emotion detection capability can be explored. Generalization capability of the models also need to be checked by trying this same model in datasets of other languages. Performance of the proposed framework can be evaluated for further improvement.

Acknowledgement. This research received funding from the ICT division of the Government of the People's Republic of Bangladesh for 2020-21 financial year (tracking no: 20FS13595).

References

1. Ahmed, A., Yousuf, M.A.: Sentiment analysis on Bangla text using long short-term memory (LSTM) recurrent neural network. In: Kaiser, M.S., Bandyopadhyay, A., Mahmud, M., Ray, K. (eds.) Proceedings of International Conference on Trends in Computational and Cognitive Engineering. AISC, vol. 1309, pp. 181–192. Springer, Singapore (2021). https://doi.org/10.1007/978-981-33-4673-4_16
2. Al Banna, M.H., et al.: Attention-based bi-directional long-short term memory network for earthquake prediction. IEEE Access **9**, 56589–56603 (2021)
3. Al Banna, M.H., Ghosh, T., Taher, K.A., Kaiser, M.S., Mahmud, M.: An earthquake prediction system for Bangladesh using deep long short-term memory architecture. Intelligent Systems: In: Proceedings of ICMIB 2020, p. 465 (2020)
4. Al Banna, M.H., Ghosh, T., Taher, K.A., Kaiser, M.S., Mahmud, M.: A monitoring system for patients of autism spectrum disorder using artificial intelligence. In: Mahmud, M., Vassanelli, S., Kaiser, M.S., Zhong, N. (eds.) BI 2020. LNCS (LNAI), vol. 12241, pp. 251–262. Springer, Cham (2020). https://doi.org/10.1007/978-3-030-59277-6_23
5. Al Banna, M.H., Haider, M.A., Al Nahian, M.J., Islam, M.M., Taher, K.A., Kaiser, M.S.: Camera model identification using deep CNN and transfer learning approach. In: 2019 International Conference on Robotics, Electrical and Signal Processing Techniques (ICREST), pp. 626–630. IEEE (2019)
6. Al Banna, M.H., Taher, K.A., Kaiser, M.S., Mahmud, M., Rahman, M.S., Hosen, A.S., Cho, G.H.: Application of artificial intelligence in predicting earthquakes: state-of-the-art and future challenges. IEEE Access **8**, 192880–192923 (2020)
7. Nahian, M.J.A., Raju, M.H., Tasnim, Z., Mahmud, M., Ahad, M.A.R., Kaiser, M.S.: Contactless fall detection for the elderly. In: Ahad, M.A.R., Mahbub, U., Rahman, T. (eds.) Contactless Human Activity Analysis. ISRL, vol. 200, pp. 203–235. Springer, Cham (2021). https://doi.org/10.1007/978-3-030-68590-4_8
8. Al Nahian, M.J., et al.: Towards an accelerometer-based elderly fall detection system using cross-disciplinary time series features. IEEE Access **9**, 39413–39431 (2021)

9. Al Nahian, M.J., et al.: Social group optimized machine-learning based elderly fall detection approach using interdisciplinary time-series features. In: 2021 International Conference on Information and Communication Technology for Sustainable Development (ICICT4SD), pp. 321–325. IEEE (2021)
10. Alam, T., Khan, A., Alam, F.: Bangla text classification using transformers (2020). arXiv preprint arXiv:2011.04446
11. Azmin, S., Dhar, K.: Emotion detection from Bangla text corpus using naïve bayes classifier. In: 2019 4th International Conference on Electrical Information and Communication Technology (EICT), pp. 1–5. IEEE (2019)
12. Bhowmik, N.R., Arifuzzaman, M., Mondal, M.R.H., Islam, M.: Bangla text sentiment analysis using supervised machine learning with extended lexicon dictionary. Nat. Lang. Proces. Res. **1**(3–4), 34–45 (2021)
13. Bojanowski, P., Grave, E., Joulin, A., Mikolov, T.: Enriching word vectors with subword information (2016). arXiv preprint arXiv:1607.04606
14. Das, A., Iqbal, M.D.A., Sharif, O., Hoque, M.M.: BEmoD: development of Bengali emotion dataset for classifying expressions of emotion in texts. In: Vasant, P., Zelinka, I., Weber, G.-W. (eds.) ICO 2020. AISC, vol. 1324, pp. 1124–1136. Springer, Cham (2021). https://doi.org/10.1007/978-3-030-68154-8_94
15. Das, A., Sharif, O., Hoque, M., Sarker, I.: Emotion classification in a resource constrained language using transformer-based approach (2021)
16. Das, D., Roy, S., Bandyopadhyay, S.: Emotion tracking on blogs - a case study for Bengali. In: Jiang, H., Ding, W., Ali, M., Wu, X. (eds.) IEA/AIE 2012. LNCS (LNAI), vol. 7345, pp. 447–456. Springer, Heidelberg (2012). https://doi.org/10.1007/978-3-642-31087-4_47
17. Ghosh, T., Abedin, M.M.H.Z., Chowdhury, S.M., Tasnim, Z., Karim, T., Reza, S.S., Saika, S., Yousuf, M.A.: Bangla handwritten character recognition using mobilenet v1 architecture. Bull. Electr. Eng. Inf. **9**(6), 2547–2554 (2020)
18. Ghosh, T., Al Banna, H., Mumenin, N., Yousuf, M.A., et al.: Performance analysis of state of the art convolutional neural network architectures in Bangla handwritten character recognition. Patt. Recogn. Image Anal. **31**(1), 60–71 (2021)
19. Ghosh, T., Al Banna, M.H., Al Nahian, M.J., Taher, K.A., Kaiser, M.S., Mahmud, M.: A hybrid deep learning model to predict the impact of Covid-19 on mental health form social media big data (2021)
20. Ghosh, T., Chowdhury, S.M., Yousuf, M.A., et al.: A comprehensive review on recognition techniques for Bangla handwritten characters. In: 2019 International Conference on Bangla Speech and Language Processing (ICBSLP), pp. 1–6. IEEE (2019)
21. Hassan, A., Amin, M.R., Al Azad, A.K., Mohammed, N.: Sentiment analysis on Bangla and romanized Bangla text using deep recurrent models. In: 2016 International Workshop on Computational Intelligence (IWCI), pp. 51–56. IEEE (2016)
22. Mikolov, T., Sutskever, I., Chen, K., Corrado, G., Dean, J.: Distributed representations of words and phrases and their compositionality (2013). arXiv preprint arXiv:1310.4546
23. Nabi, M.M., Altaf, M.T., Ismail, S.: Detecting sentiment from Bangla text using machine learning technique and feature analysis. Int. J. Comput. Appl. **153**(11), 28–34 (2016)
24. Pennington, J., Socher, R., Manning, C.D.: Glove: Global vectors for word representation. In: Empirical Methods in Natural Language Processing (EMNLP), pp. 1532–1543 (2014). http://www.aclweb.org/anthology/D14-1162

25. Rahman, M., Seddiqui, M., et al.: Comparison of classical machine learning approaches on Bangla textual emotion analysis (2019). arXiv preprint arXiv:1907.07826
26. Ruposh, H.A., Hoque, M.M.: A computational approach of recognizing emotion from Bengali texts. In: 2019 5th International Conference on Advances in Electrical Engineering (ICAEE), pp. 570–574. IEEE (2019)
27. Sarkar, K.: Using character n-gram features and multinomial naïve bayes for sentiment polarity detection in Bengali tweets. In: 2018 Fifth International Conference on Emerging Applications of Information Technology (EAIT), pp. 1–4. IEEE (2018)
28. Tripto, N.I., Ali, M.E.: Detecting multilabel sentiment and emotions from Bangla Youtube comments. In: 2018 International Conference on Bangla Speech and Language Processing (ICBSLP), pp. 1–6. IEEE (2018)

Analysing, Representing and Classifying Neuroscience Questions Using Ontologies

Aref Eshghishargh(✉) and Kathleen Gray

University of Melbourne, Melbourne, Australia
kgray@unimelb.edu.au

Abstract. Neuroscience is an important area of research due to the nature of the brain and its diseases. Scientists in this field tend to ask complicated questions which are time-consuming to answer and need several resources. Analysing, representing and finally, classifying these questions assist question resolution systems to be able to tackle them more easily.

To achieve its objectives, this study contains three different tasks, including an ontology-based question analysis approach to find question dimensions for representing questions and shaping categories for them; and two approaches in classifying questions, including one ontology-based and a set of statistical approaches.

Keywords: Ontologies · Question classification · Question representation · Neuroinformatics · Neuroscience

1 Introduction

Neuroscience is an important area of research. There are many questions regarding brain structure and its function. Neuroscientists usually have complicated questions that are hard and time consuming to analyse and answer. Analysing, reducing and classifying these questions helps in answering them automatically.

Resolving neuroscience questions requires domain knowledge. Ontologies are one of many tools and techniques that can be used to develop and enhance question classification [5,30]. An automated system such as the system described in [12–14], or a neuroscientist, should be able to distinguish between different types of questions to be able to suggest appropriate answers; tackle questions in a systematic manner; and in some instances, avoid working on repetitive questions.

Question classification is a vital part of the question analysis and processing module of systems designed for resolving questions, since it reveals information about the question and its answer types by assigning categories (classes) to them, and paves the way for other modules of systems for resolving questions [4,31,32].

Being able to represent questions is very important, since the quality of breaking down and representing questions has direct effects on question classification and therefore, resolving them. Moreover, by doing this, questions would be simplified which is important for finding answers [9,25].

M. Mahmud et al. (Eds.): BI 2021, LNAI 12960, pp. 257–266, 2021.
https://doi.org/10.1007/978-3-030-86993-9_24

In the remainder of this paper, a quick review of question classification and its significance is given in Background section. Methods demonstrate how questions were represented, analysed and classified; while Results shows the process of doing so. Results are further explained in the Discussion section alongside with a comparison of this research with similar works.

2 Background

Question classification is the task of assigning categories to questions [31,38]. It directly affects the performance of question answering systems. Statistical techniques have some shortcomings while working with classifying text [5,26]. Training data must be large to train the classifier; most traditional techniques used in this technique have not considered semantic relationships, making it harder to improve the accuracy; and finally, issues arise when language changes.

Studies such as [26,28,39], emphasise the importance and effectiveness of using domain taxonomy or ontology in text classification. Moreover, as Tomas et al. [31] discusses, semantic information is more useful than syntactic information in question classification. Ontologies can also prevent problems such as polysemy and synonymy [5]. Figure 1 demonstrates the focus and scope of this study and how ontologies are applied into the study.

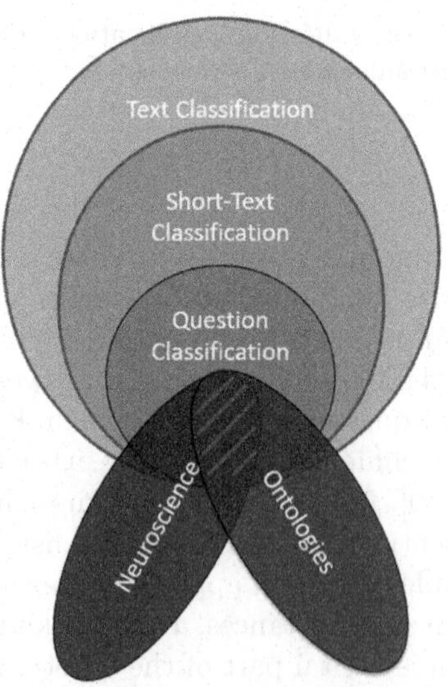

Fig. 1. An overview of the domain of this study

This paper discusses the pre-processing module of the system described in [13,14] in more detail. It is unique, based on the approach, domain, and the size of the ontology used. Here, question classification is performed based on a question hierarchy (question categorization) because of two reasons. First, as Ambert and Cohen [1] state, one of the questions that neuroinformatics is seeking an answer for, is to make sure that neuroscientists do not repeat themselves and are not answering the same sorts of questions. Second, as Tsatsaronis and Balikas [32] explain, the quality of an answer depends on the difficulty of the question. A hierarchy of questions can help addressing these issues.

3 Methods

The data-set comprised of 32 questions posed by domain experts and gathered from literature and then, validated by an expert. The data-set and more details on their collection process is available from https://github.com/Aref-cs/neuroQuestions.

Analysing questions is performed to create a representation for questions. Half of the questions were parsed manually and individually deconstructed to their language building blocks (tokens) after matching with the ontology. This, was to avoid bias while finding dimensions and the other half was used in testing the dimensions. In addition, stemming was done. Consequently, stop-words were removed. Then, tokens were visually inspected and placed into separate clusters according to their role in questions. If a new token did not match any previous cluster, a new cluster was assigned to it. This process continued until no token remained to be fitted in a cluster, a state known as theoretical saturation [7]. After that, clusters were named according to their tokens and were referred to as dimensions (features), and used in representing questions as coarse-grained [18] categories (classes).

Two approaches, namely ontology-based and statistical approached, were used in this paper. The focus in ontology-based approach was to use neuroscience domain ontologies with a partially rule-based [3,16] mechanism and finding dimensions in questions as demonstrated in Fig. 2. In this approach, first, questions were tokenized and stopwords were removed. Then the lemmatization was done according to the NIFSTD ontology. Lemmatization [26], is to map a term to its original form (lemma), based on a vocabulary or dictionary. A neuroscientist was consulted to resolve potential ambiguities. Please note that lemmatization is different with stemming. Second, ontology was search for terms in the question and their parent and ancestor nodes were found. If the parent node is the term one level above another term in the ontology hierarchy, the ancestor term would be the highest parent node in that branch.

The statistical approach, designed to test against ontology-based results and figure out its effectiveness, used four different supervised statistical techniques. This approach was performed on a dataset of 16 and 32 questions. The Weka [15] application was used as the classification platform. The classifiers used in Weka were respectively Naïve-Bayes, SMO (SVM), Lazy-IBK (KNN) and Random Forrest. The first step in the statistical approach, was to feed the questions to Weka. Then, lower case conversion, tokenization and stemming [33] were done. Feature selection is the task of selecting appropriate dimensions from the training

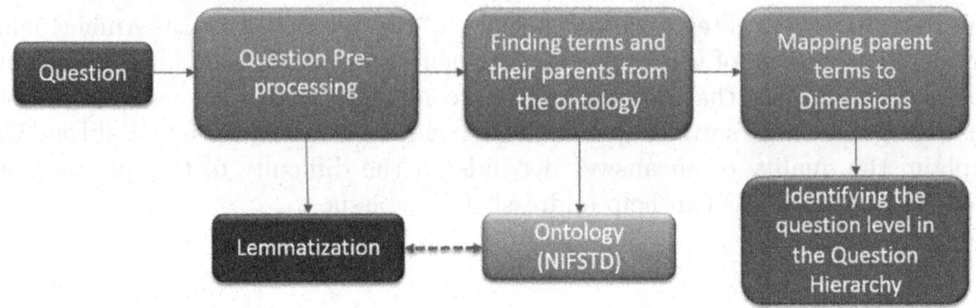

Fig. 2. Ontology-based classification diagram

dataset for use in text classification. Weka has a tool for finding features, but using dimensions as features provided better results. Then, the classification was performed, using leave-one-out cross-validation that uses one instance from the dataset as the validation set (test dataset) and other instances as the training dataset. Therefore, all questions were used as test and train sets in turns, to prevent problems such as over-fitting. Figure 3 demonstrates a high-level view of question classification methods used in this research.

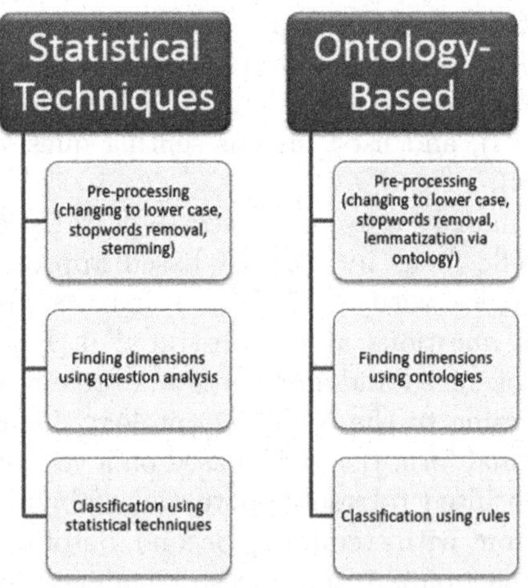

Fig. 3. The approaches toward question classification

4 Results

As the first step towards finding dimensions in questions, 14 questions were parsed manually and deconstructed to tokens as described in the Sect. 3, stop-words were omitted, and words were changed to their initial form. A sample result of this phase was:

1. synonym/hippocampus
2. parts/precentral gyrus/active/schizophrenia/healthy volunteers/data
3. relationship/telencephalon/diencephalon
4. positive/effect/aspirin/brains/elderly/people
5. how many/subject/extra/volume/subpart/diencephalon/data
6. ...

In the second step, tokens were placed into clusters based on their nature and similarities until theoretical saturation [7] was reached; meaning no token was left without being placed in a cluster. Non-repetitive tokens were assigned to clusters and new clusters were created upon facing new token types. A sample of clusters were as follows:

- Cluster A: synonyms, volume, description, ...
- Cluster B: hippocampus, precentral gyrus, superior longitudinal fasciculus, inferior parietal lobule, telencephalon, diencephalon, left amygdala, ...
- Cluster C: less, more, most common, how many, change, positive, ...
- Cluster ...

Then, similar clusters were merged, appropriate names were given to clusters, and subsequently referred to as dimensions (features). Table 1 demonstrates the list of dimensions.

Table 1. Question dimensions

Dimension	Example
Entities	Hippocampus, precentral gyrus
Domain-specific phrases	Activation, curvature
Aggregation-statistical phrases	Summary, total
Data references	Data, ontology
Conditional phrases	Elderly, connected

The rest of the data-set were used to test the coverage of dimensions in representing neurosciene questions. After they tested successful, a hierarchy of questions was created based on the number of dimensions involved in a question in a way that as levels of the hierarchy increased, the complexity of questions increased with them:

- Level 0: Questions with only entities in them.
- Level 1: Level 0 plus domain-specific phrases.
- Level 2: Level 1 plus references to data.
- Level 3: Level 2 plus aggregation/statistical phrases.
- Level 4: level 3 plus conditions, comparisons or changes.

In the ontology-based approach, the pre-processing step, including tokenization and lemmatization, were performed on questions. Multiple-word terms were checked against the ontology before tokenization and if found to be a dimension, they were counted as one token, such as the token ‘superior longitudinal fasciculus’. Also, ambiguities were resolved through information from the NIFSTD ontology and consulting a neuroscience expert.

Then, and based on question dimensions and the question hierarchy, level of each questions were identified. For example, “Which part of the precentral gyrus is active in these data?” was a level 2 question. The classification using the NIFSTD ontology, resulted in 87.5% accuracy. It is worth reminding that ontology-based classification, needed expert consultation for devising rules. In the statistical approach, first, questions were fed to the Weka, along with dimensions and hierarchy levels. Questions were then tokenized using the ‘StringToWordVector’ filter. Also, tasks such as tokenization and stop-word removal were done. Stemming was done using the Snowball stemmer. Weka provided a tool for selecting features, and using them resulted mostly in low classification percentages, but using dimensions resulted in a better outcome.

In the next step, a baseline and upper-bound was created to mark the lowest and highest accuracy; then, each classifier was applied on the dataset. As can be seen from Table 2, Naïve-Bayes and SVM classifiers scored the highest baseline percentages with 43.75%, and the upper-bound was 96% correct classification.

The third step consisted of running classifiers on half of the data-set, which resulted in a significant increase in accuracy; especially, the Random Forrest technique, with respectively 52.32% and 77.27% correct classifications. There are three different parameters for each classification including precision, recall and f-measure [23]. Precision is to see how many instances are relevant; recall is to examine how many relevant instances were selected; and f-measure, is a combination of both previous parameters.

In the final step, classifications were done on the whole dataset. The Naïve-Bayes classifier scored 0.69 on precision, 0.55 on recall and 0.57 on f-measure. The SVM scored 0.72 on precision, 0.66 on recall and 0.66 on f-measure. KNN scored 0.76 on precision, 0.55 on recall and 0.52 on f-measure. Random Forrest scored 0.54 on precision, 0.62 on recall and 0.56 on f-measure. Table 2 demonstrates the overall results.

Table 2. Results of different question classification experiments

	Naive-Bayes	SVM	KNN	Random Forrest
No dimensions (baseline)	43.75	43.75	25	31.25
With dimensions (16 questions)	46.15	46.15	46.15	52.32
With dimensions (32 questions)	54.54	72.72	68.18	77.27
Upper bound	96			

5 Discussion

Based on Table 2, while dimensions were not used, the best classification rate was 43.75%. However, using dimensions, classification rate increased up to 72.72% and improved results by at least 8.57%, and up to 28.97%.

Ontologies allow semi-supervised or even unsupervised classifications to some extents, since training data can be minimized while using ontologies. Moreover, it can assist with term and ambiguity resolution, as it was done in this study by lemmatization techniques.

Research papers such as [26] claim that ontology decreases the accuracy; especially, if it is too fine-grained [34]. Studies such as [11], suggest that using ontology increases the accuracy on main categories, but decreases the overall accuracy. However, with the introduction of dimensions alongside the ontology and matching fine-grained ontology terms with the coarse-grained or abstract dimensions, the accuracy increased and benefits of detailed information was preserved, while the accuracy did not suffer.

Using ontologies can lead to an increase of the computational cost without using techniques such as modularizing or generating specific views [27] from them. It can also lead to other costs due to issues like needing domain expertise. Statistical techniques are easy, since most are pre-designed, and do not need ongoing consultations and are much faster. Therefore, using an ontology-based approach is a choice between accuracy versus speed and ease of use.

Related works could be viewed from different aspects, including the question classification aspect with research like [16,22,31,39]. These are discussed in the following sections according to their focus, approach and domain.

Taxonomy application in text, short-text and question classification, can be seen in [10,16,19,31,36,39,40], while a few incorporated ontologies, including [6, 17,22,26,30]. Among ontology-based studies, three focused on general question and text classification and the other four have used ontologies for classification of web documents, news and operational (occupational) health and safety.

In case of domain related research in neuroscience, few papers are related to health and medicine text, or question classification including [24]. Another aspect was the question complexity. In general domain, few systems have discussed the complexity of questions, including [16,35,36]. Stevens et al. [29] had worked towards 'complex query formulation', but did not address the complexity of queries. Aqualog [20,21] dealt with complexity and used RDF triples as complexity elements and focused on computational complexity. Research such as [16,36] used Bloom's taxonomy [2] to represent questions. Veeraraghavan and Miller [35] used four groups of complexity, including simple, compound, specialized and complex. Yan and Tourangeau [37] considered the complexity of questions in response time. Bu et al. [8] suggested a taxonomy for representing general questions. Roberts et al., [25] discussed annotating general medical questions and decomposing them using UMLS. Another research paper that worked on representing questions, is [9], which studied complex question decomposition.

This study had some limitations. Addressing them, leads to future work. The data-set was not very large. It is fine with the focus of this study, which was covering different questions types, instead of optimization. However, it might be argued this had an effect on statistical methods performance. Of course, the study compensated for the number of training dataset and maximized the accuracy of statistical classification techniques by using the leave-one-out cross-validation (K-fold) technique; using the most suitable stemmer and other optimization tasks. Still, expanding the data-set and performing follow up experiments with other new types of classification techniques would be a future direction.

Classification based on other factors such as the user type or resource can be another future direction. By understanding who is posing the question, tailored answers can be provided. Also, knowing the resource type, decreases costs.

Designing automated answering systems based on the question hierarchy, which was pursued in [12]; using dimensions for annotation purposes; including other ontologies such as the RadLex in classification; and creating automated lemmatization algorithms for neuroscience are other potential future directions.

6 Conclusion

First, questions were gathered. Then, through an ontology-based analysis process, dimensions which presented questions were created and tested. A question hierarchy were created according to the dimensions. Then, ontology-based question classification was performed. It achieved 87.5% correct classification. Following that, the statistical approach was performed and was demonstrated that the ontology-based approach provided competitive results.

All in all, it was shown that ontologies are successful in analysing, representing and classifying neuroscience questions. Furthermore, ontology-based question classification might achieve better results than pure statistical techniques, while it can increase the cost of system design and run-time.

References

1. Ambert, K., Cohen, A.: Text-mining and neuroscience. Int. Rev, Neurobiol. **103**, 109–132 (2012)
2. Anderson, L., Krathwohl, D., Bloom, B.: A taxonomy for learning, teaching, and assessing: a revision of Bloom's taxonomy of educational objectives (2001)
3. Asghar, M.Z., Khan, A., Bibi, A., Kundi, F.M., Ahmad, H.: Sentence-level emotion detection framework using rule-based classification. Cogn. Comput. **9**(6), 868–894 (2017)
4. Athenikos, S.J.S., Han, H.: Biomedical question answering: a survey. Comput. Methods Program Biomed. **99**(1), 1–24 (2010)
5. Baharudin, B., Lee, L., Khan, K.: A review of machine learning algorithms for text-documents classification. Colloq. Inf. Sci. Technol. (CIST) (2010)
6. Besbes, G., Baazaoui-Zghal, H., Moreno, A.: Ontology-based question analysis method. In: International Conference on Flexible Query Answering Systems, pp. 100–111. Springer (2013)

7. Bowen, G.A.: Naturalistic inquiry and the saturation concept: a research note. Qual. Res. **8**(1), 137–152 (2008)
8. Bu, F., Zhu, X., Hao, Y., Zhu, X.: Function-based question classification for general QA. In: EMNLP 2010 - Conference on Empirical Methods in Natural Language Processing, Proceedings of the Conference, pp. 1119–1128 (2010)
9. Chali, Y., Hasan, S.A., Imam, K.: Learning good decompositions of complex questions. In: Proceedings of the 17th International Conference on Applications of Natural Language Processing and Information Systems, pp. 104–115 (2012)
10. Chen, M., Jin, X., Shen, D.: Short text classification improved by learning multi-granularity topics. In: Proceedings of the Twenty-Second International Joint Conference on Artificial Intelligence (IJCAI) (2011)
11. Dridan, R., Baldwin, T.: What to classify and how: experiments in question classification for Japanese. In: Proceedings of the 10th Conference of the Pacific Association for Computational Linguistics, pp. 333–341 (2007)
12. Eshghishargh, A., Gray, K., Kolbe, S.C.: Resolving neuroscience questions using ontologies and templates. In: Mahmud, M., Vassanelli, S., Kaiser, M.S., Zhong, N. (eds.) BI 2020. LNCS (LNAI), vol. 12241, pp. 141–150. Springer, Cham (2020). https://doi.org/10.1007/978-3-030-59277-6_13
13. Eshghishargh, A., Gray, K., Milton, S.K., Kolbe, S.C.: A semantic system for answering questions in neuroinformatics. In: ACM International Conference Proceeding Series, pp. 1–5. ACM Press, New York (2018)
14. Eshghishargh, A., et al.: An ontology-based semantic question complexity model and its applications in neuroinformatics. Front. Neurosci. **9** (2015)
15. Hall, M., Frank, E., Holmes, G., Pfahringer, B., Reutemann, P., Witten, I.H.: The WEKA data mining software. ACM SIGKDD Explor. Newslett. **11**(1), 10 (2009)
16. Haris, S.S., Omar, N.: A rule-based approach in Bloom's taxonomy question classification through natural language processing. In: Proceedings - 2012 7th International Conference on Computing and Convergence Technology (ICCIT, ICEI and ICACT), ICCCT 2012, pp. 410–414 (2012)
17. Janik, M., Kochut, K.: Training-less ontology-based text categorization. In: Workshop on Exploiting Semantic Annotations (2008)
18. Li, X., Roth, D.: Learning question classifiers: the role of semantic information. Natural Lang. Eng. **12**(03), 229 (2006)
19. Liu, Z., Yu, W., Chen, W., Wang, S., Wu, F.: Short text feature selection for micro-blog mining. In: 2010 International Conference on Computational Intelligence and Software Engineering (CiSE 2010) (2010)
20. Lopez, V., Fernandez, M., Stieler, N., Motta, E.: PowerAqua : supporting users in querying and exploring the Semantic Web content. Seman. Web J. **3**,249–265 (2011)
21. Lopez, V., Uren, V., Motta, E., Pasin, M.: AquaLog: an ontology-driven question answering system for organizational semantic intranets. Web Seman. **5**(2), 72–105 (2007)
22. Magnini, B., Speranza, M., Kumar, V.: Towards interactive question answering: an ontology-based approach. In: IEEE International Conference on Semantic Computing (ICSC 2009), pp. 612–617. IEEE (2009)
23. Powers, D.: Evaluation: from precision, recall and F-measure to ROC, informedness, markedness and correlation (2011)
24. Ribadas, F.J., De Campos, L.M., Darriba, V.M., Romero, A.E.: Two hierarchical text categorization approaches for BioASQ semantic indexing challenge. In: CEUR Workshop Proceedings 1094 (2013)

25. Roberts, K., Masterton, K., Fiszman, M., Kilicoglu, H., Demner-Fushman, D.: Annotating question decomposition on complex medical questions. In: Proceedings of the 9th International Conference on Language Resources and Evaluation (LREC 2014), pp. 2598–2602 (2014)
26. Sanchez-Pi, N., Martí, L., Garcia, A.: Improving ontology-based text classification: an occupational health and security application. J Appl. Logic **17**, 48–58 (2015)
27. Shaw, M., Detwiler, L.T., Noy, N., Brinkley, J., Suciu, D.: vSPARQL: a view definition language for the semantic web. J. Biomed. Inform. **44**(1), 102–117 (2011)
28. Sriram, B., Fuhry, D., Demir, E., Ferhatosmanoglu, H., Demirbas, M.: Short text classification in twitter to improve information filtering. In: Proceedings of the 33rd International ACM SIGIR Conference on Research\r\nand Development in Information Retrieval, pp. 841–842 (2010)
29. Stevens, R., et al.: Complex query formulation over diverse information sources in TAMBIS. In: Bioinformatics: Managing Scientific Data. Morgan Kaufmann (2003)
30. Tenenboim, L., Shapira, B., Shoval, P.: Ontology-based classification of news in an electronic newspaper. In: International Conference on "Intelligent Information and Engineering Systems" (INFOS 2008) (2008)
31. Tomás, D., Vicedo, J.L.: Minimally supervised question classification on fine-grained taxonomies. Knowl. Inf. Syst. **36**(2), 303–334 (2012)
32. Tsatsaronis, G., et al.: An overview of the BIOASQ large-scale biomedical semantic indexing and question answering competition. BMC Bioinform. **16**(1), 138 (2015)
33. Uysal, A.K., Gunal, S.: The impact of preprocessing on text classification. Inf. Proces. Manag. **50**(1), 104–112 (2014)
34. Van Zaanen, M., Pizzato, L.A., Molla, D.: Classifying sentences using induced structure. Lecture Notes in Computer Science (including subseries Lecture Notes in Artificial Intelligence and Lecture Notes in Bioinformatics) 3772 LNCS, pp. 139–150 (2005)
35. Veeraraghavan, H., Miller, J.V.: Faceted visualization of three dimensional neuroanatomy by combining ontology with faceted search. Neuroinformatics **12**(2), 245–259 (2014)
36. Yahya, A.A., Osman, A.: Automatic classification of questions into bloom's classification. In: Proceedings of the International Arab Conference on Information Technology, pp. 1–6 (2011)
37. Yan, T., Tourangeau, R.: Fast times and easy questions: the effects of age, experience and question complexity on web survey response times. Appl. Cogn. Psychol. **22**(1), 51–68 (2008)
38. Yu, H., Sable, C., Zhu, H.R.: Classifying medical questions based on an evidence taxonomy. AAAI Workshop - Technical Report WS-05-10, pp. 27–35 (2005)
39. Yu, Z., Su, L., Li, L., Zhao, Q., Mao, C., Guo, J.: Question classification based on co-training style semi-supervised learning. Patt. Recogn. Lett. **31**(13), 1975–1980 (2010)
40. Zhang, D., Lee, W.S.: Question classification using support vector machines. In: Proceedings of the 26th Annual International ACM SIGIR Conference on Research and Development in Information Retrieval, pp. 26–32 (2003)

Movie Identification from Electroencephalography Response Using Convolutional Neural Network

Dhananjay Sonawane[1], Pankaj Pandey[1], Dyutiman Mukopadhyay[2], and Krishna Prasad Miyapuram[3(✉)]

[1] Computer Science and Engineering, Indian Institute of Technology Gandhinagar, Gujarat 382355, India

[2] Experimental Psychology, University College London, London, UK

[3] Centre for Cognitive and Brain Sciences, Indian Institute of Technology Gandhinagar, Gujarat 382355, India

kprasad@iitgn.ac.in

Abstract. Visual, audio, and emotional perception by human beings have been an interesting research topic in the past few decades. Electroencephalography (EEG) signals are one of the ways to represent human brain activity. It has been shown, that different brain networks correspond to processes corresponding to varieties of emotional stimuli. In this paper, we demonstrate a deep learning architecture for the movie identification task from the EEG response using Convolutional Neural Network (CNN). The dataset includes nine movie clips that span across different emotional states. The EEG time series data has been collected for 20 participants. Given one second EEG response of particular participant, we tried to predict its corresponding movie ID. We have also discussed the various pre-processing steps for data cleaning and data augmentation process. All the participants have been considered in both train and test data. We obtained 80.22% test accuracy for this movie classification task. We also tried cross participant testing using the same model and the performance was poor for the unseen participants. Our result gives insight toward the creation of identifiable patterns in the brain during audiovisual perception.

Keywords: EEG · Classification · CNN · Neural entrainmment · Brain signals

1 Introduction

Neurocinematics is a field of study that aims to identify similarities and subjective experiences, while participants view structured movies [6]. Scenes embedded in the movie evoke various emotions. This forms a class of naturalistic audiovisual stimuli which in turn creates an opportunity to study brain responses corresponding to emotions. Few film-based studies have been performed to understand

M. Mahmud et al. (Eds.): BI 2021, LNAI 12960, pp. 267–276, 2021.
https://doi.org/10.1007/978-3-030-86993-9_25

the emotional and functional responses of the brain. However these studies are primarily grounded on the western classification of emotions comprising fear, sadness, anger, surprise, disgust, and happiness. Indian system classifies emotional states according to an ancient Indian treatise on the performing arts known as 'Natyasastra', which lays its foundation in 2nd Century AD [4]. The Rasa theory as described in 'Natyasastra', defines eight Rasas or sentiments which are: Karuna (pathetic), Bibhatsa (odious), Sringara (erotic), Adbhuta (marvelous), Veera (heroic), Bhayanaka (terrible), Hasya (comic), Raudra (furious), and lately ninth Rasa was introduced known as Santa (peace). The Navarasas are widely expressed in classical Indian performing arts. To date, one behavioral study has been performed investigating the Navarasas [7]. The present paper is based on a collection of movie clips selected from Bollywood movies based on the Nine Rasas representing different emotions.

EEG (Electroencephalogram) recordings contain high temporal resolution and an extensive array of challenges, the most common of which is a low signal-to-noise ratio. Artifacts from eye movement, head movement, and electrical line noise are examples of diverse sorts of noise. EEG data are not readily available unlike images, videos, or texts for computer vision (CV) and natural language processing (NLP). Sophisticated and efficient approaches are required to extract meaningful information from EEG data. Traditional machine learning methods have been demonstrated to be significantly outperformed by deep learning techniques. Deep learning-based methods have successfully recognized the patterns in brain activity, captured from functional MRI, Electro- and Magneto-Encephalo Graphy (EEG, MEG) etc. For example, predicting meditation expertise [12], classification of songs based on brain responses [13], and other several deep learning applications in brain imaging data [9]. Previous studies on emotion classification have primarily focused on contrasting states, such as positive-negative-neutral, threat-safety, and sadness-happiness [8,11]. The current study is concerned about stimulus-correlated activity observed through EEG while perceiving naturalistic audiovisual stimuli [3]. Based on the movie clips shown to the participants, the present research aims to identify nine different emotions.

2 Methods

This study aims to develop a procedure which can classify EEG signals corresponding to the respective movie clip. In this section, we describe the data acquisition, preprocessing, CNN deep learning architecture, training and testing process in detail.

2.1 Data Acquisition

The brain activities were captured through 128 channel recordings of viewing movie clips corresponding to the nine Rasas classified according to Indian Natyasastra. A total of 20 participants' data was collected on nine audiovisual stimuli. Movie clips used in the experiment are listed in Table 1. The sampling rate of EEG 250 Hz. Detailed description of dataset is available in the article [14].

Table 1. Movie clips used in EEG data collection

Movie ID	Rasa genre	Film name	Director	Year	Duration	Start time	End time
1	Adbhutam	Mr. India	Shekhar Kapur	1987	1 m 48 s	1 h 1 m 40 s	1 h 3 m 28 s
2	Bhayanakam	Bhoot	Ram Gopal Varma	2003	1 m 34 s	1 h 2 m 57 s	1 h 4 m 31 s
3	Bibhatsam	Rakhta Charitra	Ram Gopal Varma	2010	1 m 12 s	43 m 55 s	45 m 7 s
4	Hasyam	3 Idiots	Rajkumar Hirani	2009	2 m 33 s	59 m 55 s	1 h 2 m 28 s
5	Karunayam	Kal Ho Naa Ho	Nikhil Advani	2003	2 m 37 s	2 h 47 m 41 s	2 h 50 m 18 s
6	Raudram	Ghajini	A.R. Murugadoss	2008	2 m 9 s	2 h 38 m 43 s	2 h 40 m 52 s
7	Santam	Zindagi Na Milegi Dobara	Zoya Akhtar	2011	2 m 22 s	48 m 22 s	50 m 44 s
8	Sringaram	Umrao Jaan	Muzaffar Ali	1981	42 s	43 m 08 s	43 m 50 s
9	Veeram	Lagaan: Once Upon a Time in India	Ashutosh Gowariker	2001	2 m 3 s	2 h 10 m 57 s	2 h 13 m

2.2 Data Preprocessing

Raw EEG recordings contain noise including eye blinks and high-frequency components. As a result, before employing EEG data for any application, it must be cleaned. The preprocessing steps were carried out using the EEGLAB [2]. Continuous EEG data was segmented into different movie clips. Subsequently, the artifact subspace reconstruction method was used to clean continuous data [1]. In traditional event related potential designs, participants are presented with the

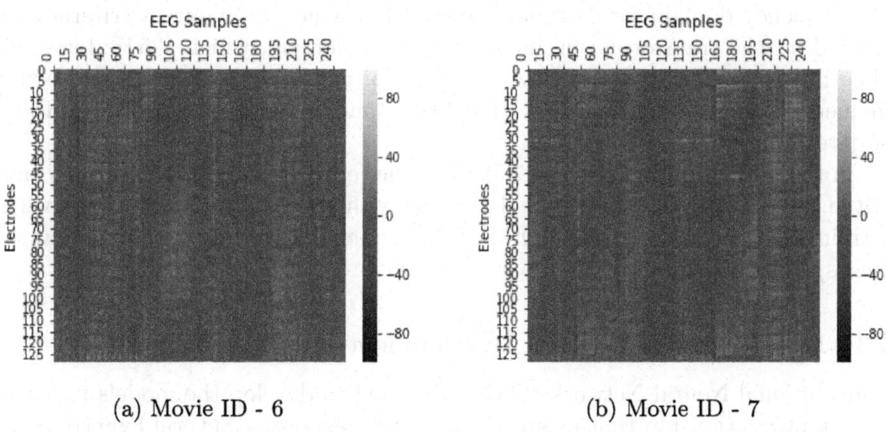

(a) Movie ID - 6 (b) Movie ID - 7

Fig. 1. Time domain representation of 26th second for participant ID 3

same stimulus multiple times. This was not the case in our study. Each movie clip was presented only once. Further continuous data that could not be corrected for artifacts is traditionally discarded. We could not discard the data in order to keep the dimensions of data the same across all participants.

For identifying patterns, a deep learning model requires abundant training examples with shorter and sensible dimensionality. The processed data consisted of 180 EEG recordings from 20 participants and nine video clips, with nearly 27000 samples captured in each electrode for EEG response at a sampling rate 250 Hz.

We employed the data augmentation technique to enhance the amount of instances in the dataset. Each participant's EEG response was separated into chunks of the 1-second length window for each video. Thus, we obtained a 2D matrices of dimension 129 (electrodes) * 250 (samples per second). Each chunked window was referred to as "movie image" and labeled with the associated movie. This approach enhanced the examples in the dataset while also allowing us to utilize 2D and 3D convolution networks. In the temporal domain, Fig. 1 exhibits the movie pictures of the 26th second of two separate movies for one of the participants. The design criteria was window size, and determining the best window size was challenging. With a larger window size, the dimensionality of the movie image increased but the overall number of samples was reduced. As a result, the data augmentation's aim was compromised. With high-dimensional input to Convolution Neural Network (CNN), the number of trainable parameters risen significantly, as long as the remainder of the architecture remained unchanged. We may lose pattern information with smaller window sizes, and CNN may perform badly. Window size, dataset, and CNN model performance all have to be balanced. In a further section, we have discussed the varying window sizes on the test accuracy of the classification task. More dimensionality reduction but not at the cost of the performance was achieved by converting EEG responses to a frequency domain. For each participant, we computed the Fast Fourier Transform (FFT) of all nine movie responses. We transformed time-domain signals to the frequency domain for each one second EEG window. Nyquist's criteria was applied for the transformation in the frequency domain, which 125 Hz for sampling rating 250 Hz. Figure 2 shows the transformation of data from time to the frequency domain. We developed models for time and frequency representation of data.

In the frequency domain, Fig. 3 depicts the representation of the 26th second of the two movies. We developed the model with the test-train split of 0.3 with a training (70%) and testing (30%) of data, including 0.2 part of the training data split for validation.

2.3 Experiment and Model Development

Convolutional Neural Network (CNN) was used to develop the models to learn the latent relationship that existed in the EEG responses. Several hyperparameters were carefully selected. We tested our model on both encodings of time and frequency domain. While applying on the time and frequency domain, only

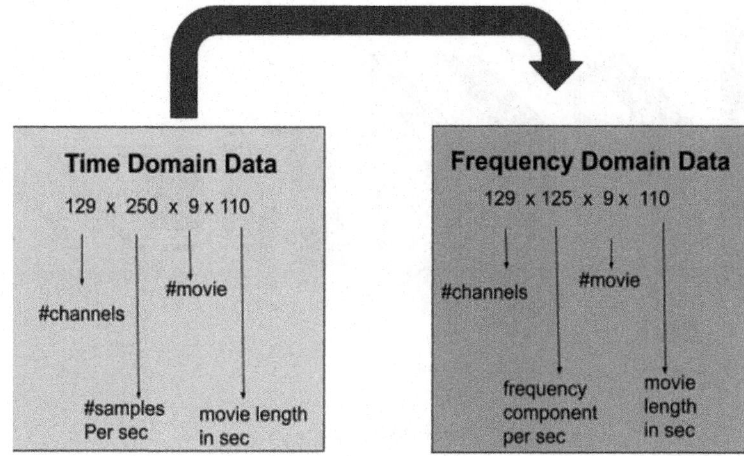

Fig. 2. Transformation of data from time to the frequency domain.

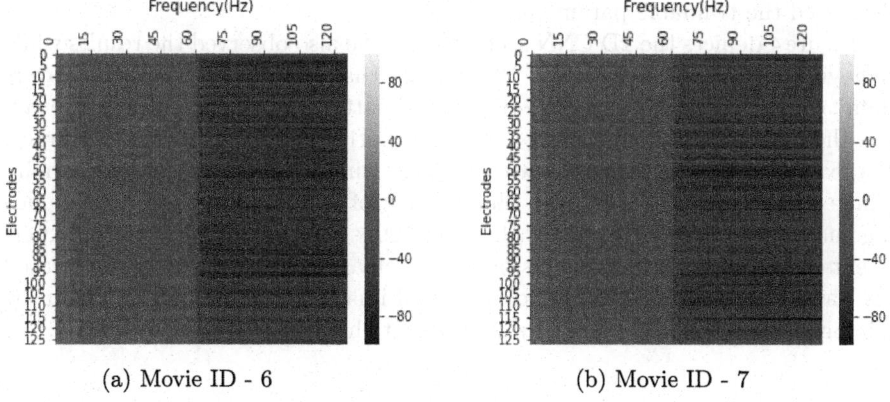

(a) Movie ID - 6 (b) Movie ID - 7

Fig. 3. Frequency domain representation of 26th second for participant ID 3

the initial layer where input was provided, was appropriately changed as per the dimension of the data.

We first hypothesized that each audiovisual stimulus might create different patterns in EEG responses. Therefore, to investigate our hypothesis, we included all participant's data with a limit. We varied the train and test split for each participant to observe the accuracy of prediction. We considered 20% to 90% of the train-test split. In the model, three layers of CNN were utilized for feature extraction and the last two dense layers for classification. Each layer included the ReLu [10] activation function except the last output layer. ReLU introduces non-linearity to identify complex representations. Softmax activation function was used for the output layer including categorical cross-entropy loss function and Adam optimizer. Each convolution layer had 16 filters with the kernel of size

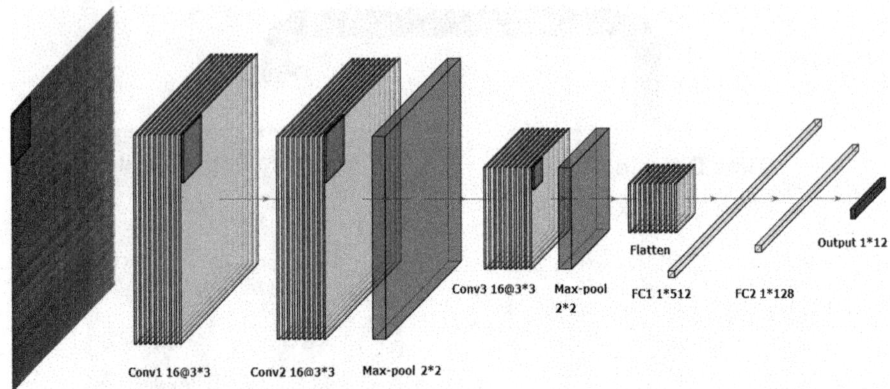

Fig. 4. 2D CNN architecture

3 × 3. Two and Three CNN layers included the max-pooling layer. Max pooling decreased the trainable parameter.

Figure 4 depicts the 2D CNN architecture. We also observed the results while removing the one or two layers. We noticed that the models excluding layers didn't perform and failed to learn the desired pattern. And if we added more layers, the model showed overfitting and significantly dropped in the test accuracy. We examined the performance with varying window size in the time domain. Three datasets were tested with the window of 1, 2, and 3 s and corresponding shapes were 129 × 250, 129 × 500, and 129 × 750. We didn't perform experiments on the other window sizes because increasing the window size decreased the dataset size. We created a 3-dimensional image in the frequency domain by joining a few seconds of responses as different channels.

Table 2. Performance of the CNN models

CNN model	Domain	Movie image shape	Total number of movie images	CNN trainable parameters	Train accuracy (%)	Test accuracy (%)
1	Time	129 * 250	13,946	3,398,089	99.22	80.22
2	Time	129 * 500	6,937	6,953,417	11.91	11.91
3	Time	129 * 750	4,597	10,623,433	11.64	12.58
4	Time	129 * 126	17,934 Cross participant	3,398,089	99.34	11.65
5	Frequency	128 * 126	13,820	1,677,769	97.06	77.61
6	Frequency	128 * 126	17,772 Cross participant	1,677,769	87.50	6.44
7	Frequency	128 * 126 * 10 3D input	1771 Cross participant	60,047,081	15.40	12.63

There is enormous individual variability and to address this, we hypothesized that each audio stimulus would generate a different pattern for each individual. To investigate this, we employed the leave one out strategy, where one participant was used for testing and the remaining for training. We iterated over all the participants one by one to include them in a test dataset, and the remaining participants were included in the training dataset. By doing so, we eliminated the effect of individual perception of audiovisual stimuli on the corresponding generated EEG signal. We tried to increase the performance using the 3D CNN model. We created 3D image by stacking ten consecutive response images and provided as input to 3D CNN model. This was primarily experimented with to consider the temporal dependency in the responses. This model was similar to 2D, with a slight change in kernel and max-pooling, which were $3 \times 3 \times 3$ and $2 \times 2 \times 2$. After some run, we observed ten was the optimum choice. We used 30 epochs with batch size 16 for training the CNN. The network architecture that we have demonstrated was also tested on our previous work [13]. Keras framework [5] was employed for all the experiments and initially, the weights of the models were randomly assigned. We used GPU NVIDIA GTX 1050 with four GB of memory.

3 Result and Discussion

We obtained outstanding results including each participant's response in the train and test set. We achieved (CNN model 1) training accuracy of 99.22% and test accuracy of 80.22%. Figure 6a shows the confusion matrix. This depicts that the test samples are balanced across all nine classes and also reflects the correct prediction. Figure 5b describes the accuracy with varying epoch. The complete accuracy information is tabulated in Table 2.

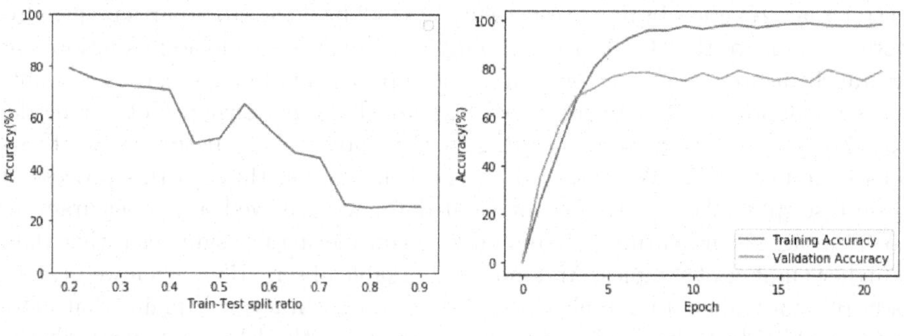

(a) Test accuracy for several train-test splits

(b) Training and validation curve

Fig. 5. Accuracy plots

The model trained on time domain dataset performed well when all the participants were taken into account, and the time window was 1 s (model 1). After increasing the time window, CNN's performance was drastically decreased in the

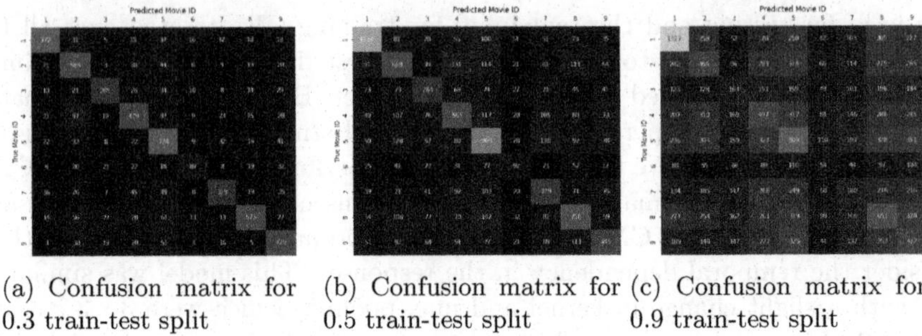

(a) Confusion matrix for 0.3 train-test split (b) Confusion matrix for 0.5 train-test split (c) Confusion matrix for 0.9 train-test split

Fig. 6. Confusion matrices

time domain (model 2, model 3). This was because the input movie image dimension was also increased, thereby increasing the number of CNN trainable parameters. And the number of training examples were decreased. CNN model became more sophisticated, resulting in poor performance. The same CNN architecture performed equally well when trained on the frequency domain dataset as compared to time domain dataset (model 5). We suggested that this learning could happen because of temporal dependencies in EEG responses and could include the common pattern in participants' responses. Hence, to understand this, we employed the leave one out strategy, in which we had 19 participants for training and one for testing. We achieved overfitted model, which can easily be understood by observing the differences in train and test accuracy of model 4 in the time domain. In the frequency domain, we found the overfitted model (model 6) and obtained very low test accuracy, and 3D CNN (model 7) performed slightly better than 2D and obtained test accuracy of 12.63% for cross-participant. Our findings indicate that CNN utilized temporal features for movie prediction and neural signatures generated for each movie clip varied individually, thus accounting for individualistic perception. We examined the performance of our model based on varying the train-test split. Figure 5a indicates the performance of various train-test splits. We observed an excellent finding through this process of train-test split. With only 40% of total data, we achieved a test accuracy of 55.48%. Significant learning existed only by considering few samples rather than a higher number of samples. And more remarkable observation, when we utilized only 10% for train data and obtained 25.42% test accuracy. It explains that more data would help to learn more complex patterns in the EEG responses. Therefore, we observed that only a few samples could outperform a random guess of 11.11% for this nine-class classification problem. Three train-test split ratios with their respective confusion matrices are shown in the Fig. 6a–c. Intermediate CNN outputs are shown in Fig. 7, which visualizes 3rd convolution layer of model 5. Participant 1 and Participant 5 learned different features for the same movie. Filter3, Filter8, Filter16 show distinct patterns in Fig. 7a,b. Hence, we support our 2nd hypothesis that EEG patterns demonstrate the individual variability arising from watching the same audiovisual clip.

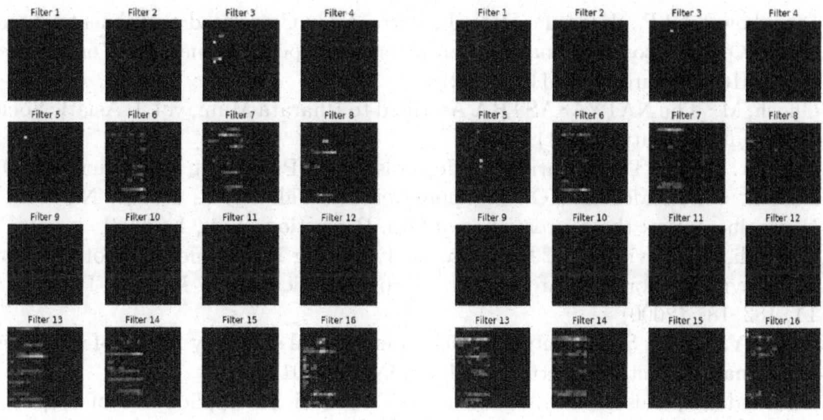

(a) Subject ID: 1, Movie ID:9 (b) Subject ID: 5, Movie ID:9

Fig. 7. Output of CNN layer 3

4 Conclusion

We exhibited several CNN models for identifying the movie clip based on brain activity captured while watching it. We used EEG responses consisting of 20 participants and nine movie clips having diverse Rasa or emotions. We explored the time and frequency domain and showed a remarkable classification performance only utilizing one second of brain responses. This study demonstrates an efficient three layers CNN model for classification. We present two significant findings from this study a) EEG responses generated from movie watching reflect the audiovisual entrainment b) the same movie clip generates the different EEG patterns in different brains. We experiment with several train-test splits of data to understand the complex pattern for the classification task. We achieve high test accuracy when including all participant's data in the train and test set and low in cross-participant settings. The possible reason for low performance could be people focused on different aspects of scenes, thereby reducing performance for cross-participant movie identification task. Thus, as future work, we aim at identifying preprocessing methods and CNN architectures to improve accuracy for across participant data. However, the findings of this article are extremely encouraging and represent a significant leap toward accomplishing the mind-reading goal.

References

1. Chang, C.Y., Hsu, S.H., Pion-Tonachini, L., Jung, T.P.: Evaluation of artifact subspace reconstruction for automatic artifact components removal in multi-channel EEQ recordings. IEEE Trans. Biomed. Eng. **67**(4), 1114–1121 (2019)
2. Delorme, A., Makeig, S.: EEGLAB: an open source toolbox for analysis of single-trial EEQ dynamics including independent component analysis. J. Neurosci. Methods **134**(1), 9–21 (2004). https://doi.org/10.1016/j.jneumeth.2003.10.009

3. Dmochowski, J.P., Sajda, P., Dias, J., Parra, L.C.: Correlated components of ongoing EEQ point to emotionally laden attention-a possible marker of engagement. Front. Hum. Neurosci. **6**, 112 (2012)
4. Ghosh, M.: The NATYASASTRA Ascribed to Bharata Muni, vol. I. Asiatic Society of Bengal,, Calcutta (1951)
5. Gulli, A., Pal, S.: Deep Learning with Keras. Packt Publishing Ltd., Mumbai (2017)
6. Hasson, U., Landesman, O., Knappmeyer, B., Vallines, I., Rubin, N., DJ., H.: Neurocinematics: the neuroscience of film. Projections **1**(2), 1 (2008)
7. Hejmadi, A., Davidson, R.J., Rozin, P.: Exploring Hindu Indian emotion expressions: evidence for accurate recognition by Americans and Indians. Psychol. Sci **11**, 183–187 (2000)
8. Lee, Y.Y., Hsieh, S.: Classifying different emotional states by means of EEQ-based functional connectivity patterns. PLoS ONE **9** (2014)
9. Mahmud, M., Kaiser, M.S., Hussain, A., Vassanelli, S.: Applications of deep learning and reinforcement learning to biological data. IEEE Trans. Neural Netw. Learn. Syt. **29**(6), 2063–2079 (2018)
10. Nair, V., Hinton, G.E.: Rectified linear units improve restricted boltzmann machines. In: Proceedings of the 27th International Conference on Machine Learning (ICML2010), pp. 807–814 (2010)
11. Nie, D., Wang, X.W., Shi, L.C., Lu, B.L.: EEQ-based emotion recognition during watching movies. Neural Eng.(NER) **2011**(5), 667–670 (2011)
12. Pandey, P., Miyapuram, K.P.: Brain2depth: Lightweight CNN model for classification of cognitive states from EEQ recordings (2021). arXiv preprint arXiv:2106.06688
13. Sonawane, D., Miyapuram, K.P., Rs, B., Lomas, D.J.: Guessthemusic: song identification from electroencephalography response. In: 8th ACM IKDD CODS and 26th COMAD, pp. 154–162 (2021)
14. Tripathi, R., Mukhopadhyay, D., Singh, C.K., Miyapuram, K.P., Jolad, S.: Characterization of functional brain networks and emotional centers using the complex networks techniques. In: International Conference on Complex Networks and Their Applications, pp. 854–867 (2019)

Searching for Unique Neural Descriptors of Primary Colours in EEG Signals: A Classification Study

Sara L. Ludvigsen, Emma H. Buøen, Andres Soler(✉), and Marta Molinas

Department of Engineering Cybernetics, Norwegian University of Science and Technology (NTNU), Trondheim, Norway
{sarall,emmahb}@stud.ntnu.no,
{andres.f.soler.guevara,marta.molinas}@ntnu.no

Abstract. Identifying unique descriptors for primary colours in EEG signals will open the way to Brain-Computer Interface (BCI) systems that can control devices by exposure to primary colours. This study is aimed to identify such unique descriptors in visual evoked potentials (VEPs) elicited in response to the exposure to primary colours (RGB: red, green, and blue) from 31 subjects. For that, we first created a classification method with integrated transfer learning that can be suitable for an online setting. The method classified between the three RGB classes for each subject, and the obtained average accuracy over 23 subjects was 74.48%. 14 out of 23 subjects were above the average level and the maximum accuracy was 93.42%. When cross-session transfer learning was evaluated, 86% of the subjects tested showed an average variation of 5.0% in the accuracy comparing with the source set.

Keywords: RGB colours · Riemannian classifier · Transfer learning

1 Introduction

Electroencephalography (EEG) signals are obtained from electrodes placed on the scalp recording the macroscopic neural activity. It is a non-intrusive method for recording brain signals, and in BCI systems it can be used by individuals with extreme motor disabilities to manipulate their surroundings. Colour recognition is a novel approach in this area, but has the advantage of being easily applied to control the surroundings. A smart home using colour cues to turn on and off light, open doors, etc. is an example of how to provide more freedom for individuals in their everyday life. Classifying the neural activity evoked by the RGB colour exposure can be enabled by identifying the key features that represent the evoked activity, however, they are often hidden in noise that can come from external sources (artifacts) and the background brain activity. Previous attempts have been made for RGB colour recognition. In [4], the authors identified the EEG signatures

S. Ludvigsen and E. H. Buøen—Equal contribution.

M. Mahmud et al. (Eds.): BI 2021, LNAI 12960, pp. 277–286, 2021.
https://doi.org/10.1007/978-3-030-86993-9_26

produced by the visual exposure to RGB colours. They observed that the difference in frequency response is a good classification signature. In [10] the intrinsic mode functions (IMFs) for Empirical mode decomposition (EMD) were used to identify features in the brain signals that describe the colour activity. The IMFs were used as input to classifiers such as Random Forest (RF) and Naive Bayes. Convolutional Neural Networks (CNNs) were also tried, but not with IMFs as input. Colour vs. none-colour was classified with an accuracy of up to 99% using EMD. The maximum accuracy obtained classifying between RGB colours was 63%, and the maximum average accuracy of 46% using CNNs. A similar attempt was conducted in [9] characterising the signals using discrete wavelet transform and EMD separately. The goal was to classify idle state versus colour exposure. Support vector machine (SVM) and RF were used as classifiers. The most consistent result was obtained using EMD-based features, classifying with an 92.3% accuracy. Another experiment was presented in [5], where a headband with 4 EEG dry electrodes (AF7, AF8, TP9, TP10) was used on eight subjects. The EEG signals were transformed using Morlet transformation and forward feature selection. It achieved an average accuracy of 72.0%, and the highest accuracy of 80.6% when classifying between the RGB colours with a RF classifier.

The scope of this work is to present a method that can be used in an online setting. The focus was therefore to find a methodology that is both fast and accurate in classifying among the RGB colours. EMD and Independent Component Analysis are time consuming operations, and were therefore not evaluated. The decision to use a Morlet wavelet to transform the data was made based on the analysis in Sect. 2.4. This technique was found advantageous to extract the peaks of several frequencies in the range 2–23 Hz as features. Recording EEG data requires expertise and time. If transfer learning is successful, it allows the reuse of data from previous recordings. Transfer learning across sessions was tested, it was done based on the Riemannian geometry classifiers that have been found suitable for transfer learning [6].

2 Materials and Methods

2.1 Data Recording and Protocol

The data used in this paper was recorded at the Aalto NeuroImaging facility at Aalto University (Finland). It was recorded using wet EEG electrodes in a high-end 3-layered magnetically shielded room. MEG measurements were recorded simultaneously, but not used in the results presented in this work. 64 electrodes were located on the head, four of which were EOG channels. Two of the EOG channels were placed on the front part of the head, one bipolar EOG channel was placed on the forehead, and below the left eye. The rest of the 60 channels were EEG channels located across the scalp. The placement was done using the international 10/10 system using a 64-channel cap from ANTNeuro, in https://www.ant-neuro.com/products/waveguard/electrode-layouts the 64 channel cap layout can be found. For all electrodes, the impedance was kept below 5k Ohm before recording. The subjects were placed in front of a screen that altered between presenting a RGB colour and a grey screen. The RGB colours were presented in a randomised order for 1.3 s each, and the grey screen was presented in a varying length of time to prevent adaptation of the brain. For each subject, at least 140 epochs of each colour were recorded. The subject also had three breaks during the recording, lasting one minute each. All the colours were presented in full-screen mode, and only during grey colour was a cross presented in the middle to keep the eyes of the subjects focused in the same area. Additionally, the subjects were asked to avoid blinking in the colours and try to blink only during grey.

2.2 Dataset

In total, 31 subjects were recorded. For the first recording of subjects 1–18 and subject 26, two of the occipital channels, Oz and O2, were flat. Therefore a second session with all the channels registering was recorded for these participants. The second session was no later than a week after the first session. The remaining 12 subjects participated only in one session. The following requirements were defined to include the subject in the dataset for classification.

1. None of the channels placed over the visual cortex is flat.
2. The subject had a correct behaviour during recording (e.g. looked at the screen, and kept its eyes open).
3. After pre-processing the data (see Sect. 2.3), and removing bad epochs, at least 60 epochs of each colour remains.

This resulted in the dataset consisting of 23 subjects in Table 1. 10-Fold cross-validation was used when calculating classification accuracy. For each subject, 90% of the epochs were used for training, and 10% for testing.

2.3 Data Pre-processing

The data was filtered between 0.1–40 Hz using a band-pass filter, the baseline for each epoch was chosen to be from −100 to 0 ms before stimuli were presented, and the data was re-referenced to the common average over all channels. All epochs containing a signal with an amplitude larger than 120 µV in the EEG channels and 150 µV in the EOG channels were rejected as bad epochs in order to remove artifacts such as blinks and muscular movement from the dataset. Additionally, the subjects were manually inspected for bad channels that were removed if found. The absolute value of the sample with the lowest value in an epoch was added to all samples in the epoch in order to shift the epoch above zero. If the lowest value was positive, it was subtracted from all samples in the epoch. As a final part of the pre-processing, the epochs were cropped to only contain the data between 50 and 450 ms after stimuli for feature extraction. All parameters used in pre-processing are listed in Table 2.

2.4 Analysis of Visual Evoked Potentials

The Visual Evoked Potentials (VEP) were extracted and visually inspected for each participant before shifting the epoch above zero. An example of a VEP is

Table 1. The dataset used in this project

Subject	Session	Red epochs	Green epochs	Blue epochs
02	2	134	135	135
03	2	129	124	120
05	2	83	81	82
06	2	134	137	133
07	2	108	110	102
08	2	119	116	115
11	2	122	127	123
13	2	132	129	131
14	2	128	126	126
15	2	103	108	101
16	2	118	126	129
18	2	140	139	139
19	1	114	96	94
20	1	135	137	136
21	1	76	66	69
23	1	125	125	120
24	1	106	113	106
25	1	116	104	108
26	2	120	119	127
28	1	136	136	133
29	1	120	121	117
30	1	117	118	115
31	1	139	135	133

shown in Fig. 1 where the plots correspond to the VEP of red colour from subject 2 session 2. Figure 1a shows the evoked response of all channels with corresponding topological-plots for the peaks at 82, 122, and 212ms. It can be seen that there are positive peaks in the nearest channels to the visual cortex, as well as negative peaks in the frontal channels. The strongest peaks were found in the channels at the occipital and parietal regions. This strong activation in those regions was seen for most colours in most subjects. It was, therefore, decided to only use channels P7, PO7, O1, POz, Oz, PO8, P8, and O2 when classifying. Figure 1b presents the VEPs of channel Oz of red colour. The black line represents the evoked of all red epochs, and the image above is the power plot of the activity evoked by red stimuli. There is an identifiable trend for the first 300 ms of the signals, where the peaks were found consistent throughout all epochs. These time ranges where the peaks are presented, were selected as the time region of interest for extracting features for classification. The features were extracted by transforming the EEG data with a Morlet wavelet of several frequencies, which is further explained in Sect. 2.5.

2.5 Feature Extraction

Only eight channels were used for feature extraction and classification. The channels are listed in Table 2. The preprocessed data in each channel was decomposed

Table 2. Parameters

Filter	0.1–40 Hz
Reject criteria	EEG: 120e−6, EOG: 150e−6
Baseline	−0.1–0.0 s
Crop	0.05–0.45 s
Channels	P7, PO7, O1, POz, Oz, PO8, P8, O2
Frequencies (Hz) used in CWT	2, 5, 8, 11, 14, 17, 20, 23
Number of cyclet in morlet wavelet	0.5

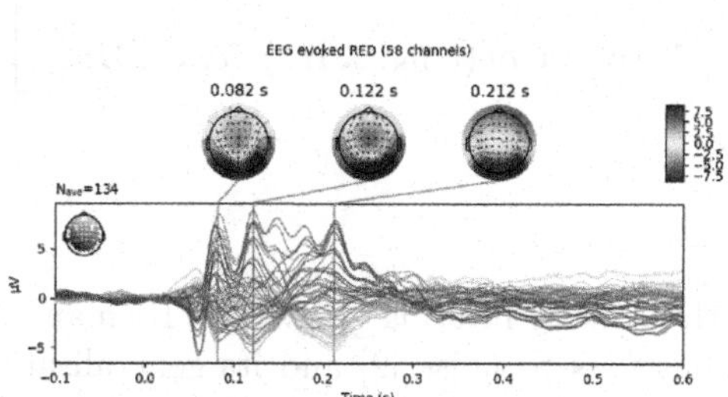

(a) Butterfly plot of the VEPs of red epochs for all channels

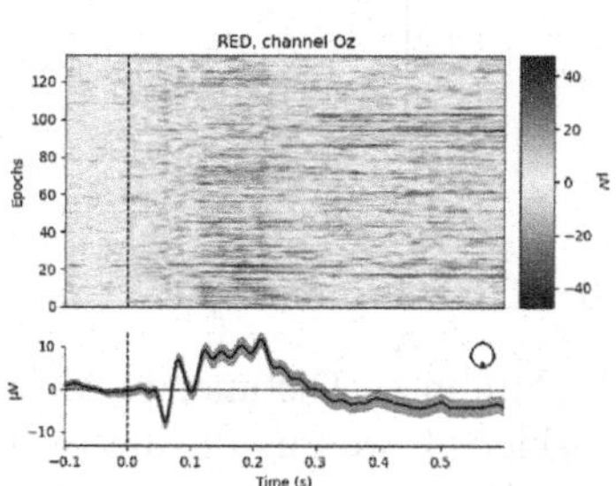

(b) VEPs of red epochs on channel Oz

Fig. 1. VEPs of subject 2 session 2 (Color figure online)

using a continuous wavelet transform (CWT) with a 0.5 cycles Morlet wavelet as the mother wavelet. The correlation between the signal and wavelet was calculated as follows.

$$CWT(a, b) = \frac{1}{|a|^{1/2}} \int_{-\infty}^{\infty} x(t)\psi(\frac{t-b}{a})dt \quad (1)$$

The decomposition was done using a built-in function in the MNE python library [7]. This function calculates the Morlet wavelet as follows.

$$\text{oscillation} = \exp(2j\pi ft) \quad (2) \qquad \text{gaussian envelope} = \exp(-t^2/(2\sigma^2) \quad (3)$$

$$w(t, f) = \text{oscillation} * \text{gaussian envelope} \quad (4)$$

With the normalisation factor given by

$$A = (\sqrt{0.5}\|w\|)^{\frac{-1}{2}} \quad (5)$$

$$w(t, f) = A\exp(2j\pi ft)\exp(-t^2/(2\sigma^2)) \quad (6)$$

The frequencies used are specified in Table 2. Each frequency decomposition in each channel was used as an input for a covariance matrix. Resulting in a 64 × 64 matrix (Eq. (9)). Where the covariance is defined as

$$Cov(X,Y) = E[(X - E[X])(Y - E[Y])] \quad (7) \qquad E[X] = \int_{-\infty}^{\infty} xf(x) \quad (8)$$

$$\mathbf{CVM} = \begin{bmatrix} Cov((ch_1, 2Hz), (ch_1, 2Hz)) & \dots & Cov((ch_1, 2Hz), (ch_8, 23Hz)) \\ Cov((ch_1, 5Hz), (ch_1, 2Hz)) & \dots & Cov((ch_1, 5Hz), (ch_8, 23Hz)) \\ \vdots & \ddots & \vdots \\ Cov((ch_2, 2Hz), (ch_1, 2Hz)) & \dots & Cov((ch_2, 2Hz), (ch_8, 23Hz)) \\ Cov((ch_2, 5Hz), (ch_1, 2Hz)) & \dots & Cov((ch_2, 5Hz), (ch_8, 23Hz)) \\ \vdots & \ddots & \vdots \\ Cov((ch_8, 23Hz), (ch_1, 2Hz)) & \dots & Cov((ch_8, 23Hz), (ch_8, 23Hz)) \end{bmatrix} \quad (9)$$

2.6 Classification

The Minimum Distance to Mean with geodesic filtering (FgMDM) Riemannian classifier [3] was used, due to its robustness to noise [2] and its generalisation capabilities [6].

In [6], the Riemannian distance (δ_G) was defined as the length of the geodesic between two symmetric positive definite matrices, $\mathbf{C}_1$ and $\mathbf{C}_2$, on a Riemannian manifold:

$$\delta_G(\mathbf{C}_1, \mathbf{C}_2) = \left\| \mathrm{Log}(\mathbf{C}_1^{-1/2}\mathbf{C}_2\mathbf{C}_1^{-1/2}) \right\|_F \quad (10)$$

where $\mathrm{Log}(\cdot)$ is the matrix logarithm. The Riemannian distance is invariant under congruence and invariant under inversion, which means that

$$\delta_G(\mathbf{X}\mathbf{C}_1\mathbf{X}^T, \mathbf{X}\mathbf{C}_2\mathbf{X}^T) = \delta_G(\mathbf{C}_1, \mathbf{C}_2) = \delta_G(\mathbf{C}_1^{-1}, \mathbf{C}_2^{-1}) \quad (11)$$

2.7 Transfer Learning

A challenge in BCI systems is to accurately classify one session data based on data from another session. This is due to the changes in impedance and electrode positioning is likely to vary each time the subject participates in a session.

The EEG signal, $\mathbf{x}(t)$, can be written as a linear combination of the sources of the signal, $\mathbf{s}(t)$:

$$\mathbf{x}(t) = \mathbf{A}\mathbf{s}(t), \quad (12)$$

where $\mathbf{A}$ is the mixing matrix [6]. The mixing matrix $\mathbf{A}$ is dependent upon the impedance and electrode placement. Let the covariance matrices $\mathbf{C}_i = \mathbf{A}\mathbf{S}_i\mathbf{A}^T$ and $\mathbf{C}_j = \mathbf{A}\mathbf{S}_j\mathbf{A}^T$ be representing class i and j, taken from the same session and subject. Let $\mathbf{Q}_i = \tilde{\mathbf{A}}\mathbf{S}_i\tilde{\mathbf{A}}^T$ and $\mathbf{Q}_j = \tilde{\mathbf{A}}\mathbf{S}_j\tilde{\mathbf{A}}^T$ be the covariance matrices taken from another session, with the same subject. Note that $\mathbf{A} \neq \tilde{\mathbf{A}}^T$, because the impedance level and electrode placement varies from session to session. These changes cause a shift in the EEG recording, which makes transfer learning difficult. Due to the congruence invariance property of the Riemannian distance between a pair of symmetric positive definite matrices, the distance between the covariance matrices in the source space are equal for both sessions, as shown in [6]:

$$\delta_G(\mathbf{C}_i, \mathbf{C}_j) = \delta_G(\mathbf{Q}_i, \mathbf{Q}_j) \tag{13}$$

The methods described in this section were implemented and tested in python by using `pyriemann` [1], `scikit-learn` [8] and `mne` [7] libraries.

3 Results

The accuracy of the classification in the results is described as a number between 0 and 1, with 1 as the highest accuracy. The standard deviation of the accuracy is included as "std" in the tables. All results were obtained when classifying between the three classes {Red, Green and Blue}.

3.1 RGB Classification

The RGB classification results are presented in Table 3, where the results correspond to the subjects in Table 1 that fulfilled all the criteria set Sect. 2.2. The average obtained across participants was 74.48% with a standard deviation of 7.5%, where more than 60% of the subjects obtained an accuracy value over the average. Where subject 14 obtained the highest accuracy of 93.42% and subject 31 the lowest with 54.02%. All the subjects obtained scores over the chance level. In addition, Table 4 shows the classification accuracy of all subjects with two sessions, where the channels Oz and O2 are excluded, as these channels were flat in session 1 for all subjects. The subjects still had to fulfill criteria 2) and 3) explained in Sect. 2.2.

3.2 Cross-Session Transfer Learning

Cross session transfer learning was evaluated for all subjects in Table 4 where both sessions had an accuracy above 60%. The subjects and results for transfer learning are presented in Table 5. Average accuracy was computed considering both sessions for the subject in Table 4, and the same procedure was done for standard deviation. The column marked "s1–s2" represents the accuracy obtained when session 1 is used for training, and session 2 is used for testing. Vice versa for the column marked "s2–s1". "diff is the difference between the average accuracy of both sessions, and the best performance for transfer learning.

Table 3. Result of RGB classification of subjects that fulfil all criteria.

Subject	FgMDM	std
s14r2	0.9342	0.056747
s02r2	0.9255	0.050247
s13r2	0.9208	0.021501
s21r1	0.8959	0.05084
s06r2	0.8515	0.050616
s29r1	0.8294	0.065617
s30r1	0.8158	0.0963
s26r2	0.8023	0.088092
s07r2	0.7813	0.108253
s19r1	0.7632	0.050098
s24r1	0.7564	0.085264
s11r2	0.7550	0.092997
s18r2	0.7512	0.09483
s23r1	0.7459	0.109585
s05r2	0.7318	0.084454
s20r1	0.7104	0.077408
s25r1	0.6705	0.110448
s08r2	0.6514	0.064902
s03r2	0.6351	0.07554
s28r1	0.5754	0.067562
s15r2	0.5451	0.096332
s16r2	0.5410	0.065429
s31r1	0.5404	0.061623
Average	**0.7448**	**0.0750**

Table 4. Results of RGB classification of all subjects with two sessions. Not including channel Oz and O2.

Subject	FgMDM	std
s02r1	0.8417	0.0493
s02r2	0.8142	0.0213
s03r1	0.5647	0.0561
s03r2	0.5526	0.0976
s04r1	0.5139	0.0780
s06r1	0.7625	0.0740
s06r2	0.7398	0.0489
s07r1	0.6493	0.1020
s07r2	0.7156	0.0963
s08r1	0.5471	0.0546
s08r2	0.6400	0.0769
s11r1	0.5857	0.0528
s11r2	0.6447	0.0987
s13r1	0.8188	0.0714
s13r2	0.8722	0.0680
s14r1	0.7125	0.0731
s14r2	0.7289	0.1085
s15r1	0.4232	0.0569
s15r2	0.5030	0.0626
s16r1	0.5209	0.0926
s16r2	0.4925	0.0786
s18r1	0.6379	0.0485
s18r2	0.7154	0.0713
s26r1	0.6439	0.0681
s26r2	0.6203	0.0487

Table 5. Results of cross-section transfer learning.

Subject	Avr. accuracy	Avr. std	s1–s2	s2–s1	diff.
02	0.8216	0.0471	0.8119	0.7825	0.0097
06	0,7487	0,0644	0,7253	0,7044	0,0234
07	0.6734	0.1010	0.6000	0.5138	0.0734
13	0.8416	0.0710	0.7679	0.7402	0.0737
14	0.7234	0.09825	0.6474	0.5843	0.0760
18	0.6765	0.0574	0.3373	0.4698	0.2067
26	0.6322	0.0605	0.6066	0.6108	0.0214

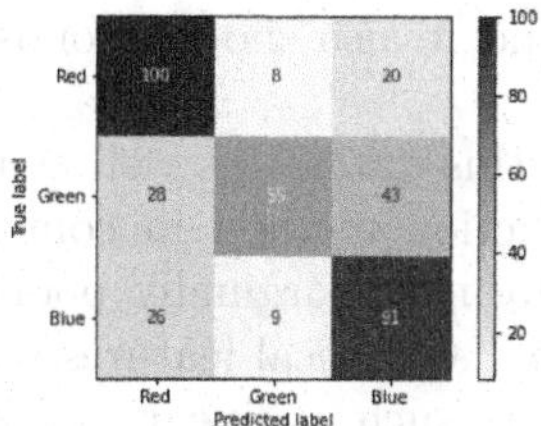

(a) Source = session 1, target = session 2.

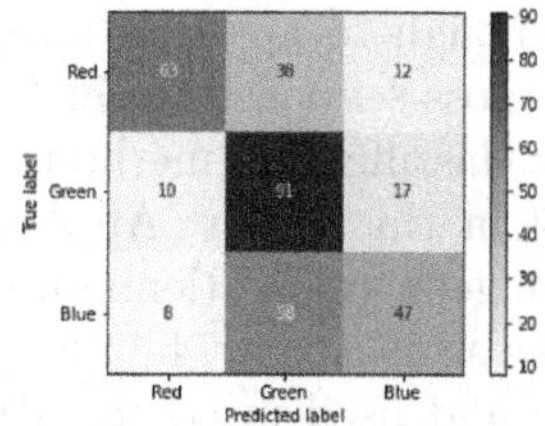

(b) Source = session 2, target = session 1.

Fig. 2. Session to session classifying for subject 14. (Color figure online)

4 Discussion and Conclusion

The results obtained show that using the correlation of the wavelet decomposition with the FgMDM Riemannian classifier for the VEP allowed to separate the colours in most of the subjects. All subjects scored above the chance level 33%, with the accuracy of the lowest performing subject at 54.04%. The average accuracy of 74.48%, which is significantly above the chance level. It clearly states that the features presented can be used to separate the responses of the RGB colours. By analysing the accuracy we can identify that from the subjects that scored at approximately 55%[1], the classifier might have been able to recognise at least *one* of the colours, and was guessing between the three classes on the remaining epochs. Similarly, the subjects that scored at approximately 77%[2], the classifier might have been able to recognise *two* of the colours, and guessing at the remaining 33% of the epochs.

The transfer learning test showed that the cross-session model can be used for classifying a different session. Six out of seven subjects obtained a difference lower than 7% when comparing training and testing between sessions with the use of the same session for training and testing. Even with the limited number of subjects with two sessions, we consider that the model is not guessing when classifying a session based on the training on the other. We consider that this aspect should be explored with more subjects in future works. When looking at the confusion matrix in Fig. 2a, it can be seen the classifier performed better at separating red and blue, while in Fig. 2b the classifier performed better when separating green. If training on both session 1 and session 2, testing on a session 3 might actually increase performance. Hence, transfer learning using more sessions should be explored as well. It is especially interesting that not any modification of the signal is needed when using a Riemannian FgMDM classifier for testing across-session, making it very convenient for offline modelling and online testing. From the features presented in this paper, the FgMDM classifier does separate between colours using EEG electrodes in a BCI model. It should

[1] Accuracy = $33\% + \frac{1}{3}66\% = 55\%$.
[2] Accuracy = $66\% + \frac{1}{3}33\% = 77\%$.

be easy enough to apply in an online setting, and it also shows promising for applying cross-session transfer learning.

Other classification methods were applied to this dataset as well as the one presented in this paper. An equal feature extraction method in combination with a tangent space Riemannian classifier performed marginally poorer with an average accuracy of 74.43%. Energy, fractal and statistical features were also extracted and used in combination with classifiers such as linear discriminant analysis with shrinkage (LDAs), RF and SVM. Of these, LDAs gave the highest average accuracy of 67.07%.

The accuracy obtained when classifying RGB-colours in this paper are higher than the accuracy obtained in [10] and [5] with an average accuracy of 46% and 70.2% respectively. However, the equipment for recording this dataset used gel based electrodes and impedance was controlled, contrary to [10] and [5], where dry electrodes were used.

References

1. Barachant, A., King, J.R.: pyriemann v0.2.2, June 2015. https://doi.org/10.5281/zenodo.18982
2. Barachant, A., Bonnet, S., Congedo, M., Jutten, C.: Riemannian geometry applied to BCI classification. In: Vigneron, V., Zarzoso, V., Moreau, E., Gribonval, R., Vincent, E. (eds.) LVA/ICA 2010. LNCS, vol. 6365, pp. 629–636. Springer, Heidelberg (2010). https://doi.org/10.1007/978-3-642-15995-4_78
3. Barachant, A., Bonnet, S., Congedo, M., Jutten, C.: Classification of covariance matrices using a Riemannian-based kernel for BCI applications. Neurocomputing **112**, 172 – 178 (2013). https://doi.org/10.1016/j.neucom.2012.12.039. Advances in artificial neural networks, machine learning, and computational intelligence
4. Bjørge, L.E., Emaus, T.: Identification of EEG-based signature produced by visual exposure to the primary colours RGB. Ph.D. thesis, NTNU (07 2017)
5. Chaudhary, M., Mukhopadhyay, S., Litoiu, M., Sergio, L., Adams, M.: Understanding brain dynamics for color perception using wearable EEG headband. In: Proceedings of 30th Annual International Conference on Computer Science and Software Engineering 2020 (08 2020)
6. Congedo, M., Barachant, A., Bhatia, R.: Riemannian geometry for EEG-based brain-computer interfaces; a primer and a review. Brain Comput. Interfaces **4**(3), 155–174 (2017). https://doi.org/10.1080/2326263X.2017.1297192
7. Gramfort, A., et al.: MEG and EEG data analysis with MNE-Python. Front. Neurosci. **7**(267), 1–13 (2013). https://doi.org/10.3389/fnins.2013.00267
8. Pedregosa, F., et al.: Scikit-learn: machine learning in Python. J. Mach. Learn. Res. **12**, 2825–2830 (2011)
9. Torres-García, A., Moctezuma, L., Molinas, M.: Assessing the impact of idle state type on the identification of RGB color exposure for BCI (02 2020). https://doi.org/10.5220/0008923101870194
10. Åsly, S.: Supervised learning for classification of EEG signals evoked by visual exposure to RGB colors. Ph.D. thesis, NTNU (06 2019). https://doi.org/10.13140/RG.2.2.13412.12165

Comparison Between Active and Passive Attention Using EEG Waves and Deep Neural Network

Sumit Chakravarty[1(✉)], Ying Xie[2], Linh Le[2], John Johnson[3], and Michael Hales[3]

[1] SPCEET Kennesaw State University, Kennesaw, USA
sumit.chakravarty@kennesaw.edu
[2] College of Computing and Software Engineering, Kennesaw State, Kennesaw, USA
[3] Wellstar College, Kennesaw State University, Kennesaw, USA

Abstract. A person's state of attentiveness can be affected by various outside factors. Having energy, feeling tired, or even simply being distracted all play a role in someone's level of attention. The task at hand can potentially affect the person's attention or concentration level as well. In terms of students who take online courses, constantly watching lectures and conducting these courses solely online can cause lack of concentration or attention. Attention can be considered in two categories: passive or active. Conducting active and passive attention-based trials can reveal different states of attentiveness. This paper compares active and passive attention trial results of the two states, wide awake and tired. This has been done in order to uncover a difference in results between the two states. The data analyzed throughout this paper was collected from DSI 24 EEG equipment, and the generated EEG is processed through a 3D Convolutional Neural Network (CNN) to produce results. Three passive attention trials and three active attention trials were performed on seven subjects, while they were wide awake and when they were tired. The experiments on the preprocessed data results in accuracies as high as 81.78% for passive attention detection accuracy and 63.67% for active attention detection accuracy, which shown a clear ability to separate between the two attention categories.

Keywords: Active attention · Classification · Electroencephalogram (EEG) waves · Passive attention · Preprocessing

1 Introduction

EEG has been used to study brain disorders [1], look at the attention levels of students [2], and assess a subject's mental workload [3]. Attention specific research in conjunction with EEG has also been conducted within recent studies. One way this research has been further developed was through the classification of attention using EEG. In [2], a protocol was developed in order to be able to classify human attention into states of attention and non-attention. This study resulted in classification accuracies as high as 92.8% and 92.4% [2]. Similarly, [4, 6] observed student attentiveness in order to

M. Mahmud et al. (Eds.): BI 2021, LNAI 12960, pp. 287–298, 2021.
https://doi.org/10.1007/978-3-030-86993-9_27

determine if students are actually attentive during class and resulted in classifications of attentive or inattentive. The study conducted in [4] found that when looking at attentive vs. inattentive, attentiveness is easier to classify and detect than inattentiveness. Focusing specifically on students and attention levels, [6] discovered a positive correlation that revealed students who participated more had a higher attention level. Another way attention and EEG research has been developed involves using convolutional neural networks to assess mental workload (active) tasks [3, 7]. These studies proposed the use of neural networks to allow for mental workload assessment classifications.

A review of previous experiments uncovered a gap in the study of attention/concentration, EEG, and neural networks. The results of mental workload assessments have never been compared to results of passive attention assessments or tasks when considering two states of attentiveness: wide awake and tired.

When considering a student's attentiveness while taking online courses, it is known that they tend to lose focus or get distracted at some point during the lecture. It is said that humans are supposed to learn in active environments [8]. Watching a lecture from a screen is considered a passive task. Combining that with another factor, like fatigue, decreases attention even more. Keeping students in mind, this paper was developed in order to ultimately help students in online courses maintain a high level of attention. Positive results should encourage students to take breaks during passive tasks or even completely stop and return to it another day in order to produce optimal results on their studies.

The main contribution of this paper is a comparison of active and passive tasks at different levels of concentration: wide awake and tired. This paper will analyze different datasets from active attention-based tasks (also referred to as "mental work-load tasks") and passive attention-based tasks ("attention tasks"). During data processing, functions of frequency analysis and time analysis will be applied and compared. Frequency analysis is achieved through the implementation of Fourier transformation. On the other hand, time analysis is performed by considering temporal vectors. Both analyses will also be combined through implementing Wigner Ville Transformation/Distribution (WVD) into the 3DCNN. In addition to frequency and time analysis, experiments consisting of selecting specific sensor channels from the data will be performed. The experiments discussed previously will be applied to the data in order to extend our research. A comparison of the EEG waves, produced by performing mental workload and attention tasks, will uncover a difference between the results of the two types of tasks while for the two states: wide awake and tired.

Both active and passive attention-based trials will be held to gather data. The active attention trial will be held while a subject is wide awake and again when the subject is tired. The same will be done for the passive attention trials. We will then use a 3DCNN to process and categorize the data. The data categories include: Active-Sleepy, Active-Awake, Passive-Sleepy, and Passive-Awake. We postulate that the results of the active attention trials will remain stable, whether the subject is wide awake or tired, whereas the passive attention trial results will have a noticeable difference. This is verified by the obtained results.

The following sections outline the remainder of this paper: first, the methods used to conduct this research, such as signal processing and data collection are discussed. The next section describes the different experiments performed on datasets ranging from raw data and preprocessed data. Section 4 provides an explanation of the results. Lastly, the conclusion closes out the paper.

2 Methods

2.1 Motivation

The focus of this project is to create a deep neural network that can accurately identify the perspective of attention of subjects. Specifically, the project calls for varying levels of difficulty in a range of tasks in order to gauge the attention level required for such tasks. The chosen method of testing the hypothesis for this project begins with creation of the methodology of data collection. The data collection plan, as shown in Fig. 8, consists of the following, each lasting for a duration of thirty seconds:

- A recording of mouse movement on a blank document
- An excerpt of Embraceable You by Sarah Vaughn
- An instructional video on creating functions in Python
- Three computer games that challenge memory, mathematical computation, and visual identification

The purpose of using the three computer games challenging various skills is to put stress on the subject's mental workload, which is "the amount of mental or cognitive resources required to meet the current task demands" [9]. Conducting tests that promote mental activity is also supported by [10], in which a study of ten subjects performing mathematical equations demonstrated that mental or motor activity spurs an alpha-blocking phenomenon. As the device records data, it is imperative that subjects remain still and try not to blink. Auxiliary movements such as these create artifacts in the data [15] that affect post analysis of the signals. These artifacts should be removed from the data through preprocessing before the data is used in an analytical capacity.

3 Data Preprocessing

Signal preprocessing is the preparation of signal data for analysis. It is believed that preprocessing data is crucial for "achieving high classification accuracy" [7] Recent studies that use raw EEG data have found much better performance that their counterparts using preprocessed data [13]. This project has been able to train the model and run tests with both, noticing a major difference in performance between tests with preprocessed data and tests with raw data. The following techniques are often used to achieve clean data:

3.1 Denoising

When collecting EEG data, there are a variety of variables that affect the signal. According to [7], it is crucial that EEG features are removed from data. This includes events like eye blinks, ECGs, and EOGs. For EEG signal recording specifically, blinking artifacts are a significant problem area [16]. Eye blinks are one of the most disruptive signal events to occur in EEG recordings, as found in a study on the sensitivity of EEG results from preprocessing methods [17]. The LARG approach to ICA is developed to remove blink artifacts, however its amplitude ratio of less than one creates the concern that "too much EEG signal has been removed" [17]. Blink artifacts can also become indistinguishable from regular data when evaluated by epochs [17].

3.2 Filtering

Filtering is a significant tool for preprocessing data because it allows interfering events to be easily identified and separated from the data points of actual interest. There are two types of filtering: adaptive and nonadaptive. Adaptive noise cancellers require a quality reference signal. For example, to cancel out noise created by eye blinks, strong data must be collected that reflects the signals from eye blinks by the subject. This data can then be used as a reference for the noise canceller.

A basic filter for EEG data is a low pass filter of about 50–70 Hz and a high pass filter less than or equal to 0.5 Hz. High-pass filtering is beneficial for removing EOG's because they typically occur at low frequencies [11]. Similar studies use a high pass filter of 1 Hz [18, 9], as recommended by EEGLAB.

3.3 Feature Extraction

Feature extraction is the classification and removal of informative features from the dataset. The features that can be removed are temporal, frequency domain, and time- frequency features. For temporal feature extractions, the methods used include amplifying raw EEG signals, autoregressive parameters, and Hjorth parameters [20].

3.4 Re-referencing

Re-referencing is a form of preprocessing that is used specifically for EEG data by averaging the signals from opposite nodes. This method is used to counteract the appearance of asymmetric spatial distribution with signals that are symmetric.

The main idea of re-referencing is that when the reference nodes are added together, they result in 0. This is based on Ohm's law and is attributed to the idea that for a positive current from the electrical source, there is a responding negative current [21]. For EEG data collection electrodes, the nodes that are most used to create this optimal average reference include Cz, TP10, or earlobe links.

3.5 Deep Learning

The core of this project is to design and exploit the ability of the 3DCconvolutional Neural Network to accurately identify the data sets according to the state of consciousness of the subjects and whether the task they were performing was active or passive. Deep learning is a form of representation learning, which is "a set of methods that allows a machine to be fed with raw data and to automatically discover the representations needed for detection or classification" [22]. For this project, the 3DCNN consisted of six intermediate layers and one output layer as enumerated below (Fig. 1):

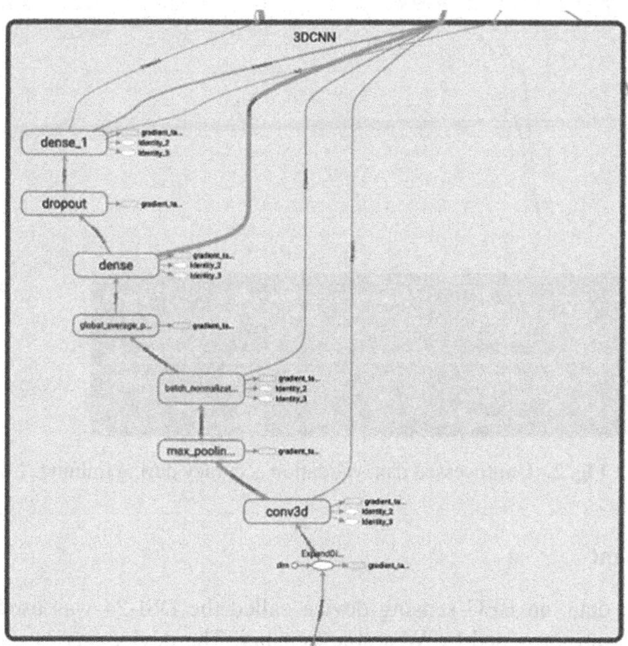

Fig. 1. – 3DCNN model.

3D Convolution (64 Filters, Input Kernel Size, ReLU)
3D max pooling
Batch normalization
3D global average pooling
512-unit Dense (ReLU)
Dropout
Output layer: Dense (Sigmoid)

Layers can go from four to thirty-two in number; However, it has been found that EEG data is best reviewed in deep learning algorithms with shallow neural networks [13]. The neural network used in this project is a convolutional neural network (CNN). For this project, the 3DCNN performs classification on its own, receiving previously preprocessed data exported from the EEGLAB module (Fig. 2).

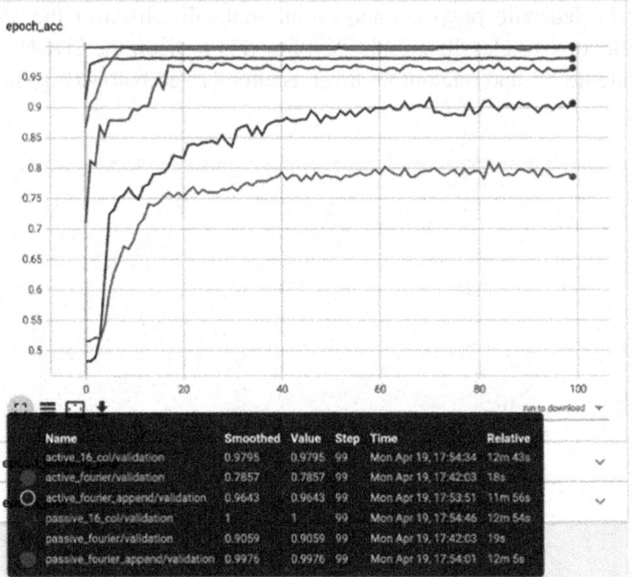

Fig. 2. Unprocessed data validation accuracy during training.

3.6 Equipment

To collect the data, an EEG sensing device called the DSI-24 was used along with recording software provided by Wearable Sensing. The device has 21 electrodes and provides coverage from the forehead to just above the nape of the neck.

4 Experiments

Experiments were conducted on several subjects. Subject were non-linear in identity and belong in the age range from 18–22 years old. A similar study pointed out that variations in gender and educational background could affect the outcome of the data. For example, "female skulls have light skull structures" which can result in a stronger signal for female subjects, when compared to male subjects [9]. Each of the subject's voluntarily agreed to participate and provided a signature as written consent. Recruitment for the study was done through oral transmission. The details of the experiment were explained to each subject before beginning and subjects were frequently asked to provide verbal feedback on their comfort level. Subjects completed all tasks in a seat position, about 2–3 feet away from the device displaying the stimulation material. The full data collection plan was followed with each subject under two separate states of mind: once as they were alert, and once again when they reported that they felt tired. The state of a subjects' consciousness during recording is subjective as it was self-reported. The test conducted can be broken into the four groups: Active Sleepy vs Active Awake, Passive Sleepy vs Passive Awake, and Comparison of Active vs Passive (Fig. 3).

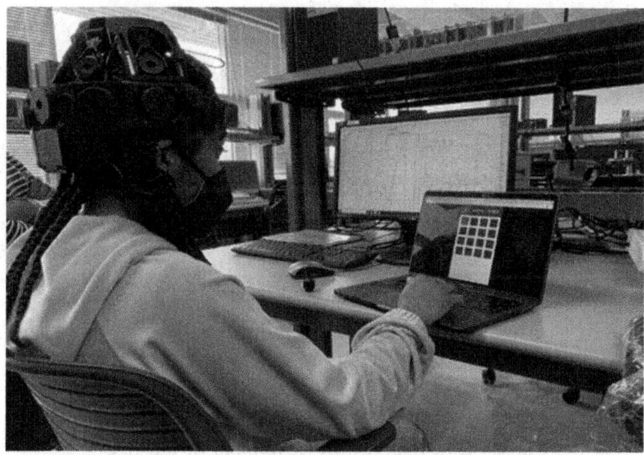

Fig. 3. A subject conducting an active attention-based trial.

5 Results

Different experiments performed on both raw and preprocessed data. The results explained below were retrieved from the following experiments: Active Sleepy vs Active Awake, Passive Sleepy vs Passive Awake, and Comparison of Active vs Passive.

5.1 Raw Data Results

To start off, experiments were first performed on raw unprocessed data. Throughout the process of model development, several tests were conducted on the raw data. These tests included reducing the number of sensor channels, selecting nodes from specific regions on the headset, expanding the Fourier transformation bands, and implementing the Wigner Ville Transformation/Distribution (WVD).

When reducing the sensor channels, tests went from using 20 nodes to 16, 12, 9, 6, 4, all the way down to only 3 nodes. The nodes used in these experiments were chosen randomly. After testing all these different sensor channel ranges, we found that the using 16 nodes produced the highest accuracy from our model: 97.75% Active Validation Accuracy and 100% Passive Validation Accuracy. These were some of the highest accuracies seen among all tests. The lowest Active accuracy percent came from only using four nodes, while the lowest Passive accuracy occurred with three nodes. See Fig. 4 for additional results.

Other tests included choosing nodes from specific regions, like the front, back, left, and right areas of the headset. For these experiments, groups of two and four nodes from each section was chosen and ran through the model. Amongst these experiments, the highest accuracy came from intentionally using two nodes from the front area. These percentages include 80.49% Active Validation Accuracy and 81.35% Passive Validation Accuracy, as shown in Fig. 5.

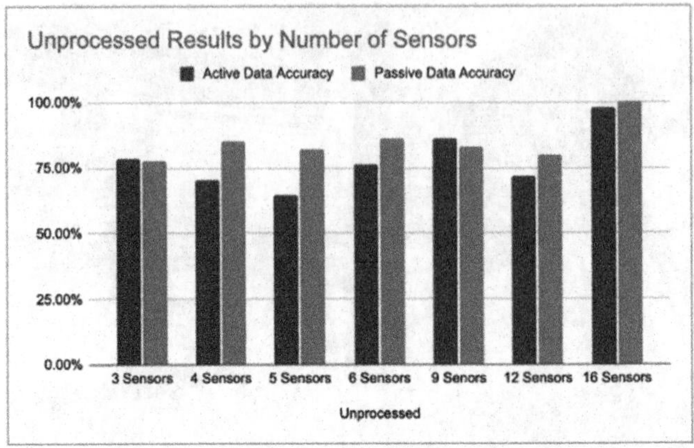

Fig. 4. Raw data results by number of sensors.

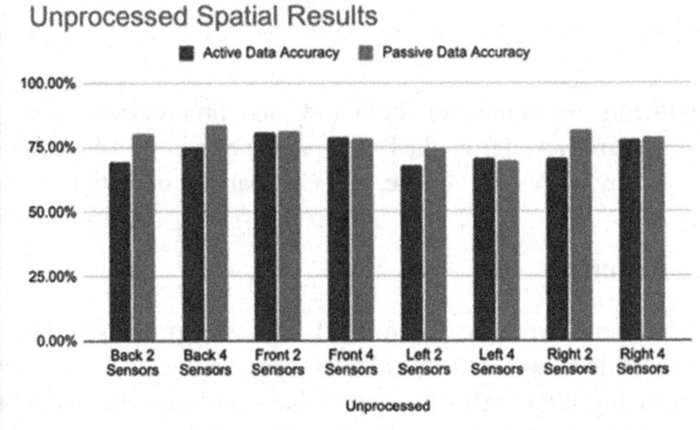

Fig. 5. Raw data spatial results.

The last experiment conducted on the raw data involved implementation of the Wigner Ville Transformation/Distribution (WVD). This transformation was implemented in order to see if it produced more accurate results than the Fourier transformation. WVD had a percentage of 56.96% Active Validation Accuracy and 56.99% Passive Validation Accuracy. Compared to the tests ran on Fourier transformation, WVD is more accurate than Fourier transformation. The WVD results can be seen in the "Time-Frequency" section of the graph in Fig. 6.

5.2 Preprocessed Data Results

The preprocessed data was tested after all raw data experiments were performed. Preprocessed data experiments covered the same areas as raw data. To reiterate, these experiments included reducing the number of sensor channels, selecting nodes from specific

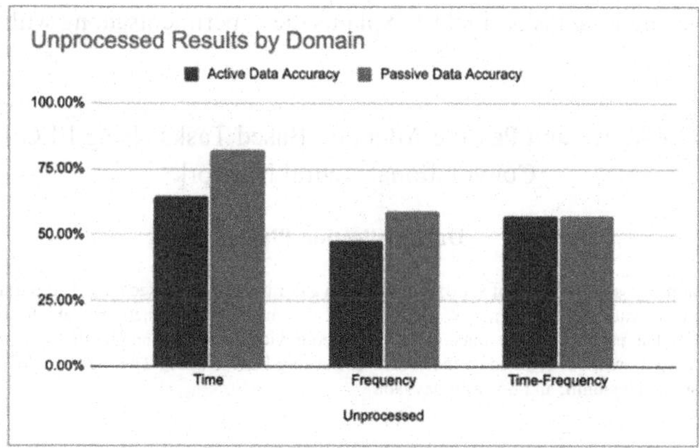

Fig. 6. Raw data domain results.

regions on the headset, expanding the Fourier transformation bands, and implementing the Wigner Ville Transformation/Distribution (WVD).

Reducing the number of sensor channels provided similar results in both raw and preprocessed data. Like the raw data results, preprocessed data performed the best with the use of 16 nodes. The percentages for 16 sensor channels were 80.15% Active Validation Accuracy and 88.42% Passive Validation Accuracy. For additional results, refer to Fig. 7.

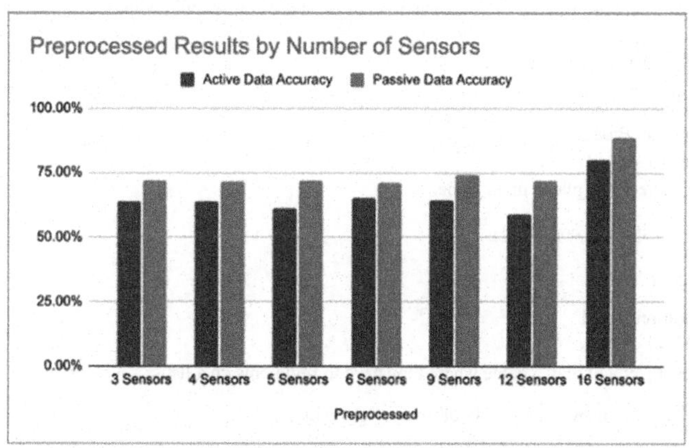

Fig. 7. Preprocessed data results by number of sensors.

5.3 Overall Results

The experiments conducted in our study covered a wide range of topics related to EEG and attention, in order to test what could be done with the data we collected. The experiments outlined in Index 1 are the main focus of our research: comparing active attention tasks to passive attention tasks. Table 1 explains the experiments along with their results in detail.

Comparison of Active and Passive Attention Based Tasks Using EEG Waves with Convolutional Neural Network

Data Collection Plan

Our data collection process will consist of six trials, each with a duration of thirty seconds. These trials are broken up into two categories: Attention and Mental Workload to test various everyday functions that will trigger brain activity. We will conduct each trial twice, once in a state of being wide awake and another in the state of being sleepy. The brain activity will be recorded by the Wearable Sensing EEG headset. The trials will be conducted by Alyssa Myers, Jasmine Hemphill, and Sowmya Javvadi.

Attention Trials

Trial 1 – Eye Tracking

- Concentration Based
- Duration: 30 seconds
- The test subject will look at a white screen and follow the movements of a computer mouse.

Trial 2 – Listening to Music

- Concentration Based
- Duration: 30 seconds
- The test subject will listen to a song with their eyes closed.

Trial 3 – Watching a Video

- Concentration Based
- Duration: 30 seconds
- The test subject will watch a video explaining how to write a program (coding)

Mental Workload Trials

Trial 4 – 2048 Game

- Concentration Based
- Duration: 30 seconds
- The test subject will play a math game.

(https://www.coolmathgames.com/0-2048)

Trial 5 – I Spy Game

- Concentration Based
- Duration: 30 seconds
- The test subject will play a game where they have to find items on a list.

(https://www.sporcle.com/games/Stanford0008/i-spy-4-clickable)

Trial 6 – Memory Cards

- Concentration Based
- Duration: 30 seconds
- The test subject will watch a pattern flash across the screen, and they have to try and repeat that pattern.

(https://www.assessmentday.com/free/gamified/memory-cards/memory-cards.html)

Fig. 8. Data collection plan.

Table 1. Explanation of research experiments with results

Index experiment	Result
1. Active attention state differentiation versus passive attention state	Models were better able to differentiate passive task energy state than active task energy state
2. Effect of the number of sensors on the accuracy of model prediction results	As the number of sensors decreased so did model accuracy. However, even with as few as three sensors, models maintained acceptable accuracy
3. Effect of the location of groups of sensors on the accuracy of model	The sensors at the front of the head
4. Effect of band size on the accuracy of models trained using Fourier transformed data	For unprocessed data, fewer bands yielded greater accuracy. For processed data, the number of bands had little effect on accuracy
5. Effect of preprocessing used on the accuracy of model results	Data processed using MNE-Python yielded greater accuracy
6. Effect of the number of subjects on the accuracy of model prediction results	For unprocessed data, fewer subjects resulted in greater accuracy. For preprocessed data, the number of subjects had little effect on accuracy

5.4 Conclusion

Whether a subject is alert or fatigued, the mental workload will still use the same amount of resources during tasks that require active attention. The mental workload seems to be exacerbated during passive tasks when a subject is tired. This is understood by the accuracy of the 3DCNN when classifying the data. The 3DCNN has a more difficult time deciphering between active tasks that were performed when the subject was alert versus when they were sleepy, than the passive task counterpart. From this result, it can be understood that students who are watching lectures or performing other passive tasks will see a decrease in efficient learning when they are tired. However, students who are performing active tasks will be more engaged whether they are tired or wide awake. It is still recommended that students get plenty of rest each night, as there are major wellness benefits associated with obtaining more than 6 h of sleep.

Appendix

A GitHub repository has been created for the 3DCNN code and data used throughout this study. Please visit the following link to view: https://github.com/mkwarman/Active-Passive-Attention-3DCNN-Classification.

References

1. Hassan, R.: Human attention recognition with machine learning from brain-EEG signals. In: 2nd IEEE Eurasia Conference on Biomedical Engineering, Healthcare, and Sustainability (2020)
2. Alirezaei, M., Sardouie, S.H.: Detection of human attention using EEG signals. In: 24th National and 2nd International Iranican Conference on Biomedical Engineering, pp. 1–5
3. Zhang, P.: (2019)
4. Liu, N.: (2013)
5. Shi, L., Ko, M.L., Ko, G.Y.P.: Retinoschisin facilitates the function of L-type voltage-gated calcium channels (2017)
6. Sezer, M.: Avârız Kayıtlarına Göre XVII. ve XVIII. Yüzyıllarda Karinabad Kazâsı (2018)
7. P: (2019). https://news.harvard.edu/gazette/story/2019/09/study-shows-that-students-learn-more-when-taking-part-in-classrooms-that-employ-active-learning-strategies/Accessed
8. Elsayed, N., Saad, Z., Bayoumi, M.: Brain computer interface: EEG signal preprocessing issues and solutions. Int. J. Comput. Appl. **169**(3), 12–16 (2017). https://doi.org/10.5120/ijca2017914621
9. Roy, Y.: Deep learning-based electroencephalography analysis: a systematic review. J. Nueral Eng.
10. Motomura, S., Tanaka, H., Nakamura, S.: Sequential attention-based detection of semantic incongruities from EEG while listening to speech. In: 42nd Annual International Conference of the IEEE Engineering in Medicine & Biology Society, pp. 268–271 (2020)
11. Subramaniyam, N.: (2018). https://sapienlabs.org/pitfalls-of-filtering-the-eeg-signal/
12. Arvaneh, M., Tanaka, T.: (2018)
13. Delorme, A., Makeig, S.: EEGLAB: an open source toolbox for analysis of single- trial EEG dynamics including independent component analysis. J. Neurosci. Methods **134**(1), 9–21 (2004)
14. Luazon, F.Q.: An introduction to deep learning. In: 11th International Conference on Information Sciences, Signal Processing and their Applications: Special Sessions (2012)
15. Gupgta, S., Singh, H.: Preprocessing EEG signals for direct human-system interface. In: Proceedings IEEE International Joint Symposia on Intelligence and Systems (1996)

An Image-Enhanced Topic Modeling Method for Neuroimaging Literature

Lianfang Ma[1,2,3], Jianhui Chen[1,2,3](✉), and Ning Zhong[1,2,3,4]

[1] Faculty of Information Technology, Beijing University of Technology, Beijing 100124, China
[2] Beijing International Collaboration Base on Brain Informatics and Wisdom Services, Beijing 100124, China
[3] Beijing Key Laboratory of MRI and Brain Informatics, Beijing 100124, China
chenjianhui@bjut.edu.cn
[4] Department of Life Science and Informatics, Maebashi Institute of Technology, Maebashi, Gunma 371-0816, Japan

Abstract. Topic modeling based on neuroimaging literature is an important approach to aggregate world-wide research findings for decoding brain cognitive mechanism, as well as diagnosis and treatment of brain and mental diseases, artificial intelligence researches, etc. However, existing neuroimaging literature mining only focused on texts and neglects brain images which contain a large amount of topic information. Following the writing and reading habits combining images with texts, we present in this paper an image-enhanced LDA (Latent Dirichlet Allocation), which extracts literature topics from both neuroimaging images and full texts. Combining topics from fMRI brain regions activation images with topics from full texts to model neuroimaging literatures more accurately. On the one hand, topics related brain cognitive mechanism can be pertinently extracted from activated brain images and their descriptions. On the other hand, topics from activated brain images can be integrated with topics from full text to model neuroimaging literature more accurately. The experiments based on actual data has preliminarily proved effectiveness of proposed method.

Keywords: Topic modeling · Literature mining · Image-enhanced LDA

1 Introduction

A series of important brain projects, such as Human Connectome Project [1], Adolescent Brain and Cognitive Development (ABCD) [2], and UK Biobank [3], have been launched to harness brain big data, especially neuroimaging data, for modeling cognitive functions of the brain. However, creating a detailed map of brain cognitive mechanism is involved with characterization of numerous entities, and it is difficult to be completed only depending on a data-driven approach in a or several laboratories. It is necessary to aggregate world-wide research findings.

M. Mahmud et al. (Eds.): BI 2021, LNAI 12960, pp. 299–309, 2021.
https://doi.org/10.1007/978-3-030-86993-9_28

Neuroimaging literature mining provides a practical approach to realize such an aggregation. In recent year, neuroimaging articles are growing fast. Taking only fMRI (functional Magnetic Resonance Imaging) as an example, there are 482 relevant articles have been published in the journal PLoS One in 2018. Many researches [4–7] have focused on knowledge or information extraction from neuroimaging literature for systematically decoding brain cognition. Related researches have brought enormous influences in psychology, neuroscience and artificial intelligence. For example, the statistical data on the Neurosynth platform shows that 14371 Neurosynth-based articles had been published by July 2018.

However, existing researches of neuroimaging literature mining only focus on texts. A large number of neuroimaging images in literature are neglected. In fact, these images are closely related to literature topics. Extracting information from neuroimaging images and their description texts is very important for not only decoding brain cognition but also modeling literature topics. Based on the above observations, this paper proposes a new image-enhanced topic modeling method of neuroimaging literature, called Image-enhanced LDA, which combines neuroimaging images and full texts to extract literature topics. The rest of the paper is structured as follows: Previous work related to topic modeling is outlined in Sect. 2. The proposed the image-enhanced LDA method is detailed in Sect. 3. Experiments are performed to evaluate the effectiveness of proposed method in both systematically decoding brain cognition and modeling literature topics in Sect. 4. There is a briefly conclusion in Sect. 5.

2 Related Work

Topic modeling learns meaningful expressions of texts from document sets [8] and is basic work in text semantic analysis [9] and text mining [10]. The LDA model [11] is the most widely used probabilistic topic model. It detects the global semantic topic structure and gives topics of each document in the form of probability distribution. In order to effectively use the word order and textual structure for document modeling, various improved LDA models have been developed. SentenceLDA [12] introduced the information of textual structures and word dependence into topic modeling for achieving the higher topic granularity. LFTM (Latent Feature Topic Modeling) [13] integrated quantitative contextual information to extend the traditional LDA and DMM (Dirichlet Multinomial Mixture) models for improving the topic consistency evaluation. The generative topic embedding model [14] mined word collocation patterns from both the global document and the local context for generating coherent topics. In order to improve semantics and comprehensibility of topics, domain knowledge was integrated into topic modeling. Probase-LDA [15] combined LDA with the large-scale probabilistic knowledge base to improve semantic consistency and accuracy of topics. MicroASM (Micro Aspect Sentiment Model) [16] introduced the external seed dictionary into topic modeling for obtaining rich semantic topics.

In recent years, topic modeling based on deep neural network has become a research hot spot. Related researches used the deep neural network to model the context for overcoming various shortcomings of traditional probabilistic topic models, including poor model scalability, poor topic semantic coherence, insufficient feature expression ability [17]. TopicRNN (Recurrent Neural Network) used RNN to capture remote semantic dependency between potential topics for generating reasonable topics. TE-LSTM+SC (Topic-Enhanced LSTM neural network model with topic similarity constraint) [18] used LSTM (longCshort-term memory) to capture contextual features of textual sequences for obtaining potential semantic topics as diverse as possible.

Topic modeling is also a core research issue of neuroimaging literature mining. Neurosynth [19] recognized domain terms based on frequency. Poldrack et al. [4] identified literature topics by using LDA. Alhazmi et al. [6] extracted topic words based on frequency and constructed relations between semantic spaces of topics and brain activated regions by using correspondence analysis and hierarchical clustering.

Recognizing brain cognitive mechanism, including cognitive functions, activated brain regions and their relations, are the primary purpose of topic modeling on neuroimaging literature. Though information is mainly contained in neuroimaging images and related descriptions, existing researches on topic modeling of neuroimaging literature only focused on literature texts. Because abstracts and full texts of literature describe the whole research, topics obtained by performing probabilistic topic models on texts often contain information unrelated to brain cognitive mechanism. This led that further processing has to be added after topic modeling. For example, Poldrack et al. used the terms of Cognitive Atlas (http://www.cognitiveatlas.org) to filter the topics obtained by LDA. Furthermore, the topic information contained in neuroimaging images and their descriptions is also crucial to understand the whole literature. Hence, it should be combined with topics obtained from full texts for modeling neuroimaging literature.

3 Methodology

Based on the above observations, this paper proposes the image-enhanced LDA which extracts literature topics from both neuroimaging images and full texts. As shown in Fig. 1, the whole method includes two steps: topic learning from images is to extract topics related to activated brain areas from neuroimaging images, other steps is that topic learning from texts is to extract topics from texts in literature. The details will be introduced in the following subsections.

3.1 Topic Learning from Images

Topic learning from images is to extract topics related to activated brain areas from neuroimaging images in literature. This paper adopts the image caption generation technology [20] to complete this step. The overall architecture is shown in Fig. 2 and includes the following two phases.

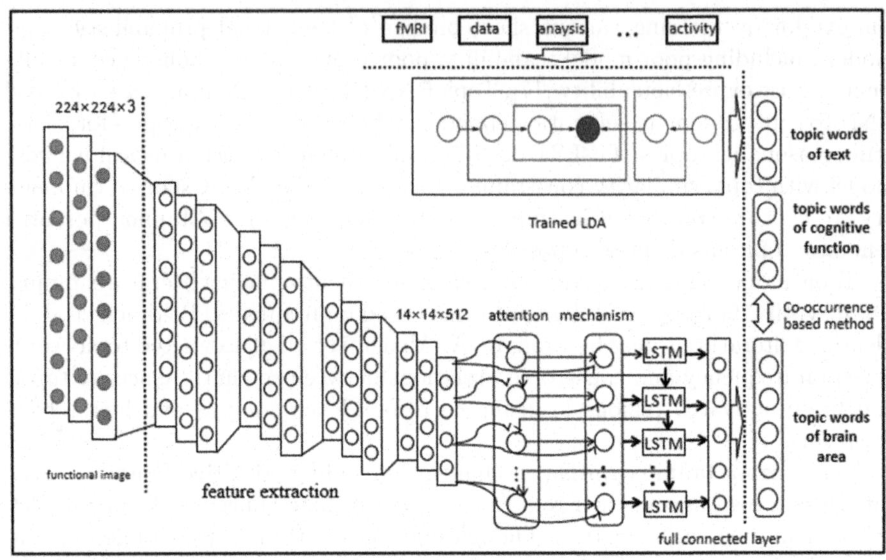

Fig. 1. The architecture of image-enhanced LDA.

The first phase is encoding which extracts a group of feature vectors from the input neuroimaging image I to represent different parts of image. CNN is used to realize this extraction. After encoding, I can be transformed into the following D-dimension feature vectors:

$$I = \{i_1, i_2, \cdots, i_L\},\ i_i \in R^D \tag{1}$$

where i denotes the ith feature vectors, L denotes total number of extracts feature vectors.

The second phase is decoding which generates a caption for each input fMRI brain image. A caption can be encoded as a sequence of $1 - of - K$ encoded words:

$$C = \{c_1, c_2, \cdots, c_L\},\ c_i \in R^K \tag{2}$$

where K is the size of the vocabulary and L is the length of the caption. As shown in Fig. 2, this paper adopts the architecture combining the attention and LSTM to generate the caption C based on I. The process can be described as follows:

$$\begin{pmatrix} i_t \\ f_t \\ o_t \\ g_t \end{pmatrix} = \begin{pmatrix} \sigma \\ \sigma \\ \sigma \\ \tanh \end{pmatrix} T_{D+m+n,n} \begin{pmatrix} Ec_{t-1} \\ h_{t-1} \\ \hat{z}_t \end{pmatrix} \tag{3}$$

$$c_t = f_t \odot c_{t-1} + i_t \odot g_t \tag{4}$$

$$h_t = o_t \odot \tanh(c_t) \tag{5}$$

where i_t, f_t, o_t, g_t, h_t are the input, forget, memory, output, and hidden state of LSTM, m and n denote the dimensionality of embedding and LSTM, $E \in R^{m\times K}$ is an embedding matrix. $\hat{z} \in R^D$ is the context vector capturing the visual information associated with a particular input location. $\hat{z}_t$ is a dynamic representation of the relevant part of the image input at time t and can be calculated as follows:

$$\hat{Z}_t = \phi(\{i_i\}, \{\alpha_i\}) \tag{6}$$

where α_i is the weight of i_i and computed by an attention model, and ϕ is a function that returns a single vector given the set of feature vectors and corresponding weight value. They are calculated by using deterministic "Soft" attention [20].

Based on the generated captions of neuroimaging images in literature, the topic word related to activated brain region can be collected to construct a topic word set of activated brain regions as follows:

$$Bra = \{bra_1 \cdots bra_p\} \tag{7}$$

where each bra_1 is a topic word of activated brain region. Because there are standard terminology dictionaries about brain regions, recognizing entities about activated brain regions from image captions can directly adopt the dictionary-based method.

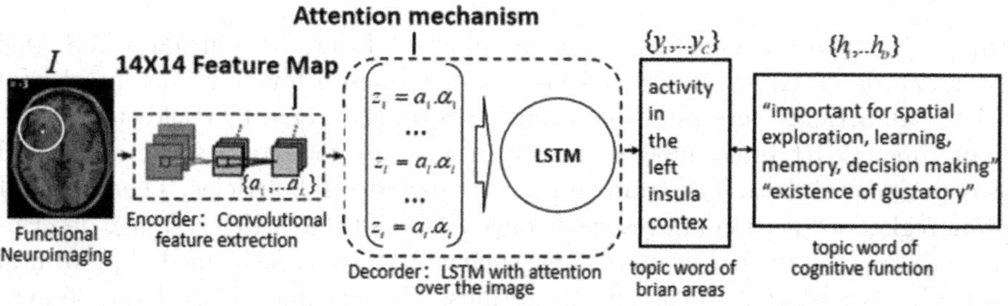

Fig. 2. The flow diagram of topic learning from images.

3.2 Topic Learning from Texts

Topic learning from texts is to extract topics from texts in literature. It includes two sub-steps: topic learning from image descriptions and topic learning from full texts.

Topic learning from image descriptions is to extract topics from the description texts corresponding to neuroimaging images. As stated above, recognizng brain cognitive mechanism are the primary purpose of topic modeling on neuroimaging literature. Topics obtained from fMRI brain image contain information about activated brain regions. The corresponding cognitive states are often contained in image descriptions. This paper adopts the co-occurrence-based method [5] to extract topics related to cognitive states from description texts. The co-occurrence window is set as a single sentence and the connected words include "reflect", "activate", "denote", etc. Different from brain regions, cognitive states lack a complete term dictionary. This paper uses the BiLSTM-CNN (Convolutional Neural Networks) model [21] to recognize entities of cognitive states. And then, a topic word set of cognitive states can be constructed as follows:

$$Cog = \{cog_1 \cdots cog_q\} \tag{8}$$

where cog_j is a topic word of cognitive state. Topic learning from full texts is to extract topics from the full texts of literature. LDA is adopted to obtain the following topics:

$$T = \{t_1 \cdots t_k\} \tag{9}$$

where each t_l is a topic words. Finally, the image-enhanced literature topics can be obtained by combining three types of topic words:

$$LiteratureTopics = \{Bra, Cog, T\} \tag{10}$$

4 Experiments and Evaluation

4.1 Experimental Data

Functional neuroimaging articles were crawled from the journal PLoS One by keywords "fMRI", "functional magnetic resonance imaging" or "functional MRI". All articles were published from 2018 to 2019. Select articles with more than three fMRI brain images. Finally, there are 130 articles were collected as experimental data. The training data set includes 100 articles. There are 314 brain regions activation images were collected from these articles. Image description related to activated brain regions, such as "Activity in the medial prefrontal cortex", were selected as the image captions. The test data set includes 30 articles with 108 brain regions activation images and their descriptions.

4.2 Baseline Methods

This paper chose four probabilistic topic models, including LDA, MicroASM, LF-LDA (Latent Feature-LDA) and LF-DMM, as baseline methods to verify the effectiveness of the proposed method on improving probabilistic topic modelling of neuroimaging literature. All baseline methods were performed on the full text of literature.

4.3 Experimental Result

Topic Learning from Images and Corresponding Descriptions. Different from existing probabilistic topic models, the proposed image-enhanced LDA extracts topic from images and corresponding descriptions. Topic learning from images can generate captions of fMRI brain regions activation images, which describe the topic information about activated brain regions. Topic words of brain regions can be extracted from these captions by using the dictionary-based method. Figure 3 gives the part of generated captions of activated brain regions [22,23]. Based on these captions, a groups of topic words about brain regions can be obtained. As shown in Fig. 3, not only a single activated brain region, such as "ventral striatum", "amygdala", but also multiple activated brain regions, such as "superior temporal gyrus, lingual gyrus" can be identified. Finally, captions of 64 images can be generated correctly. The precision rate is 59.3%.

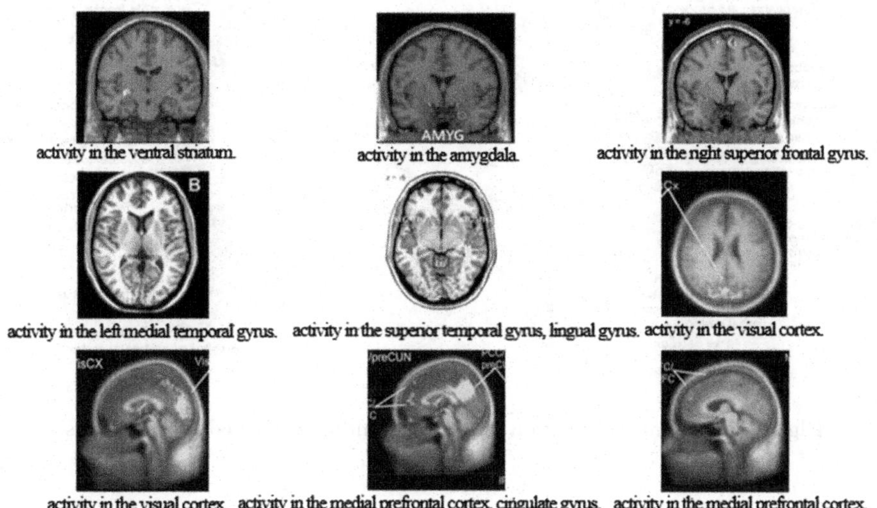

Fig. 3. The captions of brain activation regions generated by topic learning from images.

Topic learning from descriptions can extract topics about cognitive function states and identify relations between cognitive function and activated brain regions. The part of results is shown in Fig. 4. The information of brain cognitive mechanism is the primary purpose of topic modeling on neuroimaging literature. As shown in Fig. 4, a systematic view of brain cognition can be obtained by combining topic learning from images and corresponding descriptions. It shows the brain areas in the right, and some cognitive function or related elements (cognitive experiment elements)in the left. It suggests that the processed method can be effective to extract topics related brain cognitive mechanism by mining mixed neuroimaging literature.

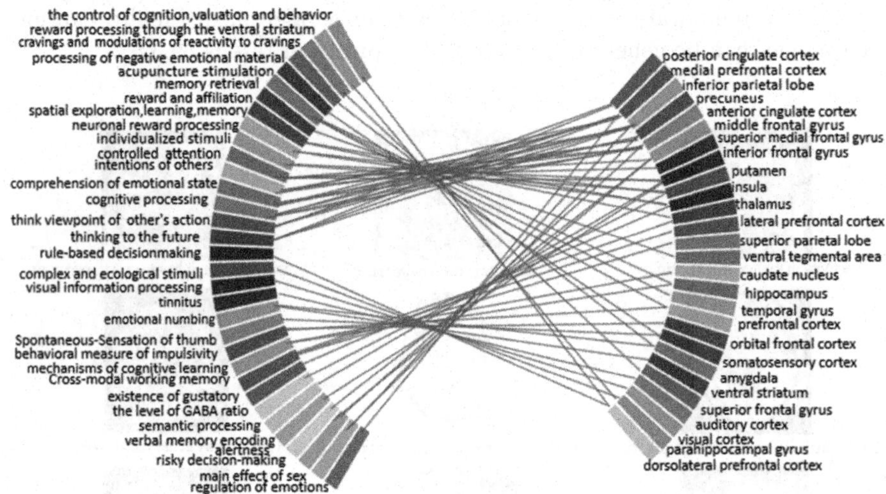

Fig. 4. The cognitive function and corresponding activated brain regions.

Topic Learning from Literature. Different from existing probabilistic topic models, the proposed image-enhanced LDA combines topics from images and corresponding descriptions with LDA topics from full texts. In order to verify the effectiveness of the combination, this paper chose four typical probabilistic topic models as baseline methods. However, how to evaluate the obtained topics became a difficulty. In this paper, all of the 30 test articles are related to brain cognitive researches based on fMRI. They have the similar topics. A good topic modeling method should be able to capture this similarity. Using this as the evaluation criterion, a variance analysis was performed on topic vectors, which were obtained by the proposed method and baseline methods. Topic vectors were constructed by using the average value of word2vec (word to vector) vectors of topic words. The experimental results are shown in Table 1. Based on the 30 test articles, the set of topic words obtained by the LFLDA has the largest variance value. The set of topic words obtained by the proposed image-enhanced LDA has the smallest variance value. Obviously, the proposed image-enhanced LDA can capture the similarity of test articles better than other baseline methods.

Table 1. Variance analysis of topic words.

Method	Image-enhanced LDA	LDA	MicroASM	LFLDA	LFDMM
Variance	2.79×10^{-6}	3.39×10^{-6}	1.091×10^{-5}	3.17×10^{-3}	4.0272×10^{-3}

5 Conclusion

Currently, neuroimaging literature has become a valuable source of knowledge. The method of neuroimaging literature mining is playing an important role on aggregate world-wide research findings for decoding brain cognitive mechanism, as well as diagnosis and treatment of brain and mental diseases, artificial intelligence researches, etc. This paper proposes the image-enhanced LDA to extract the topics of neuroimaging literature by fusing images and texts. There are two main contributions: Firstly, this paper proposes a feasible method to extract topics related brain cognitive mechanism. This effectively solves the problem that topics obtained by existing topic modeling methods of neuroimaging literature are mixed and need to be further processed. Second, this paper combines topics from fMRI brain regions activation images with topics from full texts to model neuroimaging literatures more accurately. The variance analysis shows the topic words obtained by the proposed method can better express neuroimaging than that obtained by other typical probabilistic topic models. There are also some limitations that it can add error about the influences of different brain map templates and image sharpness in extracting literature. In the future, it is interesting to use for the neural mechanisms of cognitive function. Moreover, it is also interesting to study the knowledge graph of the cognitive function by the method.

Acknowledgements. The work is supported by the JSPS Grants-in-Aid for Scientific Research of Japan (19K12123), the National Natural Science Foundation of China (61420106005), the National Basic Research Program of China (2014CB744600), the National Key Research and Development Project of China (2020YFC2007300, 2020YFC2007302) and the Key Research Project of Academy for Multi-disciplinary Studies of Capital Normal University (JCKXYJY2019019), the National Key Research and Development Program of China (Grant No. 2020YFB2104402).

References

1. Van Essen, D.C., Smith, S.M., Barch, D.M., Behrens, T.E., Yacoub, E., Ugurbil, K.: The wu-minn human connectome project: an overview. NeuroImage **80**, 62–79 (2013). https://doi.org/10.1016/j.neuroimage.2013.05.041, mapping the Connectome

2. Casey, B., et al.: The adolescent brain cognitive development (ABCD) study: Imaging acquisition across 21 sites. Dev. Cogn. Neurosci. **32**, 43–54 (2018). https://doi.org/10.1016/j.dcn.2018.03.001
3. Miller, K.L., et al.: Multimodal population brain imaging in the UK biobank prospective epidemiological study. Nat. Neurosci. **19**(11), 1523 (2016)
4. Poldrack, R., Mumford, J., Schonberg, T., Kalar, D., Barman, B., Yarkoni, T.: Discovering relations between mind, brain, and mental disorders using topic mapping. PLoS Comput. Biol. **8**, e1002707 (2012). https://doi.org/10.1371/journal.pcbi.1002707
5. French, L., Lane, S., Xu, L., Siu, C., Kwok, C., Chen, Y., Krebs, C., Pavlidis, P.: Application and evaluation of automated methods to extract brain connectivity statements from free text. Bioinformatics (Oxford, England) **28**, 2963 (2012). https://doi.org/10.1093/bioinformatics/bts542
6. Alhazmi, F.H., Beaton, D., Abdi, H.: Semantically defined subdomains of functional neuroimaging literature and their corresponding brain regions. Hum. Brain Map. **39**(7), 2764–2776 (2018). https://doi.org/10.1002/hbm.24038
7. Abacha, A.B., de, Herrera, A.G.S., Wang, K., Long, L.R., Antani, S., Demner-Fushman, D.: Named entity recognition in functional neuroimaging literature, pp. 2218–2220 (2017). https://doi.org/10.1109/BIBM.2017.8218002
8. Larochelle, H., Lauly, S.: A neural autoregressive topic model. Adv. Neural Inf. Process. Syst. **4**, 2708–2716 (2012)
9. Rakesh, V., Ding, W., Ahuja, A., Rao, N., Sun, Y., Reddy, C.K.: A sparse topic model for extracting aspect-specific summaries from online reviews. In: Proceedings of the 2018 World Wide Web Conference, pp. 1573–1582 (2018). https://doi.org/10.1145/3178876.3186069
10. Xu, Y., Yin, J., Huang, J., Yin, Y.: Hierarchical topic modeling with automatic knowledge mining. Expert Syst. Appl. **103**, 106–117 (2018). https://doi.org/10.1016/j.eswa.2018.03.008
11. Blei, D.M., Ng, A.Y., Jordan, M.I.: Latent dirichlet allocation. J. Mach. Learn. Res. **3**, 993–1022 (2003)
12. Balikas, G., Amini, M.R., Clausel, M.: On a topic model for sentences. In: Proceedings of the 39th International ACM SIGIR Conference on Research and Development in Information Retrieval, pp. 921–924 (2016). https://doi.org/10.1145/2911451.2914714
13. Nguyen, D.Q., Billingsley, R., Du, L., Johnson, M.: Improving topic models with latent feature word representations. Trans. Assoc. Comput. Linguist. **3**, 299–313 (2015). https://doi.org/10.1162/tacl_a_00140
14. Li, S., Chua, T.S., Zhu, J., Miao, C.: Generative topic embedding: a continuous representation of documents, pp. 666–675 (2016). https://doi.org/10.18653/v1/P16-1063
15. Yao, L., Zhang, Y., Wei, B., Qian, H., Wang, Y.: Incorporating probabilistic knowledge into topic models. In: Cao, T., Lim, E.-P., Zhou, Z.-H., Ho, T.-B., Cheung, D., Motoda, H. (eds.) PAKDD 2015. LNCS (LNAI), vol. 9078, pp. 586–597. Springer, Cham (2015). https://doi.org/10.1007/978-3-319-18032-8_46
16. Amplayo, R.K., Hwang, S.W.: Aspect sentiment model for micro reviews. In: 2017 IEEE International Conference on Data Mining *ICDM*, pp. 727–732 (2017). https://doi.org/10.1109/ICDM.2017.83
17. Zhu, J.: Research on topic modeling method based on deep learning. Wuhan University (2017)

18. Zhang, W., Li, Y., Wang, S.: Learning document representation via topic-enhanced LSTM model. Knowl. Based Syst. **174**, 194–204 (2019). https://doi.org/10.1016/j.knosys.2019.03.007
19. Yarkoni, T., Poldrack, R.A., Nichols, T.E., Van Essen, D.C., Wager, T.D.: Large-scale automated synthesis of human functional neuroimaging data, vol. 8, no. 8, pp. 665–670. https://doi.org/10.1038/nmeth.1635
20. Xu, K., et al.: Show, attend and tell: Neural image caption generation with visual attention. In: Proceedings of the 32nd International Conference on International Conference on Machine Learning, vol. 37 (2015)
21. Sheng, Y., Lin, S., Gao, J., He, X., Chen, J.: Research sharing-oriented functional neuroimaging named entity recognition. In: 2019 IEEE International Conference on Bioinformatics and Biomedicine *BIBM*, pp. 1629–1632 (2019). https://doi.org/10.1109/BIBM47256.2019.8982952
22. Chen, Z., et al.: Visual cortex neural activity alteration in cervical spondylotic myelopathy patients: a resting-state fMRI study. Neuroradiology **60**(9), 921–932 (2018). https://doi.org/10.1007/s00234-018-2061-x
23. Andersson, P., Ragni, F., Lingnau, A.: Visual imagery during real-time FMRI neurofeedback from occipital and superior parietal cortex. NeuroImage **200**, 332–343 (2019). https://doi.org/10.1016/j.neuroimage.2019.06.057

Frequency Bands Selection for Seizure Classification and Forecasting Using NLP, Random Forest and SVM Models

Ziwei Wang[1] and Paolo Mengoni[2](✉)

[1] Hong Kong Baptist University, Hong Kong, China
16250796@life.hkbu.edu.hk
[2] Department of Journalism, Hong Kong Baptist University, Hong Kong, China
pmengoni@hkbu.edu.hk

Abstract. Individualized treatment is crucial for epileptic patients with different types of seizures. The difference among patients impacts the drug choice as well as the surgery procedure. With the advance in machine learning, automatic seizure detection could ease the manual time-consuming and labour-intensive procedure for diagnose seizure in the clinical setting. In this paper, we propose a electroencephalography frequency bands selection method that exploits Natural Language Processing (NLP) features from individual's condition and patients with same seizure types. We used Temple University Hospital (TUH) EEG seizure corpus and conducted experiments with various input data for different seizure types classified using Random Forest (RF) and Support Vector Machine (SVM). The results show that with reduced frequency bands the performance slightly deviates from the whole frequency bands, thus leading to possible resource-efficient implementation for seizure detection.

Keywords: Seizure · Electroencephalography · Frequency bands selection · Natural Language Processing · Classification

1 Introduction

Epileptic seizure affects around 1% of world's population [18], it is one of the most common neurologic disorder like Alzheimer's disease and stroke. Despite treatment of antiepileptic drug, one-third of patients still suffer from intractable seizures, and much less can be cured by brain surgery [5]. Epilepsy is a brain spectrum disorder that is characterized by unprovoked and recurrent seizures [18]. Seizures are burst alterations of neurologic regulation triggered by abnormal electrical neurons discharge that temporarily interrupts normal electrical brain function, which could be triggered by psychological, sociological and biological consequences [19]. Medically intractable seizures severely impact individual's quality of life and result in social isolation. Furthermore, refractory seizures

M. Mahmud et al. (Eds.): BI 2021, LNAI 12960, pp. 310–320, 2021.
https://doi.org/10.1007/978-3-030-86993-9_29

crucially augment individual's safety threat in daily life, they are more likely to experience lacerations, burns, and even sudden unforeseen death.

Scalp electroencephalography (EEG) are neuroelectrophysiologic signals collected from implanted subdural electrodes. Electrical recordings of brain neurons provide information about activities passing through brain areas. Currently, the gold-standard of identifying seizure is visual inspection of EEG data to determine the abnormal electrical behaviors from electrodes and thus found the surrounding pathological tissue. But this manual procedure is time-consuming and costly in the clinical setting. Therefore, fast and accurate seizure forecasting could ease the task of medical practitioner and allow patients to plan ahead and avoid risks. Seizure prediction algorithm will enable the therapeutic and alerting process and help to prevent or even suppress seizures.

In this work, we introduce a novel technique for seizure classification that use frequency domain signals where the background signal bands are extracted from clinical reports using Natural Language Processing (NLP). In Sect. 2, we discuss related works of using features from frequency domain for seizure detection and features of background frequency activities of neurologic disorder. In Sect. 3, we introduce in detail the dataset used for this work. In Sect. 4, we discuss the method and the design thinking process, pre-processing steps, machine learning algorithms. Section 5 reports the experiment results and in Sect. 6 we draw conclusions and introduce future works.

2 Related Works

Automated seizure detection from EEG recordings have been pursued by researchers since 1970s. The models typically consist of two steps: feature engineering and classifier evaluation, where the inter-ictal/ictal (negative/positive) signals are being classified. Discriminative features from various aspects are tested in studies, including morphology [7,11], biologically [2], and time-frequency or combined domain based [10,23]. Further, in the frequency domain, background activities have been studied to find out the difference between normal and abnormal phases of neurologic disorder.

Zhou and coauthors [23] analyzed classification result on time and frequency domain separately with raw EEG signals using Convolutional Neural Networks (Zhou et al. 2018). They did three classification experiments, two binary ones: inter-ictal vs. (preictal or ictal), and one three-class: inter-ictal vs. ictal vs. preictal. The experiments were tested on two datasets: Freiburg Database and CHB-MIT Database. The results on both datasets indicted that EEG signals in frequency domain performed better than in time domain.

Roy and coauthors [14] explored multi-class seizure type classification with two version of TUH Seizure Corpus. They first applied FFT to each data segments and then used two different pre-process methods for selecting the frequencies magnitudes. This data has been used in k-Nearest Neighbors, Stochastic Gradient Descent, XGBoost, and Convolutional Neural Networks, evaluated using cross validation. They provided a baseline for seizure type classification with patient-wise cross validation.

Abasolo and coauthors [1] analyzed the Spectral entropy and Sample entropy of EEG background activity in Alzheimer's disease patients with control groups and found that the Sample entropy values of patients significant lower than control subjects ($p < 0.01$) at specific electrodes P3, P4, O1 and O2. Their results indicated an increase of EEG regularity in Alzheimer's disease patients.

Santiago-Rodrıguez et al. [15] analyzed the absolute power, relative power and mean frequency of background EEG activity including delta, theta, alpha and beta bands of juvenile myoclonic epilepsy (JME) patients with and without antiepileptic drugs. They found an increase in absolute power of delta, alpha and beta bands in JME patients without drugs, and the evidence is more clear in frontoparietal regions.

3 Dataset

In the past, seizure prediction studies using EEG signals have been limited due to insufficient standardized and qualified data [20]. The EEG have often been acquired from intensive care unit (ICU) [6], presurgical inpatient [3], animals [13], and implantable devices [4]. The short recording duration and interictal time sampling of patients as well as concerns of animal models recording limited the utilities of data. Also, the data was held primarily at the institutions where it was acquired. Recently, the opening and sharing of longer-lasting and high-quality publicly accessible chronic EEG datasets, such as the CHB-MIT Dataset [17], the UPenn and Mayo Clinic seizure detection dataset [8], and the Temple University Hospital (TUH) Dataset [12], has made it possible to advance the seizure prediction algorithms.

EEG data in clinical setting were assembled from archival and on-going records at Temple University Hospital to build the TUH Seizure Corpus (TUSZ) [16]. This is the largest open-source corpus both in terms of quantity and heterogeneity, with rich variety of seizures morphologies in aspects of frequency, amplitude, and onsets. The TUSZ was organized by patient and session in a hierarchical filetree structure. Each of the patient folders are composed of sub-folders corresponds to their individual recording sessions. Each session has EEG signals is stored in a standard European Data Format (EDF) and corresponding clinician reports in text format (TXT) collected by certified neurologists. It is also worth noting that the EDF files includes varying quantity of channels and sampling rate [12], where channels are consisting of EEG-specific channels coupled with supplemental channel information such as detected bursts and photic stimuli, and EEG may sample 250 Hz, 256 Hz, 400 Hz, 512 Hz.

3.1 EEG Data

TUSZ v1.5.2 released in May 2020 comprises 3050 seizure events. Normal EEGs are measurable both qualitatively and quantitatively, normal EEG activities appears when people is not affected by any disease. Seizure events consist of abnormal EEG, formally known as interictal epileptiform discharges (IED), are unusual waveforms and deviation of normal EEG from certain limits on EEG characteristic like frequency, amplitude, morphology, localization, and reactivity. IED is the abnormal synchronous electrical discharge originate in epileptic focus with a group of misfunctioning neurons [22]. Figure 1 displays ten seconds of normal and seizure EEG.

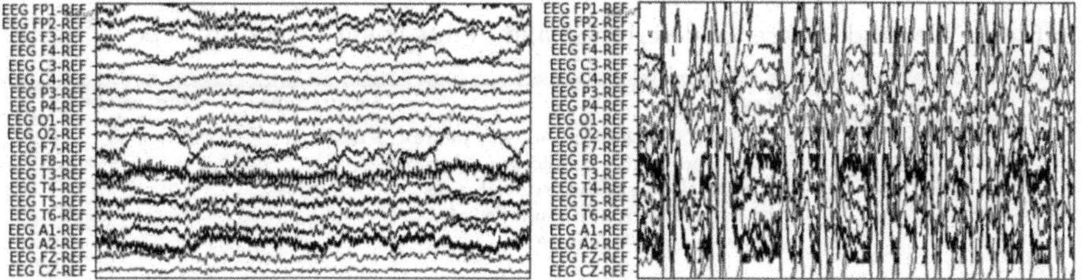

Fig. 1. Normal sample for ten seconds (left), seizure sample for ten seconds (right)

Seizure events could be further divided by different seizure types and subtypes as shown in Table 1. Generalized seizures arise in bilateral distributed neuro networks, it could be further divided into absence, myoclonic, tonic, and tonic-clonic seizure. Focal seizures originate in part of neuronal networks in part of cerebral hemisphere, the subtype include simple partial seizure and complex partial seizure. A plausible progression of seizures is to transfer from partial to generalized, i.e. to start with part of alteration in neuronal network and later became whole disfunction of neuronal network.

Table 1. Seizure type description and events count in TUSZ.

Seizure types	Description	Seizure events
Generalized Non-Specific Seizure (GNSZ)	Generalized seizures which cannot be specified further by below subtype	583
Absence Seizure (ABSZ)	Short and brief disturbance of consciousness, close resemble as daydreaming in child	99
Myoclonic Seizure (MYSZ)	Brief and sudden jerks of one or several muscles, could lead to fall and injury	3
Tonic Seizure (TNSZ)	Short, abduction of the upper limbs with expansion of the legs	62
Tonic-Clonic Seizure (TCSZ)	Final stage of seizure propagation, bilateral symmetric convulsive movements of limbs with impediment of awareness	48
Focal Non-Specific Seizure (FNSZ)	Focal seizures which cannot be specified further by below subtype	1836
Simple Partial Seizure (SPSZ)	Patients retain awareness and are able to describe motor and sensory	52
Complex Partial Seizure (CPSZ)	Consciousness is damaged and patients not able to respond to tactile/verbal stimuli	367

TUSZ consist of three type of electrode reference all constructed from neutral record listed in Table 2. Since the signal conduction through the brain with nonlinear and noisy process, the electrode locations on the scalp will significantly impact the electrical signals recorded [21]. And further have impact on classification performance [9].

Table 2. Electrode reference description and events count by seizure type in TUSZ.

Electrode reference	Description	Seizure types	Seizure events
01_tcp_ar	Based on the assumption that neural spreading in an isotropic way in a perfect layered spherical head, uses the average of a finite number of electrodes as a reference	ABSZ	2
		CPSZ	138
		FNSZ	1070
		GNSZ	428
		MYSZ	1
		SPSZ	52
		TCSZ	28
		TNSZ	62
02_tcp_le	Based on the assumption that due to the sites lack electrical activity, the average of the potentials recorded is close to zero or neutral between two ears, electrode often implemented using only one ear	ABSZ	97
		CPSZ	83
		FNSZ	231
		GNSZ	87
		MYSZ	2
		TCSZ	16
03_tcp_ar_a	The same as 01_tcp_ar, without electrode A1, A2 that connected to left ear and right ear, respectively	CPSZ	146
		FNSZ	535
		GNSZ	68
		TCSZ	4

3.2 TEXT Data

The clinical reports along with the signal file provide by TUH is unique of its kind and it is critical for seizure diagnosis. However, no other dataset beside TUH corpus has provided the information of history clinical impression from doctors that contains patient introduction, clinical history, medications, record description and seizure impression. Thus, to utilize the information in the reports, Natural Language Processing (NLP) and Term Frequency–Inverse Document Frequency (TF-IDF) have been applied to calculate pairwise similarity and list top frequency words among different seizure types. The similarity matrix heatmap of seizure types by clinical reports is shown Fig. 2.

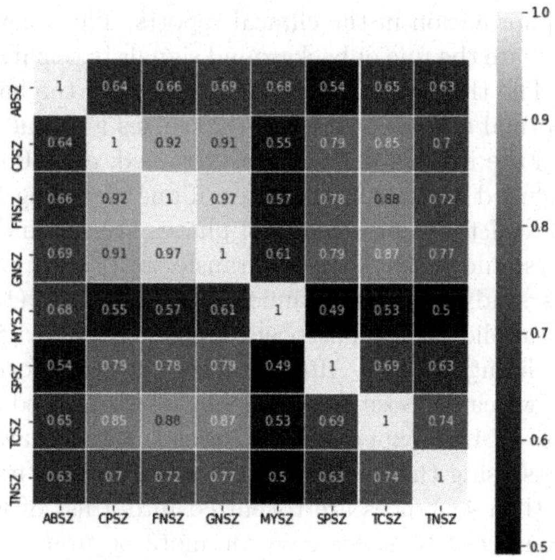

Fig. 2. Similarity matrix heatmap of seizure types by clinical reports.

For every seizure type, keywords are listed and compared. Four common observations can be extracted: 1) General words like seizure, activity, eeg, clinical, record/recording, etc.; 2) Descriptive words of seizures like spike, sharp, complex, discharge, etc.; 3) Locational words like right, left, hemisphere, posterior, anterior, etc.; 4) Background signal frequency: alpha, beta, theta, delta.

4 Method

It is broadly recognized that abnormal waveforms are signs of seizures like the spike and sharp waves. An approach to build the seizure detection algorithm is by using the waveforms of normal and abnormal EEG as training dataset. In this case the algorithm would be able to recognize the seizure when it happens. However, when the signal become abnormal, it is too late for practical seizure forecasting.

The purpose of this study is seizure prediction before seizure happens to timely warn or even suppress the seizure. Thus, with the aim of detecting seizure at the onset state, the design thinking is differentiating subtle changes in background EEG of alpha, beta, theta, delta and gamma bands. Experiments have been designed with three types of designated input data:

1. Input selected frequency bands extracted from clinical reports;
2. Input background frequency bands (alpha, beta, theta, delta, gamma);
3. Input whole frequency range without any selection.

The first type of inputs is the novel approached that we designed with aim to see the classification power of predominate frequency bands for each individual selected by using information in the clinical reports. The second type of inputs are designed to evaluate the role of background signals in seizure condition and in normal condition. The third type of input data includes the background signals together with abnormal seizure waveforms like spikes and sharps.

For each file, all the ictal recordings are extracted, and 60 s before start and end of ictal are included as inter-ictal phases, if one recording file have multiple ictal phases, the inter-ictal in between ictal phases are also included.

Sliding windows and Fast Fourier Transform (FFT) are used for pre-processing. In this study, a sliding window of one second (1 s) without overlapping have been applied. FFT has been applied to the original data after it was segmented by sliding window. After this step that transform the data in the frequency domain, we can choose the frequency bands needed for input.

For the purpose of first experiment, frequency bands have been extracted from clinical reports using the following NLP steps. Firstly, noise like punctuation are removed, then sentences are tokenized into a list of words. After that each token was converted to lower case for more accurate selection purpose. Finally, the frequency bands are selected if they are present in the text report. As a result, for each patient we will select specific frequency bands given their own clinical description.

With the extracted frequency bands list from text file and the guidance of frequency range alpha (8–12 Hz), beta (12–30 Hz), theta (5–8 Hz), delta (0.1–5 Hz), and gamma (30–50 Hz), we extract the corresponding frequency ranges from the EDF files.

The input for the second experiment only select background frequency bands range alpha, beta, theta, delta and gamma after pre-processing and the third experiment contains the whole frequency range without any selection.

The features are then fed into Random Forest (RF) and Support Vector Machine (SVM) classifiers. The parameters have been optimized to a constant value for all experiments as follows: SVM cost parameter set to 1000, gamma of 1e−09 and RBF kernel - RF with 100 estimators and minimal number of split samples set to 5.

5 Experiment Results

The results have been evaluated using accuracy (ACC), area under curve (AUC), sensitivity (TPR), and specificity (TNR) scores. The data subject used are shown in Table 2, with samples recorded by reference of 01_tcp_ar is used. FNSZ and GNSZ seizure types are the board type that do not reflect the actual seizure characteristic, thus have been excluded from the experiments.

The number of samples of EEG data fed into classifier may vary given that the data may have been sampled 250 Hz, 256 Hz, 400 Hz, 512 Hz (as stated in dataset description) and the selected bands for each patient are different. Take one patient numbered 00006546_s024_t000 in SPSZ as an example: the data for 156 s of input has 512 samples for the selected bands, 1024 samples for the background bands, and 5376 samples for whole frequency. This leads to a more simple and faster model to execute in real-time.

The resulting performance matrix is shown in Table 3. The highlighted number indicated the input of selected bands have greater or equal performance than using the background signal bands and using whole frequency as inputs. In the case of MYSZ and SPSZ the performance gap is within few percentage points from the best performing approach.

In Table 4 we report the comparison between SVM and RF classifiers with selected bands input, where highlighted number suggest better performance. In general, the Random Forest technique works better than the Support Vector Machine for all the seizure types except ABSZ.

Table 3. Seizure-wise performance with SVM and RF classifier.

		SVM				RF			
		ACC	AUC	TPR	TNR	ACC	AUC	TPR	TNR
ABSZ	selected_bands	0.96	0.94	0.72	0.99	**0.96**	**0.94**	0.63	**0.99**
	background_bands	0.98	0.95	0.78	1	0.99	0.98	0.88	1
	whole_frequency	0.98	0.99	0.83	1	0.96	0.94	0.73	0.99
CPSZ	selected_bands	**0.86**	**0.93**	**0.88**	0.83	**0.88**	**0.95**	0.88	**0.89**
	background_bands	0.85	0.92	0.84	0.85	0.88	0.95	0.89	0.87
	whole_frequency	0.88	0.95	0.88	0.88	0.92	0.97	0.93	0.91
MYSZ	selected_bands	0.89	0.91	0.70	0.70	0.91	0.91	0.37	**0.99**
	background_bands	0.96	1	0.77	0.98	0.96	0.98	0.70	1
	whole_frequency	0.98	1	0.80	0.99	0.98	1	0.87	0.99
SPSZ	selected_bands	0.77	0.84	0.66	0.85	0.82	0.91	0.73	0.89
	background_bands	0.82	0.89	0.76	0.86	0.86	0.93	0.80	0.90
	whole_frequency	0.82	0.87	0.72	0.89	0.89	0.95	0.83	0.93
TCSZ	selected_bands	**0.95**	**0.98**	0.92	**0.97**	**0.97**	**0.99**	**0.94**	**0.98**
	background_bands	0.94	0.98	0.93	0.94	0.95	0.99	0.94	0.96
	whole_frequency	0.96	0.99	0.95	0.97	0.97	1	0.96	0.98
TNSZ	selected_bands	**0.89**	0.78	0.28	0.98	**0.9**	0.79	**0.29**	**0.99**
	background_bands	0.89	0.80	0.29	0.99	0.90	0.80	0.29	0.99
	whole_frequency	0.90	0.83	0.33	0.99	0.90	0.83	0.31	0.99

Table 4. Performance comparison between SVM and RF classifiers with selected bands input.

	SVM				RF			
	ACC	AUC	TPR	TNR	ACC	AUC	TPR	TNR
ABSZ	**0.96**	**0.94**	**0.72**	**0.99**	0.96	0.94	0.63	0.99
CPSZ	0.86	0.93	0.88	0.83	**0.88**	**0.95**	**0.88**	**0.89**
MYSZ	0.89	0.91	**0.70**	0.70	**0.91**	**0.91**	0.37	**0.99**
SPSZ	0.77	0.84	0.66	0.85	**0.82**	**0.91**	**0.73**	**0.89**
TCSZ	0.95	0.98	0.92	0.97	**0.97**	**0.99**	**0.94**	**0.98**
TNSZ	0.89	0.78	0.28	0.98	**0.90**	**0.79**	**0.29**	**0.99**

6 Conclusions and Future Works

In this work, we introduce a novel classification technique that investigates different seizure types using Natural Language Processing. The proposed seizure detection method makes use of background frequency bands and further select the background bands basing on clinical reports. The results are in line with the state-of-the-art techniques but using less data samples. As seizure is a biological process emerge gradually using selected frequency bands could lead to a possible implementation for detecting/predicting seizures in real-life, real-time setting.

To the best of our knowledge, this is the first time that selected EEG bands has been used to detect seizure for every individual patient among different seizure types. This could lead to a patient-specific seizure detection method. Furthermore, the algorithm is computationally efficient with reduced power consumption and could maintain longer operation time, making it possible for implementing in resource-limited device.

For further directions, channel selection of different seizure types could be added, because different type of seizures directly related to the area of the brain cortex where seizures are generated, and it could construct by the electrode placements as method of channel-based detection. Channel selection for seizure detection often reduces the number of channels to focus on the most informative ones to be fed into classifier. Thus, channel selection has high potential for detecting/predicting onset of epileptic seizures with a higher accuracy algorithm due to remove of noise from redundant channels.

Acknowledgments. The authors would like to thank Dr. Lan Liang for the useful discussion. This work is partly supported by the "Teaching Development Grant" - Hong Kong Baptist University, Hong Kong, China

References

1. Abásolo, D., Hornero, R., Espino, P., Alvarez, D., Poza, J.: Entropy analysis of the EEG background activity in Alzheimer's disease patients. Physiol. Meas. **27**(3), 241 (2006)

2. Altenburg, J., Vermeulen, R.J., Strijers, R.L., Fetter, W.P., Stam, C.J.: Seizure detection in the neonatal EEG with synchronization likelihood. Clin. Neurophysiol. **114**(1), 50–55 (2003)
3. Chung, J.M., et al.: Utility of invasive ictal EEG recordings in pre-surgical evaluation of patients with medically refractory temporal lobe epilepsy and normal MRI. Int. J. Epilepsy **2**(2), 66–71 (2015)
4. Davis, K.A., et al.: A novel implanted device to wirelessly record and analyze continuous intracranial canine EEG. Epilepsy Res. **96**(1–2), 116–122 (2011)
5. French, J.A.: Refractory epilepsy: clinical overview. Epilepsia **48**, 3–7 (2007)
6. Gardner, A.B., Krieger, A.M., Vachtsevanos, G., Litt, B., Kaelbing, L.P.: One-class novelty detection for seizure analysis from intracranial EEG. J. Mach. Learn. Res. **7**(6) (2006)
7. Gotman, J.: Automatic recognition of epileptic seizures in the EEG. Electroencephalogr. Clin. Neurophysiol. **54**(5), 530–540 (1982)
8. Kaggle: UPenn and mayo clinic's seizure detection challenge (2014). https://www.kaggle.com/c/seizure-detection
9. Lopez, S., Gross, A., Yang, S., Golmohammadi, M., Obeid, I., Picone, J.: An analysis of two common reference points for EEGs. In: 2016 IEEE Signal Processing in Medicine and Biology Symposium (SPMB), pp. 1–5. IEEE (2016)
10. Mursalin, M., Zhang, Y., Chen, Y., Chawla, N.V.: Automated epileptic seizure detection using improved correlation-based feature selection with random forest classifier. Neurocomputing **241**, 204–214 (2017)
11. Nishida, S., Nakamura, M., Ikeda, A., Shibasaki, H.: Signal separation of background EEG and spike by using morphological filter. Med. Eng. Phys. **21**(9), 601–608 (1999)
12. Obeid, I., Picone, J.: The temple university hospital EEG data corpus. Front. Neurosci. **10**, 196 (2016)
13. Raghunathan, S., Gupta, S.K., Ward, M.P., Worth, R.M., Roy, K., Irazoqui, P.P.: The design and hardware implementation of a low-power real-time seizure detection algorithm. J. Neural Eng. **6**(5), 056005 (2009)
14. Roy, S., Asif, U., Tang, J., Harrer, S.: Seizure type classification using EEG signals and machine learning: setting a benchmark. In: 2020 IEEE Signal Processing in Medicine and Biology Symposium (SPMB), pp. 1–6. IEEE (2020)
15. Santiago-Rodríguez, E., Harmony, T., Cárdenas-Morales, L., Hernández, A., Fernández-Bouzas, A.: Analysis of background EEG activity in patients with juvenile myoclonic epilepsy. Seizure **17**(5), 437–445 (2008)
16. Shah, V.: The temple university hospital seizure detection corpus. Front. Neuroinform. **12**, 83 (2018)
17. Shoeb, A.H., Guttag, J.V.: Application of machine learning to epileptic seizure detection. In: Proceedings of the 27th International Conference on Machine Learning (ICML 2010), pp. 975–982 (2010)
18. Sirven, J.I.: Epilepsy: a spectrum disorder. Cold Spring Harbor Pers. Med. **5**(9), a022848 (2015)
19. Stafstrom, C.E., Carmant, L.: Seizures and epilepsy: an overview for neuroscientists. Cold Spring Harbor Persp. Med. **5**(6), a022426 (2015)
20. Wagenaar, J.B., Worrell, G.A., Ives, Z., Dümpelmann, M., Litt, B., Schulze-Bonhage, A.: Collaborating and sharing data in epilepsy research. J. Clin. Neurophysiol. Official Publ. Am. Electroencephalogr. Society **32**(3), 235 (2015)
21. Yao, D., Qin, Y., Hu, S., Dong, L., Vega, M.L.B., Sosa, P.A.V.: Which reference should we use for EEG and ERP practice? Brain Topogr. **32**(4), 530–549 (2019)

22. Zacharaki, E.I., Mporas, I., Garganis, K., Megalooikonomou, V.: Spike pattern recognition by supervised classification in low dimensional embedding space. Brain Inform. **3**(2), 73–83 (2016). https://doi.org/10.1007/s40708-016-0044-4
23. Zhou, M., et al.: Epileptic seizure detection based on EEG signals and CNN. Front. Neuroinform. **12**, 95 (2018)

Using Tools for the Analysis of the Mental Activity of Programmers

Rozaliya Amirova[1], Gcinizwe Dlamini[1(✉)], Vladimir Ivanov[1], Sergey Masyagin[1], Aldo Spallone[2], Giancarlo Succi[1], and Herman Tarasau[1]

[1] Innopolis University, Innopolis, Russia
g.dlamini@innopolis.university
[2] Rudn University, Moscow, Russia

Abstract. Programmers are the most important part of software production and individual developers are hard to substitute. The essential part of the knowledge intensive development process is the developers mind state. Understanding the mental states of software developers has become a main interest of software production companies since it is the most valuable resource for software development. However the main challenge in analysing the software developers mental states is that most precise equipment, such as fMRI, is extremely expensive and not portable. Thus, fMRI approximation from EEG readings tools such as MNE, have been developed over the years. The idea of recreating the fMRI based on EEG signal is the main motivation for the current work. This research explains how we used this tool in our studies.

Keywords: EEG · MNE · BCI · Software development

1 Introduction

Multi-channel EEG is a tool for monitoring brain electrical activity. This tool plays a main role in experimentation, as it supports more advanced analysis than the typical single-channeled EEG device. Such advances give motivation to develop the tools to optimize the intellectual work of computer science engineers.

The greater part of a software developers work part is in their mind. The increasing interest in modeling the behaviour and the mind state of developers has lead to development of two research branches: The first is about the cognitive structure of the developers, from psychological profiles [65] to the overall mind state [1,3,4,34,44,59] with emotions included [26,80]. Also, this studies are true in the context of agile development [9,17,21,33,37,71], or in the case of open source development, where different motivations are sought [18,22,39,57,61,64,74]. The emotional state is considered, especially in the case of people collaboration [10,16,54,58,75]. The second regards the concrete analysis of the signals coming from the mind of developers, and it is the core of this work.

M. Mahmud et al. (Eds.): BI 2021, LNAI 12960, pp. 321–337, 2021.
https://doi.org/10.1007/978-3-030-86993-9_30

A precise method for brain activity analysis is fMRI (functional magnetic resonance imaging). However, fMRI is challenging for developers as they have to work lying and see the screen using mirrors, a hardly comparable conditions to the real one, therefore alternative less disruptive approaches would be preferable. There have been works employing single channel EEG devices. Fritz et al. [81] and Müller and Fritz [53] have collected, among others, once channel EEG signals. However, the single channel electroencephalogram device was used, which may result in an error of up to fifty percent [47].

There have been recent works using multi channel EEG signals [6,7,41], which indeed provide a more comprehensive view of what happens in the brain, still using wearable devices, so being able to record the activities in quite standard working situations. Moreover, the technical development of computed analysis of spectral EEG data has allowed quali-quantitative assessment of localized brain functional areas as well as of connectivity networks [42,77], a fact which indicates that the objective evaluation specific brain functional capacity, both in physiological and in pathological conditions.

In comparison to other robust neuroimaging methods such as fMRI, EEG provides a sufficient real-time imaging about brains activity of all brain areas [32]. This would suggest that high-intellectual activity tasks, such as software conception and implementation, can be objectively measured and compared between different individuals, as well as in the same individual albeit in different moments in which emotional and psychological conditions can change [31]. There are recent reports of EEG demonstration of specific brain areas deactivation (following transient global amnesia for example) and reactivation a few days after the clinical recovery which again could indicate that memory, as well as social cognition, can be objectively screened. Moreover, default-mode network (DMN), a well-known pattern of resting state studies of brain connectivity, could also be utilizied for evaluating high-task brain activities since it is closely related to high intellectual processes such as mind/mentalization and long-term memory [29].

Indeed, the EEG description given by the activations of the brain is, mostly, less accurate that the fMRI. But, the medical discipline as a whole, has developed the new approaches and tools in past 20 years. Such tools provide the fMRI-like description from EEG activation signal. This research is focused on demonstrating the practicality of such tools in the software engineering domain. A specific tool discussed in this paper is MNE (Minimum Norm Estimates) [25]. From our experience, these set of tools gives accurate analysis, with the usage of comfortable, multichannel EEG device. The role of such tool is pivotal, as it gives the opportunity to analyse, otherwise impossible data, thus providing the basis for the followup development and research.

As a matter of fact it is very important to emphasize that on the base of such modeling, tools could be developed to supply the developers what they need in terms of information, instruments, feedback. Using an analogy, now cars have mechanisms detecting when a driver is falling a sleep and providing a signal to wake up, for instance on the steering wheel or on the dashboard; likewise, we could imagine mechanisms to alert developers that they are loosing concentration and are likely to inject mistakes in their code or to loose their productivity significantly. As mentioned, the initial modeling of the work of the mind requires quite refined tools, the simplest being EGG devices with at least a dozen of sensors, but it is not difficult to hypothesize that after the initial modeling, to spot specific state of minds requiring feedback, like the lack of attention, simpler devices could be employed, such as one channel EEG, simple galvanic skin response, or simple eye tracking devices: all tools that could cost something of the order of 7.000 roubles or 100 euros. Even more, we could hypothesize further that, after modeling, suitable correlations could be made by levels of attention and how keystrokes occur or the mouse is moved, and then using such information as input for the tools.

The paper is organized as follows. Section 2 summarizes the current approaches in measuring the activity of the brain. Section 3 provides description of background for data collection process and used software. Section 4 provides details of research settings. Section 5 outlines analysis results. Sections 6 describes possible limitations and provides some conclusions.

2 Measuring the Brain Activity

Currently, many studies use biological signal measurements and questionnaires to measure the brain activity. However, there is a lack of research related to the analysis of the mind of programmers and their concentration. In this section we briefly summarize methods used elsewhere, but applicable to programmers.

There are a lot of studies using he EEG as a primary method for measuring brain activities. In [43] researches used EEG signals for Attention Recognition (AR) and extended previous research that used other techniques such as eye-gaze, face-detection, head pose and distance from the monitor to track the subject's attention. AR is a promising field that can be applied in many areas such as e-learning, driving, and most relevant - in measuring awareness during video conferences, which is import for the current study, because some programmers participate in multiple video conferences per day. Bin et al. [27] used to EEG to determine the attention level, while the subject was performing a learning task. In [5] EEG was used to estimate alertness in real-time, which could be applicable during coding. In [38] the researchers presented the usage a single channel wireless EEG device to detect a fatigue level of a driver in real-time on a mobile devices.

Apart from brain signals measured using EEG, attention can be derived from heart rate variability, galvanic skin response, pupil diameter, eye blink frequency and brain activity measured by other neuroimaging tools such as ECoG (electrocorticogram), fNIRS (functional near-infrared spectroscopy), fMRI, MEG (Magnetoencephalogram), etc. [36,66].

Among tests to measure the brain activity, Conner's Continuous Performance Test (CPT) and test of variables attention (TOVA) are the popular techniques that have been proposed by researchers over the years. CPT is a technique where reaction is expected only on rare signal [11]. TOVA is a simple computerized neuropsychological assessment of impulsivity and attention [23].

3 EEG Device and Software Background

The electrical activity coming from various parts of the brain is reflected by EEG recordings from the scalp. The operation of Scalp EEG suggests oscillations at a range of frequencies. Such oscillations are transformed into frequency ranges, such as delta, theta, alpha, beta, and gamma. A large number of electrically charged neurons travel inside the central nervous system and trigger small electrical currents to produce this electrical activity. Volume conduction, i.e. the electromagnetic properties of the tissues inside the brain, characterizes the amount of current flow. It has been noted that EEG frequency bands have some biological significance and can be correlated with different brain functioning states [29,31]. There is still confusion about precisely where different frequencies are produced. On the contrary, evidence about the triggered areas within the areas is largely recognized. So far, several algorithms have been developed in order to process these signals better and to generate a graphical representation of them, comparable to MRI and fMRI for ease of use, starting around 30 years ago [20].

3.1 LORETA

One of the first software that used Electroencephalography to map the brain functions is low resolution electromagnetic tomography (LORETA) [46]. In 1994 Marqui et al. [46] proposed LORETA as a an answer to the issue of localizing electrical sources in the brain from brain surface recordings with the usage of multi-channel EEG.

LORETA computes a three-dimensional distribution of 2394 voxels of $7 \times 7 \times 7$ mm of the generated electric neuronal activity in the grey matter. It enables to estimate the activity distributed throughout the brain volume by decomposing the overlapping EEG voltage patterns into their underlying sources and by localizing them within the brain. A great advantage of this technique is that it is not restricted to a certain number of electrodes or electrode locations, therefore it self-adapts to almost every electrode set-up and EEG measuring device. LORETA analysis of limited frequency bands can be used to determine which regions of the brain are activated during different states or mental tasks.

LORETA helps to find not only the source, but also gives you the time courses of each source. LORETA uses Voxels, which are located in fixed positions inside the gray matter of the brain. The main purpose of voxels is to analyze not only the single voxel activation, but the entire region associated with brain functions.

Since the beginning of 2001 LORETA has also been used for Neurofeedback and its use is expanding. So far studies based on EEG recordings are replicating others obtained using fMRI in either voluntaries either clinical populations, and they appear to be more cost-effective than fMRI for investigating deep cortical structures.

Since the creation of LORETA, it has been used for Neurofeedback tasks. The studies based on EEG are trying to replicate expensive fMRI clinical trials.

Thus, EEG and LORETA appears to be more affordable in different field of studies.

There are two different kinds of LORETA:

- sLORETA: standardized low resolution brain electromagnetic tomography [40,56], that has no localization bias in the presence of measurement and biological noise.
- eLORETA: exact low resolution brain electromagnetic tomography [2,28]. The first ever 3D, discrete, distributed linear solution to the inverse problem of EEG/MEG with exact localization (zero localization error).

In order to use LORETA for source estimation, several steps should be done:

1. *Valid head coordinates:* Valid head coordinates (standard or realistic) are needed, matching the international 10–20 electrode system or it's derivatives, such as 10-10. Moreover, the research community has recommended a minimum of 64 electrode with uniform distribution throughout the scalp [49]. However studies have been published with using also 32 channels EEG recordings (i.e. [30])
2. *Accurate voltage measurements in the EEG data:* The most important prerequisite which is highly specific for LORETA. Only timed-domain voltage values are valid input for the algorithm. Also, high signal-to-noise ratio will give better source analysis quality, thus it is crucial to use well-processed data. There are two different domains in the analysis:
   (a) Electrode space: where you have the voltage measurements;
   (b) Signal source space: where the electrical current sources are confined inside the brain.

   LORETA computes the electrical potentials based on the information about channel coordinates from the electrode space and the source parameters (position, orientation and magnitude of the neuronal current sources) from the source space.
3. *Source model:* The source space should be predeifned, as it is crucial for model. The source space should be limited to the regions with cortical gray matter and hippocampus in the Talairach atlas. Then, the space are divided into 2394 voxels at 7 mm spatial resolution. The dipoles with equivalent current are modeled with sources.
4. *Volume conductor model:* The model describes the geometrical and conductive properties of the head. A standard brain model which is based on the MNI-305 brain template (Evans AC, et al. 1993) could be used. The MNI images are co-registered to the Talairach brain atlas in order to map the detailed brain structures into the MNI space.

Once all these steps are completed the lead-field matrix is ready to be analyzed by computing. This matrix is a mapping mechanism from the neuronal current sources within the brain which are recorded by the electrical potentials on the head surface.

3.2 MNE Library

MNE is a software package that is used in clinical practice [24,25] and is still receiving upgrades and improvements together. MNE also includes an Python API (MNE Python) [19,35]. Better pre-processing techniques are introduced in latest version of the library and are used in current study.

Python MNE library allows several type of analysis including

1. Time-frequency
2. Non-parametric
3. Connectivity analysis.

The data artifacts are cleaned by using signal space separation technology [76]. The signal-to-noise ratio is optimized by analyzing Pre-stimulus intervals in the evoked responses in observations. By utilizing current dipole in EEG and MEG, MNE software chooses sources to be amplified. Small number of ECDs (equivalent current dipoles) show a spatial recognition of the original source in the brain when the setting of time-varying dipole assures a proper analysis of time-related signal. MNE allows a to record either complex cognitive processes and resting or "cool" state.

By analyzing current distribution, MNE can choose the best representative from the all given currents. This technique allows best spatial and temporal resolution in one.

Sensor-space and source-space frequencies are processed simultaneously, and artifacts are then eliminated by using some signal analysis techniques [67]. MNE software allows free-surface analysis of power spectrum with FFT (fast Fourier Transform) for better analysis. The result of such analysis is spatial reconstruction of activated areas of the brain in real-time.

In order to study brain activations - fMRI, MRI and EEG techniques are used. Magnetic resonance (MR) techniques give researchers possibility to record internal activations of the brain. Also, fMRI and MRI provide high-resolution images. The problem with MR techniques is that subject need to lay down and be still in the scanner. Such positions of subject is mostly not convenient for writing code.

To overcome these problem EEG could be used, as it is portable and non-invasive tool. Moreover, EEG signal can be transform in MRI-like images [25]. Such transformation could encourage detailed vision of brain processes.

The main focus of the research is to clarify the possible usages of MNE tool [25] on EEG signal collected from developers programmers in different environmental situation. In addition, we try to give explanation to differences in activation patterns of brain during coding.

4 Experimental Settings

The settings used in this research were created in order to find remarkable differences in brain waves. The signals were collected in three different environmental conditions:

1. Coding while listening to music
2. Coding in Open Spaces
3. Pair programming.

We have also tried to connect the structure of brain waves to the different mental states. Thus, we could find best scenario in which programmers can code.

4.1 Preparation and Experimental Procedure

First, the subjects have answered questions about their working space and programming experience in form of quiz. The subjects were divided into 3 groups by their experience: beginners, intermediate and advanced. After that, subjects solved the programming tasks depended on their experience.

The EEG device was then calibrated for each subject by making the subjects spend two minutes eyes closed and two minutes eyes opened before solving any task. After the four minutes of calibration, the subjects start solving specific task. The average task solving time was between 10–20 min. Time limit for solving the task was fixed to 20 min and if a tests subject exceeds the time limit, the experiment was terminated.

4.2 Tools

Different software tools were utilized:

- Recording software: Mitsar EEG Studio (1.23.1),
- Pre-processing, analysis and visualizations: MNE 0.19.2 on Python 3.7.4,
- Working environment: Jupyter Notebook 6.0.1.

Also, MNE can work with magnometer and gradiometer, which could be applied for studying Event-related potentials, and electrooculgram, which could be useful to eye artifacts detection.

5 What We Achieved Using MNE

The MNE is reported to be quite effective in our work mostly because:

- It gives opportunity to analysis raw data. Such data could be collected in the same programming environment as programmers are acquainted, unlike the fMRI that requires the subject be lie still in the machine, without opportunity to conduct research during typical working setup.
- MNE gives opportunity to work with raw EEG data. The data is gathered from subjects during their work and represent current state of brain, unlike MR-based solutions, which require lying still in the sensor.
- Easy to install as the documentation and tutorials are available online.
- Tutorials with clear instructions are provided.
- EEG could be visualized in three-dimensional fMRI-like representation. Such visualization is created with built-in averaged brain structure.

5.1 MNE Workflow

MNE tool provides workflow summarized on its webpage. In current work, we will use raw EEG data and go through the following steps: preprocessing, epoched data, averaged data, source estimate (Fig. 1).

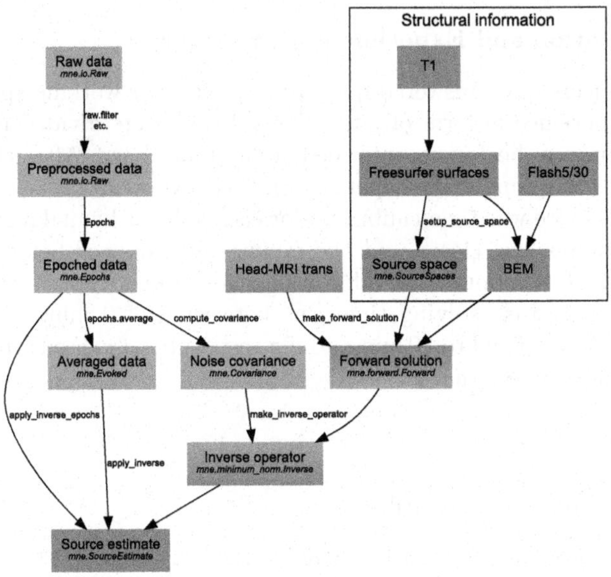

Fig. 1. Workflow of the MNE software. Picture inspiration source: https://mne.tools/stable/overview/cookbook.html

5.2 Importing Data

MNE supports importing data from various formats, such as

1. Elekta NeuroMag (`.fif`)
2. European Data Format (`.edf`)
3. General data format (`.gdf`).

We are using EDF format with events labeling form calibration, experimentation part. The MNE save function automatically splits data and convert it to `.fif` format

Exported EDF data from EEG Mitsar studio does not contain information about electrodes positions. We added positions manually using the class `mne.channels.Montage` class and its method `set_montage()`.

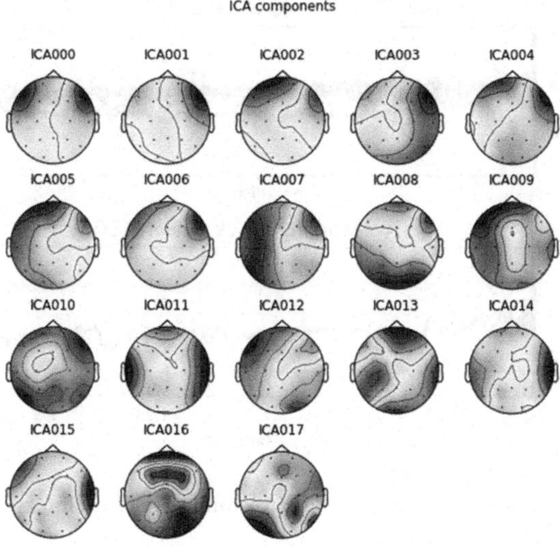

Fig. 2. Visualisation of channels after ICA

5.3 Pre-processing

One of most known EEG problems is the different artifacts, mostly, biological in origin. In order to find independent sources of signal from recording, different pre-processing techniques could be applied. In our case, PCA-based pre-processing could not be used as the signal source is non-Gaussian distributed. Therefore the most suitable algorithm for our EEG preprocessing stage is ICA(Independent component analysis) which is already available in MNE tool.

After fitting the ICA, the components produced correspond to individual, independent EEG sensors. They could be visualized as in Fig. 2. From picture (Fig. 2), we may see that EOG (eye blinks) is captured by the first component (ICA000). In next sections, different approaches of choosing Independent components are presented.

Moreover, we can plot an overlay of the original signal against the reconstructed signal with the artifactual ICs excluded (Fig. 3).

After we know which component we can exclude, we use the call `ica.apply(reconst_raw)` to exclude it.

5.4 Epoching Data

The data segments, called Epochs, could be extracted from the recording using IDs of event. The user also can build up the even hierarchy by using tags. During data collection, we marked each event in recording using labels in Mitsar studio (e.g., "eyes opened," "eyes closed" for calibration). This information could be extracted directly from raw data.

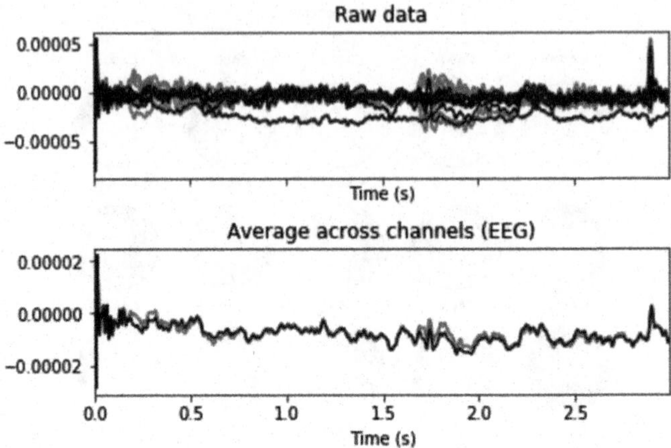

Fig. 3. Signals before (red) and after (black) cleaning EOG artifacts using MNE (Color figure online)

5.5 Averaging Data

The evoked data is taken from epoched data. Then topological maps are printed as on Fig. 4a.

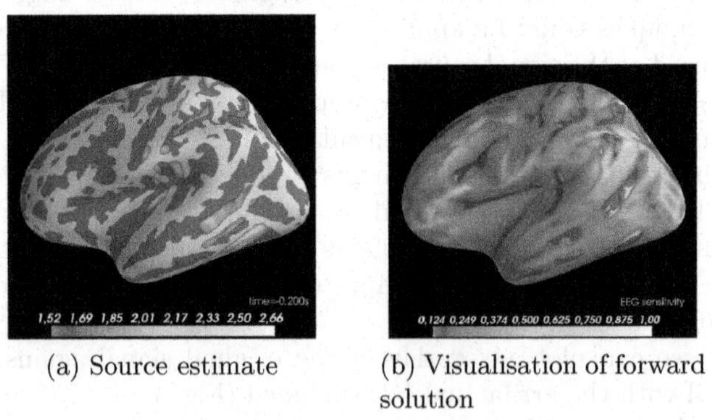

(a) Source estimate

(b) Visualisation of forward solution

Fig. 4. MNE visualization

5.6 Source Estimate

EEG cap used in the current experiment provides whole-head coverage data with accurate electrodes' locations and time source distribution. The forward problem is focused on the understanding of the potentials and magnetic fields that result from primary current sources. Then, the inverse problem is about estimation of the location of these primary current sources [52]. Processing of anatomical MRI images implemented in MNE based on the FreeSurfer package [52]. MNE provides an implementation of forward and inverse solutions to reconstruct source from EEG data. The forward solution takes as arguments EEG data, transformation and Boundary element method (BEM) solution surfaces. The BEM surfaces are the triangulations of the interfaces between different tissues needed for forward computation [25]. Since we do not have fMRI data of our subjects, we used the standard template MRI subject fsaverage. To make inverse solution we used mne.minimum_norm.make_inverse_operator method, which takes raw file info, forward solution and noise-covariance matrix, which could be computed in two ways: auto or using "empty room" (EEG/MEG cap without a subject) data [25]. Then inverse operator was applied to evoked data and result visualized in Fig 5. The MNE software calculates the inverse operator by computation Singular value decomposition (SVD) calculation. The SVD calculation approach helps brings about the ability to easily adjust regularization parameter ('SNR') when the Dynamic statistical parametric maps and final source estimates are computed (Fig. 4b).

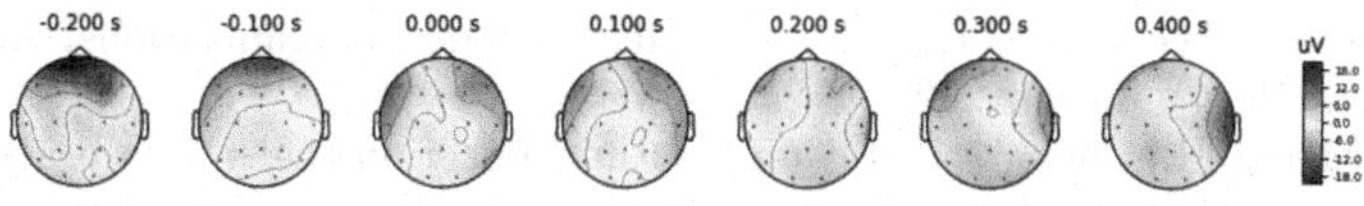

Fig. 5. Topological maps of Evoked data

6 Conclusions

The MR-based solutions provide highly accurate model of brain functioning, but the experimental settings are very restricted. The physical constraint and the cost of equipment is the most problematic part of experimental design process. This paper describes how we may model the brain activity by the means of EEG, but in format similar to fMRI. The data was collected from software developers during their work. We focused ourselves to investigating the MNE tool. The software was used for pre-processing, analysis and the reconstruction of images.

MNE provides capabilities allowing us to recreate fMRI-like images of brain activations, but using low-cost EEG device instead of expensive MRI machine. AS the test subjects does not lie down in the machine, the new possibility opens for us. The experiments in various environments and different body positions could give more precise information about brain functioning. Moreover, the EEG sampling frequency is much higher than fMRI. Thus, we may capture wider range of frequencies and give better explanations of inner brain processes.

Also, MNE provides clear workflow, detailed documentation and many training tutorials. These aspects are critically important for from non-medical researchers, who not necessarily very familiar with neurological images. Additionally, MNE provides interfaces to work with different data formats, gives different algorithms and averaged examples.

Indeed, additional research are needed, in order to provide the better tool's suitability understanding. It would be interesting also to consider the effect of different programming approaches [8,45,72,73,78], platforms [12–15,48], and even the use of metrics [50,51,55,60,62,63,68–70,79]. However, the goal of the research is about the possible usages and application of such tool and in order to achieve such goal, the significant amount of the field research is needed.

References

1. Amabile, T.M.: Creativity and innovation in organizations. Harvard Business School Background Note, pp. 396–239 (1996)
2. Aoki, Y., et al.: Detection of EEG-resting state independent networks by eLORETA-ICA method. Front. Hum. Neurosci. **9**, 31 (2015). https://doi.org/10.3389/fnhum.2015.00031. https://www.frontiersin.org/article/10.3389/fnhum.2015.00031
3. Baas, M., De Dreu, C., Nijstad, B.: A meta-analysis of 25 years of mood-creativity research: hedonic tone, activation, or regulatory focus? Psychol. Bull. **134**, 779–806 (2008)
4. Barsade, S.G., Gibson, D.E.: Why does affect matter in organizations? Acad. Manage. Pers. **21**(1), 36–59 (2007)
5. Bi, L., Zhang, R., Chen, Z.: Study on real-time detection of alertness based on EEG. In: 2007 IEEE/ICME International Conference on Complex Medical Engineering, pp. 1490–1493. IEEE (2007)
6. Brown, J.A., Ivanov, V., Rogers, A., Succi, G., Tormasov, A., Yi, J.: Toward a better understanding of how to develop software under stress – drafting the lines for future research. In: Proceedings of the 13th International Conference on Evaluation of Novel Approaches to Software Engineering, ENASE 2018, Funchal, Madeira, Portugal, March 2018
7. Busechian, S., et al.: Understanding the impact of pair programming on the minds of developers. In: Proceedings of the 40th International Conference on Software Engineering Companion, ICSE-NIER 2018. ACM, Gothenburg, May–June 2018
8. Clark, J., et al.: Selecting components in large cots repositories. J. Syst. Softw. **73**(2), 323–331 (2004)
9. Cockburn, A., Highsmith, J.: Agile software development, the people factor. Computer **34**(11), 131–133 (2001)
10. Coman, I.D., Robillard, P.N., Sillitti, A., Succi, G.: Cooperation, collaboration and pair-programming: field studies on backup behavior. J. Syst. Softw. **91**, 124–134 (2014). https://doi.org/10.1016/j.jss.2013.12.037. http://dx.doi.org/10.1016/j.jss.2013.12.037
11. Conners, C.K., Epstein, J.N., Angold, A., Klaric, J.: Continuous performance test performance in a normative epidemiological sample. J. Abnorm. Child Psychol. **31**(5), 555–562 (2003)
12. Corral, L., Georgiev, A.B., Sillitti, A., Succi, G.: A method for characterizing energy consumption in Android smartphones. In: 2nd International Workshop on Green and Sustainable Software (GREENS 2013), pp. 38–45. IEEE, May 2013. https://doi.org/10.1109/GREENS.2013.6606420. http://dx.doi.org/10.1109/GREENS.2013.6606420

13. Corral, L., Georgiev, A.B., Sillitti, A., Succi, G.: Can execution time describe accurately the energy consumption of mobile apps? An experiment in Android. In: Proceedings of the 3rd International Workshop on Green and Sustainable Software, pp. 31–37. ACM (2014)
14. Corral, L., Sillitti, A., Succi, G.: Software assurance practices for mobile applications. Computing **97**(10), 1001–1022 (2015)
15. Corral, L., Sillitti, A., Succi, G., Garibbo, A., Ramella, P.: Evolution of mobile software development from platform-specific to web-based multiplatform paradigm. In: Proceedings of the 10th SIGPLAN Symposium on New Ideas, New Paradigms, and Reflections on Programming and Software, Onward! 2011, pp. 181–183. ACM, New York (2011)
16. Corral, L., Sillitti, A., Succi, G., Strumpflohner, J., Vlasenko, J.: DroidSense: a mobile tool to analyze software development processes by measuring team proximity. In: Furia, C.A., Nanz, S. (eds.) TOOLS 2012. LNCS, vol. 7304, pp. 17–33. Springer, Heidelberg (2012). https://doi.org/10.1007/978-3-642-30561-0_3
17. Denning, P.J.: Moods. Commun. ACM **55**(12), 33–35 (2012)
18. Di Bella, E., Sillitti, A., Succi, G.: A multivariate classification of open source developers. Inf. Sci. **221**, 72–83 (2013)
19. Esch, L., et al.: MNE: software for acquiring, processing, and visualizing MEG/EEG data. In: Magnetoencephalography: From Signals to Dynamic Cortical Networks, pp. 355–371 (2019)
20. Evans, A.C., Collins, D.L., Mills, S.R., Brown, E.D., Kelly, R.L., Peters, T.M.: 3d statistical neuroanatomical models from 305 MRI volumes. In: 1993 IEEE Conference Record Nuclear Science Symposium and Medical Imaging Conference, vol. 3, pp. 1813–1817, October 1993. https://doi.org/10.1109/NSSMIC.1993.373602
21. Feldt, R., Angelis, L., Torkar, R., Samuelsson, M.: Links between the personalities, views and attitudes of software engineers. Inf. Softw. Technol. **52**(6), 611–624 (2010)
22. Fitzgerald, B., Kesan, J.P., Russo, B., Shaikh, M., Succi, G.: Adopting Open Source Software: A Practical Guide. The MIT Press, Cambridge (2011)
23. Forbes, G.B.: Clinical utility of the test of variables of attention (TOVA) in the diagnosis of attention- deficit/hyperactivity disorder. J. Clin. Psychol. **54**, 461–476 (1998)
24. Gramfort, A., et al.: MEG and EEG data analysis with MNE-Python. Front. Neurosci. **7**, 267 (2013). https://doi.org/10.3389/fnins.2013.00267
25. Gramfort, A., et al.: MNE software for processing MEG and EEG data. Neuroimage **86**, 446–460 (2014)
26. Graziotin, D., Fagerholm, F., Wang, X., Abrahamsson, P.: Unhappy developers: bad for themselves, bad for process, and bad for software product. In: 2017 IEEE/ACM 39th International Conference on Software Engineering Companion (ICSE-C), pp. 362–364. IEEE (2017)
27. Hu, B., Li, X., Sun, S., Ratcliffe, M.: Attention recognition in EEG-based affective learning research using CFS+ KNN algorithm. IEEE/ACM Trans. Comput. Biol. Bioinf. **15**(1), 38–45 (2016)
28. Ikeda, S., et al.: Automated source estimation of scalp EEG epileptic activity using eLORETA kurtosis analysis. Neuropsychobiology **77**(2), 101–109 (2019). https://doi.org/10.1159/000495522. https://www.karger.com/DOI/10.1159/000495522
29. Imperatori, C., et al.: Modification of EEG power spectra and EEG connectivity in autobiographical memory: a sLORETA study. Cogn. Process. **15**(3), 351–361 (2014). https://doi.org/10.1007/s10339-014-0605-5. https://doi.org/10.1007/s10339-014-0605-5

30. Imperatori, C., et al.: Default mode network alterations in alexithymia: an EEG power spectra and connectivity study. Sci. Rep. **6**(1), 1–11 (2016)
31. Imperatori, C., et al.: Default mode network alterations in individuals with high-trait-anxiety: an EEG functional connectivity study. J. Affect. Disord. **246**, 611–618 (2019). https://doi.org/10.1016/j.jad.2018.12.071. http://www.sciencedirect.com/science/article/pii/S0165032718321761
32. Imperatori, C., et al.: Modifications of EEG power spectra in mesial temporal lobe during n-back tasks of increasing difficulty. A Sloreta study. Front. Hum. Neurosci. **7**, 109 (2013)
33. Janes, A., Succi, G.: Lean Software Development in Action. Springer, Heidelberg (2014)
34. Janes, A.A., Succi, G.: The dark side of agile software development. In: Proceedings of the ACM International Symposium on New Ideas, New Paradigms, and Reflections on Programming and Software, Onward! 2012, pp. 215–228. ACM, New York (2012). https://doi.org/10.1145/2384592.2384612. http://doi.acm.org/10.1145/2384592.2384612
35. Jas, M., et al.: A reproducible MEG/EEG group study with the MNE software: recommendations, quality assessments, and good practices. Front. Neurosci. **12**, 530 (2018). https://doi.org/10.3389/fnins.2018.00530. https://www.frontiersin.org/article/10.3389/fnins.2018.00530
36. Katona, J.: Examination and comparison of the EEG based attention test with CPT and TOVA. In: 2014 IEEE 15th International Symposium on Computational Intelligence and Informatics (CINTI), pp. 117–120. IEEE (2014)
37. Kivi, J., Haydon, D., Hayes, J., Schneider, R., Succi, G.: Extreme programming: a university team design experience. In: 2000 Canadian Conference on Electrical and Computer Engineering. Conference Proceedings. Navigating to a New Era (Cat. No.00TH8492), vol. 2, pp. 816–820, May 2000. https://doi.org/10.1109/CCECE.2000.849579
38. Ko, L.W., et al.: Single channel wireless EEG device for real-time fatigue level detection. In: 2015 International Joint Conference on Neural Networks (IJCNN), pp. 1–5. IEEE (2015)
39. Kovács, G.L., Drozdik, S., Zuliani, P., Succi, G.: Open source software for the public administration. In: Proceedings of the 6th International Workshop on Computer Science and Information Technologies, October 2004
40. Lantz, G., et al.: Extracranial localization of intracranial interictal epileptiform activity using LORETA (low resolution electromagnetic tomography). Electroencephalogr. Clin. Neurophysiol. **102**(5), 414–422 (1997). https://doi.org/10.1016/s0921-884x(96)96551-0
41. Lee, S., Matteson, A., Hooshyar, D., Kim, S., Jung, J., Nam, G., Lim, H.: Comparing programming language comprehension between novice and expert programmers using EEG analysis. In: Proceedings of the IEEE 16th International Conference on Bioinformatics and Bioengineering (BIBE), pp. 350–355 (2016)
42. Lehembre, R., et al.: Electrophysiological investigations of brain function in coma, vegetative and minimally conscious patients. Archives italiennes de biologie **150**, 122–39 (2012). https://doi.org/10.4449/aib.v150i2.1374
43. Li, X., Hu, B., Dong, Q., Campbell, W., Moore, P., Peng, H.: EEG-based attention recognition. In: 2011 6th International Conference on Pervasive Computing and Applications pp. 196–201. IEEE (2011)
44. Lyubomirsky, S., King, L., Diener, E.: The benefits of frequent positive affect: does happiness lead to success? Psychol. Bull. **131**(6), 803–855 (2005)

45. Marino, G., Succi, G.: Data structures for parallel execution of functional languages. In: Fasel, J.H., Keller, R.M. (eds.) PARLE 1989. LNCS, vol. 279, pp. 346–356. Springer, Heidelberg (1989). https://doi.org/10.1007/3-540-18420-1_65
46. Marqui, R.P., Michel, C.M., Lehmann, D.: Low-resolution electromagnetic tomography-a new method for localizing electrical activity in the brain. Int. J. Psychophysiol. **18**, 49–65 (1994)
47. Maskeliunas, R., Damasevicius, R., Martisius, I., Vasiljevas, M.: Consumer-grade EEG devices: are they usable for control tasks? PeerJ **4**, e1746 (2016)
48. Maurer, F., Succi, G., Holz, H., Kötting, B., Goldmann, S., Dellen, B.: Software process support over the internet. In: Proceedings of the 21st International Conference on Software Engineering, ICSE 1999, pp. 642–645. ACM, May 1999
49. Michel, C.M., Murray, M.M., Lantz, G., Gonzalez, S., Spinelli, L., de Peralta, R.G.: EEG source imaging. Clin. Neurophysiol. **115**(10), 2195–2222 (2004)
50. Moser, R., Pedrycz, W., Succi, G.: A comparative analysis of the efficiency of change metrics and static code attributes for defect prediction. In: Proceedings of the 30th International Conference on Software Engineering, ICSE 2008, pp. 181–190. ACM (2008)
51. Moser, R., Pedrycz, W., Succi, G.: Analysis of the reliability of a subset of change metrics for defect prediction. In: Proceedings of the Second ACM-IEEE International Symposium on Empirical Software Engineering and Measurement, ESEM 2008, pp. 309–311. ACM (2008)
52. Mosher, J., Leahy, R., Lewis, P.: EEG and MEG: forward solutions for inverse methods. IEEE Trans. Bio-med. Eng. **46**, 245–59 (1999). https://doi.org/10.1109/10.748978
53. Müller, S.C., Fritz, T.: Stuck and frustrated or in flow and happy: sensing developers' emotions and progress. In: International Conference on the IEEE/ACM 37th IEEE Software Engineering (ICSE), vol. 1, pp. 688–699. IEEE (2015)
54. Murgia, A., Tourani, P., Adams, B., Ortu, M.: Do developers feel emotions? An exploratory analysis of emotions in software artifacts. In: Proceedings of the 11th Working Conference on Mining Software Repositories, pp. 262–271 (2014)
55. Musílek, P., Pedrycz, W., Sun, N., Succi, G.: On the sensitivity of COCOMO II software cost estimation model. In: Proceedings of the 8th International Symposium on Software Metrics, pp. 13–20. METRICS 2002. IEEE Computer Society, June 2002
56. Pascual-Marqui, R.D., Esslen, M., Kochi, K., Lehmann, D., et al.: Functional imaging with low-resolution brain electromagnetic tomography (LORETA): a review. Methods Find. Exp. Clin. Pharmacol. **24**(Suppl C), 91–95 (2002)
57. Paulson, J.W., Succi, G., Eberlein, A.: An empirical study of open-source and closed-source software products. IEEE Trans. Software Eng. **30**(4), 246–256 (2004)
58. Pedrycz, W., Russo, B., Succi, G.: A model of job satisfaction for collaborative development processes. J. Syst. Softw. **84**(5), 739–752 (2011)
59. Pedrycz, W., Russo, B., Succi, G.: Knowledge transfer in system modeling and its realization through an optimal allocation of information granularity. Appl. Soft Comput. **12**(8), 1985–1995 (2012). https://doi.org/10.1016/j.asoc.2012.02.004. http://dx.doi.org/10.1016/j.asoc.2012.02.004
60. Pedrycz, W., Succi, G.: Genetic granular classifiers in modeling software quality. J. Syst. Softw. **76**(3), 277–285 (2005)
61. Petrinja, E., Sillitti, A., Succi, G.: Comparing OpenBRR, QSOS, and OMM assessment models. In: Ågerfalk, P., Boldyreff, C., González-Barahona, J.M., Madey, G.R., Noll, J. (eds.) OSS 2010. IAICT, vol. 319, pp. 224–238. Springer, Heidelberg (2010). https://doi.org/10.1007/978-3-642-13244-5_18

62. Ronchetti, M., Succi, G., Pedrycz, W., Russo, B.: Early estimation of software size in object-oriented environments a case study in a CMM level 3 software firm. Inf. Sci. **176**(5), 475–489 (2006)
63. Rossi, B., Russo, B., Succi, G.: Modelling failures occurrences of open source software with reliability growth. In: Ågerfalk, P., Boldyreff, C., González-Barahona, J.M., Madey, G.R., Noll, J. (eds.) OSS 2010. IAICT, vol. 319, pp. 268–280. Springer, Heidelberg (2010). https://doi.org/10.1007/978-3-642-13244-5_21
64. Rossi, B., Russo, B., Succi, G.: Adoption of free/libre open source software in public organizations: factors of impact. Inf. Technol. People **25**(2), 156–187 (2012). https://doi.org/10.1108/09593841211232677
65. Rowan, T.C.: Psychological tests and selection of computer programmers. J. ACM (JACM) **4**(3), 348–353 (1957)
66. Samima, S., Sarma, M., Samanta, D.: Correlation of p300 ERPS with visual stimuli and its application to vigilance detection. In: 2017 39th Annual International Conference of the IEEE Engineering in Medicine and Biology Society (EMBC), pp. 2590–2593. IEEE (2017)
67. Schoffelen, J.M., Gross, J.: Source connectivity analysis with MEG and EEG. Hum. Brain Map. **30**, 1857–65 (2009). https://doi.org/10.1002/hbm.20745
68. Scotto, M., Sillitti, A., Succi, G., Vernazza, T.: A relational approach to software metrics. In: Proceedings of the 2004 ACM Symposium on Applied Computing, SAC 2004, pp. 1536–1540. ACM (2004)
69. Scotto, M., Sillitti, A., Succi, G., Vernazza, T.: A non-invasive approach to product metrics collection. J. Syst. Architect. **52**(11), 668–675 (2006)
70. Sillitti, A., Janes, A., Succi, G., Vernazza, T.: Measures for mobile users: an architecture. J. Syst. Archit. **50**(7), 393–405 (2004). https://doi.org/10.1016/j.sysarc.2003.09.005. http://dx.doi.org/10.1016/j.sysarc.2003.09.005
71. Sillitti, A., Succi, G., Vlasenko, J.: understanding the impact of pair programming on developers attention: a case study on a large industrial experimentation. In: Proceedings of the 34th International Conference on Software Engineering, ICSE 2012, pp. 1094–1101. IEEE Press, June 2012
72. Sillitti, A., Vernazza, T., Succi, G.: Service oriented programming: a new paradigm of software reuse. In: Gacek, C. (ed.) ICSR 2002. LNCS, vol. 2319, pp. 269–280. Springer, Heidelberg (2002). https://doi.org/10.1007/3-540-46020-9_19
73. Succi, G., Benedicenti, L., Vernazza, T.: Analysis of the effects of software reuse on customer satisfaction in an RPG environment. IEEE Trans. Software Eng. **27**(5), 473–479 (2001)
74. Succi, G., Paulson, J., Eberlein, A.: Preliminary results from an empirical study on the growth of open source and commercial software products. In: EDSER-3 Workshop, pp. 14–15 (2001)
75. Succi, G., Pedrycz, W., Marchesi, M., Williams, L.: Preliminary analysis of the effects of pair programming on job satisfaction. In: Proceedings of the 3rd International Conference on Extreme Programming (XP), pp. 212–215 (2002)
76. Taulu, S., Simola, J.: Spatiotemporal signal space separation method for rejecting nearby interference in meg measurements. Phys. Med. Biol. **51**(7), 1759–1768 (2006)
77. Teplan, M.: Fundamentals of EEG measurement. Meas. Sci. Rev. Sect. **2**, 1–11 (2002)
78. Valerio, A., Succi, G., Fenaroli, M.: Domain analysis and framework-based software development. SIGAPP Appl. Comput. Rev. **5**(2), 4–15 (1997)

79. Vernazza, T., Granatella, G., Succi, G., Benedicenti, L., Mintchev, M.: Defining metrics for software components. In: Proceedings of the World Multiconference on Systemics, Cybernetics and Informatics, vol. XI, pp. 16–23, July 2000
80. Wrobel, M.R.: Emotions in the software development process. In: 2013 6th International Conference on Human System Interactions (HSI), pp. 518–523. IEEE (2013)
81. Züger, M., Fritz, T.: Interruptibility of software developers and its prediction using psycho-physiological sensors. In: Proceedings of the 33rd Annual ACM Conference on Human Factors in Computing Systems, pp. 2981–2990. ACM (2015)

Informatics Paradigms for Brain and Mental Health Research

Explainable Boosting Machine for Predicting Alzheimer's Disease from MRI Hippocampal Subfields

Alessia Sarica[1(✉)], Andrea Quattrone[2], and Aldo Quattrone[1,3]

[1] Neuroscience Research Center, Department of Medical and Surgical Sciences, Magna Graecia University, 88100 Catanzaro, Italy
sarica@unicz.it

[2] Institute of Neurology, Department of Medical and Surgical Sciences, Magna Graecia University, 88100 Catanzaro, Italy

[3] Neuroimaging Research Unit, Institute of Molecular Bioimaging and Physiology, National Research Council, 88100 Catanzaro, Italy

Abstract. Although automatic prediction of Alzheimer's disease (AD) from Magnetic Resonance Imaging (MRI) showed excellent performance, Machine Learning (ML) algorithms often provide high accuracy at the expense of interpretability of findings. Indeed, building ML models that can be understandable has fundamental importance in clinical context, especially for early diagnosis of neurodegenerative diseases. Recently, a novel interpretability algorithm has been proposed, the Explainable Boosting Machine (EBM), which is a *glassbox* model based on *Generative Additive Models plus Interactions* GA^2Ms and designed to show optimal accuracy while providing intelligibility. Thus, the aim of present study was to assess – for the first time – the EBM reliability in predicting the conversion to AD and its ability in providing the predictions explainability. In particular, two-hundred brain MRIs from ADNI of Mild Cognitive Impairment (MCI) patients equally divided into stable (sMCI) and progressive (pMCI) were processed with Freesurfer for extracting twelve hippocampal subfields volumes, which already showed good AD prediction power. EBM models with and without pairwise interactions were built on training set (80%) comprised of these volumes, and *global* explanations were investigated. The performance of classifiers was evaluated with AUC-ROC on test set (20%) and *local* explanations of four randomly selected test patients (sMCIs and pMCIs correctly classified and misclassified) were given. EBMs without and with pairwise interactions showed accuracies of respectively 80.5% and 84.2%, thus demonstrating high prediction accuracy. Moreover, EBM provided practical clinical knowledge on why a patient was correctly or incorrectly predicted as AD and which hippocampal subfields drove such prediction.

Alzheimer's Disease Neuroimaging Initiative—Data used in preparation of this article were obtained from the Alzheimer's Disease Neuroim-aging Initiative (ADNI) database (adni.loni.usc.edu). As such, the investigators within the ADNI contributed to the design and implementation of ADNI and/or provided data but did not participate in analysis or writing of this report. A complete listing of ADNI investigators can be found at: http://adni.loni.usc.edu/wp-content/uploads/how_to_ap-ply/ADNI_Acknowledgement_List.pdf.

M. Mahmud et al. (Eds.): BI 2021, LNAI 12960, pp. 341–350, 2021.
https://doi.org/10.1007/978-3-030-86993-9_31

Keywords: Explainable boosting machine · Alzheimer's disease · Hippocampal subfields · MRI

1 Introduction

Machine learning (ML) is widely and increasingly applied to biological data [1, 2] as well as to neuroimaging data [3], especially for the early diagnosis of neurodegenerative diseases [4, 5]. In particular, high classification performance were reached for predicting Alzheimer's disease (AD) [6, 7]. However, most ML algorithms – the so called *blackbox* models - could not provide an accurate and immediate interpretability of the findings [8]. Indeed, the application of ML in the clinical and biomedical field must find an acceptable tradeoff between the accuracy and interpretability [9], where the best algorithms in terms of accuracy (e.g., SVM or Random Forest) are often not intelligible, while the most intelligible models could show poor performance (e.g., logistic regression or Naïve-Bayes) [10]. Recently, a new ML approach was introduced, the Explainable Boosting Machine (EBM) [11], a *glassbox* model based on the *Generative Additive Models* (GAMs) [12], which demonstrated comparable accuracy to the state-of-the-art ML methods by also providing the contribution of each feature to the final prediction. EBM algorithm was successfully applied in the Healthcare context for predicting pneumonia risk and hospital readmission [11], but it was never applied in Neuroimaging and moreover it was never used for predicting AD. For this reason, in the present work, EBM was trained on brain data from Magnetic Resonance Imaging (MRI) scans, where the cohort consisted of two hundred Mild Cognitive Impairment (MCI) patients, equally divided into stable and progressive MCI. The MRI images were pre-processed with Freesurfer [13] for extracting the volume of twelve subfields of the hippocampus, which already showed good classification accuracies in the prediction of conversion to AD [14–17]. Then, these volumes were used for training the EBM for distinguishing between the two diagnoses, for investigating the overall feature importance, as well as for assessing the explanation of the outcome predictions. Furthermore, pairwise interactions between variables were added to the standard GAMs through the model *Generalized Additive Models plus Interactions*, GA^{2}Ms [18].

The main contributions of the present work are: (i) to assess – for the first time - the performance of a *glassbox* model, the EBM, on Neuroimaging data; (ii) to evaluate the reliability of EBM in predicting the conversion to AD; (iii) to compare EBM classifiers without and with interactions between features; (iv) to provide the interpretability of the outcomes and the contribution of each hippocampal subfield to the prediction of the conversion from MCI to AD.

2 Materials and Methods

2.1 Participants

Data used in the preparation of this article were obtained from the Alzheimer's Disease Neuroimaging Initiative (ADNI) database (adni.loni.usc.edu). A total of two-hundred subjects were selected from ADNI, where 100 patients had a diagnosis of stable MCI (sMCI) and 100 MCI patients converted to Alzheimer's (pMCI) within 36 months from the baseline diagnosis. Demographical and clinical data of the cohort were reported in Table 1.

Table 1. Demographical and clinical data of patients as mean ± standard deviation or percentage.

	sMCI (n = 100)	pMCI (n = 100)
Age	72.27 ± 7.71	72.47 ± 6.89
Female (%)	49%	50%
Education (years)	16.38 ± 2.69	15.9 ± 2.84
CDRSB	1.22 ± 0.72	2.21 ± 1.02
MMSE	28.05 ± 1.72	27.34 ± 1.86

Abbreviation: sMCI = stable Mild Cognitive Impairment; pMCI = progressive Mild Cognitive Impairment; CDRSB = Clinical Dementia Rating Scale Sum of Boxes; MMSE = Mini Mental State Examination.

The two groups were age- and sex matched as statistically evaluated respectively by an analysis on variance (ANOVA) and a Chi-squared test (p-value > 0.05). No statistical differences existed also in the education level, CDRSB and MMSE (p-value > 0.05).

2.2 MRI Pre-processing

The MRIs of the selected cohort were downloaded from ADNI and then processed with Freesurfer 6.0 [13] using the standard cross-sectional pipeline (*recon-all*) and the automated segmentation of the hippocampus to its twelve subfields per hemisphere [19]: parasubiculum, presubiculum, subiculum, CA1, CA3, CA4 (cornu ammonis areas), granule cells in the molecular layer of the dentate gyrus (GC-ML-DG), hippocampal-amygdaloid transition area (HATA), fimbria, molecular layer, hippocampal fissure, and hippocampal tail. The detailed procedure and the mean values of each hippocampal subfields volume per diagnosis could be found elsewhere [16].

2.3 Explainable Boosting Machine (EBM)

The EBM algorithm [10] is based on GAMs, which are considered the gold standard for intelligibility. Given $D = \{(x_i, y_i)\}_1^N$ a training dataset of size N, $x_i = (x_{i1}, \ldots, x_{ip})$ the feature vector with p features, and y_i the target, the GAMs take the form:

$$g(E[y]) = \beta_0 + \sum f_j(x_j), \tag{1}$$

where x_j denotes the jth variable in the feature space, g is the *link function* that adapts the GAM to regression (e.g., g = identity) or classification (e.g., g = logistic), and f_j is the feature function. EBM presents several improvements over traditional GAMs by using bagging and gradient boosting. The boosting is applied in a round-robin fashion for training on one feature at a time with a very low learning rate with the aim of ignoring the feature order. EBM iterates through the features for mitigating the co-linearity, for learning the best feature function f_j for each feature and for providing the feature contribute to the prediction. In particular, each function f_j is used as a lookup table, where the term contribution is added and sent through the link function g to make individual predictions. Thanks to the concept of additivity and modularity, the contributions can be ranked and visualized to show which feature had the higher impact on the individual prediction [20]. Another strength of the EBM is the possibility to improve the accuracy by adding pairwise interactions to standard GAMs [18], which take the name of GA^2Ms and have the form:

$$g(E[y]) = \beta_0 + \sum f_j(x_j) + \sum f_{ij}(x_i, x_j), \tag{2}$$

where the two-dimensional interaction $f_{ij}(x_i,x_j)$ could be rendered as heatmap on the two-dimensional x_i,x_j-plane, still providing high intelligibility. First, GA^2M builds the best GAM and then finds all the possible pairs of interactions in the residuals and orders them by importance. Finally, the top k pairwise interactions are included in the model, where k is obtained by cross-validation [10].

2.4 Machine Learning Analysis

Machine Learning analysis was conducted with Python 3.7 and the package InterpretML 0.2.4 [20] on a MacOS 10.14.6 (2.9 GHz, 32 GB of RAM). First, training and test sets were randomly split with a percentage respectively of 80% and 20% with a static seed maintaining the balance in the distribution of classes. Six binary EBM classifiers – sMCI (class *1*) vs pMCI (class *0*) – were built on the training set by automatically varying the number of pairwise interactions in a range from zero (no interactions) to 5. Indeed, since this is the first application of EBM on Neuroimaging data, no information exists about the influence of the pairwise interactions on the model for predicting AD. Although a higher number of feature interactions might produce higher accuracy, searching for the optimal number of pairs is computationally expensive and GA^2M showed robustness to excess variable pairs [18].

The performance of each EBM classifier was evaluated on the test set with the Area under the Curve of the Receiver Operating Characteristic (AUC-ROC), and only the model with the highest AUC was considered for further analysis. The overall importance ranking (*global* explanation) of hippocampal subfields was obtained by ordering their average absolute contribution in the prediction of the training data [20]. Regarding the *local* explanation, four patients from the test set were randomly selected (two sMCIs and two pMCIs, where two patients were correctly classified and two were misclassified) for investigating the importance of the hippocampal subfields in the single outcome, calculated as logit (odds ratio) from the logistic link function g [11, 18].

3 Results

The AUC-ROC accuracies of the six EBM models obtained by varying the number of pairwise interactions were reported in Table 2. When the EBM classifier was trained without pairwise interactions, the AUC-ROC (depicted in Fig. 1.A) was 0.805, and its overall importance, ranking the first fifteen features, was reported in Fig. 1.A. The highest AUC-ROC 0.842 (Fig. 1.B) was reached with a number of pairwise interactions equal to four. The best EBM model found that the first four most predictive features were the interactions *left hippocampal fissure x right HATA*, *left hippocampal fissure x right subiculum*, *left CA3 x right presubiculum*, and *left parasubiculum x right presubiculum* (overall importance reported in Fig. 1.B).

Table 2. AUC-ROC accuracies of the six EBM binary models - sMCI vs pMCI - obtained by varying the number of pairwise interactions (in bold the best result).

#interactions	0	1	2	3	**4**	5
AUC-ROC	0.805	0.777	0.782	0.76	**0.842**	0.712

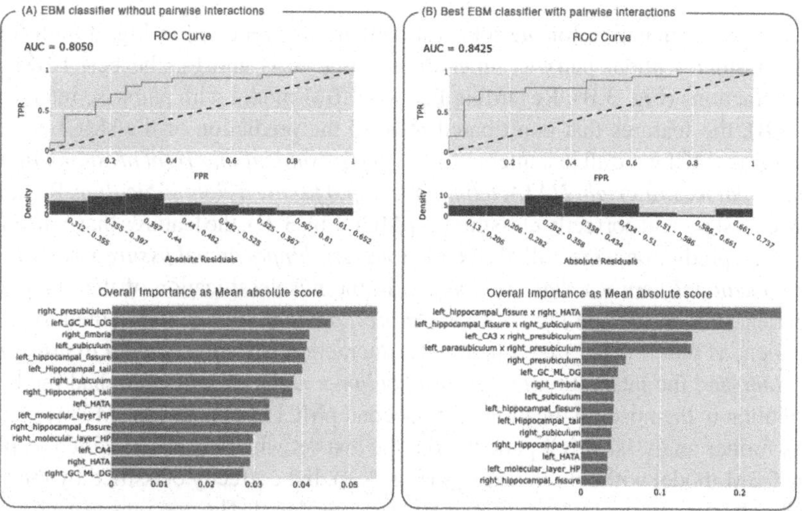

Fig. 1. Findings of (A) the EBM classifier without pairwise interactions and (B) the best (highest AUC) EBM classifier with four pairwise interactions. Upper plots are the ROC Curves (on test set) and densities of the absolute residuals, bottom plots are the rankings of the overall feature importance (first fifteen features) as mean absolute score (on training set).

The heatmaps of the four pairwise interactions – found as the most predictive features for distinguishing sMCI from pMCI patients in the overall importance ranking of the best EBM classifier - are depicted in Fig. 2.

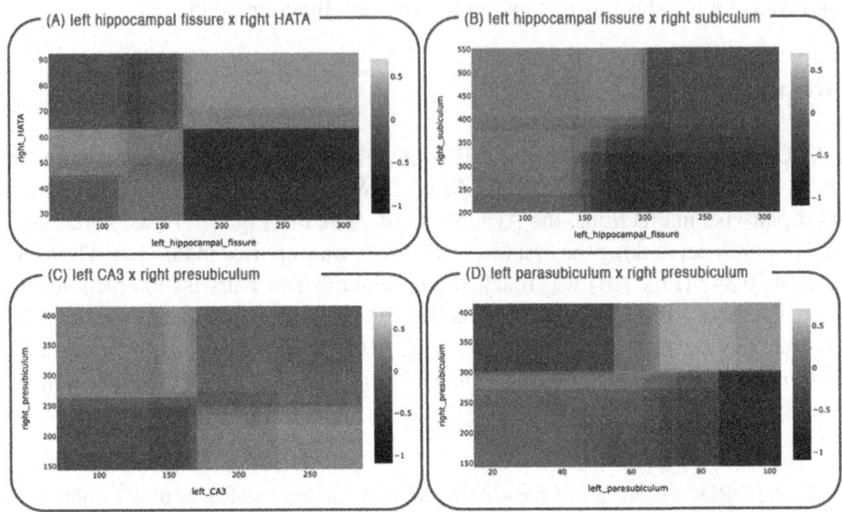

Fig. 2. Heatmaps of the four pairwise interactions between: (A) left hippocampal fissure and right HATA; (B) left hippocampal fissure and right subiculum; (C) left CA3 and right presubiculum; (D) left parasubiculum and right presubiculum. The scores are logits (log odds), where sMCI is class *1* (yellow) and pMCI is class *0* (purple). (Color figure online)

The local explanation for the four test patients was reported in Fig. 3 both for the EBM classifier without pairwise interactions (Fig. 3.A) and for the best EBM with four interactions (Fig. 3.B). Regarding the best EBM model with pairwise interactions (Fig. 3.B), the features that contributed most to the prediction of the sMCI correctly classified as sMCI were all just interactions: *left parasubiculum x right presubiculum, left hippocampal fissure x right HATA, left hippocampal fissure x right subiculum.* Regarding the pMCI test patient correctly classified as pMCI (Fig. 3. B), the features that contributed most to the prediction were still all interactions: *left hippocampal fissure x right HATA, left hippocampal fissure x right subiculum.* In the misclassification of the other sMCI test patient, the interaction *left CA3 x right presubiculum* highly contributed to predict this patient as pMCI (Fig. 3.B). Finally, the interaction *left hippocampal fissure x right subiculum*, and the interaction *left parasubiculum x right presubiculum* had the higher contribution in the misclassification of the second pMCI test patient as sMCI (Fig. 3.B).

As further analysis, sMCI patient from the test set who was misclassified as pMCI by the EBM model without interactions (Fig. 4.A), but correctly classified by the EBM model with four pair interactions (Fig. 4.B) was considered. The rankings of each feature contribution of the two models (Fig. 4) were compared and it was found that the two variables that contributed to the correct classification of this test patient were the two interactions *left CA3 x right presubiculum* and *left hippocampal fissure x right subiculum.*

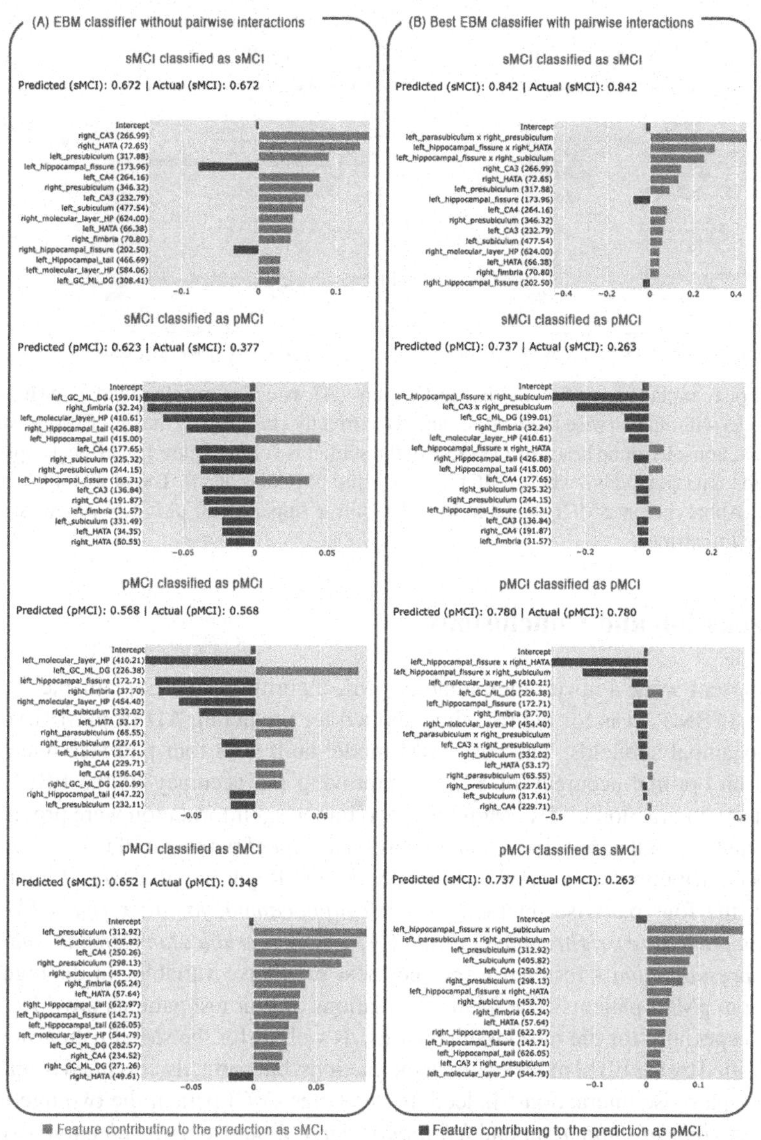

Fig. 3. Local explanation of four test patients - randomly selected from the test set - obtained by (A) the EBM classifier without pairwise interactions and (B) the best EBM classifier with four pairwise interactions. From top to bottom the classification of: an sMCI as sMCI, an pMCI as pMCI, an sMCI as pMCI, an pMCI as sMCI. In round brackets the value of the subfields volume [mm^3]. The local explanation scores are logits (log odds), where sMCI is class *1* and pMCI is class *0*. The probabilities are also reported. Abbreviation: sMCI = stable Mild Cognitive Impairment; pMCI = progressive Mild Cognitive Impairment.

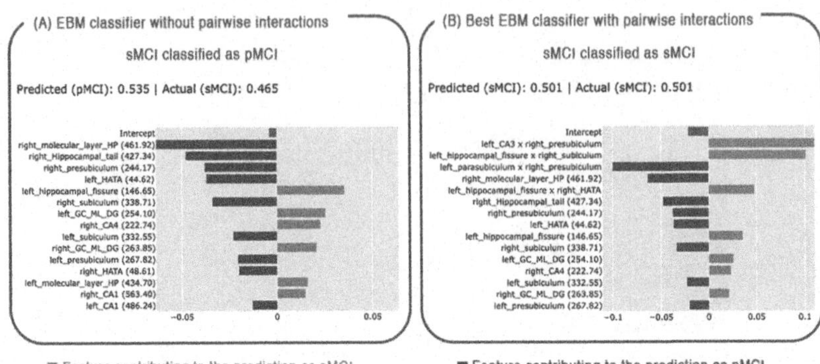

Fig. 4. Local explanation of one sMCI test patient (A) who was misclassified as pMCI by the EBM model without pairwise interactions and (B) correctly classified by the best EBM model with four interactions. In round brackets the value of the subfields volume [mm^3]. The local explanation scores are logits (log odds), where sMCI is class *1* and pMCI is class *0*. The probabilities are also reported. Abbreviation: sMCI = stable Mild Cognitive Impairment; pMCI = progressive Mild Cognitive Impairment.

4 Discussion and Conclusions

In the present work a novel interpretability ML algorithm - the Explainable Boosting Machine (EBM) - was for the first time applied for predicting AD from MRI volumes of hippocampal subfields. The best EBM model built with four pairwise interactions showed an optimal accuracy of 84.2%, improving the accuracy of the EBM model without any interaction by 5%. Moreover, two important information were provided: an *overall* ranking of the most important features and a *local* ranking of the most important features contributing to the single patient prediction. Regarding the *overall* importance ranking, the four pairwise interactions - *left hippocampal fissure x right HATA, left hippocampal fissure x right subiculum, left CA3 x right presubiculum, left parasubiculum x right presubiculum* - resulted to be the most predictive variables in distinguishing sMCI from pMCI patients. The *local* explanations of four test patients provided useful insight, especially for the misclassified cases, as well as for the sMCI patient who was misclassified by the EBM model without interactions, but correctly classified by the EBM with four pairwise interactions. Indeed, in this latter sMCI patient the two interactions *left CA3 x right presubiculum* and *left hippocampal fissure x right subiculum* were the two features that contributed to its correct classification, thus demonstrating further that considering the pairwise interactions in the EBM improved the performance while still providing the intelligibility of the model.

The volumes of the hippocampal subfields already showed their ability in predicting the progression from MCI to AD, as demonstrated by [14] and [15], given their involvement in the alterations of the mnesic profile of AD patients [17]. In particular, Khan et al. [14] found that subfields volumes were more accurate than total hippocampal volume in predicting the conversion to AD by using Orthogonal Partial Least Squares as classification approach, reaching an accuracy of 81.1%. Vasta et al. [15] confirmed the results of Khan et al. [14] through a Neural Networks classifier for distinguishing sMCI from pMCI patients, with an accuracy of 72.7%. The present EBM model with pairwise interactions, not only improved the classification accuracy of unintelligible ML methods [14, 15] trained on the same data here used, but it was also able to give practical clinical knowledge on why a test patient was correctly or incorrectly classified and which specific hippocampal subfields drove such classification.

Several limitations of the current study must be recognized. First, the small sample size could have somehow reduced the generalizability of the findings, although the bagging and boosting procedures of EBM may have been able to minimize this issue. Secondly, the tuning of the number of interactions in the GA^2M was limited to a maximum of five, thus it is not possible to know whether the accuracy might be improved with a higher number of pairs interactions considered as features. A methodological issue should be reported regarding the local explanation. Indeed, although EBM provides accurate explainability of the predictions, these are based on correlation [10], thus the explanation model could not be totally faithful when it is not possible to exclude the presence of heavy multicollinearity or of non-linearity around a prediction. Finally, further studies are needed for investigating the possible biological meaning of the hippocampal subfields interactions found, which, while being highly intelligible, should demonstrate a clinical correlate for being considered as reliable biomarkers of AD.

In conclusions, this first attempt of using EBM on brain MRI data for the prediction of AD showed high accuracy and good explainability of the outcomes, thus encouraging the further application of such *glassbox* model also in the Neuroimaging field.

References

1. Mahmud, M., Kaiser, M.S., Hussain, A., Vassanelli, S.: Applications of deep learning and reinforcement learning to biological data. IEEE Trans. Neural Netw. Learn Syst. **29**, 2063–2079 (2018)
2. Mahmud, M., Kaiser, M.S., McGinnity, T.M., Hussain, A.: Deep learning in mining biological data. Cognit. Comput. **13**, 1–33 (2021)
3. Jollans, L., et al.: Quantifying performance of machine learning methods for neuroimaging data. Neuroimage **199**, 351–365 (2019)
4. Noor, M.B.T., Zenia, N.Z., Kaiser, M.S., Mamun, S.A., Mahmud, M.: Application of deep learning in detecting neurological disorders from magnetic resonance images: a survey on the detection of Alzheimer's disease. Parkinson's disease and schizophrenia. Brain Inform. **7**, 11 (2020)
5. Mahmud, M., Vassanelli, S., Kaiser, M.S., Zhong, N. (eds.): BI 2020. LNCS (LNAI), vol. 12241. Springer, Cham (2020). https://doi.org/10.1007/978-3-030-59277-6
6. Sarica, A., Cerasa, A., Quattrone, A.: Random forest algorithm for the classification of neuroimaging data in Alzheimer's disease: a systematic review. Front. Aging Neurosci. **9**, 329 (2017)
7. Sarica, A., Cerasa, A., Quattrone, A., Calhoun, V.: Editorial on special issue: machine learning on MCI. J. Neurosci. Method **302**, 2 (2018)
8. Arrieta, A.B., et al.: Explainable Artificial Intelligence (XAI): Concepts, taxonomies, opportunities and challenges toward responsible AI. Inf. Fusion **58**, 82–115 (2020)
9. Ahmad, M.A., Eckert, C., Teredesai, A.: Interpretable machine learning in healthcare. In: Proceedings of the 2018 ACM International Conference on Bioinformatics, Computational Biology, and Health Informatics, pp. 559–560 (2018)

10. Caruana, R., Lou, Y., Gehrke, J., Koch, P., Sturm, M., Elhadad, N.: Intelligible models for healthcare: predicting pneumonia risk and hospital 30-day readmission. In: Proceedings of the 21th ACM SIGKDD International Conference on Knowledge Discovery and Data Mining, pp. 1721–1730 (2015)
11. Lou, Y., Caruana, R., Gehrke, J.: Intelligible models for classification and regression. In: Proceedings of the 18th ACM SIGKDD International Conference on Knowledge Discovery and Data Mining, pp. 150–158 (2012)
12. Hastie, T.J., Tibshirani, R.J.: Generalized Additive Models. CRC Press, Boca Raton (1990)
13. Fischl, B., et al.: Whole brain segmentation: automated labeling of neuroanatomical structures in the human brain. Neuron **33**, 341–355 (2002)
14. Khan, W., et al.: Automated hippocampal subfield measures as predictors of conversion from mild cognitive impairment to Alzheimer's disease in two independent cohorts. Brain Topogr. **28**, 746–759 (2015)
15. Vasta, R., et al.: Hippocampal subfield atrophies in converted and not-converted mild cognitive impairments patients by a markov random fields algorithm. Current Alzheimer Res. **13**, 566–574 (2016)
16. Sarica, A., et al.: MRI asymmetry index of hippocampal subfields increases through the continuum from the mild cognitive impairment to the Alzheimer's disease. Front. Neurosci. **12**, 576 (2018)
17. Novellino, F., et al.: Relationship between hippocampal subfields and category cued recall in AD and PDD: a multimodal MRI study. Neuroscience **371**, 506–517 (2018)
18. Lou, Y., Caruana, R., Gehrke, J., Hooker, G.: Accurate intelligible models with pairwise interactions. In: Proceedings of the 19th ACM SIGKDD International Conference on Knowledge Discovery and Data Mining, pp. 623–631 (2015)
19. Iglesias, J.E., et al.: A computational atlas of the hippocampal formation using ex vivo, ultra-high resolution MRI: application to adaptive segmentation of in vivo MRI. Neuroimage **115**, 117–137 (2015)
20. Nori, H., Jenkins, S., Koch, P., Caruana, R.: Interpretml: a unified framework for machine learning interpretability. arXiv preprint arXiv:1909.09223 (2019)

A Matlab-Based Open-Source Toolbox for Artefact Removal from Extracellular Neuronal Signals

Marcos Fabietti[1], Mufti Mahmud[1,2,3](✉), and Ahmad Lotfi[1]

[1] Department of Computer Science, Nottingham Trent University, Clifton Lane, Nottingham NG118NS, UK
mufti.mahmud@ntu.ac.uk

[2] Medical Technologies Innovation Facility, Nottingham Trent University, Clifton Lane, Nottingham NG118NS, UK

[3] Computing and Informatics Research Centre, Nottingham Trent University, Clifton Lane, Nottingham NG118NS, UK

Abstract. The neural recordings in the form of local field potentials offer useful insights on higher-level neural functions by providing information about the activation and deactivation of neural circuits. But often these recordings are contaminated by multiple internal and external sources of noise from nearby electronic systems and body movements. However, to facilitate knowledge extraction from these recordings, identification and removal of the artefacts are empirical, and various computational techniques have been applied for this purpose. Here we report a new module for artefact removal, an extension of the toolbox named SANTIA (SigMate Advanced: a Novel Tool for Identification of Artefacts in Neuronal Signals) which allows for fast application of deep learning techniques to remove said artefacts without relying on data from other channels.

Keywords: Computational neuroscience · Artefact detection · Machine learning

1 Introduction

Local Field Potentials (LFP) are neural signals recorded from the extracellular region surrounding the neurons, recorded from within the cortical tissue, and low-pass filtering the signal to under 100–300 Hz. The filtering retains only the slow fluctuations produced by the more sustained currents in the tissue, such as the synaptic and somato-dendritic currents and voltage-gated membrane oscillations. The obtained signal represents the contribution of several different neuronal processing pathways, and is related to the single-unit activity [32].

During the signal acquisition, other sources of electrical activity can be mixed in. These are known as artefacts in the literature and are typically classified as physiological or external. Electrical activity throughout the body, for example,

M. Mahmud et al. (Eds.): BI 2021, LNAI 12960, pp. 351–365, 2021.
https://doi.org/10.1007/978-3-030-86993-9_32

heartbeat, muscular activity, ocular movements, and blinking, etc. belong to the first group. Transmission lines, cellphone signals and light stimulation origin, electrode's poor contact, popping and lead movement in the other one. Furthermore, LFP can be contaminated with stimulation artefacts during experiments or spiking activity of local neurons and other distal electrical activity in the brain may be present in the recording. Due to artefact presence in recordings, adversary effects of the likes of misdiagnosis, disturbance of the study of the brain activity or causing a brain-machine interface device to be mistakenly operated can happen. Thus, it is imperative to detect and remove them in order to make use of them effectively.

Table 1. Open source toolboxes and noise detection and removal functionalities.

	ML art. det.\Rem.	Digital filtering	Data visual.	Spectral analysis	Stim. art. removal	File oper.	Multiple formats
Brainstorm [39]	X	✓	✓	✓	X	X	✓
BSMART [6]	X	X	✓	✓	X	X	✓
Chronux [4]	X	X	✓	✓	X	X	X
Elephant [41]	X	X	✓	✓	X	X	✓
Fieldtrip [34]	X	✓	✓	✓	X	X	✓
Klusters, NeuroScope, NDManager [13]	X	✓	✓	✓	X	✓	✓
Neo [12]	X	X	✓	X	X	✓	✓
NeuroChaT [14]	X	X	✓	✓	X	X	✓
Spycode [5]	X	✓	✓	✓	X	X	✓
SANTIA	✓	✓	✓	✓	✓	✓	✓

Legends: Machine learning based Artefact Detection and Removal, Data Visualization, Stimulation Artefact Removal and File Operations (i.e. file splitting, concatenation, column rearranging)

Artefact removal can be carried out via filtering, computational methods, or rejecting segments. Filtering is done by employing a band-pass filter on frequencies which it is known a priory to be affected by artefacts, such as the transmission lines at 50 Hz. However, many artefacts appear in a broad spectrum, which make them difficult to filter without removing neuronal information. Computational methods, such as independent component analysis, depend on an expert reviewing the neural recordings and removing contaminated components. This involves a great deal of experience in the study of neural recordings and a considerable amount of time. The base toolbox, SigMate [16–18], deals with LFP artefact detection and incorporates standard methods to analyze spikes and electroencephalography (EEG) signals, and in-house solutions for LFP analysis. The functionalities provided by SigMate include: artefact removal for both fast [23] and slow [21] artefacts, angular tuning detection [20], noise characterization [22], cortical layer activation order detection and network decoding [15,19,25,26], sorting of single trial LFP [27–30], etc. Even advanced toolboxes which offer these advanced artefact removal options (including filtering, electrical line noise removal, bad channel rejection, independent component analysis with automated component rejection, etc.) still rely on discarding segment of a channel in a corrupted epoch nonetheless. This leads to the undesired loss of information, due to the integrity of the data as well as the cost associated with it. Instead, advanced methods such as machine learning techniques could be used to recover the original signal to preserve the information. The aforementioned toolboxes for LFP data have been compiled in Table 1, where the main characteristics are listed, indicating the advantages of the SANTIA toolbox.

Machine learning techniques are algorithms that learn from patterns in data and are able to make predictions of new data based on it. These algorithms have been applied in diverse fields such anomaly detection [7–9], biological data mining [24], disease detection [33], elderly monitoring [2], financial forecasting [35], image analysis [3,37], natural language processing [36,40], patient monitoring [1,38]. Among them, deep neural networks stand out, which are composed of multiple layers of neurons for processing non-linear information and were inspired by how the human brain works. When dealing with time series analysis and forecast, the variant named recurrent neural networks (RNN) is widely used. These networks have the characteristic that they contain feed-back connections, which allows them to store information about the past states and process variable-length sequences of inputs. Therefore, they are applied in cases such as temporal processing and learning sequences. However, these models suffer the vanishing gradient problem, which makes them hard to train, caused by the re-application of the hidden layer's weight to themselves during back-propagation. Long-Short Term Memory (LSTM) is a sub-type of RNN that can overcome this problem [9].

The aim of this research is to report an artefact removal module, which complements a previously developed artefact detection tool, for individual channel LFP recordings based on the LSTM neural network architecture. The remainder of this paper is organised in 5 sections: Sect. 2 presents the utilised methods, Sect. 3 explains the apps modules and their usage, Sect. 4 contains the achieved results on a testing open-access data set and lastly, Sect. 5 concludes the report.

2 Method

By training an LSTM network to accurately forecast artefact-free data, we hypothesise is that it can effectively be used to replace artefactual segments of the signals when information of other channels have been compromised and can't be used to approximate its true behaviour. The LSTM network was trained to forecast normal behaviour via a sliding window approach, which takes the data from a time t and uses it to forecast the time $t+1$, which in turn is incorporated when making the prediction for $t+2$.

This architecture was chosen because of the capability of LSTM and RNN in recognising patterns from sequential data. The LSTM cells used in this work include a forget gate which decides what information is kept and what information is discarded from the cell state. If the value of the forget gate f_t or $f(t)$ is 1, all information are saved, but if the value of the forget gate is 0, it is forgotten. Equation set 1 shows how this specific LSTM cell can be mathematically expressed.

$$\begin{aligned} f_t &= \sigma(W_{fh}h_{t-1} + W_{fx}x_t + b_f), \\ i_t &= \sigma(W_{ih}h_{t-1} + W_{ix}x_t + b_i), \\ \tilde{c}_t &= tanh(W_{\tilde{c}h}h_{t-1} + W_{\tilde{c}x}x_t + b_{\tilde{c}}), \\ c_t &= f_t \cdot c_{t-1} + i_t \cdot \tilde{c}_t, \\ o_t &= \sigma(W_{oh}h_{t-1} + W_{ox}x_t + b_o), \\ h_t &= o_t \cdot tanh(c_t) \end{aligned} \tag{1}$$

where the variable x_t is the input vector, W are the weights, b is the bias and σ is the sigmoid function. Additionally, f_t is the forget gate, i_t is the update gate, $\tilde{c}_t$ is the cell input, c_t is the cell state, o_t is the output gate and h_t the hidden state or output vector of the cell at time t. For evaluating its performance, we used the root mean squared error (RMSE), as defined in Eq. 2, between the network's prediction and the actual values of a sub-set of the data (i.e. test set).

$$RMSE = \sqrt{\frac{\sum_{i=1}^{N}(x_i - \hat{x}_i)^2}{N}} \tag{2}$$

To construct and train the network of LSTM cells, the Deep Learning Toolbox from Matlab [31] was used. The models were composed of the input layer, a hidden layer of one-tenth of the input and finally the output layer equal to the number of predicted points. The optimisation algorithm used was Adam, with an initial learning rate of 0.1, momentum of 0.9 and a batch size of 516. The loss function of the regression layer was the half-mean-squared-error of the predicted responses for each time step, not normalised by N:

$$loss = \frac{1}{2S}\sum_{i=1}^{S}\sum_{j=1}^{N}(x_{ij} - \hat{x}_{ij})^2 \tag{3}$$

where S is the output sequence length.

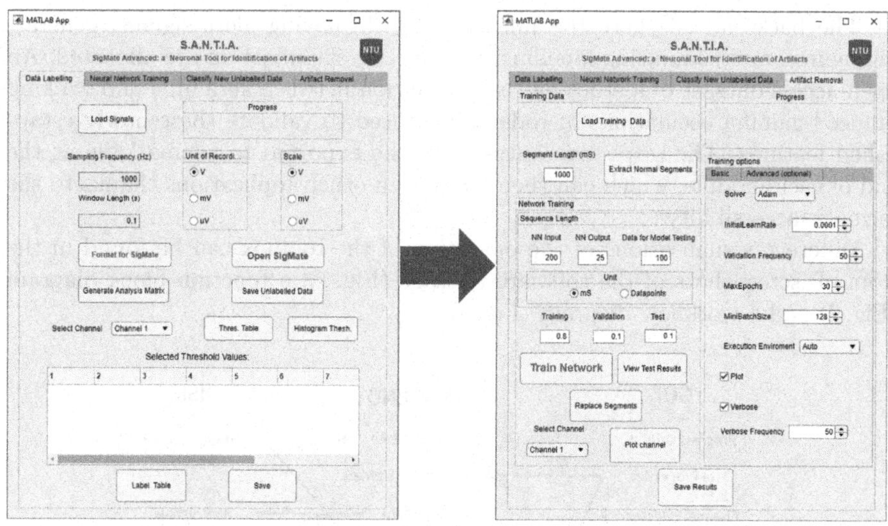

Fig. 1. Screenshots of the SANTIA toolbox graphical user interface: Data Labelling and Artefact Removal.

3 Operation

The toolbox is available for download directly from the Github repository[1]. Having launched the toolbox, the GUI provides easy access to all modules. It's important to note that SANTIA is a generic environment built on a single interface with individual features implemented, rather than a library of functions with a GUI added to make access easier.

The app is divided into four modules, each of which performs a different process and analysis on neuronal signal files. The app consists of four modules which perform various processes and analysis on neuronal signal files. For artefact removal, only the first module which labels the data and the fourth module which performs the removal are used. The first one's major functionalities are as follows: data loading, scaling, reshaping, channel selection, labelling, saving and 2D display. The fourth module is composed of: data loading, normal segments extraction, hyper-parameter setting, network train, test set visualisation, replace segments, plot replaced channels and saving.

The user communicates with the GUI by selecting functions, settings, and keyboard inputs, which are handled in the back-end. Before running any function, a check routine runs to ensure that the user has not missed a process or failed to include all of the required inputs or parameter selections. This reduces the likelihood of human error as well as the amount of time spent. When the cursor has hovered over a component of the GUI, tool-tips with a short clarification appear in case the user has doubts.

[1] https://github.com/IgnacioFabietti/SANTIAtoolbox.

The back-end is where the functions for displaying alert signals, generating figures, and computing labelling, training, or classification are allocated. An open-access dataset of a study of the correlation between ketamine and walking induced gamma oscillations in rodents was used to validate these newly established features. The respective outputs can be exported to a '.mat' file at the end of each module, which can then be used in other applications thanks to the format's accessibility.

Different visualisations of the operation of the toolbox can be found in the from of: screenshots of the software package (Fig. 1), a function block diagram (Fig. 2) and a workflow diagram (Fig. 3).

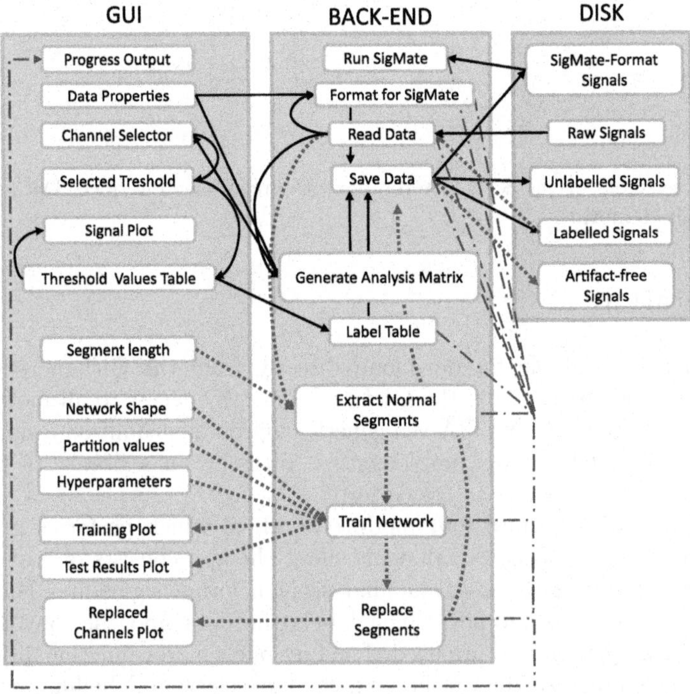

Fig. 2. Functional block diagram of the Toolbox. Arrows in black correspond to the "Data Labeling" module, in red to the "Artefact Removal" module and the purple arrows indicate the progress output. (Color figure online)

3.1 Data Labelling

The process starts with the 'Load Signals' button in the first module, which launches the import wizard to load the neural recordings as an $m \times n$ matrix, where m is the number of channels and n is the number of data points for each channel. Among the formats that are compatible are ASCII-based text (.txt, .dat, .out, .csv), spreadsheets files (.xls, .xlsx, .xlsm) and Matab files (.set, .mat).

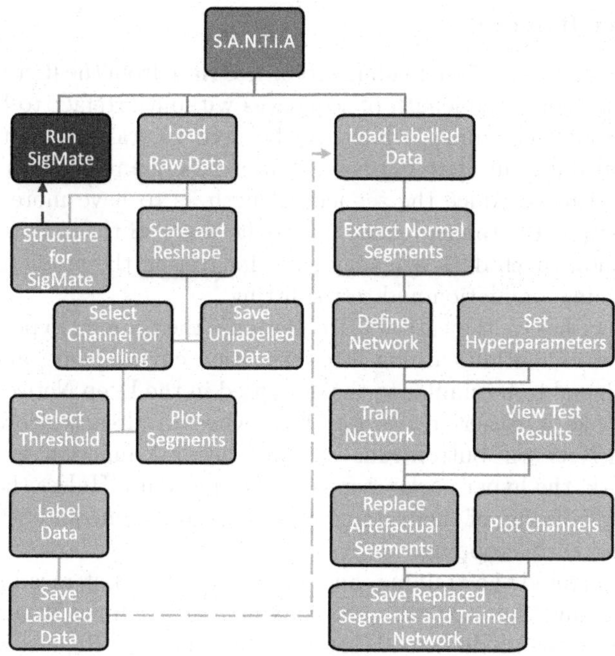

Fig. 3. Workflow of the SANTIA toolbox, where the "Data Labeling" modules are coloured yellow, and "Artefact removal" modules in green. (Color figure online)

The user must specify the sampling frequency in Hz and the window length in seconds for analysis. In addition, the recording unit and the ability to scale are included, as often errors occur as a result of inaccurate magnitude annotations.

The 'Generate Analysis Matrix' function will format the data for posterior analysis, when all of these parameters have been filled in. This is followed by the labelling of data, which consists of assigning a binary label to segments whose power exceeds that of a threshold defined by the user. This can be done via a table which allows to plot each segment and select its value as the threshold, or by a histogram plot of the segments' power, where with a slider they can set the separation of normal from artefactual or visualise a segment.

In another manner, the user can manually input threshold values in the main app's table, and once he has completed it for all channels, the data can be labelled and saved as a standardised struct, which contains the original filename, the structured data with its labels, the sampling frequency, window length, the scale, and the threshold values. This information allows researchers to quickly identify different matrices they create and wish to compare. An aid in form of text in the 'Progress' banner allows the users to know when each step has been completed, and it is replicated throughout each module.

3.2 Artefact Removal

The fourth module starts with loading structured data from the first module. The user is asked to define the length of sequences without artefact to be extracted from the neuronal recordings, which will be used to train the network. After extracting said data, an alert notifies the user how many examples there are, in case they wish to reduce the sequence length as to have more of them for training. Subsequently, the user must define the shape of the network (i.e. input and output), how much data will they leave for testing the predictions and the values for training, validation and test splitting.

If the user wishes to, they are able to customise the training hyper-parameters such as the solver, initial learning rate, execution environment, among others. These are designed to be similar to the ones used in the Deep Network Designer, in order to make it easier to use for those who are already acquainted with it. The 'Train Network' button runs the train network function which uses the defined network, the hyper parameters and the split data. Unless the user specifies otherwise, a display of the training process occurs immediately, allowing for monitoring and early stopping.

Having completed the training, an alert notifies the root mean square error of the test set, and the user can view the different examples from the set and compare them to the predictions. If satisfied, by using the 'Replace Segments', a routine which replaces each window labelled as artefact from the original recordings is run. Its results can also be visualised by first choosing which channel to plot, and using the 'Plot Channel' Button. Finally, 'Save Results' creates a struct with data's filename, the trained network, the training information, the test set's RMSE, the test set original and replaced segments and the data with the artefactual data removed.

4 Testing

Table 2. Guide to determine best channels and epochs to use of baseline walk and rest recordings in medial prefrontal cortex (mPFC) and the mediodorsal (MD) thalamus, as mentioned in the file named "Coherence Phase Plot Guide". The first column is the rat identification, column 2 and 3 the selected two best channels of the mPFC recordings and 4 and 5 of the MD recordings. Finally, column 6 shows the range of artefact free epochs during walking and column 7 during resting, respectively [10]

Rat	mPFC chan1	mPFC chan2	MD chan1	MD chan2	Walk epoch	Rest epoch
KF9	5	6	3	7	960–1160	3780–3820
KF10	3	4	3	8	670–860	1260–1390
KF14	2	6	5	7	740–940	3350–3550
KF15	3	4	5	7	450–640	1600–1700

In order to test the toolbox, a publicly available dataset was used [10]. The article linked to the dataset contains an extensive report of the recordings and the experiments [11]. The signals were obtained from male Long Evans rats, weighing from 280 to 300 g, that were trained to walk on a circular treadmill. These recorded LFP signals were acquired at a sampling rate of 2 kHz, followed by a low-pass filtering and lastly amplified times a thousand and band-pass filtered from 0.7 150 Hz.

A sub-section of the data consisting of the baseline recordings (i.e. prior to ketamine injection) were employed to test the toolbox. At least two five-minute counter-clockwise walking loops on a slow-moving treadmill and two 40-s rest periods without artefacts were included in the baseline recordings. Visual evaluation and videotaped motor activity were used to classify artefact-free periods of 100 s in treadmill-on epochs and 40 to 100 s periods in treadmill-off epochs, which are detailed in Table 2. The threshold power value for each channel was calculated using these labelled artefact-free epochs. It was chosen as the maximum power of the windows in those intervals for a window size of 50 ms, which was chosen based on previously obtained classification results.

For each of the rodents, one-second artefact free segments were extracted and then split into training (80%), validation (10%) and testing (10%) sets. In addition, a model fed with their combined data was also trained. From each one second segment, the first 200 ms were used as information for the model to forecast the subsequent data point and in the test set 100 ms were used to calculate the RMSE. The optimisation algorithm used was Adam, with an initial learning rate of 0.01, momentum of 0.9 and a batch size of 128. The results of the models are captured in Table 3, where the number of examples, validation set loss and test set RMSE for each one is shown. Overall all the individual models achieve low RMSE, in particular that of K10, however this might be attributed to having a smaller sample size. The global model shows a poorer performance due to differences between the rodent's neural recording, but still is an effective forecaster.

Table 3. Number of examples, validation set loss and test set RMSE of different rodents and a global model

Rodent	Examples	Validation loss	Test RMSE
K9	15780	9.00E−08	0.119
K10	6127	7.69E−09	0.076
K14	38034	3.16E−08	0.117
K15	39321	2.97E−08	0.162
All	99262	1.19E−05	0.189

In order to evaluate further that the replaced segment behaves accordingly like the original ones, an analysis of their frequency must be done. To that end, Fig. 4 contains exemplary two-seconds segments of a channel without and with artefact, and the same segment after its removal, along with their corresponding

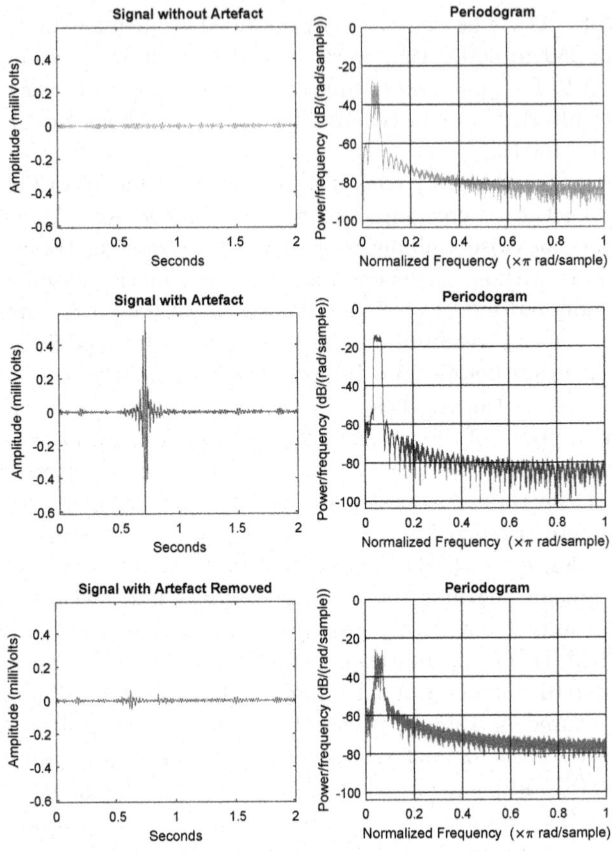

Fig. 4. Exemplary segments of channels without and with artefact, and the same segment after its removal, along with their corresponding periodogram.

periodogram. This allows to identify frequency bands in which the artefact manifests and with how much intensity, as well as how accurate the restored signal is compared to the original.

The signal resulting of the removal is closer both in shape and power per frequency to the artefact free signal, an indication of the success of the method. The presence of the artefact is noticeable in the lower frequencies, where the power of the signal exceeds the −20 dB, while the artefact free signal and the corrected signal are in the order of −30 dB.

Another comparison was carried out by training an LSTM network as a classifier of normal and artefactual segments of 100 ms from the same dataset. The segments had been already been labelled (see Sect. 3.1), and the network was trained using the artefact detection module of the toolbox. The model was trained with a balanced dataset of 21,014 examples and achieved 90% accuracy on the test set. The forecasted 100 ms of the test set belonging to the forecasting global model

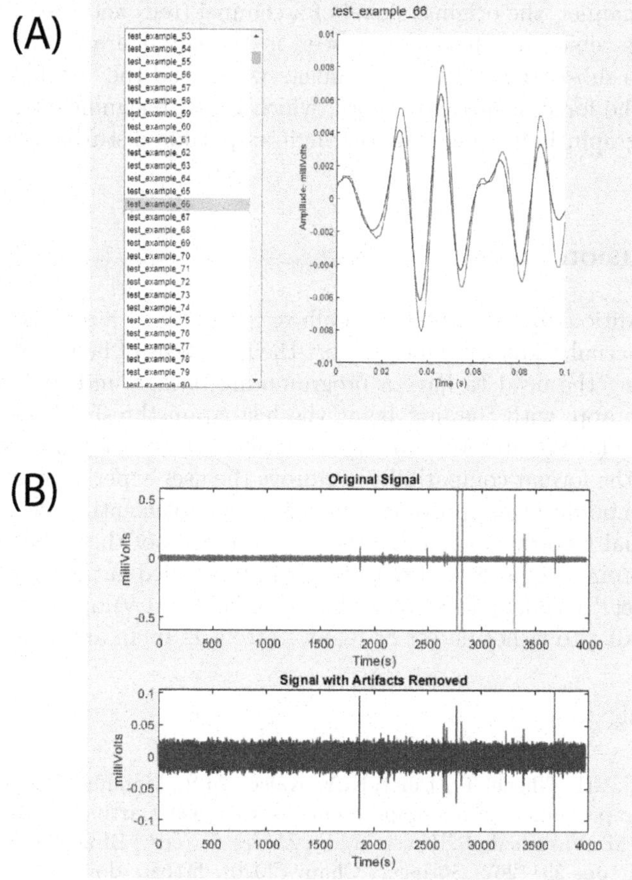

Fig. 5. Outputs of the artefact removal module: visualisation of the test set (A) and comparison of the original signal with artefacts removed (B). In both outputs the original signal is coloured in red, and the prediction or the artefact removed signal in blue. (Color figure online)

were classified with a sensitivity of 100%, indicating that the forecasted segments don't deviate from normal LFP.

4.1 Outputs

The toolbox generates outputs for the user to evaluate the performance of the network, allowing them to adjust parameters or its shape in order to improve it. In Fig. 5, the outputs of 'View Test Results' (sub-figure A) and 'Plot Channel' (sub-figure B) are shown. An example of the test set (red) and the prediction of the network (blue) can be seen in the sub-figure A. In it, the network has shown the ability to mimic the behaviour of the signal, both in shape and amplitude.

In a similar manner, the original signal of a channel (red) and the same channel with artefacts removed (blue) can be seen in the sub-figure (B). The removal of each 50 ms sub-portion of these segments which had the 'artefact' label was replaced by the forecast of the network, which leads to significantly reduce the scale of the graph, indicating that the high amplitude disturbances have been removed.

5 Conclusion

This new addition to the SANTIA toolbox is meant to aid those looking to replace artefactual segments which distort their analysis of neuronal recordings, without having the need to have a programming background. It is the second update of the app, with the first being the histogram threshold selector of the labelling module. We are still looking to improve it with features such as the expansion of the format compatibility, improve the user experience and allow the use of multi-modality to improve the models by complementing the information of the neuronal recordings, among others. The results of the publicly available dataset are promising, and further testing will be carried out with a bigger, but private dataset. To conclude, SANTIA has been further developed as a useful tool for those looking to either detect or remove artefacts in an automatic manner.

References

1. Al Banna, M.H., Ghosh, T., Taher, K.A., Kaiser, M.S., Mahmud, M.: A monitoring system for patients of autism spectrum disorder using artificial intelligence. In: Mahmud, M., Vassanelli, S., Kaiser, M.S., Zhong, N. (eds.) BI 2020. LNCS (LNAI), vol. 12241, pp. 251–262. Springer, Cham (2020). https://doi.org/10.1007/978-3-030-59277-6_23
2. Al Nahian, M.J., Ghosh, T., Uddin, M.N., Islam, M.M., Mahmud, M., Kaiser, M.S.: Towards artificial intelligence driven emotion aware fall monitoring framework suitable for elderly people with neurological disorder. In: Mahmud, M., Vassanelli, S., Kaiser, M.S., Zhong, N. (eds.) BI 2020. LNCS (LNAI), vol. 12241, pp. 275–286. Springer, Cham (2020). https://doi.org/10.1007/978-3-030-59277-6_25
3. Ali, H.M., Kaiser, M.S., Mahmud, M.: Application of convolutional neural network in segmenting brain regions from MRI data. In: Liang, P., Goel, V., Shan, C. (eds.) BI 2019. LNCS, vol. 11976, pp. 136–146. Springer, Cham (2019). https://doi.org/10.1007/978-3-030-37078-7_14
4. Bokil, H., Andrews, P., Kulkarni, J.E., Mehta, S., Mitra, P.P.: Chronux: a platform for analyzing neural signals. J. Neurosci. Methods **192**(1), 146–151 (2010)
5. Bologna, L.L., et al.: Investigating neuronal activity by SPYCODE multi-channel data analyzer. Neural Netw. **23**(6), 685–697 (2010)
6. Cui, J., Xu, L., Bressler, S.L., Ding, M., Liang, H.: BSMART: a Matlab/C toolbox for analysis of multichannel neural time series. Neural Netw. **21**(8), 1094–1104 (2008)

7. Fabietti, M., Mahmud, M., Lotfi, A.: Effectiveness of employing multimodal signals in removing artifacts from neuronal signals: an empirical analysis. In: Mahmud, M., Vassanelli, S., Kaiser, M.S., Zhong, N. (eds.) BI 2020. LNCS (LNAI), vol. 12241, pp. 183–193. Springer, Cham (2020). https://doi.org/10.1007/978-3-030-59277-6_17
8. Fabietti, M., et al.: Adaptation of convolutional neural networks for multi-channel artifact detection in chronically recorded local field potentials. In: Proceedings of SSCI, pp. 1607–1613 (2020)
9. Fabietti, M., et al.: Artifact detection in chronically recorded local field potentials using long-short term memory neural network. In: Proceedings of AICT, pp. 1–6 (2020)
10. Furth, K.: Replication data for: neuronal correlates of ketamine and walking induced gamma oscillations in the medial prefrontal cortex and mediodorsal thalamus (2017). https://doi.org/10.7910/DVN/MIBZLZ
11. Furth, K.E., McCoy, A.J., Dodge, C., Walters, J.R., Buonanno, A., Delaville, C.: Neuronal correlates of ketamine and walking induced gamma oscillations in the medial prefrontal cortex and mediodorsal thalamus. PLoS ONE **12**(11), e0186732 (2017)
12. Garcia, S., et al.: Neo: an object model for handling electrophysiology data in multiple formats. Front. Neuroinform. **8**, 10 (2014)
13. Hazan, L., Zugaro, M., Buzsáki, G.: Klusters, NeuroScope, NDManager: a free software suite for neurophysiological data processing and visualization. J. Neurosci. Methods **155**(2), 207–216 (2006)
14. Islam, M.N., Martin, S.K., Aggleton, J.P., O'Mara, S.M.: NeuroChaT: a toolbox to analyse the dynamics of neuronal encoding in freely-behaving rodents in vivo. Wellcome Open Res. **4**, 196 (2019)
15. Mahmud, M., et al.: An automated method for characterization of evoked single-trial local field potentials recorded from rat barrel cortex under mechanical whisker stimulation. Cogn. Comput. **8**(5), 935–945 (2016). https://doi.org/10.1007/s12559-016-9399-3
16. Mahmud, M., Bertoldo, A., Girardi, S., Maschietto, M., Pasqualotto, E., Vassanelli, S.: SigMate: a comprehensive software package for extracellular neuronal signal processing and analysis. In: Proceedings of NER, pp. 88–91 (2011). https://doi.org/10.1109/NER.2011.5910495
17. Mahmud, M., Bertoldo, A., Girardi, S., Maschietto, M., Vassanelli, S.: SigMate: a MATLAB-based neuronal signal processing tool. In: Proceedings of IEEE EMBC, pp. 1352–1355 (2010)
18. Mahmud, M., Bertoldo, A., Girardi, S., Maschietto, M., Vassanelli, S.: SigMate: a Matlab-based automated tool for extracellular neuronal signal processing and analysis. J. Neurosci. Methods **207**(1), 97–112 (2012). https://doi.org/10.1016/j.jneumeth.2012.03.009
19. Mahmud, M., Bertoldo, A., Maschietto, M., Girardi, S., Vassanelli, S.: Automatic detection of layer activation order in information processing pathways of rat barrel cortex under mechanical whisker stimulation. In: Proceedings of EMBC, pp. 6095–6098 (2010). https://doi.org/10.1109/IEMBS.2010.5627639
20. Mahmud, M., Girardi, S., Maschietto, M., Pasqualotto, E., Vassanelli, S.: An automated method to determine angular preferentiality using LFPs recorded from rat barrel cortex by brain-chip interface under mechanical whisker stimulation. In: Proceedings of EMBC, pp. 2307–2310 (2011). https://doi.org/10.1109/IEMBS.2011.6090580

21. Mahmud, M., Girardi, S., Maschietto, M., Rahman, M.M., Bertoldo, A., Vassanelli, S.: Slow stimulus artifact removal through peak-valley detection of neuronal signals recorded from somatosensory cortex by high resolution brain-chip interface. In: Dössel, O., Schlegel, W.C. (eds.) World Congress on Medical Physics and Biomedical Engineering. IFMBE, vol. 25/4, pp. 2062–2065. Springer, Heidelberg (2009). https://doi.org/10.1007/978-3-642-03882-2_547
22. Mahmud, M., Girardi, S., Maschietto, M., Rahman, M.M., Vassanelli, S.: Noise characterization of electrophysiological signals recorded from high resolution brain-chip interface. In: Proceedings of ISBB, pp. 84–87 (2009)
23. Mahmud, M., Girardi, S., Maschietto, M., Vassanelli, S.: An automated method to remove artifacts induced by microstimulation in local field potentials recorded from rat somatosensory cortex. In: Proceedings of BRC, pp. 1–4 (2012)
24. Mahmud, M., Kaiser, M.S., Hussain, A., Vassanelli, S.: Applications of deep learning and reinforcement learning to biological data. IEEE Trans. Neural Netw. Learn. Syst. **29**(6), 2063–2079 (2018)
25. Mahmud, M., Maschietto, M., Girardi, S., Vassanelli, S.: A Matlab based tool for cortical layer activation order detection through latency calculation in local field potentials recorded from rat barrel cortex by brain-chip interface. In: Proceedings of BRC, pp. 1–4 (2012). https://doi.org/10.1109/BRC.2012.6222170
26. Mahmud, M., Pasqualotto, E., Bertoldo, A., Girardi, S., Maschietto, M., Vassanelli, S.: An automated method for detection of layer activation order in information processing pathway of rat barrel cortex under mechanical whisker stimulation. J. Neurosci. Methods **196**(1), 141–150 (2011). https://doi.org/10.1016/j.jneumeth.2010.11.024
27. Mahmud, M., Travalin, D., Bertoldo, A., Girardi, S., Maschietto, M., Vassanelli, S.: A contour based automatic method to classify local field potentials recorded from rat barrel cortex. In: Proceedings of CIBEC, pp. 163–166 (2010). https://doi.org/10.1109/CIBEC.2010.5716087
28. Mahmud, M., Travalin, D., Bertoldo, A., Girardi, S., Maschietto, M., Vassanelli, S.: An automated classification method for single sweep local field potentials recorded from rat barrel cortex under mechanical whisker stimulation. J. Med. Biol. Eng. **32**(6), 397–404 (2012). https://doi.org/10.5405/jmbe.923
29. Mahmud, M., Travalin, D., Hussain, A.: Decoding network activity from LFPs: a computational approach. In: Huang, T., Zeng, Z., Li, C., Leung, C.S. (eds.) ICONIP 2012. LNCS, vol. 7663, pp. 584–591. Springer, Heidelberg (2012). https://doi.org/10.1007/978-3-642-34475-6_70
30. Mahmud, M., et al.: Single LFP sorting for high-resolution brain-chip interfacing. In: Zhang, H., Hussain, A., Liu, D., Wang, Z. (eds.) BICS 2012. LNCS (LNAI), vol. 7366, pp. 329–337. Springer, Heidelberg (2012). https://doi.org/10.1007/978-3-642-31561-9_37
31. Matlab: MATLAB. Deep Learning Toolbox R2020a (2017)
32. Mazzoni, A., Logothetis, N.K., Panzeri, S.: Information content of local field potentials. In: Principles of Neural Coding, pp. 411–429 (2013)
33. Noor, M.B.T., Zenia, N.Z., Kaiser, M.S., Mahmud, M., Al Mamun, S.: Detecting neurodegenerative disease from MRI: a brief review on a deep learning perspective. In: Liang, P., Goel, V., Shan, C. (eds.) BI 2019. LNCS, vol. 11976, pp. 115–125. Springer, Cham (2019). https://doi.org/10.1007/978-3-030-37078-7_12
34. Oostenveld, R., Fries, P., Maris, E., Schoffelen, J.M.: FieldTrip: open source software for advanced analysis of MEG, EEG, and invasive electrophysiological data. Comput. Intell. Neurosci. **2011** (2011)

35. Orojo, O., Tepper, J., McGinnity, T.M., Mahmud, M.: A multi-recurrent network for crude oil price prediction. In: Proceedings of IEEE SSCI, pp. 2953–2958 (2019)
36. Rabby, G., et al.: TeKET: a tree-based unsupervised keyphrase extraction technique. Cogn. Comput. **12**(5), 811–833 (2020). https://doi.org/10.1007/s12559-019-09706-3
37. Ruiz, J., Mahmud, M., Modasshir, Md., Shamim Kaiser, M., For the Alzheimer's Disease Neuroimaging Initiative: 3D DenseNet ensemble in 4-way classification of Alzheimer's disease. In: Mahmud, M., Vassanelli, S., Kaiser, M.S., Zhong, N. (eds.) BI 2020. LNCS (LNAI), vol. 12241, pp. 85–96. Springer, Cham (2020). https://doi.org/10.1007/978-3-030-59277-6_8
38. Sumi, A.I., Zohora, M.F., Mahjabeen, M., Faria, T.J., Mahmud, M., Kaiser, M.S.: *f*ASSERT: a fuzzy assistive system for children with autism using Internet of Things. In: Wang, S., et al. (eds.) BI 2018. LNCS (LNAI), vol. 11309, pp. 403–412. Springer, Cham (2018). https://doi.org/10.1007/978-3-030-05587-5_38
39. Tadel, F., Baillet, S., Mosher, J.C., Pantazis, D., Leahy, R.M.: Brainstorm: a user-friendly application for MEG/EEG analysis. Comput. Intell. Neurosci. **2011** (2011)
40. Watkins, J., Fabietti, M., Mahmud, M.: SENSE: a student performance quantifier using sentiment analysis. In: Proceedings of IJCNN, pp. 1–6 (2020)
41. Yegenoglu, A., et al.: Elephant-open-source tool for the analysis of electrophysiological data sets. In: Proceedings of Bernstein Conference, pp. 134–135 (2015)

D3mciAD: Data-Driven Diagnosis of Mild Cognitive Impairment Utilizing Syntactic Images Generation and Neural Nets

Md. Mahmodul Hasan[1], Md. Asaduzzaman[2], Mohammad Motiur Rahman[1](✉), Mohammad Shahadat Hossain[3], and Karl Andersson[4]

[1] Department of Computer Science and Engineering, Mawlana Bhashani Science and Technology University, Tangail, Bangladesh
{ce180601,motiurcse}@mbstu.ac.bd

[2] Department of Computer Science and Engineering, BGC Trust University Bangladesh, Chattogram, Bangladesh
asaduzzaman@bgctub.ac.bd

[3] Department of Computer Science and Engineering, University of Chittagong, Chattogram, Bangladesh
hossain_ms@cu.ac.bd

[4] Department of Computer Science, Electrical and Space Engineering, Luleå University of Technology, Skellefteå, Sweden
karl.andersson@ltu.se

Abstract. Alzheimer's disease, an incurable chronic neurological disorder (NLD) that affects human memory and demises cognitive thinking ability with shrinkage of the brain area. Early detection of Alzheimer's disease (AD) is the only hope to delay its effect. This study designed a computer-aided automated detection method that can detect mild cognitive impairment for AD from magnetic resonance image scans. The data-driven solution approach requires an extensive quantity of annotated images for diagnosis. However, obtaining a large amount of annotated data for medical application is a challenging task. We have exploited a deep convolutional generative adversarial network (DCGAN) for synthesizing high-quality images to increase dataset size. A fine-tuned CNN (VGG16 architecture) model works on images to extract the intuitive features for early diagnosis. The extracted features of images by VGG16 feed into the support vector machine for classification. This research has conducted copious experiments to validate the proposed method outperformed relative baselines on public datasets.

Keywords: Mild cognitive impairment · Alzheimer's disease · GAN · Early detection

1 Introduction

Worldwide nearly fifty million people have dementia, with around ten million newly found cases annually [1]. Alzheimer's is considered one of the lead-

M. Mahmud et al. (Eds.): BI 2021, LNAI 12960, pp. 366–377, 2021.
https://doi.org/10.1007/978-3-030-86993-9_33

ing causes of dementia as it contributes to approximately 70% of cases [2]. Alzheimer's disease – a human brain disorder with progressive nature that affects the brain and deteriorates the cognitive function of the patients. Memory loss, disability of thinking, uncontrolled emotion, impairment in learning and judgement etc., are the most common symptoms commonly found among older adults with AD [3]. These symptoms may also be seen among cognitively normal (CN) people. In these cases, detection and prediction are crucial to differentiate an AD patient from a CN one. Although the disease is incurable, medication can slow down the progress by preventing neuron damages at its mild stage [4]. For these reasons, physicians always emphasize the early detection of AD to ensure the treatment plan optimization [5,6].

Early detection of the progress of Alzheimer's disease is significant to reduce the impacts on the cognitive system before dementia as it may be in a long-term asymptomatic stage. The advancement in modern imaging technologies and technical development in analyzing complex biological data provide insight into disease diagnosis [7]. Among various medical images, MRI scan is being widely used to implement Computer-Aided Brain Diagnosis (CABD) [8].

Researchers from several distinct disciplines have focused on the severity level and risk factors of the progression to AD [9]. Among several schemes, deep learning implementation for automatic detection using magnetic resonance image (MRI) has become one of the best computer-aided diagnosis processes nowadays [10]. Massive development in the learning techniques to detect NLD like Alzheimer's Disease (AD), Schizophrenia (SZ), Parkinson's Disease (PD) etc., has been made in the field of neuroimaging data analysis due to the availability of massive datasets [11]. These large datasets also contribute to implementing learning models with better accuracy. On the other hand, the inadequacy of the MRI data for MCI detection has made further scopes of researches focusing on the challenges of improving accuracy level utilizing syntactic images generation techniques. These large datasets also contribute to implementing models with better accuracy. On the other hand, the inadequacy of the MRI data for MCI detection has made further scopes of researches focusing on the challenges of improving accuracy level utilizing syntactic images generation techniques.

Over the last decades, various studies have been carried out to detect AD analyzing MRI data using different Deep Learning (DL) methods [5,10]. As a DL method, Convolutional Neural Network (CNN) and several modified CNN architectures are being extensively used for learning from training datasets [11–13]. Table 1 describes such research contributions in deep neural networks based on the early diagnosis of AD. There are not many dedicated studies on MCI for AD detection. This study is entirely focused on the diagnosis of MCI for AD with GAN-based image augmentation.

The main contributions of our proposed Data-Driven Diagnosis for Mild Cognitive Impairment of AD (D3mciAD) method are listed as:

1. An early diagnosis of mild cognitive impairment – the first stage of AD using data-driven automated detection algorithms.

2. Applications of generative adversarial network-based syntactic images generation for medical diagnosis to compensate limited datasets.
3. Transfer learning-based single image detection mechanisms of Alzheimer's disease to make a collective decision with improved diagnosis performance.

Table 1. Contributions of researchers towards early detection (MCI vs CN).

References	Methods	Dataset	Performance
[10]	3D DenseNet	ADNI	AC = 94.12% SN = 94.33% PR = 94.56%
[14]	CNN + Multi-kernel SVM	ADNI	AC = 83.75% SN = 83.55% PR = 83.95%
[15]	DemNet – Modified VGG16	ADNI	AC = 91.67% SN = 92.22% PR = 91.11%
[16]	Sparse Autoencoders + 3D CNN	ADNI	AC = 92.11%
[17]	NN + SoftMax Regression	ADNI	AC = 91.10%
[18]	CNN + Fusion SVMs	ADNI	AC = 90.60%
	Ensemble of 5 Transfer Learning		AC = 83.20%
	AlexNet		AC = 84.20%
	ResNet101		AC = 82.20%
[19]	3D CNN	ADNI	AC = 87.10% SN = 87.80% SP = 86.50%
		ADNI + Milan	AC = 87.70% SN = 87.30% SP = 88.10%
[20]	3D CNN	ADNI + CADDementia	AC = 94.20% SN = 97.10% SP = 91.40%
[21]	3D DenseNet	ADNI	AC = 86.00% SN = 86.00% SP = 86.00%
[22]	DenseNet + K-Means Clustering	ADNI	AC = 73.80% SN = 86.60% SP = 51.50%

*AC = Accuracy; SP = Specificity; SN = Sensitivity; PR = Precision

The rest of the article includes several organized and substantial sections, e.g., Sect. 2 consists of the elaborative methods of the proposed work. In Sect. 3, we have analyzed and discussed the outcome of the study. The performance parameters of the proposed method have also been compared to some existing research works in that section. Finally, Sect. 4 concludes the study and future scopes have also been discussed there.

2 Methodology

This section contains the steps of the intelligent early Alzheimer's disease detection methodology. The block diagram of our proposed method in Fig. 1 shows the high-level overview of the process. This section contains the designing process of synthesized image generation technique generative adversarial network and the descriptions of fine-tuned feature extraction model.

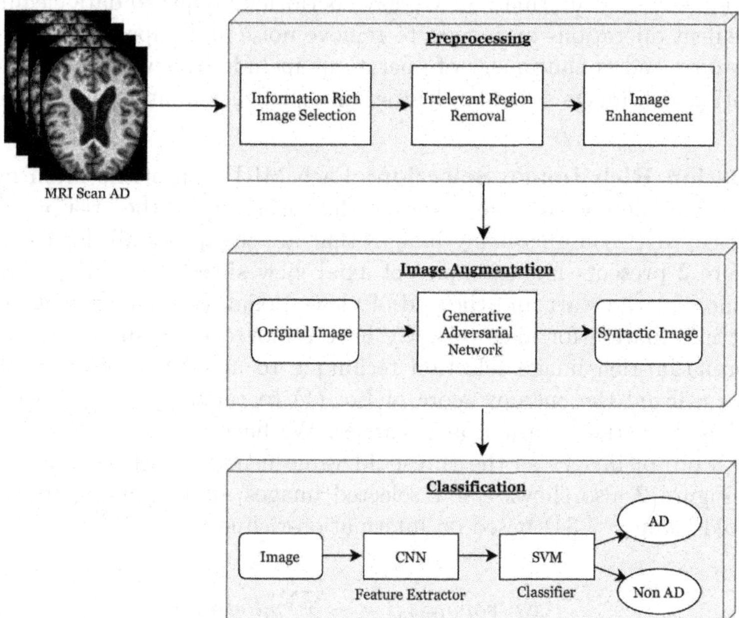

Fig. 1. Block diagram of our proposed method for Alzheimer's detection at earlier stages

2.1 Dataset Description

We have collected magnetic resonance imaging scans from the repositories - Alzheimer's Disease Neuroimaging Initiative (ADNI) and Open Access Series of Imaging Studies (OASIS) [23]. We have trained the deep learning models using the ADNI dataset. Also, models were validated and tested using the ADNI dataset using the validation and hold-out test set. The generalization performance of our method has been studied on the OASIS dataset. The training dataset contains MRI scans of 245 individuals. Each subject has been examined multiple times to track the progression of the disease.

The splitting of the available data for train, test and validation is crucial to building a generalized model to perform well during inference. We have randomly split the collected MRI scans from the ADNI dataset based on patients into three sets with a ratio of 70%, 20% and 10%, respectively, for train, test, and validation. This distribution based on patients ensures the integrity of data by putting data of the same patient be on the same set.

2.2 Data Processing

Data processing plays a vital role in feature extraction by reducing irrelevant information from data. The MRI data used in our study contains a different form of unnecessary information. We have performed required data cleaning and enhancement operations on images to remove noise and improve image quality. The cleaning and enhancement of operations include irrelevant region removal, information-rich image selection, histogram equalization, and noise removal.

Information Rich Image Selection: Each MRI scan of the brain may not have the same number of images due to the variability of the area of the skull. In practice, MRI contains many images that are inappropriate for the diagnosis. Figure 2 presents few examples of axial view slices of an MRI scan. Most of the slices at the start and the end of views (axial, coronal, sagittal) have no relevant information for diagnosis. We have removed those images by applying an information-rich image selection technique to avoid the addition of noise. We have utilized the entropy score of Eq. (1) to calculate the effectiveness of a slice based on the information it carries. We have selected the 30th highest entropy score of images as the threshold value using the trial-and-error mechanism. Figure 2 also shows a few selected images after applying thresholding (threshold value = 5.84) based on information-richness.

$$Entropy_{Image} = -\sum_{i=0}^{n-1} p_i log_2 p_i \tag{1}$$

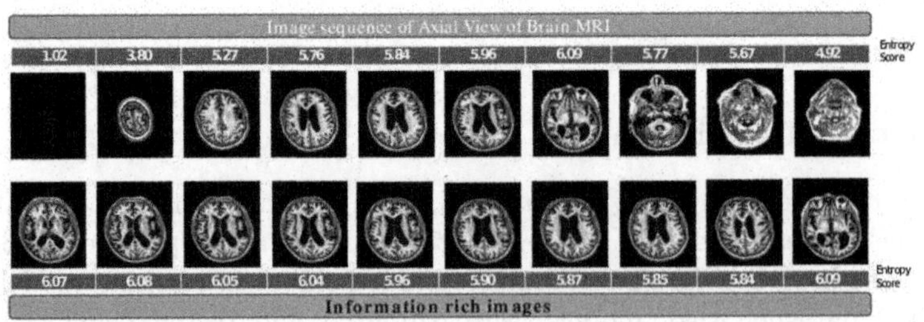

Fig. 2. Information rich images of axial view

Irrelevant Region Removal: The brain region in MRI scans differs from person to person. The shape and size of the skull create this variability and introduce blank areas, in other words, irrelevant information. Removal of those unnecessary information helps to extract improved features. We have calculated the ratio of non-black pixels (pixel value greater than 20) per column/row to remove the column/row from the image. The process was performed from four sides (top, left, right, bottom) of the image and continued until a column/row having a ratio less than sixty.

Image Enhancement and Noise Reduction: Image enhancement techniques help to prepare an image for problem-specific tasks. However, noises in the image create vulnerabilities to extract useful features. Different factors may be responsible for the introduction of noise in the image. This work has utilized multiple methods, specifically Wiener, Gaussian and median filtering, to reduce noise. Besides, we have applied Contrast Limited Adaptive Histogram Equalization (CLAHE) approach to enhance the contrast of images.

2.3 Syntactic Image Generation

Supervised DL algorithm, CNN requires large amounts of labelled data for training. The image augmentation technique helps to reduce the effect of overfitting with slight performance improvement. As available usable images of early detection of AD are inadequate for training deep models. We have utilized GAN to produce syn-tactic images from existing real images. These syntactic images help to increase the total number of images to achieve better performance and reduce overfitting [24].

We have used a deep convolution network for the generator and discriminator of the GAN architecture [25]. Figure 3 shows the visual architecture of the generator and discriminator with the dimension of layers. We have tuned the architecture several times to attain the expected outcome. The initial weights of the networks were sampled from the normal distribution. The generator network collects thousand random values as input and generates images of size 128 $\times$ 128. Then the discriminator and generator played minimax games to find the optimum parameters. Instead of using hard labels for real and fake images, we have used soft labels. Soft labels for real images were between 0.8 to 1.2 and between 0.0 to 0.3 for fake images. We have applied Adam optimizer to update the weights of parameters using the binary cross-entropy loss function.

2.4 Design of CNN Architecture

We have examined several well-known CNN architectures to extract high-level features from images. The model architectures were fine-tuned as the requirements of our task of early diagnosis. The feature vectors retrieved from distinct deep learning models vary dramatically from architecture to architecture. From our experiments, we have found that pretrained VGG16 architecture attained the best performance measures in action.

The architecture of the CNN model consists of sixteen trainable layers [26]. The architecture of the network is initialized with the weights of the ImageNet dataset. The neural network segment of the architecture contains two fully

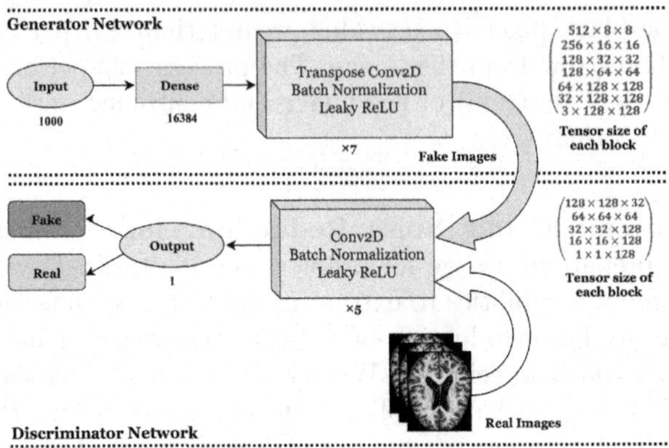

Fig. 3. The architecture of generative adversarial network

connected layers. We have tuned the output layer with one neuron to perform the diagnosis of AD from MRI images. The fine-tuned process was conducted by changing different parameters and hyperparameters of the model. We have experimented with different optimization algorithms to find the most effective for this study, and Adam gave the best results. The Adam optimizer started with an initial learning rate (ILR) of 0.01. It changed gradually to a factor of 0.1 after every seven epochs of training. The model's training was monitored using the validation loss to stop the training process for the next repeating of the same or increased validation loss for five epochs. Figure 4 presents the visual representation of the fine-tuned VGG16 architecture.

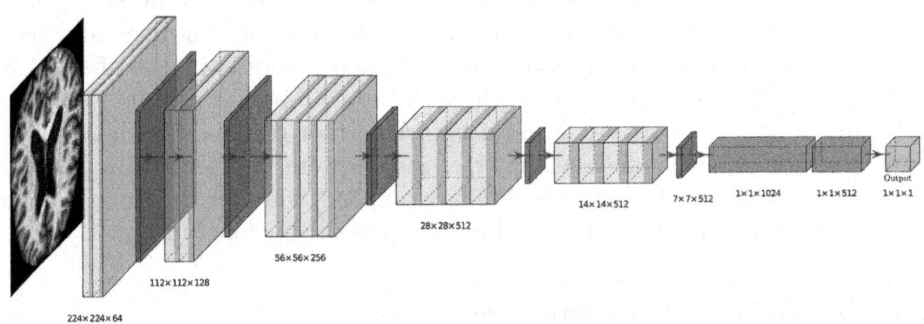

Fig. 4. Fine-tuned architecture of VGG16 network

The neural network segment of the architecture was modified to 1024 and 512 neurons on two fully connected layers. We have employed dropout mechanisms to reduce the effect of overfitting for each fully connected layer. The model was trained for thirty epochs before model training stopped execution. The output layer has used the sigmoid activation function. The remaining layers have utilized the ReLU function to work with nonlinearity.

2.5 Classification of Features

Instead of using the output of the VGG16 model, we adopted it as a high-level feature extraction method. The features of the first fully connected layer have been classified using multiple classification algorithms. We have experimented with sup-port vector machine (SVM), random forest, logistic regression, and decision tree. The SVM performed significantly better than others. The outcome of the SVM was also outperformed the VGG16 results. We have evaluated each informative slice of MRI and found the class of each image belongs. The diagnosis result of the MRI scan is the class (MCI or CN) with the maximum total number of slices.

3 Results and Discussion

This section illustrates the result of our method. We have performed our experiments on an Intel-powered central processing unit (CPU) @3.60 GHz clock speed with Nvidia's RTX 2070 Super 8 GB VRAM and 16 GB of RAM. The method was implemented using python 3.7 with Keras and scikit-learn frameworks [27,28].

In this work, the performance of the early detection of AD using the proposed method from brain MRI images are validated using five performance metrics named accuracy, specificity, sensitivity (recall), false diagnosis rate (FDR) and precision [29,30].

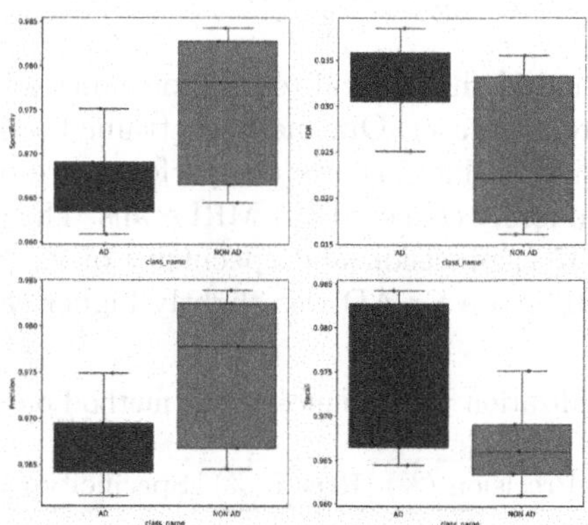

Fig. 5. The five-fold cross-validation performance of proposed method

Image augmentation technique GAN creates images using the data distribution of the primary dataset instead of performing operations (ex. rotation, cropping, shearing, and others) on the original images. The GAN-based augmentation adds diversity to the training dataset from the same data distribution. This increasing dataset technique helped to train a robust model for classification and boosted the generalized classification performance. GAN-generated images have nearly equal entropy to the original images. This information richness validates the generated image character.

We have generated 25000 images using a generator network. However, the entire set of images are not eligible to use for training. We have taken 7500 images from each category for augmentation. The images were selected based on the entropy values of the image and manual checking of the standard visual structure of the brain.

The performance of the classification method was evaluated using k-fold validation, hold-out test set and generalized performance on an entirely new dataset. Figure 5 shows the k-fold validation performance of our proposed method on the training set of the ADNI dataset.

The performance of our method on the hold-out test set has presented in Table 2. Our method performed significantly on the hold-out test set. The precision score of our method was 96%, with only 4.00% of errors on accurate MCI for AD predictions. This false diagnosis of MCI for AD as heathy was 4.17%. The accuracy of our method was 95.92% on the test set. The specificity and recall measures were 95.83% and 96%, respectively.

Table 2. Performance of our method on hold-out test set of ADNI

Accuracy (%)	Precision (%)	Recall (%)	Specificity (%)	FDR (%)
95.92	96.00	96.00	95.83	4.17 (CN)
				4.00 (MCI)

We have also evaluated the generalized performance analysis of our method on a completely different dataset. Our method attained a similar level of performance on generalization. Table 3 shows the performance of our method on the OASIS3 dataset of randomly collected 101 MRI scans. The metrics on evaluation were accuracy of 93.07%, precision and specificity of 92.16%. The recall score was 94%, and the FDR score for AD was slightly higher than not AD cases.

Table 3. Generalization performance of our method on OASIS3 dataset

Accuracy (%)	Precision (%)	Recall (%)	Specificity (%)	FDR (%)
93.07	92.16	94.00	92.16	6.00 (CN)
				7.83 (MCI)

The comparative analysis of our results with existing investigations from literature is presented in Table 4. Our proposed method has outperformed existing methods with improved performance scores. The use of proper preprocessing techniques and syntactic images with multi-level classification methods attained significant performance.

Table 4. Performance comparisons with existing methods on ADNI dataset

References	Recall (%)	Specificity (%)	Accuracy (%)
[10]	94.33	94.56	94.12
[15]	-	-	91.10
[16]	-	-	90.60
[17]	87.80	86.50	87.10
[19]	86.00	86.00	86.00
[20]	86.60	51.50	73.80
Proposed D3mciAD	96.00	95.83	95.92

4 Conclusion

Our proposed method performed significantly on early detection of Alzheimer's disease from MRI scans. The adaptation of syntactic images using generative adversarial networks facilitated to accomplish better score and reduced the risk of overfitting. Besides, the preprocessing steps performed on images eliminated noises and enhanced image quality for better feature extraction. The fine-tuned VGG16 as a feature extractor with SVM for classification captured the intuitive classification features for early Alzheimer's detection. The performance metrics of k-fold cross-validation, hold-out test set, generalization test on OASIS3 were better than methods in the literature. In future, stages of Alzheimer's disease can be studied to illustrate the severity level of the disease. In case of uncertainty, knowledge-driven approaches like belief-rule-based (BRB) expert system can also be implemented further as applied in [31–36].

Acknowledgements. Data used in preparation of this article were obtained from the Alzheimer's Disease Neuroimaging Initiative (ADNI) database (adni.loni.usc.edu). As such, the investigators within the ADNI contributed to the design and implementation of ADNI and/or provided data but did not participate in analysis or writing of this report. A complete listing of ADNI investigators can be found at: http://adni.loni.usc.edu/wp-content/uploads/how_to_apply/ADNI_Acknowledgement_List.pdf.

References

1. Dementia. https://www.who.int/news-room/fact-sheets/detail/dementia. Accessed 20 July 2021
2. Li, T.R., Wang, X.N., et al.: Extracellular vesicles as an emerging tool for the early detection of Alzheimer's disease. Mech. Ageing Dev. **184**, 111175 (2019). https://doi.org/10.1016/j.mad.2019.111175
3. Abrol, A., Bhattarai, M., et al.: Deep residual learning for neuroimaging: an application to predict progression to Alzheimer's disease. J. Neurosci. Methods **339**, 108701 (2020). https://doi.org/10.1016/j.jneumeth.2020.108701

4. Bron, E.E., Smits, M., et al.: Standardized evaluation of algorithms for computer-aided diagnosis of dementia based on structural MRI: the CADDementia challenge. Neuroimage **111**, 562–579 (2015). https://doi.org/10.1016/j.neuroimage.2015.01.048
5. Mofrad, S.A., Lundervold, A., Lundervold, A.S.: A predictive framework based on brain volume trajectories enabling early detection of Alzheimer's disease. Comput. Med. Imaging Graph. **90**, 101910 (2021). https://doi.org/10.1016/j.compmedimag.2021.101910
6. Siemers, E.R., Sundell, K.L., et al.: Phase 3 solanezumab trials: secondary outcomes in mild Alzheimer's disease patients. Alzheimer's Dement. **12**(2), 110–120 (2016). https://doi.org/10.1016/j.jalz.2015.06.1893
7. Mahmud, M., Kaiser, M.S., et al.: Applications of deep learning and reinforcement learning to biological data. IEEE Trans. Neural Networks Learn. Syst. **29**(6), 2063–2079 (2018). https://doi.org/10.1109/TNNLS.2018.2790388
8. Acharya, U.R., Fernandes, S.L., et al.: Automated detection of Alzheimer's disease using brain MRI images– A study with various feature extraction techniques. J. Med. Syst. **43**, 302 (2019). https://doi.org/10.1007/s10916-019-1428-9
9. Ballard, C., Khan, Z., et al.: Nonpharmacological treatment of Alzheimer disease. Can. J. Psychiatry **56**(10), 589–595 (2011). https://doi.org/10.1177/070674371105601004
10. Wang, H., Shen, Y., et al.: Ensemble of 3D densely connected convolutional network for diagnosis of mild cognitive impairment and Alzheimer's disease. Neurocomputing **333**, 145–156 (2019). https://doi.org/10.1016/j.neucom.2018.12.018
11. Noor, M.B.T., Zenia, N.Z., Kaiser, M.S., et al.: Application of deep learning in detecting neurological disorders from magnetic resonance images: a survey on the detection of Alzheimer's disease. Parkinson's disease and schizophrenia. Brain Inform. **7**, 11 (2020). https://doi.org/10.1186/s40708-020-00112-2
12. Zisad, S.N., Hossain, M.S., et al.: An integrated neural network and SEIR model to predict Covid-19. Algorithms **14**(3), 94 (2021). https://doi.org/10.3390/a14030094
13. Kabir, S., Islam, R.U., et al.: An integrated approach of belief rule base and deep learning to predict air pollution. Sensors (Switzerland) **20**(7), 1956 (2020). https://doi.org/10.3390/s20071956
14. Wee, C.Y., Yap, P.T., Shen, D.: Prediction of Alzheimer's disease and mild cognitive impairment using cortical morphological patterns. Hum. Brain Mapp. **34**(12), 3411–3425 (2013). https://doi.org/10.1002/hbm.22156
15. Billones, C.D., Demetria, O.J.L.D., et al.: DemNet: a convolutional neural network for the detection of Alzheimer's disease and mild cognitive impairment. In: IEEE Region 10 Annual International Conference, Proceedings/TENCON, pp. 3724–3727. IEEE, Singapore (2017). https://doi.org/10.1109/TENCON.2016.7848755
16. Payan, A., Montana, G.: Predicting Alzheimer's disease a neuroimaging study with 3D convolutional neural networks. arXiv:1502.02506 (2015)
17. Razavi, F., Tarokh, M.J., Alborzi, M.: An intelligent Alzheimer's disease diagnosis method using unsupervised feature learning. J. Big Data. **6**, 32 (2019). https://doi.org/10.1186/s40537-019-0190-7
18. Nanni, L., Interlenghi, M., et al.: Comparison of transfer learning and conventional machine learning applied to structural brain MRI for the early diagnosis and prognosis of Alzheimer's disease. Front. Neurol. **11**, 1345 (2020). https://doi.org/10.3389/fneur.2020.576194
19. Basaia, S., Agosta, F., et al.: Automated classification of Alzheimer's disease and mild cognitive impairment using a single MRI and deep neural networks. NeuroImage Clin. **21**, 101645 (2019). https://doi.org/10.1016/j.nicl.2018.101645

20. Asl, E.H., Ghazal, M., et al.: Alzheimer's disease diagnostics by a 3D deeply supervised adaptable convolutional network. Front. Biosci. Landmark **23**(3), 584–596 (2018). https://doi.org/10.2741/4606
21. Solano-Rojas, B., Villalón-Fonseca, R.: A low-cost three-dimensional DenseNet neural network for Alzheimer's disease early discovery†. Sensors (Switzerland) **21**(4), 1302 (2021). https://doi.org/10.3390/s21041302
22. Li, F., Liu, M.: Alzheimer's disease diagnosis based on multiple cluster dense convolutional networks. Comput. Med. Imaging Graph. **70**, 101–110 (2018). https://doi.org/10.1016/j.compmedimag.2018.09.009
23. LaMontagne, P.J., Benzinger, T.L.S., et al.: OASIS-3: longitudinal neuroimaging, clinical, and cognitive dataset for normal aging and Alzheimer disease. medRxiv (2019). https://doi.org/10.1101/2019.12.13.19014902
24. Mahmud, M., Kaiser, M.S., et al.: Deep learning in mining biological data. Cogn. Comput. **13**, 1–33 (2021). https://doi.org/10.1007/s12559-020-09773-x
25. Radford, A., Metz, L.: Unsupervised Representation Learning with Deep Convolutional Generative Adversarial Networks. arXiv:1511.06434 (2015)
26. Simonyan, K., Zisserman, A.: Very deep convolutional networks for large-scale image recognition. In: 3rd International Conference on Learning Representations. arXiv:1409.1556 (2015)
27. Chollet, F.: Keras (2013). https://keras.io
28. Pedregosa, F., Varoquaux, G., et al.: Scikit-learn: machine learning in Python. J. Mach. Learn. Res. **12**, 2825–2830 (2011)
29. Nahar, N., Hossain, M.S., Andersson, K.: A machine learning based fall detection for elderly people with neurodegenerative disorders. In: Mahmud, M., Vassanelli, S., Kaiser, M.S., Zhong, N. (eds.) BI 2020. LNCS (LNAI), vol. 12241, pp. 194–203. Springer, Cham (2020). https://doi.org/10.1007/978-3-030-59277-6_18
30. Zisad, S.N., Hossain, M.S., Andersson, K.: Speech emotion recognition in neurological disorders using convolutional neural network. In: Mahmud, M., Vassanelli, S., Kaiser, M.S., Zhong, N. (eds.) BI 2020. LNCS (LNAI), vol. 12241, pp. 287–296. Springer, Cham (2020). https://doi.org/10.1007/978-3-030-59277-6_26
31. Hossain, M.S., Rahaman, S., Kor, A., et al.: A belief rule based expert system for datacenter PUE prediction under uncertainty. IEEE Trans. Sustain. Comput. **2**, 140–153 (2017). https://doi.org/10.1109/TSUSC.2017.2697768
32. Hossain, M.S., Rahaman, S., Mustafa, R., et al.: A belief rule-based expert system to assess suspicion of acute coronary syndrome (ACS) under uncertainty. Soft Comput. **22**, 7571–7586 (2018). https://doi.org/10.1007/s00500-017-2732-2
33. Islam, R.U., Hossain, M.S., Andersson, K.: A novel anomaly detection algorithm for sensor data under uncertainty. Soft Comput. **22**, 1623–1639 (2018). https://doi.org/10.1007/s00500-016-2425-2
34. Hossain, M.S., Ahmed, F., Fatema-Tuj-Johora, K., et al.: A belief rule based expert system to assess tuberculosis under uncertainty. J. Med. Syst. **41**, 43 (2017). https://doi.org/10.1007/s10916-017-0685-8
35. Karim, R., Andersson, K., Hossain, M.S., et al.: A belief rule based expert system to assess clinical bronchopneumonia suspicion. In: 2016 Future Technologies Conference (FTC), pp 655—660 (2016). https://doi.org/10.1109/FTC.2016.7821675
36. Hossain, M.S., Habib, I.B., Andersson, K.: A belief rule based expert system to diagnose dengue fever under uncertainty. In: 2017 Computing Conference, pp. 179—186 (2017). https://doi.org/10.1109/SAI.2017.8252101

Mental Healthcare Chatbot Using Sequence-to-Sequence Learning and BiLSTM

Afsana Binte Rakib[1(✉)], Esika Arifin Rumky[1], Ananna J. Ashraf[1], Md. Monsur Hillas[1], and Muhammad Arifur Rahman[2]

[1] Department of ECE, North South University, Dhaka, Bangladesh
afsana.rakib@northsouth.edu, esika.rumky@northsouth.edu, ananna.ashraf@northsouth.edu, monsur.hillas@northsouth.edu

[2] Department of Physics, Jahangirnagar University, Dhaka, Bangladesh
arif@juniv.edu

Abstract. Mental health is an important aspect of an individual's well-being which still continues to remain unaddressed. With the rise of the COVID-19 pandemic, mental health has far continued to decline, especially amongst the younger generation. The aim of this research is to raise awareness about mental health while simultaneously working towards removing the societal stigma surrounding it. Thus, in this paper, we have created an integrated chatbot that is specifically geared towards mentally ill individuals. The chatbot responds empathetically which is built using a Sequence-to-Sequence (Seq2Seq) encoder-decoder architecture. The encoder uses Bi-directional Long Short Term Memory (BiLSTM). To compare the performance, we used Beam Search and Greedy Search. We found Beam Search decoder performs much better, providing empathetic responses to the user with greater precision in terms of BLEU score.

Keywords: Depression · Chatbot · BiLSTM · RNN · Encoder · Decoder · Greedy · Beam

1 Introduction

Mental health issues have continued to prevail among the population for decades. According to [11], the rate of annual self-harm by girls was found to be 37.4 and 12.3 in boys. However, most of the participants have no record of following up with mental health services. Although this study was carried out in a limited scope, it sheds light on the need for immediate intervention to help and support the myriads of people suffering in silence in a manner that is both sensible and affordable. Furthermore, studies have shown that there is an increase in Artificial Intelligence (AI) based chatbots to promote mental well-being, among which Wysa is one such example where a high percentage of the users have shown to

M. Mahmud et al. (Eds.): BI 2021, LNAI 12960, pp. 378–387, 2021.
https://doi.org/10.1007/978-3-030-86993-9_34

develop improved moods [7]. Therefore, it is evident that AI-based conversational agents can work towards the improvement of overall mental well-being. This is where our chatbot comes into play. Our bot integrates Machine Learning and executes it in a practical manner by communicating very closely with the users through a specialized algorithm. Through a Sequence-to-Sequence Learning mechanism, our model has a conversation with the user by generating appropriate responses. To evaluate the performance, we have a conversation with the bot using sentences as user inputs and calculate the BLEU score for each generated model, which uses Beam and Greedy Decoder architectures, respectively. The contribution of the paper is as follows:

- Treating mental health is costly and societal stigma bars individuals from seeking help.
- Mentally ill individuals will be benefitted from this chatbot as it will provide empathetic responses whenever they feel the need for someone to listen.
- For future improvements, we can use the data of the conversation to diagnose a patient with any disorder they may have.

2 Literature Review

According to [2], the most common barriers when it comes to seeking mental health services were attitudinal, lack of finance, and availability. This raises an immediate need for a system that acts as a supplementary support system in place of healthcare professionals in the field. This is where artificial-enabled conversational technologies come into play as an empathetic virtual support system. This is evident in the study conducted by [19] which reveals that a person discloses deeper emotions from the conversations with real-time mental healthcare chatbots. This is because of the fact that the users do not receive any judgmental attitudes which can be usually expected in the case of human-to-human interactions.

Authors Prakash et al. collaborated to build a chatterbot using an RNN Encoder–Decoder composed of two RNNs. The proposed model of the chatbot is implemented by using the Sequence-To-Sequence (Seq2Seq) model with transfer learning [20]. The fixed-size context vector generated by the encoder is given as the input to the decoder of RNN. For the dataset, the model uses a movie dialog corpus of 220,579 conversational exchanges. Long Short Term Memory (LSTM) consists of two activation functions-*Sigmoid* and *tanh*. The *Sigmoid* function generates the correct details of the memory with the new input but cannot remove the memory. The *tanh* function controls the values across the network by which conversations go on. LSTM based encoder-decoder structure has been demonstrated to be more vigorous, cleaner, and quicker than an Artificial Neural Network (ANN) model. Moreover, this model has shown to generate further accurate grammar as compared to other generative models.

Yin et al. proposed a deep learning chatbot, Evebot, that uses Seq2Seq model through LSTM in order to diagnose negative user emotions and prevent depression. The proposed system combines BiLSTM network, Seq2Seq neural network, and Maximum Mutual Information (MMI) model [25]. This system was primarily targeted towards campus students as a means of virtual psychological therapy. The chatbot using the sentiment analysis model analyzes the user emotion throughout the conversation while the classifier model is responsible for the responses of the chatbot. The BiLSTM model was used to classify the user responses into two categories - positive and negative. The BiLSTM model provided a 90.91% precision of the test set. The Seq2Seq model was built on the MMI method which analyzes the mutual dependence between the input and output. However, this system cannot remember the previous topic of conversation and generate different responses to questions of the same topic. This may confuse the users. To solve this problem, some elements of a rule-based chatbot could be added.

3 Methodology

Our model is based on a Seq2Seq encoder-decoder architecture. The encoder uses Bi-directional Long Short Term Memory (BiLSTM) units which is a variation of LSTM networks. LSTM is an extension of Recurrent Neural Network (RNN) which can control the overall flow of information within the network. LSTM primarily helps in preserving the error so that it can be dealt with through back-propagation in different time and layers [12,13,23]. LSTM contains an input gate, an output gate and a forget gate [24]. The gates have an additional layer by the name of the Sigmoid neural network layer. Since the gates control the flow of information, the Sigmoid layer is crucial as it produces outputs between the numbers zero and one, where zero represents "letting no information through" while one represents "letting all the information pass" [14]. The input gate chooses the values to be updated and the tanh layer generates a vector of new candidate values which are then added as additional information to the cell state. However, in the model used, BiLSTM is considered for making

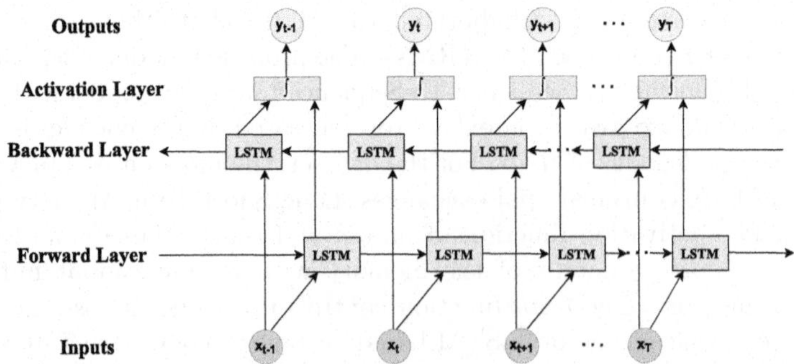

Fig. 1. BiLSTM Architecture: BiLSTM networks have two side-by-side layers of LSTMs where the actual input sequence is given as an input to the first layer and the reversed version of the input sequence is provided as an input to the second layer [17]. BiLSTMs, therefore, essentially increase the quantity of information that is available to the network which further improves the contexts of the algorithm.

fast predictions in real-time [16]. It has internal memory and can use the input to predict the next state. Since the chatbot is reliant on sequential data such as speech, it is helpful to develop an upgraded model. The encoder uses BiLSTM units which generates better results than unidirectional LSTM as it considers the embeddings of both the previous words and the next words suitable for predicting the target variable [26]. Furthermore, since the general Seq2Seq decoder has a possibility of information loss, we use the attention mechanism as proposed in [3] where the output is not solely dependent on the encoder's context vector. Rather, the decoder also pays attention to certain parts of the input. The attention is computed by taking the encoder's outputs and the current hidden state of the decoder. Here, the shape of the output attention weights matches that of the input sentence; hence, we can multiply them by the encoder outputs. This generates a weighted sum that guides the decoder to pay attention to the parts of the encoder's output. The BiLSTM architecture is shown in Fig. 1.

The Sequence-to-Sequence model with attention mechanism is given in Fig. 2. A typical Sequence-to-Sequence (Seq2Seq) model consists of the following three components [15]:

i) Embedding – The embedding layer converts the input sentence into a vector of numbers.
ii) Encoder – The encoder has BiLSTM units. The embeddings of inputs - variable-length vectors - are processed to convert into fixed-length vectors.
iii) Decoder – The decoder has a Gated Recurrent Unit (GRU) network which is a variation of LSTM. GRU merges both the forget and input gates of the network into one single gate known as the "update gate" [6].

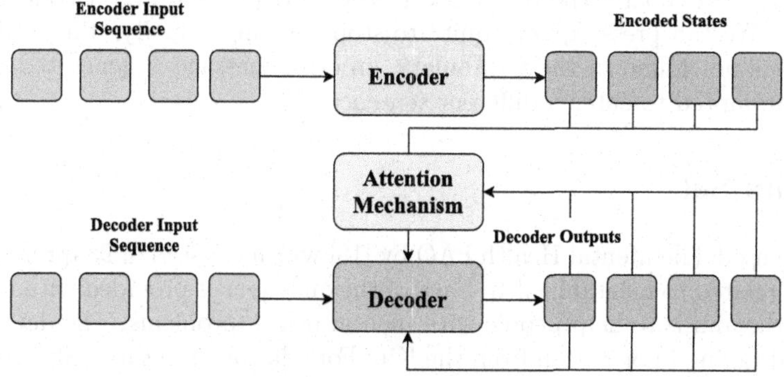

Fig. 2. Sequence-to-Sequence Model with Attention Mechanism: The encoder input sequence is passed into the encoder to receive the encoded states. Then, the encoded states from each time step are forwarded to the attention mechanism in order to choose the important encodings needed for the decoder [8]. During decoding, both the decoder and encoder states are passed into the feed-forward network which returns weights for each of the encoder states.

As our dataset consists of sentences that are sequences of words, we mapped each unique word to an index value using a vocabulary class. This class adds words to the vocabulary and counts the frequency of the words. The questions and answers from the dataset used functions as sentence pairs. To reduce the complexity of the function and to achieve faster convergence, we trim rare words which are repeated infrequently and filter out the sentences containing these rare words. The non-letter characters are also removed and the words are formed into tokens. After mapping, the encodings are then given as input to the neural network. To aid in convergence while training, the sentences having a length of greater than 1000 words are filtered out.

At each time step, we manually feed the input batch to the decoder. Based on the decoder's tensors, we calculate the masked loss. The average negative log-likelihood is calculated for those elements that correspond to a 1 in the mask tensor. For a single training iteration, a single batch of inputs is trained. RNNs are usually prone to vanishing gradient [9,10]. However, since we used LSTM, we implement gradient clipping to solve the vanishing gradient problem, thus, we prevent the gradients from growing exponentially. This also aids in convergence. We also use teacher forcing to aid in further efficient training. Here, the current target word is used as the next input of the decoder rather than using the decoder's current prediction. This model uses softmax function as its activation function:

$$p_{\mathrm{i}} = \frac{e^{\mathrm{a_i}}}{\sum_{k=1}^{N} e_k^a} \tag{1}$$

where p_i is a layer and a is the input vector to the ith layer; $a = [a_1, a_2 \ldots .., a_N]$.

For the evaluation of a string input, we created a user interface for the chatbot where the user can communicate with the chatbot through text. After pressing Enter on the keyboard, the text is fed to the model to obtain a decoded output sentence. We can press "q" or "quit" to stop chatting. Finally, if a word in the sentence is not found in the vocabulary, an error message is generated and the user is prompted to enter a different sentence.

4 Data Set

We have used The Mental Health FAQ by [18] which consists of 98 questions and answers related to mental health. Each of the questions is provided with a unique ID and the aim is to help people with mental health problems. The dataset was compiled taking information from the Kim Foundation, Mental Health America, Wellness in Mind, and here to help organizations. This dataset was collected from Kaggle.

The other dataset is solely dedicated to creating a model showing the conversation between a client and a therapist based on grounded theory analysis [22]. The main idea proposed here is a model of the therapist's inner conversation consisting of four positions. Using this idea, the conversation between the therapist and the client is conducted and we have incorporated these conversations as the dataset for training. The dataset mostly functions as a platform where the therapist performs their task in treating the client (patient) by listening to the client's story. Based on the analysis, the therapist responds to the client. As such, our chatbot is designed to function in a similar manner, opting to listen to the user vent about their innermost fears and issues.

5 Results and Analysis

During the preprocessing of data, we set a threshold of maximum length of sentences and filtered out which were longer than the threshold in order to aid in training convergence. The learning rate is kept 0.0001. To achieve faster convergence during the training process, we trimmed the least used words out of the vocabulary. Here, the current target word is used as the next input of the decoder rather than using the decoders current prediction. The model uses the softmax as its activation function and it is used in parallel with the cross-entropy loss function. The paper compares the models developed with Beam Search decoder and Greedy Search decoder respectively while other conditions such as the learning rates, number of iterations, teacher forcing ratio, and the data sets are kept constant. With Greedy search, the algorithm selects the most frequently appearing words at each time-step in the output sequence [5]. On the other hand, Beam search is an expansion of the Greedy search which returns the output sequences which are most likely to occur.

Table 1. An example of a conversation between the user and the chatbot using the Beam decoder model.

User	Chatbot
Hi	Hello..
I feel like a loser, what do I do?	Many people find peer support a helpful tool that can aid in their recovery. There are variety of organizations that that offer support groups for their family members members members members and and support groups are peer led while led by by by mental mental health health health health
Why do not my parents talk to me?	I don good talk. Mentioned it it they do to to to

The performance of our chatbot model can be further improved and the slow training rate can be overcome given larger data sets and GPU architecture. We further noticed that with increasing iterations, the chatbot's performance increases. This was expected as training a neural network model typically requires many iterations. The downside is that running the model is more time-consuming which is not efficient in the long run. Tables 1 and 2 show the results

Table 2. An example of a conversation between the user and the chatbot using the Greedy decoder model.

User	Chatbot
Hi	..
I feel like a loser, what do I do?	Many many many peer support their their. A variety of consumers their and may may may may may may may may may . . professional
Why do not my parents talk to me?	Now that you mentioned it it they they do to me

obtained from chatting with the bot using a model with Beam Search Decoder and Greedy Search Decoder respectively.

A set of questions were formed based on the data sets used and both the models were presented with the same questions. As expected, it was observed that the model using the Beam decoder provided better responses than the one with the Greedy decoder. However, the Greedy decoder is faster in terms of responses as it takes less time to respond.

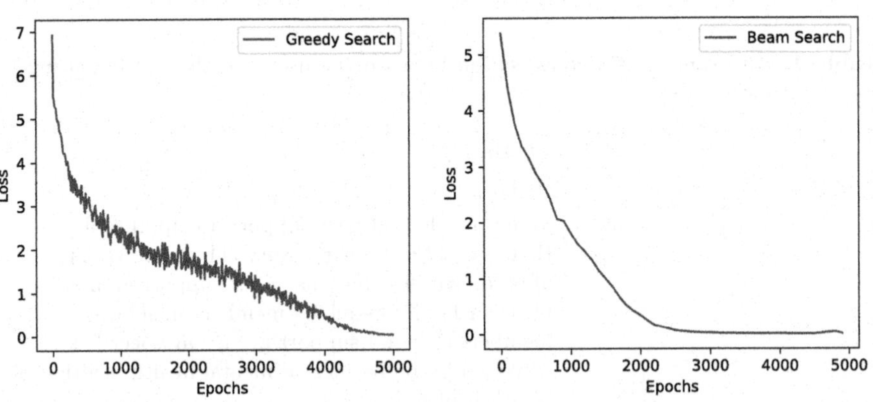

Fig. 3. It is observed that the curve for the Greedy model has a lot of spikes with a gentler slope. There is a considerable reduction in loss values with increasing iterations. The curve for the Beam model has comparatively fewer fluctuations; hence, it is smoother. However, it is slightly steeper than the other one. In both the models, the learning rate is kept 0.0001 with 5000 epochs.

Figure 3 shows the loss values with increasing iterations during the training process. In both the curves, loss values decrease significantly with an increasing number of iterations. This is expected since the loss should decrease as the predicted probability converges to the actual label. The model using the Greedy search decoder runs faster than the Beam one. Hence, it can be observed that as we increase the number of iterations in tandem with the precision of the learning rate, the model will learn better and be more efficient in the long run and the errors will also decrease considerably.

We further calculated the individual Bilingual Evaluation Understudy (BLEU) score for both models. The BLEU score is a measure of how similar the candidate text and the reference texts are. This score ranges from 0.0 to 1.0 with values closer to 0.0 indicating less precision and values closer to 1.0 indicating greater precision [4]. The BLEU score for 1-gram on testing pairs and 2-gram on testing pairs were generated for each of the models where 1-gram represents a single word and 2-gram represents word pairs. Figure 4 shows the BLEU score comparison between the Beam search and the Greedy search models.

Although both models provide a good level of precision, the model implementing the Beam search decoder generates a better precision than the Greedy one for 1-gram while they perform with a similar precision for 2-gram on testing pairs. Moreover, even though Greedy is fast, the model with the Beam search decoder provides relatively optimal responses than the Greedy one when evaluating the quality of the final output received from the conversation with the chatbot. Therefore, Beam is a heuristic search algorithm that performs better than the Greedy model. Yet, we believe that there might be a slight deviation of the results as shown by [1] if we select a different set of data set or a non parametric model setup like Gaussian process [21].

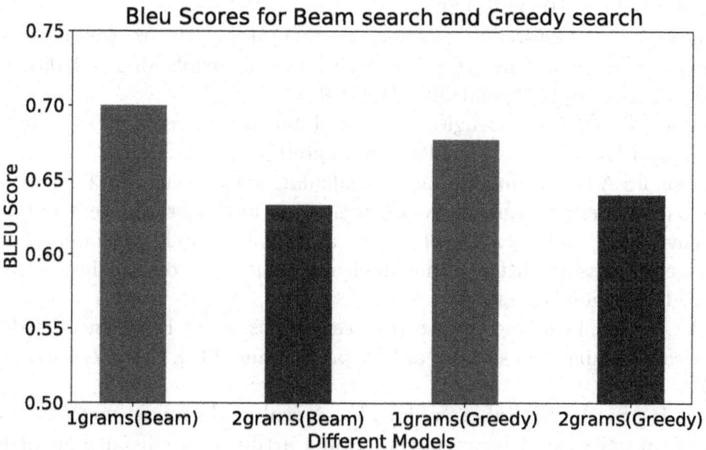

Fig. 4. For the model with the Beam search decoder, the BLEU score for 1-gram on testing pairs was 0.700 and the score for 2-gram on testing pairs was 0.634. For the model with the Greedy search decoder, the BLEU score for 1-gram on testing pairs was 0.678 and the score for 2-gram on testing pairs was found to be 0.640.

6 Conclusion

One of the main takeaways of this paper is for everyone to be aware of mental health as a whole more and to put importance into it, rather than casting it aside. In a society where mental health is considered taboo, perhaps an artificially inspired brain is a better listener than an actual person. In this paper, we built a chatbot that uses a Sequence-to-Sequence (Seq2Seq) encoder-decoder architecture where the encoder uses BiLSTM. Then we compared the performance of the model; we used two decoder architectures - one using Beam Search and the other using Greedy Search. Between two of the benefited models, the model using the Beam search decoder performs much better with empathetic responses, which is the primary aim of the chatbot. However, it should be noted that it is by no means the end of advancement. Through further training, it can be made more empathetic to cover various emotional scenarios. The model has gained considerable precision and will continue to do so as we expand the dataset and train it further. In addition to that, we can create separate logs for each user to be of use therapeutically. Through daily human interactions, it can learn more and increase its precision through reinforcement learning.

References

1. Adiba, F.I., Islam, T., Kaiser, M.S., Mahmud, M., Rahman, M.A.: Effect of corpora on classification of fake news using Naive Bayes classifier. Int. J. Autom. AI Mach. Learn. Canada **1**, 80–92 (2020)
2. Andrade, L.H., Alonso, J.: Barriers to mental health treatment: results from the who world mental health (WMH) surveys. Psychol. Med. **44**(06), 15 (2013). https://doi.org/10.1017/S0033291713001943
3. Bahdanau, D., Cho, K., Bengio, Y.: Neural machine translation by jointly learning to align and translate. arXiv 1409, 15, September 2014
4. Brownlee, J.: A gentle introduction to calculating the bleu score for text in python. https://machinelearningmastery.com/calculate-bleu-score-for-text-python/
5. Brownlee, J.: How to implement a beam search decoder for natural language processing. https://machinelearningmastery.com/beam-search-decoder-natural-language-processing/
6. Cho, K., et al.: Learning phrase representations using RNN encoder-decoder for statistical machine translation. arXiv, p. 15, June 2014. https://doi.org/10.3115/v1/D14-1179
7. Inkster, B., Sarda, S., Subramanian, V.: A real-world mixed methods data evaluation of an empathy-driven, conversational artificial intelligence agent for digital mental wellbeing. JMIR Mhealth Uhealth **6**, 14 (2018). https://doi.org/10.2196/12106
8. Lintz, N.: Sequence modeling with neural networks (part 2): Attention models. https://indico.io/blog/sequence-modeling-neural-networks-part2-attention-models/
9. Mahmud, M., Kaiser, M.S., McGinnity, T.M., Hussain, A.: Deep learning in mining biological data. Cogn. Comput. **13**(1), 1–33 (2020). https://doi.org/10.1007/s12559-020-09773-x

10. Mahmud, M., et al.: A brain-inspired trust management model to assure security in a cloud based IoT framework for neuroscience applications. Cogn. Comput. **10**, 864–873 (2018)
11. Morgan, C., Webb, R.T.: Incidence, clinical management, and mortality risk following self harm among children and adolescents: cohort study in primary care. BMJ Clin. Res. **359**, 9 (2017). https://doi.org/10.1136/bmj.j4351
12. Nasrin, F., Ahmed, N.I., Rahman, M.A.: Auditory attention state decoding for the quiet and hypothetical environment: a comparison between BLSTM and SVM. In: Proceedings of TCCE, Advances in Intelligent Systems and Computing (2020)
13. Noor, M.B.T., Zenia, N.Z., Kaiser, M.S., Mamun, S.A., Mahmud, M.: Application of deep learning in detecting neurological disorders from magnetic resonance images: a survey on the detection of Alzheimer's disease, Parkinson's disease and schizophrenia. Brain Inform. **7**(1), 1–21 (2020). https://doi.org/10.1186/s40708-020-00112-2
14. Olah, C.: Understanding LSTM networks. http://colah.github.io/posts/2015-08-Understanding-LSTMs/
15. Palasundram, K., Sharef, N.M., Nasharuddin, N.A., Kasmiran, K.A., Azman, A.: Sequence to sequence model performance for education chatbot. Int. J. Emerg. Technol. Learn. (iJET) **14**(24), 56 (2019). https://doi.org/10.3991/ijet.v14i24.12187
16. Papers with Code: Bidirectional LSTM. https://paperswithcode.com/method/bilstm
17. Papers with Code: Long short-term memory. https://paperswithcode.com/method/lstm
18. Prabhavalkar, N.: Mental health FAQ. https://www.kaggle.com/narendrageek/mental-health-faq-for-chatbot
19. Prakash, A.V., Das, S.: Intelligent conversational agents in mental healthcare services: a thematic analysis of user perceptions. Pacific Asia J. Assoc. Inf. Syst. **12**, 34 (2020). https://doi.org/10.17705/1pais.12201
20. Prakash, K.B., Nagapawan, Y., Kalyani, N.L., Kumar, V.P.: Chatterbot implementation using transfer learning and LSTM encoder-decoder architecture. Int. J. Emerg. Trends Eng. Res. **8**, 7 (2020). https://doi.org/10.30534/ijeter/2020/35852020
21. Rahman, M.A.: Gaussian process in computational biology: covariance functions for transcriptomics. Ph.D. thesis, University of Sheffield (2018)
22. Rober, P., Ellliott, R., Buysse, A., Loots, G., Corte, K.D.: Positioning in the therapist's inner conversation: a dialogical model based on a grounded theory analysis of therapist reflections. J. Marital Fam. Ther. **34**(3), 16 (2008). https://doi.org/10.1111/j.1752-0606.2008.00080.x
23. Sadik, R., Reza, M.L., Noman, A.A., Mamun, S.A., Kaiser, M.S., Rahman, M.A.: Covid-19 pandemic: a comparative prediction using machine learning. Int. J. Autom. AI Mach. Learn. Canada **1**, 1–16 (2020)
24. Sak, H., Senior, A., Beaufays, F.: Long short-term memory based recurrent neural network architectures for large vocabulary speech recognition. In: Proceedings of the Annual Conference of the International Speech Communication Association, Interspeech, p. 5, February 2014
25. Yin, J., Chen, Z., Zhou, K., Yu, C.: A deep learning based chatbot for campus psychological therapy. arXiv 8, 31, October 2019
26. Yin, W., Kann, K., Yu, M., Schütze, H.: Comparative study of CNN and RNN for natural language processing. arXiv p. 7, February 2017

A Belief Rule Base Approach to Support Comparison of Digital Speech Signal Features for Parkinson's Disease Diagnosis

Shafkat Raihan[1], Sharif Noor Zisad[1], Raihan Ul Islam[2], Mohammad Shahadat Hossain[1](✉), and Karl Andersson[2]

[1] Department of Computer Science and Engineering, University of Chittagong, Chittagong, Bangladesh
snzisad.cse@std.cu.ac.bd, hossain_ms@cu.ac.bd

[2] Department of Computer Science, Electrical and Space Engineering, Luleå University of Technology, Skellefteå, Sweden
{raihan.ul.islam,karl.andersson}@ltu.se

Abstract. Parkinson's disease is a neurological disorder. It affects the structures of the central and peripheral nervous system that control movement. One of the symptoms of Parkinson's disease is difficulty in speaking. Hence, analysis of speech signal of patients may provide valuable features for diagnosing. Previous works on diagnosis based on speech data have employed machine learning and deep learning techniques. However, these approaches do not address the various uncertainties in data. Belief rule based expert system (BRBES) is an approach that can reason under various forms of data uncertainty. Thus, the main objective of this research is to compare the potential of BRBES on various speech signal features of patients of parkinson's disease. The research took into account various types of standard speech signal features such MFCCs, TQWTs etc. A BRBES was trained on a dataset of 188 patients of parkinson's disease and 64 healthy candidates with 5-fold cross validation. It was optimized using an exploitive version of the nature inspired optimization algorithm called BRB-based adaptive differential evolution (BRBaDE). The optimized model performed better than explorative BRBaDE, genetic algorithm and MATLAB's FMINCON optimization on most of these features. It was also found that for speech based diagnosis of Parkinson's disease under uncertainty, the features such as Glottis Quotient, Jitter variants, MFCCs, RPDE, DFA and PPE are relatively more suitable.

Keywords: CNN · Speech emotion · RAVDESS · MFCC · Data augmentation

1 Introduction

Parkinson's disease is a long-term neurological disorder of the central nervous system. It affects mainly the motor system. Parkinson's disease is the second

M. Mahmud et al. (Eds.): BI 2021, LNAI 12960, pp. 388–400, 2021.
https://doi.org/10.1007/978-3-030-86993-9_35

most conventional neurodegenerative infection seen in over 60 years old people [5]. It is largely associated with the extinction of brain cells that generate dopamine. However, early detection of Parkinson's disease is quite difficult. Previous studies have shown that diagnosis results of Parkinson's disease are unsatisfactory [24]. No specific test is known for diagnosing this disease and medical professionals have to rely on possible signs and symptoms. However, there are significant cases of misdiagnosis of patients. Sometimes it is difficult to distinguish parkinsonian features from essential tremor [2].

In our study, we explored the potential of artificial intelligence techniques that can reason under uncertainty for diagnosing Parkinson's disease based on various kinds of speech signal features. We have selected disjunctive belief rule based expert system (BRBES) technique because it can reason under various kinds of uncertainty like imprecision, ambiguity, vagueness, incompleteness, ignorance and randomness. As per our knowledge, no previous work has applied BRBES in the diagnosis of Parkinson's disease. We have trained our model using various optimization algorithms such as BRB-based Adaptive Differential Evolution, genetic algorithm and MATLAB's FMINCON. We found that an exploitive version of BRBaDE performs better than its explorative counterpart, genetic algorithm and FMINCON. Among the features, Glottis Quotient, Jitter variants, MFCCs, RPDE, DFA and PPE exhibited relatively more promising result than the other features.

2 Related Work

In this section, some recent works on the Parkinson's diseases is presented.

R. Das [4] has compared different type of classification methods for diagnosing the Parkinson's diseases effectively. They got the highest classification score for the neural network and it was 92.9%. They also compared their result with some machine learning models. However, the process of hyper parameter optimization is not presented in the research. N. Imtiaz et al. [12] has organized question answer section to find out the wideness of Parkinson disease. They have shown 62% male population has the prevalence of Parkinson's diseases while 26% female population has the Parkinson's diseases. However, the survey was only organized in an specific area of Pakistan. D. Joshi et al. [14] has applied wavelet transformation to identify Parkinson's diseases. They have shown the combination of wavelet analysis and support vector machine has produced better accuracy. The classification accuracy was 90.32%. The subject group that was considered from the dataset was not matched with age, height and gender. S. A. Mostafa et al. [20] has extracted features from the recorded voice of patients and utilized them with some machine learning models. They have proposed a new approach MFEA for the multi agent system. They achieved 15.22% accuracy for Naive-Bayes classifier and 9.13% accuracy for SVM. However, they have not linked the dataset with the feature of MFEA evaluation method. M. A. Nalls et al. [21] has developed a new model for Parkinson's diseases classification with the data of PPMI (Parkinson's Progression Marker Initiative). The new model has achieved

0.903 specificity. However, the model cannot identify preclinical and prodromal Parkinson's disease. Mahmud et al. [17] reviewed various deep learning architectures as well as open source deep learning tools on their performance in data mining from medical image, signal and sequence data. Deep learning methods geometrically transform one data manifold to another under the assumption that there exist learnable transfer function to perform the mapping. However, when the relationships among the data are causal or very complex, deep learning methods do not perform up to the mark, despite the size of the dataset. Mahmud et al. [18] have performed a survey of various deep learning, reinforcement learning and deep reinforcement learning techniques to mine biological data arriving from various application domains such as Omics, Bioimaging, Medical Imaging as well as [Brain/Body]-Machine Interfaces. DL and RL require high computation power and memory, hence, they are not appropriate for moderate sized datasets. It is not possible to use all nonlinear approximators to represent action-value pairs in reinforcement learning, which may result in instability or divergence. Noor et al. [22] have compared the performance of various deep learning methods in detection of neurological - with focus on Alzheimer's disease, Parkinson's disease and schizophrenia. They used Magnetic Resonance Imaging (MRI) data for this purpose. They have pointed out that better performance of deep learning techniques depends on large training datasets, lack of which is an obstacle in application of deep learning in neuroimaging. They have also noted that deep learning techniques are black box approaches are interpretable, but not explainable. Also, deep learning does not consider the uncertainty of imprecision associated with Parkinson's disease. Belief rule based expert systems (BRBES) are proficient in addressing the uncertainties in data. In various previous researches, BRBES has been applied to design AI based diagnosis systems for various diseases and medical conditions [1,6,8,9,11,16]. BRBES can be trained using optimization algorithms. In [26], MATLAB-based optimization function fmincon was used for training single objective BRB systems. However, fmincon uses gradient based algorithms prone to problems related to local optima. Also, the problem addressed in the aforementioned research work used conjunctive BRB. Conjunctive BRB becomes computationally expensive. The problem of exponential growth can be solved using Disjunctive BRB [3]. Yet, the problem of local optima remains. [27] showed the efficiency of differential evolution (DE) in parameter optimization of BRBES. However, traditional DE lacks the mechanism to find an optimal value for its control parameters. The optimal values are essential so that exploration and exploitation of the search space is balanced. This has been addressed in [13] where a new optimization algorithm, BRBES-Based Adaptive Differential Evolution (BRBaDE) has been used to optimize a BRBES for power usage effectiveness (PUE) prediction of data centers.

In summary, disjunctive BRBES can address uncertainty in real-world data without exponential complexity and it can be optimized using gradient free algorithms. Therefore, in the next section we explore how BRBES performs on various kinds of speech signal features of patients of parkinson's disease.

3 Methodology

3.1 BRBES

Expert systems comprise of two major parts - a knowledge base and an inference engine. A BRBES uses a belief rule base (BRB) as knowledge base and evidential reasoning (ER) as inference engine. While BRBES can represent uncertain knowledge, evidential reasoning can make inference on uncertain and heterogenous data. Unlike assertive IF-THEN rule base, BRBES can address complex non-linear causality under uncertainty. BRB has two main components - antecedent and consequent. Some referential values are associated with each antecedent attribute. A distribution of belief degrees is assigned to the consequent attribute. The rule is considered complete if sum of the degrees of belief is one. The rule is considered incomplete if it is less than one. This indicates the presence of ignorance or incompleteness in data. Antecedents and consequent attribute are connected through linear causal relationship in traditional IF-THEN rule. But in case of a belief rule, this relation is non-linear. Since the example rule uses the conjunction operator (AND), it represents a conjunctive BRB. There are disjunctive BRBs as well that use the disjunctive operator (OR). The relationship between antecedents and consequents in a BRB can be represented with a BRB tree. An example BRB Tree for jitter features is shown in Fig. 1. Digital speech signals can have uncertainty of measurements. Besides, patients of Parkinson's disease have

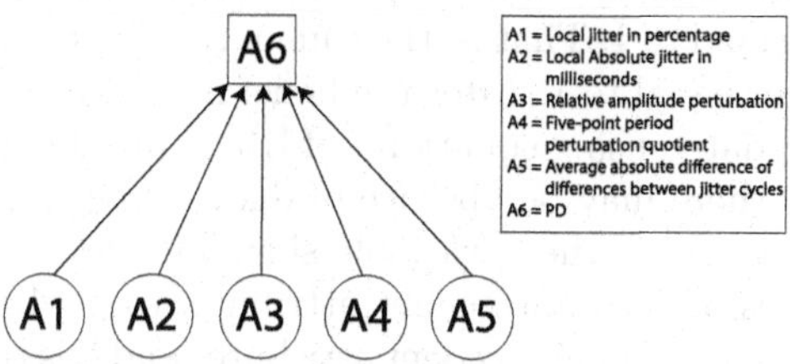

Fig. 1. A BRB tree representing the Parkinson's Disease diagnosis framework using Jitter Variant data

difficulty in speaking. Due to this, the speech signals can vary to uncertain extents. Also the relationship between these parameters is nonlinear. Thus, belief rules are suitable for representing the data effectively. ER has the ability to handle heterogeneous data and various types of uncertainties such as incompleteness, ignorance, imprecision, vagueness and randomness. ER comprises of - input transformation, matching degree calculation, rule activation weight calculation, belief update, and rule aggregation which are depicted in Fig. 2. Input transformation distributes the input antecedent attribute value over the referential values of that antecedent attribute. These transformed values are known as matching degrees. Input transformation can be performed using the equation 1 and 2 shown in [1]. The rules are generated by using multiplication or addition operation on the individual matching degrees based on whether it is conjunctive belief rule base or a disjunctive one, respectively. If there are n attributes where the i-th attribute has m_i referential values, then in conjunctive BRBES, total number of rules generated is $\sum_{i=1}^{n} m_i$. If all the attributes have the same number of referential values m, then number of rules generated in the conjunctive BRBES is m^n. However, disjunctive BRBES requires that all the attributes have the same number of referential values and the number of rules generated is always equal to m. Due to this disjunctive BRBES can address uncertainty in real-world data without exponential complexity. After input transformation operation, total matching degrees (α_k where k = 1, ... , L and L is the number of rules) are obtained for each rule. Each of the total matching degrees represents a rule in the rule base. With matching degrees assigned, the rules then become active. For conjunctive BRBES, total matching degrees are calculated using equation 5 of [1]. For disjunctive BRBES, it is to be calculated using equation 6 of [1]. Next, the activation weight (w_k) of the rule is calculated using the total matching degrees (α_k) and relative rule weights (θ_k) using equation 7 of [1]. If a rule is not activated, it will have zero activation weight. The sum of the rule activation weights of a rule base should be one. The next operation is belief update. For this operation, an initial belief matrix is generated using random number of range [0, 1] which contains degrees of belief corresponding to the consequent attribute of each rule. If there are L rules and the consequent attribute has M referential values, then the belief matrix will be a table with L columns and N rows. The value at l-th column and m-th row represents the degree of belief assigned to the m-th referential value of the consequent attribute of the l-th rule. The matrix is initialized in such a way that the sum of the values along every column is less than or equal to 1. That is, the sum of the degrees of belief of each rule has to be less than or equal to 1. After the belief matrix has been generated, the belief degrees are updated using equation 7 of [16]. Updating the degrees of belief is essential because there may be absence of data for any antecedent attributes because of ignorance. Using the τ variable shown in the equation 7 of [16] and the matching degrees of each antecedent attribute, (α_{ik} where i = 1, ... , N and k = 1 ... , L. N is the number of antecedent attributes and L is the number of rules), belief update operation addresses this uncertainty of ignorance or incompleteness in data. Lastly, evidential reasoning is used to aggregate all the rules and to calculate the output for the input antecedent attributes using equation 8 of [1]. The output value will be in a fuzzy form. This means that it will be distributed over the consequent referential values. Then a crisp or numerical value is obtained from the fuzzy form. It can be done in multiple ways. One of them is using equation 8 of [13]. In this work, we have used disjunctive BRBES since in disjunctive BRBES the parameter space does not explode exponentially. For all antecedent and consequent attributes, three referential values were selected - Low (L), Medium (M) and High (H). The utility values of low and high were selected based on the lowest and highest values of the attribute in the dataset. The Medium utility value was computed as the middle point of the two bounds.

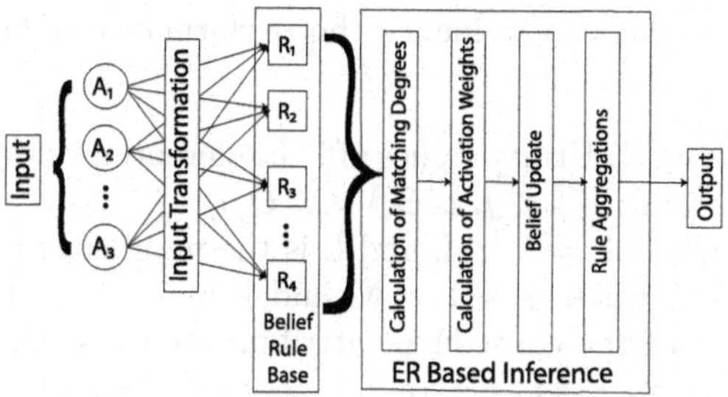

Fig. 2. Working process of a BRBES

3.2 Optimization with BRBaDE

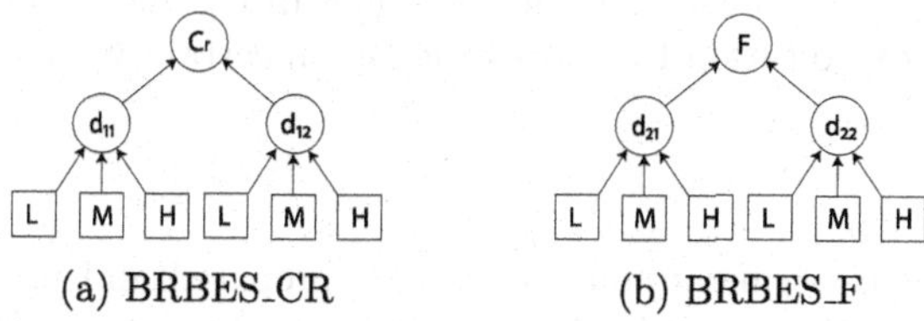

Fig. 3. BRBES for calculating verifying crossover and mutation factors in BRBaDE.

Then, optimization is performed using BRBaDE. Differential Evolution (DE) is a vector based metaheuristic algorithm. It uses both exploration and exploitation in the forms of crossover (C_r) and mutation (F) operations respectively. However, in traditional DE the C_r and F are constant. BRBaDE considers the uncertainties in C_r and F. In BRBaDE the C_r and F change per iteration based on the change in solution vector and fitness values. The change in solution population is denoted by PC and change in fitness value is denoted by FC which can be calculated using equations 15 and 16 of [13] respectively. They can be normalized using equations 17 and 18 of [13] to get the variables d_{11} and d_{12} respectively. The objective function to be optimized is constructed using equations 7–9 of [13]. Two conjunctive BRBES' are used here - BRBES_CR and BRBES_F. d_{11} and d_{12} are sent as antecedent attributes in BRBES_CR. Whereas, $d_{21} = 2d_{11}$ and $2d_{22} = 2d_{12}$ are sent as antecedent attributes in BRBES_F. The former outputs C_r as consequent attribute and the latter outputs F. All attributes (both antecedent and consequent) have three referential values i.e. Low (L), Medium (M) and High (H). Although [13] used F $\in$ [0, 2], F $\in [0, 1]$ is proven to be more efficient [28]. Thus, we have only used d_{11} and d_{12} for both BRBES_CR and BRBES_F. The boundary values among the consequent utilities were selected based on the recommendations made in [28]. The middle point of the boundary values was selected as the middle utility value. The BRB tree of these two BRBES' has been shown in Fig. 3. The parameters optimized here are the fundamental values that can influence the performance of the BRBES. These parameters are:

1. $\mu(O_j)$ $(0 \leq \mu(O_j) \leq 1$. Utility values of j-th referential value of the consequent attribute. Constraint: If $i < j$, $\mu(O_i) < \mu(O_j))$.
2. θ_k $(0 \leq \theta_k \leq 1$ where k = 1 ..., L and L is the number of rules).
3. β_{jk} $(0 \leq \beta_{jk} \leq 1$ where j = 1 ..., M and k = 1 ..., L. M is the number of referential values of the consequent attribute and L is the number of rules. Constraint: $\sum_{j=1}^{n} \beta_{jk} \leq 1)$.

Activation weight w_k is a derived quantity that depends on relative rule weight θ_k and total matching degree α_k as shown in equation 4 of [9]. Also, in joint optimization [27], the matching degrees α_{ij} are also optimized, which in turn optimizes the total matching degree. In this research, joint optimization has not been used but θ_k has been optimized, which in turn optimizes w_k. Finally, using two separate BRBES' to calculate newer values of C_r and F provides balanced exploration and exploitation by addressing the uncertainty.

3.3 Dataset

We have run our experiments on the dataset prepared and used in [25]. They provided a comparative analysis of various machine learning methods on various speech signal features. For this they collected speech data of 188 adult patients of PD as well as data of 64 healthy patients. Speech of each candidate was sampled three times. Thus, the dataset has 756 data points. Various digital speech signal features were extracted from the speech data and collected in a CSV file. The features are divided into various classes such as baseline features, time frequency features, Mel Frequency Cepstral Coefficients (MFCCs), Wavelet Transform based Features, Vocal Fold Features and tunable Q-factor wavelet transform (TQWT) features. Again, the baseline features include subclass of features such jitter variants, shimmer variants, fundamental frequency parameters, harmonicity parameters, Recurrence Period Density Entropy (RPDE), Detrended Fluctuation Analysis (DFA) and Pitch Period Entropy (PPE). Time frequency features include the subclasses intensity Parameters, formant frequencies and bandwidth features. Vocal Fold Features are also divided into subclasses such as Glottis Quotient (GQ), Glottal to Noise Excitation (GNE), Vocal Fold Excitation Ratio (VFER) and Empirical Mode Decomposition (EMD). We trained our BRBES on each of these subclass features as well as MFCC, TQWT and Wavelet Transforms. So a BRB-tree was prepared for the subclass features, MFCC features, TQWT features and wave transform features. The BRB tree for jitter subclass has been shown in Fig. 1. The subclasses RPDE, DFA and PPE each contained only one feature each. So they were considered as a joint subclass which we labeled "R-D-P". Each of these three represented an attribute in the BRB tree of R-D-P.

4 Result and Discussion

The disjunctive BRBES was trained using BRBaDE optimization algorithm. The original BRBES algorithm uses exploration operator for creating the donor vector. However, there are variants of differential evolution algorithm that use exploitation operator to create the donor vector. Therefore, we have trained two types of BRBaDE here. The exploitation based BRBaDE has been labeled as "BRBaDE Best" as it creates the donor vector using the current best solution. The exploration based BRBaDE has been labeled as "BRBaDE r1" as it creates the donor vector using the a random solution r1 from the solution population. To make our model capable of providing decision regarding diagnosis, we calculate a decision variable by setting a threshold of 0.5. Predicted crisp outputs greater than this threshold were mapped to 1. Otherwise they were mapped to 0. Various classification metrics have been used in this research to compare the diagnosis performance of the algorithms. Accuracy shows the number of correctly classified samples. Exactness of the model can be represented by precision metric and completeness can be expressed using recall metric, also known as sensitivity. F1 score is a metric that balances precision and recall of the prediction. It is very effective when the dataset has class imbalance such as the dataset we used. The true negative (recognition) rate is represented by specificity. AUC is the area under curve (AUC) of a Receiver Operator Curve (ROC). It is a measure of how capable a classifier is to distinguish between classes. The higher the AUC, the higher the capability. If a model has AUC less than 50% then it is no better than random guess. Mean square error (MSE) is a standard measure of error. The lower the MSE, the better the performance. MSE is also part of standard objective functions used in BRBES optimization. The performances of the models on various features have been shown for fold-4 in Table 1. Of the five folds, fold-4 has been shown here because it contained the most distinguished scores of performances.

In this work, we have used 5-fold cross validation on the whole dataset. The reason behind conducting the cross-validation on the whole dataset instead of just the training dataset is to avoid over-fitting or selection bias. And number of folds was selected as five based on better results obtained in previous works of speech data classification for neurological disorder [30]. In Tables 1, scores values that were within top five and which did not get repeated for more than ten times have been highlighted. Features that performed most well in all the five folds are GQ features, harmonicity features, intensity features, jitter features, MFCCs, R-D-P features, shimmer features and TQWT features. 81% accuracy was achieved by all four models in fold-4 for R-D-P. For jitter features, all models except "BRBaDE r1" achieved *geq* 80% accuracy in fold 4. The lowest MSE obtained in this research is 0.14990. It was obtained by "BRBaDE Best" in fold-4 for jitter features. F1-score creates a balance between exactness (precision) and completeness (sensitivity) of the model. 89% and 88% F1-score was obtained on R-D-P in fold-2 and fold-3. Shimmer and jitter features also obtained 81% F1-score in fold-4. AUC represents the ratio between true positive rate (sensitivity) and false positive rate. 80% AUC was achieved on MFCCs in fold-5 by all four models.

Table 1. Performance evaluation of various optimization algorithms on various types of speech signal features

Algorithms	BRBaDE best					BRBaDE r1					FMINCON					GA				
Features	Acc	Spec	F1 score	AUC	MSE	Acc	Spec	F1 score	AUC	MSE	Acc	Spec	F1 score	AUC	MSE	Acc	Spec	F1 score	AUC	MSE
Bandwidth	0.75	0.08	0.85	0.51	0.18801	0.75	0.08	0.85	0.54	0.18781	0.75	0.08	0.85	0.51	0.18802	0.74	0.03	0.85	0.57	0.18749
EMD	0.75	0.00	0.86	0.63	0.18081	0.75	0.00	0.86	0.62	0.18380	0.75	0.00	0.86	0.62	0.18123	0.75	0.00	0.86	0.62	0.18222
Form. Freq	0.75	0.03	0.86	0.60	0.18249	0.75	0.00	0.86	0.60	0.18288	0.76	0.05	0.86	0.60	0.18200	0.75	0.00	0.86	0.60	0.18321
Fund. Freq	0.75	0.03	0.86	0.52	0.18547	0.75	0.03	0.86	0.54	0.18576	0.75	0.00	0.86	0.54	0.18698	0.75	0.00	0.86	0.54	0.18952
NE	0.77	0.18	0.87	0.65	0.17168	0.76	0.11	0.86	0.62	0.17453	0.77	0.18	0.87	0.65	0.17167	0.77	0.16	0.87	0.63	0.17236
GQ	0.78	**0.26**	0.87	0.72	0.16213	0.77	0.16	0.87	0.70	0.16420	**0.79**	**0.24**	0.87	0.71	0.16456	**0.79**	**0.26**	0.87	0.71	0.16215
Harmonicity	0.75	0.00	0.86	**0.74**	0.16744	0.75	0.00	0.86	**0.74**	0.17126	0.75	0.00	0.86	**0.74**	0.16757	0.75	0.00	0.86	0.73	0.17032
Intensity	0.75	0.00	0.86	**0.76**	0.16478	0.75	0.00	0.86	**0.75**	0.16474	0.75	0.00	0.86	**0.75**	0.16562	0.75	0.00	0.86	**0.76**	0.16542
Jitter	**0.81**	**0.29**	**0.88**	**0.75**	**0.14990**	**0.79**	**0.24**	**0.88**	**0.75**	**0.15023**	**0.80**	**0.26**	**0.88**	**0.75**	**0.15142**	**0.80**	**0.26**	**0.88**	**0.75**	0.15474
MFCC	0.74	0.03	0.85	**0.77**	0.15913	0.74	0.08	0.85	**0.77**	0.15891	0.74	0.03	0.85	**0.77**	0.15947	0.75	0.00	0.86	**0.77**	0.16370
R-D-P	**0.81**	**0.32**	**0.89**	**0.76**	**0.15010**	**0.81**	**0.32**	**0.89**	**0.75**	0.15174	**0.81**	**0.32**	**0.89**	**0.75**	**0.15131**	**0.81**	**0.29**	**0.88**	**0.76**	0.15469
Shimmer	**0.79**	0.18	**0.88**	0.68	0.16790	**0.79**	0.16	**0.88**	0.69	0.16900	**0.79**	0.18	**0.88**	0.67	0.16850	0.78	0.16	0.87	0.69	0.16876
TQWT	0.75	0.00	0.86	0.72	0.17280	0.75	0.00	0.86	0.72	0.17899	0.75	0.00	0.86	0.67	0.18086	0.75	0.00	0.86	0.66	0.17973
VFER	0.78	0.13	0.87	0.62	0.17593	0.76	0.05	0.86	0.62	0.17728	0.78	0.13	0.87	0.62	0.17585	0.78	0.13	0.87	0.62	0.17571
Wave transform	0.75	0.03	0.86	0.62	0.18369	0.74	0.00	0.85	0.63	0.18422	0.75	0.00	0.86	0.63	0.18437	0.75	0.00	0.86	0.47	0.18834

Table 2. Number of metrics where the subclass of features performed the highest across all the models

Fold	Bandwidth	EMD	Form. Freq.	Fund. Freq.	GNE	GQ	Harmonicity	Intensity	Jitter	MFCC	R-D-P	Shimmer	TQWT	VFER	Wave transform
1	0.05	0.20	0.20	0.20	0.45	0.10	0	0.20	0.20	0.05	**0.55**	0	0.20	0	0.20
2	0.20	0.20	0.20	0.20	0.20	**0.50**	0.15	0.20	0	0.35	**0.60**	0.15	0.20	0.20	0.15
3	0.20	0.20	0.15	0.20	0.10	0.20	0	0.20	**0.95**	0.10	0	0	0.20	0	0.05
4	0	0.20	0.20	0.20	0	0	0.20	0.20	0.10	0.05	**0.90**	0.05	0.20	0.20	0.15
5	0	0.20	0.10	0.20	0.30	**0.70**	0.20	0.20	0	**0.60**	0	0	0.20	0	10
Average	0.09	0.20	0.17	0.20	0.21	**0.30**	0.11	0.20	0.25	**0.27**	**0.41**	0.04	0.20	0.08	0.13
Best	0.20	0.20	0.20	0.20	0.45	**0.70**	4	4	**0.95**	**0.60**	**0.90**	0.15	0.20	0.20	0.20

Table 3. Number of metrics where the models performed the highest across all the subclass features

Fold	BRBaDE Best	BRBaDE r1	FMINCON	GA
1	**0.63**	0.58	0.57	0.51
2	**0.76**	0.57	0.54	0.5
3	**0.65**	0.53	0.46	0.46
4	**0.70**	0.48	0.53	0.43
5	**0.60**	0.60	0.38	0.56
Average	**70**	58	$52.2 \approx 52$	$51.8 \approx 52$
Best	**0.67**	0.55	0.50	0.49

The BRBES approach used in this article has achieved maximum specificity of 32% on R-D-P features in fold-4 and GQ in fold-5. It was achieved by "BRBaDE Best" in fold-5 and all models except GA in fold-4. We think the reason behind a lower specificity is the class imbalance in the dataset as it contains more instances of patients of Parkinson's disease than healthy candidates. Training on a larger dataset with more samples of healthy candidates might improve the specificity. Table 2 visualizes the comparative performance of the feature subclasses. It can be seen that GQ, Jitter, MFCC and R-D-P have the topmost scores in the table. This suggests that these subclasses of features can represent valuable information that can be used to diagnose Parkinson's disease under uncertainty. A similar comparison has been shown for the models trained as well in Table 3. It can be seen that both BRBaDEs have shown promising results compared to GA and FMINCON. And among the two BRBaDEs, exploitive BRBaDE (BRBaDE Best) performed better than explorative BRBaDE (BRBaDE r1). The results above suggest that exploitive BRBaDE is a highly suitable candidate for diagnosis of Parkinson's disease based on speech signal features. It also suggests that for diagnosis of Parkinson's disease under uncertainty, the most promising speech signal features are GQ features, jitter variants, MFCCs, RPDE, DFA and PPE. They can be considered as relatively more suitable than other speech signal features for diagnosing Parkinson's disease under uncertainty.

5 Conclusion

The main aim of this research was to conduct a comparative analysis of various speech signal features for diagnosing Parkinson's disease using disjunctive BRBES [15,19,29] with optimization. It was observed that exploitive BRBaDE outperforms explorative BRBaDE, Genetic Algorithm and FMINCON in this task. Among the speech features, GQ, jitter variants, MFCCs, RPDE, DFA and PPE provided the best predictions. However, the performance of this BRBES approach still requires improvement, especially in specificity. This can be achieved by training on a larger dataset. In the previous works, deep convolutional neural networks (CNN) have shown better results on speech signal features of patients with neurological disorder [30]. Though CNN is an unexplainable technique based on backpropogation, integrating [31] it with BBRES can overcome this limitation. BRBES [7,10,23] and CNN can assist each other in a symbiotic fashion. Therefore, in future we will integrate BRBES with CNN to improve the current results.

References

1. Ahmed, F., Hossain, M.S., Islam, R.U., Andersson, K.: An evolutionary belief rule-based clinical decision support system to predict Covid-19 severity under uncertainty. Appl. Sci. **11**(13), 5810 (2021)
2. Buchert, R., Buhmann, C., Apostolova, I., Meyer, P.T., Gallinat, J.: Nuclear imaging in the diagnosis of clinically uncertain parkinsonian syndromes. Dtsch. Arztebl. Int. **116**(44), 747 (2019)
3. Chang, L., Zhou, Z., You, Y., Yang, L., Zhou, Z.: Belief rule based expert system for classification problems with new rule activation and weight calculation procedures. Inf. Sci. **336**, 75–91 (2016)
4. Das, R.: A comparison of multiple classification methods for diagnosis of Parkinson disease. Expert Syst. Appl. **37**(2), 1568–1572 (2010)
5. De Rijk, M.d., et al.: Prevalence of Parkinson's disease in Europe: a collaborative study of population-based cohorts. Neurologic diseases in the elderly research group. Neurology **54**(11 Suppl 5), S21–3 (2000)
6. Hossain, M.S., Ahmed, F., Andersson, K., et al.: A belief rule based expert system to assess tuberculosis under uncertainty. J. Med. Syst. **41**(3), 43 (2017)
7. Hossain, M.S., Al Hasan, A., Guha, S., Andersson, K.: A belief rule based expert system to predict earthquake under uncertainty. J. Wirel. Mobile Netw. Ubiquit. Comput. Depend. Appl. **9**(2), 26–41 (2018)
8. Hossain, M.S., Habib, I.B., Andersson, K.: A belief rule based expert system to diagnose dengue fever under uncertainty. In: 2017 Computing Conference, pp. 179–186. IEEE (2017)
9. Hossain, M.S., Khalid, M.S., Akter, S., Dey, S.: A belief rule-based expert system to diagnose influenza. In: 2014 9th International Forum on Strategic Technology (IFOST), pp. 113–116. IEEE (2014)
10. Hossain, M.S., Monrat, A.A., Hasan, M., Karim, R., Bhuiyan, T.A., Khalid, M.S.: A belief rule-based expert system to assess mental disorder under uncertainty. In: 2016 5th International Conference on Informatics, Electronics and Vision (ICIEV), pp. 1089–1094. IEEE (2016)
11. Hossain, M.S., Rahaman, S., Mustafa, R., Andersson, K.: A belief rule-based expert system to assess suspicion of acute coronary syndrome (ACS) under uncertainty. Soft. Comput. **22**(22), 7571–7586 (2018)
12. Imtiaz, N., et al.: Study of prevalence of Parkinson's disease in elderly population in Rawalpindi, Pakistan (2016)
13. Islam, R.U., Ruci, X., Hossain, M.S., Andersson, K., Kor, A.L.: Capacity management of hyperscale data centers using predictive modelling. Energies **12**(18), 3438 (2019)
14. Joshi, D., Khajuria, A., Joshi, P.: An automatic non-invasive method for Parkinson's disease classification. Comput. Methods Programs Biomed. **145**, 135–145 (2017)

15. Kabir, S., Islam, R.U., Hossain, M.S., Andersson, K.: An integrated approach of belief rule base and deep learning to predict air pollution. Sensors **20**(7), 1956 (2020)
16. Karim, R., Andersson, K., Hossain, M.S., Uddin, M.J., Meah, M.P.: A belief rule based expert system to assess clinical bronchopneumonia suspicion. In: 2016 Future Technologies Conference (FTC), pp. 655–660. IEEE (2016)
17. Mahmud, M., Kaiser, M.S., McGinnity, T.M., Hussain, A.: Deep learning in mining biological data. Cogn. Comput. **13**(1), 1–33 (2021)
18. Mahmud, M., Kaiser, M.S., Hussain, A., Vassanelli, S.: Applications of deep learning and reinforcement learning to biological data. IEEE Trans. Neural Netw. Learn. Syst. **29**(6), 2063–2079 (2018)
19. Monrat, A.A., Islam, R.U., Hossain, M.S., Andersson, K.: A belief rule based flood risk assessment expert system using real time sensor data streaming. In: 2018 IEEE 43rd Conference on Local Computer Networks Workshops (LCN Workshops), pp. 38–45. IEEE (2018)
20. Mostafa, S.A., et al.: Examining multiple feature evaluation and classification methods for improving the diagnosis of Parkinson's disease. Cogn. Syst. Res. **54**, 90–99 (2019)
21. Nalls, M.A., et al.: Diagnosis of Parkinson's disease on the basis of clinical and genetic classification: a population-based modelling study. Lancet Neurol. **14**(10), 1002–1009 (2015)
22. Noor, M.B.T., Zenia, N.Z., Kaiser, M.S., Al Mamun, S., Mahmud, M.: Application of deep learning in detecting neurological disorders from magnetic resonance images: a survey on the detection of Alzheimer's disease, Parkinson's disease and schizophrenia. Brain Inform. **7**(1), 1–21 (2020)
23. Rahaman, S., Hossain, M.S.: A belief rule based (BRB) system to assess asthma suspicion. In: 16th International Conference Computer and Information Technology, pp. 432–437. IEEE (2014)
24. Rizzo, G., Copetti, M., Arcuti, S., Martino, D., Fontana, A., Logroscino, G.: Accuracy of clinical diagnosis of Parkinson disease: a systematic review and meta-analysis. Neurology **86**(6), 566–576 (2016)
25. Sakar, C.O., et al.: A comparative analysis of speech signal processing algorithms for Parkinson's disease classification and the use of the tunable q-factor wavelet transform. Appl. Soft Comput. **74**, 255–263 (2019)
26. Yang, J.B., Liu, J., Xu, D.L., Wang, J., Wang, H.: Optimization models for training belief-rule-based systems. IEEE Trans. Syst. Man Cybern. Part A Syst. Hum. **37**(4), 569–585 (2007)
27. Yang, L.H., Wang, Y.M., Liu, J., Martinez, L.: A joint optimization method on parameter and structure for belief-rule-based systems. Knowl.-Based Syst. **142**, 220–240 (2018)
28. Yang, X.S.: Nature-Inspired Optimization Algorithms. Academic Press, Boston (2020)
29. Zisad, S.N., Chowdhury, E., Hossain, M.S., Islam, R.U., Andersson, K.: An integrated deep learning and belief rule-based expert system for visual sentiment analysis under uncertainty. Algorithms **14**(7), 213 (2021)
30. Zisad, S.N., Hossain, M.S., Andersson, K.: Speech emotion recognition in neurological disorders using convolutional neural network. In: Mahmud, M., Vassanelli, S., Kaiser, M.S., Zhong, N. (eds.) BI 2020. LNCS (LNAI), vol. 12241, pp. 287–296. Springer, Cham (2020). https://doi.org/10.1007/978-3-030-59277-6_26
31. Zisad, S.N., Hossain, M.S., Hossain, M.S., Andersson, K.: An integrated neural network and SEIR model to predict Covid-19. Algorithms **14**(3), 94 (2021)

Towards Autism Subtype Detection Through Identification of Discriminatory Factors Using Machine Learning

Tania Akter[1,2], Mohammad Hanif Ali[1], Md. Shahriare Satu[3], Md. Imran Khan[2], and Mufti Mahmud[4(✉)]

[1] Department of Computer Science and Engineering, Jahangirnagar University, Savar, Dhaka 1342, Bangladesh
[2] Department of Computer Science and Engineering, Gono Bishwabidyalay, Savar, Dhaka 1344, Bangladesh
[3] Department of Management Information Systems, Noakhali Science and Technology University, Sonapur, Noakhali 3814, Bangladesh
[4] Department of Computing and Technology, Nottingham Trent University, Clifton Campus, Clifton, Nottingham NG11 8NS, UK
mufti.mahmud@ntu.ac.uk

Abstract. Autism spectrum disorder (ASD) is a neuro-developmental disease that has a lifetime impact on a person's ability to interact and communicate with others. Early discovery of autism can assist to prepare a plan for suitable therapy and reduce its impact on patients at an appropriate time. The aim of this work is to propose a machine learning model which generates autism subtypes and identifies discriminatory factors among them. In this work, we use Quantitative Checklist for Autism in Toddlers-10 (Q-CHAT-10) of toddler and Autism Spectrum Quotient-10 (AQ-10) datasets of child, adolescent, and adult screening datasets respectively. Then, only autism records are merged and implemented k-means algorithm to extract various autism subtypes. According to Silhoutte score, we select the best autism dataset and balance its subtypes using random oversampling (ROS) and synthetic minority oversampling technique for numeric and categorical values (SMOTENC). Afterwards, various classifiers are employed into both primary dataset and its balanced subtypes. In this work, logistic regression shows the highest result for primary dataset. Also, it achieves the greatest results for ROS and SMOTENC datasets. Hence, shapely adaptive explanation (SHAP) technique is used to rank features and scrutinized discriminatory factors of these autism subtypes.

Keywords: Autism · K-means clustering · Machine learning · SHAP analysis · Discriminatory factors

1 Introduction

ASD is a neurological disorder that impacts on communication, interaction, and learning processes of affecting individuals [12]. It is a lifetime ailment that cannot

M. Mahmud et al. (Eds.): BI 2021, LNAI 12960, pp. 401–410, 2021.
https://doi.org/10.1007/978-3-030-86993-9_36

be totally healed. But, many significant traits of this disorder are often observed to the children. Thus, instant diagnosis and treatment (i.e. therapy and medicine) is useful to reduce multifarious complexity of this disease more precisely.

Non clinical screening tools such as AQ, Q-CHAT, Social Communication Questionnaire (SCQ), and Modified Checklist for Autism in Toddler (M-CHAT), M-CHAT/Revised with Follow-Up (RF) are more effective to detect autism at early stages [13]. However, these tools are more efficient because autistic patient or their guardians (i.e., parents, teachers, and others) can directly use them without any specific qualification. Therefore, physicians identify autism and provide proper treatment using different red flags. However, machine learning is an useful technique to investigate previous records and detect autism automatically. In many existing works, various machine learning methods were applied into Q-CHAT-10 and AQ-10 datasets to detect autism. Thabtah et al. [16] provided a computational intelligence (CI) technique named Variable Analysis (VA) that lessen several features of ASD screening datasets to predict autism more efficiently. Further, Akter et al. [4] generated several transformed datasets from Q-CHAT-10 and AQ-10 datasets where individual classifiers shows best performance. Then, these datasets were used to identify significant ASD risk factors for toddler, child, adolescent and adult subjects using various feature selection methods respectively. Thabtah and Peebles [17] represented rules based machine learning approach that detects autism traits and extracts rules to understand the reasons of this disorder. Akyol [5] identified many significant attributes for detecting autism using recursive feature elimination and stability selection methods. Wiratsin et al. [18] proposed a feature selection technique and extracted significant attributes of child, adolescent, and adult, respectively. Hossain et al. [10] evaluated these datasets with various state-of-the-art methods to find out the best classifier and feature set for Toddler, Child, Adolescent and Adult subjects respectively. Baadel et al. [7] proposed clustering based autistic trait classification (CATC) for AQ-10 datasets where they optimized input and identified relevant features based on similarity measures. Again, Akter et al. [3] used correlation based analysis to eliminate highly co-linear features of autism and investigated the predictivity of different classifiers using data transformation methods. In the application of Q-CHAT-10 and AQ-10 datasets, researchers were inspected their characteristics for both case and controls, respectively. However, the exploration of different ASD subtypes are required to realize major discriminatory characteristics of autism and ensure proper therapy of it.

In this study, we amalgamated only autism records from Q-CHAT-10 of toddler and AQ-10 datasets of child, adolescent, and adult, respectively. Then, several state-of-the-art methods were used to identify autism subtypes and investigate discriminative factors of them. This effort is beneficiary for numerous scientists and ASD welfare organizations. The most important contributions of this work are:

- Propose a machine learning model that extracts possible autism subtypes and characterizes this disorder more precisely.

- Explore these subtypes using various widely used machine learning methods (i.e., clustering, data transformation, classification, and feature selection) to evaluate this work.
- Use explainable machine learning methods to determine which features are important for getting the best result.
- Identify the key characteristics of autism subtypes by investigating discriminative factors.

2 Materials and Methods

2.1 Dataset Description

Baron-Cohen et al. [8] formulated Autistic-Spectrum (AQ) screening method to detect autism. Then, Allison et al. [6] proposed a shorten version of AQ (i.e. Q-CHAT 10, AQ-10 Child, AQ-10 Adolescent, and AQ-10 Adult) for identifying autism of different types of people respectively. Further, Thabtah et al. [14] developed a smart phone based app named ASDTests based on AQ-10 method for detecting ASD at early stage. Then, there were gathered individual's instances between 18–36 months, 4–11 years old, 12–16 years old and above 16 years respectively. However, two versions of AQ-10 dataset versions were gathered where version-1 contains 20 attributes and version-2 has 23 attributes (i.e., except Q-CHAT-10 Toddler dataset which hold 18 attributes). But, version-1 dataset is unavailable for Toddler. Besides, several questionnaires (A1 to A10) remain same in both versions where version-2 has more records than version-1 [10]. Moreover, child and adolescent datasets have similar queries while toddler and adult consume some particular questions. In this study, we work with version-2 based toddler (N = 1054), child (N = 509), adolescent (N = 248) and adults (N = 1118) screening datasets [7]. For every dataset, the class value "No" indicates this record have no ASD (i.e., control). Additionally, the instance having ASD denotes as class value "Yes". These values are assigned based on the responses of AQ-10 questions. When the final score of them is less than or equal to 7, then the class value is declared as "No", otherwise "Yes".

2.2 Proposed Autism Subtype Detection Model

In this Section, proposed autism subtypes detection model is described step by step briefly as follows (see details in Fig. 1).

- **Data Preprocessing:** There are merged only autism instances of toddler, child, adolescent, and adult from Q-CHAT-10 (i.e. for toddler) and AQ-10 datasets respectively. This work is completely used the attribute notation of following works [7,10,17]. Then, severa missing values of features are replaced with mean values. According to the Hossain et al. [10], we remove some irrelevant attributes [10] such as "Case", "Used App Before", "User (who completed the screening)", "Language", "Why taken the screening", "Age Description", "Screening Type", and "Score". In this work, some features

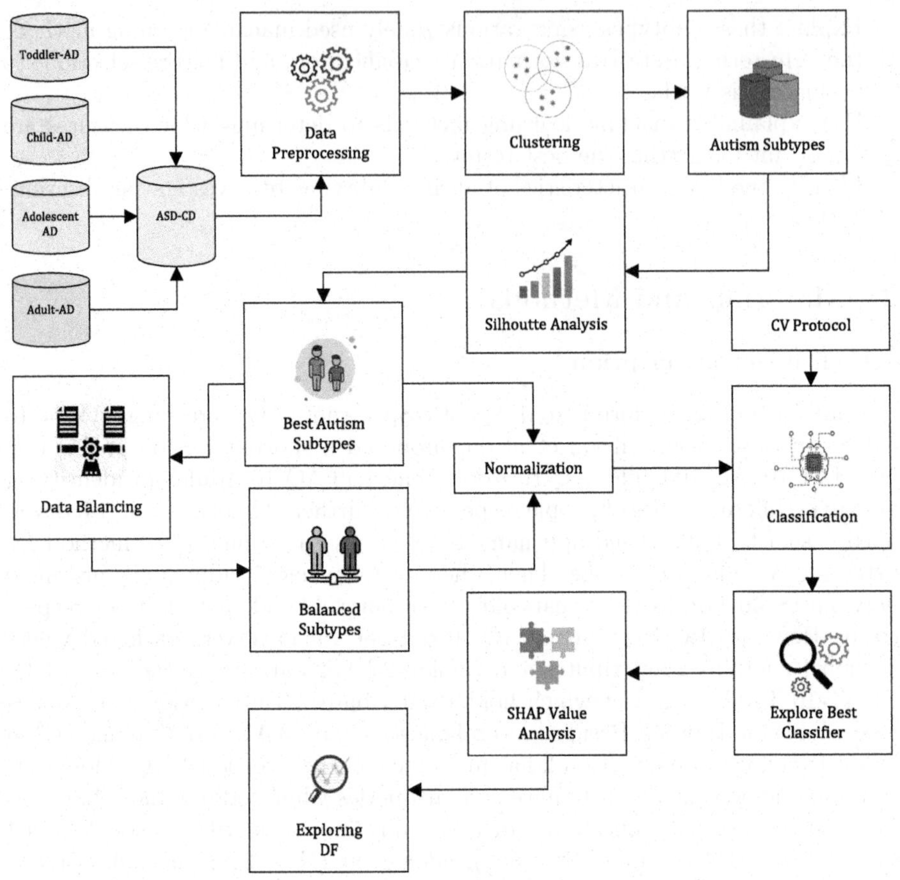

Fig. 1. Proposed autism subtype model

such as Sex, Jaundice, "Family_ASD" are encoded into numeric format where toddler age group has been converted from month to years.

- **Applying Clustering Technique:** Cluster analysis is used to generate similar groups from individual instances according to the data characteristics [1]. Consequently, k-means algorithm is created various clusters by calculating the distances among different records. However, we apply this method into combined autism dataset and generate various autism sub-types by changing the values of k from 2 to 10 in each iteration. Later, these subtypes are considered as individual "class labels" to reveal the predictability of proposed model.
- **Silhouette Analysis:** The estimation of the detachment gap and data consistency are measured in the individual clusters using silhouette analysis [1]. If this value is high, the object is well matched to its own cluster. In this work, this method is implemented on different autism subtypes in each iteration (i.e., depending on the value of k) to identify the best group.

- **Data Balancing:** In the best autism subtypes, the instances of majority and minority clusters are not equal and need to balance these subtypes for further investigation. In this work, we employ Random OverSampling (ROS) and Synthetic Minority Oversampling Technique for Nominal and Categorical Features (SMOTE-NC) and generate two balanced datasets. ROS randomly identifies various examples from minority class with replacement and appends them to the training dataset. On the other hand, SMOTENC is used to estimate class distribution by casually increasing minority instances for both continuous and categorical attributes.
- **Normalization:** Data transformation method is converted into another value to integrate and manage relevant features for machine learning analysis. In this work, we normalize (i.e. applying Z-Score method) baseline (i.e., autism subtypes) and its balanced datasets into suitable structures.
- **Classification Approaches:** Then, we apply several widely used classifiers [12,15] such as Decision Tree (DT), Naïve Bayes (NB), K Nearest Neighbor (KNN), Support Vector Machine (SVM), Logistic Regression (LR), Random Forest (RF), Extreme Gradient Boosting (XGB) and Gradient Boost (GB) on normalized baseline, ROS and SMOTENC dataset. These classifiers which are implemented in this investigation have been widely used in earlier works relating to autism [11]. Then, the best classifier have been determined for each dataset where all classifier's results are justified using some evaluation metrics like accuracy, f-measure and AUC (see details in Sect. 2.3).
- **Exploring Significant Features:** In a nutshell, SHapley Additive exPlanations (SHAP) is a game theoretic approach where shapley values evaluate the degree of contribution of each feature for the comprehensive machine learning model. In this work, we implement SHAP method to manipulate the priority of individual features of each autism dataset employing the best classifier. Afterwards, the discriminatory factors of autism subtypes are determined by counting frequency of individual items for both primary and balanced dataset, respectively.

2.3 Evaluation Metrics

In this work, several evaluation metrics such as accuracy, area under the curve (AUC), f-measure are implemented to evaluate the performance of various classifiers. These metrics are enumerated by true positive (TP), true negative (TN), false positive (FP) and false negative (FN), which are defined as follows:

$$\text{Accuracy} = \frac{TP + TN}{TP + FN + FP + TN} \tag{1}$$

$$\text{F-Measure} = 2 \times \frac{\text{precision} \ \times \ \text{recall}}{\text{precision} \ + \ \text{recall}} = \frac{TP}{TP + \frac{1}{2}(FP + FN)} \tag{2}$$

$$\text{AUC} = \frac{\text{TP rate} + \text{TN rate}}{2} \tag{3}$$

3 Result and Discussion

In this study, we have implemented k-means and its silhouette analysis using Orange data mining toolkit version 3.29. Then, data balancing, and classification process (i.e., apply DT, NB, KNN, SVM, LR, RF, XGB and GB using 10 fold cross validation) have been employed using scikit-learn library [2] and feature interpretation has been done using SHAP library. Without clustering, all experiments are employed at Google Colaboratory in python [9].

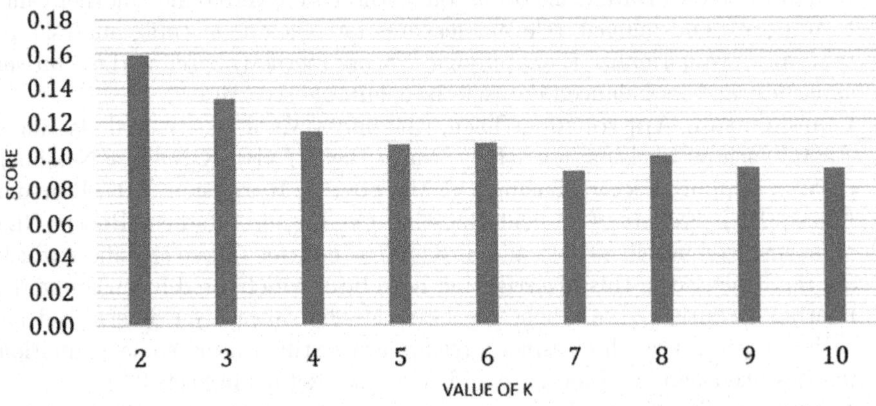

Fig. 2. Silhouette score for individual clusters depending on the values of k (for k = 2 to 10)

In this model, different autism subtypes are formulated depending on k values of k-means algorithm. In Fig. 2, we observe the silhouette values of generated clusters for k = 2 to 10, respectively. Then, the highest score 0.159 is obtained for k = 2 autism subtypes. Besides, other scores are gradually reduced for different k based autism subtypes. So, we take k = 2 subtypes as the best group for further machine learning analysis. These subtypes are denoted as subtype-1 and subtype-2, respectively.

3.1 Comparison of Performance of Individual Classifiers

Primary k = 2 autism subtypes (baseline) are balanced with ROS and SMOTENC methods and formulated two datasets. Then, various classifiers which is mentioned in Sect. 2.2 are used to investigate these datasets. Several evaluation metrics like accuracy, f-measure and AUC are used to justify the results (see Table 1). In this experiment, all classifiers produce high result (i.e. above 90%) where LR shows the highest 99.25% accuracy, 99.25% F-Measure, and 99.16% AUC, for baseline. On the other hand, these classifiers also provide good results (i.e. above 90%) for ROS and SMOTENC dataset respectively. Again, LR outperforms other classifiers where it shows 98.80% accuracy, 98.80% F-Measure

Table 1. Experimental results of individual datasets

	Baseline			ROS Dataset			SMOTE Dataset		
	Accuracy	F-Measure	AUC	Accuracy	F-Measure	AUC	Accuracy	F-Measure	AUC
DT	97.35	97.37	97.37	98.61	98.61	98.61	98.06	98.06	98.06
NB	94.08	94.23	95.40	93.02	92.99	93.02	88.72	88.64	88.72
KNN	92.52	92.44	89.38	91.27	91.25	91.27	93.62	93.62	93.62
SVM	97.76	97.77	97.57	98.11	98.10	98.11	98.01	98.01	98.01
LR	***99.25***	***99.25***	***99.16***	***98.80***	***98.80***	***98.80***	***99.03***	***99.03***	***99.03***
RF	98.03	98.03	97.83	98.61	98.61	98.61	98.57	98.57	98.57
XGB	97.76	97.76	97.48	98.48	98.47	98.48	98.75	98.75	98.75
GB	97.62	97.62	96.89	98.11	98.10	98.11	98.29	98.29	98.29

and 98.80% AUC for ROS dataset. Also, this classifier presents 99.03% accuracy, 99.03% F-Measure and 99.03% AUC for SMOTENC dataset. Besides, the performance of almost all classifiers for balanced datasets are comparatively well than baseline.

3.2 Interpretation of Features for Discriminatory Factors

In primary autism subtypes, the ranks of shapely values of existing features (i.e. implying LR [15]) has been shown at Fig. 3(a). According to this illustration and statistical analysis, the identification of age group is the most significant discriminatory factor to distinguish its subtypes. Hence, the ages of subtype-1 are less than 12 years old and subtype-2 represent its age group greater than 11 years old. Then, Sex is considered as the second discriminatory factors where the number of female is greater than male in subtype-2. Therefore, shapely values of another features are prioritized from high to low values and explained how LR achieves the best performance in this work (see Fig. 3(a)). Besides, both subtypes contain more autistic traits than controls. However, subtype-1 shows more instances (i.e., yes/no responses) than subtype-2 (i.e., not found more DFs between two subtypes). In this experiment, "Pretending Capability (A8)", "Sound Sense (A1)", "Making Friends (A10)", and "Interpreting Conversation (A5)" can be taken as next prior features for both subtypes (see Details in Fig. 3(a)). However, jaundice and "family_ASD" are not so such useful to distinguish autism subtypes.

Then, we determine shapely values to extract significant factors applying best performing LR for ROS and SMOTENC dataset which are shown at Fig. 3(b) and (c). Almost all autistic features (i.e., except A6 and A7) including no jaundice and "family_ASD" are oversampled to the minor subtype-2 for both data balancing techniques. In this case, subtype-1 contains more records than subtype-2. Like primary autism subtypes, age group is found as the most discriminatory factor for both balanced datasets. Therefore, the age group of subtype-1 is less than 22 years old and subtype-2 is more than 11 years old. Then, sex is the second best discriminatory factor where the female samples are also increased into subtype-2. Therefore, it preserve almost similar ranking of autistic features (i.e. "Pretending Capability (A8)", "Character's Intention (A7)", "Making Friends (A10)", "Sound Sense (A1)", and "Interpreting Conversation (A5)")

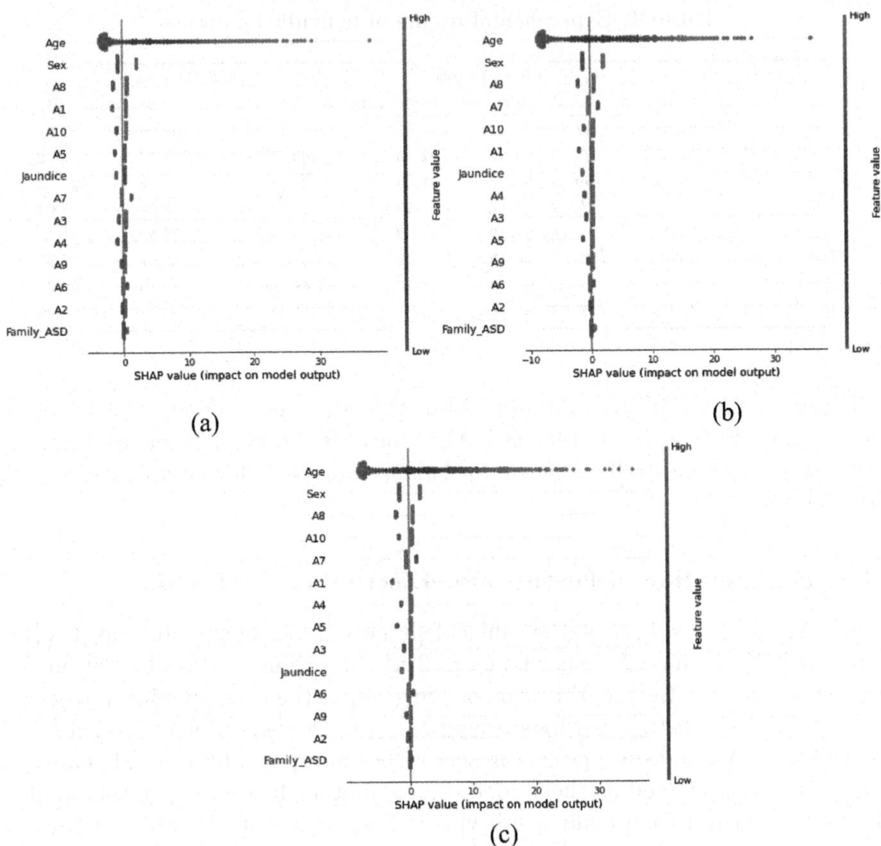

Fig. 3. SHAP values analysis using best performing LR for (a) primary, (b) ROS, and (c) SMOTENC generated autism subtypes

like primary subtypes (see details Fig. 3(b) and (c)). Then, "track conversation (A3)", "back to the activities (A4)" are found as the medium level discriminative factors. Afterwards, "Social Chit-Chat (A6)", "eye contact (A2)", and "Family_ASD" do not more significant discriminatory factor in this analysis.

3.3 Comparative Studies and Implication

Many researchers investigated Q-CHAT-10 and AQ-10 datasets to explore significant outputs for autistic cases and some of them are briefly described at Sect. 1. In that works, they investigated common features between autistic and normal cases. However, the variation of autism can be determined by exploring autism subtypes. Nevertheless, previous models didn't concern about these issue. In this work, we have separated only autism data from controls and extracted subtypes from Q-CHAT-10 and AQ-10 based datasets. Then, the best autism subtypes are formulated and different significant features are prioritized to explore discriminative factors between two subtypes. This key characteristics are useful to understand the level of autism among various types of patients that ensure proper treatments of them. It enhances technical skills and managerial strategy of clinicians to detect real features. In addition, the economical cost of patients are reduced because of detecting discriminatory factors more quickly.

4 Conclusion and Future Work

We integrate and preprocess only autistic cases to categorize them into different groups and explore the best autism subtypes. Then, different classifiers have been applied into the best autism subtypes where LR demonstrates the best results (99.25% accuracy, 99.25% f-measure and 99.16% AUC) for baseline, (98.80% accuracy, 98.80% f-measure, and 98.80% AUC) for ROS, and (99.03% accuracy, 99.03%f-measure and 99.03% AUC) for SMOTENC datasets. The rapid identification of autism subtypes is useful for clinicians and psychiatrists to realize distinguished factors and specify proper therapy for them. Further, it helps to produce relevant drugs and cure various abnormal behaviors of ASD patients. Besides, Q-CHAT-10 and AQ-10 datasets which are used in this study are not huge. In future, we will collect more records about autism and use more advanced machine learning techniques (i.e., deep/reinformcement learning approaches) to increase performance of detecting autism subtypes.

References

1. Akter, T., et al.: Improved transfer-learning-based facial recognition framework to detect autistic children at an early stage. Brain Sci. **11**(6), 734 (2021)
2. Akter, T., Ali, M.H., Khan, M.I., Satu, M.S., Moni, M.A.: Machine learning model to predict autism investigating eye-tracking dataset. In: 2021 2nd International Conference on Robotics, Electrical and Signal Processing Techniques (ICREST), pp. 383–387. IEEE (2021)
3. Akter, T., Khan, M.I., Ali, M.H., Satu, M.S., Uddin, M.J., Moni, M.A.: Improved machine learning based classification model for early autism detection. In: 2021 2nd International Conference on Robotics, Electrical and Signal Processing Techniques (ICREST), pp. 742–747. IEEE (2021)
4. Akter, T., et al.: Machine learning-based models for early stage detection of autism spectrum disorders. IEEE Access **7**, 166509–166527 (2019)
5. Akyol, K.: Assessing the importance of autistic attributes for autism screening. Exp. Syst. **37**(5), e12562 (2020)
6. Allison, C., Auyeung, B., Baron-Cohen, S.: Toward brief "red flags" for autism screening: the short autism spectrum quotient and the short quantitative checklist in 1,000 cases and 3,000 controls. J. Am. Acad. Child Adolesc. Psychiatr. **51**(2), 202–212 (2012)
7. Baadel, S., Thabtah, F., Lu, J.: A clustering approach for autistic trait classification. Inf. Health Soc. Care **45**(3), 309–326 (2020)

8. Baron-Cohen, S., Wheelwright, S., Skinner, R., Martin, J., Clubley, E.: The autism-spectrum quotient (AQ): evidence from asperger syndrome/high-functioning autism, malesand females, scientists and mathematicians. J. Autism Dev. Disord. **31**(1), 5–17 (2001)
9. Bisong, E.: Building machine learning and deep learning models on Google cloud platform. Springer, Berkeley (2019). https://doi.org/10.1007/978-1-4842-4470-8
10. Hossain, M.D., Kabir, M.A., Anwar, A., Islam, M.Z.: Detecting autism spectrum disorder using machine learning techniques. Health Inf. Sci. Syst. **9**(1), 1–13 (2021). https://doi.org/10.1007/s13755-021-00145-9
11. Hyde, K.K., et al.: Applications of supervised machine learning in autism spectrum disorder research: a review. Rev. J. Autism Dev. Disord. **6**(2), 128–146 (2019)
12. Omar, K.S., Mondal, P., Khan, N.S., Rizvi, M.R.K., Islam, M.N.: A machine learning approach to predict autism spectrum disorder. In: 2019 International Conference on Electrical, Computer and Communication Engineering (ECCE), pp. 1–6. IEEE (2019)
13. Tartarisco, G., et al.: Use of machine learning to investigate the quantitative checklist for autism in toddlers (q-chat) towards early autism screening. Diagnostics **11**(3), 574 (2021)
14. Thabtah, F.: An accessible and efficient autism screening method for behavioural data and predictive analyses. Health Inform. J. **25**(4), 1739–1755 (2019)
15. Thabtah, F., Abdelhamid, N., Peebles, D.: A machine learning autism classification based on logistic regression analysis. Health Inf. Sci. Syst. **7**(1), 1–11 (2019). https://doi.org/10.1007/s13755-019-0073-5
16. Thabtah, F., Kamalov, F., Rajab, K.: A new computational intelligence approach to detect autistic features for autism screening. Int. J. Med. Inform. **117**, 112–124 (2018)
17. Thabtah, F., Peebles, D.: A new machine learning model based on induction of rules for autism detection. Health Inf. J. **26**(1), 264–286 (2020)
18. Wiratsin, I.O., Narupiyakul, L.: Feature selection technique for autism spectrum disorder. In: Proceedings of the 5th International Conference on Control Engineering and Artificial Intelligence, pp. 53–56 (2021)

Indoor Navigation Support System for Patients with Neurodegenerative Diseases

Milon Biswas[1(✉)], Ashiqur Rahman[1], M. Shamim Kaiser[2,3], Shamim Al Mamun[2,3], K. Shayekh Ebne Mizan[2], Mohammad Shahidul Islam[2], and Mufti Mahmud[4]

[1] Department of Computer Science and Engineering, Bangladesh University of Business and Technology, Mirpur-02, Dhaka 1216, Bangladesh
milon@ieee.org, ashiqur@bubt.edu.bd

[2] Institute of Information, Jahangirnagar University, Savar, Dhaka 1342, Bangladesh
{mskaiser,shamim,sislam}@juniv.edu

[3] Applied Intelligence and Informatics (AII) Lab, Wazed Miah Science Research Centre, Jahangirnagar University, Savar, Dhaka 1342, Bangladesh

[4] Medical Technologies Innovation Facility, Nottingham Trent University, Clifton, Nottingham NG11 8NS, UK
mufti.mahmud@ntu.ac.uk

Abstract. A handheld device (such as a smartphone/wearable) can be used for tracking and delivering navigation within a building using a wireless interface (such as WiFi or Bluetooth Low Energy), in situations when a traditional navigation system (such as a global positioning system) is unable to function effectively. In this paper, we present an indoor navigation system based on a combination of wall-mounted wireless sensors, a mobile health application (mHealth app), and WiFi/Bluetooth beacons. Such a system can be used to track and trace people with neurological disorders, such as Alzheimer's disease (AD) patients, throughout the hospital complex. The Contact tracing is accomplished by using Bluetooth low-energy beacons to detect and monitor the possibilities of those who have been exposed to communicable diseases such as COVID-19. The communication flow between the mHealth app and the cloud-based framework is explained elaborately in the paper. The system provides a real-time remote monitoring system for primary medical care in cases where relatives of Alzheimer's patients and doctors are having complications that may demand medical care or hospitalization. The proposed indoor navigation system has been found to be useful in assisting patients with Alzheimer's disease (AD) while in the hospital building.

Keywords: Alzheimer's disease · IoT · Bluetooth beacon · Smart care · Sensor

1 Introduction

One of the major illnesses that contribute to dementia instances is neurodegenerative diseases (ND), such as Alzheimer's disease (AD) [1,2]. Alzheimer's disease

M. Mahmud et al. (Eds.): BI 2021, LNAI 12960, pp. 411–422, 2021.
https://doi.org/10.1007/978-3-030-86993-9_37

primarily affects those over the age of 65. It's a long-term neurological disease that generally develops slowly. Over time, it worsens. Alzheimer's disease is a chronic neurological illness that affects people as they become older and causes gradual memory loss. At this time, more than 50 million individuals worldwide are affected by Alzheimer's disease. Alzheimer's patients have health problems such as headaches, mood changes, memory loss, and lack of judgment as a result of the disease's impact on the human brain [3–6]. They also have difficulty going from one direction to another in most parts of their daily lives. When they are at home, they usually have family members to support them in navigating from one place to another. But when they go outside (i.e. hospital), it is impossible for the hospital authorities to provide them with a one-on-one caregiver for their support in navigating inside the hospital. To help them and assist those patients IoT [7–10] is one of the powerful communication paradigms. Different types of modern devices, monitoring cameras, home appliances, and sensors interact with the help of IoT [11]. The IoT promises to have a tremendous impact on every aspect of everyday life and will ultimately be able to identify, track, and communicate with almost every object on the planet [12–14].

Positioning, location, and navigation (PLAN) technologies have been extensively researched and efficiently commercialized in a variety of applications, including mobile phones and unmanned systems. With PLAN inside technology, new Micro Electromechanical System (MEMS) sensors, Big Data location and Artificial Intelligence (AI) technology, as well as growing public interest and social possibilities, are becoming increasingly important. Indoor navigation technology is required to enable people with neurodegenerative disease or visually impaired people to move about with ease. Navigating within buildings is a challenging task since the Global Positioning System or GPS reception is usually non - existent [15–17]. Different positioning methods are used when autonomous positioning is necessary. A handheld mobile phone can include a mobile application and a large number of sensors which can be used for health, wellbeing and positioning. In this situation, Wi-Fi or beacons (Bluetooth Low Energy, BLE) are typically utilized to establish a so-called "indoor GPS." However, contrary to GPS, they also allow a smartphone user to determine the exact level of the floor. In most applications, an "indoor routing" feature is required, guiding individuals precisely through buildings through an interior navigation application and determining their position automatically.

We deploy indoor navigation technology in an IoT-based healthcare system to assist alzheimer's patients in navigating within a hospital. We have utilized bluetooth beacon technology for contact tracing and wifi technology for indoor navigation. The following are the study's contributions:

- For assisting older patients, a simple smartphone application is implemented.
- Regular health updates, tips and health recommendations are available.
- Bluetooth beacon technology for contact tracing.
- Wi-fi technology to guide elderly patients inside the hospital.

The remainder of the paper is arranged as follows: Sect. 2 discusses the related works; Sect. 3 includes discussion about the proposed model; Sect. 4 details about the implementations; Sect. 5 is all about challenges and future research and finally, Sect. 6 is conclusion.

2 Related Work

Artificial intelligence and mobile application developers focus on this Neurodegenerative disease issue and there are some existing applications available. On the other hand WiFi and Bluetooth Low Energy (BLE) technologies are the most frequently used wireless indoor PLAN technology [18] (positioning, location and navigation) for consumer electronics. RSS [19] is widely utilized, and the typical positioning precision is on the meter. WiFi systems have a key benefit in being able to leverage existing communication infrastructure. On the other hand, BLE is versatile and easy to use. New capabilities have been introduced to WiFi and BLE technologies to suit the future Internet-of-Things (IoT) and accurate localization needs. WiFi HaLow and Bluetooth long range (Bluetooth 5) were added to the signal repertoire, while WiFi RTT (IEEE 802.11 mc) (IEEE 2020) and Bluetooth direction (Bluetooth 5.1) have been released to enable accurate placement. The objective of this research [20] was to find all viable indoor navigation technologies and to create a small prototype. Augmented Reality utilized its built-in features for indoor navigation to detect an individual's location and give the required navigation instruction.

In addition, high-precision measurement researchers, such as CSI [21], RTT, and AoA have extracted. These measures are suitable for PLAN decimeters or even centimeters. The authors [22] examined several DL architectures' applications to this data, focusing on the use of DL to analyze patterns in data from various biological areas. This is followed by a look of open-access data sources for the three data kinds, as well as prominent open-source DL tools that may be used with them. Comparative analyses of these tools are also offered from qualitative, quantitative, and benchmarking viewpoints. They [23] also assessed and compared current deep learning (DL)-based techniques for identifying neurological diseases using MRI data obtained using a variety of modalities, including functional and structural MRI, with an emphasis on Alzheimer's disease, Parkinson's disease, and schizophrenia. Researchers [24,25] developed different IoT based control system consisting of a prototype, a smart healthcare system for health monitoring. Smart first aid kit with wireless internet connectivity helps patients receive regular health care. It helps patients to communicate with a doctor virtually and has an alert module to help the patient with medications.

There is an application called Mind Mate [26] and Balance: Alzheimer's Caregiving Application [27] both contain the same service in different ways. In another article [28] authors primarily described the localization and positioning of users (patients) and their devices. In contrast with the existing surveys, they also evaluate different systems from the perspective of energy efficiency, availability, cost, reception range, latency, scalability, and tracking accuracy.

In the early diagnosis of mild cognitive impaiments (MCIs) and AD, the extraction from magnetic resonance imaging is important for the management of this condition (MRI). This [29] article offers a 4 way grading of 3D MRI images using a 3D Densely Connected Convolutionary Networks model (3D DenseNets). The objective of this [30] work was an upgraded step detection method, a periodic attitude remedying approach and a new PCA-based motion direction estimation technique, to improve and extend the short term dependability of PDR systems for smartphones as standalone systems. Tests have shown that the proposed system (S-PDR) offers a solid shorter-term solution with a definitive positioning mistake of up to 6 m in 3 min. In another article authors [9] suggested an emotion-aware fall monitoring framework based on IoT, AI algorithms, and big data analytics, which will deal with elderly people's emotion detection, health status forecasts, and real-time fall monitoring. In the event of an emergency, the suggested framework notifies the designated caregiver of the circumstance. A smart ambulance or mobile clinic will arrive at the site of the elderly person in the shortest possible period.

3 Proposed Model

3.1 Scenario

Older people worldwide are growing, and average life expectancies in human history are higher than ever before. And majority of these seniors suffered from neurological conditions such as AD. Common signs of a patient with a neurological disease tend to forget things that are important. Often they receive assistance from family members or personal caregivers during their stay at home but in hospitals it is difficult for hospital authorities to supply one-to-one support and it's expensive. On this basis, we have thus proposed a Bluetooth and WiFi systems to enable patients navigate the hospital. When a patient reaches the hospital complex area (Fig. 1), a connection will be established in between hospital network and the patient through our mobile application. Then the patient can navigate inside the hospital by selecting the desired destination.

3.2 Indoor Navigation Model

The indoor navigation system is one of the latest technology used to tackle complex challenges in shopping malls, hospitals, retails stores, etc. Patients and visitors benefit from indoor navigation throughout the hospital since it reduces interruptions from medical personnel asking for directions. Patients, visitors, and employees will always be given the best path to their destination. We have developed an android app that helps the elderly people by navigating inside the hospital using Wifi and Bluetooth beacon technology. When elderly people enter inside a hospital, he will need to connect with the hospital network. After that, he will need to select his destination inside the hospital. Then our app will guide him/her to reach his destination inside the hospital Fig. 2.

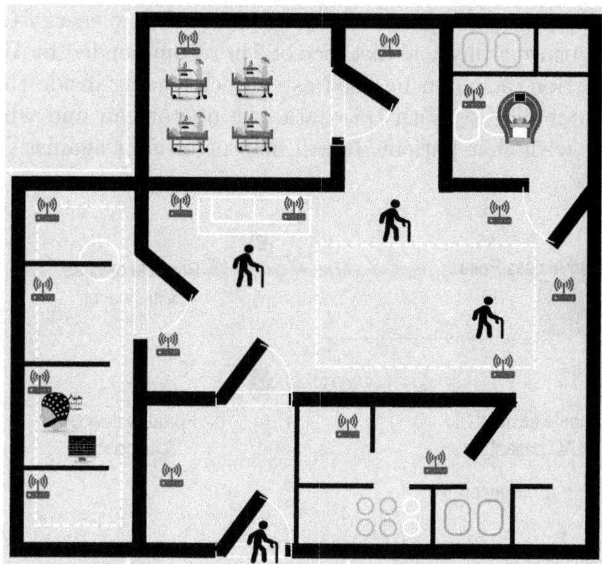

Fig. 1. Indoor Navigation Scenario for patient having Alzheimer disease (AD). A mobile app can produce indoor navigation maps of a hospital using augmented reality (AR) technologies as well as Bluetooth beacons which can assist AD patient.

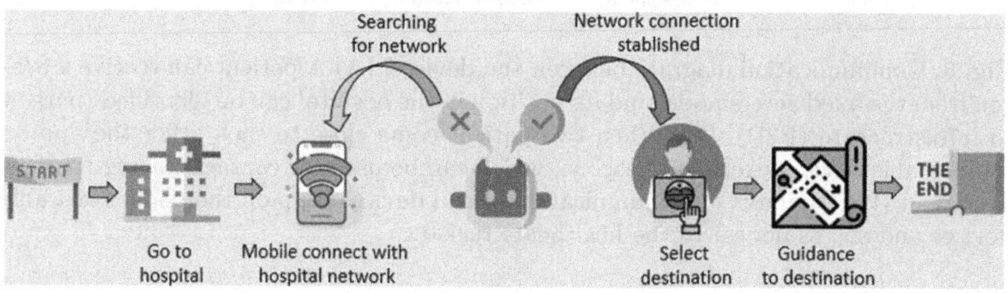

Fig. 2. Basic Communication model. App connect with hospital network and assist AD patient to reach the destination.

3.3 Communication Flow

Most elderly people have dementia, Alzheimer's, and so on. Beacon, in Fig. 3 a smart indoor localization technology that can communicate with the smartphone in close range. Bluetooth Low Energy Beacon devices send out data packets at a regular gap. We can also perform contact tracing operation by using this technology. All these data are reserved in the cloud database so the doctor can check the list he needed and find out the person list who is being closed with that patient. When elderly people enter in a hospital, the triangulation method is used to find out the location of the elderly people and sends the message to the caregiver and patient for instruction inside the hospital. This device also exchanges data with other patient using a bluetooth low energy transceiver. It can be used to ensure a physical distance of 2 m recommended by WHO to avoid COVID-19 infection, also can be used as contact tracing inside the hospital as well as any indoor places. With this data, the doctor can find which person is in close contact with that patient. It will help us to fight against COVID-19.

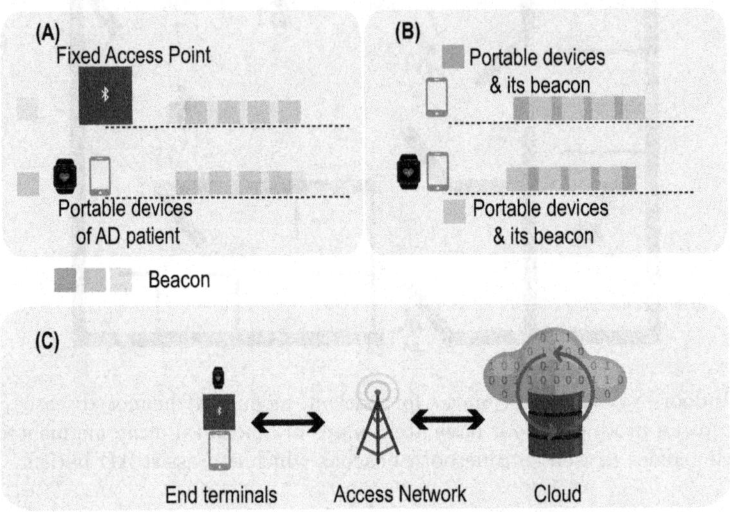

Fig. 3. Communication diagram between end devices. (A) A patient can receive a beacon from the fixed access node, and its position in the hospital can be identified (patient to infrastructure (P2I)); (B) When two patient come close to each other the app on the portable devices exchange beacons, which can be used for contact tracing (patient to patient (P2P)) and (C) Communication of end devices (app on the phone/wearable devices and access nodes) to the healthcare register

3.4 Patient Assessment

In this paper, we mainly focus on elderly patient. A common disease of an elderly patient is that they tend to forget everything. In this patient assessment module we try to collect patients' health related data and update the patients' regular health related issues to his doctor, relatives and caregiver. We have divided our patient assessment module into three different parts. For patient assessment, we first need to know the patients' health condition. And for this we need patients' health related data. To obtain this, we have developed an android app that will help to collect the data. These data includes: Fall detection, movement, temperature, blood pressure etc. All this collected data are passed through the internet using a data gateway. There are API, APP, and plugins that are used to pass those data to the cloud server. If the patient has heart disease, what type of food he will have, and how he will make himself healthy, the app user will be get notified by getting daily health tips (Fig. 4).

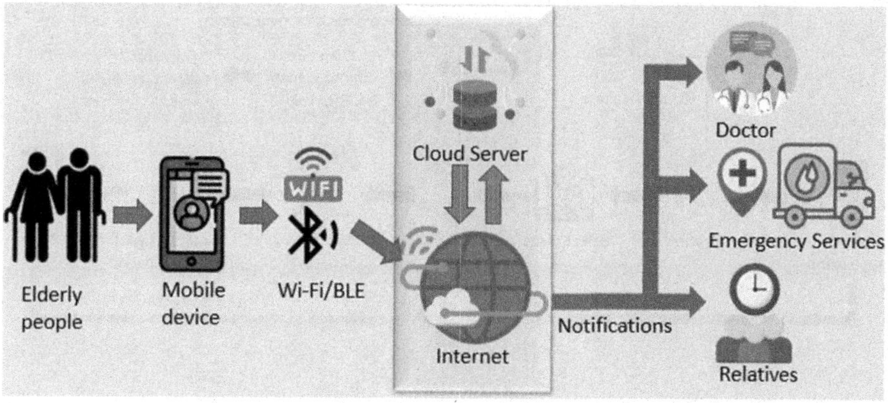

Fig. 4. Patient assessment phases: a flow diagram of user with our mobile app and the notification system. How elderly people are connected with the mobile application, where all those data stores and how the notification works.

4 Implementation

4.1 Indoor Navigation and Positioning

The user initially registers by mobile phone number. The appropriate area in the app will then be selected. The specified user location will be uploaded into the cloud database with a unique user id. This improves user monitoring and security. The user then uses the Bluetooth and Wi-Fi on the device. BLE tags are put at different locations in the chosen interior location, generating and disseminating signals that each signal represents each point range. The app scans the Wi-Fi and BLE signals in the vicinity. In order to solve the overlapping signal problems (Fig. 5), the app will shift amongst the received signals using RSSI values and only get the highest RSSI value signal. The placement is made inside. The user then clicks the direction button on the tap. An algorithm works with the intended destination and signal received which results in the user's navigation or next moving direction. The user reaches hence his chosen destination. The voice command and message for the user to navigate will be shown in this environment. Command to move north, for example. A virtual compass is utilized in this context for the direction. For the compass application on android OS, the magnetometer sensor is employed. In addition, the line map shows the selected indoor locations and a green point that makes the user's current situation easier to use and more transparent.

4.2 Assessment

We have implemented our idea into an android application and our interface will look like Fig. 6. When the app user clicks on the regular health checkup button he will see his blood pressure, sugar, temperature, etc. When he clicks

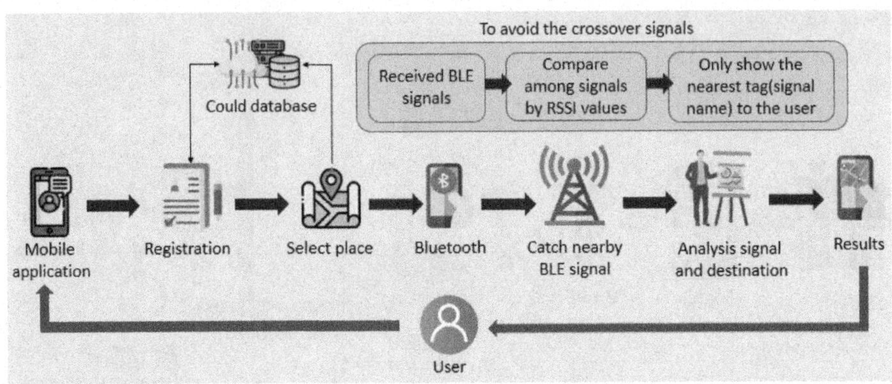

Fig. 5. Flow of indoor positioning and navigation: how users use our mobile app-registration process to navigation map as result is shown as well as how to avoid the crossover signal is also shown.

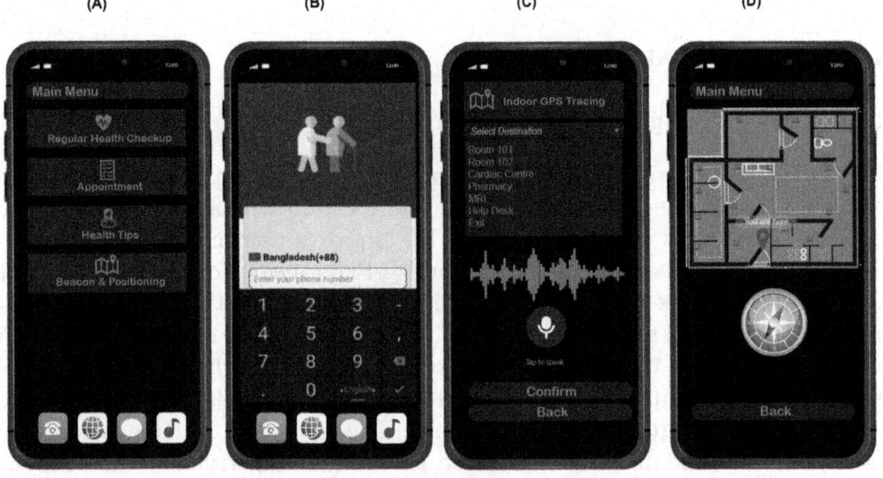

Fig. 6. Indoor navigation user interface. (A) The main menu of the app includes regular health checkup, appointment with the doctor, personalized health tips and Indoor navigation, (B) App registration with cell phone number, (C) Selection of a destination using voice command or dropdown menu selection, and (D) Indoor navigation map and position. A compass on the app guide the user to reach the exact destination.

the appointment button, he will check his upcoming appointment. And after clicking on the health tips button, he will see different health-related advice such as how to diet, how to keep himself healthy, how to make himself safe during pandemic situations, etc. The mobile application willl collect the information for health assessments and BLE (bluetooth low energy) technology collects the information for contact tracing and all these information will be stored into cloud server and notify doctors and relatives if needed.

5 Challenges and Future Research

Measuring Errors in RSS. When there are many tags present, the distance between the tags is critical in determining which tag is the closest to the other. It has been found that the method of determining distances is based on Radio Signal Strength (RSS), which is not accurate when utilizing Bluetooth Low Energy (BLE)/WiFi. The machine learning-based methods can be utilized to improve the positioning accuracy in the building during navigation with BLE/WiFi tags.

Bandwidth Interference. Wireless fidelity (WiFi) and Bluetooth (Bluetooth Low Energy) will work simultaneously in the proposed system to give services to a large number of customers operating on the same 2.4 GHz frequency. If there are other WiFi networks in our neighborhood that are all using the same WiFi channel, the network may run slower as a result of the congestion. It was necessary to implement an adaptive channel management method in order to resolve this issue. Furthermore, the 5 GHz WiFi frequency must be used in order to minimize interference with Bluetooth, which operates at the 2.4 GHz frequency.

Security and Privacy. Bluesnarfing, eavesdropping, denial of service, viruses, and worms are all possible security flaws in the system. As a result, network monitoring in real time is essential. In addition to this, refusing pairing requests from unrecognized devices; and keeping firmware up to date. Over time, the tracing of Bluetooth low-energy device is diminished due to the use of an address randomization function that changes the Bluetooth device address on a regular basis. The device address (called private address) must be resolved by the other device to reconnect with recognized devices when employing the privacy function. The device identity resolve key can be used to generate a private address which was exchanged during the pairing operation.

6 Conclusion

Mobile devices (phones/wearables) can track and deliver navigation within buildings utilizing wireless interfaces (such as WiFi or Bluetooth Low Energy) when traditional navigation systems (such as global positioning systems) are not working. This study describes an interior navigation system which can be used to track and trace patients with neurological illnesses, such as Alzheimer's disease. Contact tracing uses Bluetooth low-energy beacons to detect and track persons who may have been exposed to contagious diseases like COVID-19. The study elaborates on the communication flow between the mHealth app and the cloud-based infrastructure. For families of Alzheimer's patients and doctors, the device provides real-time remote monitoring for primary medical care.

The planned indoor navigation system has been found to help Alzheimer's sufferers navigate the facility. In future, the detail analysis is required to check the exact positing of a AD patient in hospital. In addition, such system can be used to detect fall detection and measurement of physiological signaling using an add-on in the USB port

References

1. Noor, M.B.T., Zenia, N.Z., Kaiser, M.S., Mahmud, M., Al Mamun, S.: Detecting neurodegenerative disease from MRI: a brief review on a deep learning perspective. In: Liang, P., Goel, V., Shan, C. (eds.) BI 2019. LNCS, vol. 11976, pp. 115–125. Springer, Cham (2019). https://doi.org/10.1007/978-3-030-37078-7_12
2. Alam, M.E., Kaiser, M.S., Hossain, M.S., Andersson, K.: An IoT-belief rule base smart system to assess autism. In: 2018 4th International Conference on Electrical Engineering and Information & Communication Technology (iCEEiCT), pp. 672–676. IEEE (2018)
3. Al Banna, M.H., Ghosh, T., Taher, K.A., Kaiser, M.S., Mahmud, M.: A monitoring system for patients of autism spectrum disorder using artificial intelligence. In: Mahmud, M., Vassanelli, S., Kaiser, M.S., Zhong, N. (eds.) BI 2020. LNCS (LNAI), vol. 12241, pp. 251–262. Springer, Cham (2020). https://doi.org/10.1007/978-3-030-59277-6_23
4. Sumi, A.I., Zohora, M.F., Mahjabeen, M., Faria, T.J., Mahmud, M., Kaiser, M.S.: *f*ASSERT: a fuzzy assistive system for children with autism using Internet of Things. In: Wang, S., et al. (eds.) BI 2018. LNCS (LNAI), vol. 11309, pp. 403–412. Springer, Cham (2018). https://doi.org/10.1007/978-3-030-05587-5_38
5. Ali, H.M., Kaiser, M.S., Mahmud, M.: Application of convolutional neural network in segmenting brain regions from MRI data. In: Liang, P., Goel, V., Shan, C. (eds.) BI 2019. LNCS, vol. 11976, pp. 136–146. Springer, Cham (2019). https://doi.org/10.1007/978-3-030-37078-7_14
6. Nahiduzzaman, M., Tasnim, M., Newaz, N.T., Kaiser, M.S., Mahmud, M.: Machine learning based early fall detection for elderly people with neurological disorder using multimodal data fusion. In: Mahmud, M., Vassanelli, S., Kaiser, M.S., Zhong, N. (eds.) BI 2020. LNCS (LNAI), vol. 12241, pp. 204–214. Springer, Cham (2020). https://doi.org/10.1007/978-3-030-59277-6_19
7. Altulayan, M.S., Huang, C., Yao, L., Wang, X., Kanhere, S.: Contextual bandit learning for activity-aware things-of-interest recommendation in an assisted living environment. In: Qiao, M., Vossen, G., Wang, S., Li, L. (eds.) ADC 2021. LNCS, vol. 12610, pp. 37–49. Springer, Cham (2021). https://doi.org/10.1007/978-3-030-69377-0_4
8. Sharma, S., Dudeja, R.K., Aujla, G.S., Bali, R.S., Kumar, N.: DeTrAs: deep learning-based healthcare framework for IoT-based assistance of Alzheimer patients. Neural Comput. Appl. 1–13 (2020). https://doi.org/10.1007/s00521-020-05327-2
9. Al Nahian, M.J., Ghosh, T., Uddin, M.N., Islam, M.M., Mahmud, M., Kaiser, M.S.: Towards artificial intelligence driven emotion aware fall monitoring framework suitable for elderly people with neurological disorder. In: Mahmud, M., Vassanelli, S., Kaiser, M.S., Zhong, N. (eds.) BI 2020. LNCS (LNAI), vol. 12241, pp. 275–286. Springer, Cham (2020). https://doi.org/10.1007/978-3-030-59277-6_25

10. Biswas, M., Whaiduzzaman, M.D.: Efficient mobile cloud computing through computation offloading. Int. J. Adv. Technol. **10**(2) (2018)
11. Ahsanul Sarkar Akib, A.S.M., Ferdous, M.F., Biswas, M., Khondokar, H.M.: Artificial intelligence humanoid bongo robot in Bangladesh. In: 2019 1st International Conference on Advances in Science, Engineering and Robotics Technology (ICASERT), pp. 1–6. IEEE (2019)
12. Kaiser, M.S., et al.: iWorksafe: towards healthy workplaces during COVID-19 with an intelligent Phealth app for industrial settings. IEEE Access **9**, 13814–13828 (2021)
13. Kaiser, M.S., et al.: Advances in crowd analysis for urban applications through urban event detection. IEEE Trans. Intell. Transp. Syst. **19**(10), 3092–3112 (2018)
14. Asif-Ur-Rahman, M., et al.: Toward a heterogeneous mist, fog, and cloud-based framework for the internet of healthcare things. IEEE Internet Things J. **6**(3), 4049–4062 (2018)
15. Kaiser, M.S., Chowdhury, Z.I., Mamun, S.A., Hussain, A., Mahmud, M.: A neuro-fuzzy control system based on feature extraction of surface electromyogram signal for solar-powered wheelchair. Cogn. Comput. **8**(5), 946–954 (2016). https://doi.org/10.1007/s12559-016-9398-4
16. Biswas, S., Akhter, T., Kaiser, M.S., Mamun, S.A., et al.: Cloud based healthcare application architecture and electronic medical record mining: an integrated approach to improve healthcare system. In: 2014 17th International Conference on Computer and Information Technology (ICCIT), pp. 286–291. IEEE (2014)
17. Paul, M.C., Sarkar, S., Rahman, M.M., Reza, S.M., Kaiser, M.S.: Low cost and portable patient monitoring system for e-health services in Bangladesh. In: 2016 International Conference on Computer Communication and Informatics (ICCCI), pp. 1–4. IEEE (2016)
18. El-Sheimy, N., Li, Y.: Indoor navigation: state of the art and future trends. Satell. Navig. **2**(1), 1–23 (2021). https://doi.org/10.1186/s43020-021-00041-3
19. Zhuang, Y., Yang, J., Li, Y., Qi, L., El-Sheimy, N.: Smartphone-based indoor localization with bluetooth low energy beacons. Sensors **16**(5), 596 (2016)
20. Sayapogu, T., Dsa, K., Kaul, P.: AR smart navigation system. In: 2021 2nd International Conference for Emerging Technology (INCET), pp. 1–4. IEEE (2021)
21. Halperin, D., Hu, W., Sheth, A., Wetherall, D.: Tool release: gathering 802.11 n traces with channel state information. ACM SIGCOMM Comput. Commun. Rev. **41**(1), 53–53 (2011)
22. Mahmud, M., Kaiser, M.S., McGinnity, T.M., Hussain, A.: Deep learning in mining biological data. Cogn. Comput. **13**(1), 1–33 (2021). https://doi.org/10.1007/s12559-020-09773-x
23. Noor, M.B.T., Zenia, N.Z., Kaiser, M.S., Al Mamun, S., Mahmud, M.: Application of deep learning in detecting neurological disorders from magnetic resonance images: a survey on the detection of Alzheimer's disease. Parkinson's disease and schizophrenia. Brain Inform. **7**(1), 1–21 (2020). https://doi.org/10.1186/s40708-020-00112-2
24. Tsuchiya, L.D., Braga, L.F., de Faria Oliveira, O., de Bettio, R.W., Greghi, J.G., Freire, A.P.: Design and evaluation of a mobile smart home interactive system with elderly users in Brazil. Pers. Ubiquit. Comput. **25**(2), 281–295 (2020). https://doi.org/10.1007/s00779-020-01408-0
25. Adardour, H.E., Hadjila, M., Irid, S.M.H., Baouch, T., Belkhiter, S.E.: Outdoor Alzheimer's patients tracking using an IoT system and a Kalman filter estimator. Wirel. Pers. Commun. **116**(1), 249–265 (2020). https://doi.org/10.1007/s11277-020-07713-4

26. McGoldrick, C., Crawford, S., Evans, J.J.: MindMate: a single case experimental design study of a reminder system for people with dementia. Neuropsychol. Rehabil. **31**(1), 18–38 (2021)
27. Aljehani, S.S., Alhazmi, R.A., Aloufi, S.S., Aljehani, B.D., Abdulrahman, R.: iCare: applying IoT technology for monitoring Alzheimer's patients. In: 2018 1st International Conference on Computer Applications Information Security (ICCAIS), pp. 1–6 (2018)
28. Zafari, F., Gkelias, A., Leung, K.K.: A survey of indoor localization systems and technologies. IEEE Commun. Surv. Tutor. **21**(3), 2568–2599 (2019)
29. Ruiz, J., Mahmud, M., Modasshir, Md., Shamim Kaiser, M., For the Alzheimer's Disease Neuroimaging Initiative: 3D DenseNet ensemble in 4-way classification of Alzheimer's disease. In: Mahmud, M., Vassanelli, S., Kaiser, M.S., Zhong, N. (eds.) BI 2020. LNCS (LNAI), vol. 12241, pp. 85–96. Springer, Cham (2020). https://doi.org/10.1007/978-3-030-59277-6_8
30. Khedr, M., El-Sheimy, N.: S-PDR: SBAUPT-based pedestrian dead reckoning algorithm for free-moving handheld devices. Geomatics **1**(2), 148–176 (2021)

A Parallel Machine Learning Framework for Detecting Alzheimer's Disease

Sean A. Knox[1], Tianhua Chen[1(✉)], Pan Su[2], and Grigoris Antoniou[1]

[1] University of Huddersfield, Queensgate, Huddersfield HD1 3DH, UK
{sean.knox2,t.chen,g.antoniou}@hud.ac.uk

[2] School of Control and Computer Engineering, North China Electric Power University, Baoding, China
supan@ncepu.edu.cn

Abstract. This paper proposes a parallel machine learning framework for detecting Alzheimer's disease through T1-weighted MRI scans localised to the hippocampus, segmented between the left and right hippocampi. Feature extraction is first performed by 2 separately trained, unsupervised learning based AutoEncoders, where the left and right hippocampi are fed into their respective AutoEncoder. Classification is then performed by a pair of classifiers on the encoded data from the AutoEncoders, to which each pair of the classifiers are aggregated together using a soft voting ensemble process. The best averaged aggregated model results recorded was with the Gaussian Naïve Bayes classifier where sensitivity/specificity achieved were 80%/81% respectively and a balanced accuracy score of 80%.

Keywords: Machine learning · Alzheimer's disease · Autoencoder · Multi-layer perceptron · Support vector machine · Gaussian Naïve Bayes

1 Introduction

Dementia is a syndrome that causes a more than normal deterioration in cognitive function to that caused by the usual affects of aging. Dementia is chronic and/or progressive in nature. Globally an estimated 50 million people have some form of dementia ca. 2020, according to the WHO (World Health Organisation) [24].

Alzheimer's Disease (AD) is the most common form of dementia contributing around 60–70% of all dementia cases globally [24]. AD is predominantly found in the aged population (65+), with the risk of AD doubling every 5 years after [1]. While AD is not currently curable, the symptoms of AD can be lessened with the aid of prescription drugs: Acetylcholinesterase (AChE) inhibitors (early- to mid-stage), Memantine (late-stage), antipsychotics (behavioural and psychological symptoms of dementia (BPSD)) [17]. There are also therapies and activities that are beneficial to patients diagnosed with AD [17], therefore it is pivotal

M. Mahmud et al. (Eds.): BI 2021, LNAI 12960, pp. 423–432, 2021.
https://doi.org/10.1007/978-3-030-86993-9_38

that patients are diagnosed accurately and as early, in the stages of their AD, as possible. The earliest clinical stage to detect progression to either dementia, in general or specifically AD, is Mild Cognitive Impairment (MCI) [14]. MCI is the "transitional stage between age-related cognitive decline and AD" [15].

AD is defined by the "observation of specific pathological lesions" [16], these pathological lesions include: intracellular neurofibrillary tangles, extracellular β-amyloid senile plaques and blood vessel deposits, and synaptic degradation and neuronal atrophy of the brain [16]. As these pathological lesions are found in a specific pattern associated with AD, it is possible with the use of Magnetic Resonance Imaging (MRI) to detect the signs, or the absence of signs, of AD in a patient. "MRI has attracted a significant interest in AD related studies because of its completely non-invasive nature, high availability, high spatial resolution and good contrast between different soft tissues" [15].

In recognition of the challenges diagnosing dementia and the potentials of utilising recent machine learning techniques to facilitate clinical decision support, this paper proposes a parallel machine learning architecture where feature extraction and classification are trained in pairs (left/right hippocampi). Decisions from these pairs are then aggregated together using a soft voting ensemble algorithm. In particular, the feature extraction is performed by an unsupervised learning AutoEncoder and classification is performed by 3 different classifiers (Multi-layer Perceptron, Support Vector Machine, and Gaussian Naïve Bayes). Experimental results suggest this research is able to achieve comparable performance when compared to other proposed solutions which require more data points, than what is required for the proposed solution in this paper.

The reminder of this paper is organised as follows. Section 2 introduces the related works. Section 3 describes data set and the proposed pipeline. Section 4 presents and discusses the experimental outcomes. Section 5 concludes the paper and outlines ideas for further development.

2 Related Works

Recent advances in machine learning (ML) have lead to many successes in the healthcare domain [3,4,22]. Numerous models [7–9,11,12,18,21] have been proposed for ML driven AI for the detection of signs of AD, ranging from the binary style classification of AD or CN (Cognitive normal), to multi-class classification of AD, MCI (progressive MCI (pMCI), stable MCI (sMCI)), and CN. Models that concentrate on multi-class classification introduce the capability of predicting the likelihood of a patient transitioning through MCI-to-AD in a given time frame.

While binary classifiers offer less granularity in their classification (i.e. MCI patients are usually coupled with AD), they do typically offer greater accuracy than those found with multi-class classification, around 80–95% according to [20]. The popular OASIS dataset classifies any patient with greater than 0 Clinical Dementia Rating (CDR) as having AD, whereas the alternative ADNI repository would classify a patient with a CDR of 0.5 as having MCI not AD [13]. This stipulation would mean that the OASIS dataset would have a generally higher sensitivity than other datasets, as it is more likely to predict AD than CN.

The capability of predicting when/if a patient is transitioning through MCI-to-AD, allows for the patient to take quality of life improvements/preparations for when they do transition into AD. While preventative measures are not proven to work, cognitive stimulation therapy, has been proven to improve memory and problem-solving skills [17]. As such, the multi-class classification is one of the most researched areas in AI detection of AD, with it's added granularity that enables the ability to predict when a patient is going through the transition of MCI-to-AD.

The popular machine learning methods used in AD classification include Convolutional Neural Networks (CNN), which was originally designed for objective detection, and is able to learn image features of most importance that allow for correctly classifying the image as an image of a patient with AD or CN. In extension to the multiple types of neural networks, deep learning neural networks are also used in AD classification, these deep neural networks have achieved high performances e.g. some GoogleNet and ResNet models have achieved accuracies in the 97.9% on 3 way class classification tasks [18]. In regards to a binary classification task, AD vs CN, as used in this paper, deep neural network-based utilizing a sparse AutoEncoder and CNN for subjects only 75 and over have achieved 89.47% [18,19].

Another machine learning method showing promise in AD classification is the utilisation of an AutoEncoder to perform unsupervised learning on feature extraction. An AutoEncoder's architecture is very similar to that of a CNN except that it performs encoding (takes the data and encodes it to reduce it's size) and then decodes (takes the reduced data and tries to reconstruct the data to be as close to the original input as possible).

Although AutoEncoders may have a vanishing gradient problem, which can be mitigated by only allowing for the k highest hidden units to be active in any given hidden layer, an AutoEncoder is promising choice for AD classification, with its dimensionality reduction - it reduces the chance of data in the image, that is not important to AD classification, from influencing the classifier as much. This also inspires the underlying research to utilise AutoEncoders as a feature extraction technique, followed by the use of powerful classifiers to construct predictive models.

3 Method

3.1 Data Subjects, Acquisition, and Pre-processing

All data used during the experimentations relating to this paper were acquired from the OASIS-1: Cross-sectional MRI Data in Young, Middle Aged, Nondemented and Demented Older Adults dataset [13]. OASIS-1 contains 416 unique subjects, age ranging from 18–96, with 100 of those subjects being older than 60 and have been clinically diagnosed with very mild to moderate Alzheimer's disease. OASIS-1 contains age, education level (if present), CDR, MRI T1-weighted scans, and sex for each unique subject.

Table 1. OASIS-1 dataset [13] after stage 1 pre-processing [23]

	N	Age	%SexF	Education	MMS	CDR = 0	CDR = 0.5	CDR = 1	CDR = 2
AD	73	77.5 ± 7.4	63.0	2.7 ± 1.3	22.7 ± 3.6	0	45	26	2
CN	304	44.0 ± 23.3	62.2	3.5 ± 1.2	29.7 ± 0.6	124	0	0	0

The dataset used had been pre-processed according to the methods set out by [23], in which bias field correction was performed to reduce any bias field corruption in the images, each image is then registered to the MNI space using a linear algorithm. Once the MNI space is registered the images were then cropped to remove the background, finally each image went through quality control where a probability score was produced on how accurate the MNI registration was, any images below .5 were removed automatically and images below .7 were manually reviewed. During this quality control phase 39 non-usable data subjects were removed as their MRI scans were not viable for use in ML (Table 1), during this pre-processing stage the dataset was split into separate training and validation sets (80/20% split). After the pre-processing performed by [23], another pre-processing stage was undertaken which primary goal was to separate and crop the left and right hippocampus (Fig. 1), this allowed for the Neural Network to train only on the hippocampi and effectively doubled the dataset, allowing for a parallel computing approach where the left and right hippocampus are fed into the two separate models with an aggregation process at the end which will then calculate the prediction.

3.2 Feature Extraction

Feature extraction is performed by unsupervised learning with an AutoEncoder, two separate AutoEncoders are trained, left hippocampus and right hippocampus models. The AutoEncoder performs feature extraction by reducing the size of the data, it does this by removing detail in the image that are not of importance to the classification layer.

Both AutoEncoders used in this paper were trained using the Mean Squared Error loss function with reduction set to summation, i.e., Sum Squared Error:

$$\mathcal{L}(x, y) = \sum_{i=1}^{n} (\mathcal{Y}_i - \widehat{\mathcal{Y}}_i)^2 \tag{1}$$

where $\mathcal{Y}_i$ is the target image which in the case of AutoEncoder's is the input image, as an AutoEncoder's performance is evaluated by how closely the recreated image is to the original image. Adam was used as the algorithm optimiser. Each AutoEncoder had a starting learning rate of 10^{-3}, each AutoEncoder was trained using mini-batch gradient descent with an epoch of 50.

Since this is an unsupervised learning algorithm it is possible that the AutoEncoder will fixate on the wrong area of the image. To ensure that the AutoEncoder has fixated on the important details of the respective left and

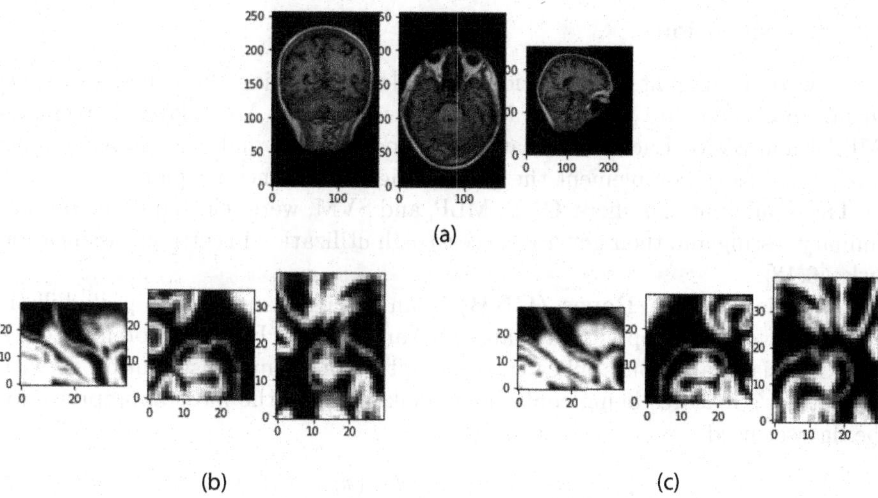

Fig. 1. MRI Slices of subject sub-OASIS10003 after stage 1 and stage 2 pre-processing. Where a shows the centre slices after stage 1 pre-processing on MRI image of subject sub-OASIS10003 and b and c shows the left and right hippocampus slices, respectively, after stage 2 pre-processing on MRI image of subject sub-OASIS10003

right hippocampus, the AutoEncoders and all the classifiers were trained 10 times with the average of the aggregation layer being recorded.

Both AutoEncoders had the same architecture, with the encoder starting with a 3D convolutional layer, a 3D batch normaliser, leaky ReLU process followed by a 3D pad max pool (custom operation that ensures no loss of data), repeating 3 times (Fig. 2).

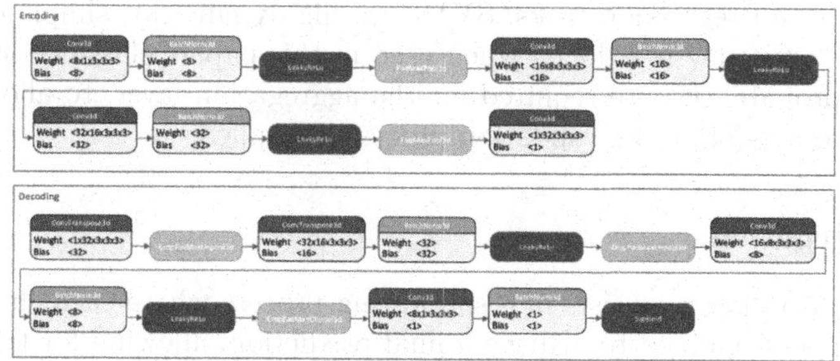

Fig. 2. AutoEncoder architecture used for feature extraction

3.3 Classification

There were 3 different classification methods used during the course of experimentation, these are Gaussian Naïve Bayes (GNB), Multi-layer Perceptron (MLP), and SVM. Each classification method had left and right hippocampus pairs, this was to complement the left and right AutoEncoder pairs.

The 3 different classifiers, GNB, MLP, and SVM, were selected based on preliminary testing and their general success/high utilization in certain classification tasks [6,18].

Gaussian Naïve Bayes (GNB) is an efficient, supervised, probabilistic learning algorithm applying a Gaussian variation on Bayes' theorem (Eq. 2). The Gaussian variation applies the assumption of normal distribution as with the dataset's features being continuous, making GNB the most appropriate for the dataset used.

$$P(x_i|y) = \frac{1}{\sqrt{2\pi\sigma_y^2}} exp\left(-\frac{(x_i-\mu_y)^2}{2\sigma_y^2}\right) \tag{2}$$

Multi-layer Perceptron (MLP) is a feedforward artificial neural network used for classification and regression tasks. MLPs consist of multiple hidden layers with multiple hidden nodes in each layer, they are often trained using back-propagation, back-propagation was chosen to train the model as this enabled supervised learning. During the training of the MLP the Adam optimizer and the ReLu activation function were used.

Adam optimizer is seen as the best of both worlds as it combines parts of RMSProp and Stochastic Gradient Descent (SGD) with momentum optimizers, from RMSProp it uses squared gradients to scale the learning rate, and from SGD with momentum it uses the moving average of the gradient instead of the gradient itself [10].

Support Vector Machine (SVM) is a supervised learning algorithm for classification and regression tasks. SVMs are highly efficient, simple classifiers, however the efficiency is reduced when used in this papers classification task as prediction probabilities are required for the aggregation layer, to allow for this an expensive five-fold cross validation process is applied.

3.4 Aggregation

The aggregation layer consists of a soft voting process where each classification method pair is combined to achieve a final prediction, allowing for the left and right hippocampi to have equal influence on the final prediction. The soft voting process is the average of each of the models probabilities with the class with the highest probability being chosen (Eq. 3).

$$\widehat{y} = \arg\max_i \sum_{j=1}^{m} w_j p_{ij} \tag{3}$$

4 Results and Discussions

4.1 Results

Each classification method was run 10 times with the average of each methods being recorded. As can be seen in Table 2, the accuracy of the models are fairly consistent at 83% ± 9% over both training and validation sets, while sensitivity (true positive rate) is concerning with 2 of the classification methods, MLP and SVM, leaving an average percentage error of 53% ± 33% over both training and validation sets.

As can be seen in Table 3 the AUC values for each classification methods are extremely good for both the left and right hippocampus, this shows that the models, before aggregation, are highly capable of differentiating between both classes.

Table 2. Average results over 10 runs foreach of the classification methods

Model	MLP		SVM		GNB	
	Train	Valid	Train	Valid	Train	Valid
Acc (Avg)	.82	.87	.85	.90	.74	.81
Sen (Avg)	.20	.52	.26	.59	.81	.80
Spe (Avg)	.96	.95	.99	.98	.72	.81
BAcc (Avg)	.58	.73	.63	.78	.76	.80

Table 3. Area Under Curve (AUC) Snapshot of 10th run of the classification methods

Model	MLP		SVM		GNB	
	Train	Valid	Train	Valid	Train	Valid
AUC (Left)	.93	.90	.99	.89	.93	.88
AUC (Right)	.94	.91	.99	.92	.93	.89

The performance of the aggregated MLP model is highly biased to specificity (true negative rate) with an average of 96%, while sensitivity suffers at 20% on the training set, the model does perform much better on the validation set with sensitivity/specificity at 52%/95%. The balanced accuracy - a metric that is the average of sensitivity and specificity to adjust for the imbalance in the dataset - achieves 53%/73% in the training/validation sets.

The performance of the aggregated SVM model are slightly better with accuracy reaching 85%/90% on the train/validation set. Sensitivity/specificity also peak at 59%/98% respectively on the validation set. Balanced accuracy, influenced by the increased sensitivity compared to MLP, achieved 63%/78% on the training/validation sets.

The aggregated GNB out performed MLP and SVM with sensitivity/specificity reaching and average 80%/81% on the validation set. Accuracy at an average of 74%/81% has been sacrificed compared to MLP and SVM, whereas balanced accuracy, influenced by the more higher sensitivity and specificity scores, is higher at 76%/80% training/validation sets.

4.2 Discussions

Feature extraction has been successful using the unsupervised learning based AutoEncoders, this is evident by the AUC scores in Table 3 where each of the models seem to have, almost, excellent performance in differentiating between the AD and CN classes. The AutoEncoders never once fixated on the wrong features in the MRI images supplied this is most likely due to the highly localised cropping of the images before the unsupervised learning process (Fig. 1b and 1c).

While Pre-aggregation classification full results were not recorded a snapshot of AUC were recorded, through the AUC scores some partial assessments can be made of the performance of the models at this point. It is evident that the left and right hippocampi models pre-aggregation perform extremely well in their classification task, whereas once the aggregation layer has performed it's task the MLP and SVM aggregated models started to decline in accuracy.

Post-aggregation, the MLP and SVM aggregated models started to produce a high bias towards CN classification, it is probable that this happened due to the imbalance in the dataset where the training/validation sets have 4.17/4.13 times as many CN records as AD records, respectively. It is also probable that the pre-aggregation SVM models were mis-reporting the prediction probabilities, as SVM does not natively support prediction probabilities and this functionality was artificially introduced to the SVM. With regards to the GNB aggregated models, they didn't seem to have the same issues as MLP or SVM, as they kept both high sensitivity and specificity scores.

5 Conclusion

This paper has proposed a parallel machine learning framework where feature extraction (by AutoEncoder) and classification (by Multi-layer Perceptron, Support Vector Machine, and Gaussian Naïve Bayes) are trained in pairs through the left/right hippocampi of an image, before aggregating decisions through a soft voting ensemble algorithm.

Overall the performance of the best averaged post-aggregation GNB model is able to match, and succeed in some cases, that of other models proposed [6–8, 19] in the same area while only taking into account the single data point of T1-weighted MRI scans localised to the hippocampi and not discounting training data of those 74 and under. With the post-aggregation GNB model proposed in this paper achieving exceedingly high sensitivity score, it is highly beneficial to the medical field where an incorrectly predicted positive result is much more detrimental than an incorrectly predicted negative result.

Future work may considering incorporating fuzzy logic system [2,5] to enhance the capability of working with imprecision and uncertainly that commonly exist in the medical imaging.

Acknowledgements. The authors are grateful to the reviewers for their constructive comments, which have helped elevate this piece of work significantly. The first author would also like to thank the University of Huddersfield for providing the PhD scholarship in support of their research. Part of this piece of work is also supported by the Santander International Research Funding Scheme and National Natural Science Foundation of China under grant 61906181.

References

1. Alzheimer's Association: What Causes Alzheimer's Disease?—Alzheimer's Association. https://www.alz.org/alzheimers-dementia/what-is-alzheimers/causes-and-risk-factors
2. Chen, T., Shang, C., Yang, J., Li, F., Shen, Q.: A new approach for transformation-based fuzzy rule interpolation. IEEE Trans. Fuzzy Syst. **28**, 1 (2019). https://doi.org/10.1109/TFUZZ.2019.2949767
3. Chen, T., Antoniou, G., Adamou, M., Tachmazidis, I., Su, P.: Automatic diagnosis of attention deficit hyperactivity disorder using machine learning. Appl. Artif. Intell. **43**, 1–13 (2019)
4. Chen, T., et al.: A decision tree-initialised neuro-fuzzy approach for clinical decision support. Artif. Intell. Med. **111**, 101986 (2021)
5. Chen, T., Shang, C., Su, P., Shen, Q.: Induction of accurate and interpretable fuzzy rules from preliminary crisp representation. Knowl. Based Syst. **146**, 152–166 (2018)
6. Cho, Y., Seong, J.K., Jeong, Y., Shin, S.Y.: Individual subject classification for Alzheimer's disease based on incremental learning using a spatial frequency representation of cortical thickness data. NeuroImage **59**, 2217–2230 (2012)
7. Chupin, M., et al.: Fully automatic hippocampus segmentation and classification in Alzheimer's disease and mild cognitive impairment applied on data from ADNI. Hippocampus **19**(6), 579–587 (2009). https://doi.org/10.1002/hipo.20626, http://doi.wiley.com/10.1002/hipo.20626
8. Coupé, P., Eskildsen, S.F., Manjón, J.V., Fonov, V.S., Collins, D.L.: Simultaneous segmentation and grading of anatomical structures for patient's classification: application to Alzheimer's disease. NeuroImage **59**(4), 3736–3747 (2012). https://doi.org/10.1016/j.neuroimage.2011.10.080, https://linkinghub.elsevier.com/retrieve/pii/S1053811911012444
9. Gaser, C., Franke, K., Klöppel, S., Koutsouleris, N., Sauer, H.: BrainAGE in mild cognitive impaired patients: predicting the conversion to Alzheimer's disease. PLoS One **8**(6), e67346 (2013). https://doi.org/10.1371/journal.pone.0067346, https://dx.plos.org/10.1371/journal.pone.0067346
10. Kingma, D.P., Ba, J.L.: Adam: a method for stochastic optimization. In: 3rd International Conference on Learning Representations, ICLR 2015 - Conference Track Proceedings. International Conference on Learning Representations, ICLR, December 2015. https://arxiv.org/abs/1412.6980v9

11. Mahmud, M., Kaiser, M.S., McGinnity, T.M., Hussain, A.: Deep learning in mining biological data. Cogn. Comput. **13**(1), 1–33 (2021). https://doi.org/10.1007/s12559-020-09773-x, http://link.springer.com/10.1007/s12559-020-09773-x
12. Mahmud, M., Kaiser, M.S., Hussain, A., Vassanelli, S.: Applications of deep learning and reinforcement learning to biological data. IEEE Trans. Neural Networks Learn. Syst. **29**(6), 2063–2079 (2018). https://doi.org/10.1109/TNNLS.2018.2790388, https://ieeexplore.ieee.org/document/8277160/
13. Marcus, D.S., Fotenos, A.F., Csernansky, J.G., Morris, J.C., Buckner, R.L.: Open access series of imaging studies: longitudinal MRI data in nondemented and demented older adults. J. Cogn. Neurosci. **22**(12), 2677–2684 (2010). https://doi.org/10.1162/jocn.2009.21407, https://direct.mit.edu/jocn/article/22/12/2677-2684/4983
14. Markesbery, W.R.: Neuropathologic alterations in mild cognitive impairment: a review. J. Alzheimer's Disease JAD **19**(1), 221–228 (2010). https://doi.org/10.3233/JAD-2010-1220, http://www.ncbi.nlm.nih.gov/pubmed/20061641
15. Moradi, E., Pepe, A., Gaser, C., Huttunen, H., Tohka, J.: Machine learning framework for early MRI-based Alzheimer's conversion prediction in MCI subjects. NeuroImage **104**, 398–412 (2015). https://doi.org/10.1016/j.neuroimage.2014.10.002
16. Mosconi, L., Brys, M., Glodzik-Sobanska, L., De Santi, S., Rusinek, H., de Leon, M.J.: Early detection of Alzheimer's disease using neuroimaging. Experimental Gerontol. **42**(1–2), 129–138 (2007). https://doi.org/10.1016/j.exger.2006.05.016
17. National Health Service (NHS): Alzheimer's disease - Treatment - NHS (2018). https://www.nhs.uk/conditions/alzheimers-disease/treatment/
18. Noor, M.B.T., Zenia, N.Z., Kaiser, M.S., Mamun, S.A., Mahmud, M.: Application of deep learning in detecting neurological disorders from magnetic resonance images: a survey on the detection of Alzheimer's disease, Parkinson's disease and schizophrenia. Brain Inform. **7**(1), 11 (2020). https://doi.org/10.1186/s40708-020-00112-2, https://braininformatics.springeropen.com/articles/10.1186/s40708-020-00112-2
19. Payan, A., Montana, G.: Predicting Alzheimer's disease: a neuroimaging study with 3D convolutional neural networks, February 2015. http://arxiv.org/abs/1502.02506
20. Samper-González, J., et al.: Reproducible evaluation of classification methods in Alzheimer's disease: framework and application to MRI and PET data. NeuroImage **183**, 504–521 (2018). https://doi.org/10.1016/j.neuroimage.2018.08.042, https://linkinghub.elsevier.com/retrieve/pii/S1053811918307407
21. Stirling, J., Chen, T., Bucholc, M.: Diagnosing Alzheimer's disease using a self-organising fuzzy classifier. In: Carter, J., Chiclana, F., Khuman, A.S., Chen, T. (eds.) Fuzzy Logic, pp. 69–82. Springer, Cham (2021). https://doi.org/10.1007/978-3-030-66474-9_5
22. Su, P., et al.: Corneal nerve tortuosity grading via ordered weighted averaging-based feature extraction. Med. Phys. **47**(10), 4983–4996 (2020)
23. Wen, J., et al.: Convolutional neural networks for classification of Alzheimer's disease: overview and reproducible evaluation. Med. Image Anal. **63**, 75 (2019). https://doi.org/10.1016/j.media.2020.101694, http://arxiv.org/abs/1904.07773dx.doi.org/10.1016/j.media.2020.101694
24. World Health Organisation: Dementia (2020). https://www.who.int/news-room/fact-sheets/detail/dementia

Early Detection of Parkinson's Disease from Micrographic Static Hand Drawings

Nanziba Basnin[1], Tahmina Akter Sumi[2(✉)], Mohammad Shahadat Hossain[2], and Karl Andersson[3]

[1] International Islamic University Chittagong, Chittagong, Bangladesh
[2] University of Chittagong, Chittagong, Bangladesh
[3] Lulea University of Technology, Skelleftea, Sweden

Abstract. Parkinson's disease (PD) is a neurological illness that occurs by the degeneration of cells in the nervous system. Early symptoms include tremors or involuntary movements of the hands, arms, legs, and jaw. Currently, the only method to diagnose PD involves the observation of its prodromal symptoms. Moreover, detecting handwriting will work as a variable for clinitians to understand PD in patients better. With the advancement of technology, it is possible to build applications that will aid in diagnosing PD without any clinical intervention. The majority suffering from PD have handwriting abnormalities (referred to as micrographia), which is the most reported among earlier signs of the disease. So this research is undertaken by focusing on the implication of micrographia. For this purpose, handwritten images are collected from a group of 136 PD patients and 36 healthy patients. These images form a dataset of 800 images that are used to train a model which will accurately classify PD patients. To achieve this transfer learning is chosen because of its ability to produce accurate results regardless of the limited size of the dataset. Here, different models of transfer learning are trained to figure out the well-fitting model. It was observed that VGG-16 performed adequately with a training accuracy of 90.63% while a testing accuracy of 91.36%.

Keywords: Parkinson's disease · Transfer learning

1 Introduction

Parkinson's disease (PD) is the second most common neurodegenerative disorder after Alzheimer's disease [3,28] which adversely affects the central nervous system of our brain that controls our balance, body movement and posture. PD generally occurs with the loss of dopaminergic neurons [16] in the substantia nigra which is a part of our brain. Usually, the symptoms of this disease appear slowly and as it gets worse over time, the non motor symptoms like tremor, slow movement (bradykinesia), rigidity, difficulty in walking, pain, fatigue, restless legs, speech and communication issues, low blood pressure etc. appear. It also

M. Mahmud et al. (Eds.): BI 2021, LNAI 12960, pp. 433–447, 2021.
https://doi.org/10.1007/978-3-030-86993-9_39

causes the cognitive and behavioral problem for example depression, anxiety, memory difficulties and apathy. PD most commonly affects more than 1% of people older than 60 years of age [33] occurring alteration in gaits and posture which causes difficulty in movement and risk of falls.

Though Parkinson's disease is getting worse day by day, no cure has been found for it till now. The treatment of this disease generally intents to improve the current state of the patient but it can't give any permanent solution. Therefore, research in the field of Parkinson's disease diagnosis has become crucial from the aspect of medical treatment to assess the efficacy of treatment. In this case an accurate biomarker is needed to be identified first. Several studies have been published regarding the diagnosis of PD detection where speech processing were considered. But in case of audio dataset the size of database is a major problem as it is too small (less than 60 PD cases) [2,31,35]. Being a complex activity involving cognitive, sensory and perceptual-motor components [32], handwriting can be considered as a promising biomarker [4] in this case as abnormal handwriting is obvious in PD. Moreover, handwriting is a daily activity of human and so it is also easy and cost-effective to detect PD from handwritten images. A wide variety of techniques have been used till now in the sector of PD detection among which Computer Aided Systems that use machine learning, optimization, fuzzy logic methods have been fruitful with higher accuracy and efficient result.

In this paper we have used an transfer learning algorithm on handwriting dataset for the detection of Parkinson's disease as it shows better performance saveing training time and not needing a lot of data [24]. In this case, at first an image processing technique has been applied where images are converted into a two dimensional array. Each value of the array indicates the pixel value of image. Meanwhile, all the pixel values are brought within a certain range from 0 to 1 by dividing each of the value by 255. This is done to reduce the difference of the pixel values. After this pre-processing step, data augmentation has been applied so that the size of the dataset is increased and the over-fitting can be suppressed. After that, the augmented data are passed through a pretrained model of transfer learning called VGG-16 for the detection of parkinson's disease. Throughout this study, a significant contribution has been made which are as follows-

1. Two datasets have been combined to resolve the size issue of dataset noticed in previous research works regarding Parkinson detection from handwriting images.
2. Different architectures have been applied to show the comparison with our proposed model in terms of performance.
3. Performance comparison has been illustrated among different optimizers.
4. K-fold cross validation has been applied as a deep learning approach.

The next sections of the paper have been organized accordingly: Sect. 2 contains the previous works, Sect. 3 describes the methodology, Sect. 4 shows system implementation where the experimental tools used in implementing our system has been stated, Sect. 5 shows the result and discussion and finally in Sect. 6 conclusion and future work has been discussed.

2 Literature Review

In past years, several research studies have been published regarding PD diagnosis among which machine learning techniques showed promising results [29]. Zuo et al. [39] applied fuzzy k-nearest neighbors classifier and Particle Swarm Optimization for PD diagnosis achieving 97.47%.

However, most of the previous works considered signal analysis from patient's voice [17,23] as PD causes voice disorder. Few of the studies were based on MRI images [20,21]. Haller et al. [7] presented a system to aid PD detection using Magnetic Resonance Images (MRI) as MRI can detect any kind of damage in the brain. They used SVM based pattern recognition of DTI which classified PD patient with 97% accuracy. Nonetheless, collecting MRI images may be costly and for image acquisition process, a patient needs to stand still which is difficult for a PD patient. Thereafter, handwriting images are much easier and cheaper to aid the PD detection.

Pereira et al. [22] applied machine learning and computer vision techniques on their own designed handwriting dataset called "HandPD" to deal with PD recognition. Here they have used some supervised techniques such as OPF, SVM and Naive Bayes classifier (NB) to evaluate the dataset among which Naive Bayes classifier (NB) have resulted the best accuracy which is 78.9%. This accuracy is quite low and needs to be improved.

Kotsavasiloglou et al. [15] utilized a pen and tablet device to show the differences of hand-movement and the coordination of muscle between the PD patients and control subjects. The authors considered five matrices of 24 PD patients and 20 control subjects. They evaluated different classification algorithms among which they obtained the best accuracy of 88.63% and an Area Under the ROC Curve (AUC) of 93.1% for Naive Bayes. Zham et al. [36] considered ten features which include both static and dynamic data of 31 PD patients and 31 healthy subjects using NB algorithm for classification. They achieved 83.2% accuracy and 93.3% AUC. In these two papers the dataset size they considered are relatively smaller in size and also the accuracy they achieved can be improved.

Gallicchio et al. [5] used Deep Echo State Networks (DeepESNs) considering Spirals and stability movement where they acquired 89.3% accuracy. Khatamino et al. [14] have worked on PD diagnosis using AlexNet architecture of convolution neural network (CNN). Since the dataset used in this paper is smaller, they considered smaller number of layers in the implementation. The accuracy they obtained after implementation was 72.5% which is quite low. Martín et al. [6] also have used a simplified version of AlexNet but they used spectrum points as input to CNN instead of raw data. The researcher obtained a good accuracy 96.5% in this case. All these three papers used same dataset named Parkinson Disease Spiral Drawings Using Digitized Graphics Tablet dataset [8] where 62 of the participants where PD patients and 15 were control subjects which indicates a big difference in the size of two classes. This may lead a biased result.

As in most of the research works of Parkinson's detection based on handwriting dataset, the size of the dataset is a major problem so we have tried to overcome this combining two global dataset where the number of healthy subject and Parkinson subject is almost equal which reduce the biased problem. Moreover, the accuracy of most of the papers discussed above is quite low which has been improved in our model.

3 Methodology

In order to carry out this research, a dataset consisting of handwritten images of PD and non-PD patients are collected from two different sources. Firstly, the dataset is pre-processed to make it applicable for feeding into the model. Secondly, the dataset is augmented to increase its robustness. Thirdly, the dataset is split into a ratio of 7:3 for training and testing respectively. Afterwards, a VGG-16 model is employed for training the dataset, as it can effectively extract important features [30]. Afterwards the model is tested.

3.1 Dataset

The detection of Parkinson's disease is quite difficult as no medical tests for Parkinson's detection have been discovered so far. The most common symptom that is noticeable in almost every patient with Parkinson's disease is tremor which occurs change in writing. That's why we have considered the handwriting dataset in this research work. In the field of Parkinson disease detection, there are several global datasets used in different research works. But the size of the datasets is a great issue here as the number of the images is very poor. So in this paper, we have combined two global datasets to make a large dataset. One of the two datasets is collected from kaggle website and the other is HandPD dataset. After combining the two datasets, the total number of the images are 808 where 400 images for control subject and 408 images for Parkinson subject. We have splitted our dataset into 80% training and 20% testing.

3.2 Pre-processing

Pre-processing of image generally removes low frequency background noise, normalizes the intensification of the individual practical image, removes reflection of light to get rid of the image noise, and prepares the face image to better feature extraction. In our system, we have first resized the images into 96 × 96 dimension. Then We have converted the image to an array of pixel value. Each pixel value of the array is converted to float and divided by 255.0 so that all the pixel values comes to a range between 0 to 1. In Fig. 1, the whole pre-processing system has been illustrated.

3.3 Data Augmentation

Data augmentation is a technique which is used to increase the size of dataset by creating some modified copies of data which already exists in dataset.

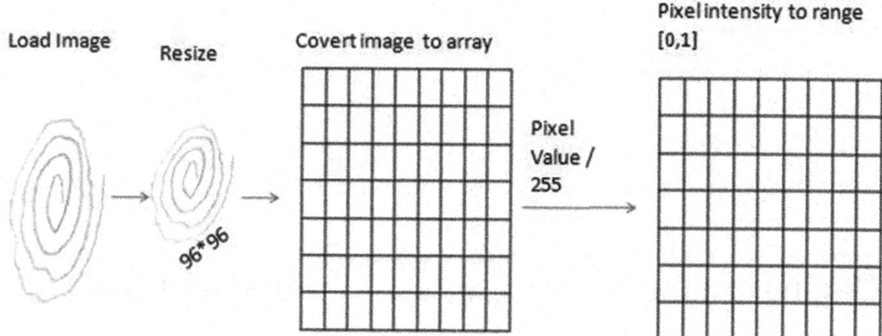

Fig. 1. Pre-processing steps

This technique is used mainly to reduce the overfitting. In this paper, the data augmentation has helped to increase the size of the existing dataset. In Fig. 2 the data augmentation has been showed.

3.4 Transfer Learning

We have evaluated our model using transfer learning based pretrained model VGG-16 for the detection of Parkinson disease. After the pre-processing and data augmentation, the pre-trained model is loaded. Thereafter the fully connected layers are interchanged with dense layers. The past convolution layers are stabled and not replaced or removed to learn strong features by the network. The softmax function has been applied as the activation function.

$$Softmax(x_i) = \frac{\exp(x_i)}{\sum_j \exp(x_j)}$$

The Fig. 3 shows the whole systematic representation of our model.

3.5 Performance Metrics

In this study, we have evaluated our model based on three performance metrics. These are precision, recall and F1-score. Precision measures positive class predictions number which belongs to the positive class in real. In case of two class classification problem, precision is counted dividing true positives by the sum of true positives and false positives. Recall measures positive class predictions number consist of all positive case in the dataset. In case of two class classification problem, recall is counted dividing true positives by the sum of true positives and false negatives. Precision or recall can't evaluate a model properly alone. One can have an excellent precision with a poor recall or an excellent recall with a poor precision. F1-score create a balance between these two with a single score. So, F1-score renders a single score which conveys a balance precision and recall by a single number.

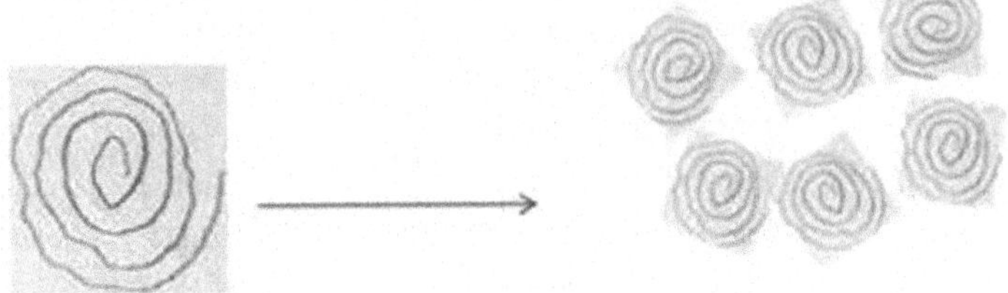

Fig. 2. Data augmentation

$$Precision = \frac{\text{TP(True Positive)}}{\text{TP(True Positive)} + \text{FN(False Negative)}}$$

$$Recall = \frac{\text{TP(True Positive)}}{\text{TP(True Positive)} + \text{FP(False Positive)}}$$

$$F1 - score = \frac{2 \times \text{Precision} \times \text{Recall}}{\text{Precision} + \text{Recall}}$$

Here, the true positive is the result where model appropriately estimates the positive class. Similarly, a true negative is the result where model appropriately estimates the negative class. A false positive is the result where the model inappropriately predicts the positive class. A false negative is an outcome where the model inappropriately predicts the negative class.

4 VGG-16 Model Architecture

The VGG-16 model consists of one input layer, thirteen convolutional layers followed by a fully connected layer. Firstly, two convolutional layers have 64 features in the kernel filters of size three by three. The dimensions of the input are transformed into 224 × 224 × 64. The corresponding output is transported along with the max-pooling layer. Secondly, two convolutional layers consists 124 features in its kernel filter of size three by three. The output from these two layers is passed down to another max-pooling layer where its dimensions are reduced to be 56 × 56 × 126. Thirdly, three convolutional layers comprise a kernel filter size of three by three, with a feature map of 256. The resulting output bypasses a third max-pooling layer. Fourthly, five convolutional layers with a kernel size of three by three alongside 512 kernel filers are followed by a max-pooling layer. Lastly, the two layers are fully connected as hidden layers which include a softmax function for output.

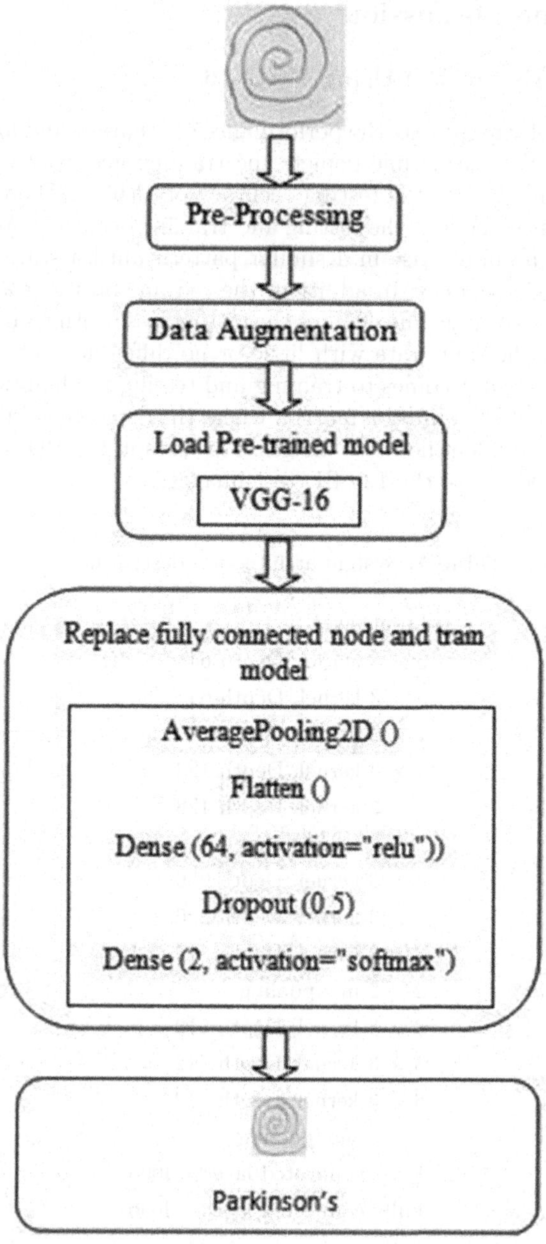

Fig. 3. Schematic representation of the whole system

5 Result and Discussion

5.1 Classification of PD Using VGG-16

Figure 4 graphically represents the performance of accuracy and loss of the VGG-16 model. Here, the purple line depicts the training accuracy which is 90.63% while the grey line depicts the testing accuracy of 91.63%. There appears to be not much difference between the testing and training accuracy. According to the graph, both the accuracy rise in a similar pattern until a state of the plateau is reached after 17.5 epochs. In addition, the red line on the graph denotes the training loss while the blue line denotes the testing loss. Both training and testing loss decreases at the same rate with little or no difference. Thus, the VGG-16 model is well-fit when it comes to training and testing the handwritten dataset. Figure 5 represents the confusion matrix, where the diagonal columns dictate the number of correctly identified test images. For instant 119 PD test images were correctly identified out of the 120 PD test images.

Table 1. System architecture description.

Input layer
3 × 3 kernel, Depth 64
3 × 3 kernel, Depth 64
2 × 2 maxpooling
3 × 3 kernel, Depth 128
3 × 3 kernel, Depth 128
2 × 2 maxpooling
3 × 3 kernel, Depth 256
3 × 3 kernel, Depth 256
3 × 3 kernel, Depth 512
2 × 2 maxpooling
3 × 3 kernel, Depth 512
3 × 3 kernel, Depth 512
3 × 3 kernel, Depth 512
2 × 2 maxpooling
Fully connected layer 1-4096
Fully connected layer 1-4096
Softmax

5.2 K-fold Cross Validation

Cross validation is a re-sampling method which is applied to assess the machine learning models on a specific data sample. In k-fold cross validation, the dataset is divided into k subsets which are equal in size. It is generally less biased because of larger training set and not expensive. In our study we have evaluated our model using K-fold cross validation as deep learning approach on our combined dataset. We have chosen the value of k = 5 here as 5 fold cross-validation.

Table 2. Different parameters

Fold	Training accuracy	Testing accuracy
1	88.89%	88.28%
2	88.89%	88.89%
3	88.39%	91.36%
4	90.63%	90.74%
5	88.75%	90.12%
Average accuracy	89.11%	89.88%
Best accuracy	90.63%	91.36%

Table 2 illustrates the result of our model where we have used the five fold cross validation also the average accuracy and the best accuracy calculated after the five fold cross-validation. Here, the average accuracy and the best accuracy are respectively 89.88% and 91.36%.

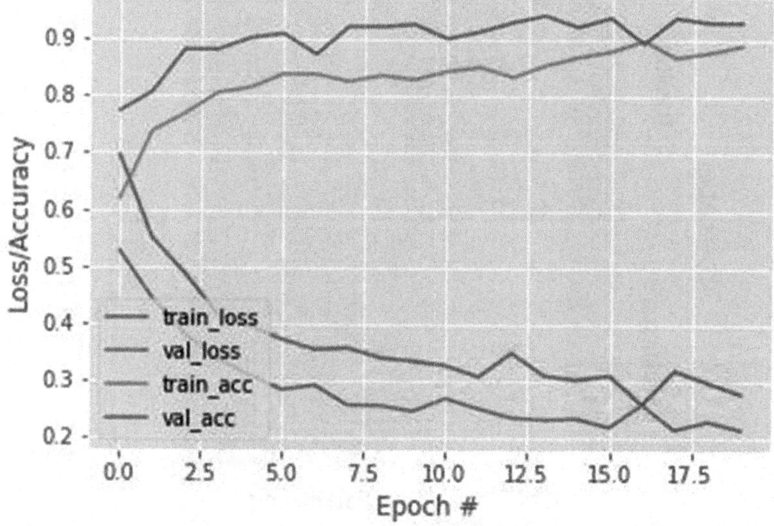

Fig. 4. Model accuracy and model loss

5.3 Performance Metrics

Researchers usually judge the overall performance and efficiency of machine learning model using different performance metrics [26]. In our model we have implemented performance metrics so that we can understand if our model is performing well on our dataset. In this study, the performances have been assessed based on three criterion- Recall, Precision and F1-score. In Table 3, the comparison of the performance metrics has been illustrated.

Table 3. Different parameters

Performance matrices	Healthy	Parkinson	Macro average
Precision	0.96	0.90	0.93
Recall	0.89	0.97	0.93
F1-score	0.93	0.93	0.93

5.4 Comparison of VGG-16 with Other Models

Table 4 illustrates a comparison between the training accuracy and loss as well as testing accuracy and loss between transfer learning models, CNN along with CNN-LSTM model. It is observed that DenseNet, ResNet, CNN-LSTM, and

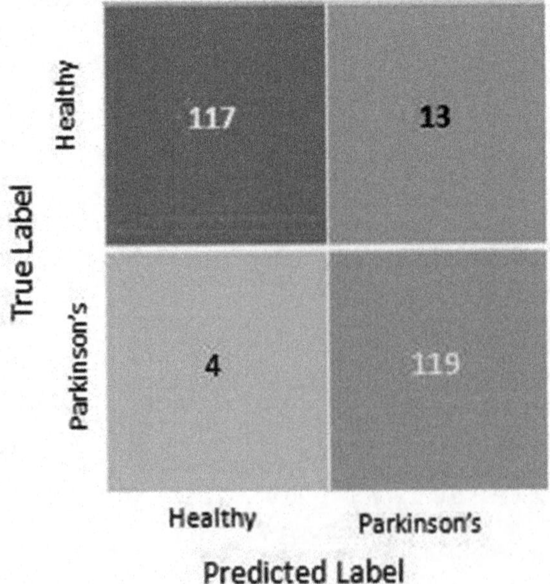

Fig. 5. Confusion matrix of Parkinson's detection

CNN are underfitting models, as their testing accuracy is greater than their training accuracy. In contrast, NASNet and InceptionV3 are overfitting models as their training accuracy is greater than their testing accuracy. On the other hand, EfficientNetB7 and EfficientNetB1 are well-fitting models because there lies a slight difference of 0.05 and 0.04 between the training and testing accuracy. However, this well-fit model cannot be acknowledged as their training (0.55, 0.54) and testing accuracy (0.5, 0.5) is much lower compared to that of the VGG-16 model proposed in this research.

However, there are some limitations noticed in the other methods. Though in the field of image classification CNN has been proved to perform as best algorithm comparing with other machine learning algorithms [1,9,27,38], but in CNN low level information are transmitted to high level neurons [18]. After that additional convolutions are executed to examine the presence of certain features. Moreover, the internal data regarding pose and orientation of object may be lose. In case of ResNet, it is quite deeper compared to VGG16. However, over-fitting problem occurs as ResNet go deeper (e.g. over 1000). But the size of ResNet model is less than VGG16 because of global average pooling instead of using fully-connected layers. This causes the reduction of the model size. Moreover another model named Inceptionv3, which is also known as point wise convolutions, generally consists of X1 filters. It is formed by convolutional layers with different filter sizes that help to learn complex features. For simple features VGG16 is more preferable than Inceptionv3. In DenseNet, each of the layers is connected to the other layers. This excessive connections decrease efficiency of computation and parameter-efficiency. Moreover, DenseNet occupies lot of memory, causes over-fitting, use excessive parameters which result low object recognition accuracy. NASNet has managed deeper neural networks using Reinforcement Learning (RE) [19] and evolutionary algorithms in the field of image processing and computer vision. But NASNet methods are costly for realistic applications. Search efficiency is another issue of NASNet. For achieving best computer vision results, it needs huge amount of GPU-days of searching.

Table 4. Comparison of results

Models	Train acc	Train loss	Test acc	Test loss
VGG-16	0.90	0.26	0.91	0.12
CNN	0.67	0.62	0.71	0.62
CNN-LSTM	0.67	0.62	0.72	0.62
InceptionV3	0.78	0.47	0.63	0.65
ResNet	0.62	0.71	0.48	0.70
NASNet	0.80	0.67	0.76	0.67
EfficientNetB7	0.54	1.19	0.5	1.19
EfficientNetB1	0.55	0.74	0.5	0.72
DenseNet	0.45	0.79	0.55	1.02

6 Conclusion and Future Work

This research enables to attain a solution for early detection of Parkinson's disease irrespective of clinical trials. Besides tremor appears to be the first symptom among patients with PD, so the focus is diverted toward studying micrographic distinctive patterns. In order to achieve this handwritten images of PD patients alongside a control group are considered while undertaking this research. The dataset is experimented upon with different transfer learning models to achieve an optimal learning model. The transfer learning model is adapted in this research because of the lack of publicly available PD handwritten datasets as well as to save training time and achieve the best performance. It was observed that the VGG-16 model generated a better performance compared to other transfer learning models.

In the future, this research aims to collect a dynamic dataset by utilizing an electronic pen-pad for samples. So that the handwriting motion and the number of frames required to complete one set of hand drawings can be evaluated. As PD debilitates the movement in the handwriting of patients. Moreover, this will make the diagnosis of PD more accurate and effective. A more efficient system can be built for PD detection using Belief Rule Based Expert Systems (BRBES) [10–13,25,34,37].

References

1. Ahmed, T.U., Hossain, S., Hossain, M.S., ul Islam, R., Andersson, K.: Facial expression recognition using convolutional neural network with data augmentation. In: 2019 Joint 8th International Conference on Informatics, Electronics & Vision (ICIEV) and 2019 3rd International Conference on Imaging, Vision & Pattern Recognition (icIVPR), pp. 336–341. IEEE (2019)
2. Belalcazar-Bolaños, E.A., Orozco-Arroyave, J.R., Vargas-Bonilla, J.F., Arias-Londoño, J.D., Castellanos-Domínguez, C.G., Nöth, E.: New cues in low-frequency of speech for automatic detection of Parkinson's disease. In: Ferrández Vicente, J.M., Álvarez Sánchez, J.R., de la Paz López, F., Toledo Moreo, F.J. (eds.) IWINAC 2013. LNCS, vol. 7930, pp. 283–292. Springer, Heidelberg (2013). https://doi.org/10.1007/978-3-642-38637-4_29
3. De Rijk, M.D., et al.: Prevalence of Parkinson's disease in Europe: a collaborative study of population-based cohorts. Neurologic diseases in the elderly research group. Neurology **54**(11 Suppl 5), S21–S23 (2000)
4. De Stefano, C., Fontanella, F., Impedovo, D., Pirlo, G., di Freca, A.S.: Handwriting analysis to support neurodegenerative diseases diagnosis: a review. Pattern Recogn. Lett. **121**, 37–45 (2019)
5. Gallicchio, C., Micheli, A., Pedrelli, L.: Deep echo state networks for diagnosis of Parkinson's disease. arXiv preprint arXiv:1802.06708 (2018)
6. Gil-Martín, M., Montero, J.M., San-Segundo, R.: Parkinson's disease detection from drawing movements using convolutional neural networks. Electronics **8**(8), 907 (2019)

7. Haller, S., Badoud, S., Nguyen, D., Garibotto, V., Lovblad, K., Burkhard, P.: Individual detection of patients with Parkinson disease using support vector machine analysis of diffusion tensor imaging data: initial results. Am. J. Neuroradiol . **33**(11), 2123–2128 (2012)
8. Isenkul, M., Sakar, B., Kursun, O., et al.: Improved spiral test using digitized graphics tablet for monitoring Parkinson's disease. In: Proceedings of the International Conference on e-Health and Telemedicine, pp. 171–5 (2014)
9. Islam, M.Z., Hossain, M.S., ul Islam, R., Andersson, K.: Static hand gesture recognition using convolutional neural network with data augmentation. In: 2019 Joint 8th International Conference on Informatics, Electronics & Vision (ICIEV) and 2019 3rd International Conference on Imaging, Vision & Pattern Recognition (icIVPR), pp. 324–329. IEEE (2019)
10. Islam, R.U., Hossain, M.S., Andersson, K.: A deep learning inspired belief rule-based expert system. IEEE Access **8**, 190637–190651 (2020)
11. Jamil, M.N., Hossain, M.S., ul Islam, R., Andersson, K.: A belief rule based expert system for evaluating technological innovation capability of high-tech firms under uncertainty. In: 2019 Joint 8th International Conference on Informatics, Electronics & Vision (ICIEV) and 2019 3rd International Conference on Imaging, Vision & Pattern Recognition (icIVPR), pp. 330–335. IEEE (2019)
12. Kabir, S., Islam, R.U., Hossain, M.S., Andersson, K.: An integrated approach of belief rule base and deep learning to predict air pollution. Sensors **20**(7), 1956 (2020)
13. Karim, R., Andersson, K., Hossain, M.S., Uddin, M.J., Meah, M.P.: A belief rule based expert system to assess clinical bronchopneumonia suspicion. In: 2016 Future Technologies Conference (FTC), pp. 655–660. IEEE (2016)
14. Khatamino, P., Cantürk, İ., Özyilmaz, L.: A deep learning-CNN based system for medical diagnosis: an application on Parkinson's disease handwriting drawings. In: 2018 6th International Conference on Control Engineering & Information Technology (CEIT), pp. 1–6. IEEE (2018)
15. Kotsavasiloglou, C., Kostikis, N., Hristu-Varsakelis, D., Arnaoutoglou, M.: Machine learning-based classification of simple drawing movements in Parkinson's disease. Biomed. Signal Process. Control **31**, 174–180 (2017)
16. Lang, A.E., Lozano, A.M.: Parkinson's disease. New Engl. J. Med. **339**(16), 1130–1143 (1998)
17. Little, M., McSharry, P., Hunter, E., Spielman, J., Ramig, L.: Suitability of dysphonia measurements for telemonitoring of Parkinson's disease. Nat. Precedings 1–1 (2008)
18. Mahmud, M., Kaiser, M.S., McGinnity, T.M., Hussain, A.: Deep learning in mining biological data. Cogn. Comput. **13**(1), 1–33 (2021)
19. Mahmud, M., Kaiser, M.S., Hussain, A., Vassanelli, S.: Applications of deep learning and reinforcement learning to biological data. IEEE Trans. Neural Netw. Learn. Syst. **29**(6), 2063–2079 (2018)
20. Noor, M.B.T., Zenia, N.Z., Kaiser, M.S., Al Mamun, S., Mahmud, M.: Application of deep learning in detecting neurological disorders from magnetic resonance images: a survey on the detection of Alzheimer's disease, Parkinson's disease and schizophrenia. Brain Inform. **7**(1), 1–21 (2020)
21. Noor, M.B.T., Zenia, N.Z., Kaiser, M.S., Mahmud, M., Al Mamun, S.: Detecting neurodegenerative disease from MRI: a brief review on a deep learning perspective. In: Liang, P., Goel, V., Shan, C. (eds.) Brain Informatics. International Conference on Brain Informatics, pp. 115–125. Springer, Cham (2019). https://doi.org/10.1007/978-3-030-37078-7_12

22. Pereira, C.R., et al.: A step towards the automated diagnosis of Parkinson's disease: analyzing handwriting movements. In: 2015 IEEE 28th International Symposium on Computer-Based Medical Systems, pp. 171–176. IEEE (2015)
23. Pereira, J.C., Schelp, A.O., Montagnoli, A.N., Gatto, A.R., Spadotto, A.A., Carvalho, L.R.D.: Residual signal auto-correlation to evaluate speech in Parkinson's disease patients. Arquivos de neuro-psiquiatria **64**, 912–915 (2006)
24. Progga, N.I., Hossain, M.S., Andersson, K.: A deep transfer learning approach to diagnose COVID-19 using x-ray images. In: 2020 IEEE International Women in Engineering (WIE) Conference on Electrical and Computer Engineering (WIECON-ECE), pp. 177–182. IEEE (2020)
25. Rahaman, S., Hossain, M.S.: A belief rule based clinical decision support system to assess suspicion of heart failure from signs, symptoms and risk factors. In: 2013 International Conference on Informatics, Electronics and Vision (ICIEV), pp. 1–6. IEEE (2013)
26. Ramteke, S.P., Gurjar, A.A., Deshmukh, D.S.: A streamlined OCR system for handwritten Marathi text document classification and recognition using SVM-ACS algorithm. Int. J. Intell. Eng. Syst. **11**(3), 186–195 (2018)
27. Rezaoana, N., Hossain, M.S., Andersson, K.: Detection and classification of skin cancer by using a parallel CNN model. In: 2020 IEEE International Women in Engineering (WIE) Conference on Electrical and Computer Engineering (WIECON-ECE), pp. 380–386. IEEE (2020)
28. Ruiz, J., Mahmud, M., Modasshir, Md., Shamim Kaiser, M., Alzheimer's Disease Neuroimaging Initiative: 3D DenseNet ensemble in 4-way classification of Alzheimer's disease. In: Mahmud, M., Vassanelli, S., Kaiser, M.S., Zhong, N. (eds.) BI 2020. LNCS (LNAI), vol. 12241, pp. 85–96. Springer, Cham (2020). https://doi.org/10.1007/978-3-030-59277-6_8
29. Sakar, B.E., et al.: Collection and analysis of a Parkinson speech dataset with multiple types of sound recordings. IEEE J. Biomed. Health Inform. **17**(4), 828–834 (2013)
30. Tammina, S.: Transfer learning using VGG-16 with deep convolutional neural network for classifying images. Int. J. Sci. Res. Publ. (IJSRP) **9**(10), 143–150 (2019)
31. Tsanas, A., Little, M., McSharry, P., Spielman, J., Ramig, L.: A decision support system to improve medical diagnosis using a combination of k-medoids clustering based attribute weighting and svm. IEEE Trans. Biomed. Eng. **59**(5), 1264–71 (2012)
32. Tseng, M.H., Cermak, S.A.: The influence of ergonomic factors and perceptual-motor abilities on handwriting performance. Am. J. Occup. Ther. **47**(10), 919–926 (1993)
33. Tysnes, O.B., Storstein, A.: Epidemiology of Parkinson's disease. J. Neural Transm. **124**(8), 901–905 (2017)
34. Uddin Ahmed, T., Jamil, M.N., Hossain, M.S., Andersson, K., Hossain, M.S.: An integrated real-time deep learning and belief rule base intelligent system to assess facial expression under uncertainty. In: 9th International Conference on Informatics, Electronics & Vision (ICIEV). IEEE Computer Society (2020)
35. Vásquez-Correa, J.C., Arias-Vergara, T., Orozco-Arroyave, J.R., Vargas-Bonilla, J.F., Arias-Londoño, J.D., Nöth, E.: Automatic detection of Parkinson's disease from continuous speech recorded in non-controlled noise conditions. In: Sixteenth Annual Conference of the International Speech Communication Association (2015)
36. Zham, P., Arjunan, S.P., Raghav, S., Kumar, D.K.: Efficacy of guided spiral drawing in the classification of Parkinson's disease. IEEE J. Biomed. Health Inform. **22**(5), 1648–1652 (2017)

37. Zisad, S.N., Chowdhury, E., Hossain, M.S., Islam, R.U., Andersson, K.: An integrated deep learning and belief rule-based expert system for visual sentiment analysis under uncertainty. Algorithms **14**(7), 213 (2021)
38. Zisad, S.N., Hossain, M.S., Andersson, K.: Speech emotion recognition in neurological disorders using convolutional neural network. In: Mahmud, M., Vassanelli, S., Kaiser, M.S., Zhong, N. (eds.) BI 2020. LNCS (LNAI), vol. 12241, pp. 287–296. Springer, Cham (2020). https://doi.org/10.1007/978-3-030-59277-6_26
39. Zuo, W.L., Wang, Z.Y., Liu, T., Chen, H.L.: Effective detection of Parkinson's disease using an adaptive fuzzy k-nearest neighbor approach. Biomed. Signal Process. Control **8**(4), 364–373 (2013)

An XAI Based Autism Detection: The Context Behind the Detection

Milon Biswas[1], M. Shamim Kaiser[2,3](✉), Mufti Mahmud[4], Shamim Al Mamun[2,3], Md. Shahadat Hossain[5], and Muhammad Arifur Rahman[3,6]

[1] Department of Computer Science and Engineering, Bangladesh University of Business and Technology, Mirpur, Dhaka 1216, Bangladesh
milon@ieee.org

[2] Institute of Information Jahangirnagar University, Savar, Dhaka 1342, Bangladesh
{mskaiser,shamim}@juniv.edu

[3] Applied Intelligence and Informatics (AII) Lab, Wazed Miah Science Research Centre, Jahangirnagar University, Savar, Dhaka 1342, Bangladesh

[4] Department of Computer Science, Nottingham Trent University, Clifton Lane, Nottingham NG118NS, UK
mufti.mahmud@ntu.ac.uk

[5] Department of Computer Science and Engineering, Chittagong University, Chittagong 4331, Bangladesh
hossain_ms@cu.ac.bd

[6] Department of Physics, Jahangirnagar University, Savar, Dhaka 1342, Bangladesh
arif@juniv.edu

Abstract. With the rapid growth of the Internet of Healthcare Things, a massive amount of data is generated by a broad variety of medical devices. Because of the complex relationship in large-scale healthcare data, researchers who bring a revolution in the healthcare industry embrace Artificial Intelligence (AI). In certain cases, it has been reported that AI can do better than humans at performing healthcare tasks. The data-driven black-box model, on the other hand, does not appeal to healthcare professionals as it is not transparent, and any biasing can hamper the performance the prediction model for the real-life operation. In this paper, we proposed an AI model for early detection of autism in children. Then we showed why AI with explainability is important. This paper provides examples focused on the Autism Spectrum Disorder dataset (Autism screening data for toddlers by Dr Fadi Fayez Thabtah) and discussed why explainability approaches should be used when using AI systems in healthcare.

Keywords: Explainable AI · Support vector machine (SVM) · Machine learning · Co-relation coefficient

1 Introduction

Autism Spectrum Disorder (ASD) is a term that refers to a group of neurodevelopmental diseases that include autism and Asperger's syndrome. The ASD

M. Mahmud et al. (Eds.): BI 2021, LNAI 12960, pp. 448–459, 2021.
https://doi.org/10.1007/978-3-030-86993-9_40

is a life-style condition that cannot be cured but should be recognized early since it allows therapies to be mitigated more effectively [10,20]. However, typical behavioral testing make the identification and diagnosis of ASD extremely difficult. ASD normally occurs about the age of two years, but may be detected later, depending on the severity of symptoms. Although ASD is discovered by a number of clinical tools as early as possible, it does include onerous diagnostic procedures that are normally not used unless there is a strong doubt or a high risk of ASD [17].

Artificial intelligence (AI)—a brain-inspired bio-network—was developed as a promising approach that imitates human intellect and can execute cognitive processes. AI has been proven its potential in engineering, process control, science, and our daily life applications. Thus, research has attempted AI for patient care especially symptom identification, diagnosis, and management. However, the data-driven black-box model does not appeal to healthcare professionals because the model is not open and any bias may impede the performance of the real-life operation prediction model. Researchers used various types of AI (such as rule based), and Machine Learning (support vector machine (SVM), decision tree (DT), Logistic regression (LR) etc.) algorithms to detect and classify various types of ASD with high accuracy.

Previous research have sought to use a variety of data modalities in conjunction with AI to produce a more objective technique of detecting ASD through assessment of major traits associated with the disease. Healthcare practitioners aspire to control and test AI (Blackbox) models. It is necessary to compare predictions [5,18,27] with reality (via split test) and evaluate the explainability (reason) in the predicted model.

In this paper, an explainable AI based Autism Detection is discussed. As a first step, we constructed an Autism Detection and Classification Model based on machine learning (e.g., SVM); as a second step, we demonstrated that the model outcome was explainable by showing a relationship between the dominating features and the model outcome.

The remaining sections of the papers are as follows: Sect. 2 contains a review of the literature on AI and explainability in the context of autism spectrum disorders (ASD), Sect. 3 discusses the methodology of this work, Sect. 4 contains the results and discussion, and Sect. 5 concludes the paper with future recommendations.

2 Literature Review

Using a variety of machine learning methodologies, many researchers have sought to identify and diagnose ASD. The authors [26] of this paper proposed utilizing Rules-based Machine Learning (RML) to evaluate ASD symptoms and observed that RML permits classifiers to perform better. Using Tree-based classifiers, Satu et al. discovered specific key characteristics of normal and autistic children in Bangladesh [22]. Abbas et al. [1] integrated the ADI-R and ADOS ML methods into a single evaluation, addressing scarcity, sparsity, and differing definitions concerns with feature knowledge of content. For robust ASD diagnoses and prognoses, researchers [12,13,24–26] employed variable analysis to reveal feature-to-class and feature-to-feature correlations, as well as computational intelligence approaches including support vector machine (SVM), decision tree (DT), and logistic regression (LR).

Duda et al. [11] used several classifiers to examine ASD data and discovered ASD from attention deficit hyperactivity disorder (ADHD). However, authors found that cluster analysis could be a superior way to capture complex factors that predict ASD phenotype and heterogeneity.

Payrovnaziri SN et al. [21] built a comprehensive scoping assessment of explanatory AI (XAI) models using electronic records of real-world health, categorize these methods into various biomedical applications, identify existing study gaps, and offer future research guidelines. The XAI assessment was determined to be improperly and formally used in medicine, according to the authors. Reproducibility is still a major issue.

The authors [3] proposed an AI-based system that uses sensor data to monitor the patient's health and changes the learning approach through interesting games and activities based on the patient's emotion and facial expression. The objective of this study was to develop a more accurate machine learning model for detecting autism. To determine the effectiveness of community-based autism screening programs, researchers [6] performed a literature review. When compared to the most important issues concerning autism, screening programs fell short on almost every criterion. There aren't enough reliable screening instruments or effective treatments, and there's no proof that such a program would do more benefit than damage. Banna et al. [4] presented an AI-based system that uses sensor data to monitor the patient's state and changes the learning approach through interesting games and activities based on the patient's emotion and facial expression. To diagnose Autism Spectrum Disorder, a hybrid method [2,7,9] based on the Internet of Things (IoT) and the Belief Rule Base (BRB) is introduced (ASD). This intelligent technology can collect sign and symptom data from diverse autistic youngsters in real-time and classify them. The suggested system outperformed both the fuzzy system and the expert system, which were both state-of-the-art at the time. An assistive system for children with autism spectrum disorder was presented in this study (C-ASD) [23]. The major goal of this method would be to help children become more independent by reducing their reliance on their caregivers and parents.

An expert system based on fuzzy logic had been developed to aid in the development of intervention methods. The authors [19] looked at methodological research articles that proposed employing deep machine learning algorithms to detect neurodegenerative illnesses only using MRI data to detect neurodegenerative diseases. The findings demonstrate that deep learning-based approaches can accurately determine the degree of chaos. At the conclusion, present difficulties are discussed, as well as some potential future research areas. This study [8] began with an introduction of Convolutional Neural Networks, the most frequently used DL approach, and its application to separate brain areas from

Magnetic Resonance Imaging, aimed at novices. It then goes on to give a quantitative analysis of the approaches under consideration, as well as a thorough discussion of their effectiveness. To analyze the trustworthiness of nodes, the authors [17] suggested TMM, which uses Adaptive Neuro-Fuzzy Inference System and weighted-additive techniques to estimate node behavioral trust and data trust, respectively. NS2 simulation results show the resilience and accuracy of the proposed TMM in identifying malicious nodes in the communication network, in contrast to current fuzzy based TMMs. Mahmud et al. [15,16] prepared reports that gives a thorough overview of the use of DL, RL, and Deep RL algorithms in biological data mining. They also compare the results of DL approaches when applied to various datasets across a variety of application areas, highlighting unresolved difficulties in this difficult research area and discussing future development prospects. Autism spectrum disorder is a permanent developmental condition in which persons with the illness exhibit repetitive behavior and have communication difficulties.

The healthcare professionals do not put their faith in black box AI models because any inaccurate or biased diagnosis can put a person in danger, which is why they are apprehensive [14]. As a result, they seek transparency and explainability in the AI model employed for disease diagnosis.

3 Methodology

3.1 Datasets

Data is crucial in the AI activity and a big number of data must be analyzed to attain substantive efficiency. Multiple resources have collected data. Dr Fadi Fayez Thabtah [25,26] has developed the dataset, called Toddler dataset, to assess autism in young children using a mobile app called ASDTests (ASDtests.com). A novel dataset relating to the autism screening of infants with influential factors for future investigation particularly for the detection of autistic characteristics and for the improvement of ASD categorization. Figure 1 shows data collection and ASD classification in the Toddler dataset. In this data collection ten behavioral traits (Q-Chat-10) are recorded, plus other characteristics of people that have shown beneficial in diagnosing ASD cases in behavioral science controls (Fig. 2). Other functionality (i.e. Age, Q-chat-10Score, Sex, Ethnicity, Born with jaundice, ASD history, Who is completing the test, Why are you taken the screening and Class variable) in the datasets are gathered in the ASDTes screening application. It is important to remember that the variable class was automatically allocated on the basis of the scoring acquired by user using the ASDTests application.

Attributes: A1-A10: Q-Chat-10 items in which possible replies are asked: "Always, Usually, sometimes, rare and never" entries are mapped on a dataset to "1" or "0" If the answer was sometimes/Rarly/Never "1" in questions 1–9 (A1-A9) in Q-CHAT-10 (A1-A9). For Question 10 (A10) however, "1" is allocated if the response was always/usually/sometimes. If you have more than 3 users Please

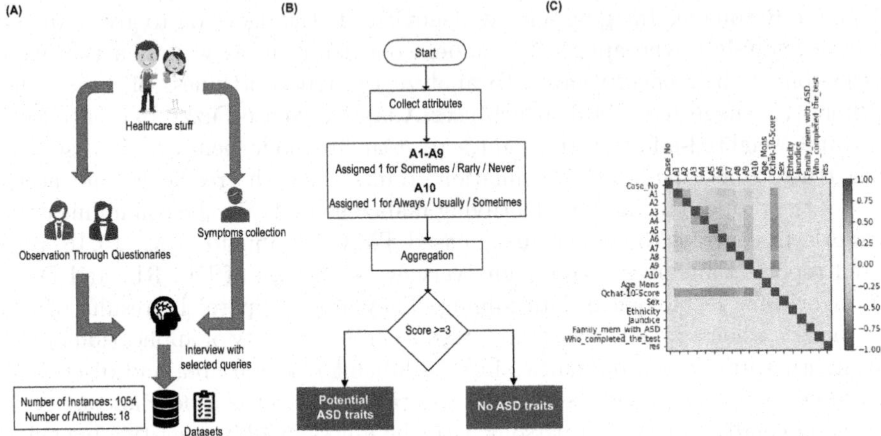

Fig. 1. Toddler dataset: (A) Data Collection process through questionnaire (B) flow chart of the ASD classification in the dataset

add points for all 10 questions together. If the kid scores greater than 3, then there are probable ASD characteristics, else no ASD characteristics are noticed.

3.2 SVM

Support Vector Machines (SVMs) are supervised data-driven learning models that attempt to differentiate between classes and find the best linear boundaries to separate those classes. Such model can also be used for regression and outlier identification. The SVM concept uses a hyperplane to generate data divisions. These aircraft could be written as:

$$\mathbf{WX} + \mathbf{B} = 0 \tag{1}$$

where the weight, denoted by $W = \{W_1, W_2, ..., W_N\}$. If X is two input attributes A_1 and A_2, training tuples are 2-D, (e.g., $X = x1, x2$, where x1 and x2 are the values of attributes A1 and A2, respectively. Thus, any points above the separating hyper-plane belong to Class A1:

$$\mathbf{WX} + \mathbf{B} > 0 \tag{2}$$

and any points below the separating hyper-plane belong to Class A2:

$$\mathbf{WX} + \mathbf{B} < 0 \tag{3}$$

The Support Vector Machine (SVM) algorithm supports a series of SVM-defined math function sets. These SVM kernels accept data as its input and convert it to the necessary form. Different forms of SVM algorithms employ different types of kernel functions and different types of SVM functions. Linear SVM, Polynomial SVM, Gauussian Radial Kernel, Sigmoid SVM Kernels are

Variable	Corresponding Q-chat-10-Toddler Features
A1	Does your child look at you when you call his/her name?
A2	How easy is it for you to get eye contact with your child?
A3	Does your child point to indicate that s/he wants some-thing?
A4	Does your child point to share interest with you?
A5	Does your child pretend? (e.g. care for dolls, talk on atoy phone)
A6	Does your child follow where you're looking?
A7	If you or someone else in the family is visibly upset, doesyour child show signs of wanting to comfort them?
A8	Would you describe your child's first words as
A9	Does your child use simple gestures? (e.g. wave goodbye)
A10	Does your child stare at nothing with no apparent pur-pose?

Fig. 2. Details of variables mapping to the Q-Chat-10 screening methods and Features Collection

the most frequently used SVM kernels. Our data does not fit the linear kernel, as one reliable answer and one or more separate variables are linear. We must figure out which SVM kernel works best with the dataset used.

Among them is the Gaussian base kernel that is more effective than the Polynomial kernel. First, we split our data between training (70%) and testing into two categories (30%). We utilized this machine classifier to identify the outcomes of the evaluation matrices after splitting the dataset. Here the ROC curves are shown according to the AUC value of the SVM kernels. The AUC value of a perfect test result is 1.0 whereas a random probability is 0.5 or below for an AUC value. Here, therefore, the best performing method and classification for this sort of datasets are the SVM Gaussian Basic Radial kernel.

3.3 XAI Model

In our view, the difficulty of explainability is not merely an algorithmic difficulty that demands a combination of best practices in data science and domain expertise. The XAI library aims to allow engineers and relevant specialists to analyze a solution from end-to-end and to uncover inconsistencies which may lead to sub-optimal performance in relation to the needed objectives. The XAI library has been built in more depth with the help of the three processes of explainable machine learning, including 1) data analysis, 2) model assessment and 3) production monitoring. Figure 3 illustrates the functional block diagram of XAI model.

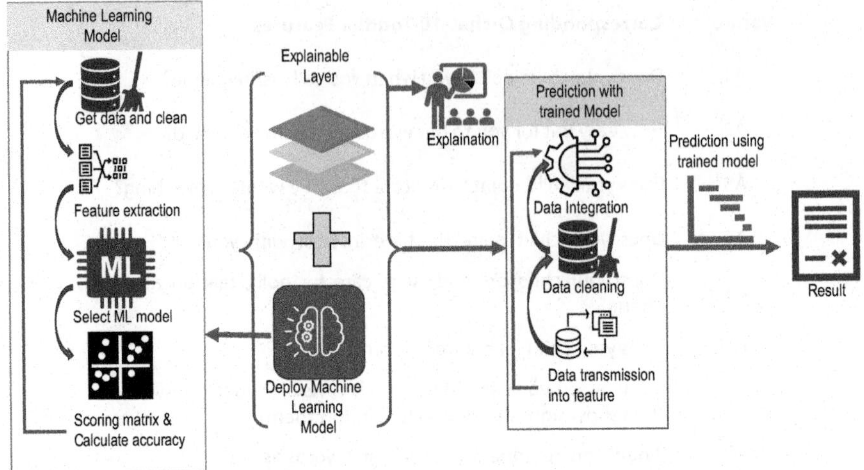

Fig. 3. A conceptual framework Machine Learning model with explainablity.

3.4 Performance Metrics

Accuracy. Consider the accuracy of the classification system when determining how often a data point is correctly classified by a machine learning classification system. More formally, it is defined as the number of true positives and true negatives divided by the number of true positives ($\mathcal{TP}$), true negatives ($\mathcal{TN}$), false positives ($\mathcal{FP}$), and false negatives ($\mathcal{FN}$).

A data point that the algorithm properly categorized as true or false is referred to as a $\mathcal{TP}$ or $\mathcal{TN}$. A $\mathcal{FP}$ or $\mathcal{FN}$, on the other hand, is a data point incorrectly classified by the algorithm.

It would be a $\mathcal{FP}$ if the algorithm classified a false data point as true. Precision and recall, two other metrics that use various ratios of true/false positives/negatives, are frequently used in conjunction with accuracy. These metrics, when combined, provide a comprehensive picture of how the algorithm classifies data points.

Mathematically, Accuracy (A) can be expressed by

$$A = \frac{\mathcal{TP} + \mathcal{TN}}{\mathcal{TP} + \mathcal{TN} + \mathcal{FP} + \mathcal{FN}} \tag{4}$$

Sensitivity. The fraction of actual positive instances that were anticipated as positive is known as sensitivity (or $\mathcal{TP}$). Recall is another name for sensitivity. This means that there will be a fraction of genuine positive cases that are wrongly projected as negative (and, thus, could also be termed as the false negative). A false negative rate can also be used to illustrate this. The total of the sensitivity and false negative rate is one. Mathematically, Sensitivity (Sen) can be written as

$$Sen = \frac{\mathcal{TP}}{\mathcal{TP} + \mathcal{FN}} \tag{5}$$

Specificity. The fraction of real negatives that were anticipated as negatives is known as specificity (or true negative). This means that a fraction of genuine negatives will be projected as positives, which might be referred to as false positives. This percentage is also known as the false positive rate. The sum of specificity and false positive rate is always 1 in this case. Mathematically Specificity (Spe) is given by

$$Spe = \frac{\mathcal{TN}}{\mathcal{TN} + \mathcal{FP}} \tag{6}$$

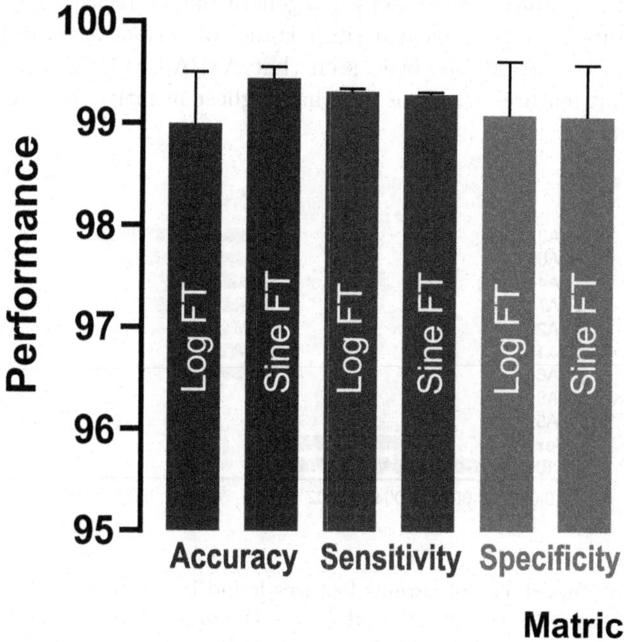

Fig. 4. The performance evaluation of SVM classifier in detecting autism from toddler dataset.

4 Results and Discussion

In this paper, the Log, and Sine FT methods were applied in toddler dataset. SVM classifier with radial basis function as a kernel is used to classify the autism. Accuracy, Sensitivity and Specificity of SVM classifier were used to justify experimental findings. It has been found that the accuracy of toddler ASD dataset has an 98.27 ± 1.12 (for Log FT method) and 98.47 ± 1.10 (Sine FT method); the sensitivity of toddler ASD dataset has an 99.29 ± 0.1 (for Log FT method) and 98.27 ± 0.1 (Sine FT method); and the specificity of toddler ASD dataset has an 98.32 ± 1.01 (for Log FT method) and 98.3 ± 1.14 (Sine FT method). Figure shows the performance evaluation of SVM classifier in detecting autism from toddler dataset.

The feature importance score is critical for explainability since it provides insight into the dataset and model. This can be useful in identifying which features are most important to the target and which features are least relevant to the target based on relative scores. Depending on the domain, this could be analyzed by a domain expert and utilized as a starting point for obtaining additional or different data. Many importance scores are calculated using a predictive model fitted to the dataset. Examining the importance score provides insight into that specific model, as well as which features are the most important and least relevant to the model when generating a forecast in that particular situation. Figure 5 shows the feature importance of various features found in the toddler ASD datasets. It has been seen that A3, A6, A4, A7 and A2 are the most important features where as A10 has highest negative feature importance in the dataset.

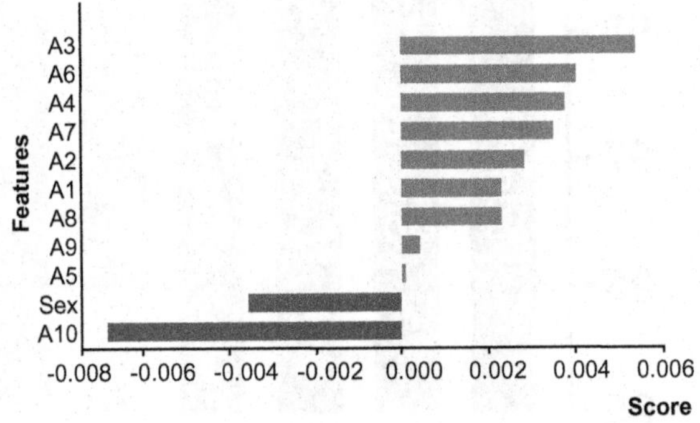

Fig. 5. Feature importance of various features found in the toddler ASD datasets. It has been seen that A3, A6, A4, A7 and A2 are the most important features where as A10 has highest negative feature importance in the dataset.

Figure 6 illustrates explainability in SVM Model and toddler ASD dataset. In Fig. 6(A), the Correlation among corresponding Q-chat-10-Toddler features in the toddler ASD data-set is shown. Figure 6(B) shows the dendrogram which shows the hierarchical relationships among the features mentioned in the toddler ASD dataset. This hierarchical clustering is essential for clustering the features. Figure 6(C) shows ASD classification based on the gender [male/female] of the subjects. Figure 6(D) shows the Visualization of Accuracy [correct/incorrect] is binned according to its probability in the Probability Bucket.

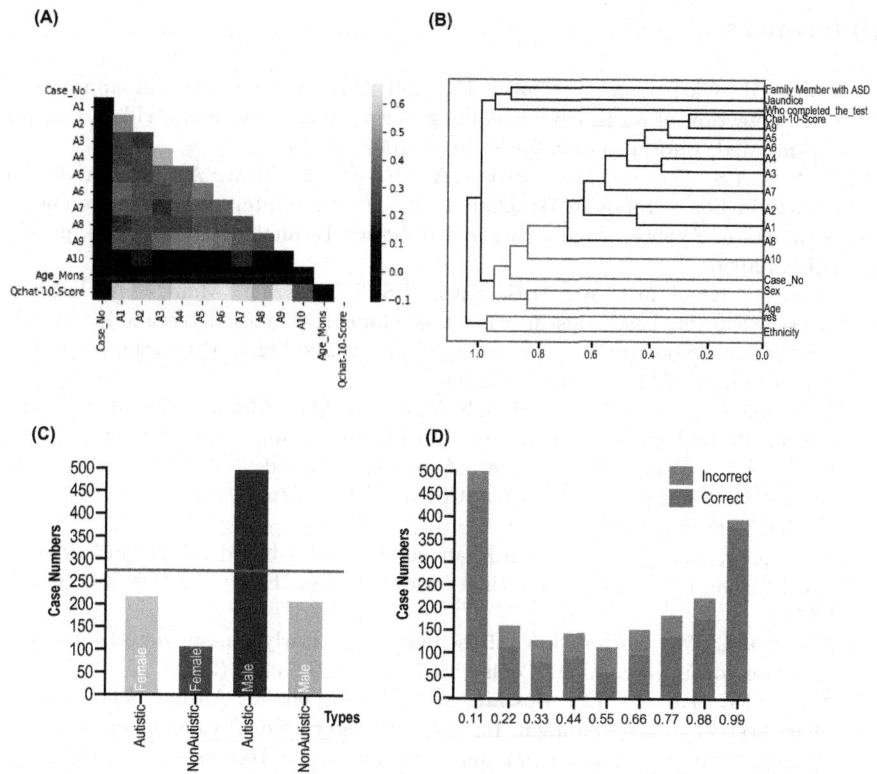

Fig. 6. Explainability in SVM Model and dataset (A) Correlation among Features in the toddler ASD data-set; (B) the hierarchical relationship among the features; (C) Gender vs ASD classification; and (D) Visualization of Accuracy [correct/incorrect] binned by the probability bucket.

5 Conclusion

In this paper, we employed an SVM model for making classification decisions on dataset named early-detected autism spectrum disorders (ASD) in toddlers. The log and sine functions transformation functions were utilized to convert the dataset to the appropriate format. We employ the XAI model to identify the most relevant aspects that would contribute to the prediction of the support vector machine. The results reveal that, when properly optimized, machine learning systems can provide accurate predictions of whether or not a person has an ASD diagnosis. It has been discovered that explainability of ML models can be achieved without sacrificing the model's performance.

References

1. Abbas, H., Garberson, F., Glover, E., Wall, D.P.: Machine learning approach for early detection of autism by combining questionnaire and home video screening. J. Am. Med. Inform. Assoc. **25**(8), 1000–1007 (2018)
2. Akib, A.A.S., Ferdous, M.F., Biswas, M., Khondokar, H.M.: Artificial intelligence humanoid bongo robot in Bangladesh. In: 2019 1st International Conference on Advances in Science, Engineering and Robotics Technology (ICASERT), pp. 1–6. IEEE (2019)
3. Akter, T., Khan, M.I., Ali, M.H., Satu, M.S., Uddin, M.J., Moni, M.A.: Improved machine learning based classification model for early autism detection. In: 2021 2nd International Conference on Robotics, Electrical and Signal Processing Techniques (ICREST), pp. 742–747. IEEE (2021)
4. Al Banna, M.H., Ghosh, T., Taher, K.A., Kaiser, M.S., Mahmud, M.: A monitoring system for patients of autism spectrum disorder using artificial intelligence. In: Mahmud, M., Vassanelli, S., Kaiser, M.S., Zhong, N. (eds.) BI 2020. LNCS (LNAI), vol. 12241, pp. 251–262. Springer, Cham (2020). https://doi.org/10.1007/978-3-030-59277-6_23
5. Al Nahian, M.J., et al.: Towards an accelerometer-based elderly fall detection system using cross-disciplinary time series features. IEEE Access **9**, 39413–39431 (2021)
6. Al-Qabandi, M., Gorter, J.W., Rosenbaum, P.: Early autism detection: are we ready for routine screening? Pediatrics **128**(1), e211–e217 (2011)
7. Alam, M.E., Kaiser, M.S., Hossain, M.S., Andersson, K.: An IoT-belief rule base smart system to assess autism. In: 2018 4th International Conference on Electrical Engineering and Information and Communication Technology (iCEEiCT), pp. 672–676. IEEE (2018)
8. Ali, H.M., Kaiser, M.S., Mahmud, M.: Application of convolutional neural network in segmenting brain regions from MRI data. In: Liang, P., Goel, V., Shan, C. (eds.) BI 2019. LNCS, vol. 11976, pp. 136–146. Springer, Cham (2019). https://doi.org/10.1007/978-3-030-37078-7_14
9. Biswas, M., Whaiduzzaman, M.: Efficient mobile cloud computing through computation offloading. Int. J. Adv. Technol. **10**(2), 32 (2018)
10. Biswas, S., Akhter, T., Kaiser, M., Mamun, S., et al.: Cloud based healthcare application architecture and electronic medical record mining: an integrated approach to improve healthcare system. In: 2014 17th International Conference on Computer and Information Technology (ICCIT), pp. 286–291. IEEE (2014)
11. Duda, M., Ma, R., Haber, N., Wall, D.: Use of machine learning for behavioral distinction of autism and ADHD. Transl. Psychiatry **6**(2), e732–e732 (2016)
12. Hossain, M.A., Islam, S.M.S., Quinn, J.M., Huq, F., Moni, M.A.: Machine learning and bioinformatics models to identify gene expression patterns of ovarian cancer associated with disease progression and mortality. J. Biomed. Inform. **100**, 103313 (2019)
13. Howlader, K.C., Satu, M.S., Barua, A., Moni, M.A.: Mining significant features of diabetes mellitus applying decision trees: a case study in Bangladesh. BioRxiv, p. 481994 (2018)
14. Kaiser, M.S., Al Mamun, S., Mahmud, M., Tania, M.H.: Healthcare robots to combat COVID-19. In: Santosh, K.C., Joshi, A. (eds.) COVID-19: Prediction, Decision-Making, and its Impacts. LNDECT, vol. 60, pp. 83–97. Springer, Singapore (2021). https://doi.org/10.1007/978-981-15-9682-7_10

15. Mahmud, M., Kaiser, M.S., McGinnity, T.M., Hussain, A.: Deep learning in mining biological data. Cogn. Comput. **13**(1), 1–33 (2021)
16. Mahmud, M., Kaiser, M.S., Hussain, A., Vassanelli, S.: Applications of deep learning and reinforcement learning to biological data. IEEE Trans. Neural Networks Learn. Syst. **29**(6), 2063–2079 (2018)
17. Mahmud, M., et al.: A brain-inspired trust management model to assure security in a cloud based IoT framework for neuroscience applications. Cogn. Comput. **10**(5), 864–873 (2018)
18. Nahiduzzaman, M., Tasnim, M., Newaz, N.T., Kaiser, M.S., Mahmud, M.: Machine learning based early fall detection for elderly people with neurological disorder using multimodal data fusion. In: Mahmud, M., Vassanelli, S., Kaiser, M.S., Zhong, N. (eds.) BI 2020. LNCS (LNAI), vol. 12241, pp. 204–214. Springer, Cham (2020). https://doi.org/10.1007/978-3-030-59277-6_19
19. Noor, M.B.T., Zenia, N.Z., Kaiser, M.S., Mahmud, M., Al Mamun, S.: Detecting neurodegenerative disease from MRI: a brief review on a deep learning perspective. In: Liang, P., Goel, V., Shan, C. (eds.) BI 2019. LNCS, vol. 11976, pp. 115–125. Springer, Cham (2019). https://doi.org/10.1007/978-3-030-37078-7_12
20. Paul, M.C., Sarkar, S., Rahman, M.M., Reza, S.M., Kaiser, M.S.: Low cost and portable patient monitoring system for e-health services in Bangladesh. In: 2016 International Conference on Computer Communication and Informatics (ICCCI), pp. 1–4. IEEE (2016)
21. Payrovnaziri, S.N., et al.: Explainable artificial intelligence models using real-world electronic health record data: a systematic scoping review. J. Am. Med. Inform. Assoc. **27**(7), 1173–1185 (2020)
22. Satu, M.S., Sathi, F.F., Arifen, M.S., Ali, M.H., Moni, M.A.: Early detection of autism by extracting features: a case study in Bangladesh. In: 2019 International Conference on Robotics, Electrical and Signal Processing Techniques (ICREST), pp. 400–405. IEEE (2019)
23. Sumi, A.I., Zohora, M.F., Mahjabeen, M., Faria, T.J., Mahmud, M., Kaiser, M.S.: *f*ASSERT: a fuzzy assistive system for children with autism using Internet of Things. In: Wang, S., et al. (eds.) BI 2018. LNCS (LNAI), vol. 11309, pp. 403–412. Springer, Cham (2018). https://doi.org/10.1007/978-3-030-05587-5_38
24. Thabtah, F.: Autism spectrum disorder screening: machine learning adaptation and DSM-5 fulfillment. In: Proceedings of the 1st International Conference on Medical and health Informatics 2017, pp. 1–6 (2017)
25. Thabtah, F.: Machine learning in autistic spectrum disorder behavioral research: a review and ways forward. Inform. Health Soc. Care **44**(3), 278–297 (2019)
26. Thabtah, F., Kamalov, F., Rajab, K.: A new computational intelligence approach to detect autistic features for autism screening. Int. J. Med. Inform. **117**, 112–124 (2018)
27. Zohora, M.F., Tania, M.H., Kaiser, M.S., Mahmud, M.: Forecasting the risk of type ii diabetes using reinforcement learning. In: 2020 Joint 9th International Conference on Informatics, Electronics and Vision (ICIEV) and 2020 4th International Conference on Imaging, Vision and Pattern Recognition (icIVPR), pp. 1–6. IEEE (2020)

Brain-Machine Intelligence and Brain-Inspired Computing

EEG Seizure Prediction Based on Empirical Mode Decomposition and Convolutional Neural Network

Jianzhuo Yan[1,2], Jinnan Li[1,2], Hongxia Xu[1,2(✉)], Yongchuan Yu[1,2], Lexin Pan[3], Xuerui Cheng[4], and Shaofeng Tan[5,6]

[1] Beijing University of Technology, Beijing, China
{yanjianzhuo,xhxcclv,yuyongchuan}@bjut.edu.cn, lijinnanjn@emails.bjut.edu.cn

[2] Engineering Research Center of Digital Community, Ministry of Education, Beijing, China

[3] School of Mechatronical Engineering, Beijing Institute of Technology, Beijing, China

[4] Mount Pisgah Christian School, Johns Creek, USA

[5] Join Lab of Digital Health, Beijing University of Technology and Beijing Pinggu Hospital, Beijing, China

[6] Information Center of Beijing Pinggu Hospital, Beijing, China

Abstract. Epilepsy is a common neurological disease characterized by recurrent seizures. Electroencephalography (EEG), which records neural activity, is commonly used to diagnose epilepsy. This paper proposes an Empirical Mode Decomposition (EMD) and Deep Convolutional Neural Network epileptic seizure prediction method. First, the original EEG signals are segmented using 30 s sliding windows, and the segmented EEG signal is decomposed into Intrinsic Mode Functions (IMF) and residuals. Then, the entropy features which can better express the signal are extracted from the decomposed components. Finally, a deep convolutional neural network is used to construct the epileptic seizure prediction model. This experiment was conducted on the CHB-MIT Scalp EEG dataset to evaluate the performance of our proposed EMD-CNN epileptic EEG seizure detection model. The experimental results show that, compared with some previous EEG classification models, this model is helpful to improving the accuracy of epileptic seizure prediction.

Keywords: EEG · Epilepsy · Empirical Mode Decomposition · Convolutional neural network

1 Introduction

Epilepsy is a chronic disease, in which symptoms are sudden onset of brain neurons by abnormal discharge, leading to transient cerebral dysfunction. Currently, according to the statistical report of the World Health Organization, about 50

M. Mahmud et al. (Eds.): BI 2021, LNAI 12960, pp. 463–473, 2021.
https://doi.org/10.1007/978-3-030-86993-9_41

million patients are suffering from epilepsy, which has become one of the most common neurological diseases in the world [1]. The characteristics of epilepsy are repetitive and paroxysmal. During the period of epilepsy, patients will involuntarily produce symptoms such as general convulsions, loss of consciousness, and cognitive impairment, which have a great impact on the normal life of patients. Electroencephalogram (EEG) directly records the electrical activity of brain neurons through electrodes attached to the scalp and is the most effective method for diagnosing epilepsy [2]. However, the reading and analysis of EEG need to be handled by experienced neurology experts, which not only increases the burden on doctors but also easily leads to subjective judgment errors. Therefore, it is of great significance to design a reliable automatic epileptic detection technology for clinical application and research [3]. In the past few decades, machine learning has gained extensive attention in epileptic seizure detection of EEG signals.

Over the last decades, machine learning has attracted extensive attention in epileptic seizure detection based on EEG signals. The automatic detection technology of epilepsy EEG data includes two parts: feature extraction and classification. For feature extraction, it is mainly divided into linear analysis and nonlinear analysis methods. The common linear analysis methods are divided into time-domain analysis [4,5], frequency domain analysis [6], and time-frequency domain analysis [7,8]. The brain is a nonlinear dynamic system, so more and more scholars are interested in the nonlinear characteristics of EEG signals. Among them, the commonly used nonlinear characteristics of EEG signals mainly include correlation dimension [9], Lyapunov exponent [10,11], entropy [12], and other nonlinear dynamic indexes. By adopting the effective feature extraction method and then putting the extracted features into the classification model, the automatic classification detection of EEG signals can be realized. Recently, deep learning models have made some important progress in the analysis of time-series signals, especially EEG signals. You et al. proposed an automatic detection of epilepsy method by using a Generative Adversarial Network (GAN) combined with Gram matrix for anomaly detection [13]. Abbasi et al. used Long Short-Term Memory Network (LSTM) as a deep learning model to detect epilepsy in Electroencephalography (EEG) signals, and its performance was better than that of traditional recurrent neural networks (RNN) [14] Besides, convolutional neural networks play an important role in the analysis of EEG data. For the first time, Acharya et al. used a 13-layer deep convolutional neural network (CNN) to analyze EEG to detect seizure events [15].

The main purpose of this research is to propose an effective feature extraction method that is based on time-frequency and nonlinear analysis, and combined with a deep convolutional neural network to classify the preictal and interictal periods of EEG data. The application of our proposed epileptic seizure prediction model can enable patients and doctors to be prepared before the onset of an epileptic seizure. This paper proposes a nonlinear analysis feature extraction method based on Empirical Mode Decomposition. We decompose the original EEG signals into different IMF components, then calculate their entropies as feature vectors. Finally, we classified the Epilepsy EEG signals by deep convolution network and obtained good results.

2 Materials and Methods

2.1 Dataset

The epilepsy EEG dataset used in this article is derived from the CHB-MIT Scalp EEG database of Boston Children's Hospital [16], which is available at https://physionet.org [17]. It contains EEG records of pediatric patients with refractory seizures. Table 1 shows the basic situation of the database. The dataset was sampled 256 Hz sampling rate and 16-bit resolution from the electrodes, which are placed in the international 10–20 system of EEG electrode positions. The total duration of the EEG recording was nearly 983 h, of which 198 seizures were manually noted by experts. We define the interictal period as the period between 4 h before each seizure and 4 h after the end of the seizure, and the period between 33 min before each seizure and 3 min before the seizure is defined as the preictal period. We extracted the EEG data of the interictal and preictal in the CHB-MIT dataset to verify the effectiveness of the proposed prediction model.

In the experiment, we chose the cases with 23 channels in the EEG dataset and the same placement of electrode position for research. Since our classification task is aimed at the interictal and preictal phases, according to the previous definition, we have selected those patients who are more than 33 min between two seizures as the dataset of our experiment. After screening, we selected 8 patients' EEG signals to experiment. The basic situation of our experiment data is shown in Table 1.

Table 1. Summary of the datasets used in this work.

Dataset	EEG type	Patients	Number of channels	Number of seizures
CHB-MIT dataset	Scalp	8 patients	23	47

2.2 Empirical Mode Decomposition

The Empirical Mode Decomposition (EMD) method was proposed by Norden E. Huang [18], which is an adaptive time-frequency localization analysis method. It can decompose the original signals continuously and obtain the Intrinsic Mode Functions (IMF) components under certain conditions. Suppose the signal is x(t), EMD will decompose the signal into

$$x(t) = \sum_{i=1}^{n} c_i(t) + r_n(t) \tag{1}$$

Where $c_i(t)$ is the i-th IMF component obtained by the EMD decomposition; $r_n(t)$ is the residual component of the signal after n IMF components are decomposed and screened, which often represents the DC component or the trend of the signal.

Norden E. Huang believes that any signal can be divided into the sum of several intrinsic mode functions, and an IMF has two constraints:

1) In the entire data sequence, the difference between the number of extreme points and the number of zero-crossing points cannot exceed one at most.
2) At any point in time, the mean value of the upper envelope determined by the local maximum and the lower envelope determined by the local minimum is zero, that is, the upper and lower envelopes are locally symmetric concerning the time axis.

EMD is a non-stationary signal analysis method, but it is different from FFT. EMD is suitable for any data, it is decomposed based on the data itself, and no basis function is needed.

2.3 Feature Extraction

Feature extraction is very important for representing nonstationary and nonlinear EEG signals. In order to potentially improve the detection performance, we extract entropy features from the first 3 IMF components after decomposition. In this study, there are six types of entropy as features, namely permutation entropy, approximate entropy, sample entropy, Shannon entropy, spectral entropy, and singular decomposition entropy. The permutation entropy can effectively amplify the slight changes of the time series and has the advantages of easy computing and good quality in a real-time application, which has a good application prospect in the detection of signals. The approximate entropy is an important method of analyzing the complexity of time series. The sample entropy is the improvement of approximate entropy, both of them are used to measure the complexity of the time series and the probability of a new pattern generated by the sequence when the dimensionality changes. Sample entropy has the advantages of short data required, strong anti-noise ability, and good consistency within a large parameter range. Shannon entropy can fully mine the change information of the EEG signal in the time dimension, and characterize the changing intensity and change trend information of the signal in a certain period. Singular decomposition entropy is an index to measure the complexity of information and it is widely used in the fields of disease diagnosis. Spectral entropy can be used as a parameter to measure the electrophysiological activity of the brain and provide information to reflect the intensity of the activity. During the process of epileptic seizures, a large number of neuron groups discharge synchronously, a variety of complex brain functions have different degrees of inhibition. Compared with the normal brain electrical activity, the complexity of it will be reduced. Entropy is commonly used to measure the amount of disorder in the system. It can be utilized to measure the randomness of signals and to analyze complex EEG signals. Therefore, these six entropies were selected as eigenvectors to be used in the classification of epileptic EEG preictal and interictal.

1) Permutation entropy

Permutation entropy measures the complexity of time series by comparing adjacent values. It is calculated as follows:

$$PE = \sum_{k=1}^{n} s_k \log s_k \tag{2}$$

$$s_k = \frac{t_k}{N - m + 1} \tag{3}$$

Where N represents the length of the decomposed signal, t_k indicates the occurrence of the k-th symbol, s_k is the probability of the k-th permutation in the time series, and N implies the permutation order of $n \geq 2$.

2) Approximate entropy

Approximate entropy is a nonlinear dynamic parameter used to quantify the regularity and unpredictability of time series fluctuations. It can be expressed as:

$$APE = \varphi^m(r) - \varphi^{m+1}(r) \tag{4}$$

$$\varphi^m(r) = \frac{1}{N - (m-1)\tau} \sum_{i=1}^{N-(m+1)} \log C_i^m(r) \tag{5}$$

$$C_i^m(r) = \frac{1}{N - (m-1)\tau} \sum_{i=1}^{N-(m+1)} \theta(r - d(x(i), x(j))) \tag{6}$$

$$d(x(i), x(j)) =_{k=1,2,\ldots,m}^{max} | \, y(i + (k-1)\tau) - y(j + (k-1)\tau) \, | \tag{7}$$

Where m, r, τ, and N represent the embedding dimension, similarity coefficient, time delay, and the number of data points, respectively.

3) Sample entropy

The sample entropy is derived from approximate entropy, which is used to evaluate the complexity of physiological time-series signals. It can be represented as:

$$SaE = -\ln \frac{A^m(r)}{B^m(r)} \tag{8}$$

Where $B^m(r)$ is the probability of matching two sequences for m oints, while $A^m(r)$ indicates the probability of matching two sequences for $m + 1$ points.

4) Shannon entropy

Shannon entropy is a standard measure of the state of a sequence. Its formula is as follows:

$$ShE = -\sum_{i=1}^{N} p(i) \log_2 p(i) \tag{9}$$

Where i implies all observed values of EEG series data, and $p(i)$ represents the probability that value occurs in the whole EEG series.

5) Spectral entropy

Spectral entropy is the Shannon entropy of the power spectral density of the data. It is calculated as follows:

$$SpE = -\sum_{f=0} p_f \log p_f \tag{10}$$

Where p_f is the relative power of the component with frequency f.

6) Singular decomposition entropy

Singular decomposition entropy is an indicator of the number of feature vectors required to adequately interpret a dataset, which can be expressed as follows:

$$SvdE = -\sum_{i=1}^{M} \bar{\sigma}_i \log_2(\bar{\sigma}_i) \tag{11}$$

$$Y = [y_1, y_2, \ldots, y_{(N-(r-1)\tau)}]^T \tag{12}$$

$$y_i = [x_i, x(i+\tau), \ldots, x(i+(r-1)\tau)] \tag{13}$$

Where M represents the number of singular values of the embedded matrix Y. $\sigma_1, \sigma_2, \ldots, \sigma_M$ are the normalized singular values of Y, r indicates the order of permutation entropy, τ represents the time delay.

In the experiment, we segment the EEG signals by 30-s overlapping sliding windows and then divide 30-s EEG data into five fragments with 6-s each. After that, we performed Empirical Mode Decomposition on these 6-s time series and respectively took the six entropy features of the first three IMF components to form a feature vector of length $5 \times 3 \times 6 = 90$, and converted the feature vector into a two-dimensional array of (15,6), which is directly input into the deep convolutional neural network for training. Figure 1 shows the process of feature extraction.

2.4 Convolutional Neural Network

Nowadays, Convolutional Neural Network (CNN) has become one of the research hotspots in many scientific fields. It is not only used in image processing and natural language processing [19,20] but also has been successfully applied in

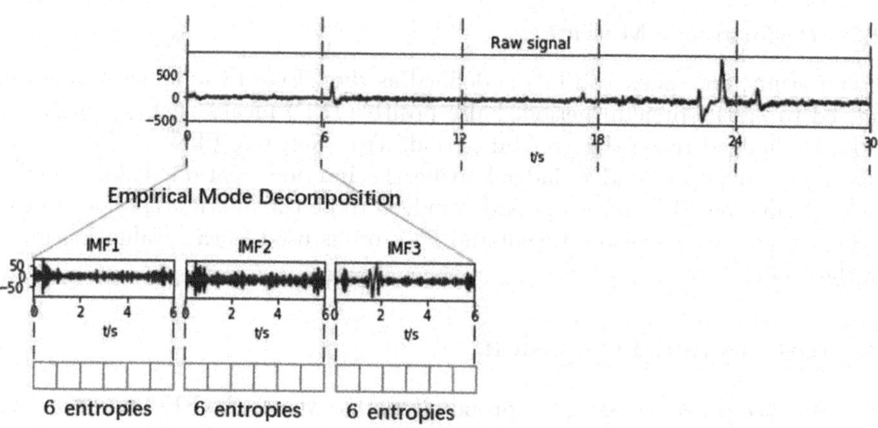

Fig. 1. The extraction process of feature vector

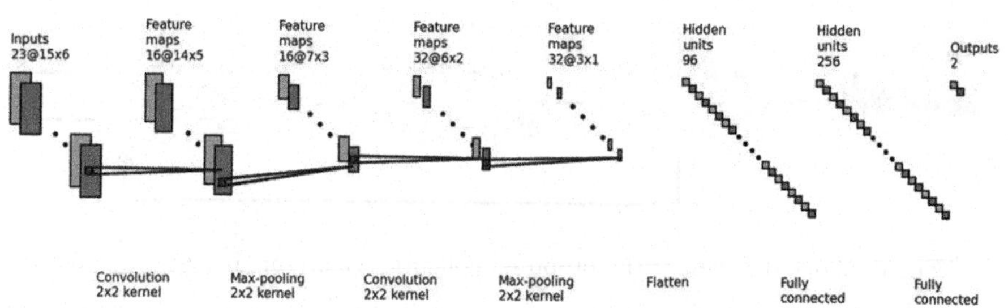

Fig. 2. Convolutional neural network architecture

many aspects of biomedical research based on physiological signals and medical image analysis [21]. In this study, we used the deep convolutional neural network shown in Fig. 2 to classify the preictal and interictal EEG signals.

There are 2 convolutional blocks in this model with 16 and 32 filters respectively. Each convolutional block consists of a two-dimensional convolutional layer with a Rectified Linear Unit (ReLU) activation function, a maximum pooling layer, and a batch normalization layer. For each convolution block, the size of the convolution kernel is $2 * 2$, and the number is 16 and 32 respectively. The size of the maximum pooling layer is $2 * 2$. The Batch Normalization layer normalizes the input of each layer to make the training process faster and more stable. After that, the features extracted by the two convolutional blocks are flattened and connected to two fully connected layers with output sizes of 256 and 2, respectively. The former fully connected layer uses a sigmoid activation function, while the latter uses a soft-max activation function, and the dropout rate is both 0.5. Our model is implemented in Python 3.7 with the use of Keras 2.0 with a Tensorflow 1.12.0 backend. The model was configured to run in parallel on three NVIDIA graphics cards.

2.5 Performance Metrics

In our study, true positive (TP) is defined as the EEG of the preictal period is judged to be the preictal period. False positive (FP) means that the interictal period is judged to be the preictal period. True Negative (TN) is the EEG of the interictal period and is judged to be the interictal period. False negative (FN) means that the preictal period is judged to be the interictal period. In this paper, Accuracy, Precision, Recall and F1-score is used as the evaluation index of the model.

3 Results and Discussion

To verify the effectiveness of the proposed model, we use the EEG monitor data of 8 cases on the CHB-MIT dataset as test samples. The experimental process of epileptic seizure prediction is shown in Fig. 3:

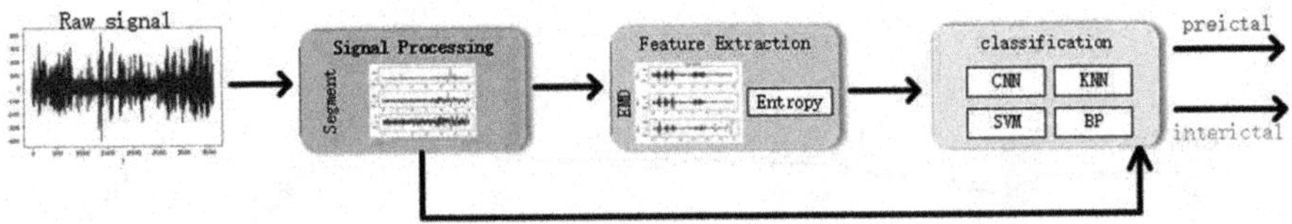

Fig. 3. Block diagram of the proposed epileptic seizure prediction method

Firstly, we segment the original EEG data of the interictal period and the preictal period. Since the EEG data of the interictal phase is much larger than that of the preictal phase, in order to balance the data samples, we adopt the method of overlapping sliding windows. Approximately 27344 30-s EEG segments were obtained in the interictal period and the preictal period. Secondly, the EMD decomposition method is used to decompose the segmented EEG data into several IMF components, and the entropy features of the first three IMF components are extracted. Finally, we input respectively the extracted features and segmented EEG data into KNN, SVM, BP neural network, and our proposed convolutional neural network for classification. In this work, the experimental data is divided into the training set and test set by 4:1. To prevent over-fitting during neural network training, we also use 20% of the training set as the validation set.

In the experiment, we first used 30 s sliding windows to segment the original EEG signals and then transmitted the segmented EEG signals directly into the CNN network for classification. Besides, we also chose BP neural network, SVM and KNN machine learning classifiers for comparative experiments. After that, we used the feature extraction method proposed in this paper to extract features of the original EEG signals and input them into the proposed CNN, SVM, KNN, and BP networks for training. Table 2 shows the classification accuracy results of these experiments.

Table 2. Classification results of original EEG windows and EEG windows after feature extraction by CNN, KNN, SVM, BP

Input	Method	Accuracy	Precision	Recall	F1-score
Origin EEG windows	SVM	0.8631	0.7717	0.7172	0.7435
	BP	0.8772	0.7768	0.7259	0.7505
	KNN	0.8356	0.6903	0.6801	0.6852
	CNN	0.8826	0.8234	0.7638	0.7925
EEG windows after feature extraction	SVM	0.8857	0.8102	0.7800	0.7948
	BP	0.9009	0.8195	0.8058	0.8126
	KNN	0.8543	0.7076	0.7293	0.7183
	CNN	0.9159	0.8586	0.8326	0.8454

As shown in Table 2, the comparison results of the various evaluation indicators between the proposed network and other classifiers show that without the feature extraction method we proposed, the convolutional neural network proposed by us has improved on Accuracy, F1 value and other indexes on model prediction compared with other classifiers. It verifies that our network has certain advantages over traditional machine learning classification algorithms and BP neural networks, which is mainly attributed to the fact that CNN can effectively learn the corresponding features from a large number of samples. After adding our feature extraction method, the prediction effect of each network and classifier has increased, which proves that our feature extraction method has a positive effect on the epileptic seizure prediction task. The results show that, compared with other methods, our model has higher Accuracy, Recall, Precision and F1-score after the feature extraction method of EMD decomposition and entropy is added. The feature extraction method we proposed effectively classifies the preictal and interictal epilepsy EEG signals.

4 Conclusion

The purpose of our research is to propose an epileptic seizure prediction model which can automatically detect the preictal and interictal period of EEG signals through technical means, so as to improve the diagnostic ability of epilepsy.This paper puts forward a feature extraction method that combines time-frequency analysis and nonlinear analysis. The EMD decomposition method is used to analyze the time-frequency domain characteristics of EEG signals. On the other hand, considering that the brain is a nonlinear dynamic system, it combines the nonlinear analysis method of EEG signals. Finally, the convolutional neural network is used to classify and predict epileptic EEG signals. The epileptic seizure prediction model has obtained good results on the EEG dataset of Boston Children's Hospital. Predicting epileptic seizures can give doctors and patients a buffer time so that they can fully prepare before the onset of epileptic seizures, treat epilepsy more effectively, and help to relieve the pain of patients during seizures.

References

1. WHO (2018) WHO report. http://www.who.int/mediacentre/factsheets/fs999/en/
2. Yuan, Q., Zhou, W., Zhang, L., et al.: Epileptic seizure detection based on imbalanced classification and wavelet packet transform. Seizure **50**, 99 (2017)
3. Hu, X., Yuan, S., Xu, F., et al.: Scalp EEG classification using deep Bi-LSTM network for seizure detection. Comput. Biol. Med. **124**, 103919 (2020)
4. Fasil, O.K., Rajesh, R.: Time-domain exponential energy for epileptic EEG signal classification. Neurosci. Lett. **694**, 1–8 (2018)
5. Hopfengärtner, R., Kerling, F., Bauer, V., Stefan, H.: An efficient, robust and fast method for the offline detection of epileptic seizures in long-term scalp EEG recordings. Clin. Neurophysiol. **118**, 2332–2343 (2007)
6. Navakatikyan, M.A., Colditz, P.B., Burke, C.J., et al.: Seizure detection algorithm for neonates based on wave-sequence analysis. Clin. Neurophysiol. **117**(6), 1190–1203 (2006)
7. Srirangan, M., Tripathy, R.K., Pachori, R.B.: Time-frequency domain deep convolutional neural network for the classification of focal and non-focal EEG signals. IEEE Sensors J. **20**, 3078–3086 (2019)
8. Ali, K.N., Sadiq, A.: A new feature for the classification of non-stationary signals based on the direction of signal energy in the time-frequency domain. Comput. Biol. Med. **100**, 10 (2018)
9. Maska, B., Saac, D., Mrh, E.: Analysis of variations of correlation dimension and nonlinear interdependence for the prediction of pediatric myoclonic seizures - a preliminary study. Epilepsy Res. **135**, 102–114 (2017)
10. Świderski, B., Osowski, S., Cichocki, A., Rysz, A.: Epileptic seizure prediction using Lyapunov exponents and support vector machine. In: Beliczynski, B., Dzielinski, A., Iwanowski, M., Ribeiro, B. (eds.) ICANNGA 2007. LNCS, vol. 4432, pp. 373–381. Springer, Heidelberg (2007). https://doi.org/10.1007/978-3-540-71629-7_42
11. Swiderski, B., Osowski, S., Rysz, A.: Lyapunov exponent of EEG signal for epileptic seizure characterization. In: Proceedings of the 2005 European Conference on Circuit Theory and Design. IEEE (2005)
12. Kannathal, N., Min, L.C., Acharya, U.R., et al.: Entropies for detection of epilepsy in EEG. Comput. Methods Programs Biomed. **80**(3), 187–194 (2005)
13. You, S., Cho, B.H., Yook, S., et al.: Unsupervised automatic seizure detection for focal-onset seizures recorded with behind-the-ear EEG using an anomaly-detecting generative adversarial network. Comput. Methods Programs Biomed. **193**, 105472 (2020)
14. Abbasi, M.U., Rashad, A., Basalamah, A., et al.: Detection of epilepsy seizures in neo-natal EEG using LSTM architecture. IEEE Access **7**, 179074–179085 (2019)
15. Acharya, U.R., Adeli, H., et al.: Deep convolutional neural network for the automated detection and diagnosis of seizure using EEG signals. Comput. Biol. Med. **100**, 270–278 (2018)
16. Shoeb, A.: Application of machine learning to epileptic seizure onset detection and treatment. Ph.D. thesis, Massachusetts Institute of Technology, September 2009
17. Goldberger, A.L., et al.: PhysioBank, PhysioToolkit, and PhysioNet: components of a new research resource for complex physiologic signals. Circulation **101**(23), e215–e220 (2000). Circulation Electronic Pages; http://circ.ahajournals.org/cgi/content/full/101/23/e215

18. Huang, N.E., Shen, Z., Long, S.R., et al.: The empirical mode decomposition and the Hilbert spectrum for nonlinear and non-stationary time series analysis. Proc. Math. Phys. Eng. Sci. **454**(1971), 903–995 (1998)
19. Zagoruyko, S., Komodakis, N.: Learning to compare image patches via convolutional neural networks. In: 2015 IEEE Conference on Computer Vision and Pattern Recognition (CVPR). IEEE (2015)
20. Johnson, R., Tong, Z.: Effective use of word order for text categorization with convolutional neural networks. Eprint Arxiv (2014)
21. Truong, N.D., Nguyen, A.D., Kuhlmann, L., et al.: Convolutional neural networks for seizure prediction using intracranial and scalp electroencephalogram. Neural Netw. **105**, 104–111 (2018). S0893608018301485

TSC-MI: A Temporal Spatial Convolution Neural Network Fused with Mutual Information for Motor Imagery Based EEG Classification

Yonghao Ren[1,2], Shuo Zhang[1,2], Jing Wang[1,2], and Runzhi Li[2](✉)

[1] School of Information Engineering, Zhengzhou University, Zhengzhou 450000, China
[2] Cooperative Innovation Center of Internet Healthcare, Zhengzhou University, Zhengzhou 450000, China
rzli@ha.edu.cn

Abstract. Electroencephalography (EEG) classification is an important part in brain-computer interface system. Motor imagery is a novel experimental paradigm that has been proved effective clinically in recognizing EEG from different limb motions. Our object is to finish motor imagery based EEG classification. Due to EEG signals followed by some features, e.g. noisy, weak signal, personalization and so on, traditional methods could encounter limit from the single feature extraction. In this work, we propose a multi-scale spatio-temporal features fusion deep learning model. Given raw EEG signals, we calculate mutual information matrix among different channels. It incorporates spatio-temporal feature extraction and mutual information matrix. We deploy experiments on two datasets that consists of the High Gamma Dataset and BCI IV 2A dataset. Experiment results show that the proposed temporal spatial convolution neural network fused with mutual information model outperform other methods.

Keywords: Motor imagery (MI) · EEG classification · Deep learning · Feature fusion

1 Introduction

Brain-computer interface (BCI) technology provides a new way to communicate between human and external devices by recognizing brain activity. It is helpful for patients who suffers severe dyskinesia, in which BCI system collects EEG signals and makes the EEG analysis and recognition from different limbs movement, and then controls external devices to assist limbs motion. For example, robotic arms and intelligent rehabilitation robot both are external devices that combine with BCI systems are applied in the field of rehabilitation [1]. It plays an important role for EEG recognition and classification in BCI systems. Motor imagery (MI) is a novel technology to be proved effective clinically in recognizing EEG from different limb motions. It means one imagines limb movements instead of actual limb movements. They have the same mechanism of action, but there is a difference in the level of muscle activation. MI produces frequency band disturbances

M. Mahmud et al. (Eds.): BI 2021, LNAI 12960, pp. 474–485, 2021.
https://doi.org/10.1007/978-3-030-86993-9_42

of μ and β rhythms when a subject imagines one limb moving. This event is called event-related desynchronization (ERD) or event-related synchronization (ERS) phenomenon [2]. In this work, we target at MI based EEG recognition and classification. It is a big challenge to finish accurate EEG recognition efficiently due to the characters of EEG signals, high signal-to-noise ratio, individualization and so on. Due to different MI tasks has different activation regions of the cerebral cortex, it forms the time-frequency domain and spatial features for MI based EEG signals. They are distinguishable. Limited by the single feature extraction, the classification performance of some related works is not ideal. Our object is to classification MI based EEG signals by extracting the spatial-time-frequency characteristics.

Based on our previous study [3], we propose a temporal spatial convolution neural network fused with mutual information (TSC-MINet) for MI based EEG recognition. For multiple channel EEG collecting, mutual information among channels reflects the whole relation for EEG signals between different channels that is a supplement to extract fully the spatio-temporal features. It consists of three core blocks. TS-Conv block extracts spatio-temporal features, DT-Conv block extracts high-level temporal features. Finally, CC-Conv block is a Channel Correlation Conv block that captures correlation features from channel mutual information matrix.

The main contributions of this paper are as follows:

(a) We propose a multi-features fusion framework that improves the spatial-time-frequency characteristics extraction to recognize MI based EEG signals.
(b) DT-Conv block is presented to extract the high-level temporal features from spatio-temporal mixed features.
(c) We design CC-Conv block calculate the mutual information features as a supplement for extracting spatial features.

The remaining part of this paper is structured as follows. Section 2 introduces related research. Section 3 gives the model framework. Section 4 describes the data processing and experimental settings. Section 5 shows the results and discussion. Finally, conclusion and future directions are provided in Sect. 6.

2 Related Work

Due to the low signal-to-noise ratio (SNR) of EEG, there are a lot of unavoidable biological noises, such as blinking (EOG), electrocardiogram (ECG), muscle movement (EMG), swallowing or power line noise interference [4]. The decoding and classification of MI based EEG is still challenging. Traditional methods extract EEG features manually based on expert experience, such as common spatial pattern algorithm (CSP) [5] and filter bank common spatial pattern (FBCSP) [6], Riemannian covariance [7], etc. Then the features used to train classifiers, such as decision trees [8], support vector machine [9] (SVMs) for the classification tasks. However, these methods ignore the further mining of EEG temporal information after extracting features.

Recently, convolutional neural networks have gained widespread attention in the fields of speech recognition and computer vision. It reduces the steps of data preprocessing and does not require manual feature extraction. Bashivan et al. employed Fast

Fourier transform (FFT) to convert the EEG recordings divided by the sliding window into 2-D images [10], and then used long short-term memory (LSTM) and ConvNets to classify the image sequence. Furthermore, B. Lei et al. extracted time-frequency features through CSP, and then classified them through deep polynomial network (DPN) [11]. Inspired by FBCSP, Schirrmeister et al. [12] proposed multiple depth convolutional networks for MI classification. The performance of ShallowConvNet is better than FBCSP. However, the increase of ConvNet depth will exacerbate gradient disappearance, and increase the parameters to be tuned. Therefore, the model performs poorly in many cases. Wang et al. combined CNN with LSTM and achieved an average kappa value of 0.64 on BCI IV 2a dataset [13]. At the cost of a large number of parameters, the performance is not ideal. In addition, insufficient mining of spatio-temporal information results in the suboptimal performance of these methods.

To tackle the above obstacles, in this paper, we proposed a temporal spatial convolution neural network fused with mutual information to improve the MI based EEG signals decoding accuracy further.

3 Method

3.1 Temporal Spatial Convolution Neural Network Fused with Mutual Information

In this work, we propose a novel Temporal spatial convolution neural network fused with mutual information (TSC-MINet) to finish MI based EEG classification. It contains three core blocks: TS-Conv block, DT-Conv block and CC-Conv block. The architecture chart is shown in Fig. 1. We extract features from the raw EEG signals. Firstly, TS-Conv block extracts the spatio-temporal mixed representation from multi-channel EEG signals. Then DT-Conv block further captures the deep temporal features. Simultaneously, CC-Conv block digs the channel correlation features from the channel mutual information matrix. They are regard as a supplement to the spatial features. Multi-scale spatio-temporal features are generated through feature fusion for the MI based EEG classification.

TS-Conv Block. As Shown in Fig. 1(a), It Consists of One 2D Temporal Convolution Layer of 8 Kernels, One Spatial Convolution of 16 Kernels, One 2D Average Pooling Layer of 16 Kernels and One Batch Normalization (BN). In Addition, We Use the Exponential Linear Unit (ELU) Inspired by Reference [14] as the Activation Function and Dropout Operation.

First, the EEG trail with the shape of $(C, T, 1)$ is fed into the first 2D temporal convolution layers with 8 layers of size $(1, 64)$ to learn the temporal features solely along the time axis, its padding strategy is "same". C indicates the number of channels, T is the number of total sampling points. In this work, EEG signals produced in 0.25 s could be regarded as quasi-stationary signals [15]. Next, we set the spatial convolutional layer with 16 kernels of size $(C, 1)$ without padding. It performs a convolution along the electrodes axis to obtain mixed spatio-temporal feature maps. The BN layers are applied to make the feature maps normally distributed after all the convolutional layers. We employ average pooling of 16 kernels with the pooling size of 8×1 to reduce the length of outputs in the temporal dimension. Furthermore, we use an ELU activation function after the second BN layer. Finally, the dropout operation (dropout rate = 0.2) is used to simplify the calculation and reduce overfitting.

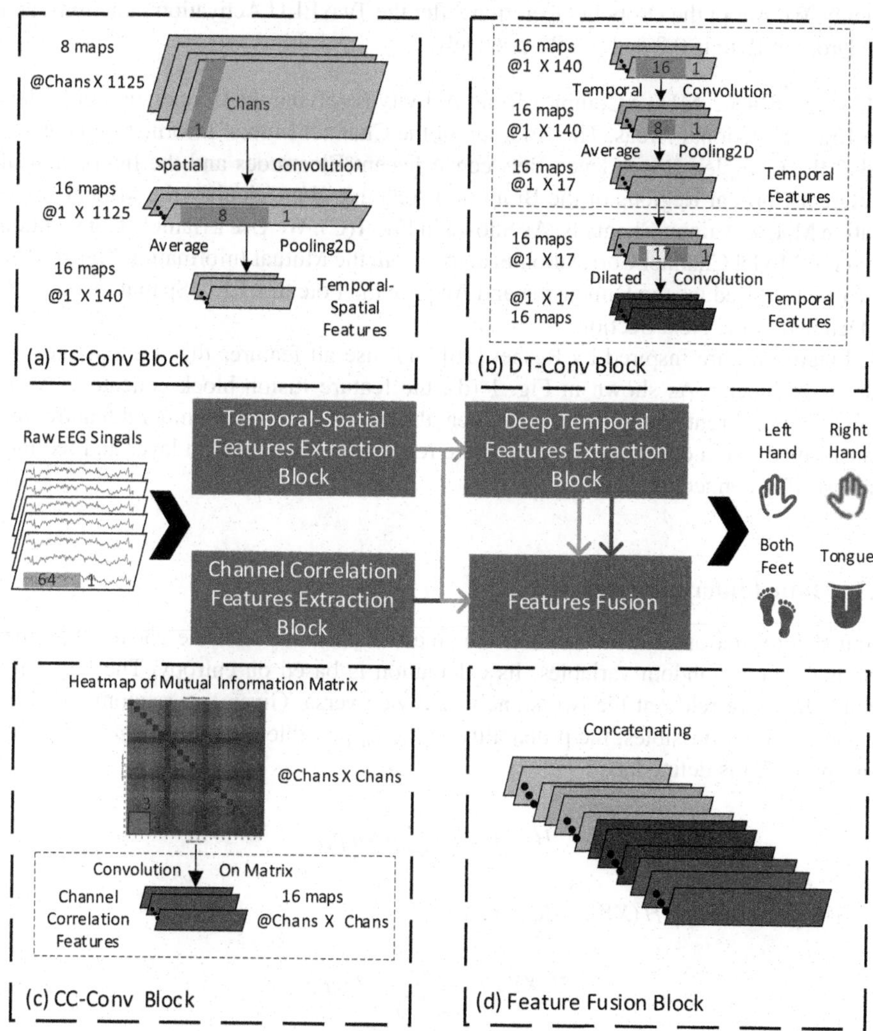

Fig. 1. The schematic of TSC-MINet architecture.

DT-Conv Block. Behind of the Spatio-Temporal Features Extraction from TS-Conv Block, Followed by DT-Conv Block that Extracts Advanced Temporal Features. It is Illustrated in Fig. 1 (B). It Consists of One Temporal Convolution Layer of 16 Kernels with Size of 1×16, One 2D Average Pooling Layer of 16 Layers with Size of 1×8, and One Dilated Convolution Layer. Due to Different Size of Convolution Kernels, This Temporal Convolution Layer Would Extract Different Scale Temporal Features from Spatio-Temporal Features Furtherly. The Output is 16 Feature Maps with Size of 1×140. We Use One Average Pooling Layer to Reduce the Length of Outputs. Thus, the

Size of One Output is 1×17. Next, We Use Dilated Convolution with Size of 1×17 to Extract the Temporal Information Implicit in the Upper Layer Further, and Dilation Rate is 2. We Insert BN Layer and ELU Activation Function After Each Convolutional Layer. Finally, We Adopt the Dropout Operation After the Two ELU Activation Functions, and the Dropout Rate is 0.2 and 0.3 Respectively.

CC-Conv Block. MI is a Complex Brain Activity Involving the Cooperation of Different Brain Functional Areas. The Addition of the Channel Mutual Information Features Takes the Complex Dependence Between Adjacent Electrodes and the Interaction of Different Cortical Regions of the Brain into Account. We Calculate the Mutual Information Matrix Among Channels. As Shown in Fig. 1(C), We Use a Sample Convolution Layer to Model Channel Correlation Features from the Mutual Information Matrix. The Purpose is to Reduce the Dimension and Acquire the Potential EEG Spatial Features. It is Detailed in the Next Section.

Finally, we are inspired by Resnet [16] and fuse all features that are extracted by the above blocks. As shown in Fig. 1 (d), the feature fusion block concatenates the above four different features together. Then, the multiscale spatio-temporal features are transformed into a one-dimensional feature representation by flatten layer and fed into the last fully connected layer.

3.2 Mutual Information Matrix

Mutual information is a measurement of the fact that one variable carries the other variable in two random variables. Its calculation is based on entropy. The larger the value, the more relevant the two signals, and vice versa. Given two random variables X and Y with n possibles, the probability of the i_{th} possible x_i in X is $p_i(p_i \geq 0)$. The entropy $H(X)$ is defined as:

$$H(X) = -\sum_{i=1}^{n} p_i logp_i \tag{1}$$

The joint entropy $H(XY)$ is defined as:

$$H(XY) = -\sum_{i,j=1}^{n} p_{ij} logp_{ij} \tag{2}$$

Then the mutual information $I(XY)$ is defined as:

$$I(XY) = H(X) + H(Y) - H(XY) \tag{3}$$

In this work, for an EEG signal trail $E = \{(E(t)_i), i = 1, 2, \cdots C\} \in \mathbb{R}^{C \times T}$, we calculate a mutual information matrix $m = \{(m_{ij}), i = 1, 2, \cdots C; j = 1, 2, \cdots, C\} \in \mathbb{M}^{C \times C}$. Where $E(t)_i$ is the signal from i-th electrode of$E$, and m_{ij} is the mutual information between $E(t)_i$ and $E(t)_j$. Thus, the mutual information matrix is an $C \times C$ upper triangle. It indicates the mutual info among different from different channels. Algorithm 1 gives the procedures. The heat map of the mutual information matrix is shown in Fig. 2.

Algorithm 1 Steps of Generating the Mutual Information Matrix

Input: E ;
Output: mutual information matrix m;
for i=1, 2, …, C **do**
  for j=1, 2, …, C **do**
    denoting the signal from i-th electrode of E as $E(t)_i$;
    denoting the signal from j-th electrode of E as $E(t)_j$;
    calculating mutual information $I(E(t)_j, E(t)_j)$ *of* $E(t)_i$ and $E(t)_j$ by (3) and $m_{ij}= I(E(t)_j, E(t)_j)$;
  end
end
return the mutual information matrix m_{ij};

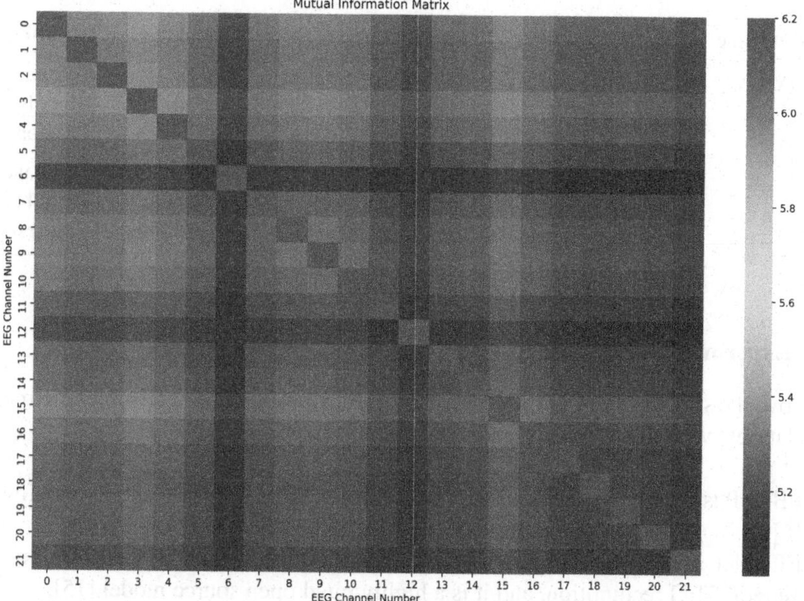

Fig. 2. The heatmap of mutual information matrix.

4 Experiments

4.1 Dataset and Implementation

We evaluate the effectiveness of our proposed model on two public datasets. The first BCI IV 2A dataset contains EEG recordings obtained from 9 healthy subjects over two sessions of two days, and the second HGD dataset is obtained from 14 subjects. The electrodes of two datasets are configured according to the international 10–20 system. The differences between the two datasets are shown in Table 1.

In BCI IV 2A dataset, three electrooculography (EOG) channels provide eye movement information. Based on the rules of BCI Competition IV-2a, we employ the dataset without EOG data. We adopt extra preprocessing: bandpass filtered between 8 Hz and 38 Hz, unify the test set and training set by normalization. We use the common fragments of [0.5,5] s (post-cue), and expand the dimensions of the fragments for 2D convolution. The final shape of each trail is (22,1125,1).

In HGD dataset, we randomly select 20% of the training set data as the validation set. In order to improve computing efficiency, we only employ 44 electrodes with a high correlation to the motor imagery tasks [19]. The detailed electrodes can be seen in [19]. We resample the signals to 250 Hz. For a fair comparison with the BCI IV 2A Dataset, 4.5 s fragments are also selected for each sample. The preprocessing is same as the BCI IV 2A Dataset. Here the final shape is (44,1125,1).

Table 1. Details of two datasets

Dataset name	Electrode numbers	Raw trail numbers	Sample rate	MI tasks
BCI IV 2A	22	288 (train) 288 (test)	250 Hz	Left hand Right hand Feet tongue
HGD	128	880 (train) 160 (test)	500 Hz	Left hand Right hand Feet rest

4.2 Experiment Setup

To prove the superiority of our model, we conduct an overall comparison experiment on two datasets with the following methods:

1) FBCSP is a widely used baseline algorithm for MI based EEG signal classification [6].
2) EEGNet is a universal and compact convolutional neural network designed for general EEG recognition, and it is a highly-cited open source model [15].
3) DeepConvNet [12] is a deep learning model with outstanding performance in a number of motor imagery datasets.
4) MI-EEGNet [20], an improved EEGNet based on the Mobile inception structure. To the best of our knowledge, the MI-EEGNet is the state-of-the-art deep learning model on HGD datasets.
Then ablation comparison was performed between Baseline, TSCNet, and TSC-MINet to verify the influence of DT-Conv block and CC-Conv block. The structure of Baseline and TSCNet is as follows:
5) Baseline is constructed without the deep temporal features extraction block and channel correlation features extraction block from TSC-MINet.
6) TSCNet drops the channel correlation features extraction block from TSC-MINet.

Models are trained and tested on a NVIDIA RTX 3090 GPU with a tensorflow environment. We use the cross-entropy loss function, employ Adam optimizer [17] to optimize the models with initial learning rate of 0.001, and adopt softmax function as classifier [18]. The models are trained for 750 epochs and a batch size of 64. In addition, we leverage grid-search and cross-validation algorithms to optimize the hyperparameters.

4.3 Metrics

In the experiments, we select Cohen's kappa coefficient (κ) [21] and accuracy (Acc) as performance metrics. They are defined as follows:

$$Acc = \frac{TP+TN}{TP+FP+TN+FN} \tag{4}$$

$$\kappa = \frac{Acc-Acc_{rand}}{1-Acc_{rand}} \tag{5}$$

where TP, FP, TN, FN represent true positive, false positive, true negative, false positive, and false negative, respectively. Acc_{rand} is the accuracy of random guessing.

5 Results and Discussion

5.1 Overall Comparison

Table 2 and Table 3 summarize the accuracy and kappa value of our proposed model. The overall comparison results derived by FBCSP, EEGNet, DeepConvNet, MI-EEGNet, TSC-Net, and TSC-MINet on two public datasets are summarized in Table 4. It appears that MI-EEGNet achieves an accuracy of 76.79% on the BCI IV 2A dataset. Especially, the proposed TSC-MINet achieves the highest accuracy of 79.03%, which is 2.24% higher than MI-EEGNet. In order to verify the robustness of our proposed model, we further evaluate these methods on HGD dataset. TSC-MINet obtains the best performance of 94.97% brought by the robust representation ability of spatio-temporal EEG. We adopt t-SNE [22] to display the features extracted by MI-EEGNet in the 2-D embedding space, which aims to demonstrate the high separability (Fig. 3). Experimental results prove that the outstanding capability of the proposed TSC-MINet for classifying MI based EEG signals.

5.2 Ablation Study

To study the impact of DT-Conv block and CC-Conv block, we build an ablation study on BCI IV 2A DATASET. Table 5 exhibits TSCNet outperforms Baseline. Due to DT-Conv block, TSCNet gains 6.52% higher accuracy and 0.1 higher kappa value than Baseline. Moreover, the accuracy of TSC-MINet further increases 1.93% benefit from the employer of CC-Conv block. With the addition of above blocks, TSC-MINet has increased by 0.12 average kappa value than Baseline. These results revalidate that DT-Conv block and CC-Conv block could indeed improve EEG classification performance.

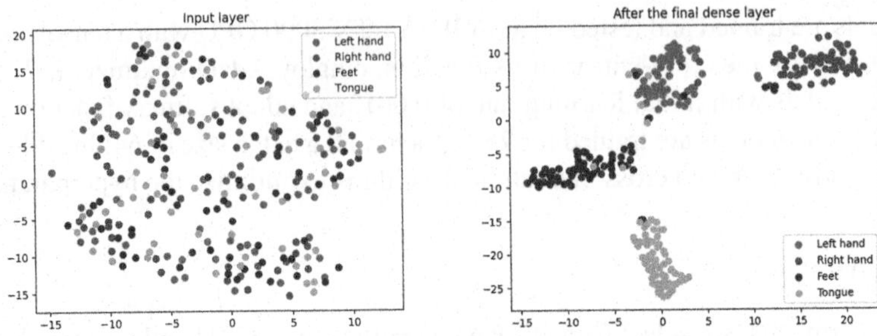

Fig. 3. t-SNE feature visualization of TSC-MINet on subject3 of BCI IV 2A.

Table 2. Classification accuracy (%) and kappa value on BCI IV 2A

Subject	S1	S2	S3	S4	S5	S6
Acc (%)	87.19	66.43	92.31	72.81	76.09	63.26
Kappa	0.85	0.55	0.90	0.66	0.68	0.51
Subject	S7	S8	S9	Mean	Std	
Acc (%)	89.53	84.13	79.55	79.03	9.62	
Kappa	0.86	0.79	0.73	0.73	0.13	

Table 3. Classification accuracy (%) and kappa value on hgd dataset

Subject	S1	S2	S3	S4	S5	S6	S7	S8
Acc (%)	93.75	95.63	99.38	98.13	97.50	92.50	93.71	93.13
Kappa	0.92	0.94	0.99	0.97	0.96	0.90	0.91	0.91
Subject	S9	S10	S11	S12	S13	S14	Mean	Std
Acc (%)	95.63	91.25	94.38	95.00	92.45	97.16	94.97	2.28
Kappa	0.94	0.89	0.93	0.93	0.90	0.96	0.93	0.03

5.3 Discussion

Compared with such well-known methods, our method seems to be ahead in the task of classification for MI based EEG signals. Ablation study demonstrates DT-Conv block could significantly improve performance. Baseline model can only extract spatio-temporal information within one scale, while DT-Conv block could capture different scale temporal information for feature fusion. It can be seen from Table 5 that with the addition of CC-Conv block, the average classification accuracy has increased by 1.93% Because the channel correlation features extracted from the channel mutual information matrix can be used as a supplement to the EEG spatial features. Thus, the model could learn multi-scale spatial features.

Our proposed approach has excellent performance compared to other methods on the two public datasets. However, in Table 2 and 3, TSC-MINet has a large difference in

Table 4. The overall comparison of classification performance

Method	Acc (%) on BCI IV 2A	Acc (%) on HGD
FBCSP	67.81	90.87
EEGNet	72.46	87.81
DeepConNet	70.91	91.40
MI-EEGNet	76.79	92.49
TSCNet	76.90	93.11
TSC-MINet	**79.03**	**94.97**

Table 5. Ablation study of our method on BCI IV 2A dataset

Subject	Baseline	TSCNet	TSC-MINet
S1	80.78 (0.75)	83.63 (0.81)	87.19 (0.85)
S2	53.71 (0.39)	64.31 (0.53)	66.43 (0.55)
S3	88.01 (0.84)	90.84 (0.88)	92.31 (0.90)
S4	63.16 (0.52)	68.86 (0.63)	72.81 (0.66)
S5	67.41 (0.57)	75.36 (0.66)	76.09 (0.68)
S6	53.95 (0.39)	61.39 (0.50)	63.26 (0.51)
S7	77.26 (0.70)	87.72 (0.84)	89.53 (0.86)
S8	76.73 (0.69)	83.03 (0.77)	84.13 (0.79)
S9	74.19 (0.65)	78.79 (0.73)	79.55 (0.73)
Average	70.58 (0.61)	77.10 (0.71)	**79.03 (0.73)**

classification performance on BCI IV 2A and HGD dataset. The average classification accuracy of 94.97% on HGD dataset is significantly higher than 79.03% on BCI IV 2A. On the one hand, it is due to the strong feature representation of our model. On the other hand, the quality and quantity of the dataset have a great impact on the motor imagery classification model. Compared with BCI IV 2A, per subject owns more EEG trails with higher data quality in HGD dataset. Besides, the motor imagery task in HGD is left and right hands, feet and rest, while the task of BCI IV 2A is left and right hands, feet and tongue. From Fig. 3, model confuses between left-hand and right-hand MIs and between tongue and feet MIs. The hand MIs generate ERD/ERS patterns which are different from them generated by feet and tongue MIs. The ERD/ERS patterns produced by tongue MIs are easily confused with feet MIs, and the rest state does not produce ERD/ERS. The above elaboration is consistent with previous research [23].

6 Conclusion and Future Directions

Temporal information and spatial information are critical to EEG signals classification. In this paper, we propose a novel neural network named TSC-MINet. TS-Conv block extracts the spatio-temporal mixed representation from multi-channel EEG signals. Then DT-Conv block further captures the deep temporal features. Simultaneously, CC-Conv block digs the channel correlation features from the channel mutual information matrix. They are regard as a supplement to the spatial features. Multi-scale spatio-temporal features are generated through feature fusion. The experimental results show that our proposed approach outperforms other methods. Therefore, the proposed approach can be regarded as a promising tool to improve the performance of MI based BCIs. However, the limitation is still involved in the current work. We only use simple dimensionality reduction to extract channel mutual information features from the channel mutual information matrix, and we lack the exploration of the interpretability of the model. Future work will consider better methods of extracting mutual information features and explore the mechanism of mutual information features to strengthen the classification performance of motor imagery.

Acknowledgements. This work was supported in part by the China Education and Research Network (CERNET) Innovation Project under Grant NGII20180708; and in part by the Program of Scientific and Technological Research of Henan Province under Contract 192102310215; and in part by the Key Science & Research Program of Henan Province under Grant 21A520044 (Corresponding author: Runzhi Li).

References

1. Ang, K.K., Guan, C.: EEG-based strategies to detect motor imagery for control and rehabilitation. IEEE Trans. Neural Syst. Rehabil. Eng. **25**(4), 392–401 (2016)
2. Jahanshahi, M., Hallett, M.: The Bereitschaftspotential || Movement and ERD/ERS. https://doi.org/10.1007/978-1-4615-0189-3. Chapter 12(2003):191–206.
3. Yang, P., et al.: MLP With riemannian covariance for motor imagery based EEG analysis. IEEE Access **8**, 139974–139982 (2020)
4. Tandle, A., Jog, N.: Classification of artefacts in EEG signal recordings and overview of removing techniques. Int. J. Comput. Appl. **975**, 8887 (2015)
5. Blankertz, B., et al.: Optimizing spatial filters for robust EEG single-trial analysis. IEEE Signal Process. Mag. **25**(1), 41–56 (2007)
6. Ang, K.K., et al.: Filter bank common spatial pattern algorithm on BCI competition IV datasets 2a and 2b. Front. Neurosci. **6**, 39 (2012)
7. Barachant, A., et al.: BCI signal classification using a Riemannian-based kernel. In: 20th European Symposium on Artificial Neural Networks, Computational Intelligence and Machine Learning (ESANN 2012), Michel Verleysen (2012)
8. Min, S., Lee, B., Yoon, S.: Deep learning in bioinformatics. Brief. Bioinformat. **18**(5), 851–869 (2017)
9. Lotte, F., et al.: A review of classification algorithms for EEG-based brain–computer interfaces: a 10 year update. J. Neural Eng. **15**(3), 031005 (2018)
10. Bashivan, P., et al.: Learning representations from EEG with deep recurrent-convolutional neural networks. *arXiv preprint* arXiv:1511.06448 (2015)

11. Lei, B., et al.: Walking imagery evaluation in brain computer interfaces via a multi-view multi-level deep polynomial network. IEEE Trans. Neural Syst. Rehabil. Eng. **27**(3), 497–506 (2019)
12. Schirrmeister, R.T., et al.: Deep learning with convolutional neural networks for EEG decoding and visualization. Hum. Brain Mapping **38**(11), 5391–5420 (2017)
13. Wang, L., et al.: Temporal-spatial-frequency depth extraction of brain-computer interface based on mental tasks. Biomed. Signal Process. Control **58**, 101845 (2020)
14. Clevert, D.-A., Unterthiner, T., Hochreiter, S.: Fast and accurate deep network learning by exponential linear units (elus). *arXiv preprint* arXiv:1511.07289 (2015)
15. Lawhern, V.J., et al.: EEGNet: a compact convolutional neural network for EEG-based brain–computer interfaces. J. Neural Eng. **15**(5), 056013 (2018)
16. He, K., et al.: Deep residual learning for image recognition. In: Proceedings of the IEEE Conference on Computer Vision and Pattern Recognition (2016)
17. Kingma, D.P., Ba, J.: Adam: a method for stochastic optimization. *arXiv preprint* arXiv:1412. 6980 (2014)
18. Hopfield, J.J., Tank, D.W.: "Neural" computation of decisions in optimization problems. Biol. Cybernet. **52**(3), 141–152 (1985)
19. Schirrmeister, R.T., et al.: Deep learning with convolutional neural networks for EEG decoding and visualization. Hum. Brain Mapp. **38**(11), 5391–5420 (2017)
20. Riyad, M., Khalil, M., Adib, A.: MI-EEGNET: a novel convolutional neural network for motor imagery classification. J. Neurosci. Methods **353**, 109037 (2021)
21. Carletta, J.: Assessing agreement on classification tasks: the kappa statistic. *arXiv preprint cmp-lg/9602004* (1996)
22. Van Der Maaten, L.: Accelerating t-SNE using tree-based algorithms. J. Mach. Learn. Res. **15**(1), 3221–3245 (2014)
23. Pfurtscheller, G., et al.: Mu rhythm (de) synchronization and EEG single-trial classification of different motor imagery tasks. Neuroimage **31**(1), 153–159 (2006)

A Novel Approach Towards Early Detection of Alzheimer's Disease Using Deep Learning on Magnetic Resonance Images

Kushpal Singh Yadav and Krishna Prasad Miyapuram(✉)

Indian Institute of Technology Gandhinagar, Gujarat, India
kprasad@iitgn.ac.in

Abstract. Magnetic Resonance Imaging (MRI) is used extensively for the diagnosis of Alzheimer's Disease (AD). Early detection of AD can help people with early intervention and alleviate the progression of disease symptoms. Previous studies have applied deep learning methods for computer-aided diagnosis of AD. In this present study, an efficient architecture has been proposed, composed of a 2D Convolutional neural network with batch normalization for the classification of AD using MRI images. The proposed model was created using 11 layers, which was obtained by experimenting with different combinations of batch normalization and activation functions. All the experiments are performed using the Alzheimer Disease Neuroimaging Initiative (ADNI) data. The novelty of our approach was that different slices of the brain, such as axial, coronal, and sagittal, were used to classify brain slices into three classes: *Cognitively Normal (NC), Mild Cognitive Impairment (MCI), and AD.* The proposed model achieved a sensitivity (SEN) of 99.73% for NC, 99.79% for MCI, and 99.96% for AD, a specificity (SPE) of 99.80% for NC, 99.90% for MCI, and 99.74% for AD, and accuracy of 99.82%. The contribution of our proposed method's classification accuracy was better than that of the recent state-of-the-art methods.

Keywords: Deep learning · MRI · Alzheimer's disease · ADNI · Batch normalization · 2D CNN

1 Introduction

Alzheimer's Disease (AD) is the most common dementia among older people. Early diagnosis of AD is essential and helps in devising intervention strategies that could delay the disease progression. The latest developments in the field of computer vision have inspired researchers to use deep learning methods for medical imaging, primarily due to the complexity involved in analyzing these images [12]. Deep learning not only focusses on finding the hidden patterns in brain images for diagnosis of AD but can also be informative about the role

M. Mahmud et al. (Eds.): BI 2021, LNAI 12960, pp. 486–495, 2021.
https://doi.org/10.1007/978-3-030-86993-9_43

played by different regions of the brain [2]. Convolutional neural networks (CNN) is a specific type of artificial neural network which is inspired by the human brains. CNN uses a series of filters and tries to automatically identify patterns that are essential features of the image identified by the weights and biases amongst different layers of the neural network. The Authors used to capture the anatomical shape variations in structural brain MRI by using 3D CNN which they claimed that it can be used to diagnose AD and achieved 94.80% accuracy for classification of AD [6]. Nevertheless, the problem is that the 3D CNN relies on high dimensional data. With fewer examples for training and testing, 3D CNN is not viable. So we proposed a novel 2D CNN architecture, which learns from the 2D slices comprising of sagittal plane of the brain. The proposed 2D CNN model thus uses data augmentation by multiple slices of the brain to handle the 3D brain images. The proposed architecture balances the learning ability and parameter-efficiency (fewer parameters) of the model. The performance of the model is examined using sensitivity (SEN), specificity (SPE), and F1-score to compare the proposed model against seven other models as benchmarks in the classification.

2 Related Work

Deep learning methods have been successfully applied for computer-aided diagnosis of AD by using medical images with different modalities [14,16]. For example, in [6], the authors used 3D-CNN, which built upon a 3D convolutional autoencoder. Further, the model was pre-trained to capture anatomical shape variations in ventricles size, hippocampus shape, cortical thickness, and brain volume. Gupta et al. [4] employed 2D Convolutional Neural Network (CNN) for the slice-wise feature extraction of MRI scans. The authors used a sparse autoencoder (SAE) to train CNN, which results in an enhancement in the classification performance. Kloppel et al. [10] used the gray matter (GM) voxels as features and trained an SVM to discriminate between the AD and cognitively normal (NC) subjects. In [10] and [18], the authors used stacked autoencoder for AD/MCI diagnosis. Payan et al. [15] proposed a 3D Convolutional Neural Network for AD diagnosis based on pre-training by SAE. Liu et al. [11] used stacked autoencoders to extract high-level features. The authors considered only 83 regions-of-interest (ROI) from MRI and PET scans and used multimodal fusion to create a set of features. Suk et al. [19] proposed a deep learning-based feature representation for AD/MCI classification with a stacked autoencoder. Zhu et al. [20] has shown that identifying brain disease and predicting clinical score are highly related to each other. The authors proposed a joint regression and prediction model for classification of AD/MCI and used Support Vector Regression (SVR) and Support Vector Classification (SVC) to build clinical scores regression models and a clinical label identification model. Billones et al. [1] modified the 16-layered VGGNet deep learning architecture to classify the three classes; NC/MCI/AD and achieved 91.85% accuracy.

3 Dataset

The dataset used in this study has been collected from ADNI database [9]. The selected data are MRI scans of 3 T collected longitudinally at baseline over a period of 3 years obtained at 6 months, 12 months, 24 months, and 36 months. The Dataset includes 21 patients with AD, 22 patients with MCI, and 27 NC patients. The total number of scans of NC patients, including all the months, are 107, for MCI 110, and for AD 86, which makes a total of 303 MRI volumes. The total number of slices after 2D conversion into sagittal, coronal, and axial planes are 27270, 36057, and 31209 of 121 × 145, 121 × 90, and 145 × 90 shape, respectively after discarding the images which do not have any information (Fig. 1).

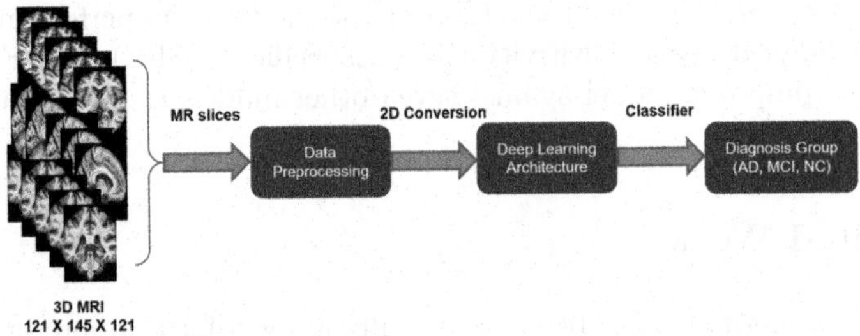

Fig. 1. Classification approach using deep learning

4 Experiments

The 2D CNN proposed model is combined with convolution, max-pooling, dense layer, flatten layer, and batch normalization (Fig. 2). The CNN is used to find a pattern in the images by using filters and updates the weights and biases of the matrix after every epoch while training the model. Max-pooling used for handling the volume size which minimize the size of the image while keeping all the necessary information of the image. A dense layer is used to combine all the features learned from previous convolutional layers where every input weight is directly connected to the output of the next layer in a feed-forward fashion [7]. Batch normalization is used to accelerate the neural network by using internal covariate shift which helps the network in training and also regularizes it [8]. Rectified Linear Unit (ReLu) activation function is used due to its advantage of non-linearity and also back-propagates the errors easily [13]. In the last level of the model, the activation function softmax is used because the model's requirement was to predict only the specific class, which results in highest probability. To find out the loss of the model, categorical cross-entropy is used.

$$H'_y(y) = -\sum_i (y'_i log(y_i) + (1 - y'_i) log(1 - y'_i)) \quad (1)$$

In the above equation, y_i represents the predicted probability and y_i' represents the ground truth probability for class i so the final cross entropy loss function is represented as $H_y'(y)$.

The block diagram of the proposed architecture is shown in (Fig. 2). In this architecture, we have used 13 layers including input and output layers.

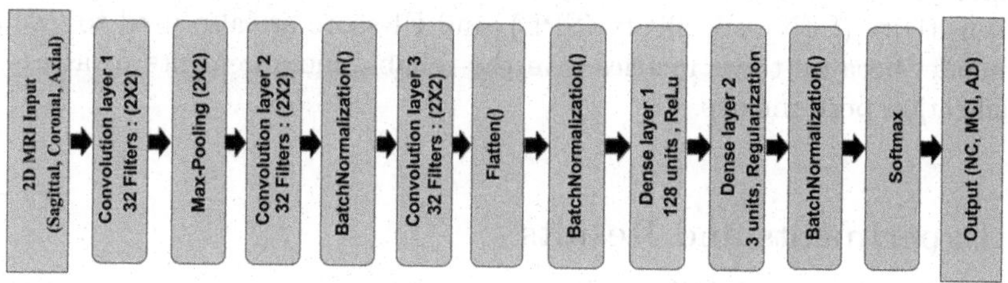

Fig. 2. Block diagram of the proposed architecture

4.1 Network Architecture

In this present study, a well known deep learning architecture ResNet50 used in order to classify AD and also to find out the features of the image. ResNet network architecture is eight times deeper than the older version of the network. The size of the model is substantially smaller due to the use of global average pooling instead of fully connected layers. This reduces the model size down to 102MB for ResNet50. In a ResNet, several layers are stacked, and the network learns several features at the end of its layers.

1. If the input and output dimensions are same then identity which is 'x' can be directly used.

$$y = F(x, \{W_i\}) + x \tag{2}$$

2. If the output and input dimensions are not same, then the identity 'x' still used by padding zero entries and projection method was used to match the dimension. It can be done by 1×1 convolution. We can relate to it by using the following equation.

$$y = F(x, \{W_i\}) + W_s x \tag{3}$$

The first equation does not add any extra parameters in the model but in the second equation some element is added in the form of W_i. Instead of trying to learn some features, it tries to learn some residuals. Residuals can be understood as subtraction of feature learned from the input of that layer. It has been proved that training these type of networks is more natural than training simple deep Convolutional Neural Networks. It also resolves the problem of degrading accuracy [5].

4.2 Evaluation Metric

Here, the evaluation metric plays an important role in order to get the correct result. The dataset contains unequal number of images in all three categories. As the dataset is imbalanced, so we used an accuracy score (ACC) as well as other evaluation metric for the model. In the present study, classes do not have equal number of slices which can lead to a false result if the ACC alone is used; so the sensitivity (SEN), specificity (SPE), and F1-score are also used to evaluate our model because these metrics give the reliable measurements to assess the classification performance.

5 Experiments and Results

5.1 Experimental Setup

In this present study, the dataset is divided into three parts (1) 70% of the dataset is used for training the model, (2) 10% of the training data is used for validating the model, and (3) 30% of the dataset is for testing the model. The trade-off of training and testing proportions of the dataset is as follows: more training data makes the classification model better, and the more test data makes the model more accurate. In this work, all the architectures are trained from scratch on data for 30 epochs with each epoch consisting of 10 batches with the GPU of 4 GB RAM (GTX 1050 Ti). The proposed network architecture is designed in the Keras framework [3] that used ten batches and adam optimizer with a learning rate of 1×10^{-5} to perform all the experiments. All the parameters used in this study are found by hyper-parameter tuning with the accurate stability of the model. The initialization of weights is assigned with some random numbers by using the Keras framework itself (Table 1).

5.2 Cross-Validation

In this work, cross-validation performed to select the deep learning architecture, which can be applied to limited data as well as extensive data and is also used to prevent overfitting and to underfit the model. Initially, when the model was trained on the training data, it has been found that the training accuracy was not getting increased, so to do that, we have applied some different types of architectures. On one of the architecture, we got high training accuracy, but when the model is tested onto the unseen data, then the model performed poorly. After trying all the self-made architectures, we have tried Billones et al. [1] architecture in which we got 92.65% accuracy for classification of all the three classes. When we trained the ResNet50 architecture from scratch, we got 98.30% accuracy on unseen data. From there, we found that the model can be improved then we introduced some new layers to our architecture, which are batch normalization and regularization, so we get the correct model for the classification of AD with different planes of the brain which maintain a good trade-off between training and validation accuracy.

Table 1. The performance of the proposed models

MODEL	CLASS	SEN (%)	SPE (%)	F1-SCORE (%)	ACC (%)
Proposed model with axial slices	NC	90.22	99.30	94.54	94.41
	MCI	97.95	90.74	94.21	
	AD	95.13	93.13	94.54	
Proposed model with coronal slices	NC	97.12	97.20	97.16	97.44
	MCI	98.81	96.66	97.72	
	AD	96.07	98.80	97.41	
ResNet50 with sagittal slices	NC	98.84	98.39	98.61	98.30
	MCI	97.09	99.57	98.31	
	AD	99.29	96.55	97.90	
Proposed model with sagittal slices	NC	99.73	99.80	99.76	**99.82**
	MCI	99.79	99.90	99.85	
	AD	99.96	99.74	99.85	

5.3 Results and Discussions

The proposed model with three different planes of the brain used to predict AD. The performance of the proposed model is evaluated in terms of accuracy (ACC), sensitivity (SEN), specificity (SPE), and F1-score. The highest accuracy of 99.82% is achieved by using the proposed model with the sagittal plane, while the model with axial plane achieved 94.41%, the model with coronal plane achieved 97.44%, and ResNet50 with sagittal plane achieved 98.30%, respectively. From the results, it has been identified that the model with sagittal slices performs exceptionally well in comparison to coronal and axial slices, perhaps because most of the functionality provided in the inter-hemispheric transfer of sensory, motor, and cognitive information [17] is better captured by the sagittal plane. To find out the activated part of the brain while predicting the particular class label for the selected network, we have used class activation maps visualization technique to find the location of pixels in the slices where the features which are related to classification. Every location of the input slices indicates that each location associated with a particular class is important for the classification of AD (Fig. 3 and 4).

5.4 Comparison with the State of Art Methods

The performance of the model is evaluated by comparing the accuracy with the state of the art methods Sect. 5.4. The present study is mainly focused on 3-way classification (NC, MCI, AD) as well as class-wise classification, where our model is compared with recent studies in which the present study shows the significant improvement in the accuracy. The authors [4] and [6] have presented the

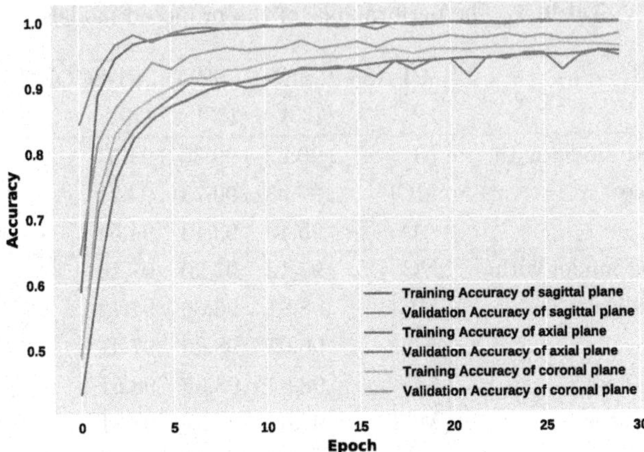

Fig. 3. The training and validation of the proposed model resulted in a very high level of accuracy of almost 100%. As seen, the validation of the sagittal plane approached almost 100% when the 30th epoch completed, and for the other planes of the brain, the accuracy rates of both the coronal and axial planes were close. However, the final accuracy of the sagittal was better than both of the planes.

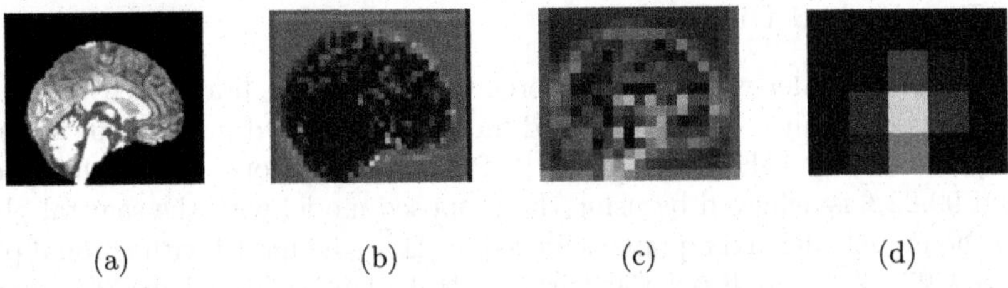

(a) (b) (c) (d)

Fig. 4. Class activation map visualization of Resnet50 at different convolutional layers (a) Random input slice, heatmaps of the learned features (b) closer to the input, (c) at middle convolutional layer, and (d) closer to the output.

class-wise performance of the models in which they achieved 85.0% and 94.6% accuracy, respectively. Although the sensitivity for AD class is better than the other existing methods, the misclassification of NC as a patient would be unacceptable in the medical field. Our model gives the best class-wise performance in comparison to the state of the art model. For example, ten slices are classified as NC out of 9900 MCI slices by our model (Table 2).

Table 2. Comparison of the proposed model to other techniques

Approach	Technique	Modalities	NC/MCI/AD (%)	NC/AD (%)	MCI/AD (%)	NC/MCI (%)
Gupta et al. [4]	2D, SAE	MRI	85.00	94.70	88.10	86.30
Hosseni et al. [6]	3D-CNN	MRI	94.80	99.30	100	94.20
Payan et al. [15]	3D-CNN, SAE	MRI	89.40	95.39	86.80	92.10
Liu et al. [11]	3D-CNN	MRI+PET	53.80	91.40	n/a	82.10
Suk et al. [19]	SAE+SVM	MRI+PET+CSF	n/a	95.90	n/a	85.00
Zhu et al. [20]	Joint Regression	MRI+PET+CSF	n/a	95.90	n/a	85.70
Billones et al. [1]	Modified VGG16	MRI	91.95	98.33	93.89	91.67
Proposed model with sagittal slices	2D CNN	MRI	**99.82**	**99.79**	**99.91**	**99.89**

6 Conclusion

In this present study, 2D CNN model is proposed for the classification of AD using MR images. We also experimented with different planes of the brain such as sagittal, coronal and axial. We successfully classified the different stages of AD with 99.82% accuracy for sagittal plane. By applying CNN on sagittal plane, we found that the architecture, which has enormous numbers of layers, might not perform well. Our results show that CNN can extract discriminative features for prediction among different stages of AD. We compared our model with other state-of-the-art methods, and the proposed method outperforms previous work including ResNet50 with higher accuracy while keeping the balance between the sensitivity and specificity. The novelty of our approach was to use 2D brain slices for data augmentation. The limitation of our approach is that we have randomly divided the training and test dataset based on 2D slices. Future work can focus on extending the classification to individual patients with 3D scans i.e. the training and test dataset can comprise of approaches such as leave K subjects out, i.e. incorporating the fact that each patient contributes to multiple 2D slices.

Acknowledgements. This research is supported by India-Trento Program for Advanced Research (Phase IV).

References

1. Billones, C.D., Demetria, O.J.L.D., Hostallero, D.E.D., Naval, P.C.: Demnet: a convolutional neural network for the detection of Alzheimer's disease and mild cognitive impairment. In: IEEE Region 10 Conference (TENCON 2016) , pp. 3724–3727 (2016)
2. Cai, Y., Wu, S., Zhao, W., Li, Z., Wu, Z., Ji, S.: Concussion classification via deep learning using whole-brain white matter fiber strains. PLoS ONE **13** (2018). https://doi.org/10.1371/journal.pone.0197992
3. Chollet, F., et al.: Keras, GitHub (2015). https://github.com/fchollet/keras

4. Gupta, A., Ayhan, M.S., Maida, A.S.: Natural image bases to represent neuroimaging data. In: Proceedings of the 30th International Conference on International Conference on Machine Learning - Volume 28, pp. III-987-III-994. JMLR.org, Atlanta (2013)
5. He, K., Zhang, X., Ren, S., Sun, J.: Deep residual learning for image recognition. In: 2016 IEEE Conference on Computer Vision and Pattern Recognition (CVPR), pp. 770–778 (2016)
6. Hosseini-Asl, E., Keynton, R., El-Baz, A.: Alzheimers disease diagnostics by adaptation of 3D convolutional network. In: 2016 IEEE International Conference on Image Processing (ICIP) (2016)
7. Huang, G., Liu, Z., van der Maaten, L., Weinberge, Q.K.: Densely connected convolutional networks. In: 2017 IEEE Conference on Computer Vision and Pattern Recognition (CVPR), pp. 2261–2269 (2017)
8. Ioffe, S., Szegedy, C.: Batch normalization: accelerating deep network training by reducing internal covariate shift. In: Proceedings of the 32nd International Conference on International Conference on Machine Learning - Volume 37, pp. 448–456. JMLR.org, Lille (2015)
9. Jack Jr, C.R., et al.: The Alzheimer's disease neuroimaging initiative (ADNI): MRI methods. J. Magn. Reson. Imaging **27**(4), 685–691 (2008)
10. Kl"oppel, S., et al.: Automatic classification of MR scans in Alzheimer's disease. Brain **131**, 681–689 (2008). https://doi.org/10.1093/brain/awm319
11. Liu, S., et al.: ADNI: multimodal neuroimaging feature learning for multiclass diagnosis of Alzheimer's disease. IEEE Trans. Biomed. Eng. **62**, 1132–1140 (2015). https://doi.org/10.1109/TBME.2014.2372011
12. Mahmud, M., Kaiser, M.S., McGinnity, T.M., Hussain, A.: Deep learning in mining biological data. Cogn. Comput. **13**(1), 1–33 (2021)
13. Nair, V., Hinton, G.E.: Rectified linear units improve restricted boltzmann machines. In: Proceedings of the 27th International Conference on Machine Learning, pp. 807–814. Omnipress, Haifa (2010)
14. Noor, M.B.T., Zenia, N.Z., Kaiser, M.S., Al Mamun, S., Mahmud, M.: Application of deep learning in detecting neurological disorders from magnetic resonance images: a survey on the detection of Alzheimers disease, Parkinsons disease and schizophrenia. Brain Inform. **7**(1), 1–21 (2020)
15. Payan, A., Montana, G.: Predicting Alzheimers disease: a neuroimaging study with 3D convolutional neural networks (2015)
16. Ruiz, J., Mahmud, M., Modasshir, Md., Shamim Kaiser, M.: 3D DenseNet ensemble in 4-way classification of Alzheimers disease. In: Mahmud, M., Vassanelli, S., Kaiser, M.S., Zhong, N. (eds.) BI 2020. LNCS (LNAI), vol. 12241, pp. 85–96. Springer, Cham (2020). https://doi.org/10.1007/978-3-030-59277-6_8
17. Sidtis, J.J., Volpe, B.T., Holtzman, J.D., Wilson, D.H., Gazzaniga, M.S.: Cognitive interaction after staged callosal section: evidence for transfer of semantic activation. Science **212**, 344–346 (1981). https://doi.org/10.1126/science.6782673
18. Suk, H.I., Lee, S.W., Shen, D.: The Alzheimer's disease neuroimaging initiative: Latent feature representation with stacked auto-encoder for ad/mci diagnosis. Brain Struct. Funct. **220**, 841–859 (2015). https://doi.org/10.1007/s00429-013-0687-3

19. Suk, H.-I., Shen, D.: Deep learning-based feature representation for AD/MCI classification. In: Mori, K., Sakuma, I., Sato, Y., Barillot, C., Navab, N. (eds.) MICCAI 2013. LNCS, vol. 8150, pp. 583–590. Springer, Heidelberg (2013). https://doi.org/10.1007/978-3-642-40763-5_72
20. Zhu, X., Suk, H.I., Shen, D.A.: novel matrix-similarity based loss function for joint regression and classification in ad diagnosis. Neuroimage **100**, 91–105 (2014). https://doi.org/10.1016/j.neuroimage.2014.05.078

Feature Selection Based Machine Learning to Improve Prediction of Parkinson Disease

Nazmun Nahar[1], Ferdous Ara[1], Md. Arif Istiek Neloy[1], Anik Biswas[1], Mohammad Shahadat Hossain[2](✉), and Karl Andersson[3]

[1] BGC Trust University Bangladesh Bidyanagar, Chandanaish, Bangladesh
nazmun@bgctub.ac.bd

[2] University of Chittagong, Chittagong, Bangladesh
hossain_ms@cu.ac.bd

[3] Lulea University of Technology, 931 87 Skellefteå, Sweden
Karl.andersson@ltu.se

Abstract. Parkinson's disease (PD) is a kind of neurodegenerative disorder characterized by the loss of dopamine-producing cells in the brain. The disruption of brain cells that create dopamine, a chemical that allows brain cells to connect with one another, causes Parkinson's disease. Control, adaptability, and rapidity of movement are all controlled by dopamine-producing cells in the brain. Researchers have been investigating for techniques to identify non-motor symptoms that show early in the disease as soon as possible, slowing the disease's progression. A machine learning-based detection of Parkinson's disease is proposed in this research. Feature selection and classification techniques are used in the proposed detection technique. Boruta, Recursive Feature Elimination (RFE) and Random Forest (RF) Classifier have been used for the feature selection process. Four classification algorithms are considered to detect Parkinson disease which are gradient boosting, extreme gradient boosting, bagging and Extra Tree Classifier. Bagging with recursive feature elimination was found to outperform the other methods. The lowest number of voice characteristics for the diagnosis in Parkinson attained 82.35% accuracy.

Keywords: Parkinson disease · Boruta · RFE · RF · Feature selection

1 Introduction

Parkinson's disease is a well-known nervous system ailment characterized by difficulties walking, maintaining body balance, and shaking. This disease also manifests itself in mental and behavioral disorders. This condition can affect both men and women. However, it appears that men are more likely to be affected by this [19]. Parkinson's disease worsens over time once it has been diagnosed. Walking and speech become increasingly difficult for the patient as time goes on.

M. Mahmud et al. (Eds.): BI 2021, LNAI 12960, pp. 496–508, 2021.
https://doi.org/10.1007/978-3-030-86993-9_44

Parkinson's disease is more likely to impact people as they get older. Though the probability of being impacted is low at a young age (5% to 10%), the risk grows considerably after the age of 60. Lewy bodies, low-level norepinephrine, hereditary variables, and other factors are some of the causes of Parkinson's disease [9]. However, Parkinson's disease is thought to be caused by a lack of dopamine. Dopamine production is reduced when nerve cells die. Dopamine is important because it keeps the brain and nerve cells linked. Researchers are still trying to figure out why brain cells are dying.

Parkinson's disease treatment is mostly determined by the patient's state. From early diagnosis through the last phase of the disease, the condition can be divided into several stages. The most prevalent drugs are Levodopa, Dopamine agonists, Amantadine, COMT inhibitors, and others, depending on the condition [15]. However, none of them can guarantee that the ailment will be cured. That is why it is so important to diagnose Parkinson's disease early. Parkinson's disease has yet to be diagnosed in a definite method. To identify Parkinson's disease in its early stages, most doctors must rely on fundamental symptoms (difficulty walking, maintaining bodily balance, shaking, and so on). As a result, the researchers are looking for strategies to identify these non-motor symptoms as early as possible throughout the disease, in order to reduce the disease's development. This is where Machine Learning enters the picture.

Machine learning (ML) is increasingly being utilized for medical diseases detection [25,26,31] due to its ease of implementation and high accuracy. Nowadays, the quantity and complexity of clinical datasets have been grown rapidly, resulting in large datasets of large dimensions. Reduction of dimensionality attempts to decrease the number of variables. For the dimensionality reduction method, both feature extraction and feature selection strategies are applied. The goal of this study is to reduce computing time by using fewer effective features, a lightweight feature selection methodology, and a classifier has been proposed. The features are derived from the speech signals, making them easier to collect than those derived from MRI or motion-based [19] approaches.

The proposed ML-based early PD diagnostic method's main contributions are mentioned below.

- For the identification of the most relevant characteristics to be employed in the classification task, Boruta, Recursive Feature Elimination (RFE) and Random Forest (RF) approaches were applied.
- The results of many popular classifiers have been analyzed and the optimal classifier for the PD diagnostic problem has been determined.
- The significance of applying FS approaches in the preprocessing step of PD patient classification has been demonstrated. Bagging classifier performance has been increased by Feature Selection by approximately 8% and Extra Tree Classifier has been increased by approximately 10%.
- The fewer speech features required to diagnose PD have been achieved with less effort, and very high accuracy detection rates (82.35%).

The remainder of this paper is organized as follows: Sect. 2 summarizes the study of the literature review on current studies in this area. The proposed framework and methodology are described in Sect. 3. Section 4 presents experimental results and comparisons between classification techniques. The conclusion and future work of the paper is defined in Sect. 5.

2 Literature Review

ML was also employed in the literature for the processing of PD.

M. AI-Sarem et al. [5] presented the detection of Parkinson's disease through a number of set methods including random forest, extreme gradient boosting (XGBoost), and CatBoost to increase accuracy. They examine the important feature for each ensemble classification using random forest and extreme gradient increase (XGBoost) and categorical boost (CatBoost).

T. J. Wronge et al. [37] proposed a Voice Activation Detection (VAD) technique for prediction of Parkinson disease. Raw audio has been extracted and background noise eliminated then sent into two distinct feature-extraction algorithms. In the end, they use an algorithm for machine learning.

K.R. Wan et al. [36] analyzed papers to be utilized for ML in brain surgery for selection of functions (FS). An ML-based technique is used to find the real region to be operated on during brain surgery for Parkinson's disease. This study focuses on investigations conducted after Parkinson's disease has been diagnosed.

F. Cavallo et al. [11] attempted to forecast Parkinson's disease based on motion data collected from people's upper limbs. The researchers implanted a device into the upper limbs of the experimental subjects (both PD patients and healthy persons) and instructed them to perform a series of activities. To get parameters, a spatiotemporal and frequency data analysis was done, and then several supervised learning approaches were employed for classification.

J.S. Almeida et al. [6] employed a variety of feature extraction and machine learning strategies to detect PD. They discovered that phonation is the most effective activity for detecting Parkinson's disease. The research examined at K-NN, Multilayer Perceptron (MLP), Optimum Path Forest, and Support Vector Machines (SVM) as classifiers.

L. Parisi et al. [32], artificial neural networks were used to minimize voice characteristics for ML-based PD diagnosis. SVM was used to classify the data. Instead of MRI, motion or speech information utilizing ML algorithms, PD was also identified using handwriting tasks [21]. Despite the fact that high classification rates were obtained in the literature from ML-based PD diagnosis. They either employed a large number of features, which increases calculation time, or the extraction of the features was difficult even when just a few features were used. As a result, the computation time is increased indirectly. The goal of this study is to reduce computing time by using fewer effective features, a lightweight feature extraction process. The features are derived from speech signals, making it easier to collect the features than other MRI-based [21] or motion-based approaches in the literature. The ML-based early Parkinson disease prediction is the main contributions.

3 Methodology

The workflow for this research is described in Fig. 1. There are various steps to the experiment. First, acquire data set from machine-learning repository of the University of California Irvine (UCI). Secondly, we use the RF, Boruta and RFE selection methods to select key features. The next is to compare the different models of machine learning for classification analysis like Gradient Boosting, Extreme Gradient Boosting, Bagging and Extra Tree Classifier. A mathematical challenge is to determine an optimum subset of features from the attributes list. Our experiment uses a recursive process to get to the root of the issue. In the classification data analysis, various models will have varied capabilities. We compare four classifier methods with various attributes to choose the best way for classifying based on each classifier's accuracy. The steps of the proposed technique are as follows.

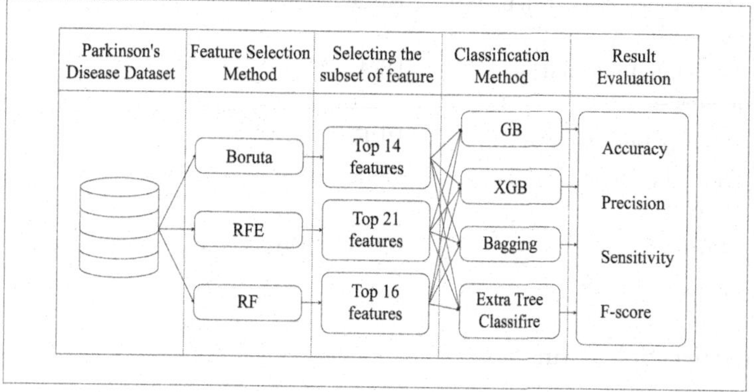

Fig. 1. Overall research workflow

3.1 Data Collection

Parkinson Dataset with replicated acoustic features [29] has been used for the training and evaluation of our methodology. A total of 80 participants over 50 years participated in the research. Forty of them were healthy: 22 (55%) male and 18 (45%) female and forty people suffered from PD: 27 (67.5%) male and 13 (32.5%) female. A total of 80 participants over 50 years participated in the research. The research is based on 44 acoustic features that may be divided into five groups. These 44 features are shown in Table 1.

Table 1. Dataset description.

SL no.	Feature group	Feature name
1	ID	Subjects's identifier
2	Recording	Number of the recording
3	Gender	0 = Man; 1 = Woman
4	Pitch local perturbation measure	Relative jitter (Jitter_rel), absolute jitter (Jitter_abs), relative average perturbation (Jitter_RAP) pitch perturbation quotient (Jitter_PPQ)
5	Amplitude perturbation measures	Local shimmer (Shim_loc), shimmer in dB (Shim_dB), 3-point amplitude perturbation quotient (Shim_APQ3), 5-point amplitude perturbation quotient (Shim_APQ5)
6	Harmonic-to-noise ratio measures	HNR05, HNR15, HNR25, HNR35, HNR38
7	Mel frequency cepstral coefficient-based spectral measures	MFCC0, MFCC1,..., MFCC12) and their derivatives (Delta0, Delta1,..., Delta12)
8	Recurrence period density entropy	RPDE
9	Detrended fluctuation analysis	DFA
10	Pitch period entropy	PPE
11	Glottal-to-noise excitation ratio	GNE
12	Status	0 = Healthy; 1 = PD

3.2 Feature Selection

The goal of feature selection is to identify the most significant features of a problem domain. The computational speed and accuracy of prediction [16] are improved. In this paper, we apply three very well-known feature selection methods to identify most relevant features. These three feature selection methods are Boruta, Recursive Feature Elimination (RFE) and Random Forest (RF).

Boruta: Boruta [22] is an algorithm for feature selection and feature ranking which work based on Random forest algorithm. The benefits of Boruta are to determine the importance of the variable and help to choose significant variables statistically. In addition, by increasing p value to 0.01, we may increase the robustness of the method. The number of times the algorithm has executed is known as nEstimator. The higher the nEstimator, the more selective the variables are to be chosen. 100 is the default. This method provides a top down approach with the comparison of the original features with relevant attributes.

Feature Feature Elimination (RFE): RFE gives an accurate approach to determine the key variables before we enter into a machine learning system. In this study we present RFE for the classification of parkinson diseases with the technique Decision Tree (DT). RFE uses all the features for building a DT model. The RFE eventually removes the irrelevant features which contribute meaninglessly to the DT model. Furthermore, RFE is a strong feature selection approach that is dependent on the learning model [34].

Random Forest (RF): In a data science approach, random forests are sometimes employed to select features. The reason for this is that random forests' tree-based methods are naturally ranked by how effectively they increase node purity [23]. This represents an overall decrease in impurity (called gini impurity). At the beginning of the trees there are nodes with the most decrease in impurity, while at the end of the trees there are nodes with the least reduction in impurity. Thus, we may build a subset of the most essential features by cutting trees below a given node.

3.3 Data Splitting

In this phase, the Parkinson disease dataset is separated into a training set of 80% and a testing set of 20%. The training set is used to develop the models, and the test set is used to assess the models.

3.4 Training Models and Evaluation Matrices

We have trained our models using four classification methods which are Gradient Boosting [30], Extreme Gradient Boosting [12], bagging [10] and Extra Tree Classifier [13]. First we train our model using 44 feature. Then we select important feature from the 44 using three feature selection method and we train our model using the selected feature. The proposed model is evaluated using a set of metrics, including accuracy, recall, precision, F-score, and others [35].

4 Result and Discussion

In this part, the experimental result of our developed classification method will be discussed. At first we predict Parkinson disease with four classifier which are Gradient Boosting, Extreme Gradient Boosting, Extra Tree Classifier and Bagging. Then we apply three feature selection method and after selecting some important feature then we apply again our above four classifier. Here, we want to show that how feature selector method effect the prediction result.

4.1 System Configuration

To execute our proposed methodology, Google Colaboratory was used. Google Colaboratory provides users with free CPU and GPU help to perform Python research projects in the cloud. The user interface of Google Colab is built on Jupiter notebooks. Our proposed technique was created using the PYTHON scikit-learn library [1]. PYTHON scikit-learn library is necessary in order to execute classification models like Gradient Boosting, Extreme Gradient Boosting, Extra Tree Classifier and Bagging algorithm and it is also necessary to execute feature selection method like RF and Recursive RFE. To implement Boruta classifier we use "Python BorutaPy" library [24]'.

4.2 Result of Classifier Before Applying Feature Selection Method

Table 2 shows the result of our proposed four classifier which are Gradient Boosting, Extreme Gradient Boosting, Extra Tree Classifier and Bagging. From the Table 1 we can see that the accuracy of Gradient Boosting is 77.21%, Extra Tree classifier accuracy is 71.91%, Bagging classifier accuracy is 75.08% and Extreme Gradient Boosting classifier accuracy is 78.08%. That means Extreme Gradient Boosting gives the best accuracy among all the classifier before applying any feature selection method.

Table 2. Accuracy of the classifier before applying feature selection method.

Classifier name	Accuracy (%)	Precision	Recall	F-Score
Gradient Boosting	77.21	0.79	0.72	0.78
Extra Tree Classifier	71.91	0.71	0.74	0.72
Bagging	75.08	0.71	0.83	0.77
Extreme Gradient Boosting	78.08	0.77	0.79	0.78

4.3 Result of Classifier After Applying Boruta Feature Selection Method

14 important features are selected by the Boruta feature selection method. We show these feature in Fig. 2. From the Fig. 2 we can see that DFE feature has the highest score and so this feature is the most important feature to predict parkinson disease.

Table 3 shows the result of our proposed four classifier after applying Boruta feature selection method which are Gradient Boosting, Extreme Gradient Boosting, Extra Tree Classifier and Bagging. From the Table 3 we can see that the accuracy of Gradient Boosting is 74.16%, Extra Tree classifier accuracy is 72.91%, Bagging algorithm accuracy is 77.08% and Extreme Gradient Boosting classifier accuracy is 75.08%. That means Bagging algorithm gives the best accuracy among all four the classifier after applying Botuta feature selection method.

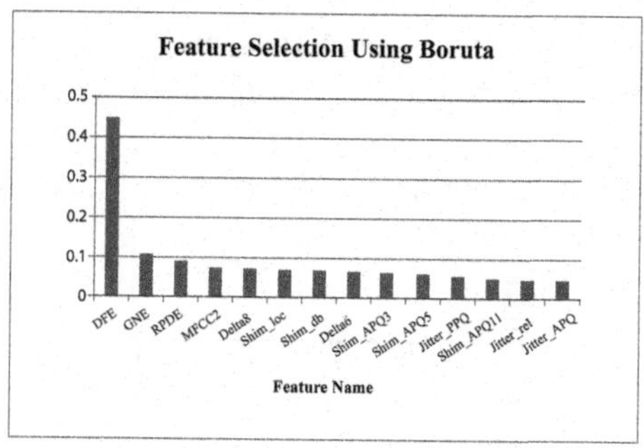

Fig. 2. Boruta feature scores

From the table we can also noticed that the Gradient Boosting and Extreme Gradient Boosting algorithm is decreased but Extra Tree Classifier and Bagging algorithm accuracy is increased after applying Boruta feature selection method.

Table 3. Accuracy of the classifier after applying Boruta method.

Classifier name	Accuracy (%)	Precision	Recall	F-Score
Gradient Boosting	74.16	0.74	0.71	0.72
Extra Tree Classifier	72.91	0.73	0.70	0.73
Bagging	77.08	0.76	0.79	0.78
Extreme Gradient Boosting	75.00	0.75	0.75	0.75

4.4 Result of Classifier After Applying Recursive Feature Elimination (RFE) Feature Selection Method

The REF feature selection approach selects 21 main features. Figure 3 depicts these features. Figure 3 shows that the HNR25 feature has the best score, indicating that it is essential for predicting Parkinson disease.

Table 4 shows the result of our proposed four classifier after applying RFE feature selection method which are Gradient Boosting, Extreme Gradient Boosting, Extra Tree Classifier and Bagging. From the Table 4 we can see that the accuracy of Gradient Boosting is 70.75%, Extra Tree classifier accuracy is 81.25%, Bagging algorithm accuracy is 82.35% and Extreme Gradient Boosting classifier accuracy is 79.16%. That means Bagging algorithm gives the best accuracy among all four the classifier after applying RFE feature selection method. From the table we can also noticed that the Gradient Boosting is decreased but Extra Tree Classifier, Bagging and Extreme Gradient Boosting algorithm accuracy is increased after applying RFE feature selection method.

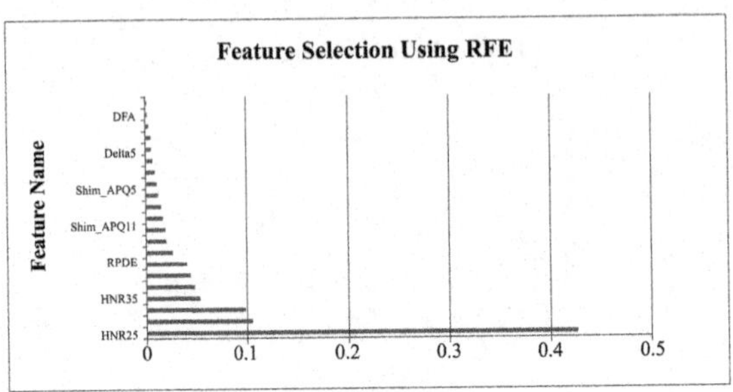

Fig. 3. RFE feature scores

Table 4. Accuracy of the classifier after applying RFE method.

Classifier name	Accuracy (%)	Precision	Recall	F-Score
Gradient Boosting	70.75	0.70	0.71	0.69
Extra Tree Classifier	81.25	0.78	0.88	0.82
Bagging	82.35	0.80	0.83	0.82
Extreme Gradient Boosting	79.16	0.75	0.88	0.81

4.5 Result of Classifier After Applying Random Forest (RF) Feature Selection Method

16 main features are chosen using the RF feature selection methodology. These features are visualized in Fig. 4. Figure 4 demonstrates that the GNE feature has the best score, showing that it is important for Parkinson's disease prediction.

Table 5 shows the result of our proposed four classifier after applying RF feature selection method which are Gradient Boosting, Extreme Gradient Boosting, Extra Tree Classifier and Bagging. From the Table 5 we can see that the accuracy of Gradient Boosting is 79.16%, Extra Tree classifier accuracy is 75.00%, Bagging algorithm accuracy is 80.21% and Extreme Gradient Boosting classifier accuracy is 78.16%. That means Bagging algorithm gives the best accuracy among all four the classifier after applying RF feature selection method. From the table we can also noticed that the all the classifier algorithm has been increased after applying RF feature selection method.

From the above implementation of three feature selection method we noticed the RFE feature selection method performs better than the other.

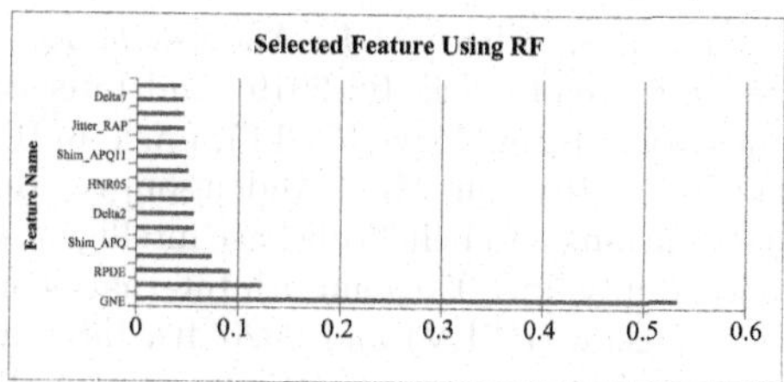

Fig. 4. RF feature scores

Table 5. Accuracy of the classifier after applying RF method.

Classifier name	Accuracy (%)	Precision	Recall	F-Score
Gradient Boosting	79.16	0.79	0.79	0.79
Extra Tree Classifier	75.00	0.73	0.79	0.76
Bagging	80.21	0.74	0.96	0.82
Extreme Gradient Boosting	78.16	0.78	0.78	0.78

5 Conclusion

In this work, a Feature selection based classification system for the early identification of Parkinson's disease was designed utilizing the characteristics of speech signals from both PD patients and healthy persons. In the experiments, various Feature Selection methods and classification techniques were employed. The major goal was to increase the model's performance and accuracy while simultaneously lowering the computing cost of the classification task. The classification techniques' accuracy' were analyzed with and without Feature Selection, and the significant impacts of feature selection was demonstrated. The results show that combining feature selection approaches with classification techniques is quite beneficial, particularly when working with voice data. The data of our Parkinson disease voice dataset is limited. In future we will collect more data to detect Parkinson disease and we will work with some deep learning method and other method [2–4,7,8,14,17,18,20,27,28,33,38]. In future, we will also work with Parkinson disease MRI Data.

References

1. Abadi, M., et al.: TensorFlow: a system for large-scale machine learning. In: 12th USENIX Symposium on Operating Systems Design and Implementation (OSDI 2016), pp. 265–283 (2016)
2. Abedin, M.Z., Akther, S., Hossain, M.S.: An artificial neural network model for epilepsy seizure detection. In: 2019 5th International Conference on Advances in Electrical Engineering (ICAEE), pp. 860–865. IEEE (2019)

3. Ahmed, T.U., Hossain, M.S., Alam, M.J., Andersson, K.: An integrated CNN-RNN framework to assess road crack. In: 2019 22nd International Conference on Computer and Information Technology (ICCIT), pp. 1–6. IEEE (2019)
4. Ahmed, T.U., Jamil, M.N., Hossain, M.S., Andersson, K., Hossain, M.S.: An integrated real-time deep learning and belief rule base intelligent system to assess facial expression under uncertainty. In: 2020 Joint 9th International Conference on Informatics, Electronics & Vision (ICIEV) and 2020 4th International Conference on Imaging, Vision & Pattern Recognition (icIVPR), pp. 1–6. IEEE (2020)
5. Al-Sarem, M., Saeed, F., Boulila, W., Emara, A.H., Al-Mohaimeed, M., Errais, M.: Feature selection and classification using CatBoost method for improving the performance of predicting Parkinson's disease. In: Saeed, F., Al-Hadhrami, T., Mohammed, F., Mohammed, E. (eds.) Advances on Smart and Soft Computing. AISC, vol. 1188, pp. 189–199. Springer, Singapore (2021). https://doi.org/10.1007/978-981-15-6048-4_17
6. Almeida, J.S., et al.: Detecting Parkinson's disease with sustained phonation and speech signals using machine learning techniques. Pattern Recogn. Lett. **125**, 55–62 (2019)
7. Basnin, N., Nahar, L., Hossain, M.S.: An integrated CNN-LSTM model for micro hand gesture recognition. In: Vasant, P., Zelinka, I., Weber, G.-W. (eds.) ICO 2020. AISC, vol. 1324, pp. 379–392. Springer, Cham (2021). https://doi.org/10.1007/978-3-030-68154-8_35
8. Basnin, N., Nahar, L., Hossain, M.S.: An integrated CNN-LSTM model for Bangla lexical sign language recognition. In: Kaiser, M.S., Bandyopadhyay, A., Mahmud, M., Ray, K. (eds.) Proceedings of International Conference on Trends in Computational and Cognitive Engineering. AISC, vol. 1309, pp. 695–707. Springer, Singapore (2021). https://doi.org/10.1007/978-981-33-4673-4_57
9. Brazier, Y.: Parkinson's disease early signs and causes (2021). https://www.medicalnewstoday.com/articles/323396#causes. Accessed 20 May 2021
10. Bühlmann, P.: Bagging, boosting and ensemble methods. In: Gentle, J., Härdle, W., Mori, Y. (eds.) Handbook of Computational Statistics, pp. 985–1022. Springer, Heidelberg (2012). https://doi.org/10.1007/978-3-642-21551-3_33
11. Cavallo, F., Moschetti, A., Esposito, D., Maremmani, C., Rovini, E.: Upper limb motor pre-clinical assessment in Parkinson's disease using machine learning. Parkinsonism Related Disord. **63**, 111–116 (2019)
12. Chen, T., Guestrin, C.: XGBoost: a scalable tree boosting system. In: Proceedings of the 22nd ACM SIGKDD International Conference on Knowledge Discovery and Data Mining, pp. 785–794 (2016)
13. Geurts, P., Ernst, D., Wehenkel, L.: Extremely randomized trees. Machine Learn. **63**(1), 3–42 (2006)
14. Gosh, S., Nahar, N., Wahab, M.A., Biswas, M., Hossain, M.S., Andersson, K.: Recommendation system for E-commerce using alternating least squares (ALS) on apache spark. In: Vasant, P., Zelinka, I., Weber, G.-W. (eds.) ICO 2020. AISC, vol. 1324, pp. 880–893. Springer, Cham (2021). https://doi.org/10.1007/978-3-030-68154-8_75
15. Holland, K.: Everything You Want to Know About Parkinson's Disease (2021). https://www.healthline.com/health/parkinsons#treatment. Accessed 20 May 2021
16. Hsu, H.H., Hsieh, C.W., Lu, M.D.: Hybrid feature selection by combining filters and wrappers. Expert Syst. Appl. **38**(7), 8144–8150 (2011)
17. Islam, R.U., Hossain, M.S., Andersson, K.: A deep learning inspired belief rule-based expert system. IEEE Access **8**, 190637–190651 (2020)

18. Islam, R.U., Ruci, X., Hossain, M.S., Andersson, K., Kor, A.L.: Capacity management of hyperscale data centers using predictive modelling. Energies **12**(18), 3438 (2019)
19. Michael, J.: Parkinson Disease (2017). https://www.nia.nih.gov/health/parkinsonsdisease#:~:text=Parkinson%27s%20disease%20is%20a%20brain. Accessed 20 May 2021
20. Kabir, S., Islam, R.U., Hossain, M.S., Andersson, K.: An integrated approach of belief rule base and deep learning to predict air pollution. Sensors **20**(7), 1956 (2020)
21. Kotsavasiloglou, C., Kostikis, N., Hristu-Varsakelis, D., Arnaoutoglou, M.: Machine learning-based classification of simple drawing movements in Parkinson's disease. Biomed. Signal Process. Control **31**, 174–180 (2017)
22. Kursa, M.B., Jankowski, A., Rudnicki, W.R.: Boruta-a system for feature selection. Fund. Inform. **101**(4), 271–285 (2010)
23. Kursa, M.B., Rudnicki, W.R.: The all relevant feature selection using random forest. arXiv preprint arXiv:1106.5112 (2011)
24. Kursa, M.B., Rudnicki, W.R., et al.: Feature selection with the boruta package. J. Stat. Softw. **36**(11), 1–13 (2010)
25. Mahmud, M., Kaiser, M.S., McGinnity, T.M., Hussain, A.: Deep learning in mining biological data. Cogn. Comput. **13**(1), 1–33 (2021)
26. Mahmud, M., Kaiser, M.S., Hussain, A., Vassanelli, S.: Applications of deep learning and reinforcement learning to biological data. IEEE Trans. Neural Netw. Learn. Syst. **29**(6), 2063–2079 (2018)
27. Nahar, N., Ara, F., Neloy, M.A.I., Barua, V., Hossain, M.S., Andersson, K.: A comparative analysis of the ensemble method for liver disease prediction. In: 2019 2nd International Conference on Innovation in Engineering and Technology (ICIET), pp. 1–6. IEEE (2019)
28. Nahar, N., Hossain, M.S., Andersson, K.: A machine learning based fall detection for elderly people with neurodegenerative disorders. In: Mahmud, M., Vassanelli, S., Kaiser, M.S., Zhong, N. (eds.) BI 2020. LNCS (LNAI), vol. 12241, pp. 194–203. Springer, Cham (2020). https://doi.org/10.1007/978-3-030-59277-6_18
29. Naranjo, L., Perez, C.J., Campos-Roca, Y., Martin, J.: Addressing voice recording replications for Parkinson's disease detection. Expert Syst. Appl. **46**, 286–292 (2016)
30. Natekin, A., Knoll, A.: Gradient boosting machines, a tutorial. Front. Neurorobot. **7**, 21 (2013)
31. Noor, M.B.T., Zenia, N.Z., Kaiser, M.S., Al Mamun, S., Mahmud, M.: Application of deep learning in detecting neurological disorders from magnetic resonance images: a survey on the detection of Alzheimer's disease, Parkinson's disease and schizophrenia. Brain Inform. **7**(1), 1–21 (2020)
32. Parisi, L., RaviChandran, N., Manaog, M.L.: Feature-driven machine learning to improve early diagnosis of Parkinson's disease. Expert Syst. Appl. **110**, 182–190 (2018)
33. Pathan, R.K., Uddin, M.A., Nahar, N., Ara, F., Hossain, M.S., Andersson, K.: Gender classification from inertial sensor-based gait dataset. In: Vasant, P., Zelinka, I., Weber, G.-W. (eds.) ICO 2020. AISC, vol. 1324, pp. 583–596. Springer, Cham (2021). https://doi.org/10.1007/978-3-030-68154-8_51
34. Richhariya, B., Tanveer, M., Rashid, A., Initiative, A.D.N., et al.: Diagnosis of alzheimer's disease using universum support vector machine based recursive feature elimination (USVM-RFE). Biomed. Sig. Process. Contr. **59**, 101903 (2020)

35. Sokolova, M., Lapalme, G.: A systematic analysis of performance measures for classification tasks. Inf. Process. Manage. **45**(4), 427–437 (2009)
36. Wan, K.R., Maszczyk, T., See, A.A.Q., Dauwels, J., King, N.K.K.: A review on microelectrode recording selection of features for machine learning in deep brain stimulation surgery for Parkinson's disease. Clin. Neurophysiol. **130**(1), 145–154 (2019)
37. Wroge, T.J., Özkanca, Y., Demiroglu, C., Si, D., Atkins, D.C., Ghomi, R.H.: Parkinson's disease diagnosis using machine learning and voice. In: 2018 IEEE Signal Processing in Medicine and Biology Symposium (SPMB), pp. 1–7. IEEE (2018)
38. Zisad, S.N., Hossain, M.S., Andersson, K.: Speech emotion recognition in neurological disorders using convolutional neural network. In: Mahmud, M., Vassanelli, S., Kaiser, M.S., Zhong, N. (eds.) BI 2020. LNCS (LNAI), vol. 12241, pp. 287–296. Springer, Cham (2020). https://doi.org/10.1007/978-3-030-59277-6_26

Feature Analysis of EEG Based Brain-Computer Interfaces to Detect Motor Imagery

Saima Akbar[1], A. M. Martinez-Enriquez[2], Muhammad Aslam[1](✉), and Rabeeya Saleem[1]

[1] Department of CS, University of Engineering and Technology, Lahore, Pakistan
maslam@uet.edu.pk, rabeeyasaleem@uet.edu.pk

[2] Department of CS, CINVESTAV, Mexico City, Mexico
ammartin@cinvestav.mx

Abstract. Brain-Computer Interfaces (BCI) is one of the alluring breakthroughs for mankind as it provides a new way of communication for the patients of neuro-muscular disorders. Electroencephalography (EEG) signals are the most studied type of signals to detect brain activities because of its non-invasive and portable nature. The major problem in the identification of neural activities from EEG signals and the presence of non-task related artifacts in the signal data. These artifacts affect the classification of feature set. With these effective techniques, BCI classifier can efficiently classify EEG signals. The proposed research deals with different motor imagery datasets for the detection of movements. An EEG based BCI system is proposed that implement a linear regression based artifact removal method for EOG processing, feature construction and recursive feature elimination with cross-validation. It achieved promising results with relatively fewer data used for training than the original competition's data, that shows the significance as compared to top leaderboard entries. The results obtained show that our approach tackles noise and artifacts in EEG signals which provides reliable features for BCI classification.

Keywords: Brain-computer interface (BCI) · Electroencephalography (EEG) · Electrooculography (EOG) · Feature selection · Motor Imagery (MI)

1 Introduction

Brain-computer interface (BCI) provide a communication system in which an individual can send messages to an external device (e.g. a computer) without using the brain's muscular. The person's intention to control or communicate initiates brain activities and the patterns from those brain activities can be detected

M. Mahmud et al. (Eds.): BI 2021, LNAI 12960, pp. 509–518, 2021.
https://doi.org/10.1007/978-3-030-86993-9_45

from electrophysiological signals [1,2]. Patients suffering from high spinal cord injuries (HSCL), amyotrophic lateral sclerosis (ALS), brainstem stroke, cerebral palsy or other neural disorders find difficulties in communication and neural prosthetics. BCI aims at resolving the difficulties of such patients and raise their standard of living [3–5].

There are different invasive and non-invasive electrophysiological signal recording methods that are being used to detect brain activities. Electroencephalography (EEG) signals are the most studied type of signals to detect brain activities because of its non-invasive and portable nature. Non-invasive methods include magneto encephalography (MEG), positron emission tomography (PET), functional magnetic resonance imaging (fMRI), and optimal imaging. These methods have expensive setup and equipment costs, they are technically more demanding, have longer time constants and less suitable for rapid communication [6,7].

When recording EEG signals, most of the electrodes are not tightly contained within the scalp therefore many environmental, electromagnetic (EM) and other surrounding sources contribute to the high noise-to-signal ratio of EEG signals. The EOG artifact is most disturbing artifact that corrupt the EEG signal because of the frequency range of EOG activity [1,8–10]. The important aspect of a BCI system is, therefore, to minimize the noise-to-signal ratio and remove the non-CNS related artifacts from the signals. High dimensional feature set reduces the accuracy of the BCI classifier by contributing more noise.

For good classification of mental tasks by a BCI system it needs to give more importance to the preprocessing and feature selection units. But constructing an efficient one and less complicated system is still a goal to achieve. Different machine learning and signal processing techniques are being explored for these preprocessing stage [11–13]. But these are quite time consuming because of heavy computations and our main target while developing a BCI system should be fine accuracy with more instantaneous attitude. So we presents a simple yet efficient model for EEG based BCI to detect motor imagery.

The main objective of our research is to deal with feature selection stage for better classification of motor imagery by EEG based BCI. The proposed system take three different dataset and process it through various experiments. It record the EEG signals from and optimized it through NAN values and separate the data into training and testing data to lower the frequency with RFECV feature selection. The system will classified the results and compare these experiments to achieve an appropriate model.

In the next section we discussed our proposed methodology and its implementation on our main observed dataset. Section 3 presents the experiment on remaining two datasets to test our model. Section 3.2 gives discussion on results of implementation and finally Sect.4 concludes this paper.

2 Proposed System Model

This section presents BCI design, which is tested through different experimentation performed on BCI motor-imagery datasets. The main component of proposed research is Butterworth low-pass filter banks method for feature construction with "Recursive Feature Elimination with Cross Validation (RFECV)". Working on Graz 2A, Graz 2B datasets [14] and Random forest classifier keeps it simple and robust. To evaluate the system, Receiver Operate characteristics (ROC) and Area Under Curve (AUC) as an evaluation matrix for 'Grasp-And-Lift' dataset [15] and Cohen's kappa score for Graz 2A and Graz 2B datasets [16]. The proposed model as shown in Fig. 1, the demand of Graz 2A and Graz 2B datasets.

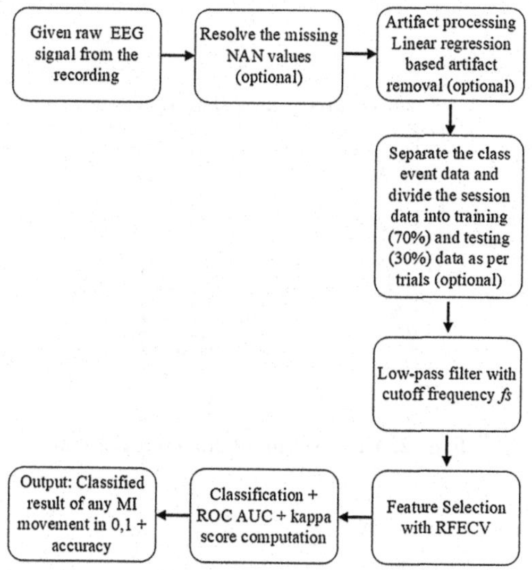

Fig. 1. BCI generalized proposed model

2.1 Design and Implementation

Before going into the design and implementation there is an important point showed in the task video of the dataset [15]. The subjects viewed a light bulb constantly, when the light bulb glows subject performs hand movements accordingly. When the bulb glows, visual evoked potential (VEP) is generated in the EEG dataset. They occur just before the hand movement [15].

We also performed a basic experiment to analyze the BCI dataset of "Grasp-and-Lift". By using the simple approach of training and testing, it achieved accuracy of 0.73 with ROC and AUC as shown in Fig. 2. This experiment showed that by only dividing the six-class problem into the two-class problem accuracy of 0.73 is achieved.

2.2 Classification Method Used

Below are the steps for training of classifier with specific approach

- For each subject S, there are 6 different classes required
- Train the classifier on class m, m = 1.6 using X as training data and Y as target labels. For U predict the class label P
- Combine all the series data and event data for subject S in X and Y
- Combine all the test series data for a subject S in U
- Compute the ROC AUC for all 6 classes and micro-average ROC AUC for all.

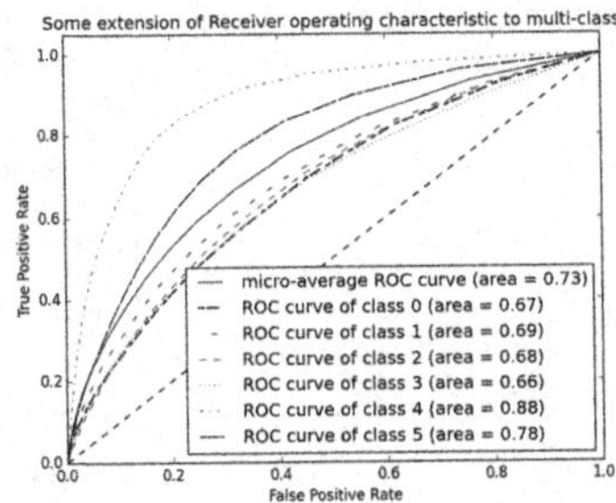

Fig. 2. EEG segment for channel Cz

2.3 Preprocessing and Feature Construction

To deal with these high frequency components, a low-pass filter should be used. Therefore, we used the Butterworth digital low-pass filter with some low cutoff frequency to attenuate the high frequency components. The EOG artifact due to eye movement and eye blinking also lies in the low frequency range from 0–4 Hz. Figures 3, 4 and 5 shows the effect of choosing different cutoff frequencies. Figure 6 shows the boost in classification accuracy described in previous section, which make use of all feature columns. Later, non-important filtered features can be excluded from the feature set by using suitable feature selection method.

2.4 Feature Selection

We filter the potential features with low-pass filter banks with five different frequency banks between 0–5 Hz. To overcome this problem, we implemented an automated features selection RFECV method. As the random forest classifier is used for feature classification so we also used it with RFECV. The accuracy score for cross-validation scoring and K = 3 for cross-validation. There are numerous possibilities in which RFECV method can be used to find optimal features.

We take the option 2 and 5 to run our model with RFECV method because option 1 might not give the optimal features for classification. Each channel has their own feature channel's importance for a particular task so option 3 is also out of consideration and Option 4 will not give the true generalization of trials. Option 5 gives the best results of all but the RFECV method take some considerable time to run.

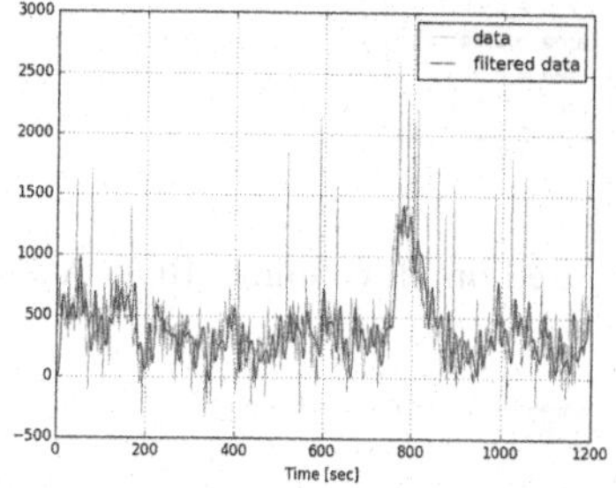

Fig. 3. Butterworth with filtering f = 0.4

Fig. 4. Butterworth with filtering f = 1

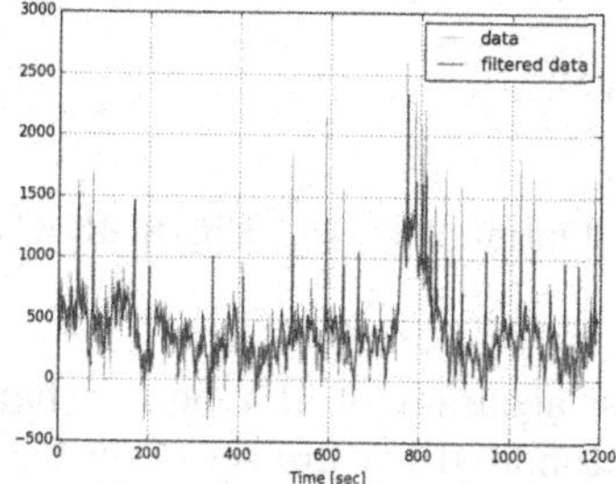

Fig. 5. Butterworth with filtering f = 2

So now we filtered all 32 EEG channels with digital Butterworth low-pass filter banks with 5 cut-off frequencies f = [0.5,1.5,2,3,20]. There are total of 32 × 5 = 160 features in the feature set. Then RFECV method is applied with option 2, 14 optimal features are reached from 160 total features with 90% accuracy, Fig. 7 represents the ROC curve using the RFECV method with option 2 for 'Grasp-and-Lift' dataset. Then we applied RFECV selection method using option 5 just like option 2. Again the 32 EEG channels are filtered with 5 low-pass filter banks of order 5 at f = [0.5,1.5,2,3,20], so there is a total of 160 features before RFECV feature selection. Figure 8 shows the ROC curve with option 5.

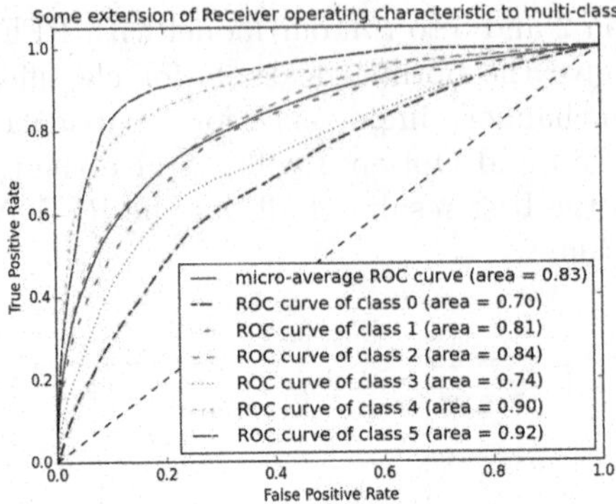

Fig. 6. ROC AUC for Butterworth low pass filter used on all columns, ROC AUC, is increased to 0.83 from 0.73

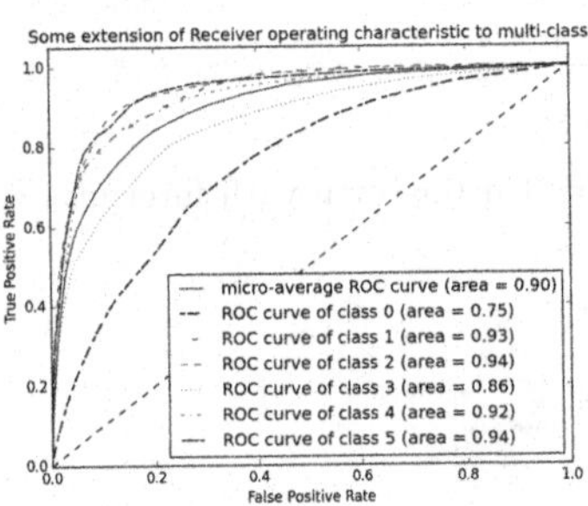

Fig. 7. ROC & AOC using Option 2

Some extension of Receiver operating characteristic to multi-class

True Positive Rate

False Positive Rate

micro-average ROC curve (area = 0.91)
ROC curve of class 0 (area = 0.79)
ROC curve of class 1 (area = 0.93)
ROC curve of class 2 (area = 0.94)
ROC curve of class 3 (area = 0.86)
ROC curve of class 4 (area = 0.93)
ROC curve of class 5 (area = 0.94)

Fig. 8. ROC & AOC using Option 5

Option 5 gives the best accuracy of 91% better than about 90% accuracy of option 2 with RFECV automated feature selection for Grasp-And-Lift dataset, but as compared to option 2, option 5 takes six times more time to run. While for option 5 RFECV method is executed for all classes separately that means RFECV method runs for six times and optimal features are found for each class separately, which are presented in Table 1.

3 Experimental Study

3.1 Implementation on Graz 2A BBCI Dataset

To confirm the performance of developed system, we have to test it with more datasets, we take the Graz dataset 2A from BBCI competition IV [16]. It is a four-class problem for the detection of motor imagery movements of left hand (class1), right hand (class2), both feet (class3) and tongue (class4). So, for each subject out of 72 trials for each class, 50 trials are used for training, and 22 trials are used for evaluation or classification. For this dataset, we performed two experiments using our proposed model.

Table 1. Optimal features selection using RFECV

Class #	Hand movement	Optimal features
1	Hand start	7
2	First digit touch	27
3	Both start load phase	45
4	Lift off	31
5	Replace	25
6	Both released	15

Experiment 1

Digital Butterworth low-pass filter banks of order 5 with 4 cut-off frequencies f = [0.5,1.5,2,3] are used. $22 \times 4 = 88$ features are given to RFECV for feature selection. Figure 9 shows the optimal number of features for this dataset against the cross-validation score. Table 2 concludes the results of experiment 1 with our approach for Graz 2A dataset and Fig. 10 shows the average ROC AUC for experiment 1.

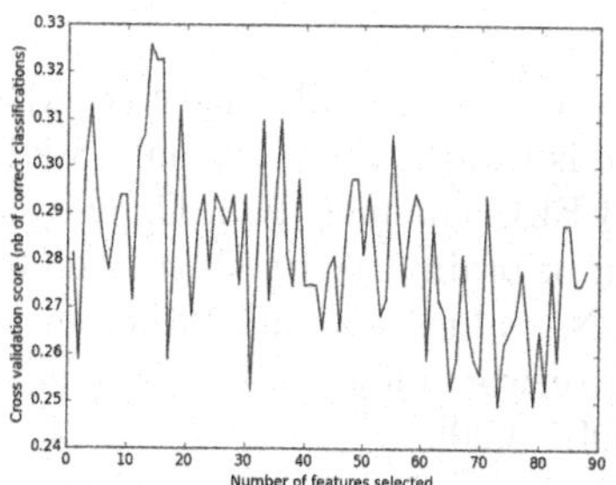

Fig. 9. Exp-1 features for Graz 2A

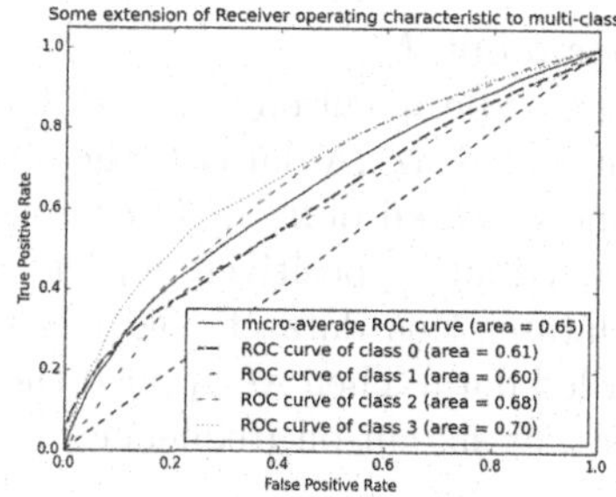

Fig. 10. Exp-1 ROC & AUC on Graz 2A

We also computed kappa score for all subjects and mean kappa score for overall experiment 1, which is 0.2155 is quite promising and competitive with the top five participants by using 50% less data for each subject.

Experiment 2

For artifact processing we implemented linear regression based artifact removal method for experiment 2 on Graz 2A BBCI dataset. The result of applying linear regression based EOG artifact removal method on subject A01 where fluctuations in EOG channels shows eye blinking which is the corrected signal as shown after EOG artifact processing. Table 2 presents the summary of experiment 2 on Graz 2A dataset using the artifact-processing unit.

Table 2. Result summary of Experiment 1 & 2 on GRAZ2A

Subject	Subject name	Experiment 1			Experiment 2		
		Optimal features	AOC ROC	Kappa score	Optimal features	AOC ROC	Kappa score
1	A01	33	0.65	0.23	34	0.77	0.40
2	A02	37	0.58	0.10	8	0.81	0.48
3	A03	37	0.68	0.26	27	0.79	0.43
4	A04	32	0.63	0.19	45	0.78	0.42
5	A05	36	0.67	0.28	50	0.79	0.45
6	A06	40	0.62	0.20	30	0.74	0.39
7	A07	45	0.67	0.25	26	0.80	0.44
8	A08	13	0.68	0.26	7	0.80	0.46
9	A09	14	0.64	0.19	23	0.76	0.38
Average			0.65	0.2155		0.78	0.42

3.2 Implementation on Graz 2B BBCI Dataset

It is a two-class problem for the detection of right and left hand motor imagery movements. For all nine subjects (B01 to B09), there are 5 sessions recorded signal, out of which 3 sessions are meant to use for training and 2 are meant to use for testing/evaluation. We performed two experiments on this Graz 2B BBCI dataset using our proposed model.

Experiment 1
For first experiment on Graz 2B dataset we used the same model just like experiment 1 of Graz 2A dataset, the only difference is that as there are only 3 EEG channels instead of 22 EEG channels and all 3 EEG channels (C3, Cz and C4) are contributing positively for the classification of brain activity. Just like Graz 2A dataset this dataset also has missing (NaN) values and idle/other events recorded data. Then we applied the Digital Butterworth low-pass filter banks of order 5 at six cut-off frequencies i.e. f = [1,2,3,4,7,9,20].

Experiment 2
For experiment 2 the missing values are resolved by averaging method. Then the signal is corrected by linear regression based artifact removal method. The signal data is filtered with Butterworth low-pass filter banks of order 5 at cut-off frequencies f = [1,2,3,4,7,9,20] just like experiment 1. For experiment 2 on Graz 2B dataset, we achieved a promising mean Cohen's kappa score of 0.61 and ROC AUC accuracy of about 93% as shown in Figs. 11 and 12. The accuracy achieved through this experiment on kappa score is quite promising.

CSP is widely used for EEG based BCI systems [17], and it shows good results. For benchmarking we applied the CSP on same datasets and kept the random forest as a classifier. The detail discussion for all three datasets experiments is presented below. Table 3 summarizes the results obtained using our proposed approach as compared to the CSP method.

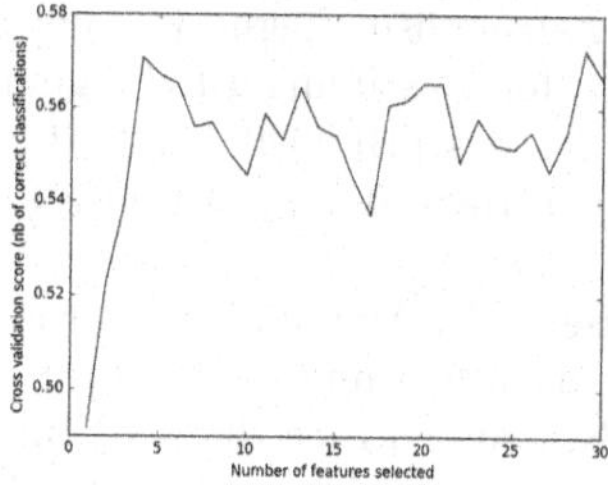

Fig. 11. Exp-1 features for Graz 2B

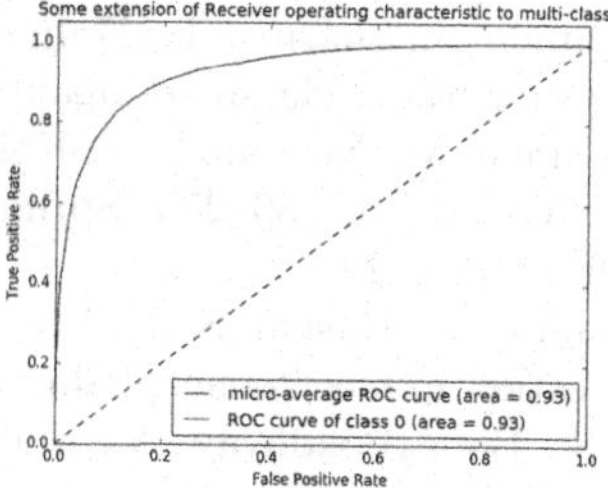

Fig. 12. Exp-1 ROC & AUC on Graz 2B

Table 3. Summary of results obtained using proposed approach

Dataset	Methods	Accuracy method	Accuracy
Grasp-And-Lift	Butterworth, RFECV, RF classifier	AUC ROC	91.3%
	CSP with RF classifier	AUC ROC	89.13%
Graz 2A Dataset	Butterworth, RFECV, RF classifier	Kappa Score	0.42
	CSP with RF classifier	Kappa Score	0.31
Graz 2B dataset	Butterworth, RFECV, RF classifier	Kappa Score	0.61
	SP with RF classifier	Kappa Score	0.60

4 Conclusion and Future Work

To compensate the noise and artifacts of EEG signals this paper presents an improved model for feature construction and feature selection and hence provide a more efficient BCI system to classify motor imagery. For 'Grasp-And-Lift' challenge we increased the accuracy to 91% from 73% using our proposed model with 25% less data for training. For Graz 2A and 2B datasets, we achieved kappa scores of 0.42 and 0.61 respectively, by using 50% and 40% reduced data. For all our experiments, we used relatively simple random classifier for feature classification. The promising results achieved by using our proposed feature construction and feature selection model shows the potential of its use for online experimentation. Further work will focus on online experiments to minimize the noise and improve the efficiency for its effectiveness.

References

1. Satu, M.S., et al.: Towards improved detection of cognitive performance using bidirectional multilayer long-short term memory neural network. In: Mahmud, M., Vassanelli, S., Kaiser, M.S., Zhong, N. (eds.) BI 2020. LNCS (LNAI), vol. 12241, pp. 297–306. Springer, Cham (2020). https://doi.org/10.1007/978-3-030-59277-6_27
2. Putz, M., et al.: Towards noninvasive hybrid brain-computer interfaces: framework, practice, clinical application, and beyond. Proc. IEEE **103**(6), 926–943 (2015)
3. Geronimo, A., Simmons, Z., Schiff, S.J.: Performance predictors of brain-computer interfaces in patients with amyotrophic lateral sclerosis. J. Neural Eng. **13**(2), 026002 (2016)

4. Rahman, S., Sharma, T., Mahmud, M.: Improving alcoholism diagnosis: comparing instance-based classifiers against neural networks for classifying EEG signal. In: Mahmud, M., Vassanelli, S., Kaiser, M.S., Zhong, N. (eds.) BI 2020. LNCS (LNAI), vol. 12241, pp. 239–250. Springer, Cham (2020). https://doi.org/10.1007/978-3-030-59277-6_22
5. Tahura, S., Hasnat Samiul, S.M., Shamim Kaiser, M., Mahmud, M.: Anomaly detection in electroencephalography signal using deep learning model. In: Kaiser, M.S., Bandyopadhyay, A., Mahmud, M., Ray, K. (eds.) Proceedings of International Conference on Trends in Computational and Cognitive Engineering. AISC, vol. 1309, pp. 205–217. Springer, Singapore (2021). https://doi.org/10.1007/978-981-33-4673-4_18
6. Tahir, A., Iqbal, J., Aized, T.: Human machine interface: robotizing the instinctive living. Int. Rob. Auto. J. **4**, 308–314 (2018)
7. Keil, A., et al.: Committee report: publication guidelines and recommendations for studies using electroencephalography and magnetoencephalography. Psychophysiology **51**(1), 1–21 (2014)
8. Mahmud, M., Kaiser, M.S., Hussain, A., Vassanelli, S.: Applications of deep learning and reinforcement learning to biological data. IEEE Trans. Neural Netw. Learn. Syst. **29**(6), 2063–2079 (2018)
9. López-Larraz, E., Bibián, C., Birbaumer, N., Ramos-Murguialday, M.: Influence of artifacts on movement intention decoding from EEG activity in severely paralyzed stroke patients. In: 2017 International Conference on Rehabilitation Robotics (ICORR), pp. 901–906. IEEE (2017)
10. Mahmud, M., Shamim Kaiser, M., McGinnity, T.M., Hussain, A.: Deep learning in mining biological data. Cogn. Comput. **13**(1) 1–33 (2021)
11. Tahernezhad-Javazm, F., Azimirad, V., Shoaran, M.: A review and experimental study on the application of classifiers and evolutionary algorithms in EEG-based brain-machine interface systems. J. Neural Eng. **15**(2), 021007 (2018)
12. Lotte, F., et al.: A review of classification algorithms for EEG-based brain-computer interfaces: a 10 year update. J. Neural Eng. **15**(3), 031005 (2018)
13. Lakshmi, M.R., Prasad, T.V., Chandra Prakash, V.: Survey on EEG signal processing methods. Int. J. Adv. Res. Comput. Sci. Softw. Eng. **4**(1) (2014)
14. Schlögl, A., Keinrath, C., Zimmermann, D., Scherer, R., Leeb, R., Pfurtscheller, G.: A fully automated correction method of EOG artifacts in EEG recordings. Clin. Neurophysiol. **118**(1), 98–104 (2007)
15. "Grasp-and-Lift EEG Detection." Kaggle. Accessed June 16, 2021. https://www.kaggle.com/c/grasp-and-lift-eeg-detection
16. Brunner, C., Leeb, R., Müller-Putz, G., Schlögl, A., Pfurtscheller, G.: BCI Competition 2008-Graz Data Set A. Institute for Knowledge Discovery (Laboratory of Brain-Computer Interfaces), Graz University of Technology, vol. 16, pp. 1–6 (2008)
17. Martín-Clemente, R., Olias, J., Thiyam, D.B., Cichocki, A., Cruces, A.: Information theoretic approaches for motor-imagery BCI systems: review and experimental comparison. Entropy **20**(1) 7(2018)
18. Grasp-and-Lift EEG Detection.: Kaggle. https://www.kaggle.com/c/grasp-and-lift-eeg-detection/leaderboard. Accessed 16 June 2021

EEG Signal Discrimination with Permutation Entropy

Youpeng Yang[1], Haolan Zhang[2], and Sanghyuk Lee[1](✉)

[1] Xi'an Jiaotong-Liverpool University, Suzhou 215123, China
Sanghyuk.Lee@xjtlu.edu.cn
[2] The Center for SCDM, NIT, Zhejiang University, Ningbo, China

Abstract. The information analysis of the electroencephalogram (EEG) signal is carried out by granulation and reciprocal entropy (PeEn). The analysis of the EEG signal is obtained by experimental activity. Due to its complexity and multichannel characteristic, together with granular computing (GrC) and PeEn are used to analyze the EEG signal. The EEG signal consists of 32 channels of data and the experimental data are used to discriminate patterns, with experimental focus on considering real and thinking actions. The time-series EEG signals were granularized according to the changes in the signal and analyzed by PeEn coding and Fuzzy C-Means (FCM) algorithm. Because there are two main actions, i.e., left-handed, and right-handed actions were clearly delineated. In addition, we provide the GrC algorithm to prove the boundary problem with the help of Hilbert-Huang transform. The obtained results show an advanced approach for analyzing EEG signals, which can be the basis for solving complex multichannel data analysis.

Keywords: EEG signal · Data uncertainty · Permutation entropy · Granulation · Granular computing

1 Introduction

Importance of information analysis for the complex system has been emphasized, and information granulation has illustrated as an interesting topic for knowledge representation and problem solving [1]. Methodology of mass data processing could be applied to many industrial areas such as application to the automation and smart factory [2]. As it pointed out, huge data including multi-channel processing methodology is one of challenge how to process massive information, specifically EEG signal processing has been carried out by numerous researchers [3, 4] and the references therein. In order to get the signal processing, the algorithm and methodologies are proposed to resolve the complexity including uncertainty [6–8].

In this paper, we focus on analyzing the EEG signal. EEG signals represent the measured brain signal, and it includes human thinking together with decision for the motion [9, 10]. EEG signal is composed of multi-channel which are dependent on measurement device and man machine interface. Widely and commonly, non-invasive scalp-recorded

M. Mahmud et al. (Eds.): BI 2021, LNAI 12960, pp. 519–528, 2021.
https://doi.org/10.1007/978-3-030-86993-9_46

EEG signal is used, it is rather easy and inexpensive to get the experimental signal. However, we face to the challenge in the analysis on EEG signal due to their multi-channel characteristics [11]. In brain signal analysis, there are many approaches such as pattern discrimination, information retrieval, action decision. Regardless of any brain signal analysis, feature extraction from EEG is one of the most important tasks. Analyzing approach includes many types of ways. First, we must differentiate for the different patterns. It is based on the fact that different thinking generates different EEG signal. Lots of methodologies has been proposed by many researchers [10–14]. In their research, classification results were obtained by using EEG signal as digitization and principal component. Another challenge to analyzing EEG signal is to get the explicit information from EEG signal. The research outcomes are still left to the open problem.

In order to analyze experimental EEG signal, signal entropy and data granulation are considered in this paper. For the time series signal discrimination, statistical approached has been carried out. However, it is believed that the information is included in data trend change and its degree. To get such information analysis with group data, piecewise data analysis has limitation, and statistical value such as average and standard deviation is not proper for recognizing accurate information. Herewith, data granulation provides good motivation to get the information from the time series data. In this paper, we have provided data granulation for EEG signal with the help of time series granulation research [5]. After dividing data group, we get the information on data rectangle with minimum and maximum values of the data granule. Due to the successive granulation process, overlap can happen with adjacent granule. Fuzzy C-Mean (FCM) methodology is considered to overcome overlap problem. Generally, entropy notice us data uncertainty. We also considered data entropy for successive data. From the entropy, flat data distribution shows low entropy value, whereas high variant data indicates high entropy. Together with data granulation, data interval for the calculation of entropy is fixed. Specifically, entropy value is calculated from all possible combination, hence data permutation is considered during data interval. In the previous research, PeEn provides time series data discrimination through calculation of the signal entropy [11, 15, 16]. With the obtained experimental EEG data, it includes two hands raising with real action and just thinking. However, information granular rectangle overlap happens, and it makes difficult to discriminate the patterns. Hence, Hilbert-Huang transformation to overcome the granular overlap.

The paper is organized as follows. In the next section, we introduce preliminary knowledge on EEG signal and granulation methodology. This provides the foundation to organize EEG data granulation. Additionally, PeEn is also illustrated with numeric calculation. In Sect. 3, data granulation and PeEn apply to the EEG signal granulation. Action classifications result also followed. In Sect. 4, Hilbert-Huang methodology is proposed to overcome the overlap in granulation. The calculation result is acceptable for wide range of sample time. Finally, paper conclusions are included in Sect. 5.

2 Data Granulation and Preliminaries

In this section, data collection procedure together with experiment conditions are introduced. Proper channel data selection, granulation background and granulation process are also introduced. Furthermore, in order to resolve data uncertainty in EEG signal, entropy theory is used with PeEn.

2.1 EEG Signal and Its Acquisition

Normally, EEG signal is obtained by the experimental unit including sensor with head cab, data logger unit. In the lab environment, non-invasive experiment would be carried out from its inexpensive cost and lots of brain-computer interface (BCI) applications Multi-channel EEG data that we obtain are dependent on experimental unit, it means 16, 32, 64 and more 128 channels are also possible. For the classification methodology, lots of approaches including time series analysis, frequency approach and heuristic approaches were proposed [17]. In the experiment, 32 channel data with 28 sensors in scalp and 2 sensors for eye motion are measured. In Fig. 1, 32 channels head cap is shown. In the experiment, we emphasized the following viewpoints: It focuses on real action and thinking for the same action. More analysis on the experiment is needed for the virtual action and control.

We collected EEG signal from 40 experiment participants. Their experiments focus on real action of raising right/left hand and just thinking of the motion. In order to discriminate each action, we paused with 5 s. And experiment participant information is blinded to protect personal information.

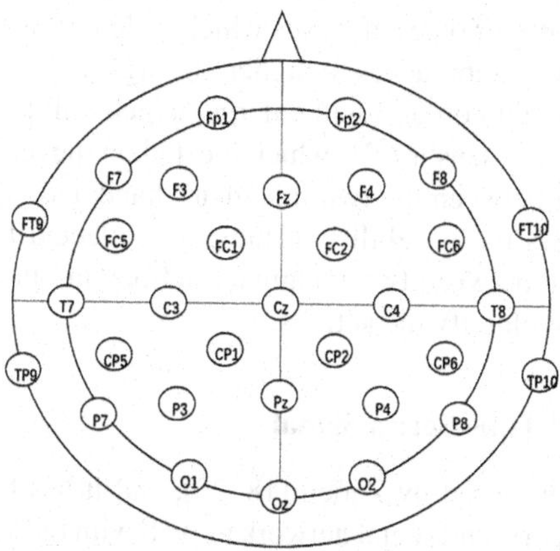

Fig. 1. EEG data collection cap

During the experiment, participants are required to image pressing the left or right arrow keys when seeing the corresponding arrow on the screen. Furthermore, the experiment of actual pressing keys is also required to finish in next step of the data collection experiment. To find the difference between the different parts of body, videos about hands and legs actions would be shown to participants in the third part of the experiment. In order to simplify the discrimination by PeEn, in this study only hand actions will be classified.

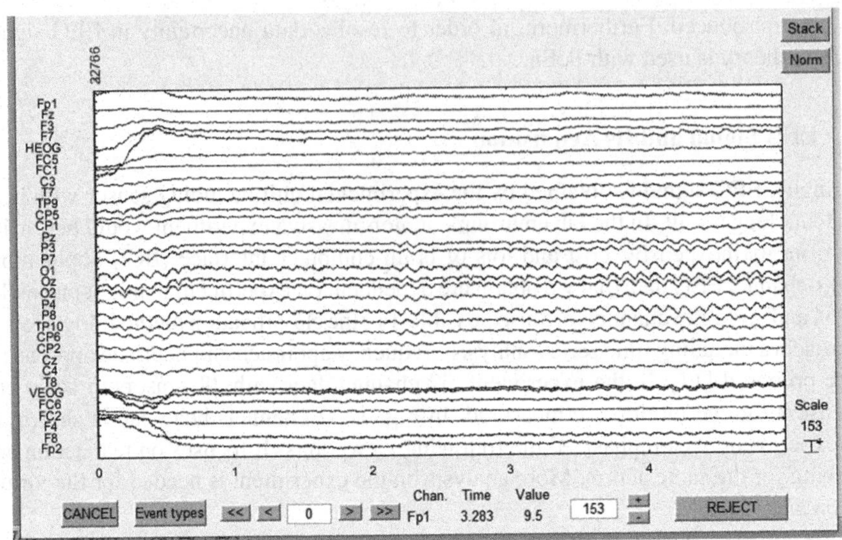

Fig. 2. Original EEG signal plotting without noise reduction.

Figure 2 shows sample of EEG signal, it composes 32 channel information. Signal last 5 s and it shows typical multi-channel data. From the conventional knowledge of EEG signal, it consists of four types of waves which called α wave, β wave, θ wave and δ wave. When the frequency approaches to higher, the signal becomes more complex and the permutation entropy with order 3 will enlarge, which will be explained in Sect. 3.

In this study, the data of sensor FP1, which located on the left front side of the cap is the most distinguishing between the two imaginary hand actions. Although the largest standard deviation shows the instability of the data collected from FP1 channel. The mean values of distance between two imaginary actions in other sensors are not large enough and it is risky to classify the actions.

2.2 Granulation with Time Series Signal

Granulation has been proposed by Zadeh [18–20], and it has been extended to signal processing, decision theory, and social network as well with the help of fuzzy and human centered information processing [4, 19–21]. For the formulation of granulation, different kind of axiomatization of granulation have been proposed such as Zermelo - Fraenkel Axiomatization, von Neumann – Bernays - Goedel Axiomatization, and Mereology [5].

In this paper, we propose information granule with the consideration of time series signal magnitude and gradient value [24]. For the time series data granulation, data granulation provides the understanding of concept on abstract knowledge by way of numerical data transformation [8]. Granulation schemes has been proposed by Bargiela and Pedrycz as time-domain, phase–space and information density granulation approaches.

From the time series data granulation methodologies, each granulation was organized through numerical data to abstract knowledge [21–23]. Fragments are assigned as Ω_k $k = 1, \ldots, m$, as to the number of fragments m. Data granulations are considered from original N data $X = \{x_1, x_2, \ldots, x_N\}$ to the set of time interval $I = \{I_1, I_2, \ldots, I_G\}$, were G is number of granules.

Granulation window $\omega_o, \omega_o G \leq N$ is satisfied. Then for the time domain granulation,

$$I_k = (min(x_i), \max(x_i)). \tag{1}$$

It means that each I_k is constituted to make set interval I. In the phase space granulation, hyper-boxes are constituted by Cartesian product together with Eq. (1) and following phase granulation. And the $grad(x_i, x_j)$ is the data slope between x_i and x_j, $norm(\cdot)$ indicates normalization for each gradient value of interval. Hence, minimum and maximum values of phase each interval expressed as:

$$J_k = \begin{cases} \min\limits_{i \neq j, i, j \in \Omega_k} (norm(grad(x_i, x_j))) \\ \max\limits_{i \neq j, i, j \in \Omega_k} (norm(grad(x_i, x_j))). \end{cases} \tag{2}$$

Then, we can obtain hyper-box with time domain granulation as $H = \{H_1, H_2, \ldots, H_G\}$ for each granule, that is expressed as Cartesian product $H_k = I_k \times J_k$.

2.3 Permutation Entropy on EEG Signals

With the various application of Permutation Entropy (PeEn) method, PeEn has been provided for the information of complexity measure for time series data by Bandit and Pompe [13]. For the set of time series value $X = \{x_1, x_2, \ldots, x_N\}$, ordinal patterns of permutation have the following structure $\mathrm{P}_N = \{\mathrm{P}_1, \mathrm{P}_2, \ldots, \mathrm{P}_{N!}\}$. For example, tuple (x_1, x_2, x_3) with different values with the height order 1, 2, 3. Then, possible outcomes have 3! with whole pattern [13],

$$P_3 = \{123, 132, 213, 231, 312, 321\}. \tag{3}$$

For the particular pattern π_t, where $\pi_t = (x_t, x_{t+\tau}, \ldots, x_{t+(m-1)\tau})$, m is order from the time series X and τ denotes distance between samples. The permutation entropy of order $2 \leq n$ can be defined as:

$$H(n) = -\sum p(\pi) logp(\pi) \tag{4}$$

Where n is the order of the permutation entropy and $p(\pi)$ is the relative frequency which can be expressed as:

$$p(\pi) = \frac{\#\{t | 0 \leq t \leq T - n, (x_t, \ldots, x_{t+n}) \text{has type } \pi)}{T - n + 1} \tag{5}$$

The permutation entropy is used as a complexity measurement of time series. It also was used in EEG data analysis [15, 16]. In granular computing, permutation entropy can be used as a new base to do the granulation. It will be discussed in the research outcome part.

3 EEG Signals Granulation

In this section, we derive EEG signal classification with granulation and PeEn. Due to inclusion of uncertainty in EEG signal, GrC and PeEn are considered together. After signal granulation, the EEG data are separated with different group through FCM clustering method. We have obtained two kind of EEG signal which show two hand actions, thinking and actual raise right and left hand separately. The action lasted for 2.5 s. The EEG data was collected 1000 times per second.

The permutation entropy of the EEG signal for the two hands are illustrated in Fig. 3. Red and blue points are raising right and left-hand thinking, respectively. From the Fig. 3, obvious discriminations start from 500 ms sample time. As sample time increase, more distinctive phenomena appeared.

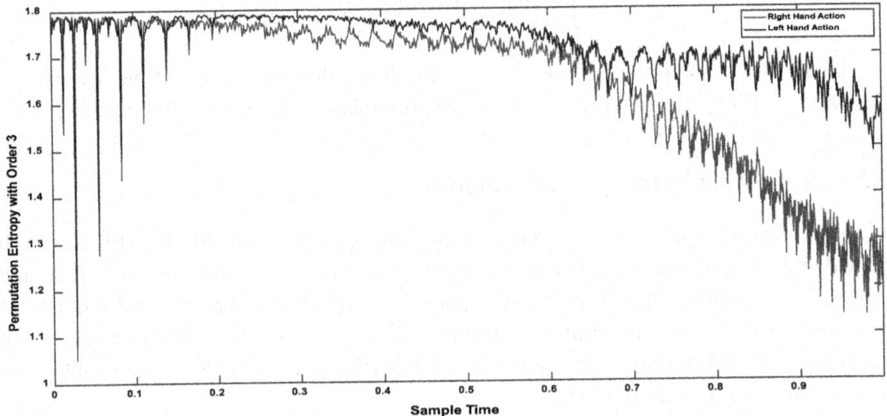

Fig. 3. Permutation entropy of two hand actions

From the Fig. 3, the two actions of different hand can be distinguished after sample time larger than 0.5 s. Meanwhile, the frequency of EEG wave is at most 40 Hz. In next step of the simulation, we only take the PeEn values with sample time greater than 0.5 s.

After calculation of the permutation entropy, we employ the FCM method to clustering the entropy data into 5 clusters. The five clusters can be seen as different waves of the EEG data. With this characteristic of different EEG waves, the permutation entropy with different sample time can be shown as the granules in the granular computing method.

Two hands actions are discriminated clearly, the boundary between two actions is also obvious. However, difference between five actions is not discriminated. Hence, we apply data granulation for the obtained each action. By the employment of FCM method, the granulation processing is shown in Fig. 4. From the result of Fig. 4, left hand raisings are separated well than right hand raising. For the right hand raising, it is rather difficult to discriminate due to its boundary overlap.

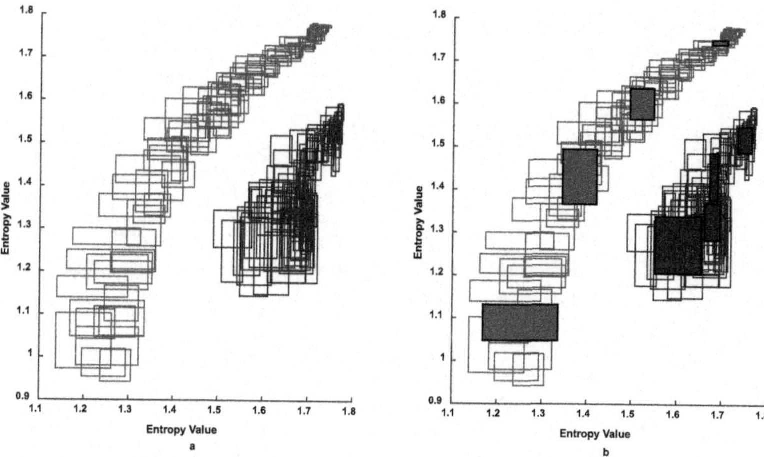

Fig. 4. Granulation result of the entropy value. a) granules of five kinds of wavs, b) granules and their center of four kinds of waves

4 Discussions

Along with the increase of sample time in Fig. 4, the PeEn decreases. According to the frequency of different wave and the granules representing different values of PeEn, there have been shown overlap in Fig. 4. The sample time intervals can be fixed as the length of specific EEG wave. From the studies [27], four kinds of EEG waves have different frequency with 8–13 Hz, 14–40 Hz, 0.5–3 Hz, and 4–7 Hz. Therefore, the sample time of PeEn can be taken as four intervals: 0.076 s to 0.140 s, 0.025 to 0.075 s, 0.300 to 1 s, and 0.142 to 0.250 s. The entropy values in each interval can be seen as the corresponding entropy values of each EEG wave. After this method, the entropy points can be drawn together with the same interval of sample time. For β wave with the highest frequency has been analyzed by previous research using the down sampling method by increasing the sample time [25, 26]. Furthermore, from the outcome in this study, low-frequency information contributes more to classification of imaginary actions. The order of PeEn can be enlarged to ensure that there is less missing for low-frequency information. However, PeEn is proposed to simplify the analysis of signal. The calculation would be more complex with the order increasing [15].

In recent research [9, 27–29], the Hilbert Huang Transform (HHT) was applied in EEG data analysis. It made a decomposition of the signal into a collection of Intrinsic Mode Function. This method of transformation can be also used to normalize the EEG data. After normalization, the data will be change smoothly. This could transform the overlapping EEG data into detached. However, the normalized data will be small quantitatively. It may make the granulation more difficult. Furthermore, the granules might overlap to each other (Fig. 5).

The Hilbert transformation can be expressed as below:

$$H(x(t)) = y(t) = \lim_{\varepsilon \to 0}[\int_{-\infty}^{0-\varepsilon} \frac{x(u)}{\pi(t-u)}du + \int_{0-\varepsilon}^{\infty} \frac{x(u)}{\pi(x-u)}du]$$

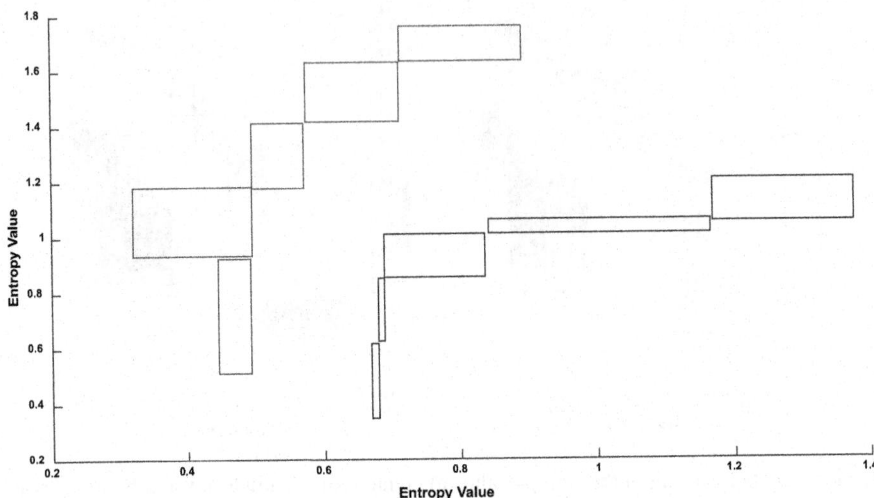

Fig. 5. Granulation result with Hilbert-Huang transformation

Hilbert-Huang transformation is introduced to reduce the overlap between same action's granules. In this regards, Hilbert-Huang transformation will also reduce the value of PeEn since the transformation will change the data into a smooth change rather than the sudden change.

5 Conclusions

Electroencephalography (EEG) signal analysis with PeEn and GrC has been carried out. EEG signal consists of 32 channel data, and the experimental data are used to discriminate the pattern. Exploring analysis method, EEG signal is coded as PeEn and illustrated by Fuzzy C-Mean (FCM) algorithm. Discriminate experiment signal for more detail, GrC is proposed and two main actions with left- and right-hand actions are divided with obviously. However, additional actions with each hand are not clear with only PeEn. Simulation result with GrC also has challenge to make more discriminate for each action due to its overlap around boundary regions. Additionally, we provide modified GrC algorithm to improve the boundary issue. The obtained result shows advanced approach to analyze EEG signal, and it could be the foundation to resolve complex, multi-channel data analysis.

References

1. Elhoseny, M., Azar, A.T., Snášel, V. (eds.): Big Data in Complex Systems: Challenges and Opportunities. Springer, Cham (2015). https://doi.org/10.1007/978-3-319-11056-1
2. Pagnon, W.: The 4th industrial revolution–a smart factory implementation guide. Int. J. Adv. Robot. Autom. (IJARA) **2**(2), 1–5 (2017)

3. Shestyuk, A.Y., Kasinathan, K., Karapoondinott, V., Knight, R.T., Gurumoorthy, R.: Individual EEG measures of attention, memory, and motivation predict population level TV viewership and Twitter engagement. PLoS One **14**(3), e0214507 (2019)
4. Wang, G., Xu, J.: Granular computing with multiple granular layers for brain big data processing. Brain Informatics **1**(1–4), 1 (2014). https://doi.org/10.1007/s40708-014-0001-z
5. Bargiela, A., Pedrycz, W.: Toward a theory of granular computing for human-centered information processing. IEEE Trans. Fuzzy Syst. **16**(2), 320–330 (2008)
6. Yao, J.T., Vasilakos, A.V., Pedrycz, W.: Granular computing: perspectives and challenges. IEEE Trans. Cybern. **43**(6), 1977–1989 (2013)
7. Oh, S.K., Kim, W.D., Park, B.J., Pedrycz, W.: A design of granular-oriented self-organizing hybrid fuzzy polynomial neural networks. Neurocomputing **119**, 292–307 (2013)
8. Pedrycz, W., Rai, P.: A multifaceted perspective at data analysis: a study in collaborative intelligent agents. IEEE Trans. Syst. Man Cybern. Part B Cybern. **39**(4), 834–44 (2009)
9. Quan, L., et al.: Frontal EEG temporal and spectral dynamics similarity analysis between propofol and desflurane induced anesthesia using Hilbert-Huang transform. BioMed. Res. Int. **2018**, 1–16 (2018)
10. Aziz, F., Shapiai, M.I., Setiawan, N.A., Mitsukura, Y.: Classification of human concentration in EEG signals using Hilbert Huang transform. Int. J. Simul. Syst. Sci. Technol. **18**(1), 10.1–10.11 (2017)
11. Miao, M., Zeng, H., Wang, A., Zhao, C., Liu, F.: Discriminative spatial-frequency-temporal feature extraction and classification of motor imagery EEG: an sparse regression and weighted Nave Bayesian classifier-based approach. J. Neurosci. Methods **278**, 13–24 (2017)
12. Bandt, C.: A new kind of permutation entropy used to classify sleep stages from invisible EEG microstructure. Entropy **19**(5), 197 (2017)
13. Berger, S., Schneider, G., Eberhard, K., et al.: Permutation entropy: too complex a measure for EEG time series? Entropy **19**, 692 (2017)
14. Zhang, H.L., Lee, S., Li, X., He, J.: EEG self-adjusting data analysis based on optimized sampling for robot control. Electronics **9**(6), 925 (2020)
15. Procházka, A., Mudrová, M., Vyšata, O., Gráfová, L., Araujo, C.P.S.: Computational intelligence in multi-channel EEG signal analysis. In: Recent Advances in Intelligent Engineering Systems. Springer, Berlin, Heidelberg (2012)
16. Bandt, C., Pompe, B.: Permutation entropy: a natural complexity measure for time series. Phys. Rev. Lett. **88**(17), 174102 (2002)
17. Quadrianto, N., Cuntai, G., Dat, T.H., Xue, P.: Sub-band Common Spatial Pattern (SBCSP) for brain-computer interface. In: International IEEE/EMBS Conference on Neural Engineering. IEEE (2007)
18. Zadeh, L.A.: Toward a theory of fuzzy information granulation and its centrality in human reasoning and fuzzy logic. Fuzzy Sets Syst. **90**(2), 111–127 (1997)
19. Zadeh, L.A.: Some reflections on soft computing, granular computing and their roles in the conception, design and utilization of information/intelligent systems. Soft Comput. **2**(1), 23–25 (1998)
20. Zadeh, L.A., Gupta, M.M., Ragade, R.K., Yager, R.R.: Fuzzy sets and information granularity (1979)
21. Hońko, P.: Association discovery from relational data via granular computing. Inf. Sci. **234**, 136–149 (2013)
22. Li, J., Mei, C., Xu, W., Qian, Y.: Concept learning via granular computing: a cognitive viewpoint. Inf. Sci. **2015**, 1–21 (2015)
23. Kundu, S., Pal, S.K.: Double bounded rough set, tension measure, and social link prediction. IEEE Trans. Comput. Soc. Syst. **PP**(99), 1–13 (2018)

24. Bargiela, A., Pedrycz, W.: Granulation of temporal data: a global view on time series. In: Fuzzy Information Processing Society, Nafips International Conference of the North American. IEEE (2003)
25. Liu, N.H., Chiang, C.Y., Chu, H.C.: Recognizing the degree of human attention using EEG signals from mobile sensors. Sensors **13**(8), 10273–10286 (2013)
26. Noachtar, S., Binnie, C., Ebersole, J., Mauguiere, F., Sakamoto, A., Westmoreland, B.: A glossary of terms most commonly used by clinical electroencephalographers and proposal for the report form for the EEG findings. Klinische Neurophysiologie **35**(1), 5–21 (2004)
27. Liu, X., Wang, G., Gao, J., Gao, Q.: A quantitative analysis for EEG signals based on modified permutation-entropy. IRBM **38**(2) (2017)
28. Feng-Fang, T., Fan, S.Z., Lin, Y.S., Huang, N.E., Jia-Rong, Y., Schmitt, F.G.: Investigating power density and the degree of nonlinearity in intrinsic components of anesthesia EEG by the hilbert-huang transform: an example using ketamine and alfentanil. PLoS One 11(12), e0168108 (2016)
29. Popov, A., Avilov, O., Kanaykin, O.: Permutation entropy of EEG signals for different sampling rate and time lag combinations. In: Signal Processing Symposium. IEEE (2013)

Human-Computer Interaction Model for Brainstorming Based on Extenics

Xingsen Li[1(✉)], Haibin Pi[2], and Haolan Zhang[3]

[1] Research Institute of Extenics and Innovation Methods, Guangdong University of Technology, Guangzhou 510006, China
lixs@gdut.edu.cn

[2] School of Electromechanical Engineering, Guangdong University of Technology, Guangzhou 510006, China

[3] Center for SCDM, NIT, Zhejiang University, Ningbo 315100, China
haolan.zhang@nit.zju.edu.cn

Abstract. Brainstorming has been used for many years and have a very good efforts, however, the brainstorm also mainly relies on human's capability of brains, especially experience and knowledge they possessed. Based on the new discipline called Extenics, we proposed a testing method to explore the process of how ideas are bring out of brains, and help people think in multi dimensions and put forward more ideas. Extenics has been applied to study the extension and transformation of things in formalized models and obtain systematic creatives to solve contradictory problems intelligently since 1983. Support with Information technology and artificial Intelligence, we collect more Information and knowledge systematically to form basic elements based on Extenics using Human-Computer Interaction model to help people find more characteristics and its value of objectives. This will compensate the limited Information and knowledge in human brains. Also, we provide a methodology to help people thinking in multi dimensions positively according to the instruction of our methods based on extension innovation method. The case study proves its effectiveness in improving the capability of innovation of college students by EGG and Data Statistics.

Keywords: Human-computer interaction · Extenics · Brainstorming · Innovative ideas

1 Introduction

Innovation is playing a more and more important role both in research and business in the 21st century [1]. However, innovation relies on novel ideas created from individuals with limited experience and background knowledge, less breakthrough on the process of how innovative ideas is produced by ordinary people which remain considered as a "black box" and difficult to be observed and modeled [2, 3].

Brainstorming is a method of stimulating creative thinking first proposed in 1938 by American scholar Alex Osborne, the founder of modern creation studies [4]. It uses intuitive thinking and divergent thinking to generate new possible solutions or ideas to

M. Mahmud et al. (Eds.): BI 2021, LNAI 12960, pp. 529–535, 2021.
https://doi.org/10.1007/978-3-030-86993-9_47

problems and has been widely used in creative thinking activities in business, teaching and other fields [5, 6]. However, the brainstorm also mainly relies on human's capability of brains, especially experience and knowledge they possessed. Today's Internet environment provides a good opportunity for innovation [7, 8]. An increasing amount of information and knowledge springs up in the World Wide Web which can be combined with Brainstorming methods to fill the gap of knowledge and information of mankind.

Extenics has been applied to study the extension and transformation of things in formalized models and obtain systematic creatives to solve contradictory problems intelligently based on extension set theory, basic element theory and extension transformation methods since 1983 [9, 10]. Based on Extenics, we proposed a testing method to explore the process of how ideas are bring out of brains, and help people think in multi dimensions and put forward more ideas.

2 Methodology Analysis

2.1 Brainstorming

The process of brainstorming is simple without much constraints. It allows people to speak freely, regardless of their rank and position. There is no much threshold requirement for participants and does not allow them to comment or evaluate their ideas in the process. So employees, managers, supervisors and senior leaders can participate in the process in various environmental scenarios. In this method, a group of people jointly explore specific topics and problems, and the process of joint exploration will be more exciting and energetic. the participants are more likely to be inspired and open up new directions for exploration [11].

However,there are several disadvantages in current Brainstorming method in its practical application. The first is that divergent thinking used in Brainstorming lacks systemicity and can often only solve relatively simple problems. It can only stimulate the original talents of the participants, and most of the ideas generated are not pioneering ideas. The second is that the average quality of a single idea is poor. The number of plans is large, but the quality is not high, and they even deviate from the topic and discussion of the issue. When communicating and discussing, it is impossible to judge whether the divergence is comprehensive, lacking in logic and structure, and ignoring the level or angle that should be paid attention to. The third is that the success of brainstorming depends on the individual's ability and the host. In the practice of many brainstorming methods, the results achieved are different, and the gap between the professional backgrounds of the group members is too large, which may not be able to cause enlightening thinking [11, 12].

Due to people's experience, knowledge and ability are limited, sometimes more innovative ideas are difficult to generate through brainstorming without the support of effective scientific methods. Extenics provides a systematic thinking method, which can effectively make up for the disadvantages of brainstorming.

2.2 Extenics

Extenics is a new crossing discipline which sets up on the foundation of mathematics, philosophy, and information science, etc. It takes contradiction problems as the research object and has been applied in many engineering fields [9]. According to the Extenics, the Basic-element theory defines basic elements of "matter-element" (all physical and non-physical existence), "affair-element" (events or actions between matters) and "relation-element" (relations between matter and matter, event and event, event and matter) for modeling the information. One dimensional basic-element is an ordered triad, consisting of object, characteristics and corresponding measures, denoted by $M = (O, c, v)$ where M represents the matter; c, the characteristics; v is the M's measure about the characteristics c, affair-element $A = (E, c, v)$ and relation-element $R = (N, c, v)$.

The basic-element theory can guide us to collect information in a systematic and uniform structure. Things change as time goes by, so we usually use dynamic matter with multiple characteristics to express information of matter as following.

$$M(t) = \begin{bmatrix} O_m(t), & c_{m1}, & v_{m1}(t) \\ & c_{m2}, & v_{m2}(t) \\ & \vdots & \vdots \\ & c_{mn}, & v_{mn}(t) \end{bmatrix} = (O_m(t),\ C_m,\ V_m(t)) \tag{1}$$

As to a given matter, its value about characteristic is unique at certain moment as shown in above equation. The basic-element guide us to think all possible directions in multi-dimensions.

3 Human-Computer Interaction Model for Brainstorming

3.1 Brainstorming Process Based on Extenics

Based on the theory of Extenics and extension innovation method [10], the Brainstorming process to obtain new ideas can be listed in Fig. 1:

We define problems from conditions and goals, then we divided all attenders into several small teams according to Extenics such as following.

Firstly, we divided all attenders into two groups. One group analysis on conditions, Call the group C and another group analysis on goals called group G. Then we divided group C into three small groups called matter element, a fair element and relation element groups. Named as C1, C2 and C3; Similarly, we divided group G into three groups such as G1, G2 and G3. each group try its best to list as much as objects, characteristics and values according to its subtopics. For example, group C3 will list as much as objectives, characteristics and values on relationships of conditions. Meanwhile, group G2 will list as much as objectives, characteristics and values on the affairs of goals.

Four extension analysis methods will support the group to thinking in higher dimensions. The four methods includes divergence analysis, correlation analysis, conjugate analysis, and implication analysis. We collect all Information together, then use human-computer interaction model to compensate more Information by a software from the world wide web. And finally, we get a multi-dimensional extended information base in the format of basic element. After we have obtained a full set extended Information base, we Reunion all groups together And Let them review all the Information on goals and conditions until no new Information will be added in the base.

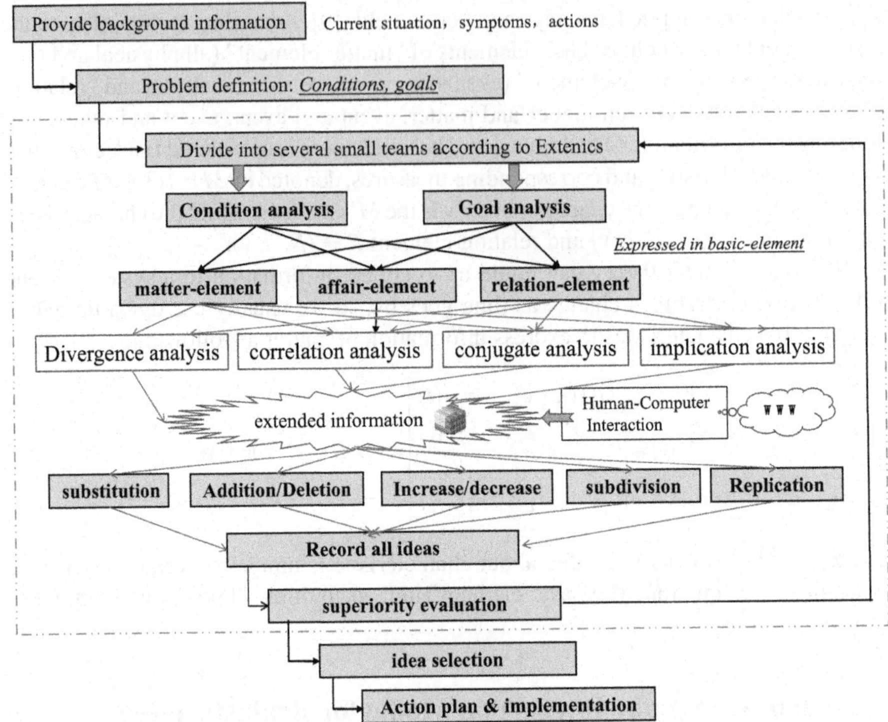

Fig. 1. A Brainstorming process based on Extenics

We Redivide them into five groups, according to five basic transformation methods Including substituting, addition/deletion, increase/decrease, subdivision and replication. Each group use one substitute transformation methods to create new ideas. If time permission, they can shift the transformation methods to get more innovative ideas, then we use superiority evolution methods to score and select the best ideas for action plan and implementation.

3.2 Human-Computer Interaction Methods

Based on the Human-Computer Interaction model, the general steps to obtain new ideas can be listed as four steps in Fig. 2:

Step 1. Collect Information and Knowledge

Collect information and tacit knowledge related to the innovation goal and practical condition from the Web, expertise by information technology such as web crawler and web mining.

Step 2. Information Processing to Build Basic Element Base

Describe and transform the information and knowledge as matter-elements, event-elements or relation-element and save them into tables or database. Then build extension information cube by conjugate analysis.

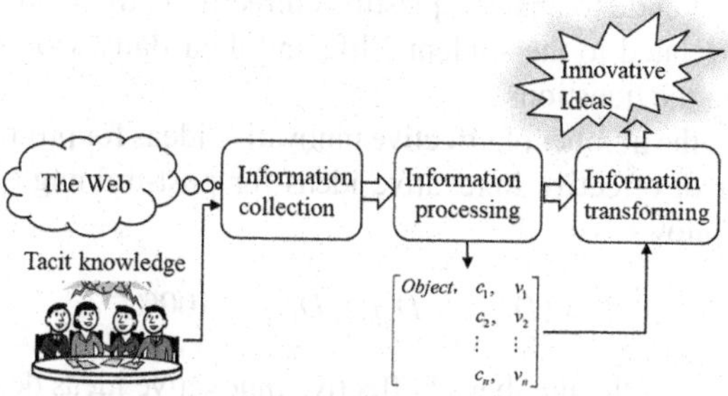

Fig. 2. Main steps to obtain new ideas based on Human-Computer Interaction

Step 3. Get Possible Ideas by Information Transforming

Apply five basic transformation methods to transform the information base in matrix of basic-elements and get possible ideas.

Step 4. Select the Novel Ideas

Select the novel ideas by AHP method or dependant function [10] from above possible ideas. The evaluation criteria are both quantitative and qualitative.

4 Case Study

We have designed some seemingly different creative thinking training topics for our new Brainstorm model. Here are four topics as example:

> "1. Some graduates plan to work in the Google company, but the score of data analysis cannot meet the requirements of qualification, please expand as much as possible actions to help it achieve this goal"
>
> "2. A key middle school student wants to be an miyoshi outstanding student, the miyoshi student requires all previous English test scores more than 85 points on average, but his English exam is only an average of 82 points, how to do?"
>
> "3. A professor's mandarin is not standard, he is not humor, but each time full of the students gathered to listen to his class, why?" You have 10 min to come up with 25 more reasonable explanations.
>
> "4. A junior high school student only got 56 score in his math exam, but his parents are very happy to treat him McDonald's, why?" Please come up with more than 20 reasonable explanations in 8 min.

This training method was compared between students of Ningbo Institute of Technology Zhejiang University in 2011–2015 and students of Guangdong University of Technology in 2015–2018 (involving 23 majors). Sixty students were randomly selected as control group. One week before training and two weeks after free learning, they were given a similar innovative training topic. In the elective course of Extension Innovative Thinking and Training, all the students from 19 majors, as the training group, also do the same innovative training topic one week before training and two weeks after free learning. In the past few years, it was written on paper, and then it was changed to scan two-dimensional code to answer questions directly on the mobile phone. Because the topic is closely related to the students' life and their daily scores, the students are enthusiastic in doing the questions.

D_{old} is defined as the number of effective innovative ideas for pre-training expansion, D_{new} is the number of effective innovative ideas for post-training expansion, and the degree of lift is as follows:

$$l = (D_{new} - D_{old})/D_{old} \times 100\% \quad (2)$$

The results show that the number of effective innovative ideas developed by trained students has a remarkable improvement proved by the statistical results.

5 Conclusion

We can't observe the innovation process well formerly so we don't know how innovative ideas is created. Based on the new discipline Extenics and Brainstorming method, we are proposing a testing method with the aid of Electroencephalography (EEG) to explore the process of how ideas are bringing out of brains [13, 14], and help people think in multi dimensions and put forward more ideas.

Support with Information technology and artificial Intelligence, we will collect more Information and knowledge systematically to form basic elements based on Extenics and use Human-Computer interaction model to help people find more characteristics and its value of objectives. This will compensate the limited information and knowledge in human brains. Also, we will provide our methodology to help people thinking in multi dimensions positively according to the instruction of our new model.

Acknowledgements. This research was supported by Humanities and Social Sciences project (18YJAZH049) of the Ministry of Education, China and Postgraduate Education Innovation Project of Guangdong Province (2018JGXM34).

References

1. Chen, J., Lv, W.: Innovation study: evolution and contribution of China. Technol. Econ. **37**(5), 1–13 (2018)
2. Martin, B.R.: Twenty challenges for innovation studies. Sci. Pub. Policy **43**(3), 432–450 (2016)
3. He, H., Liu, W., Yu, J., Li, X.: Extenics-based testing method of divergent thinking quotient. Procedia Comput. Sci. **91**, 151–157 (2016)
4. Chae, K. : Alex Osborn & brainstorming (1997). http://www.ciadvertising.org/
5. Dugosh, K.L.: Cognitive stimulation in brainstorming. J. Pers. Soc. Psychol. **79**(5), 722–735 (2020)
6. Wu, J.: Application of brainstorming in the internet. Inf. Sci. **06**, 749–751 (2004)
7. Zhuang, Y., Wu, F., Chen, C., Pan, Y.: Challenges and opportunities: from big data to knowledge in AI2.0. Front. Inf. Technol. Electron. Eng. **18**(1), 3–14 (2017)
8. Li, X., Tian, Y., Smarandache, F., Alex, R.: An extension collaborative innovation model in the context of Big Data. Int. J. Inf. Technol. Decis. Making **14**(1), 69–91 (2015)

9. Yang, C., Cai, W.: Extenics: Theory. Method and Application. Science Press, Beijing (2013)
10. Yang, C.: Extension Innovation Method. CRC Press, Cornwall (2019)
11. Litchfield, R.C., Fan, J., Brown, V.R.: Directing idea generation using brainstorming with specific novelty goals. Motivat. Emot. **35**(2), 135–143 (2011)
12. Danes, J E.; Lindsey-Mullikin, J; Lertwachara, K.: The sequential order and quality of ideas in electronic brainstorming. Int. J. Inf. Manage. **53**, 102126 (2020)
13. Zhang, H., Lee, S., Li, X., He, J.: EEG self-adjusting data analysis based on optimized sampling for robot control. Electronics **9**(6), 925 (2020)
14. Zhang, H., Liu, J., Dowens, M.: Complex brain activity analysis and recognition based on multiagent methods. Conc. Comput. Pract. Exp. **7** (2010). https://doi.org/10.1002/cpe.5855

Deep Learning Approach to Classify Parkinson's Disease from MRI Samples

Nanziba Basnin[1(✉)], Nazmun Nahar[2], Fahmida Ahmed Anika[3], Mohammad Shahadat Hossain[4], and Karl Andersson[5]

[1] International Islamic University Chittagong, Chittagong, Bangladesh
[2] BGC Trust University Bangladesh Bidyanagar, Chandanaish, Bangladesh
[3] Independent University Bangladesh, Dhaka, Bangladesh
[4] University of Chittagong, Chittagong, Bangladesh
[5] University of Technology, Skelleftea, Sweden

Abstract. Perkinson's disease is a progressive degenerative disorder that comes from a recognized clinical parkinsonian syndrome. The manifestations of Parkinson's disease include both motor and nonmotor symptoms identified as tremor, bradykinesia (slowed movements), rigidity, and postural instability. PD is marked as one of the most prevalent disorders from various researches and surveys because it has been observed in 90% of people out of 100. It is imperative to design CAD to develop an advanced model for the determination of this disease with accuracy since up to date there is no accurate clinical intervention for the diagnosis of PD. In contrast to conventional methods. Deep learning convolutional neural network tools are implied for the faster and accurate identification of PD through MRI. The purpose of this research is to contribute to the development of an accurate PD detection method. To conduct the research a public dataset NTU (National Technical University of Athens) is used. The data samples are categorized into three sets (Training, Test, and Validation). A DenseNet integrated with LSTM is applied to the MRI data samples. DenseNet is used to strengthen the feature selection ability, as each layer selects features depending on the temporal closeness of the image. The output is then fed into the LSTM layer, for discovering the significant dependencies in temporal features. The performance of the proposed DenseNet-LSTM is compared to other CNN state-of-the-art models. The proposed model outputs a training accuracy of 93.75%, testing accuracy of 90%, and validation accuracy of 93.8% respectively.

Keywords: Parkinson's Disease · CNN state-of-the-art-model · DenseNet-LSTM · MRI data samples

1 Introduction

Parkinson's Disease (PD) is a neurodegenerative disorder that is the primary stage of parkinsonism, (an idiopathic chronic disorder) usually predominant in the elderly. Approximately 1% of the world population encounters PD, From

M. Mahmud et al. (Eds.): BI 2021, LNAI 12960, pp. 536–547, 2021.
https://doi.org/10.1007/978-3-030-86993-9_48

which the majority of cases manifested complicated motor and cognitive issues. As the disease starts to develop, a prodromal phase of cognitive and behavioral symptoms inclusive of various personality changes, depressive disorders, memory dysfunction, and emotion dysregulation may become apparent. To date, clinicians still follow conventional methods to diagnose PD based on the prodromal symptoms mentioned above including slowness, stiffness, tremor, and movement difficulties. However, these symptoms tend to vary according to each individual being affected. Hence, at present, there is no particular blood test or biomarker to diagnose PD meticulously or detect prime changes as the condition rises. Researchers have perceived with the provision that changes in disease progression can be detected by brain MRI under a distinctive protocol.

PD in the primary stage can be misdiagnosed as other syndromes. PD is a most remarkable disease to be misinterpreted with abundant atypical parkinsonian disorders (APDs). For instance, progressive supranuclear palsy (PSP), multiple system atrophy (MSA), specifically the Parkinson variant of multiple system atrophy (MSA-P), and corticobasal degeneration (CBD). In addition to this, categorizing clinical entities of PD is difficult. Furthermore, classification of APDs and PD is imperative for accurate diagnosis during the prodromal phase as well as for choosing a specific intervention. MRI, a revolutionary and widespread method used in modern diagnosis, has proven to be significant for detecting PD. In general, MRI images undergo distributional differences in image resolution, contrast, signal to noise ratio due to hardware acquisitions, or techniques used in scanning. All these factors impact the composition of such images, in turn influencing the performance of training models.

In this research, we are adapting Deep Learning methods because it authorizes a higher quality learning representation of MRI image data [18, 21] enabling multiple levels of abstraction, achieved through multiple processing of layers. Thus providing an optimal rate of model performance in comparison to other learning approaches. The dataset selected for this study is a public dataset NTUA (National Technical University of Athens), which is split into training, testing, and validation sets. A DenseNet Model is integrated with LSTM to train the MRI data samples. The use of learning parameters is significantly reduced in DenseNet, as the input in each layer is provided as output in the next layer. Enabling reuse, and smooth flow of prominent features throughout the layer without any loss. Further, within each layer, some mechanism exists that select features according to their temporal relatedness apt to predicting class. These selected features are passed through the LSTM layer where their temporal dependencies are discovered. This exposes the model to more complex temporal dynamics of imaging, enhancing the classification and learning of the model [11]. In addition to this LSTM handles back prop and vanishing gradient problems [3] to enable effective training of datasets. The proposed model is further compared to other CNN state-of-the-art models, namely, DenseNet, VGG19, InceptionV3, ResNet, MobileNet for further evaluation.

Thus, through this section, the motive behind this research is understood. In the following Sect. 2, other works related to this research are assessed. Section 3 illustrated the methodology. Section 4 investigates and evaluates the proposed model. Section 5 outlines the conclusion and future prospects. While Sect. 6 provides acknowledgment.

2 Literature Review

Ref. No.	Methodology	Accuracy	Limitation
[26]	A CAD-based CNN model for auto-diagnosis of PD is proposed. A T2-weighted Magnetic Resonance Imaging (MRI) data samples are used in trainning the model. The model is compared to other ML models	96%	The complex manifestations of MRI data make it difficult to select the appropriate structure of CNN
[14]	T1-weighted sMRI scans from 416 patients are included to build the OASIS 3D dataset. A 2D architecture of 3 layers of distinct configuration of CNN is proposed to build the classification system for Alzheimer's. It is compared with other CNN state-of-the-art models	93.18%	The model may stop working if the vanishing gradient is relatively small, preventing the weights from getting updated
[28]	This is a review study consisting of some experiments with different layers of CNN, CNN-RNN, DNN. It was conducted to survey different types of datasets (image, speech handwriting, sensor, DATscan, MRI) on ML and DL models. Neurodegenerative disorders such as Alzheimer's and PD were investigated	96% for CNN-LSTM	Retraining the DNN model can lead to unforgettable prior knowledge
[19]	A classification model is generated to dissimilate PD-induced olfactory dysfunction from other types of non-Parkinsonian olfactory dysfunction (NPOD) from T1-weighted axial MRI samples of 30 patients. A 4 layer of CNN architecture along with other ML models are applied to train the data samples	96.6%	The size of MRI samples are small in order to reduce bias. The proposed model suffers from the problem of overfitting
[23]	A classification model is generated to dissimilate PD-induced olfactory dysfunction from other types of non-Parkinsonian olfactory dysfunction (NPOD) from T1-weighted axial MRI samples of 30 patients. A 4 layer of CNN architecture along with other ML models are applied to train the data samples	96.6%	The size of MRI samples are small in order to reduce bias

3 Methodology

Figure 1 demonstrated the methodology which is undertaken to carry out this research. In the beginning, the dataset is preprocessed by applying normalization and other perimeters found in data augmentation, followed by segmentation using K-means algorithm. Afterwords, the dataset is split into three parts. This dataset is then fed into the training model. The training model is labeled and used to predict PD from a sample of test datasets.

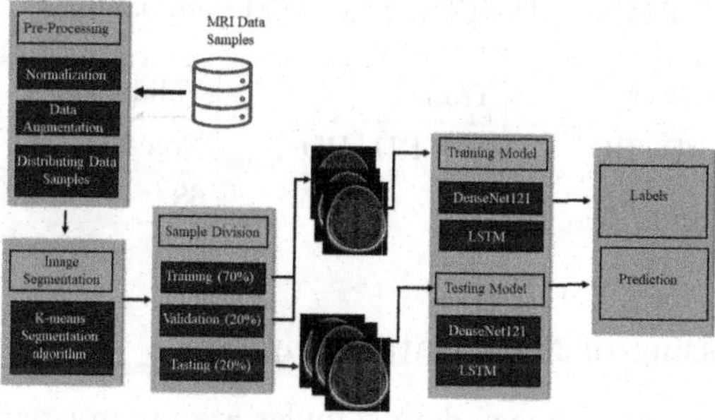

Fig. 1. Methodology

3.1 MRI Data Samples

This dataset comprises MRI examination report samples from a total of 78 individuals, 55 of which are suffering from Parkinson's Disease, 23 are healthy and serve as control subjects. This dataset is made accessible for the public, which includes the epidemiological, clinical and paraclinical data sample of patients, and is named as the 'National Technical University of Athens (NTUA) Parkinson's Dataset'. This dataset contains T1, T2, and Flair MRI image samples where the frames per sequence and the resolution differ for individual images. Although the images were derived in DICOM format, which is standard in medical imaging, the images Were published in PNG format for efficient storage (Fig. 2).

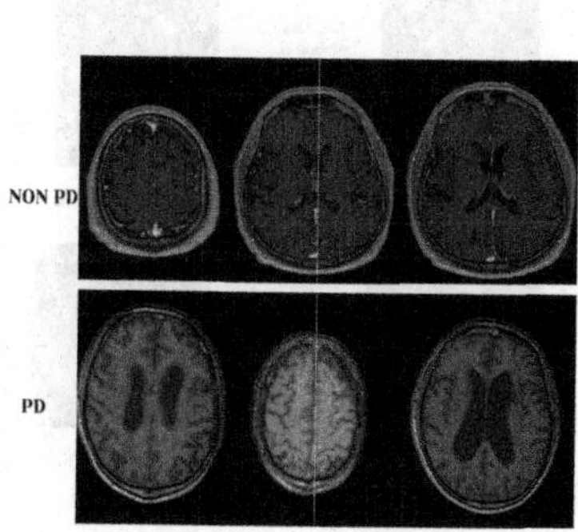

Fig. 2. Sample of NTUA MRI

The total number of data samples is 1387, of which 472 are NON PD patients and 915 PD patients. The samples were divided into three sets, Test, Training, and Validation samples respectively [28]. The Table 1 represents how the samples are distributed into sets.

Table 1. Distribution of MRI data samples

Test		Train		Validation	
Non PD	PD	Non PD	PD	Non PD	PD
35	51	369	605	68	259

3.2 Pre-processing of MRI Data Samples

In the beginning the MRI image data samples are preprocessed with an ImageDataGenerator class available in keras. The ImageDataGenerator class provides access to a wide range of pixel scaling methods and data augmentation techniques. The ImageDataGenerator class comprises three prominent methods of pixel scaling procedures. Here, the Normalization method is implied to re-scale the pixel values from a range of 0–255 to a range of 0–1. The rescale argument is invoked in order to carry out normalization of the image dataset before feeding it to the neural network for training [24]. The data augmentation increases the data quality and its robustness. Parameters such as shifting, rotation, shear and zoom, and flip are instigated. Moreover, augmented datasets aid in increasing data points by reducing the length between the testing and training dataset. Hence preventing the overfitting in the training dataset [27].

3.3 MRI Sample Segmantation

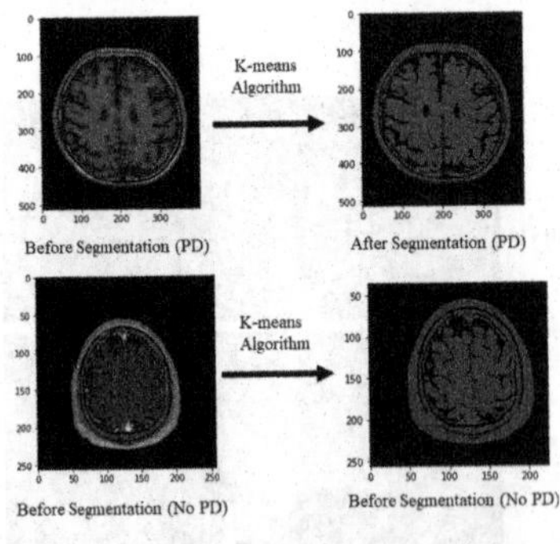

Fig. 3. Sample of MRI segmented

The MRI samples are converted to LAB color space. The adaptive K-means algorithm is employed to segment each image by a value of K which falls between a cycle two to ten. Secondly, the morphological operation is applied to transform the image into two values. Lastly, the maximum threshold is registered by iterating the process, to obtain the segmentation outcome. If the number of the outcome matches the value of K in that instant, a stop iteration command is invoked and the outcome of division becomes the final outcome.

3.4 Proposed Model Architecture

Table 2. System architecture description.

Layers	Output size
Convolution	112 × 112
Pooling	56 × 56
Dense Block (1)	56 × 56
Transitional Block (1)	56 × 56
Dense Block (2)	28 × 28
Transitional Block (2)	28 × 28
Dense Block (3)	14 × 14
Transitional Block (3)	14 × 14
Dense Block	7 × 7
ReLu	-
LSTM	(None, 148, 70)
Global Average Pooling	(None, 1024)
LSTM	(None, 70)
Concatenate	(None, 1024)
Dense	(None, 1)

DenseNet is a state-of-the-art which is the most suggested convolutional neural networks, because it can join both the previous and updraught layers. The structure offers advantages superior to existing structures like mitigating the vanishing gradient drawback, reinforcing propagation of feature, enables reuse of features, and turn down the number of parameters. In general, deep DenseNets are sets of dense blocks which is associated consecutively, with subsidiary convolutional and operations of pooling allying consecutive dense blocks. This development allows to construct a deep neural network able to constitute difficult transformations [13]. Thus, the task consists of two major obstructions: (i) Invoking CNN to deal with image sequences is inapt as CNN formerly established for static data. And leads to obtaining features from the image. These features are provided to the LSTM as it is capable of dealing with sequence data. Hence it is used to acquire image-sequence differentiation. The real image sequences are noisy and high dimensional, so it provides poor results when fed onto the LSTM Model (Table 2).

3.5 System Implementation

Google Colab was employed to generate the training module [7]. This platform expedites the implementation of programs in run time and supports deep learning libraries by providing access to robust GPU (Graphics Processing Unit) and TPU (Tensor Processing Unit). Python is compatible with the Google Colab environment. To build the programs, libraries obligatory for implementation include Tensor flow, Keras, OpenCV, PIL, sklearn, Matplotlib, Pandas, and Numpy. In this study, Tensor was implied for the backend of the system and Keras was employed to build the pre-trained models of CNN [1] because it can aid in built-in functions for the purpose of layering, optimization, and activation. OpenCV is vital for image processing [25]. Conversely, Sklearn provides access to various supervised and unsupervised algorithms [12]. A confusion matrix was implemented to build Matplotlib [12]. Image processing was carried out by the utilization of an integration tool PIL, whereas Numpy was employed to aid in the operations of arrays [10]. Callbacks are implemented to train the model. The advantage of using Callbacks includes not only overfitting which is the result of the occurrence of numerous epochs as well as circumvents under models. Check points, early stopping and lowering the learning rate on a plateau are utilized in callbacks. Checkpoints aid in the preservation of the best models by inspection of the loss within validation. Early stopping halts the training epochs, once the model exhibits no significant change in model performance. When the validation loss declines for any further enhancement, a Reducing learning rate on the plateau is invoked.

4 Experimental Result

This section evaluates the performance of the models when trained using the MRI data samples for the classification of PD.

4.1 Comparison of Results

After the MRI data samples are pre-processed, they are fed into state-of-the-art CNN models. These models are, namely, DenseNet, VGG19, ResNet, MobileNet, and Inception V3. It is observed that VGG19, ResNet, MobileNet have a training accuracy of 1.0 with very insignificant loss, in contrast, their testing accuracy is 0.81, 0.93, and 0.84. Whereas, these models have a validation accuracy of 0.82, 0.96, and 0.94 respectively. Since the training accuracy is 100%, the model is likely to be an overfitted model. In order to justify this cross-validation needs to be carried out for VGG-19, ResNet, and MobileNet.

Table 3. Comparison of result

Transfer learning model	Training accuracy	Training loss	Testing accuracy	Testing loss	Validation accuracy	Validation loss
DenseNet	0.93	0.061	0.87	0.10	0.94	0.023
VGG19	1.0	0.095	0.8125	0.07	0.828	0.114
ResNet	1.0	0.00028	0.93	0.07	0.96	0.038
MobileNet	1.0	0.0018	0.84	0.114	0.94	0.067
InceptionV3	0.95	0.038	0.843	0.112	0.90	0.0431

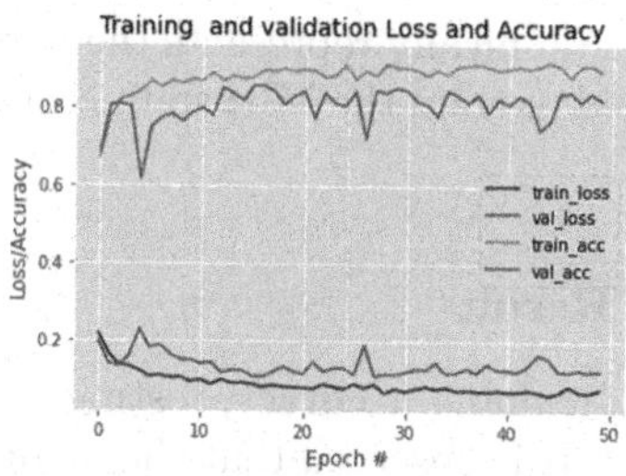

Fig. 4. Performance curve of InceptionV3

On the other hand, InceptionV3 has a training accuracy of 0.95, a testing accuracy of 0.84, and a validation accuracy of 0.94. Since there is an 11% difference between the training and testing. Furthermore, it can be said that the model suffers from overfitting. In the case of DenseNet, the model has a relatively close training and testing accuracy as well as shows little or no significant difference between the validation and training accuracy. Thus, this model can be taken into account for further experimenting.

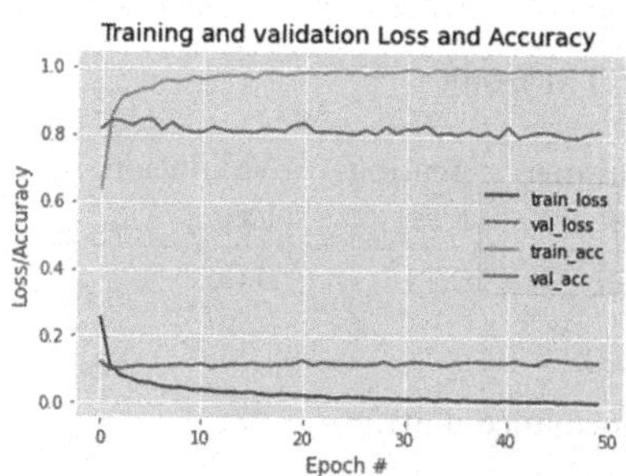

Fig. 5. Performance curve of DenseNet

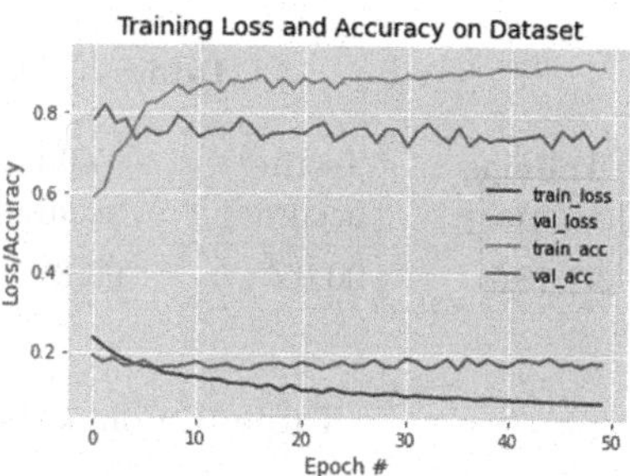

Fig. 6. Performance curve of VGG19

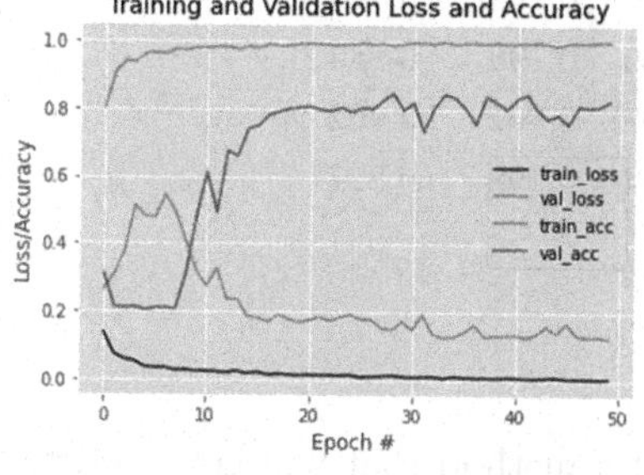

Fig. 7. Performance curve of ResNet

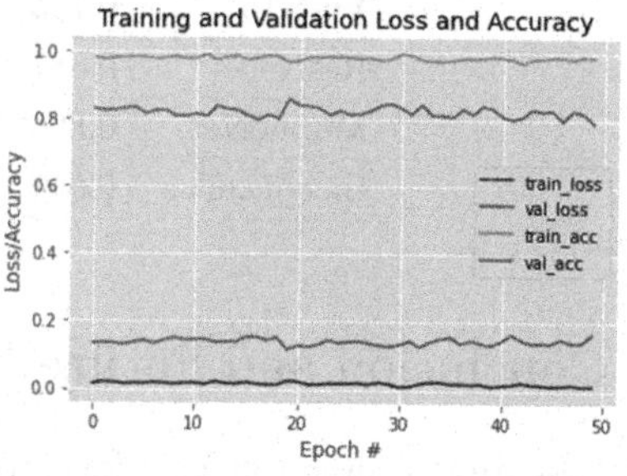

Fig. 8. Performance curve of MobileNet

Figures 3, 4, 5, and, 6 graphically represents the performance curve of all the state of the art model aplied to train the MRI samples for the classification of PD (Fig. 7).

4.2 Proposed Model Result

Table 3, demonstrates the training accuracy, testing accuracy as well as validation accuracy of the model. It is observed that the model is a well-fit model since there is not any significant differences between, testing, training and validation. Figures 8 and 9 represents the Model accuracy and that Model loss. In Fig. 8 the red line depicts the training accuracy which is observed to increase after 20 epochs while the blue line depicts the validation accuracy. Both the red line and the blue line is observed to meet at a particular point after 30 epochs. On the other hand, in Fig. 9 the blue line represents the validation loss which is slightly less than the training loss represented by the red line .

4.3 Performance Matrix of Various Deep Learning Models

To evaluate each models used in this research, the performance matrices such as precision, recall, f1-score, AUC are used (Tables 4 and 5).

Table 4. DenseNet-LSTM result

Training accuracy	Testing accuracy	Validation accuracy	Training loss	Testing loss	Validation loss
93.75%	90.0%	93.8%	0.06	0.11	0.06

Table 5. Comparison of performance matrices

Model	Precision	Recall	f1-score	AUC
DenseNet121	0.865	0.902	0.798	0.907
VGG16	0.793	0.886	0.798	0.829
ResNet	0.881	0.769	0.798	0.882
MobileNet	0.860	0.902	0.802	0.902
InceptionV3	0.817	0.844	0.798	0.827

5 Conclusion and Future Work

This research is aimed at the development of a method that will help to determine and differentiate PD with precision as well as without the interference of traditional approaches. To detect PD early, it is crucial to use an application that can segment the data sample image for better visualization and image resolution. With the emergence of various applications, in the modern era, MRI plays an important role as it can aid in the segmentation of images for a vivid understanding of the target affected side, leading to the recognition of PD while in the prodromal stage. To build an optimal learning model, DenseNet integrated with the LSTM model is trained with the publicly available NTUA dataset. This model is deployed for this research because it is better at learning and storing significant features within layers. The LSTM layers benefit by sorting the features according to their dependencies to be more relatable to predictable targets. The performance is further evaluated against other CNN state-of-the-art models in order to find which model is more appropriate for the data sample. However, the downside of Deep learning approaches adhered to in this research is that it is inadequate for in-depth comprehension as these models used are similar to a "Black-box" [17]. So to remove prior intuitive interpretations, explainable Artificial Intelligence can be introduced in near future. Further, this model can be enhanced to classify other syndromes like PD and we use other model to predict PD[?] [2,4–6,8,9,14,15,20,22,29].

References

1. Abadi, M., et al.: TensorFlow: a system for large-scale machine learning. In: 12th USENIX Symposium on Operating Systems Design and Implementation (OSDI 16), pp. 265–283 (2016)
2. Abedin, M.Z., Akther, S., Hossain, M.S.: An artificial neural network model for epilepsy seizure detection. In: 2019 5th International Conference on Advances in Electrical Engineering (ICAEE), pp. 860–865. IEEE (2019)
3. Ahmed, T.U., Hossain, M.S., Alam, M.J., Andersson, K.: An integrated CNN-RNN framework to assess road crack. In: 2019 22nd International Conference on Computer and Information Technology (ICCIT). pp. 1–6. IEEE (2019)
4. Ahmed, T.U., Jamil, M.N., Hossain, M.S., Andersson, K., Hossain, M.S.: An integrated real-time deep learning and belief rule base intelligent system to assess facial expression under uncertainty. In: 2020 Joint 9th International Conference on Informatics, Electronics & Vision (ICIEV) and 2020 4th International Conference on Imaging, Vision & Pattern Recognition (icIVPR), pp. 1–6. IEEE (2020)
5. Basnin, N., Nahar, L., Hossain, M.S.: An integrated CNN-LSTM model for micro hand gesture recognition. In: Vasant, P., Zelinka, I., Weber, G.-W. (eds.) ICO 2020. AISC, vol. 1324, pp. 379–392. Springer, Cham (2021). https://doi.org/10.1007/978-3-030-68154-8_35
6. Basnin, N., Nahar, L., Hossain, M.S.: An integrated CNN-LSTM model for Bangla lexical sign language recognition. Proceedings of International Conference on Trends in Computational and Cognitive Engineering ,pp. 695–707 (2021). https://doi.org/10.1007/978-981-33-4673-4_57
7. Carneiro, T., Da Nóbrega, R.V.M., Nepomuceno, T., Bian, G.B., De Albuquerque, V.H.C., Reboucas Filho, P.P.: Performance analysis of google colaboratory as a tool for accelerating deep learning applications. IEEE Access **6**, 61677–61685 (2018)
8. Chowdhury, R.R., Hossain, M.S., Hossain, S., Andersson, K.: Analyzing sentiment of movie reviews in Bangla by applying machine learning techniques. In: 2019 International Conference on Bangla Speech and Language Processing (ICBSLP), pp. 1–6. IEEE (2019)

9. Chowdhury, R.R., Hossain, M.S., ul Islam, R., Andersson, K., Hossain, S.: Bangla handwritten character recognition using convolutional neural network with data augmentation. In: 2019 Joint 8th International Conference on Informatics, Electronics & Vision (ICIEV) and 2019 3rd International Conference on Imaging, Vision & Pattern Recognition (icIVPR), pp. 318–323. IEEE (2019)
10. Diez, P.: Smart Wheelchairs and Brain-Computer Interfaces: Mobile Assistive Technologies. Academic Press, London (2018)
11. Donahue, J., et al.: Long-term recurrent convolutional networks for visual recognition and description. In: Proceedings of the IEEE Conference on Computer Vision and Pattern Recognition, pp. 2625–2634 (2015)
12. Greenfield, P., Miller, J.T., Hsu, J., White, R.L.: numarray: a new scientific array package for python. PyCon DC (2003)
13. Huang, G., Liu, Z., Van Der Maaten, L., Weinberger, K.Q.: Densely connected convolutional networks. In: Proceedings of the IEEE Conference on Computer Vision and Pattern Recognition, pp. 4700–4708 (2017)
14. Islam, J., Zhang, Y.: Brain MRI analysis for Alzheimer's disease diagnosis using an ensemble system of deep convolutional neural networks. Brain Inf. **5**(2), 1–14 (2018)
15. Islam, R.U., Hossain, M.S., Andersson, K.: A deep learning inspired belief rule-based expert system. IEEE Access **8**, 190637–190651 (2020)
16. Islam, R.U., Ruci, X., Hossain, M.S., Andersson, K., Kor, A.L.: Capacity management of hyperscale data centers using predictive modelling. Energies **12**(18), 3438 (2019)
17. Mahmud, M., Kaiser, M.S., McGinnity, T.M., Hussain, A.: Deep learning in mining biological data. Cogn. Comput. **13**(1), 1–33 (2021)
18. Mahmud, M., Kaiser, M.S., Hussain, A., Vassanelli, S.: Applications of deep learning and reinforcement learning to biological data. IEEE Trans. Neural Netw. Learn. Syst. **29**(6), 2063–2079 (2018)
19. Mei, J., Tremblay, C., Stikov, N., Desrosiers, C., Frasnelli, J.: Differentiation of Parkinson's disease and non-parkinsonian olfactory dysfunction with structural MRI data. In: Medical Imaging 2021: Computer-Aided Diagnosis. vol. 11597, p. 115971E. International Society for Optics and Photonics (2021)
20. Nahar, N., Hossain, M.S., Andersson, K.: A machine learning based fall detection for elderly people with neurodegenerative disorders. In: Mahmud, M., Vassanelli, S., Kaiser, M.S., Zhong, N. (eds.) BI 2020. LNCS (LNAI), vol. 12241, pp. 194–203. Springer, Cham (2020). https://doi.org/10.1007/978-3-030-59277-6_18
21. Noor, M.B.T., Zenia, N.Z., Kaiser, M.S., Al Mamun, S., Mahmud, M.: Application of deep learning in detecting neurological disorders from magnetic resonance images: a survey on the detection of Alzheimer's disease, Parkinson's disease and schizophrenia. Brain Inform. **7**(1), 1–21 (2020)
22. Pathan, R.K.: Gender classification from inertial sensor-based gait dataset. In: Vasant, P., Zelinka, I., Weber, G.-W. (eds.) ICO 2020. AISC, vol. 1324, pp. 583–596. Springer, Cham (2021). https://doi.org/10.1007/978-3-030-68154-8_51
23. Pugalenthi, R., Rajakumar, M., Ramya, J., Rajinikanth, V.: Evaluation and classification of the brain tumor MRI using machine learning technique. J. Control Eng. Appl. Inform. **21**(4), 12–21 (2019)
24. Reisfeld, D., Yeshurun, Y.: Preprocessing of face images: detection of features and pose normalization. Comput. Vis. Iimage Understand. **71**(3), 413–430 (1998)
25. Samal, B., Behera, A.K., Panda, M.: Performance analysis of supervised machine learning techniques for sentiment analysis. In: 2017 Third International Conference on Sensing, Signal Processing and Security (ICSSS), pp. 128–133. IEEE (2017)

26. Shah, P.M., Zeb, A., Shafi, U., Zaidi, S.F.A., Shah, M.A.: Detection of Parkinson disease in brain MRI using convolutional neural network. In: 2018 24th International Conference on Automation and Computing (ICAC), pp. 1–6. IEEE (2018)
27. Shorten, C., Khoshgoftaar, T.M.: A survey on image data augmentation for deep learning. J. Big Data **6**(1), 1–48 (2019)
28. Tagaris, A., Kollias, D., Stafylopatis, A., Tagaris, G., Kollias, S.: Machine learning for neurodegenerative disorder diagnosis-survey of practices and launch of benchmark dataset. Int. J. Artif. Intell. Tools **27**(03), 1850011 (2018)
29. Zisad, S.N., Hossain, M.S., Andersson, K.: Speech emotion recognition in neurological disorders using convolutional neural network. In: Mahmud, M., Vassanelli, S., Kaiser, M.S., Zhong, N. (eds.) BI 2020. LNCS (LNAI), vol. 12241, pp. 287–296. Springer, Cham (2020). https://doi.org/10.1007/978-3-030-59277-6_26

Automatic Pose and Shape Initialization via Multiview Silhouette Images

Yifan Lu(✉), Guanghui Song, and Haolan Zhang

Ningbo Institute of Technology, Zhejiang University, Ningbo, China
{Yifan.Lu,Guanghui.Song,Haolan.Zhang}@nit.zju.edu.cn

Abstract. Automatic pose and shape initialization is the first step to conquer the problem of human tracking, acquiring prior knowledge about the tracking subject. It is crucial for accomplishing a successful tracking. In this paper, we present a simple and effective framework to automatically calibrate the human pose and shape by integrating a data driven shape parameterization into the skeletal animation pipeline and optimizing the template body model against multiview silhouette images to acquire the tracking subject shape and pose information. A PCA based approach is proposed to summarize the space of human body variations in height, weight, muscle tone, gender, body shape. Multiview analysis by synthesis optimization in the hierarchial order is employed to realize pose and shape calibration. Finally, experiments on HumanEvaII and Human3.6m dataset demonstrate our approach is very effective and robust to real world situations.

Keywords: Human body modeling · Human pose estimation · Human body parametrization · Human computer interaction

1 Introduction

Human tracking has gain tremendous attentions in the research community, as it opens up a broad range of real world applications. Let us start with a question regarding general tracking: how much information about the target is necessary to achieve accurate tracking, and is it possible to track the target without knowing anything about it? To a certain extent, the information of the tracking subject in advance determines the tracking accuracy. For example, if there is no prior information about the human body, the tracking result can only identify the human body as a general object. Considering tracking as an inference process, the goal is to infer the current state of a subject through available information which is often hidden in both observations and prior knowledge. How much effort should be put into extracting information from observations and prior knowledge is situationally dependent. Sometimes, it is easier to extract the current state directly from observations even without prior knowledge. On the other hand, if observations are entangled or information contained in prior knowledge is easier to be extracted, it is wise to put more efforts to exploit prior

M. Mahmud et al. (Eds.): BI 2021, LNAI 12960, pp. 548–557, 2021.
https://doi.org/10.1007/978-3-030-86993-9_49

knowledge. We believe human tracking belongs to the latter case in which the relationship between the current posture and image observations is a complicated function in high dimensional space. Thus, incorporating more prior knowledge, such as building a subject specific appearance model, is a sensible way to solve this problem.

The appearance model can be learned online and updated dynamically through the tracking process. This is an ideal scenario for many tracking problems. However, this scenario introduces much more computational burden online, and tracking errors are easily accumulated in the appearance model, compromising its tracking accuracy. On the other hand, subject specific modelling is a one-time effort that pre-builds a high resemblance model of the tracking subject (possibly in a controlled environment). Such precision and details are not achievable with online learning methods. One-time modelling transfers the expensive online computations to the initialization stage and provides sound prior knowledge, so that the tracking becomes more robust and accurate. This paper begins with reviewing some related studies in human body modelling, and describes general articulated human body skeleton and its 3D joint rotation parameterizations in the form of the axis angle and exponential map. A body shape parameterization will be then described in details. Finally, an automatic initialization is proposed to simultaneously estimate the body shape and initial posture through a novel optimization method.

2 Related Works

Tremendous efforts have been made to study how to model the human body so that its digital version can be processed and utilized in different scenarios. For example, in the field of computer graphics, researchers are concerned with the automatic generation and animation of realistic human models. The applications of a system that simultaneously models pose and body shape include crowd generation for movie or game projects, creation of custom avatars for visual assistants, and usability testing of virtual prototypes. The studies in this category [1–3,6,9,11,13] often use a general data driven approach to build a parameterized template model. In this, hundreds of high resolution 3D human body scans are fit with a template model mesh to register correspondences. Subsequently, the parameterization is derived for non-rigid surface deformation as a function of pose, body shape, or some combination, and solved by a nonlinear optimizer under correspondence constraints. The established parameterization allows the template model to simulate a great variety of distinctive individual shapes and poses in realistic details.

To model body shape variation across different people, Allen et al. [1] morph a generic template shape into 250 3D scans of different humans in the same pose. The variability of human shape is captured by performing principal component analysis (PCA) over displacements of the template points. The model is used for hole-filling of scans and fitting a set of sparse markers for people captured in standard poses. Thalmann and Seo [11] introduced a framework for collecting and managing a set of range scan data to build a modeler that synthesizes the realistic appearance of the body model directly from the control parameters. The developed tools are used to help annotate landmarks, automatically estimate skeletal structures for animations, and establish correspondences within the population of captured data. Their modeler then uses this structurally annotated data to synthesize new body models by blending different models in a way that statistics are implicitly exploited. Consequently, their technique offers a time-saving generation of realistic, animatable body models with high realism, primarily for real-time applications. The SCAPE (Shape Completion and Animation of People) model [3] represents both articulated and non-rigid deformation of the human body. The pose deformation model captures how the body shape of a person varies as a function of their pose and is parameterized by a set of 3D rotations of skeletal bones. The shape deformation model captures the variability in body shape across different people by shape parameters–a coefficient vector corresponding to a point in a low-dimensional shape space obtained by Principal Component Analysis. Later, Allen et al. in [2] presented a method that learns skinning weights for corrective enveloping from 3D scans using a maximum a posteriori estimation for solving a highly nonlinear function which simultaneously describes the pose, skinning weights, bone parameters, and vertex positions. The weight or height of a character can be changed during the animation and muscle deformation looks significantly more realistic than with linear blend skinning. A fully differential model describing the pose and shape has been presented by [6]. The representation is uniform in pose and shape but involves solving two equation systems to reconstruct one mesh. Since pose and shape variations are expressed by a differential encoding invariant to rotation and translation, the main drawback of this approach is that the pose and shape cannot be analysed independently. Loper et al. [9] propose SMPL, a skinned vertex-based model that more accurately captures correlations in human shapes across the population. Comparing to the triangle-based approach, it achieves superior accuracy in terms of vertex based errors between the alignment model and the registered mesh. However, SMPL has a huge number of parameters resulting from its use of global blend shapes, capturing unnecessary long-range correlations between vertices and joints. To address this, Osman et al. [13] define per-joint pose correctives and learn the subset of mesh vertices that are influenced by each joint movement, significantly reducing the number of model parameters to 20% of SMPL.

3 Generic Human Body Skeleton

From simple stick figures, boxes, spheres and articulated cylinders to complex superquadric spheres, meshes and the more advanced deformable Laplacian mesh, various human body models has been used for markerless motion capture research. As a consequence of such diversity in body models, outcomes of different research groups have become very difficult to evaluate and compare with each other. Our approach emphasizes on building a generic skeleton-based body model with a small number of changeable parameters. Any specific body

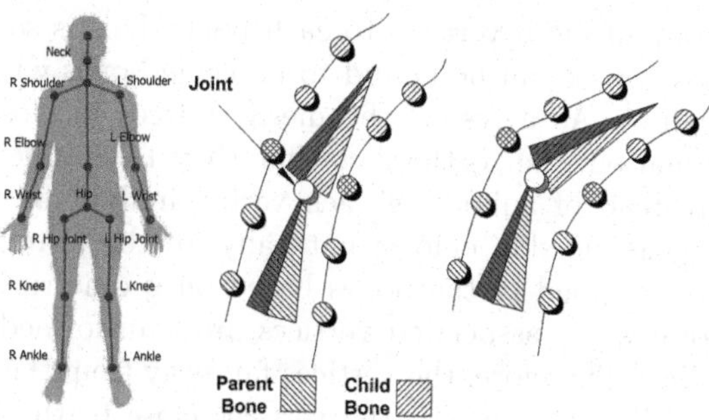

Fig. 1. a) Human skeleton parameterized by articulated bone segments with corresponding joint angles. b) Vertex blending. The bones are drawn as triangular solids, vertices are drawn as circles. Vertices are shaded according to their associated bones. The movements of bones drive the vertices to be transformed in a manner scaled by vertex weights, ultimately leading to skin deformation.

shape and posture can be adapted by adjusting the corresponding parameters without the need to modify the basic body skeleton structure. As illustrated in Fig. 1, an articulated skeleton has a total of 17 joints and 54 degrees of freedom (DOFs). To avoid overcomplication, only 10 articulated segments (ankle and wrist joints are optional) and 25 DOFs are considered important and modeled for estimation. The translation and orientation of the entire model are described by 6 DOFs. The remaining 19 DOFs are used to describe the joint angles of limbs. Thereby, any point ${}^{b}P$ in a local kinematic coordinate frame b can be transformed to the point ${}^{w}P$ in the world coordinate frame w by:

$$^{w}P = \prod_{i}^{N} T(\theta_i)^{b}P \tag{1}$$

where, N is the number of transformations. $T(\theta_i)$ is a homogeneous transformation matrix specified by θ_i, a particular set of joint angles and a translation. The joint angle estimation involves the three DOF rotation parameterization, which is non-Euclidean in nature. The axis angel representation (ω, θ) is used to parameterize the joint rotation using the Rodrigues formula:

$$exp(\theta, \omega) = I + \hat{\omega}\sin\theta + \hat{\omega}^2(1 - \cos\theta) \tag{2}$$

where I is the identity matrix and $\hat{\omega}$ is the skew symmetric matrix of the axis vector ω.

4 Human Body Shape

In standard computer graphics animation, the human body is often represented by two parts: a skin mesh used to render the human body, and a set of hierarchical bones used in animation. The skin mesh can be associated to hierarchical bones by assigning a group of mesh vertices to each bone. This is sometimes referred to as rigging. Each vertex can be bound to multiple bones with scaling factors called vertex weights[1]. As a result, the mesh vertices in close proximity can have subtle deformation due to the fact that they have different effects from multiple bones. Instead of animating each vertex individually, the skeleton is manipulated to make the skin deform naturally. In the example illustrated in Fig. 1, vertices are assigned to the bones based on geometric distances. When the child bone rotates, its associated vertices are transformed with respect to vertex weight scaling. Therefore, the vertices far away from the parent bone will be transformed further. Conversely, the vertices close to the parent bone will remain close to their previous positions. This is formally stated in the Skeletal Subspace Deformation (SSD) algorithm [10] which is based on weighted blending of affine transformations for each joint by:

$$v_d = (\sum_{i=1}^{M} w_i T(\theta_i))v_0 \tag{3}$$

where, M is the number of joints, v_d is a vertex after deformation, w_i is a vertex weight and v_0 is a vertex in the registered initial pose. Although SSD suffers from the inherent limitations of linear blending [8] (known as the "collapsing joints" and "twisting elbow" problem, where in general, the mesh deformed by SSD loses volume as the joint rotation increases), this simple algorithm still remains the most popular deformation scheme because of its computational efficiency.

4.1 Data-Driven Body Shape Parameterization

A PCA based approach used in this section is similar to the method proposed in [1]. The major difference between our approach and [1] is that we use software to generate a variety of synthetic human humanoids, instead of human body scan data. This allow great flexibility in simulating body shape variations and registering the mesh with the articulated skeleton. The open source software packages MakeHuman [12] and Blender [5] are used to create the synthetic dataset. A script is used to generate 6561 models corresponding to different combinations of eight properties: gender, age, muscle tone, height, weight, chest circumference, waist circumference and hip circumference. Each model is also associated with a feature vector $\mathbf{f}$ that defines height, weight, muscle tone, gender, body shape and a flag component. All models have an identical number of vertices n_v, and the same posture. For each model, we put all vertex positions in a single shape vector $\mathbf{a}_i$, which has $3n_v$ coordinates in a single column. The index i ranges from 1 to $N = 6561$. Initially, the mean $\bar{\mathbf{a}}$ of the example vectors is calculated by $\bar{\mathbf{a}} = \frac{1}{N}\sum_{i=1}^{N}\mathbf{a}_i$. Then, a matrix $\mathbf{A}$ is defined by assigning its ith column equal to $\mathbf{a}_i - \bar{\mathbf{a}}$. The principal components is obtained by multiplying $\mathbf{A}$ by the eigenvectors of $\mathbf{A}^T\mathbf{A}$. Each principal component corresponds to a variance σ_i^2, or a eigenvalue. The eigenvectors are usually sorted in order of decreasing σ_i^2. As the mean are subtracted from all models, there are $N - 1$ components with

[1] Vertex weights are often assigned by graphics software or artists.

variance greater than zero at most. It turns out that the overall shape of the body can be captured reasonably well with as few as 25 components. Therefore, we use only the 25 most significant components to represent the template model.

Principal component analysis is able to characterize the space of human body variation, but it lacks a direct way to change body shapes in an human-readable manner (e.g. weight and height). Blanz and Vetter [4] used linear regression to realize such controls for single variables. Below, we perform linear regression to learn a mapping $\mathbf{M}$ between the controls and the PCA weights. Assuming there are l such controls, the mapping $\mathbf{M}$ is denoted by an $(N-1) \times (l+1)$ matrix (where l is 6 in this case):

$$\mathbf{Mf} = \mathbf{p} \tag{4}$$

where f_i are the feature values of an individual, and $\mathbf{p}$ are the corresponding PCA weights. The last component 1 of the feature vector $\mathbf{f}$ allowing the feature values to be set to zeros and still keep $\mathbf{p}$ positive. Let $\mathbf{F}$ denote a $(l+1) \times N$ feature matrix constructed by stacking all feature vectors for all models, the $\mathbf{M}$ can be solved by:

$$\mathbf{M} = \mathbf{PF}^{\dagger} \tag{5}$$

where $\mathbf{F}^{\dagger}$ is the pseudoinverse of $\mathbf{F}$, and $\mathbf{P}$ is a PCA weights matrix whose ith column corresponds ith individual. The distinctive individuals then can be created by specifying different feature vectors with various heights, weights and so on. In this way, the user can edit features independently, or together. In addition to synthesizing generic models according to feature values, The existing models can be modified by creating delta-feature vectors of the form: $\Delta = [\Delta f_1, ..., \Delta f_l, 0]$ where Δf_i denotes the difference between a target feature and the actual feature for an individual. By adding $\Delta \mathbf{p} = \mathbf{M}\Delta \mathbf{f}$ to the PCA weights, We can modify the individual feature appearances. For instances, control them gain or lose weight, and/or make them taller or shorter. The examples of body deformation are shown in Figs. 2.

5 Automatic Initialization

A silhouette-based analysis-by-synthesis approach is performed to search the optimal anthropomorphic shape and pose parameters in order to maximize the overlap between the silhouettes of the re-projected model and the image silhouettes in all camera views. The energy function that evaluates this overlap by performing binary XOR operations on the image and model silhouettes from all camera perspectives. Automatical initialization is designated to handle relatively large variations in both shape and pose parameters. For general non-self-occluding gestures, skeleton translation offset[2] within 5-m-side-length bounding box and the shape dimension difference ratio[3] within the range $[0.1, 10]$, our automatical initialization procedure is able to drive the "T" gesture template model converging to the reasonable initial pose.

[2] The skeleton root offset between the true posture and the template model.

[3] The shape dimension difference ratio is defined by the subject body height divided by the template body height.

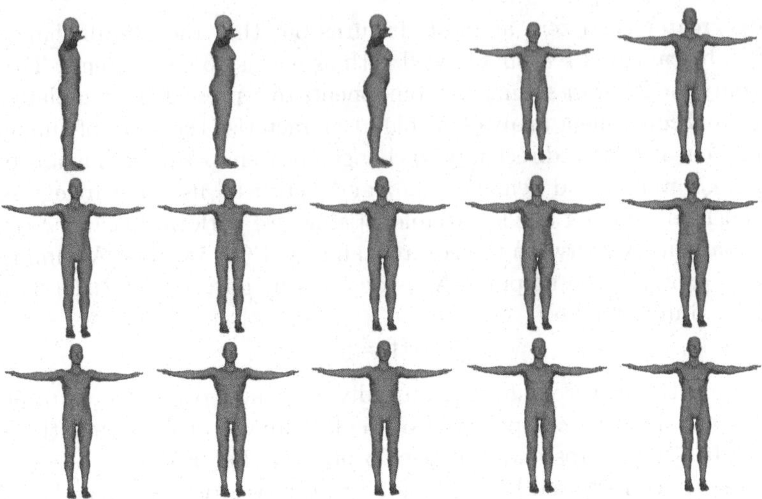

Fig. 2. Body deformations in gender, height, weight, shape and muscular tone

Given a pose and shape configuration, we can generate a human model with corresponding appearance. The skeleton kinematical structure implies that the pose optimization by nature is constrained to a hierarchical order. For instance, it is futile to estimate the other pose and shape parameters before the torso position is reasonably estimated. Making use of these hierarchical constraints to avoid the curse of dimensionality, we perform the Powell's dog leg method [14] to estimate the torso position at first, and then proceeding in the order of the hierarchical skeleton structure. Further, to make the energy function behave better, the silhouettes are distance transformed as shown in Fig. 3. As a result, the descending direction points to the original silhouette more clearly, and the optimization is less likely to become trapped in local optimums. After the torso has reasonably aligned with the silhouettes, the position and rotation of the torso are optimized simultaneously using normal multiview silhouettes. The subsequent optimization is applied to the rest body segments in the hierarchical order, respectively. At this stage, the whole body model should then already be posed reasonably close to the optimal posture. So we fix the pose parameters and only estimate the

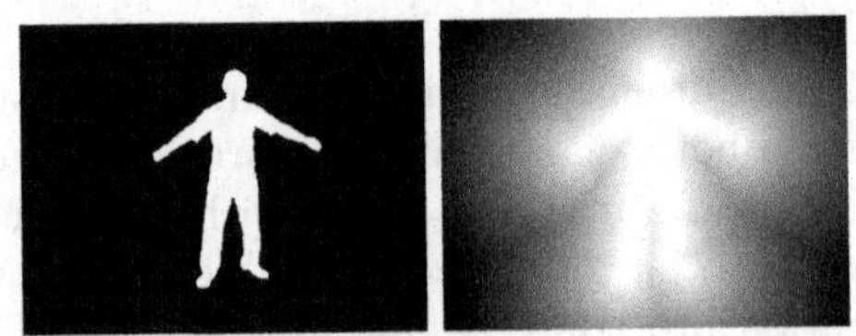

Fig. 3. The left diagram is the silhouette. The right diagram is the distance transformed silhouette, which helps the energy function be well behaved, making errors progressively concentrate around the area of the silhouette.

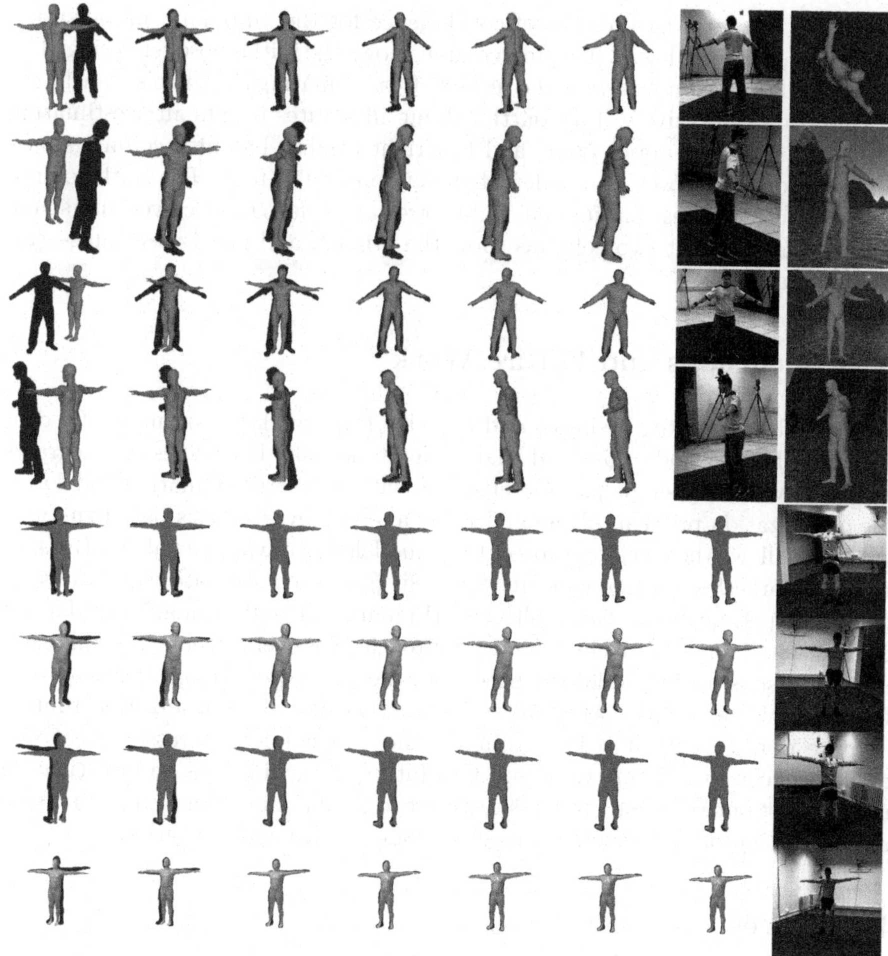

Fig. 4. The sequence of images from four camera views illustrates progressive convergence of results on HumanEvalI and Human3.6m

shape configuration. Finally, the shape and pose configurations are re-estimated with smaller ranges of motion to refine the result.

6 Experiments

Experiments were performed on the HumanEvalI [15] and Human3.6m [7] dataset that contains 4 colour calibrated image sequences synchronized with Mocap data 60 Hz. The 4 view silhouettes were handcrafted and undistorted according to the camera calibration parameters. Experiments were conducted on a desktop computer with Intel i7 10700F CPU and single Nvidia GeForce GTX 3080 GPU. It takes around 3 s to do 100 evaluations on four 256 by 256 silhouette images. The progress of convergence for the automatic initialization are demonstrated in Fig. 4. The first column shows the initial pose rendering. The second and third columns show the results after estimating the torso's translation and rotation respectively. The fourth column illustrates results after estimating the head, left/right upper arms, and left/right thighs. The fifth column shows estimates of height, weight, gender, shape and muscular tone. The sixth column shows results after estimating left/right lower arms, left/right calves and shape parameters. The last two columns show the original and novel view images(for HumanEvalI).

7 Conclusions and Future Work

We have demonstrated a simple and effective framework to automatically calibrate the human body pose and shape simultaneously. It seamlessly integrates a data-driven body shape parameterization with character animation and solves the optimization problem in the multiview analysis by synthesis paradigm. Our approach allows the tracking subject to be modeled in advance, enabling the subsequent markerless motion capture to benefit from such accurate template body model. Experiments on the multiview HumanEvalI and Human3.6m dataset demonstrated the effectiveness of our approach. However, when a tracking subject has a substantially different pose from the "T" pose, the optimization may fail to converge to the correct pose. This is because the optimization routine is quite easy to trap into local minima and can not leap across a great distance between two distinctive poses. Our future work will focus on investigating more robust optimization methods resistant to local minima, and explore texture reconstruction of the tracking subject on more challenging scenarios.

References

1. Allen, B., Curless, B., Popović, Z.: The space of human body shapes: reconstruction and parameterization from range scans. In: SIGGRAPH 2003: ACM SIGGRAPH 2003 Papers, pp. 587–594. ACM Press, New York (2003). https://doi.org/10.1145/1201775.882311. http://grail.cs.washington.edu/projects/digital-human/pub/allen03space.pdf
2. Allen, B., Curless, B., Popović, Z., Hertzmann, A.: Learning a correlated model of identity and pose-dependent body shape variation for real-time synthesis. In: SCA 2006: Proceedings of the 2006 ACM SIGGRAPH/Eurographics Symposium on Computer Animation, pp. 147–156. Eurographics Association, Aire-la-Ville (2006). http://portal.acm.org/citation.cfm?id=1218084
3. Anguelov, D., et al.: SCAPE: shape completion and animation of people. ACM Trans. Graph. **24**(3), 408–416 (2005)
4. Blanz, V., Vetter, T.: A morphable model for the synthesis of 3d faces. In: Rockwood, A. (ed.) SIGGRAPH 1999, Computer Graphics Proceedings, pp. 187–194. Addison Wesley Longman, Los Angeles (1999). http://citeseerx.ist.psu.edu/viewdoc/summary?doi=10.1.1.27.8314

5. Blender: Blender is the free open source 3d content creation suite (2020). http://www.Blender.org
6. Hasler, N., Stoll, C., Sunkel, M., Rosenhahn, B., Seidel, H.P.: A statistical model of human pose and body shape. In: Dutr'e, P., Stamminger, M. (eds.) Computer Graphics Forum (Proceedings of the Eurographics 2008), Munich, Germany, vol. 2, March 2009
7. Ionescu, C., Papava, D., Olaru, V., Sminchisescu, C.: Human3.6M: large scale datasets and predictive methods for 3d human sensing in natural environments. IEEE Trans. Pattern Anal. Mach. Intell. **36**(7), 1325–1339 (2014). https://doi.org/10.1109/TPAMI.2013.248, 3D
8. Lewis, J.P., Cordner, M., Fong, N.: Pose space deformation: a unified approach to shape interpolation and skeleton-driven deformation. In: SIGGRAPH, pp. 165–172 (2000)
9. Loper, M., Mahmood, N., Romero, J., Pons-Moll, G., Black, M.J.: SMPL: a skinned multi-person linear model. ACM Trans. Graph. (Proc. SIGGRAPH Asia) **34**(6), 248:1–248:16 (2015)
10. Magnenat-Thalmann, N., Laperrière, R., Thalmann, D.: Joint-dependent local deformations for hand animation and object grasping. In: Proceedings on Graphics Interface 1988, pp. 26–33. Canadian Information Processing Society (1988)
11. Magnenat-Thalmann, N., Seo, H.: Data-driven approaches to digital human modeling. In: 3DPVT, pp. 380–387 (2004)
12. MakeHuman: Open source tool for making 3d characters (2020). http://www.makehuman.org
13. Osman, A.A.A., Bolkart, T., Black, M.J.: STAR: sparse trained articulated human body regressor. In: Vedaldi, A., Bischof, H., Brox, T., Frahm, J.-M. (eds.) ECCV 2020. LNCS, vol. 12351, pp. 598–613. Springer, Cham (2020). https://doi.org/10.1007/978-3-030-58539-6_36
14. Powell, M.J.D.: A hybrid method for nonlinear equations. Numerical Methods for Nonlinear Algebraic Equations (1970). https://ci.nii.ac.jp/naid/10006528967/en/
15. Sigal, L., Balan, A., Black, M.: HUMANEVA: synchronized video and motion capture dataset and baseline algorithm for evaluation of articulated human motion. Int. J. Comput. Vis. **87**, 4 (2010)

The Necessity of Leave One Subject Out (LOSO) Cross Validation for EEG Disease Diagnosis

Sajeev Kunjan[1(✉)], T. S. Grummett[1], K. J. Pope[1], D. M. W. Powers[1], S. P. Fitzgibbon[3], T. Bastiampillai[2], M. Battersby[2], and T. W. Lewis[1]

[1] College of Science and Engineering, Flinders University, Adelaide, Australia
{chat0068,tyler.grummett,kenneth.pope,david.powers, trent.lewis}@flinders.edu.au

[2] College of Medicine and Public Health, Flinders University, Adelaide, Australia
{tarun.bastiampillai,malcolm.battersby}@flinders.edu.au

[3] Oxford Centre for Functional MRI of the Brain, University of Oxford, Oxford, UK
sean.fitzgibbon@ndcn.ox.ac.uk

Abstract. High variability between individual subjects and recording sessions is a known fact about scalp recorded EEG signal. While some do, the majority of the EEG based machine learning studies do not attempt to assess performance of algorithms across recording sessions or across subjects, instead studies use the whole data-set available for training and testing, using an established k-fold cross validation technique and thus missing performance in a real-life setting on an unseen subject. This study primarily aimed to show how important is to have a leave-one-subject-out (LOSO) evaluation done for any scalp recorded EEG based machine learning. This study also demonstrates effectiveness of a Multilayer Perceptron (MLP) in getting good LOSO accuracy from balanced, clean EEG data, without any pre-processing in comparison with traditional machine learning algorithms. The study used data from participants diagnosed with schizophrenia, as well as a group of participants with no known neurological disorder. Classification was done using traditional methods and MLP to classify the participants as belonging to disease or control subjects. Results shows that 85% accuracy on unseen subject was achievable from a clean data-set. MLP is seen to be effective in finding features by which schizophrenia could be detected from clean EEG data. LOSO evaluation done with this proven MLP configuration using carefully and intentionally corrupted data clearly indicate that for disease diagnosis, the k-fold classification result is misleading. Therefore, evaluation of any scalp recorded EEG based disease classification method *must* use a LOSO style cross-validation.

This work was supported by the National Health and Medical Research Council, the Flinders Medical Centre Foundation, the Clinician's Special Purpose Fund of the Flinders Medical Centre, and an equipment grant from the Wellcome Trust, London, U.K.

M. Mahmud et al. (Eds.): BI 2021, LNAI 12960, pp. 558–567, 2021.
https://doi.org/10.1007/978-3-030-86993-9_50

Keywords: EEG · MLP · Machine learning · Classification · Cross-subject classification · Leave one subject out · LOSO

1 Introduction

Schizophrenia is a neurological disorder with a strong hereditary component that has been found to affect 1% of the population [2,13]. Symptoms include challenges in perception or perception of reality and, more broadly, are characterised as 'positive' and 'negative'. Positive symptoms of schizophrenia include conceptual disorganisation, suspiciousness, delusions, or hallucinatory behaviour. Negative symptoms of schizophrenia include lack of motivation and lack of movement. Research suggests that social and psychological factors, neurobiological, early environmental and genetic factors could be contributing to this condition [2,13]. Most of the neurological disorder or disease classification studies uses traditional machine learning algorithms like Support Vector Machine (SVM), Bayesian Gaussian-process logistic regression models and discriminant analysis [1,5,10,15,16,19,21].

In this study, we use a multilayer perceptron (MLP) to show importance of Leave-One-*Subject*-Out (LOSO) cross validation machine learning and how MLP is effective in making use of clean EEG data in mining out the features important for disease classification. While many studies [3,7,17,18] uses LOSO as cross validation, the majority [11,12] do not use any kind of leave subject out cross validation techniques to understand the effectiveness of the classifier in a real-life situation. To our knowledge there is no other study that objectively demonstrates the importance and necessity of leave subject out cross validation in EEG classification studies. In non-trivial EEG applications like disease diagnosis and safety-critical BCI applications, this approach is important in demonstrating the validity and generalisability of the method under investigation.

2 Data EEG Acquisition and Pre Processing

2.1 Participants

Data for this study were previously collected and described in detail in [9]. The participants were recruited from the Flinders Medical Centre and recorded during 2003–2006. All participants signed written, informed consent. The Flinders Clinical Research Ethics Committee approved the reanalysis of the pre-existing EEG records. The study had 632 participants and each performed 10 different tasks whilst recording EEG. A subset of the data from 30 subjects (15 from a Schizophrenia sub-group and 15 from matched control group) were selected for the study described in this paper. The size of the data-set was limitted by number of subject with schizophrenia condition. Data from eyes-closed and maze tasks only was used in this study.

2.2 Data Acquisition

An EEG system with 128 channels (Compumedics, Victoria, Australia) and the Neuroscan 'Quick cap' (Quick-Cap, Neuromedical Supplies, El Paso, TX) or the Falk Minnow 'Easy-cap' (Falk Minow Services, Germany) were used to record the EEG data from participants at a sampling rate 2000 Hz with 500 Hz low-pass filter. The data from the Quick-cap were interpolated to match with the 10–20 positioning of the Easy-cap electrodes. This enabled the data from both caps to be analysed together. A linked-ear reference was used. To minimise electromagnetic noise, participants were seated in a Faraday cage. Visual and auditory instructions were presented using Presentation (version 9.2 NBS http://www.neurobs.com) on a computer screen and speakers. A custom-built response panel (Biomedical Engineering, Flinders University) was used to record participants' manual responses. This linked the Presentation software and acquisition software to ensure accurate timing. EEG was recorded while subjects undertook mental tasks.

The current study includes data from two mental tasks: resting eyes-open and maze. For eyes-open task, participants were looking at a black screen with a white cross positioned one metre in front of them with their eyes-open for 40 s. The white cross was to aid fixation and reduce eye movement. For the maze task, participants were asked to learn and memorise a hidden pathway embedded within a maze presented on a computer screen. Participants moved the hidden cursor with directional-buttons. The task ended when the participant correctly traversed the maze twice in succession, or six minutes elapsed.

2.3 Artefact Removal

All the automatic direct current corrections applied by the EEG recording system were marked out before any further processing and data was resampled 2000 Hz 1000 Hz. The recorded EEG was also detrended using the SIFT toolbox [6,14]. This is a linear piecewise method, with a time segment length of 0.33 s and a step size of 0.082 s. EEG was then re-referenced using the common average reference. Faulty channels were determined using three different methods: probabilistic (threshold = 5), kurtosis (threshold = 5), and spectra (threshold = 2, 20 75 Hz).

The probabilistic method uses joint probability on the data from each channel separately to calculate the entropy of the data. The joint probability values are then normalised via the subtraction of the mean, and the division of the standard deviation. If the resulting normalised joint probability values (one per channel) exceed a threshold, then the corresponding channels are labelled for rejection.

The kurtosis method uses the same methodology as the probabilistic method, but uses discrete kurtosis rather than joint probability. The spectra method performs a spectral analysis using Welch's [20] modified periodogram. In contrast to the latter two methods, the probabilistic method was used to permanently remove faulty EEG channels, whereas the kurtosis and spectra methods were only utilised for the subsequent artefact correction step as these methods were subjectively determined to be overly sensitive and would reject too many channels. Artefact contaminated EEG data was then rejected by separating the data into epochs and flagging data as being artefactual, if two contiguous epochs exceeded a threshold (threshold = 10, Hamming taper).

The data was then demeaned again to account for the artefact correction. This data is referred as "clean" data and used for this study.

2.4 Data-Set for Current Study

Based on the quality of the data acquired some subjects were discarded making the effective data-set as shown in the table below for respective tasks. To make the data-set balanced, an equal (or comparable) number of control subject data was considered for the study.

Table 1. Properties of the data-set being considered for the study.

Task	Pre process	No of subjects	No of elec-trodes	No of fre-quency bands	No of features	No of samples	Subject count (disease)	Subject count (control)
Eyes open	Pruned	30	45	5	225	207	16	14
Maze	Clean	22	39	5	195	1181	11	11

In eyes open task, there were 30 subjects. Each subject had 5 to 8 non-overlapping, 5 s epochs making the total data points 207. The number epochs varied due to the rejection of epochs with bad data from the 40 s task. Importantly, each epoch was non-overlapping, that is each epoch was unique and there was no data leakage between each epoch.

Data from 45 electrodes in 5 bands (delta: 1–4 Hz, theta: 4–8 Hz, alpha: 8–13 Hz, beta: 13–25 Hz and gamma: 25 Hz) was used and this results in 225 (45×5) features. This make the data-set dimension 207×225. Output classes are 0 (control) and 1 (disease). Similarly, maze task data is of shape 1181×195 (39 electrodes, 5 channel, 22 subjects) as shown in Table 1. Number of subjects and channels vary between tasks slightly based on data quality.

For the leave one subject out (LOSO) classification experiment, all data from all subjects was used for training except one, which was used for testing purposes. Where as for K-fold entire data set was split into 9:1 ration for each fold of training and testing.

3 Method

3.1 Multi-Layer Perceptron

A Multi-Layer Perceptron (MLP) is a basic deep learning architecture [8]. It uses a supervised learning process called back propagation to train the model. It is a feed forward network consists of input layer, output layer and an arbitrary number of layers in between called hidden layers. Nodes of each hidden layer of an MLP are connected to every node in the previous and following layer. None of the nodes are connected to any other node of the same layer. The weights carried by these connections represents the strength of the connection. These weights are typically initialized randomly. Learning is a process by which MLP network determines which network connection weights best reduce the difference between true and calculated outputs. The nonlinear relationship between input of the node to the node output is defined by an activation function. A MLP with 4 layers was used in this study. An input layer, 2 hidden layers, with 12 and 8 hidden units respectively and an output layer were used for this study. The ReLU was used as the activation function for input and hidden layers. The sigmoid was the activation function used for the output layer. The Loss function used was the binary-cross entropy and Adam as the optimizer. The learning environment used Python (3.6.6), Anaconda (5.3.0), Keras (2.2.4), Tensorflow (1.11.0) and sklearn (0.22.1). Experiments were conducted with various numbers of hidden layers, hidden units other activation functions like softmax, tanh and Leaky ReLU, but the results were not in anyway better than that of ReLU and Sigmoid.

3.2 Machine Learning Method

The study was aiming at finding the effectiveness of each method to correctly identify if a new subject has Schizophrenia. The study has two parts: the first part was testing the effectiveness of MLP and the second part evaluating the necessity of LOSO cross validation. Models were created from the data-set over two task: maze and eyes-open for the first and the second part of the study, respectively. The study used Random Forest (RF), Logical Regression (LR), Linear discriminant analysis (LDA), Support vector machine (SVM) with linear and RBF kernel to confirm the study findings.

The cleaned and epoched EEG was standardised by removing the mean and scaling to unit variance. The training set was randomized for each round to ensure that model was not learning from any particular order of data input. No seed was used to enable random initialization of the weights each time the model was created (i.e. for each round and for each subject). Since a balanced data-set was used for all experiments in this study, accuracy was chosen to measure classification effectiveness.

As a prerequisite to the experiments, the initial step was to undertake MLP configuration and tune the hyper-parameters (hidden layers, hidden units, optimiser, activation functions, epochs, batch size). This was done by empirically analysing the results with different configurations. Best performance was found with: 2 hidden and output layers with, respectively, 12, 8 and 1 units, Adam optimizer, ReLU and sigmoid as activation functions for hidden layers and output layer, respectively, 150 epochs and a batch size of 10. In addition, RF parameters like number of trees in the forest and maximum depth of the tree were also determined empirically. LR, LDA, SVM-Linear and SVM-RBF used the default configurations from sklearn, without any further tuning. A separate data subset was not used for parameter tuning in this study due to small size of data. Since the purpose of the experiments are to compare the differences in performance in algorithms and, importantly, cross validation methods, tuning parameter on the same data as training/testing is not seen as problem.

The first part of the study was to understand how effective MLP is in identifying people with Schizophrenia using the scalp recorded EEG. Primarily, the maze task data was used for this part as there were more samples for maze compared with eyes open data task. The same data-set was used for classification using the ensemble method Random Forest (RF) [4] and the results were compared with that of MLP. Later LR, LDA, SVM with linear and RBF kernel were used to confirm the results.

The second and main part of the study was to determine differences in performance of a classification algorithm when k-fold cross validation and LOSO cross validation were used. The eyes-open task was used for this part of the study. To begin with, data was used on MLP based disease classification where 10-fold cross validation was employed. Then the same data was used to train an MLP using LOSO cross validation.

In order to confirm that the MLP model is learning the disease condition and not simply the subject (and hence the disease condition), the model was trained and tested with *corrupted label-data.* Two types of corruption where explore: 1) subject-wise data corruption, where the whole set of labels for each subject were interchanged and 2) sample-wise data corruption, where individual instance labels are randomly changed. Subject-wise could result in all the data samples for a subject being mislabelled whilst sample-wise would have parts of a subject mislabelled.

For leave one subject out (LOSO) cross validation experiment, all data from all subjects was used for training except one, which was used for testing purpose. The size of training and testing data-set is approximately 200:7, equal to the cumulative number of epochs (5 to 8) of the selected subject data (29 for training 1 for testing). This process was repeated for each subject being kept aside for testing purposes constituting one round. To get an average measure of accuracy, 100 rounds of such training and testing were completed. For K-fold cross validation data samples were separated in 9:1 ratio where 90% samples (approx. 185) were used for training and 10% (approx. 20) were used for testing in each fold until every data is used for testing in one of the fold, this process repeated for 100 rounds for an average result. In both LOSO and K-fold experiments the input was randomised, for each round.

4 Results

4.1 Effectiveness of MLP in Disease Classification

This part was completed using data "clean" data from the maze task. RF, LDA, SVM-L and SVM-RBF were used for comparing the result with an MLP. LOSO cross validation method was used for classification and 100 rounds of training were executed to get the mean accuracy and standard deviation. Pairwise T-test was conducted to see whether MLP performance was significantly different from others at a significance level of 0.05. Results are shown in Table 2.

Table 2. Classification accuracy for MLP, RF, LDA, SVM-L and SVM-RBF when maze data used. * indicates significantly different from MLP ($p < 0.05$)

Algorithm	Mean accuracy
MLP	85% ± 19
RF	82% ± 02*
LR	81% ± 32
LDA	63% ± 37*
SVM linear	80% ± 32
SVM RBF	80% ± 34

4.2 LOSO Versus K-Fold Cross-Validation

This part of the study was also performed using "clean" data from the eyes open task. Only the MLP algorithm was used for all classification. Five classification experiments were done to show the need for of LOSO when evaluating disease classification algorithms. First, 10-fold cross validation was used to show the accuracy in which data from all subjects were used in training, such that even though the individual data instances were distinct, the same subject appears in both training AND testing data. The second exercise was done with LOSO cross-validation. In order to determine if the algorithm was learning from the disease features, rather than subject features, an experiment with corrupted class labels (sample wise corruption and subject wise corruption) was undertaken. Corrupted labels were used for both k-fold and LOSO evaluation. Results from these evaluations are tabulated in Table 3.

Table 3. Classification accuracy comparison for LOSO and k-fold cross validation experiments. * indicates significantly different from LOSO on Original Data ($p < 0.05$)

Cross validation method	Label status	Accuracy
LOSO	Original data	70% ± 36
K-fold	Original data	98% ± 03*
LOSO	Subjectwise corrupted	30% ± 36*
K-fold	Subjectwise corrupted	98% ± 03*
K-fold	Each sample corrupted	37% ± 10*

5 Discussion

The effectiveness of MLP in disease learning was evaluated in the first part of the study (Table 2). In this, clean schizophrenia maze data was processed using 4 layer MLP. The result shows that with clean data, the MLP classifier is able to discern the disease group subjects from the control group based on EEG. From the t-test results, it can be seen that MLP is significantly better than RF and LDA, and comparable with LR, SVM-L and SVM-RBF results. In general, MLP and other deep learning architectures perform better with bigger data-sets. Considering the data-set used in this study was smaller (20 subjects, 195 features and 1181 samples) compared to what deep learning normally deals with, this result from MLP is promising.

Most importantly, the necessity of LOSO evaluation methodology was evaluated in the second part of the study (Table 3). Results from k-fold evaluation shows that if data from all subjects are used for training the model almost certainly (98%) can detect subjects with disease. In this case, training and testing data is not separated in terms of subjects, leaving data related to a subject in both places. As result shows, it can yield a high level of accuracy. A more realistic scenario, what is required is to classify a new unseen subject into one of the classes. With all other experimental aspects remaining the same, when the k-fold validation technique is changed to LOSO the accuracy decreased significantly to 70%. This likely means that in the case of k-fold where a subject data is in both training and testing partitions, the algorithm is learning the subject rather than the disease condition.

In order to confirm this inference, additional experiments were done by corrupting the outcome variable both subject-wise and sample-wise. From the t-test results, it is clear that LOSO results from original data is significantly different from rest of the results. The data (label) was first corrupted subject-wise and fed through the same training and testing procedure with k-fold cross validation. This resulted in an accuracy of 98%. Same corrupted data was then fed through (LOSO) classifier and the result was significantly lower at 30%. These two results show that standard machine learning evaluation methodology of k-fold learns the subject specific features rather than the disease related features. The last row in Table 3 shows the outcome, when k-fold learning was applied to label data corrupted at the level of each sample. The accuracy of 37% indicates that the classification is by chance. This result is expected as there is no subject related feature that consistently used by the algorithm to identify corresponding subject since labels are corrupted for each sample, that is a single subject has been labelled as both disease and control. Table 3 also shows that there is high standard deviation in the LOSO results, as some subjects were difficult to classify and thus accuracy on those subjects were too low. The k-fold results are distributing these difficult to classify subjects across test sets and therefore gives a false indication about overall result. These results clearly indicate that for disease diagnosis, the k-fold classification result is misleading. Therefore, evaluation of any scalp recorded EEG based disease classification method *must* use a LOSO style cross-validation.

Acknowledgements. We thank Prof Michael Baigent and Dr Randall Long (Department of Psychiatry and Flinders University and Medical Centre), Dr Cate Houen (Central Adelaide Local Health Network, SA Psychiatry Training Unit), Dr Emma Whitham and Prof John Willoughby (Department of Neurology, Flinders University and Medical), for their contributions in collecting and classifying the clinical material and providing the clinical background.

References

1. Arribas, J.I., Calhoun, V.D., Adali, T.: Automatic Bayesian classification of healthy controls, bipolar disorder, and schizophrenia using intrinsic connectivity maps from fMRI data. IEEE Trans. Biomed. Eng. **57**(12), 2850–2860 (2010)
2. Başar, E., Güntekin, B.: A review of brain oscillations in cognitive disorders and the role of neurotransmitters. Brain Res. **1235**, 172–193 (2008)
3. Boostani, R., Sadatnezhad, K., Sabeti, M.: An efficient classifier to diagnose of schizophrenia based on the EEG signals. Expert Syst. Appl. **36**(3), 6492–6499 (2009)
4. Breiman, L.: Random forests. Mach. Learn. **45**(1), 5–32 (2001). https://doi.org/10.1023/A:1010933404324
5. Challis, E., Hurley, P., Serra, L., Bozzali, M., Oliver, S., Cercignani, M.: Gaussian process classification of Alzheimer's disease and mild cognitive impairment from resting-state fMRI. Neuroimage **112**, 232–243 (2015)
6. Delorme, A., et al.: EEGLAB, SIFT, NFT, BCILAB, and ERICA: new tools for advanced EEG processing. Comput. Intell. Neurosci. **2011**, 5–6 (2011)
7. Fazli, S., Popescu, F., Danóczy, M., Blankertz, B., Müller, K.R., Grozea, C.: Subject-independent mental state classification in single trials. Neural Netw. **22**(9), 1305–1312 (2009)
8. Goodfellow, I., Bengio, Y., Courville, A., Bengio, Y.: Deep Learning, vol. 1. MIT Press, Cambridge (2016)
9. Grummett, T.: Analytical complexity required for diagnosing bipolar disorder, schizophrenia, and dementia. Ph.D. thesis, College of Science and Engineering, Flinders University, South Australia, December 2018
10. Jamal, W., Das, S., Oprescu, I.A., Maharatna, K., Apicella, F., Sicca, F.: Classification of autism spectrum disorder using supervised learning of brain connectivity measures extracted from synchrostates. J. Neural Eng. **11**(4), 046019 (2014)
11. Karimi, S., Mijani, A., Talebian, M., Mirzakuchaki, S.: Comparison of the P300 detection accuracy related to the BCI speller and image recognition scenarios. arXiv preprint arXiv:1912.11371 (2019)
12. Khan, K.A., Shanir, P., Khan, Y.U., Farooq, O.: A hybrid local binary pattern and wavelets based approach for EEG classification for diagnosing epilepsy. Expert Syst. Appl. **140**, 112895 (2020)
13. Merikangas, K.R., et al.: Lifetime and 12-month prevalence of bipolar spectrum disorder in the national comorbidity survey replication. Arch. Gen. Psychiatry **64**(5), 543–552 (2007)
14. Mullen, T., Delorme, A., Kothe, C., Makeig, S.: An electrophysiological information flow toolbox for EEGLAB. Biol. Cybern. **83**, 35–45 (2010)
15. Peters, H., et al.: More consistently altered connectivity patterns for cerebellum and medial temporal lobes than for amygdala and striatum in schizophrenia. Front. Hum. Neurosci. **10**, 55 (2016)

16. Rashid, B., et al.: Classification of schizophrenia and bipolar patients using static and dynamic resting-state fMRI brain connectivity. Neuroimage **134**, 645–657 (2016)
17. Ravi, K., Palaniappan, R.: Leave-one-out authentication of persons using 40 Hz EEG oscillations. In: EUROCON 2005-The International Conference on "Computer as a Tool", vol. 2, pp. 1386–1389. IEEE (2005)
18. Sabeti, M., Katebi, S., Boostani, R.: Entropy and complexity measures for EEG signal classification of schizophrenic and control participants. Artif. Intell. Med. **47**(3), 263–274 (2009)
19. Watanabe, T., Kessler, D., Scott, C., Angstadt, M., Sripada, C.: Disease prediction based on functional connectomes using a scalable and spatially-informed support vector machine. Neuroimage **96**, 183–202 (2014)
20. Welch, P.: The use of fast Fourier transform for the estimation of power spectra: a method based on time averaging over short, modified periodograms. IEEE Trans. Audio Electroacoust. **15**(2), 70–73 (1967)
21. Zhu, M., Jie, N., Jiang, T.: Automatic classification of schizophrenia using resting-state functional language network via an adaptive learning algorithm. In: Medical Imaging 2014: Computer-Aided Diagnosis, vol. 9035, p. 903522. International Society for Optics and Photonics (2014)

Author Index

Printed in the United States
by Baker & Taylor Publisher Services

Printed in the United States
by Baker & Taylor Publisher Services